**WileyPLUS** helps today's students succeed in the classroom using resources relevant to their everyday lives and to the workplace that will help make them globally competitive. With the complete e-book plus a variety of interactive tools, **WileyPLUS** makes teaching, learning, and retaining the material easier, more relevant, and more exciting than ever.

*"I wish all my classes had WileyPLUS linked to their textbooks so I could study better in all my classes"*
**- Student David Delgado**

Instructors using **WileyPLUS** easily choose all of the resources they need to effectively design and deliver their courses with maximum impact and minimum preparation time. Conveniently organized and highly integrated resources include the Instructor's Manual, Test Bank, PowerPoint slides, Cases, Videos, and more.

**WileyPLUS** links students directly from homework assignments to specific portions of the online text for the contextual help they need - when they need it.

# See and try *WileyPLUS* in action!
## • www.wileyplus.com •

# CONTEMPORARY STRATEGY ANALYSIS

To Sue

# SEVENTH EDITION
# CONTEMPORARY STRATEGY ANALYSIS

## ROBERT M. GRANT

John Wiley & Sons, Ltd

First published by Blackwell Publishing Ltd 1991, 1995, 1998, 2002, 2005, 2008
Copyright © Robert M. Grant

This edition Copyright © 2010 Robert M. Grant
Published by John Wiley & Sons Ltd

*Registered office*
John Wiley & Sons Ltd, The Atrium, Southern Gate, Chichester, West Sussex, PO19 8SQ, United Kingdom

For details of our global editorial offices, for customer services and for information about how to apply
for permission to reuse the copyright material in this book please see our website at www.wiley.com.

The right of Robert M. Grant to be identified as the author of this work has been asserted in accordance
with the U.K. Copyright, Designs and Patents Act 1988.

Reprinted with corrections January 2010, July 2010, November 2010, April 2011

*Library of Congress Cataloging-in-Publication Data*

Grant, Robert M., 1948-
  Contemporary strategy analysis/Robert M. Grant.–7th ed.
      p. cm.
  Includes bibliographical references and index.
  ISBN 978-0-470-74710-0
1. Strategic planning.    I. Title.
  HD30.28.G72 2009
  658.4'012–dc22

                                        2009025382

A catalogue record for this book is available from the British Library.

ISBN: 978-0-470-74710-0

Set in 10/12pt Classical Garamond by Thomson Digital, India
Printed in Italy by Printer Trento S.r.l.

I wrote *Contemporary Strategy Analysis* to equip managers and students of management with the concepts, frameworks and techniques needed to make better strategic decisions. I wanted a strategy text that would reflect the dynamism and intellectual rigor of this fast-developing field of management. At that time, the existing texts failed to incorporate either the enormous advances taking place in strategy research or the strategic management practices of leading-edge companies.

The result is a strategy text that endeavors to be both rigorous and relevant. While embodying the latest thinking in the strategy field, *Contemporary Strategy Analysis* aims to be accessible to students from different backgrounds and with varying levels of experience. I achieve this accessibility by combining clarity of exposition with concentration on the fundamentals of value creation and an emphasis on practicality.

These same objectives are unchanged in this seventh edition of *Contemporary Strategy Analysis*. My approach is simultaneously analytical and practical. If strategic management is all about managing to achieve outstanding success then the essential tasks of strategy are to identify the sources of superior business performance and to formulate and implement a strategy that exploits these sources of superior performance.

The seventh edition also reflects the developments that have occurred since 2007 both in the business environment and in strategy analysis. With regard to the former, the dominant feature is the global recession that followed the financial crisis of 2008–9. I view this financial crisis less as an isolated event than one in a series of shocks that have afflicted the twenty-first century business environment. Looking ahead, I anticipate that turbulence, unpredictability, and intense competition will continue to dominate the global business environment.

The principal implications I draw are, first, that strategy will become increasingly important to firms as they navigate a challenging and unpredictable business environment and, second, that a determined focus on the fundamentals of value creation will be critical to firm survival and prosperity. Despite the reaction against shareholder value maximization for its inducement to short-termism and crass materialism, strategy analysis must focus on the pursuit of long-run profitability. This requires a penetrating understanding of customer needs, competitive forces and the firm's strengths and weaknesses.

Achieving profitability in the face of intense competition means that competitive advantage must be the central focus of strategy. This new edition places a stronger emphasis on the primary sources of competitive advantage: the resources and capabilities of the enterprise.

This edition also places a greater emphasis on strategy implementation. Establishing competitive advantage in a complex and unpredictable business environment requires that firms reconcile scale economies with entrepreneurial flexibility, innovation with cost efficiency and globalization with local responsiveness. This creates new challenges for the design of organizational structures and management systems. At the same time I have maintained an integrated approach to strategy formulation and strategy implementation recognizing their codependence. A strategy that is formulated without regard to its implementation is likely to be fatally flawed. It is through the process of implementation that strategies adapt and emerge.

As well as emphasizing the fundamentals of strategy analysis, I draw upon promising new approaches to strategy analysis including the role of complementarity, the use of real options to analyze flexibility, the nature of complexity and the potential for self-organization, and the role of legitimacy and its relevance to corporate social responsibility.

There is very little in this book that is original—I have plundered mercilessly the ideas, theories and evidence of fellow scholars. My greatest debts are to my colleagues and students at the business schools where this book has been developed and tested— notably Georgetown University and Bocconi University. This edition has also benefitted from feedback and suggestions from professors and students in other schools where *Contemporary Strategy Analysis* is used. I am particularly grateful to Andrew Campbell for assisting with Chapters 16 and 17. With the enhanced Web-based support being provided by the publisher, I look forward to closer interaction with users.

The success of *Contemporary Strategy Analysis* owes much to the professionalism and enthusiasm of the editorial, production and sales and marketing teams at John Wiley & Sons, Ltd. I am especially grateful to Steve Hardman, Deborah Egleton, Catriona King and Rosemary Nixon.

*Robert M. Grant*
*London*

Guide to the Instructor and Student resources to accompany Contemporary Strategy Analysis

Visit www.contemporarystrategyanalysis.com to access all the teaching and learning materials that accompany this text.

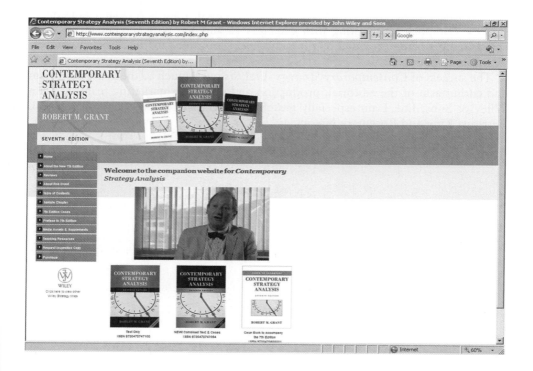

Students can see video clips of the author summarising and extending the learning in each chapter. There are also self-test quizzes and case study activities, including case-related video clips with questions.

Instructors can access the password-protected resources including the Instructor's Manual, case teaching notes, PowerPoint slides and a Test Bank with over 1500 questions.

Contemporary Strategy Analysis is also accompanied by a WileyPLUS course

**WileyPLUS** is an online teaching and learning environment that integrates the **entire digital textbook** with the most effective instructor and student resources to fit every learning style.

**With** *WileyPLUS:*

- Students achieve concept mastery in a rich, structured environment that is available 24/7.
- Instructors personalize and manage their course more effectively with assessment, assignments, grade tracking, and more.

*For Students* - **Personalize the learning experience**

Different learning styles, different levels of proficiency, different levels of preparation—each of your students is unique. *WileyPLUS* empowers them to take advantage of their individual strengths:

- Students receive timely access to resources that address their demonstrated needs, and get immediate feedback and remediation when needed.
- Integrated, multi-media resources provide multiple study-paths to fit each student's learning preferences and encourage more active learning.

*For Instructors* - **Personalize the teaching experience**

*WileyPLUS* empowers you with the tools and resources you need to make your teaching even more effective:

- With *WileyPLUS* you can identify those students who are falling behind and intervene accordingly, without having to wait for them to come to you in office hours.
- *WileyPLUS* simplifies and automates such tasks as student performance assessment, creating assignments, scoring student work, keeping grades, and more.

# I

# INTRODUCTION

1    The Concept of Strategy

# 1 The Concept of Strategy

*Strategy is the great work of the organization. In situations of life or death, it is the Tao of survival or extinction. Its study cannot be neglected.*

—SUN TZU, *THE ART OF WAR*

## OUTLINE

# Introduction and Objectives

Strategy is about winning. This chapter explains what strategy is and why it is important to success—both for organizations and individuals. We will distinguish strategy from planning. Strategy is not a detailed plan or program of instructions; it is a unifying theme that gives coherence and direction to the actions and decisions of an individual or an organization.

The principal task of this chapter will be to introduce the basic framework for strategy analysis that underlies this book. I will introduce the two basic components of strategy analysis: analysis of the external environment of the firm (mainly industry analysis) and the analysis of the internal environment (primarily analysis of the firm's resources and capabilities).

By the time you have completed this chapter, you will be able to:

◆ appreciate the contribution that strategy can make to successful performance, both for individuals and for organizations;

◆ recognize the key characteristics of an effective strategy;

◆ comprehend the basic framework of strategy analysis that underlies this book;

◆ become familiar with the major trends in the development of business strategy during recent decades;

◆ understand how strategy is made within organizations and the role played by strategic planning systems.

Since the purpose of strategy is to help us to win, we start by looking at the role of strategy in success.

## The Role of Strategy in Success

Strategy Capsules 1.1, 1.2, and 1.3 outline examples of success in three very different arenas: Madonna in popular entertainment, General Giap and the North Vietnamese armed forces in warfare, and Lance Armstrong in cycling. Can the success of these diverse individuals and the organizations they led be attributed to any common factors?

### STRATEGY CAPSULE 1.1

# Madonna

The fifty-first birthday of Madonna Louise Veronica Ciccone on August 16, 2009 offered no respite from her hectic work schedule. The day before she had performed the 71st concert in her *Sweet and Sticky* world tour; a tour that would gross over $400 million. For yet another year it seemed unlikely that Madonna would be displaced in the *Guinness Book of Records* as the world's top-earning female entertainer and most successful female recording artist of all time.

In the summer of 1978, aged 19, Madonna arrived in New York with $35 to her name. After five years of struggle, she landed a recording contract. *Madonna* (1983) ultimately sold 10 million copies worldwide, while *Like a Virgin* (1984) topped 12 million copies. Between 1985 and 1990, six further albums, three world tours, and five movie roles had established Madonna with an image and persona that transcended any single field of entertainment: she was rock singer, actor, author, and pinup. Yet, she was more than this—as her website proclaims, she is "icon, artist, provocateur, diva, and mogul." She has also made a great deal of money.

What is the basis of Madonna's incredible and lasting success? Certainly not outstanding natural talent. As a vocalist, musician, dancer, songwriter, or actress, Madonna's talents seem modest. Few would regard her as an outstanding beauty.

She possesses relentless drive. Her wide range of activities—records, concerts, music videos, movies, books, and charity events—are unified by her dedication to a single goal: the quest for superstar status. "Even as a little girl, I knew I wanted the whole world to know who I was." She is widely regarded as a workaholic who survives on little sleep and rarely takes vacations: "I am a very disciplined person. I sleep a certain number of hours each night, then I like to get up and get on with it. All that means that I am in charge of everything that comes out."

She has drawn heavily on the talents of others: writers, musicians, choreographers, and designers. Many of her personal relationships have been stepping stones to career transitions. Her transition from dance to music was assisted by relationships, first, with musician Steve Bray, then with disc jockey John Benitex. Her entry into Hollywood was accompanied by marriage to Sean Penn and an affair with Warren Beatty. Most striking has been continuous reinvention of her image. From the street-kid look of the early 1980s, to the hard-core sexuality of the 90s, to the Madonna-with-children spirituality of the past decade, her fans have been treated to multiple reincarnations. As Jeff Katzenberg of Dreamworks observed: "She has always had a vision of exactly who she is, whether performer or businesswoman, and she has been strong enough to balance it all. Every time she comes up with a new look it is successful. When it happens once, OK, maybe it's luck, but twice is a coincidence, and three times it's got to be a remarkable talent. And Madonna's on her fifth or sixth time."

She was quick to learn the ropes both in Tin Pan Alley and in Hollywood. Like Evita Perón, whom Madonna portrayed in *Evita*, Madonna has combined determination, ambition, social acumen, and mastery of the strategic use of sex. As a self-publicist she is without equal, using nudity, pornography, bisexuality, spirituality and philanthropy as publicity tools. She is also astute at walking the fine line between the shocking and the unacceptable. Through Maverick Inc., a joint venture with Time Warner, she has been able to control her own creative output and also manage and develop younger entertainers and musicians. Her 2007, $120 million contract with Live Nation revealed her understanding of the shifting of economic power from recorded music to live performances.

---

## STRATEGY CAPSULE 1.2
# General Giap and the Vietnam Wars, 1948–75

*As far as logistics and tactics were concerned, we succeeded in everything we set out to do. At the height of the war the army was able to move almost a million soldiers a year in and out of Vietnam, feed them, clothe them, house them, supply them with arms and ammunition and generally sustain them better than any army had ever been sustained in the field . . . On the battlefield itself, the army was unbeatable. In engagement after engagement the forces of the Vietcong and the North Vietnamese Army were thrown back with terrible losses. Yet, in the end, it was North Vietnam, not the United States that emerged victorious. How could we have succeeded so well yet failed so miserably?*

Despite having the largest army in Southeast Asia, North Vietnam was no match for South Vietnam so long as the south was backed by the world's most powerful military and industrial nation. South Vietnam and its U.S. ally were defeated not by superior resources but by a superior strategy. North Vietnam achieved what Sun Tzu claimed was the highest form of victory: the enemy gave up.

The master of North Vietnam's military strategy was General Vo Nguyen Giap. In 1944, Giap became head of the Vietminh guerrilla forces. He was commander-in-chief of the North Vietnamese Army until 1974 and Minister of Defense until 1980. Giap's strategy was based on Mao Tse Tung's three-phase theory of revolutionary war: first, passive resistance to mobilize political support; second, guerrilla warfare aimed at weakening the enemy and building military strength; finally, general counteroffensive. In 1954, Giap's brilliant victory over the French at Dien Bien Phu fully vindicated the strategy. Against the U.S., the approach was similar.

> Our strategy was . . . to wage a long-lasting battle . . . Only a long-term war could enable us to utilize to the maximum our political trump cards, to overcome our material handicap, and to transform our weakness into strength. To maintain and increase our forces was the principle to which we adhered, contenting ourselves with attacking when success was certain, refusing to give battle likely to incur losses.

The strategy built on the one resource where the communists had overwhelming superiority: their will to fight. As Prime Minister Pham Van Dong explained: "The United States is the most powerful nation on earth. But Americans do not like long, inconclusive wars . . . We can outlast them and we can win in the end." Limited military engagement and the charade of the Paris peace talks helped the North Vietnamese prolong the conflict, while diplomatic efforts to isolate the U.S. from its Western allies and to

sustain the U.S. peace movement accelerated the crumbling of American will.

The effectiveness of the U.S. military response was limited by two key uncertainties: what the objectives were and who the enemy was. Was the U.S. role one of supporting the South Vietnamese regime, fighting Vietcong terrorism, inflicting a military defeat on North Vietnam, conducting a proxy war against the Soviet Union, or combating world communism? The consistency and strength of North Vietnam's strategy allowed it to survive errors in implementation. Giap was premature in launching his general offensive. Both the 1968 Tet Offensive and 1972 Easter Offensive were beaten back with heavy losses. By 1974, U.S. resistance had been sapped by the Watergate scandal. On April 29, 1975, Operation Frequent Wind began evacuating all remaining Americans from South Vietnam, and the next morning North Vietnamese troops entered the Presidential Palace in Saigon.

**Sources**: Col. Harry G. Summers Jr., *On Strategy* (Novato, CA: Presidio Press, 1982): 1; Vo Nguyen Giap, *Selected Writings* (Hanoi: Foreign Language Publishing House, 1977); J. Cameron, *Here Is Your Enemy* (New York: Holt, Rinehart, Winston, 1966).

## STRATEGY CAPSULE 1.3

# Lance Armstrong and the Tour de France

On July 24, 2005, Lance Armstrong became the first person to win the Tour de France seven times. His achievement was all the more remarkable for the fact that he had recovered from testicular cancer that had spread to his lungs and brain.

Even without cancer, Lance Armstrong was not an obvious candidate for title of the

greatest cyclist ever. Despite certain natural advantages—notably a heart 30% larger than normal with an abnormally slow beat rate (32 times per minute while at rest)—Armstrong's aerobic rate was less than that of cycling greats such as Miguel Indurain and Greg LeMond. For most of his career, Armstrong was not the world's pre-eminent cyclist. He won the world championship just once (1993) and his Olympic best was a bronze medal in the 2000 Sydney games.

Armstrong's seven-year dominance of the Tour de France resulted from a combination of factors, not least of which was his single-minded focus, not just on cycling, but on a single race: between his seven Tour de France victories, Armstrong won only five other races.

Armstrong raised planning for the Tour to new levels of sophistication: with meticulous attention to training, diet and calorific intake and expenditure. His all-round abilities as a cyclist, mental resilience, and mastery of bluff and psychological warfare were well suited to the requirements of the Tour. His feigning exhaustion at critical junctures before devastating his rivals with a powerful breakaway has been deemed "worthy of a Hollywood Oscar." However, it was in team planning and coordination where the major differences between Armstrong and his competitors were most evident.

The principal prize in the Tour de France is for the individual who achieves the fastest overall time, but cyclists compete within teams. Team coordination and the willingness of the other team members (*domestiques*) to sacrifice themselves for the leader is critical to individual success. Armstrong's U.S. Postal Service team (which became the Discovery Channel team for the 2005 Tour) was remarkable not just for the quality of other team members but for the willingness of these world-class cyclists to serve their leader. Olympic gold medal winner Viatcheslav Ekimov—"The Russian Power House"—was critical to pulling Armstrong through the flatter stages of the Tour. Roberto Heras and Jose Asevedo defended Armstrong in the mountains—shielding him from the wind and supporting him during breakaways. George Hinkapie rode in all seven of Armstrong's Tour victories as a versatile all-rounder. Why did the team show a unique degree of loyalty to their team leader? Part was Armstrong's infectious commitment; part was his willingness to pay bonuses out of his own pocket to other riders, but also important was reciprocity—while team members gave total support to Armstrong on the Tour de France, in other competitions the roles were reversed and Armstrong served as a *domestique* to other team members.

The team's master planner was director, Johan Bruyneel, whose unrivaled knowledge of the Tour spanned sports physiology, game theory, psychology, and tactics. As well as team selection, role assignment, and discipline, Bruyneel managed a network of secret agreements with other teams. In return for financial support, other teams agreed to support Armstrong should he find himself split from his own team members. Bruyneel gave particular attention to team dynamics: fostering loyalty, camaraderie discussion, and shared emotions to overcome the notorious individualism of professional cyclists.

Armstrong's decision to come out of retirement electrified the 2009 Tour. In the Astana team, Armstrong rejoined Bruyneel and other former USPS/Discovery riders—but with one difference: Alberto Contador was team leader, not Armstrong. Contrador duly won the 2009 Tour de France; Lance Armstrong in third place.

For none of these three examples can success be attributed to overwhelmingly superior resources:

- Madonna possesses vitality, intelligence and magnetism, but lacks outstanding talents as a vocalist, musician or actress.

- The military, human, and economic resources of the Vietnamese communists were dwarfed by those of the U.S. and South Vietnam. Yet, with the U.S. evacuation from Saigon in 1975, the world's most powerful nation was humiliated by one of the world's poorest.

- Lance Armstrong possessed a powerful combination of physical and psychological attributes. Yet these endowments were not markedly superior to other top-class cyclists—especially after Armstrong's near-death encounter with cancer.

Nor can their success be attributed either exclusively or primarily to luck. For all three, lucky breaks provided opportunities at critical junctures. None, however, was the beneficiary of a consistent run of good fortune. More important than luck was the ability to recognize opportunities when they appeared and to have the clarity of direction and the flexibility necessary to exploit these chances.

My contention is that the key common ingredient in all three success stories was the presence of a soundly formulated and effectively implemented *strategy*. These strategies did not exist as a plan; in most the strategy was not even made explicit. Yet, in all three, we can observe a consistency of direction based on a clear understanding of the "game" being played and a keen awareness of how to maneuver into a position of advantage.

- Underpinning Madonna's many years as a superstar has been a strategy built on dedication, opportunism, reinvention of herself and a well-coordinated multimarket presence.

- The victory of the Vietnamese communist forces over the French and then the Americans is a classic example of how a sound strategy pursued with total commitment over a long period can succeed against vastly superior resources. The key was Giap's strategy of a protracted war of limited engagement. With the U.S. constrained by domestic and international opinion from unleashing its full military might, the strategy was unbeatable once it began to sap the willingness of the U.S. government to persevere with a costly, unpopular foreign war.

- Lance Armstrong's domination of the Tour de France from 1999 to 2005 was because he and his team did the most effective job of analyzing the requirements for success in the race, developing a strategy around those requirements and executing it almost faultlessly.

We can go further. What do these examples tell us about the characteristics of a strategy that are conducive to success? In all three stories, four common factors stand out (see Figure 1.1):

1 *Goals that are simple, consistent, and long term.* All three individuals displayed a single-minded commitment to a clearly recognized goal that was pursued steadfastly over a substantial part of their lifetime.
   - Madonna's career featured a relentless drive for stardom in which other dimensions of her life were absorbed within her career.
   - North Vietnamese efforts were unified and focused on the ultimate goal of reuniting Vietnam under communist rule and expelling a foreign army

**FIGURE 1.1** Common elements in successful strategies

from Vietnamese soil. By contrast, U.S. efforts in Vietnam were bedeviled by confused objectives.

● On his return to professional cycling in 1998, Lance Armstrong committed to a single goal: winning the Tour de France.

**2** *Profound understanding of the competitive environment.* All three individuals designed their strategies around a deep and insightful appreciation of the arena in which they were competing.

● Fundamental to Madonna's continuing success has been a shrewd understanding of the ingredients of stardom and the basis of popular appeal. This extends from the basic marketing principle that "sex sells" to recognition of the need to manage gatekeepers of the critical media distribution channels. Her periodic reincarnations reflect an acute awareness of changing attitudes, styles, and social norms.

● Giap understood his enemy and the battlefield conditions where he would engage them. Most important was appreciation of the political predicament of U.S. presidents in their need for popular support in waging a foreign war.

● Lance Armstrong and team director Johan Bruyneel took analysis of the requirements for success in the Tour de France to unprecedented levels of detail and sophistication.

**3** *Objective appraisal of resources.* All three strategies were effective in exploiting internal strengths, while protecting areas of weakness.

● By positioning herself as a "star," Madonna exploited her abilities to develop and project her image, to self-promote and to exploit emerging trends while avoiding being judged simply as a rock singer or an actress. Her live performances rely heavily on a large team of highly qualified dancers, musicians, vocalists, choreographers and technicians, thus compensating for any weaknesses in her own performing capabilities.

● Giap's strategy was carefully designed to protect against his army's deficiencies in arms and equipment while exploiting the commitment and loyalty of his troops.

- Armstrong's campaign to win the Tour de France was based on two key strengths: unmatched determination to win and superior team-building capability.

**4** *Effective implementation.* Without effective implementation, the best-laid strategies are of little use. Critical to the success of Madonna, Giap, and Armstong was their effectiveness as leaders in terms of their capacity to reach decisions, energy in implementing them, and ability to foster loyalty and commitment among subordinates. All three built organizations that allowed effective marshaling of resources and capabilities and quick responses to changes in the competitive environment.

These observations about the role of strategy in success can be made in relation to most fields of human endeavor. Whether we look at warfare, chess, politics, sport, or business, the success of individuals and organizations is seldom the outcome of a purely random process. Nor is superiority in initial endowments of skills and resources typically the determining factor. Strategies that build on the basic four elements almost always play an influential role.

Look at the "high achievers" in any competitive area. Whether we review the world's political leaders, the CEOs of the Fortune 500, or our own circles of friends and acquaintances, those who have achieved outstanding success in their careers are seldom those who possessed the greatest innate abilities. Success has gone to those who managed their careers most effectively—typically by combining the four strategic factors mentioned above. They are goal focused; their career goals have taken primacy over the multitude of life's other goals—friendship, love, leisure, knowledge, spiritual fulfillment—which the majority of us spend most of our lives juggling and reconciling. They know the environments within which they play and tend to be fast learners in terms of understanding the keys to advancement. They know themselves in terms of both strengths and weaknesses, and they implement their career strategies with commitment, consistency and determination. As the late Peter Drucker observed: "we must learn how to be the CEO of our own careers."[4]

There is a downside, however. Focus on a single goal may lead to outstanding success, but may be matched by dismal failure in other areas of life. Many people who have reached the pinnacles of their careers have led lives scarred by poor relationships with friends and families and stunted personal development. These include Howard Hughes and Jean Paul Getty in business, Richard Nixon and Joseph Stalin in politics, Marilyn Monroe and Elvis Presley in entertainment, Joe Louis and O. J. Simpson in sport, and Bobby Fischer in chess. Fulfillment in our personal lives is likely to require broad-based lifetime strategies.[5]

These same ingredients of successful strategies—clear goals, understanding the competitive environment, resource appraisal and effective implementation—form the key components of our analysis of business strategy.

## The Basic Framework for Strategy Analysis

Figure 1.2 shows the basic framework for strategy analysis that we shall use throughout the book. The four elements of a successful strategy shown in Figure 1.1 are recast into two groups—the firm and the industry environment—with strategy forming a link between the two. The firm embodies three sets of these elements:

**FIGURE 1.2** The basic framework: strategy as a link between the firm and its environment

goals and values ("simple, consistent, long-term goals"), resources and capabilities ("objective appraisal of resources"), and structure and systems ("effective implementation"). The industry environment ("profound understanding of the competitive environment") is defined by the firm's relationships with customers, competitors and suppliers.

This view of strategy as a link between the firm and its industry enviroment has close similarities with the widely used, but inferior, SWOT Framework (see strategy capsule 1.4).

The task of business strategy, then, is to determine how the firm will deploy its resources within its environment and so satisfy its long-term goals, and how to organize itself to implement that strategy.

## STRATEGY CAPSULE 1.4
# What's Wrong with SWOT?

Distinguishing between the external and the internal environment of the firm is common to most approaches to strategy analysis. The best known and most widely used of these approaches is the "SWOT" framework, which classifies the various influences on a firm's strategy into four categories: Strengths, Weaknesses, Opportunities, and Threats. The first two—strengths and weaknesses—relate to the internal environment; the last two—opportunities and threats—relate to the external environment.

Which is better, a two-way distinction between internal and external influences or the four-way SWOT taxonomy? The key issue is whether it is sensible and worthwhile to classify internal factors into strengths and weaknesses and external factors into opportunities and threats. In practice, such distinctions are difficult:

- Is Steve Jobs a strength or a weakness for Apple? As both founder and reincarnator of Apple, few major companies owe so much to a single person. Yet, having suffered pancreatic cancer and the subject of continuing health concerns, Jobs is also a critical source of vulnerability for Apple.

- Is global warming a threat or an opportunity to the world's automobile producers? Global warming may encourage governments to raise taxes on motor fuels and support public transport, thereby threatening the demand for private motoring. At the same time, these circumstances create an opportunity for developing new, fuel-efficient cars that may encourage consumers to scrap their gas-guzzlers.

The lesson here is that an arbitrary classification of external factors into opportunities and threats, and internal factors into strengths and weaknesses, is less important than a careful identification of these external and internal factors followed by an appraisal of their implications. My approach to strategy analysis favors a simple two-way classification of *internal* and *external* factors. What will characterize our strategic appraisal will be the rigor and depth of our analysis of these factors, rather than a superficial categorization into strengths or weaknesses, and opportunities or threats.

## Strategic Fit

Fundamental to this view of strategy as a link between the firm and its external environment is the notion of *strategic fit*. For a strategy to be successful, it must be consistent with the firm's external environment, and with its internal environment— its goals and values, resources and capabilities, and structure and systems. As we shall see, the failure of many companies is caused by lack of consistency with either the internal or external environment. General Motors' long-term decline is a consequence of a strategy that has failed to break away from its long-established ideas about multibrand market segmentation and adapt to the changing market for automobiles. In other cases, many companies have failed to align their strategies to their internal resources and capabilities. A critical issue for Nintendo in the coming years will be whether it possesses the financial and technological resources to continue to compete head-to-head with Sony and Microsoft in the market for video game consoles.

As you will discover, the notion of *strategic fit* extends beyond the simple notion that strategy must fit with the external and the internal environment of the firm. The principles of strategic fit extend to organizational design—what is called *contingency theory* (see Chapter 7) and the view of the firm as a system of interlinked activities (see the discussion of *contextuality* in Chapter 8 and *complementarity* in Chapter 11).

## A Brief History of Business Strategy

## Origins and Military Antecedents

Enterprises need business strategies for much the same reasons that armies need military strategies—to give direction and purpose, to deploy resources in the most effective manner and to coordinate the decisions made by different individuals. Many of the concepts and theories of business strategy have their antecedents in military strategy. The term *strategy* derives from the Greek word *strategia*, meaning "generalship." However, the concept of strategy did not originate with the Greeks. Sun Tzu's classic *The Art of War*, written circa 500 BC, is regarded as the first treatise on strategy.[6]

Military strategy and business strategy share a number of common concepts and principles, the most basic being the distinction between strategy and tactics. *Strategy* is the overall plan for deploying resources to establish a favorable position; a *tactic* is a scheme for a specific action. Whereas tactics are concerned with the maneuvers necessary to win battles, strategy is concerned with winning the war. Strategic decisions, whether in military or business spheres, share three common characteristics:

- they are important
- they involve a significant commitment of resources
- they are not easily reversible.

Many of the principles of military strategy have been applied to business situations. These include the relative strengths of offensive and defensive strategies; the merits of outflanking over frontal assault; the roles of graduated responses to aggressive initiatives; the benefits of surprise and the potential for deception, envelopment, escalation and attrition.[7] At the same time, the differences between business competition and military conflict must be recognized. The objective of war is (usually) to defeat the enemy. The purpose of business rivalry is seldom so aggressive: most business enterprises limit their competitive ambitions, seeking coexistence rather than the destruction of competitors.

The tendency for the principles of military and business strategy to develop along separate paths indicates the absence of a general theory of strategy. The publication of Von Neumann and Morgenstern's *Theory of Games* in 1944 gave rise to the hope that a general theory of competitive behavior would emerge. During the subsequent six decades, game theory has revolutionized the study of competitive interaction, not just in business but in politics, military conflict and international relations as well. Yet, as we shall see in Chapter 4, game theory has achieved only limited success as a practical and broadly applicable general theory of strategy.[8]

## From Corporate Planning to Strategic Management

The evolution of business strategy has been driven more by the practical needs of business than by the development of theory. During the 1950s and 1960s, senior executives were experiencing increasing difficulty in coordinating decisions and maintaining control in companies that were growing in size and complexity. Financial budgeting, in the form of annual financial planning and investment appraisal provided short-term control and project selection but did little to guide the long-term development of the firm. Corporate planning (also known as *long-term planning*) was developed during the late 1950s to serve this purpose. Macroeconomic forecasts provided the foundation for the new corporate planning. The typical format was a five-year corporate planning document that set goals and objectives, forecasted key economic trends (including market demand, the company's market share, revenue, costs and margins), established priorities for different products and business areas of the firm, and allocated capital expenditures. The diffusion of corporate planning was accelerated by a flood of articles and books addressing this new science.[9] The new techniques of corporate planning proved particularly useful for developing and guiding the diversification strategies that many large companies were pursuing during the 1960s. By the mid-1960s , most large U.S. and European companies had set up corporate planning departments. Strategy Capsule 1.5 provides an example of such formalized corporate planning.

---

**STRATEGY CAPSULE 1.5**

## Corporate Planning in a Large U.S. Steel Company, 1965

The first step in developing long-range plans was to forecast the product demand for future years. After calculating the tonnage needed in each sales district to provide the "target" fraction of the total forecast demand, the optimal production level for each area was determined. A computer program that incorporated the projected demand, existing production capacity, freight costs etc., was used for this purpose.

When the optimum production rate in each area was found, the additional facilities needed to produce the desired tonnage were specified. Then the capital costs for the necessary equipment, buildings, and layout were estimated by the Chief Engineer of the corporation and various district engineers. Alternative plans for achieving company goals were also developed for some areas, and investment proposals were formulated after considering the amount of available capital and the company debt policy. The Vice President who was responsible for long-range planning recommended certain plans to the President and, after the top executives and the Board of Directors reviewed alternative plans, they made the necessary decisions about future activities.

*Source:* Harold W. Henry, *Long Range Planning Processes in Forty-five Industrial Companies* (Englewood Cliffs, NJ: Prentice-Hall, 1967): 65.

---

During the 1970s and early 1980s, confidence in corporate planning and infatuation with scientific approaches to management were severely shaken. Not only did diversification fail to deliver the anticipated synergies but the oil shocks of 1974 and 1979 ushered in a new era of macroeconomic instability, combined with increased international competition from resurgent Japanese, European, and Southeast Asian firms. Faced with a more turbulent business environment, firms could no longer plan their investments, new product introductions and personnel requirements three to five years ahead, simply because they couldn't forecast that far into the future.

The result was a shift in emphasis from *planning* to *strategy making*, where the focus was less on the detailed management of companies' growth paths than on positioning the company in markets and in relation to competitors in order to maximize the potential for profit. This transition from *corporate planning* to what became termed *strategic management* was associated with increasing focus on competition as the central characteristic of the business environment and competitive advantage as the primary goal of strategy.

This emphasis on strategy as a quest for performance directed attention to the sources of profitability. During the late 1970s and into the 1980s, attention focused on sources of profit within the industry environment. Michael Porter of Harvard Business School pioneered the application of industrial organization economics to analyzing industry profitability.[10] Other studies focused on how profits were distributed between the different firms in an industry—in particular the impact of market share and experience upon costs and profits.[11] These two lines of inquiry—into interindustry and interfirm differences in profitability—were combined in the Strategic Planning Institute's PIMS (Profit Impact of Market Strategy) project.[12]

During the 1990s, the focus of strategy analysis shifted from the sources of profit in the external environment to the sources of profit within the firm. Increasingly the resources and capabilities of the firm became regarded as the main source of competitive advantage and the primary basis for formulating strategy.[13] This emphasis on what has been called the *resource-based view of the firm* represented a substantial shift in thinking about strategy. Rather than firms pursuing similar strategies, as in seeking attractive markets and favorable competitive positions, emphasis on internal resources and capabilities has encouraged firms to identify how they are different from their competitors and design strategies that exploit these differences. Michael Porter's answer to the question "What is strategy?" emphasized that: "Competitive strategy is about being different. It means deliberately choosing a different set of activities to deliver a unique mix of value."[14]

During the first decade of the twenty-first century, the principles and practice of strategy have been molded by the uniquely challenging circumstances of a new era. Technology has been a particularly potent force.[15] The beginning of the decade saw the bursting of the TMT (technology, media, telecommunications) bubble and the realization that the "new knowledge economy" and internet-based business models did not require a rewriting of the principles of strategy. Nevertheless, technology continues to reshape industries: digital technologies are associated with standards wars,[16] the emergence of "winner-take-all" markets, [17] and the potential for strategic innovation as firms seek the "blue oceans" of uncontested market space.[18]

In the face of continuous change and relentless competition, strategy becomes less about building positions of sustained competitive advantage and more about developing the responsiveness and flexibility to create successive temporary advantages. Reconfiguring resources and capabilities to achieve such responsiveness typically requires firms to collaborate within networks of strategic alliances.

The continuing traumas of the twenty-first century, including the recession of 2008–9, are encouraging new thinking about the purpose of business. Disillusion with "shareholder value capitalism" has been accompanied by renewed interest in corporate social responsibility, ethics, sustainability of the natural environment and the role of social legitimacy in long-term corporate success.

Figure 1.3 summarizes the main developments in strategic management over the past 60 years.

## Strategic Management Today

### What Is Strategy?

In its broadest sense, strategy is the means by which individuals or organizations achieve their objectives. Table 1.1 presents a number of definitions of the term strategy. Common to definitions of business strategy is the notion that strategy is focused on achieving certain *goals*; that the critical actions that make up a strategy involve *allocation of resources*; and that strategy implies some *consistency*, *integration*, or *cohesiveness* of decisions and actions.

**FIGURE 1.3** Evolution of strategic management: dominant themes

FINANCIAL BUDGETING
- DCF-based capital budgeting
- Financial control through operating budgets

CORPORATE PLANNING
- Medium-term economic forecasting
- Formal corporate planning
- Diversification and quest for synergy
- Creation of corporate planning departments

STRATEGY AS POSITIONING
- Industry analysis
- Market segmentation
- The experience curve
- PIMS analysis
- Planning business portfolios

QUEST FOR COMPETITIVE ADVANTAGE
- Analysis of resources and capabilities
- Shareholder value maximization
- Restructuring and re-engineering
- Alliances

STRATEGY FOR THE NEW ECONOMY
- Strategic innovation
- New business models
- Disruptive technologies

STRATEGY IN THE NEW MILLENNIUM
- CSR and business ethics
- Competing for standards
- Winner-take-all markets
- Global strategies

1950 1960 1970 1980 1990 2000 2009

**TABLE 1.1** Some definitions of strategy

- Strategy: a plan, method, or series of actions designed to achieve a specific goal or effect.

  —*Wordsmyth Dictionary*

- The determination of the long-run goals and objectives of an enterprise, and the adoption of courses of action and the allocation of resources necessary for carrying out these goals.

  —Alfred Chandler, *Strategy and Structure* (Cambridge, MA: MIT Press, 1962)

- Strategy is the pattern of objectives, purposes, or goals and the major policies and plans for achieving these goals, stated in such a way as to define what business the company is in or is to be in and the kind of company it is or is to be.

  —Kenneth Andrews, *The Concept of Corporate Strategy*
  (Homewood, IL: Irwin, 1971)

- Lost Boy:        "Injuns! Let's go get 'em!"
  John Darling:   "Hold on a minute. First we must have a strategy."
  Lost Boy:        "Uhh? What's a *strategy*?"
  John Darling:   "It's, er . . . it's a plan of attack."

  —Walt Disney's *Peter Pan*

Yet, as we have seen, the conception of firm strategy has changed greatly over the past half century. As the business environment has become more unstable and unpredictable, so strategy has become less concerned with detailed plans and more about the quest for success. This is consistent with the starting point to the chapter. If we think back to our three introductory examples—Madonna, General Giap and Lance Armstrong—none wrote detailed strategic plans but all possessed clear ideas of what they wanted to achieve and how they would achieve it. This shift in emphasis from strategy as plan to strategy as direction does not imply any downgrading of the role of strategy. Certainly, in a turbulent environment, strategy must embrace flexibility and responsiveness. But it is precisely in these conditions that strategy becomes more, rather than less, important. When the firm is buffeted by unforeseen threats and where new opportunities are constantly appearing, then strategy becomes a vital tool to navigate the firm through stormy seas.

In an environment of uncertainty and change, a clear sense of direction is essential to the pursuit of objectives. As Michael Porter has emphasized, strategy is not about doing things better—this is the concern of operational effectiveness—strategy is about doing things *differently*; hence, the essence of strategy is *making choices*.[19]

Strategic choices can be distilled to two basic questions:

- *Where* to compete?
- *How* to compete?

The answers to these questions also define the major areas of a firm's strategy: *corporate strategy* and *business strategy*.

## Corporate and Business Strategy

If we start from basics, the purpose of strategy is to achieve certain goals. For the firm, the basic goal is to survive and prosper. Survival, over the long term, requires

**FIGURE 1.4** The sources of superior profitability

that the firm earns a rate of return on its capital that exceeds its cost of capital. There are two possible ways of achieving this. First, the firm may locate within an industry where overall rates of return are attractive. Second, the firm may attain a position of advantage vis-à-vis its competitors within an industry, allowing it to earn a return in excess of the industry average (see Figure 1.4).

These two sources of superior performance define the two basic levels of strategy within an enterprise:

- *Corporate strategy* defines the scope of the firm in terms of the industries and markets in which it competes. Corporate strategy decisions include choice over in diversification, vertical integration, acquisitions and new ventures; and the allocation of resources between the different businesses of the firm.
- *Business strategy* is concerned with how the firm competes within a particular industry or market. If the firm is to prosper within an industry, it must establish a competitive advantage over its rivals. Hence, this area of strategy is also referred to as *competitive strategy.*

This distinction may be expressed in even simpler terms. The basic question facing the firm is: "How do we make money?" The answer to this question corresponds to the two basic strategic choices we identified above: "Where to compete?" ("In which industries and markets should we be?") and "How should we compete?"

The distinction between corporate strategy and business strategy corresponds to the organization structure of most large companies. Corporate strategy is the responsibility of the top management team and the corporate strategy staff. Business strategy is primarily the responsibility of divisional management.

As an integrated approach to firm strategy, this book deals with both business and corporate strategy. However, my primary emphasis will be business strategy. This is because the critical requirement for a company's success is its ability to establish competitive advantage. Hence, issues of business strategy precede those of corporate strategy. At the same time, these two dimensions of strategy are intertwined: the scope of a firm's business has implications for the sources of competitive advantage, and the nature of a firm's competitive advantage determines the range of businesses it can be successful in.

## Describing a Firm's Strategy

These same two questions "Where is the firm competing?" and "How is it competing?" also provide the basis upon which we can describe the strategy that a firm is pursuing. The *where* question has multiple dimensions. It relates to the industry or industries in which the firm is located, the products it supplies, the customer groups it targets, the countries and localities in which it operates and the vertical range of activities it undertakes.

Thus, Coca-Cola's strategy comprises these two elements. With regard to *where*:

- Coca-Cola competes in the soft drinks industry where it supplies concentrate for its branded carbonated drinks (such as Coca-Cola, Sprite, Fanta, Tab and Fresca) and supplies other drinks (such as Minute Maid, Hi-C and Five Alive fruit juices, and Dasani bottled water).
- Geographically, Coca-Cola competes worldwide. Its major markets are the U.S. (27% of sales) followed by Mexico, Brazil, Japan, and China.
- In terms of vertical scope, Coca-Cola's main activities are product development, brand management, and concentrate manufacture and distribution. The production and distribution of its soft drinks are undertaken by its sister company Coca-Cola Enterprises and franchised local bottlers.

With regard to *how*: Coca-Cola pursues a differentiation strategy where it relies on brand image developed through heavy advertising and promotion. It seeks market share leadership through its mass marketing and through close relationships with the leading bottlers in every country where it does business.

However, strategy is not simply about "competing for today"; it is also concerned with "competing for tomorrow." This dynamic concept of strategy involves establishing objectives for the future and determining how they will be achieved. Future objectives relate to the overall purpose of the firm (*mission*), what it seeks to become (*vision*) and specific performance targets.

In the case of Coca-Cola, this dynamic dimension of its strategy is outlined in broad terms in its statements of vision (to refresh the world) and mission which outlines goals in relation to its five Ps: people, products, planet, partners, and profit. More specific objectives are outlined in presentations to analysts: long-term volume growth of 3–4%, revenue growth of 5–6%, and operating profit growth of 6–8%. These objectives are to be achieved through growing sales of still drinks, exploiting growth opportunities in emerging markets, accelerating innovation and building core capabilities.[20]

These two dimensions of strategy—the static and the dynamic—are depicted in Figure 1.5. As we shall see, reconciling these two dimensions of strategy—what Derek Abell calls "competing with dual strategies" and Tushman and O'Reilly refer to as "the challenge of ambidexterity"—is one of the central dilemmas of strategic management.[21]

**FIGURE 1.5** Describing firm strategy: competing in the present, preparing for the future

STATIC

- *Where are we competing?*
  - Product market scope
  - Geographical scope
  - Vertical scope
- *How are we competing?*
  - What is the basis of our competitive advantage?

**COMPETING FOR THE PRESENT**

DYNAMIC

- *What do we want to become?*
  - Vision statement
- *What do we want to achieve?*
  - Mission statement
  - Performance goals
- *How will we get there?*
  - Guidelines for development
  - Priorities for capital expenditure, R&D
  - Growth modes: organic growth, M&A, alliances

**PREPARING FOR THE FUTURE**

## How Is Strategy Made? Design versus Emergence

How companies make strategy has been one of the most hotly debated issues in strategic management. Our emphasis on strategy analysis encourages the view that strategy is the result of managers engaging in deliberate, rational analysis. However, strategy may also emerge through adaptation to circumstances. In discussing Madonna's career, we discerned a consistency and pattern to her career decisions that we described as a strategy, yet there is no evidence that she engaged in any systematic strategic planning. Similarly many successful companies were not products of grand designs—for example Wal-Mart's winning strategy built on large-store formats, hub-and-spoke distribution, small-town locations and employee motivation emerged from Sam Walton's hunches and a series of historical accidents.

Henry Mintzberg is a leading critic of rational approaches to strategy design. He distinguishes *intended*, *realized* and *emergent* strategies. *Intended strategy* is strategy as conceived of by the top management team. Even here, intended strategy is less a product of rational deliberation and more an outcome of negotiation, bargaining and compromise among the many individuals and groups involved in the process. However, *realized strategy*—the actual strategy that is implemented—is only partly related to that which was intended (Mintzberg suggests only 10–30% of intended strategy is realized). The primary determinant of realized strategy is what Mintzberg terms *emergent strategy*—the decisions that emerge from the complex processes in which individual managers interpret the intended strategy and adapt to changing external circumstances.[22] According to Mintzberg, not only is rational design an inaccurate account of how strategies are actually formulated—it is a poor way of making strategy. "The notion that strategy is something that should happen way up there, far removed from the details of running an organization on a daily basis, is one of the great fallacies of conventional strategic management."[23] The emergent approaches to strategy making permit adaptation and learning though continuous interaction between strategy formulation and strategy implementation in which strategy is constantly being adjusted and revised in light of experience.

Honda's successful entry into the US motorcycle market has provided a central battleground between those who view strategy making as primarily a rational, analytical process of deliberate planning (the design school) and those that envisage strategy as emerging from a complex process of organizational decision making (the emergence or learning school of strategy).[24] Boston Consulting Group lauded Honda for its single-minded pursuit of a global strategy based on exploiting economies of scale and learning to establish unassailable cost leadership.[25] However, subsequent interviews with the Honda managers in charge of U.S. market entry revealed a different story: a haphazard entry with little analysis and no clear plan.[26] As Mintzberg observes: "Brilliant as its strategy may have looked after the fact, Honda's managers made almost every conceivable mistake until the market finally hit them over the head with the right formula."[27]

In practice, strategy making almost always involves a combination of centrally driven rational design and decentralized adaptation. The design aspect of strategy comprises a number of organizational processes through which strategy is deliberated, discussed, and decided. In larger companies these include board meetings and a formalized process of strategic planning process supplemented by more broadly participative events such as strategy workshops. I will discuss processes of strategic planning more fully in Chapter 6.

At the same time, strategy is being continually enacted through decisions that are made by every member of the organization—by middle management especially. The decentralized, bottom-up strategy emergence often precedes more formalized strategy formulation. Intel's historic decision to abandon memory chips and concentrate on microprocessors was initiated by incremental decisions taken by business unit and plant managers that were subsequently promulgated by top management into strategy.[28]

In all the companies I am familiar with, strategic planning combines design and emergence—a process that I have referred to as "planned emergence."[29] The balance between the two depends greatly upon the stability and predictability of a company's business environment. The Roman Catholic Church and the U.S. Postal Service inhabit relatively stable environments. For Google, Al Qaida and Zimbabwe Banking Corporation, strategic planning will inevitably be restricted to a few principles and guidelines; the rest must emerge as circumstances unfold.

As the business environment becomes more turbulent and less predictable, so strategy making becomes more concerned with guidelines and less with specific decisions. Bain & Company advocate the use of strategic principles— "pithy, memorable distillations of strategy that guide and empower employees"—to combine consistent focus with adaptability and responsiveness.[30] America's most successful airline, Southwest, encapsulates its strategy in a simple statement: "Meet customers' short-haul travel needs at fares competitive with the cost of automobile travel." Kathy Eisenhart and Don Sull make a similar argument when they advocate "simple rules" as the basis for successful strategies in fast-moving businesses. For example, Lego evaluates new product proposals by applying a checklist of rules: "Does the product have the Lego look?" "Will children learn while having fun?" "Does it stimulate creativity?"[31]

We shall return to the role of rules and principles to guide an organization's evolution and coordinate the decisions of its many members in our final chapter where we explore some of the implications of complexity theory for strategic management.

## Identifying a Company's Strategy

Where do we look to find a company's strategy? Strategy is located in three places: in the heads of the chief executive and senior managers, in their articulations of strategy in speeches and written documents, and in the decisions through which strategy is enacted. Only the last two are observable.

While the most explicit statements of strategy—in board minutes and strategic planning documents—are almost invariably confidential, most companies—public companies in particular—see value in communicating their strategy to employees, customers, investors, and business partners—and, inevitably, to the public at large. Collis and Rukstad identify a hierarchy of strategy statements:

- The mission statement is the basic statement of organizational purpose, it addresses "Why we exist."
- A statement of principles or values states "What we believe in and how we will behave."
- The vision statement projects "What we want to be."
- The strategy statement articulates "What our competitive game plan will be." Collis and Rukstad argue that this should comprise three definitive components of strategy: *objectives*, *scope* (where we will compete) and *advantage* (how we will compete).[32]

A version of some or all of these statements is typically found on the corporate pages of companies' websites. More detailed statements of strategy—including qualitative and quantitative medium-term targets—are often found in top management presentations to analysts which are typically included in the "for investors" pages of company websites.

More detailed information on scope (*where?*) and advantage (*how?*) can be found in companies' annual reports. For U.S. corporations, the description of the business that forms Item 1 of the 10-K annual report to the SEC is particularly informative about strategy.

Strategy capsules 1.6 and 1.7 provide summary statements of strategy by Apple Inc. and Nokia Corp.

---

**STRATEGY CAPSULE 1.6**

## Apple Computer, Inc.: Business Strategy

The Company is committed to bringing the best personal computing and music experience to students, educators, creative professionals, businesses, government agencies, and consumers through its innovative hardware, software, peripherals, services and internet offerings. The Company's business strategy leverages its unique ability, through the design and development of its own operating system, hardware, and many software applications and technologies, to bring to its customers new products and solutions with superior ease-of-use, seamless integration, and innovative industrial design. The Company believes continual investment in research and development is critical to facilitate innovation of new and improved products and technologies. Besides updates to its existing line of personal computers and related software, services, peripherals, and networking solutions, the Company continues to capitalize on the convergence of digital consumer electronics and the computer by creating innovations like the iPod and iTunes Music Store. The Company's strategy also includes expanding its distribution network to reach more of its targeted customers effectively and provide them a high-quality sales and after-sales support experience.

*Source:* Apple Computer, Inc., 10-K Report, 2005.

---

**STRATEGY CAPSULE 1.7**

# Nokia's Strategy

## VISION

Our vision is a world where everyone can be connected. Everyone has a need to communicate and share. Nokia helps people to fulfill this need and we help people feel close to what matters to them. We focus on providing consumers with very human technology—technology that is intuitive, a joy to use, and beautiful.

We are living in an era where connectivity is becoming truly ubiquitous. The communications industry continues to change and the internet is at the center of this transformation. Today, the internet is Nokia's quest.

Nokia's strategy relies on growing, transforming, and building the Nokia business to ensure its future success.

## STRATEGY

We seek to grow, transform and build the Nokia business based on our business strategies and strategic capabilities.

Our business strategies reflect the primary focus of each of Nokia's business areas as follows:

- lead and win in mobile devices
- grow consumer internet services
- accelerate adoption of business solutions
- leverage scale and transform solutions in infrastructure.

Our strategic capabilities are the priority areas where we are investing with the aim of gaining a competitive advantage. The following capabilities can be shared among our several business areas:

- consumer understanding
- brand
- technology and architecture
- channels and supply chain.

*Sources:* www.nokia.com/A4126317 (accessed July 2, 2009); U.S. Securities and Exchange Commission, Nokia Form 20-F 2007 (March 20, 2008): 27–28.

However, the usefulness of public statements of strategy is limited by their role as public relations vehicles—this is particularly evident in vision and mission statements which are frequently grandiose and platitudinous. Hence, explicit statements of strategy need to be checked against decisions and actions:

- Where is the company investing its money? Notes to financial statements provide detailed breakdowns of capital expenditure by region and by business segment.

- What technologies are the company developing? Identifying the patents that a company has filed (using the online databases of the U.S. and E.U. patent offices) indicates the technological trajectory it is pursuing.

- What new products have been released, major investment projects initiated, and top management hired? A company's press releases usually announce these strategic decisions.

To identify a firm's strategy it is necessary to draw upon multiple sources of information in order to build an overall picture of what the company says it is doing and what it is actually doing. We will return to this topic when we discuss competitive intelligence in Chapter 4.

## Multiple Roles of Strategy

The transition from corporate planning to strategic management has involved strategy moving from technocratic planning departments to the center of corporate leadership. As a result, strategy occupies multiple roles within an organization.

*Strategy as Decision Support*  I have described strategy as a pattern or theme that gives coherence to the decisions of an individual or organization. But why can't individuals or organizations make optimal decisions in the absence of such a unifying theme? Consider the 1997 "man-versus-computer" chess epic in which Garry Kasparov was defeated by IBM's "Deep Blue." Deep Blue did not need strategy. Its phenomenal memory and computing power allowed it to identify its optimal moves based on a huge decision tree.[33] Kasparov—although the world's greatest chess player—was subject to *bounded rationality*: his decision analysis was subject to the cognitive limitations that constrain all human beings.[34] For chess players, a strategy offers guidelines and decision criteria that assist positioning and help create opportunities.

Strategy improves decision making in several ways. First, strategy simplifies decision making by *constraining* the range of decision alternatives considered and by acting as a *heuristic*—a rule of thumb that reduces the search required to find an acceptable solution to a decision problem. Second, a strategy-making process permits the knowledge of different individuals to be pooled and integrated. Third, a strategy-making process facilitates the use of analytic tools—the frameworks and techniques that we will encounter in the ensuing chapters of this book.

*Strategy as a Coordinating Device*  The greatest challenge of managing an organization is coordinating the actions of different organizational members. Strategy can promote coordination in several ways. First, it is a communication device. Statements of strategy are a powerful means through which the CEO can communicate the identity, goals and positioning of the company to all organizational members. However, communication alone is not enough. For coordination to be effective, buy-in is essential from the different groups that make up the organization. The strategic planning process can provide a forum in which views are exchanged and consensus developed. Once formulated, the implementation of strategy through goals, commitments and performance targets that are monitored over the strategic planning period also provides a mechanism to ensure that the organization moves forward in a consistent direction.

*Strategy as Target*   Strategy is forward looking. It is concerned not only with how the firm will compete now but also with what the firm will become in the future. A key purpose of a forward-looking strategy is not only to establish a direction of the firm's development but also to set aspirations that can motivate and inspire members of the organization. Gary Hamel and C. K. Prahalad use the term "strategic intent" to describe the articulation of a desired leadership position. They argue that: ". . . strategic intent creates an extreme misfit between resources and ambitions. Top management then challenges the organization to close the gap by building new competitive advantages."[35] The implication they draw is that strategy should be less about fit and resource allocation, and more about *stretch* and *resource leverage*.[36] The evidence from Toyota, Virgin, and Southwest Airlines is that resource scarcity may engender ambition, innovation, and a "success-against-the-odds" culture. Jim Collins and Jerry Porras make a similar point: U.S. companies that have been sector leaders for 50 years or more—Merck, Walt Disney, 3M, IBM, and Ford—have all generated commitment and drive through setting "Big, Hairy, Ambitious Goals."[37] Striving, inspirational goals are typical of most organizations' statements of vision and mission. One of the best known is the goal set by President Kennedy for NASA's space program: ". . . before this decade is out, of landing a man on the moon and returning him safely to Earth." British Airways aspires to be "The World's Favourite Airline," while Coca-Cola's drive for growth is driven by the quest to "have a Coca-Cola within arm's reach of everyone in the world."

## The Role of Analysis in Strategy Formulation

Despite the criticism of rational, analytical approaches to strategy formulation by Henry Mintzberg and others, the approach of this book is to emphasize analytic approaches to strategy formulation. This is not because I wish to downplay the role of intuition, creativity and spontaneity—these qualities are essential ingredients of successful strategies. Nevertheless, whether strategy formulation is formal or informal, whether strategies are deliberate or emergent, systematic analysis is a vital input into the strategy process. Without analysis, strategic decisions are susceptible to power battles, individual whims, fads and wishful thinking. Concepts, theories, and analytic tools are complements not substitutes for experience, commitment and creativity. Their role is to provide frameworks for organizing discussion, processing information and opinions and assisting consensus.

This is not to endorse current approaches to strategy analysis. Strategic management is still a young field and the existing toolbox of concepts and techniques remains woefully inadequate. Our challenge is to do better. If existing analytical techniques do not adequately address the problems of strategy making and strategy implementation under conditions of uncertainty, technological change and complexity, we need to augment and extend our analytical toolkit. In the course of the book you will encounter concepts such as real options, tacit knowledge, hypercompetition, complementarity, and complexity that will help you address more effectively the challenges that firms are facing in today's turbulent business environment. We must also recognize the nature of strategy analysis. Unlike many of the analytical techniques in accounting, finance, market research, or production management, strategy analysis does not generate solutions to problems. It does not yield rules, algorithms, or formulae that tell us the optimal strategy to adopt. The strategic questions that companies face (like those that we face in our own careers and lives) are simply too complex to be programmed.

The purpose of strategy analysis is not to provide answers but to help us understand the issues. Most of the analytic techniques introduced in this book are frameworks that allow us to identify, classify and understand the principal factors relevant to strategic decisions. Such frameworks are invaluable in allowing us to come to terms with the complexities of strategy decisions. In some instances, the most useful contribution may be in assisting us to make a start on the problem. By guiding us to the questions we need to answer and by providing a framework for organizing the information gathered, strategy analysis places us in a superior position to a manager who relies exclusively on experience and intuition. Finally, analytic frameworks and techniques can improve our flexibility as managers. The analysis in this book is general in its applicability; it is not specific to particular industries, companies, or situations. Hence, it can help increase our confidence and effectiveness in understanding and responding to new situations and new circumstances. By encouraging depth of understanding in fundamental issues concerning competitive advantage, customer needs, organizational capabilities, and the basis of competition, the concepts, frameworks and techniques in this book will encourage rather than constrain innovation and flexibility.

## Summary

This chapter has covered a great deal of ground—I hope that you are not suffering from indigestion. If you are feeling a little overwhelmed, not to worry: we shall be returning to most of the themes and issues raised in this chapter in the subsequent chapters of the book.

The next stage is to delve further into the basic strategy framework shown in Figure 1.2. The elements of this framework—goals and values, the industry environment, resources and capabilities, and structure and systems—comprise the basic components of strategy analysis. The next part of the book devotes separate chapters to each. We then deploy these tools in the analysis of competitive advantage (Part III), in the formulation and implementation of business strategies in different industry contexts (Part IV), and then in the development of corporate strategy (Part V). Figure 1.6 shows the framework for the book.

**FIGURE 1.6** The structure of the book

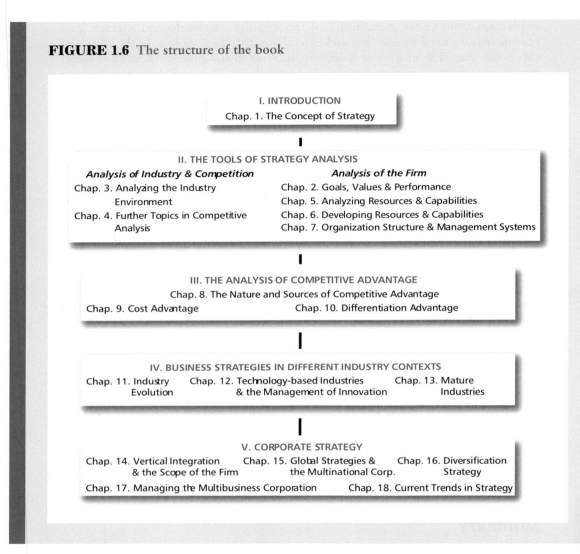

## Self-Study Questions

1   In relation to the four characteristics of successful strategies (clear, consistent, long-term objectives; profound understanding of the environment; objective appraisal of resources and effective implementation), assess the U.S. strategy towards Iraq during 2003–9.

2   The discussion of the evolution of business strategy ("From Corporate Planning to Strategic Management") established that the characteristics of a firm's strategic plans and its strategic planning process are strongly influenced by the volatility and unpredictability of its external environment. On this basis, what differences would you expect in the strategic plans and strategic planning processes of Coca-Cola Company and Google Inc.?

**3**  I have noted that a firm's strategy can be described in terms of the answers to two questions: "Where are we competing?" and "How are we competing?" Applying these two questions, provide a concise description of Madonna's career strategy (see Strategy Capsule 1.1).

**4**  Using the structure outlined in Figure 1.5, describe the strategy of the business school you attend?

**5**  What is your career strategy for the next five years? To what extent does your strategy fit with your long-term goals, the characteristics of the external environment and your own strengths and weaknesses?

**6**  In relation to each of the "multiple roles of strategy" outlined above, what use (if any) is Nokia's statement of strategy as outlined in Strategy Capsule 1.7?

# Notes

1  Col. Harry G. Summers Jr., *On Strategy* (Novato, CA: Presidio Press, 1982): 1.

2  Vo Nguyen Giap, *Selected Writings* (Hanoi: Foreign Language Publishing House, 1977).

3  J. Cameron, *Here Is Your Enemy* (New York: Holt, Rinehart & Winston, 1966).

4  P. F. Drucker, "Managing Oneself," *Harvard Business Review* (March–April 1999): 65–74.

5  Stephen Covey (*The Seven Habits of Highly Effective People*, Simon & Schuster, 1989) advises us to start at the end—to visualize our own funerals and imagine what we would like the funeral speakers to say about us and our lives. On this basis, he recommends that we develop lifetime mission statements based on the multiple roles that we occupy in life.

6  Sun Tzu, *The Art of Strategy: A New Translation of Sun Tzu's Classic "The Art of War,"* trans. R. L. Wing (New York: Doubleday, 1988).

7  See: R. Evered "So What is Strategy," *Long Range Planning* 16, no. 3 (June 1983): 57–72; E. Clemons and J. Santamaria, "Maneuver Warfare," *Harvard Business Review* (April 2002): 46–53.

8  On the contribution of game theory to business strategy analysis, see F. M. Fisher, "Games Economists Play: A Non-cooperative View," *RAND Journal of Economics* 20 (Spring 1989): 113–24; and C. F. Camerer, "Does Strategy Research Need Game Theory?" *Strategic Management Journal* 12, Special Issue (Winter 1991): 137–52.

9  During the late 1950s, *Harvard Business Review* featured a number of articles on corporate planning, for example D. W. Ewing, "Looking Around: Long-range Business Planning," *Harvard Business Review* (July–August 1956): 135–46; B. Payne, "Steps in Long-range Planning," *Harvard Business Review* (March–April 1957): 95–101.

10  M. E. Porter, *Competitive Strategy* (New York: Free Press, 1980).

11  Boston Consulting Group, *Perspectives on Experience* (Boston: Boston Consulting Group, 1978).

12  R. D. Buzzell and B. T. Gale, *The PIMS Principles* (New York: Free Press, 1987).

13  R. M. Grant, "The Resource-based Theory of Competitive Advantage: Implications for Strategy Formulation," *California Management Review* 33 (Spring 1991): 114–35; D. J. Collis and C. Montgomery, "Competing on Resources: Strategy in the 1990s," *Harvard Business Review* (July–August 1995): 119–28.

14  M. E. Porter, "What is Strategy?" *Harvard Business Review* (November–December 1996): 64.

15  C. Christensen, *The Innovator's Dilemma* (Boston: Harvard Business School Press, 1997).

16  C. Shapiro and H. R. Varian, *Information Rules* (Boston: Harvard Business School Press, 1998).

17  R. H. Frank and P. J. Cook, *The Winner-Take-All Society* (New York: Penguin, 1997).

18  W. C. Kim and R. Mauborgne, "Creating New Market Space," *Harvard Business Review* (January–February 1999): 83–93.

19  M. E. Porter, "What is Strategy?" op. cit.

20  Coca-Cola Company, Inc. Presentation to Lehman Brothers Conference, September 3, 2008 (http://media.corporate-ir.net/media_files/irol/94/94566/presentations/KO_Lehman_Conference_090308.pdf, accessed July 2, 2009).

21  D. F. Abell, *Managing with Dual Strategies* (New York: Free Press, 1993); M. L. Tushman and C. A. O'Reilly, "The Ambidextrous Organization," *Harvard Business Review* (April 2004): 74–81.

22  See H. Mintzberg, "Patterns of Strategy Formulation," *Management Science* 24 (1978): 934–48; "Of Strategies:

Deliberate and Emergent," *Strategic Management Journal* 6 (1985): 257–72; and *Mintzberg on Management: Inside Our Strange World of Organizations* (New York: Free Press, 1988).

23 H. Mintzberg, "The Fall and Rise of Strategic Planning," *Harvard Business Review* (January–February 1994): 107–14.

24 The two views of Honda are captured in two Harvard cases: *Honda [A]* (Boston: Harvard Business School, Case No. 384049, 1989) and *Honda [B]* (Boston: Harvard Business School, Case No. 384050, 1989).

25 Boston Consulting Group, *Strategy Alternatives for the British Motorcycle Industry* (London: Her Majesty's Stationery Office, 1975).

26 R. T. Pascale, "Perspective on Strategy: The Real Story Behind Honda's Success," *California Management Review* 26, no. 3 (Spring 1984): 47–72.

27 H. Mintzberg, "Crafting Strategy," *Harvard Business Review* 65 (July–August 1987): 70.

28 R. A. Burgelman and A. Grove, "Strategic Dissonance," *California Management Review* 38 (Winter 1996): 8–28.

29 R. M. Grant, "Strategic Planning in a Turbulent Environment: Evidence from the Oil and Gas Majors," *Strategic Management Journal* 14 (June 2003): 491–517.

30 O. Gadiesh and J. Gilbert, "Transforming Corner-office Strategy into Frontline Action," *Harvard Business Review* (May 2001): 73–80.

31 K. M. Eisenhardt and D. N. Sull, "Strategy as Simple Rules," *Harvard Business Review* (January 2001): 107–16.

32 D. J. Collis and M.G. Rukstad, "Can You Say What Your Strategy Is?" *Harvard Business Review* (April 2008): 63–73.

33 "Strategic Intensity: A Conversation with Garry Kasparov," *Harvard Business Review* (April 2005): 105–13.

34 The concept of bounded rationality was developed by Herbert Simon ("A Behavioral Model of Rational Choice," *Quarterly Journal of Economics* 69 (1955): 99–118).

35 G. Hamel and C. K. Prahalad, "Strategic Intent," *Harvard Business Review* (May–June 1989): 63–77.

36 G. Hamel and C. K. Prahalad, "Strategy as Stretch and Leverage," *Harvard Business Review* (March–April 1993): 75–84.

37 J. C. Collins and J. I. Porras, *Built to Last: Successful Habits of Visionary Companies* (New York: HarperCollins, 1995).

# II

# THE TOOLS
# OF STRATEGY
# ANALYSIS

# 2 Goals, Values, and Performance

*The strategic aim of a business is to earn a return on capital, and if in any particular case the return in the long run is not satisfactory, then the deficiency should be corrected or the activity abandoned for a more favorable one.*

—ALFRED P. SLOAN JR., *MY YEARS WITH GENERAL MOTORS*

## OUTLINE

- ◆ Introduction and Objectives

- ◆ Strategy as a Quest for Value
  - In Whose Interest? Shareholders versus Stakeholders
  - What Is Profit?
  - From Accounting Profit to Economic Profit
  - Linking Profit to Enterprise Value
  - Applying DCF Analysis to Valuing Companies, Businesses and Strategies

- ◆ Strategy and Real Options
  - Strategy as Options Management

- ◆ Putting Performance Analysis into Practice
  - Appraising Current and Past Performance
  - Performance Diagnosis
  - Can Past Performance Guide Strategies for the Future?
  - Setting Performance Targets

# Introduction and Objectives

Our framework for strategy analysis (Figure 1.2) comprises four components: the firm's goals and values, its resources and capabilities, its structure and management systems and its industry environment. The chapters that form Part II of the book develop these four components of strategy analysis. We begin with goals and values and, by extension, the performance of the firm in attaining its goals.

Firms possess multiple goals. However, for the purpose of strategy analysis, we focus upon a single goal: the maximization of the value of the firm. The value of the firm is determined, primarily, by the profits it earns over its lifetime—hence, business strategy becomes a quest for profit. Most of the frameworks and techniques of strategy analysis that we will cover are concerned with identifying and exploiting the sources of profitability open to the firm.

This focus on profitability and value creation means that we will draw upon some of the tools of financial analysis for the purposes of performance appraisal, performance diagnosis, and target setting. At the same time we shall recognize that, while profit is the most useful measure of firm performance, firms are motivated by goals other than profit. Indeed, the companies that are most successful in generating profits over the long run are typically those driven by ambitions other than profit. Profit is the life-blood of the organization, but it is not a goal that inspires organizational members to outstanding achievement. Moreover, for a firm to survive and generate profit over the long run requires responsiveness to, and accommodation with, its social, political, and natural environment.

By the time you have completed this chapter you will be able to:

◆ appreciate the main arguments in the debate over shareholder versus stakeholder goals for the firm;

◆ understand the relationship between profit, cash flow and value;

◆ use financial and strategic information to diagnose the sources of a company's performance problems;

◆ translate the overall goals of long-term profit maximization into meaningful performance targets that can be measured and monitored;

◆ understand the linkages between financial analysis and strategic analysis, and how they can be used to complement one another;

◆ comprehend the role of values, mission and vision in formulating and implementing strategy.

## Strategy as a Quest for Value

Business is about creating *value*. *Value* is the monetary worth of a product or asset. The purpose of business is, first, to create value for customers and, second, to extract some of that customer value in the form of profit, thereby creating value for the firm.

Value can be created in two ways: by production and by commerce. Production creates value by physically transforming products that are less valued by consumers into products that are more valued by consumers—turning clay into coffee mugs, for example. Commerce creates value not by physically transforming products but by repositioning them in space and time. Trade involves transferring products from individuals and places where they are less valued to individuals and locations where they are more valued. Similarly, speculation involves transferring products from a point in time where the product is valued less to a point in time where it is valued more. Thus, the essence of commerce is creating value through arbitrage across time and space.[1]

The difference between the value of a firm's output and the cost of its material inputs is its *value added*. Value added is equal to the sum of all the income paid to the suppliers of factors of production. Thus:

value added = sales revenue from output—cost of material inputs

= wages/salaries + interest + rent + royalties/license fees

+ taxes + dividends + retained profit

### In Whose Interest? Shareholders versus Stakeholders

The value added created by firms is distributed among different parties: employees (wages and salaries), lenders (interest), landlords (rent), government (taxes) and owners (profit). In addition, firms also create value for their customers to the extent that the satisfaction customers gain exceeds the price they pay (they derive *consumer surplus*). It is tempting, therefore, to think of the firm as operating for the benefit of multiple constituencies. This view of the business enterprise as a coalition of interest groups where top management's role to balance these different—often conflicting—interests is referred to as the *stakeholder* approach to the firm.[2]

The notion of the corporation balancing the interests of multiple stakeholders has a long tradition, especially in Asia and continental Europe. By contrast, most English-speaking countries have endorsed *shareholder capitalism*, where companies' overriding duty is to produce profits for owners. These differences are reflected in international differences in companies' legal obligations. In the U.S., Canada, the U.K. and Australia, company boards are required to act in the interests of shareholders. In continental European countries, companies are legally required to take account of the interests of employees, the state and the enterprise as a whole. Whether companies should operate exclusively in the interests of their owners or should also pursue the goals of other stakeholders is an ongoing debate. During the 1990s, "Anglo-Saxon" shareholder capitalism was in the ascendant—many continental European and Japanese companies changed their strategies and corporate governance to increase their responsiveness to shareholder interests. However, during the twenty-first century, shareholder value maximization became associated with short-termism, financial manipulation (Enron, World.com), excessive CEO compensation, and the failures of risk management that precipitated the 2008–9 financial crisis. The responsibilities of business to employees, customers, society and the natural environment are central ethical and social issues. Nevertheless, in order to make progress in developing analytical tools for designing successful strategies I shall adopt the simplifying assumption that companies operate in the interests of their owners by seeking to maximize profits over the long term. Why do I make this assumption and how do I justify it? Let me point to four key considerations:

- *Competition*. Competition erodes profitability. As competition increases, the interests of different stakeholders converge around the goal of survival. Survival requires that, over the long term, the firm earns a rate of profit that covers its cost of capital otherwise it will not be able to replace its assets. Over half of America's publicly listed companies do not cover their cost of capital.[3] Across many sectors of industry, the heat of international competition is such that few companies have the luxury of pursuing goals that diverge from profit maximization.

- *The market for corporate control*. Management teams that fail to maximize the profits of their companies will be replaced by teams that do. In the "market for corporate control" companies that underperform financially suffer a declining share price that attracts acquirers—other public companies or private equity funds. In addition, activist investors, both individuals (Carl Icahn, Kirk Kerkorian) and funds (such as California Public Employees' Retirement System, The Children's Investment Fund) put pressure on boards of directors to improve shareholder returns. One result has been increased turnover of chief executives.[4]

- *Convergence of stakeholder interests*. Even beyond a common interest in the survival of the firm, there is likely to be more community of interests than conflict of interests among different stakeholders. Profitability over the long-term requires loyalty from employees, trusting relationships with suppliers and customers, and support from governments and communities. The argument that firms require legitimacy in order to survive and prosper is reinforced by evidence that firms that pursue ethical principles and corporate social responsibility achieve superior financial performance.[5]

● *Simplicity*. A key problem of the stakeholder approach is that considering multiple goals and specifying tradeoffs between them vastly increases the complexity of decision making.[6] Virtually all the major tools of business decision making, from pricing rules to discounted cash flow analysis, are rooted in the assumption of profit maximization. Adopting stakeholder goals risks opening the door to political wrangling and management paralysis.

Assuming that firm strategy is directed primarily toward making profit doesn't mean that we have to accept that profit is the sole motivation driving business enterprises. As we noted in the previous chapter, the goals driving the architects of the world's great enterprises—Henry Ford at Ford Motor Company, Bill Gates at Microsoft, and Nicholas Hayek of Swatch—are seldom financial. The dominant drivers tend to be the fulfillment of a vision and the desire to make a difference in the world. Nevertheless, even when business goals transcend mere money making, their achievement requires enterprises that are commercially successful—this requires the adoption of strategies that generate profit.

## What Is Profit?

Thus far, we have referred to firms' quest for profit in loose terms. It is time to look more carefully at what we mean by profit and how it relates to shareholder value.

Profit is the surplus of revenues over costs available for distribution to the owners of the firm. But, if profit maximization is to be a realistic goal, the firm must know what profit is and how to measure it. Otherwise, instructing managers to maximize profit offers little guidance. What is the firm to maximize: total profit or rate of profit? Over what time period? With what kind of adjustment for risk? And what is profit anyway—accounting profit, cash flow, or economic profit? The ambiguity is apparent once we consider the profit performance of companies. Table 2.1 shows that ranking companies by profitability depends critically on how profitability is measured.

## From Accounting Profit to Economic Profit

A major problem of accounting profit is that it combines two types of returns: the *normal return to capital* that rewards investors for the use of their capital; and *economic profit*, which is the pure surplus available after all inputs (including capital) have been paid for. Economic profit represents a purer and more reliable measure of profit that is a better measure of performance. To distinguish economic profit from accounting profit, economic profit is often referred to as *rent* or *economic rent*.

A widely used measure of economic profit is *economic value added* (EVA), devised and popularized by the New York consulting firm Stern Stewart & Company.[7] Economic value added is measured as net operating profit after tax (NOPAT) less cost of capital, where cost of capital is calculated as capital employed *multiplied by* the weighted average cost of capital (WACC).

**TABLE 2.1** Performance of the world's biggest companies using different profitability measures (2007)

| Company | Market capitalization[a] ($ bn) | Net income[a] ($ bn) | Return on sales[b] (%) | Return on equity[c] (%) | Return on assets[d] (%) | Return to shareholders[e] (%) |
|---|---|---|---|---|---|---|
| ExxonMobil | 453 | 40.61 | 17.42 | 33.35 | 29.69 | 24.30 |
| PetroChina | 424 | 20.75 | 24.48 | 19.99 | 18.85 | 28.90 |
| General Electric | 370 | 22.21 | 15.40 | 19.22 | 7.46 | 2.60 |
| Gazprom | 300 | 26.11 | 38.66 | 16.11 | 10.33 | 103.50 |
| China Mobile | 298 | 12.41 | 36.21 | 23.32 | 22.02 | 21.50 |
| Microsoft | 264 | 14.07 | 39.41 | 48.73 | 30.90 | 20.80 |
| AT&T | 231 | 11.95 | 15.31 | 10.36 | 7.40 | 20.50 |
| Royal Dutch Shell | 220 | 31.33 | 14.22 | 25.28 | 15.12 | 20.10 |
| Procter & Gamble | 216 | 10.34 | 19.25 | 17.38 | 11.86 | 16.60 |
| Wal-Mart Stores | 211 | 12.73 | 5.33 | 19.70 | 13.45 | 4.70 |
| Berkshire Hathaway | 207 | 13.21 | 17.05 | 10.94 | 8.08 | 28.70 |
| Nestlé | 197 | 10.72 | 12.57 | 20.99 | 13.10 | 31.60 |

*Notes*

[a] Source: *Financial Times*.

[b] Pretax profit as a percentage of sales revenues. Source: Hoovers

[c] Net income as a percentage of (year end) shareholders' equity. Source: Hoovers.

[d] Operating income as a percentage of (year end) total assets. Source: Hoovers.

[e] Dividend + share price appreciation during 2007. Source: *Fortune*.

Economic profit has two main advantages over accounting profit as a performance measure. First, it sets a more demanding performance discipline for managers. At many capital intensive companies seemingly healthy profits disappear once cost of capital is taken into account.

Second, using economic profit improves the allocation of capital between the different businesses of the firm by taking account of the real costs of more capital intensive businesses (see Strategy Capsule 2.1).

### STRATEGY CAPSULE 2.1

# Economic Value Added at Diageo plc.

At Guinness-to-Johnny-Walker drinks giant Diageo, EVA transformed the way in which Diageo measured its performance, allocated its capital and advertising expenditures, and evaluated its managers.

Taking account of the costs of the capital tied up in slow-maturing, vintage drinks such as Talisker and Lagavulin malt whisky, Hennessey cognac, and Dom Perignon champagne showed that these high-margin drinks were often not as profitable as the company had believed. The result was that Diageo's advertising expenditures were reallocated towards Smirnoff vodka, Gordon's gin, Bailey's and other drinks that could be sold within weeks of distillation.

Once managers had to report profits after deduction of the cost of the capital tied up in their businesses, they took measures to reduce their capital bases and make their assets work harder. At Diageo's Pillsbury food business, the economic profit of every product and every major customer was scrutinized. The result was the elimination of many products and efforts

make marginal customers more profitable. Ultimately, EVA analysis resulted in Diageo selling Pillsbury to General Foods. This was followed by the sale of Diageo's Burger King chain to Texas Pacific, a private equity group.

Value-based management was extended throughout the organization by making EVA the primary determinant of the incentive pay earned by 1400 Diageo managers.

*Sources:* John McGrath, "Tracking Down Value," *Financial Times Mastering Management Review*, December 1998; www.diageo.com.

## Linking Profit to Enterprise Value

There is also the problem of time. Once we consider multiple periods of time, then profit maximization means maximizing the net present value of profits over the lifetime of the firm.

Hence, profit maximization translates into maximizing the value of the firm. The value of the firm is calculated in the same way as any other asset: it is the net present value (NPV) of the returns that the asset generates. The relevant returns are the cash flows to the firm. Hence, firms are valued using the same discounted cash flow (DCF) methodology that we apply to the valuation of investment projects. Thus, the value of an enterprise ($V$) is the sum of its free cash flows ($C$) in each year $t$, discounted at the enterprise's cost of capital ($r$).[8] The relevant cost of capital is the weighted average cost of capital ($r_{e+d}$) that averages the cost of equity ($r_e$) and the cost of debt ($r_d$):

$$V = \sum_t \frac{C_t}{(1 + r_{e+d})^t}$$

where *free cash flow* (C) is measured as:

> net operating profit + depreciation—taxes—investment in fixed and working capital

To maximize its value, a firm must maximize its future net cash flows (its *free cash flow*) while also managing its finances to minimize its cost of capital.

This value-maximizing approach implies that *cash flow* rather than *accounting profit* is the relevant performance measure. In practice, valuing companies by discounting economic profit gives the same result as by discounting net cash flows. The difference is in the treatment of the capital consumed by the business. The cash flow approach deducts capital at the time when the capital expenditure is made; the

EVA approach follows the accounting convention of charging capital as it is consumed (through charging depreciation). In principle, a full DCF approach is the most satisfactory approach to valuing companies. In practice, however, for DCF analysis to be meaningful requires forecasting cash flows several years ahead, since cash flow for a single year is a poor indicator of underlying profitability. Companies that are profitable and growing fast are likely to have negative cash flows. The preference of many financial analysts for cash-based accounting is also based on the fact that cash flows are less easily manipulated by company managers for cosmetic purposes than are accounting profits. For the same reason, operating earnings, EBIT (earnings before interest and tax) and EBITDA (earnings before interest, tax, depreciation, and amortization) are often preferred to net income as an indicator of profit.

If financial forecasts can only be made for a few years out, then economic profit is usually preferable to free cash flow as a performance indicator. Economic profit shows the surplus being generated by the firm in each year, whereas free cash flow depends on management choices over the level of capital expenditure. Thus, a firm can easily boost its free cash flow by slashing capital expenditures.

*Enterprise Value and Shareholder Value*    How does maximizing enterprise value relate to the much-lauded goal of *maximizing shareholder value*? In the 1950s, Modigliani and Miller laid the foundations of modern financial theory by showing that the value of a company's assets must equal the value of the claims against those assets.[9] Hence, for public companies, the DCF value of the firm is equal to the market value of the firm's securities (plus any other financial claims such as debt and pension fund deficits). Thus, shareholder value is calculated by subtracting the debt (and other non-equity financial claims) from the DCF value of the firm.

Does enterprise value less debt really equal the stock market value of a firm's equity? So long as full information about a firm's prospects reaches the stock market and this information is efficiently reflected in stock prices—yes. But isn't the stock market subject to bubbles, fads, and crashes? Yes—but this instability is a reflection of volatile expectations of companies' future cash flows. Our emphasis in this book will be on maximization of enterprise value rather than maximization of shareholder value. This is principally for convenience: distinguishing debt from equity is not always straightforward due to the presence of preference stock and convertible debt, while junk bonds share the characteristics of both equity and debt. Also, focusing on the value of the enterprise as a whole assists us in identifying the fundamental drivers of firm value. In practice, however, maximization of enterprise value and maximization of shareholder value mean much the same in terms of our strategy analysis.

## Applying DCF Analysis to Valuing Companies, Businesses and Strategies

*Applying DCF to Uncertain Future Cash Flows*    The biggest difficulty in using DCF analysis to value companies and business units is forecasting cash flows sufficiently far into the future. Given the level of uncertainty affecting most businesses, even one-year forecasts of profits and cash flows may be difficult. To estimate future cash flows we may need to make assumptions. For example in a stable growth business (the sole dairy in an expanding village) it may be reasonable to assume that the current year's cash flow ($C_0$) will grow at a constant rate ($g$) to infinity. In this case, the above equation becomes:

$$V = \frac{C_0}{(r_{e+d} - g)^t}$$

A slightly more sophisticated approach is to forecast free cash flow over the medium term—say five years—then to calculate a horizon value ($H$) based either on the book value of the firm at that time or on some more arbitrary forecast of cash flows beyond the medium term:

$$V = C_0 + \frac{C_1}{(1 + r)^1} + \frac{C_2}{(1 + r)^2} + \frac{C_3}{(1 + r)^3} + \frac{C_4}{(1 + r)^4} + \frac{H_4}{(1 + r)^4}$$

*Valuing Strategies* The same approach used to value companies and business units can be applied to evaluate alternative strategies. Thus, different strategy options can be appraised by forecasting the cash flows under each strategy and then selecting the strategy that produces the highest NPV.[10] Since the early 1990s, companies have increasingly integrated value analysis into their strategic planning processes. At PepsiCo, for example, value maximization provides the basis on which strategic plans are formulated, divisional and business unit targets are set and performance is monitored. A key merit of value maximization is its consistency. The same DCF methodology is used to value individual projects, individual business units, alternative business strategies and the company as a whole.

Applying enterprise value analysis to appraising business strategies involves several steps:

- Identify strategy alternatives (the simplest approach is to compare the current strategy with the preferred alternative strategy).
- Estimate the cash flows associated with each strategy.
- Estimate the implications of each strategy for the cost of capital—according to the risk characteristics of different strategies and their financing implications, each strategy will have a different cost of capital.
- Select the strategy that generates the highest NPV.

Although simple in principle, applying DCF analysis to strategy selection runs into major practical difficulties. The central problem is forecasting cash flows. A strategy that is implemented today will influence a company's cash flows long into the future. Given the unpredictability of future business conditions, forecasting the costs and revenues resulting from a particular strategy is exceedingly difficult. The problem of forecasting is compounded by the fact that choosing a strategy does not predetermine cash flows. As we discussed in the first chapter, a strategy is not a detailed plan, it is a direction and a set of guidelines. As such, a strategy will be consistent with a range of specific outcomes in terms of product introductions, output levels, prices and investments in new plans. Once we recognize that strategy is about reconciling flexibility with direction in an uncertain environment, there are two key implications for strategy analysis: first, it may be better to view strategy as a portfolio of options rather than a portfolio of investment projects; second, qualitative approaches to strategy analysis may be more useful than quantitative ones. Let me address each of these themes.

## Strategy and Real Options

The simple idea that an *option*—the choice of whether to do something or not—has value has important implications for how we value firms. In recent years, the principles of option pricing have been extended from valuing financial securities to valuing investment projects and companies. The resulting field of *real option analysis* has emerged as one of the most important developments in financial theory over the past decade, with far-reaching implications for strategy analysis. The technical details of valuing real options are complex. However, the underlying principles are intuitive. Let me outline the basic ideas of real options theory and what they mean for strategy analysis.

In November 2005, BP announced the doubling of capital expenditure at its newly formed BP Alternative Energy division. Yet, it was highly unlikely that returns to this investment would match those of BP's oil and gas businesses. How could investing in renewable energy—wind and solar power—be consistent with shareholder interests?

The answer lies in the *option value* of alternative energy investments. BP's $600 million in alternative energy represented only 0.4% of overall 2006 capital expenditure. By developing a position in solar, wind and hydrogen energy technologies, BP was buying the option to become a leading player in these energy sources should hydrocarbon use be restricted by Middle East conflict, reserve exhaustion, or environmental concerns.

In a world of uncertainty, where investments, once made, are irreversible, flexibility is valuable. Instead of committing to an entire project, there is virtue in breaking the project into a number of phases, where the decision of whether and how to embark on the next phase can be made in the light of prevailing circumstances and the learning gained from the previous stage of the project. Most large companies have a *phases and gates* approach to product development in which the development process is split into distinct phases, at the end of which the project is reassessed before being allowed through the "gate." Such a phased approach creates the options to continue the project, to abandon it, to amend it, or to wait. The growth options that a company faces are valued by the stock market and by investors. The emphasis that venture capitalists place on "scalability"—the potential to scale up or replicate a business should the initial launch be successful similarly acknowledges the value of growth options. Strategy Capsule 2.2 addresses the calculation of real option values.

### Strategy as Options Management

For strategy formulation, our primary interest is how we can use the principles of option valuation to create shareholder value. There are two types of real option: *growth options* and *flexibility options*. Growth options allow a firm to make small initial investments in a number of future business opportunities but without committing to them. Flexibility options relate to the design of projects and plants that permit adaptation to different circumstances—*flexible manufacturing systems*

## STRATEGY CAPSULE 2.2
# Calculating Real Option Value

Application of real option valuation to investment projects and strategies has been limited by the complexity of the valuation techniques. Yet, even without getting into the mathematics needed to quantify option values, we can use the basic principles involved to understand the factors that determine option values and to recognize how projects and strategies can be designed in order to maximize their option values.

The early work on real option valuation adapted the *Black–Scholes option-pricing formula* developed for valuing financial options to the valuation of real investment projects.[11] Black–Scholes comprises six determinants of option value, each of which has an analogy in the valuation of a real option:

1    Stock price = The NPV of the project: a higher NPV increases option value

2    Exercise price = Investment cost: the higher the cost, the lower the option value

3    Uncertainty: for both financial and real options, uncertainty *increases* option value

4    Time to expiry: for both financial and real options, the longer the option lasts, the greater its value

5    Dividends = Decrease in the value of the investment over the option period: lowers option value

6    Interest rate: a higher interest rate increases option value by making deferral more valuable.[12]

However, the dominant methodology used for real option valuation is the *binomial options pricing model*. By allowing the sources of uncertainty and key decision points in a project to be a modeled explicitly, the technique offers a more intuitive appreciation of the sources of option value. The analysis involves two main stages:

1    Create an event tree that shows the value of the project at each development period under two different scenarios.

2    Convert the event tree into a decision tree by identifying the key decision points on the event tree—typically the points where commitments of new funds to the project are required, or where there is the option to defer development. Incremental project values at each stage can then be calculated for each decision point by working back from the final nodes of the decision tree (using a discount factor based upon the *replicating portfolio* technique). If the incremental project value at the initial stage exceeds the initial investment, proceed with the first phase—and similarly for each subsequent phase.[13]

allow different product models to be manufactured on a single production line. Individual projects can be designed to introduce both growth options and flexibility options. This means avoiding commitment to the complete project and introducing decision points at multiple stages, where the main options are to delay, modify, scale up, or abandon the project. Merck, an early adopter of option pricing, noted, "When you make an initial investment in a research project, you are paying an entry fee for a right, but you are not obligated to continue that research at a later stage."[14]

In developing strategy, our main concern is with growth options. These might include:

- "Platform investments." These are investments in core products or technologies that create a stream of additional business opportunities.[15] 3M's investment in nanotechnology offers the opportunity to create new products across a wide range of its businesses, from dental restoratives and drug-delivery systems to adhesives and protective coatings. Google's search engine has provided the platform for a wide variety of initiatives that range from other search products (Google Maps, Google Scholar) to advertising management products, to downloadable software.[16]

- Strategic alliances and joint ventures, which are limited investments that offer options for the creation of whole new strategies.[17] Virgin Group has used joint ventures as the basis for creating a number of new businesses: with Stagecoach to create Virgin Rail, with AMP to create Virgin Money (financial services), with Deutsche Telecom to form Virgin Mobile. Shell has used joint ventures and alliances as a means of making initial investments in wind power, biodiesel fuel, solar power, and other forms of renewable energy.

- Organizational capabilities, which can also be viewed as options offering the potential to create competitive advantage across multiple products and businesses.[18] Sharp's miniaturization capability has provided a gateway to success in calculators, LCD screens, solar cells and PDAs.

## Putting Performance Analysis into Practice

Our discussion so far has established the following:

- For the purposes of strategy formulation, profit maximization is a convenient and reasonable assumption. Once we look beyond a single period, maximizing profit translates into maximizing enterprise value.

- Discounted cash flow (DCF) valuation of enterprises and strategies encounters two problems. First, it is difficult to estimate cash flows more than a few years into the future. Second, it does not take account of option value.

Given these challenges, what practical guidance can I offer about using financial analysis to appraise and develop business strategies? Let me deal with four questions. First, how can we best appraise overall firm (or business unit) performance? Second, how can we diagnose the sources of poor performance? Third, how can we select strategies on the basis of their profit prospects? Lastly, how do we set performance targets?

### Appraising Current and Past Performance

The first task of any strategy formulation exercise is to assess the current situation. This requires that we identify the current strategy of the firm and assess how well that strategy is doing in terms of the financial performance of the firm. The next stage is diagnosis—identifying the sources of unsatisfactory performance. Thus, good strategic practice emulates good medical practice: the first task is to determine the state of health of the patient, and then to determine the reasons for any sickness.

*Forward-Looking Performance Measures: Stock Market Value* If our goal is maximizing profit over the lifetime of the firm, then to evaluate the performance of a firm we need to look at its stream of profit (or cash flows) over the rest of its life. The problem, of course, is that we don't know what these will be. However, for public companies we do have a good indicator: stock market valuation, which represents the best available estimate of expected cash flows into the future. Thus, to evaluate the effectiveness of a firm's CEO, we can look at the change in the market value of the firm relative to that of competitors over the CEO's period of tenure. Of course, using stock market valuation as a performance indicator has its problems, the information upon which the stock market values companies is imperfect and expectations about a firm's future earnings tend to be volatile.

*Backward-Looking Performance Measures: Accounting Ratios* Given the volatility of performance measures based on stock market values, evaluation of firm performance for the purposes of assessing the current strategy or evaluating management effectiveness tends to concentrate on accounting-based performance. All of these are inevitably historical—financial reports appear, at minimum, three weeks after the period to which they relate.

In the light of our discussion over accounting profit versus economic profit versus cash flow, which are the best indicators to use? McKinsey & Company argue that, for practical purposes, the DCF value of the firm may be viewed as a function of three variables: the return on the firm's invested capital (ROIC), its weighted average cost of capital, and the rate at which it grows its operating profit.[19] Hence, return on invested capital, or its close relatives return on capital employed (ROCE), return on assets (ROA) and return on equity (ROE) are useful indicators of the effectiveness of the firm in generating profits from its assets. However, to evaluate a firm's return on capital, we must first compare it with cost of capital, and second take account of growth. The value of a firm is highly sensitive to the rate at which profit grows. Hence efforts to boost a firm's return on capital by cutting capital expenditure and disposing of less profitable businesses may fail to increase the value of the firm.

Different profitability measures are related. Indeed, in practice, the longer the time period under consideration, the greater their convergence.[20] Over shorter periods, the key issues are, first, to be aware of the limitations and biases inherent in any particular profitability measure and, second, to use multiple measures of profitability so that their consistency can be judged. Table 2.2 outlines some commonly used performance indicators.

Interpreting probability ratios requires benchmarks. Longitudinal comparisons examine whether a profitability ratio is improving or deteriorating. Interfirm comparisons tell us how a firm is performing relative to a competitor, relative to its industry average, or relative to firms in general (for example, the average for the Fortune 500 or FT 500). Another key benchmark is cost of capital. ROIC and ROCE should be compared with WACC, and ROE compared with the cost of equity capital.

**TABLE 2.2** Profitability ratios

| Ratio | Formula | Comments |
|---|---|---|
| Return on Invested Capital (ROIC) | $$\frac{\text{operating profit before interest after tax}}{\text{fixed assets} + \text{net current assets}}$$ | ROIC measures the return on the capital invested in the business. ROIC is also referred to as return on capital employed (ROCE). It is sometimes calculated pre-tax and sometimes post-tax. The numerator can be operating profit or earnings (EBIT). Invested capital (capital employed) can also be measured as equity *plus* debt. |
| Return on Equity (ROE) | $$\frac{\text{net income}}{\text{shareholders' equity}}$$ | ROE measures the firm's success in using shareholders' capital to generate profits that are available for remunerating investors. Net income should ideally be measured net of dividends on preferred stock. Net income is often measured net of income from discontinued operations and before any special items. |
| Return on Assets (ROA) | $$\frac{\text{operating profit}}{\text{total assets}}$$ | Different measures of the numerator are common. Ideally the numerator should be a broad-based measure of profit: operating profit, EBITDA (earnings before interest, tax, depreciation, and amortization), or EBIT (earnings before interest and tax). |
| Gross margin | $$\frac{\text{sales} - \text{cost of bought-in goods and services}}{\text{sales}}$$ | Gross margin measures the extent to which a firm adds value to the goods and services it buys in. |
| Operating margin | $$\frac{\text{operating profit}}{\text{sales}}$$ | Operating margin and net margin measure a firm's ability to extract profit from its sales, but for comparing firms' performance, these ratios reveal little because margins vary so much between different sectors (see Table 2.1). |
| Net margin | $$\frac{\text{net income}}{\text{sales}}$$ | |

*Notes*

Few accounting ratios have agreed definitions. Hence, it is always advisable to be explicit about how you have calculated the ratio you are using.

   A general guideline for rate of return ratios is that the numerator should be the profits that are available to remunerate the owners of the assets in the denominator. Profits are measured over a period of time (typically over a year).

   Assets are valued at a point of time. Hence, in rate-of-return calculations, assets and capital employed need to be averaged between the end of the period and the end of the previous period.

## Performance Diagnosis

If profit performance is unsatisfactory, we need to identify the sources of poor performance so that management can take corrective action. Diagnosis primarily involves disaggregation of return on capital in order to identify the fundamental "value drivers." A useful approach is to apply the *Du Pont Formula* to disaggregate return on invested capital into sales margin and capital turnover. We can go further: as Figure 2.1 shows, sales margin and capital productivity can be further disaggregated into their constituent items. This analysis allows us to identify the sources of poor performance in terms of specific activities.

Strategy Capsule 2.3 investigates the performance of Ford's automotive operations compared with those of the industry's top performer, Toyota. By disaggregating overall return on assets we can begin to pinpoint the sources of Ford's dismal profitability. We can also disaggregate performance by business and geographical segments. If we then combine the financial data with qualitative data on Ford's business strategy, its operations, its product strategy, the organizational issues it has faced, and the conditions in the world market for motor vehicles, we can begin to formulate hypotheses as to why Ford has performed so poorly. This can then provide the basis for identifying corrective measures.

**FIGURE 2.1**  Disaggregating return on capital employed

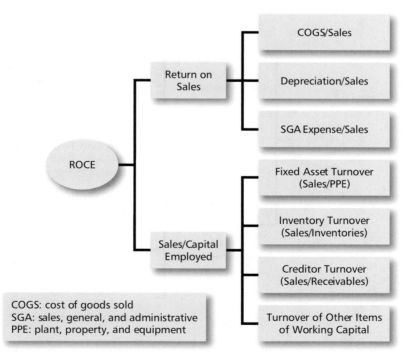

*Note:* For further discussion, see T. Koller, M. Goedhart, and D. Wessels, *Valuation*, 4th edn (New York: John Wiley & Sons, Inc., 2005): Chapter 7.

### STRATEGY CAPSULE 2.3

## Diagnosing Performance: What Ails Ford?

During the early years of the twenty-first century, Ford Motor Company continued the declining trend that had begun during the 1980s. During the five-year period 2003–7, return on equity averaged a negative 3.9% while operating losses in its automotive business totaled over $24 billion. Ford's share of the U.S. car and truck market declined from 21.8% to 16.8%. A new CEO, Alan Mulally, initiated vigorous cost cutting and asset sales, but without any significant upturn in profitability.

To understand the sources of Ford's poor financial performance, it is useful to compare Ford's automotive operations with those of the company that had displaced it as the world's second largest auto manufacturer (by volume)—Toyota. Combining data for 2006 and 2007, we can disaggregate Ford and Toyota's return on capital employed into sales margin and capital turnover, then disaggregate further into individual cost and asset productivity ratios:

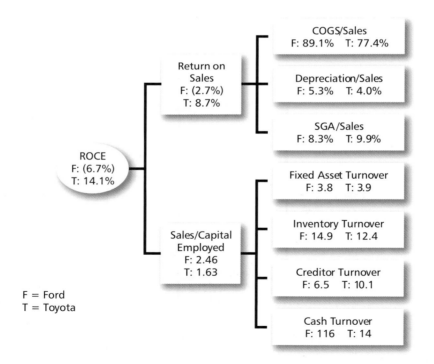

**Note:** These ratios relate to the automotive businesses only; financial services are excluded.

The analysis reveals the following:

- Ford's lower ROCE is wholly the result of a lower margin on sales than Toyota. This lower margin results from a substantially higher ratio of cost of goods sold to sales. This could be the result of higher costs (for example, of labor and parts), or lower unit prices for vehicles, or both. Additional analysis suggests that Ford's higher COGS/sales ratio is the result of lower productivity of labor—Ford produced 23.8 vehicles per employee compared with 31.9 for Toyota. Also, Toyota with just 17 manufacturing plants worldwide is likely to exploit scale economies more effectively than Ford with its 113 plants. Although Ford received more revenue per vehicle than Toyota ($22, 814 versus $21, 442), the difference seems to be accounted for by Toyota's greater emphasis on small cars. For comparable models, it appears that Toyota's prices are higher than Ford's—possibly the result of higher quality and better features.

- Ford's overall capital productivity is higher than Toyota's. Yet, when we review the disaggregated asset productivity ratios, it is difficult to find the source of this higher capital turnover. In terms of fixed asset productivity, the two are almost the same. Ford's productivity advantages stem from two sources: first, higher inventory turnover; second, Ford's fewer current assets in the form of cash and receivables.

## Can Past Performance Guide Strategies for the Future?

A probing diagnosis of a firm's recent performance—as outlined above—provides useful input into strategy formulation. If we can establish why a company has been performing badly then we have a basis for corrective actions. These corrective actions are likely to be both strategic (i.e. focused on the medium to long term) and operational (focused on the short term). The worse a company's performance, the more likely it is that management will concentrate on the short term. For companies teetering on the brink of bankruptcy, such as General Motors and LyondellBassell chemical company—long-term strategy takes a back seat; survival is the dominant concern.

For companies that are performing well, financial analysis allows us to understand the sources of superior performance so that strategy can protect and enhance these determinants of success.

However, analyzing the past only takes us so far. The world of business is one of constant change and the role of strategy is to allow the firm to adapt to change. The challenge is to look into the future and identify factors that threaten performance or create new opportunities for profit. As we have already noted, financial analysis does not allow us to forecast cash flows or profits into the future. In making strategy recommendations to Toyota, our financial analysis can tell us some of the reasons why Toyota has been doing well up until now, but Toyota wants to know what its performance is likely to be in the future and what strategy will be most effective in maximizing that performance. Here, financial analysis is of little use. To look ahead into the future Toyota needs to understand the strategic factors that are the ultimate drivers of profitability. What will be happening in the industry in terms of competition and customer demand? Which companies will possess the resources and capabilities needed to establish a competitive advantage in tomorrow's markets? Applying the tools of strategy analysis will not enable us to forecast Toyota's profits and cash flows quantitatively but it will offer qualitative indications as to the implications of Toyota sticking to its present strategy and the likely consequences of adopting alternative strategies.

## Setting Performance Targets

We noted in Chapter 1 that an important role for strategic planning systems is to drive corporate performance through setting performance goals then monitoring results against targets. To be effective, performance targets need to be consistent with long-term goals, linked to strategy, and relevant to the tasks and responsibilities of individual organizational members. The instruction to maximize long-run profits is meaningless outside the executive suite. Corporate targets need to be translated into specific goals that are meaningful for managers further down the organization. The key is to match performance targets to the variables over which different managers exert some control. Thus, for the CEO, it may make sense to set the overall goal of maximizing enterprise value. For the chief operating officer and divisional heads it makes sense to set more specific financial goals (such as maximizing ROCE on existing assets and investing in projects whose rate of return exceeds the cost of capital). More specific operating targets are preferable for functional, departmental and unit managers. Thus, in a retailing company, store managers might be given targets with regard to sales per square foot and gross margins. Warehouse managers might be required to achieve target levels of inventory turns. Purchasing managers might be required to reduce the cost of goods purchased as a percentage of sales revenue. The chief financial officer might be required to minimize average cost of capital and reduce cash balances.

The same procedure that we used to disaggregate return on capital for appraising past performance can be used to set performance targets appropriate to different levels and functions within the organization. Figure 2.2 uses the same breakout of the drivers of return on capital as Figure 2.1. The difference is that Figure 2.2 provides a basis for identifying the financial and operating ratios appropriate to managers at the different levels and in the different functions of the company.

*Balanced Scorecards*   The problem with any system of performance management is that the performance goals are long term (for example, maximizing profits over the lifetime of the company) but to act as an effective control system performance targets need to be monitored over the short term. The problem with the above financially based approach of disaggregating profitability into its constituent ratios is that the short-term pursuit of financial targets is unlikely to result in long-term profit maximization. One solution to this dilemma is to link the overall corporate goal of value maximization to strategic and operational targets to ensure that the pursuit of financial goals is not at the expense of the longer term strategic position of the company. The most widely used method for doing this is the *balanced scorecard* developed by Robert Kaplan and David Norton.[21] The balanced scorecard methodology provides an integrated framework for balancing financial and strategic goals and cascading performance measures down the organization to individual

**FIGURE 2.2** Linking value drivers to performance

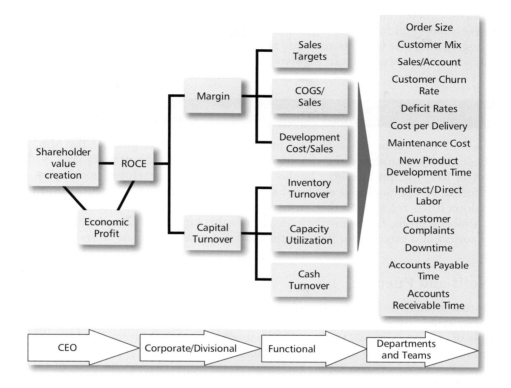

business units and departments. The performance measures combine the answers to four questions:

- *How do we look to shareholders?* The financial perspective is composed of measures such as cash flow, sales and income growth and return on equity.
- *How do customers see us?* The customer perspective comprises measures such as goals for new products, on-time delivery, and defect and failure levels.
- *What must we excel at?* The internal business perspective relates to internal business processes such as productivity, employee skills, cycle time, yield rates and quality and cost measures.
- *Can we continue to improve and create value?* The innovation and learning perspective includes measures related to new product development cycle times, technological leadership and rates of improvement.

By balancing a set of strategic and financial goals, the scorecard methodology allows the strategy of the business to be linked with the creation of shareholder value while providing a set of measurable targets to guide this process.

Mobil Corporation's North American Marketing and Refining business (NAM&R) was a pioneer of the balanced scorecard during the 1990s. Faced with pressures of unsatisfactory profit performance, the business adopted the scorecard methodology as a means of linking strategy with financial performance goals and translating these into operating objectives tailored to the circumstances of individual business units and functional departments. The scorecard provided a mechanism for disaggregating divisional strategy into specific operating goals which were linked to individuals' bonuses.[22] Figure 2.3 shows NAM&R's scorecard.

## Beyond Profit: Values and Social Responsibility

It is time to look more deeply and more realistically at the goals of the firm. In Chapter 1 we introduced the simplifying assumption that the primary goal of the firm is long-run profitability. In this chapter we have developed techniques of performance appraisal and analysis based on this assumption. Yet, lurking in the shadows is the recognition that, in reality, firms are motivated by goals other than maximizing profit. Even more worrying, such alternative goals may be better, both for society and maybe even for the firm itself. Let us address these issues directly.

### Profit and Purpose

There is more to business than making money. Profit maximization (enterprise value maximization, to be more precise) provides a convenient foundation for building our tools of strategy analysis, yet it is not the goal that inspired Henry Ford to build a business that precipitated a social revolution.

> I will build a motor car for the great multitude . . . It will be so low in price that no man making good wages will be unable to own one and to enjoy with his family the blessing of hours of pleasure in God's great open spaces . . . When I'm through, everyone will be able to afford one, and everyone will have one.[23]

Similar remarks can be made about entrepreneurs generally: they are driven less by the promise of riches as by the desire to create.

As we recognized in Chapter 1 (see *Strategy as Target*, pg 26), the world's most consistently successful companies in terms of profits and shareholder value tend to be those that are motivated by factors other than profit. A succession of studies point to the role of strategic intent, vision, and "big, hairy, ambitious goals" in driving sustained corporate success.[24] Indeed, the converse may also be true—the companies that are most focused on profitability and the creation of shareholder value are often remarkably unsuccessful at achieving those goals. The case of Boeing during the 1990s is instructive (see Strategy Capsule 2.4).

Why does the pursuit of profit so often fail to realize its goal? First, profit will only be an effective guide to management action if managers know what determines profit. Obsession with profitability can blinker managers' perception of the real drivers of superior performance. Conversely, a strategic goal "to build a motor car for the great multitude that everyone will be able to afford" (Ford), or to "build great planes" (Boeing), or to "become the company most known for changing the worldwide poor quality image associated with Japanese products" (Sony, 1950s)

**FIGURE 2.3**  Balanced scorecard for Mobil North American Marketing and Refining

| | | Strategic Objectives | Strategic Measures |
|---|---|---|---|
| **Financially Strong** | Financial | F1 Return on Capital Employed<br>F2 Cash Flow<br>F3 Profitability<br>F4 Lowest Cost<br>F5 Profitable Growth<br>F6 Manage Risk | ● ROCE<br>● Cash Flow<br>● Net Margin<br>● Full cost per gallon delivered to customer<br>● Volume growth rate vs. industry<br>● Risk index |
| **Delight the Consumer**<br><br>**Win–Win Relationship** | Customer | C1 Continually delight the targeted consumer<br><br><br>C2 Improve dealer/distributor profitability | ● Share of segment in key markets<br>● Mystery shopper rating<br><br>● Dealer/distributor margin on gasoline<br>● Dealer/distributor survey |
| **Safe and Reliable**<br><br><br><br><br><br><br><br>**Competitive Supplier**<br><br><br><br>**Good Neighbor**<br>**On Spec**<br>**On time** | Internal | I1 Marketing<br>  1. Innovative products and services<br>  2. Dealer/distributor quality<br><br>I2 Manufacturing<br>  1. Lower manufacturing costs<br>  2. Improve hardware and performance<br>I3 Supply, Trading, Logistics<br>  1. Reducing delivered cost<br>  2. Trading organization<br>  3. Inventory management<br><br>I4 Improve health, safety, and environmental performance<br>I5 Quality | ● Non-gasoline revenue and margin per square foot<br>● Dealer/distributor acceptance rate of new programs<br>● Dealer/distributor quality ratings<br>● ROCE on refinery<br>● Total expenses (per gallon) vs. competition<br>● Profitability index<br>● Yield index<br>Delivered cost per gallon vs. competitors<br>● Trading margin<br>● Inventory level compared to plan and to output rate<br>● Number of incidents<br>● Days away from work<br>● Quality index |
| **Motivated and Prepared** | Learning and growth | L1 Organization involvement<br>L2 Core competencies and skills<br>L3 Access to strategic information | ● Employee survey<br>● Strategic competitive availability<br>● Strategic information availability |

**STRATEGY CAPSULE 2.4**

## The Pitfalls of Pursuing Shareholder Value: Boeing

Boeing was one of the most financially successful members of the Dow Jones Industrial Index between 1960 and 1990. Yet, financial management received little attention at Boeing over this period. CEO Bill Allen was interested in building great planes and leading the world market with them: "Boeing is always reaching out for tomorrow. This can only be accomplished by people who live, breathe, eat and sleep what they are doing." Allen bet the company on the 747, yet when asked by non-executive director Crawford Greenwalt for financial projections on the project, Allen was utterly vague. "My God," muttered Greenwalt, "these guys don't even know what the return on investment will be on this thing."

The change came in the mid-1990s when Boeing acquired McDonnell Douglas and a new management team of Harry Stonecipher and Phil Condit took over. Mr Condit proudly talked of taking the company into "a value-based environment where unit cost, return on investment, shareholder return are the measures by which you'll be judged."

The result was lack of investment in major new civil aviation projects and diversification into defense and satellites. Under Condit, Boeing relinquished market leadership in passenger aircraft to Airbus, while faltering as a defense contractor due partly to ethical lapses by key executives. When Condit resigned on December 1, 2003, Boeing's stock price was 20% lower than when he was appointed.

*Source:* Adapted from John Kay, "Forget how the Crow Flies," *Financial Times Magazine* (January 17, 2004): 17–27.

may lead a company to direct its efforts towards the sources of competitive advantage within its industry—ultimately leading to superior long-term profitability.

The second factor concerns motivation. Success is the result of coordinated effort. The goal of maximizing the return to stockholders is unlikely to inspire employees and other company stakeholders and it's unlikely to be especially effective in inducing cooperation and unity between them. Dennis Bakke, founder of the international power company AES, offers the following analogy:

> Profits are to business as breathing is to life. Breathing is essential to life, but is not the purpose for living. Similarly, profits are essential for the existence of the corporation, but they are not the reason for its existence.[25]

A sense of purpose is a common to most new, entrepreneurial enterprises. The primary impetus driving entrepreneurs to found new businesses is typically not the quest for riches—if that was the case, most would have pursued less uncertain avenues to wealth. According to Schumpeter, "The entrepreneur-innovator's motivation includes such aspects as the dream to found a private kingdom, the will to conquer and to succeed for the sake of success itself, and the joy of creating and getting things done."[26]

But what about established companies? What happened to the sense of purpose that was presumably present at their founding? Some companies have kept alive a keen sense of purpose—it is embedded in organizational culture and implicit in strategy and in the behavior of corporate leaders. However, sustaining a sense of purpose typically requires articulation in explicit statements of mission, vision, and purpose. For example:

- Google's mission is: ". . . to organize the world's information and make it universally accessible and useful."
- "The IKEA vision is to create a better everyday life for the many people. We make this possible by offering a wide range of well-designed, functional home furnishing products at prices so low that as many people as possible will be able to afford them."
- "SAP strives to define and establish undisputed leadership in the emerging market for business process platform offerings and accelerate business innovation powered by IT for companies and industries worldwide."
- Gaia House (a Buddhist retreat center in England) "exists for the liberation of all beings from greed, hatred and delusion."

Is organizational purpose instilled at birth, or can companies choose or adapt their *raison d'être* during the course of their lives? Certainly many of the companies that are most closely identified with clarity of purpose—HP, Johnson & Johnson, Walt Disney—have a sense of mission that is little changed from that articulated by their founders. Yet, Cynthia Montgomery argues that "forging a compelling organizational purpose" is the ongoing job of the CEO—indeed, it is the "crowning responsibility of the CEO."[27] The challenge is to link change with continuity. Some of the most successful corporate turnarounds have been engineered by corporate leaders—Gerstner at IBM, Eisner at Walt Disney—who have renewed and redirected organizational purpose while appealing to continuity of tradition and values.

## Values and Principles

A sense of purpose—as articulated in statements of mission and vision—is often complemented by beliefs about how this purpose should be achieved. These company beliefs are likely to include a set of values that comprise commitments to different stakeholder groups and to ethical precepts. Company values may be articulated as a set of principles to guide the decisions and actions of organizational members. Strategy Capsule 2.5 summarizes Shell's values and business principles.

At one level, statements of values and principles may be regarded as instruments of companies' external image management. Yet, to the extent that companies are consistent and sincere in their adherence to values and principles, these ideals can be a critical component of organizational identity and an important influence on employees' commitment and propensity to collaborate. To the extent that values are shared among organizational members, they form a central component of organizational culture.

**STRATEGY CAPSULE 2.5**
# Shell's Values and Principles

## OUR VALUES

Shell employees share a set of core values— honesty, integrity and respect for people. We also firmly believe in the fundamental importance of trust, openness, teamwork and professionalism and pride in what we do.

## PRINCIPLES

1  Economic. Long-term profitability is essential to achieving our business goals and to our continued growth . . .

2  Competition. Shell companies support free enterprise. We seek to compete fairly and ethically and within the framework of applicable competition laws . . .

3  Business integrity. Shell companies insist on honesty, integrity and fairness in all aspects of our business . . .

4  Political Activities . . . Shell companies act in a socially responsible manner within the laws of the countries in which we operate in pursuit of our legitimate commercial objectives . . .

5  Health, safety, security *and the environment.* Shell companies have a

systematic approach to health, safety, security and environmental management in order to achieve continuous performance improvement.

6  Local communities. Shell companies aim to be good neighbors by continuously improving the ways in which we contribute directly or indirectly to the general wellbeing of the communities within which we work . . .

7  Communication and engagement. Shell companies recognize that regular dialogue and engagement with our stakeholders is essential. We are committed to reporting of our performance by providing full relevant information to legitimately interested parties . . .

8  Compliance. We comply with all applicable laws and regulations of the countries in which we operate.

*Source*: Extracted from Royal Dutch Shell plc *General Business Principles,* 2008(http://www.shell.com/home/content/aboutshell/who_we_are/our_values/sgbp/sgbp_30032008.html, accessed July 2, 2009).

The evidence that commitment to values and principles influences organizational performance is overwhelming. Peters and Waterman identified "shared values" as a key determinant of "excellence".[28] Jim Collins and Jerry Porras argue that "core values" and "core purpose"—the organization's most fundamental reason for being—unite to form an organization's "core ideology" which "defines an organization's timeless character" and is "the glue that holds the organization together."[29] When core ideology is put together with an "envisioned future" for the enterprise, the result is a powerful sense of strategic direction that provides the foundation for long-term success.

## The Debate over Corporate Social Responsibility

Values and principles can enhance a sense of identity and motivate employees—but this still leaves the question of *what* values and principles should companies adopt? This issue is central to the recent debate over *corporate social responsibility* (CSR). What are a company's obligations to society as a whole? In a sharp rebuttal to calls for business to address the broader problems of society, free-market economist Milton Friedman declared CSR to be both unethical and undesirable. Unethical because it involved management spending owners' money on projects that owners had not approved; undesirable because it involved corporate executives determining the interests of society. Once business enterprises accept responsibility for society, does this justify support for political activities, for religious movements, for elitist universities? According to Friedman:

> There is one and only one social responsibility of business—to use its resources and engage in activities designed to increase its profits so long as it stays within the rules of the game, which is to say, engage in open and free competition without deception or fraud.[30]

Despite these arguments, companies are increasingly accepting responsibilities that extend well beyond the immediate interests of their owners. The case for CSR is based both on ethics and efficacy. Ethical arguments about management responsibility depend, ultimately, upon what we conceive the firm to be. William Allen contrasts two different notions of the public corporation: "the property conception", which views the firm as a set of assets owned by stockholders, and the "social entity conception", which views the firm as the community of individuals that is sustained and supported its relationships with its social, political, economic and natural environment.[31] The "firm as property" view implies that management's responsibility is to operate in the interests of shareholders. The "firm as social entity" implies a responsibility to maintaining the firm within its overall network of relationships and dependencies. Charles Handy dismisses the "firm as property" view as a hangover from the nineteenth century—in the twenty-first century shareholders invest in companies but are not "owners" in any meaningful sense. To regard profit as the purpose for which companies exist, he argues, is a tragic confusion.[32]

The efficacy argument for CSR also views the firm as embedded within the ecosystem of its social and natural environments implying congruence between the interests of the firm and those of the supporting ecosystem. Thus, according to former Shell executive, Arie De Geus, long-living companies are those that build strong communities, have a strong sense of identity, commit to learning and are sensitive to the world around them. In short, they recognize they are living organisms whose lifespans depend upon effective adaptation to a changing environment.[33] A narrower view of this dependency is the sociological concept of *legitimacy*: organizations that gain social legitimacy attract resources and customers.

Michael Porter and Mark Kramer outline a more focused and pragmatic approach to CSR.[34] Putting aside ethical arguments (what they call "the moral imperative"), they identify three reasons why CSR might also be in the interests of a company: the *sustainability argument*—CSR is in firms' interests due to a mutual interest in sustaining the ecosystem; the *reputation argument*—CSR enhances a firm's reputation with consumers and other third parties; and *license-to-operate* argument—to conduct their businesses firms require the support of the constituencies upon which they depend. However, these fail to offer clear guidance as to what CSR initiatives firms should pursue. The critical task, according to Porter and Kramer, is to identify *specific intersections between the interests of the firm and those of society*: i.e. projects and activities that create competitive advantage for the firm while generating positive social outcomes—what they term *strategic CSR*. For example:

- Toyota's early efforts to address the problems of pollution and global warming resulted in its coming early to market with its Prius hybrid car—one of the most successful automobile launches of the past decade.
- To develop a dairy in the Moga, India, Nestlé established a refrigerated milk collection network and offered veterinary and nutrition services to farmers. The resulting fall in the mortality of newborn calves and rise in milk yield permitted a virtuous cycle of development of the local dairy industry that benefitted both farmers and Nestlé.

C. K. Prahalad also sees the potential for win-win relationships in the relationship between business and the world's poor: the four billion people at the "the bottom of the pyramid" living off less than \$2 a day.[35] If multinationals can stop viewing the poor as victims or as a burden and recognize them as value-conscious consumers, resilient workers, and creative entrepreneurs then a whole world of opportunity opens up. At the bottom of the pyramid there are attractive growth markets. The shanty towns of Rio de Janeiro, Johannesburg and Mumbai house millions of people, vibrant economies and substantial collective purchasing power. Lack of disposable income does not necessarily mean lack of profit. Grameen Telecom's payphones sited in Bangladeshi villages generate strong profit margins. Moreover, engaging with the world's poor creates pathways to growth—and early mover advantage in the markets of the future. Finally, through meeting the challenges of serving this market, and forging relationships with local government, aid agencies and local businesses, multinational firms can generate innovations that they can apply more widely. The wind-up, batteryless radio was developed by British inventor Trevor Bayliss to allow Third World communities access to radio broadcasts—yet, wind-up radios and other mechanically powered electrical products have sold massively to sophisticated First World consumers. The use of mobile phones to make person-to-person financial transactions in the Third World has stimulated innovative thinking among telecom multinationals about the financial services potential of wireless telecommunications.

## Summary

Chapter 1 introduced a framework for strategy analysis that provides the structure for Part II of this book. This chapter has explored the first component of that framework— the goals, values, and performance of the firm. My key assumption is that the firm operates in the interests of its owners through maximizing their returns (profits), which implies maximizing the value of the firm. Focusing upon profit and value maximization allows us to use the tools of financial analysis both in diagnosing the sources of superior or inferior performance and for setting performance targets.

At the same time, we must recognize that profit, while essential, is not the *raison d'être* for most business enterprises. Strategy is also about creating purpose and committing revenues and principles. The pursuit of wider social and environmental goals does not necessarily conflict with the interests of owners.

Financial analysis is primarily useful for analyzing past performance. Strategy's main concern is creating value in the future. This requires identifying and exploiting the fundamental drivers of firm value. That is the challenge we address in the next three chapters of the book. We begin with the industry environment of the firm.

## Self-Study Questions

1   Table 2.1 compares companies according to different profitability measures.

   (a)  Which two of the six performance measures do you think are the most useful indicators of how well a company is being managed?
   (b)  Is return on sales or return on equity a better basis on which to compare the performance of the companies listed?
   (c)  Several companies are highly profitable yet have delivered very low returns to their shareholders. How is this possible?

2   Nike, supplier of sports footwear and apparel, is interested in the idea that it could increase its stock market value by creating options for itself. Advise Nike on some of the actions it might take in order to generate option value.

3   India's Tata Group is a diversified group. Some of its largest companies are: Tata Steel, Tata Motors, Tata Consultancy Services (IT), Tata Power (electricity generation), Tata Chemicals, Tata Tea, Indian Hotels, and Tata Communications. How do you think Tata Group's recent adoption of EVA as a performance management tool is likely to influence the way in which it allocates investment among the companies listed above?

4   With regard to Strategy Capsule 2.3, what additional data would you seek and what additional cost and productivity ratios would you calculate to shed further light on the reasons for Ford's inferior ROCE relative to Toyota?

5   The CEO of a chain of pizza restaurants is interested in initiating a program of corporate social responsibility to be funded by a 5% levy on the company's operating profit. The board of directors, fearing a negative shareholder reaction, is opposed to the plan. What arguments might the CEO use to persuade the board that CSR might be in the interests of shareholders, and what types of CSR initiatives might the program include to ensure that this is the case?

# Notes

1  In this chapter, I use the term "value" in two distinct senses. Here I am referring to *economic value*, which is worth as measured in monetary units. We shall also be discussing *values* as moral principles or standards of behavior.

2  T. Donaldson and L. E. Preston, "The stakeholder theory of the corporation," *Academy of Management Review* 20 (1995): 65–91.

3  Stern Stewart & Co., "Russell 3000 Annual Ranking Data, 2003", (2004).

4  Weber Shandwick, "Global CEO Turnover Rises 10 Percent in Past 12 Months According To New Study," (March 3, 2008), www.webershandwick.com; M. Wiersema, "Holes at the Top: Why CEO Firings Backfire," *Harvard Business Review* (December 2002): 66–78; S. N. Kaplan and B. Minton, "How CEO Turnover Changed," NBER Working Paper No. 12465 (August, 2006).

5  S. L. Hart and M. B. Milstein, "Global Sustainability and the Creative Destruction of Industries," *Sloan Management Review* 41 (Fall, 1999): 23–33; M. Orlitzky, F. L. Schmidt and S. L. Rynes, "Corporate Social and Financial Performance: A Meta-Analysis," *Organization Studies* 24 (Summer, 2003): 403–41.

6  J. Figuero, S. Greco and M. Ehrgott, *Multiple Criteria Decision Analysis: State of the Art Surveys* (Berlin: Springer, 2005).

7  See www.sternstewart.com. See also: J. L. Grant, *Foundations of Economic Value Added,* 2nd edn (New York: Wiley, 2003).

8  The cost of equity capital is calculated using the capital asset pricing model: firm X's cost of equity = the risk-free rate of interest + a risk premium. The risk premium is the excess of the stock market rate of return over the risk-free rate multiplied by Firm X's beta coefficient (its measure of *systematic risk*). See T. Koller, M. Goedhart and D. Wessels, *Valuation: Measuring and Managing the Value of Companies*, 4th edn (New York: Wiley, 2005): Chapter 10.

9  F. Modigliani and M. H. Miller, "The Cost of Capital, Corporation Finance, and the Theory of Investments," *American Economic Review* 48 (1958): 261–97.

10  This "shareholder value" approach to strategy appraisal is outlined by A. Rappaport in *Creating Shareholder Value: The New Standard for Business Performance* (New York: Free Press, 1986); and "CFOs and Strategists: Forging a Common Framework," *Harvard Business Review* (May–June 1992): 84–91.

11  F. Black and M. Scholes, "The Pricing of Options and Corporate Liabilities," *Journal of Political Economy* 81 (1993): 637–54.

12  K. J. Leslie and M. P. Michaels, "The Real Power of Real Options", *McKinsey Quarterly Anthology: On Strategy* (Boston: McKinsey & Company, 2000). Also: A. Dixit and R. Pindyck, "The Options Approach to Capital Investment," *Harvard Business Review* (May–June 1995): 105–15.

13  This approach is developed in T. Copeland and P. Tufano, "A Real-world Way to Manage Real Options" *Harvard Business Review,* March, 2004. See also: T. Copeland, *Developing Strategy Using Real Options,* Monitor Company (October 2003).

14  N. Nichols, "Scientific Management at Merck: An Interview with CFO Judy Lewent," *Harvard Business Review* (January–February, 1994): 89–105.

15  B. Kogut and N. Kulatilaka, "Options Thinking and Platform Investments: Investing in Opportunity," *California Management Review* (Winter, 1994): 52–69.

16  A. Gower and M. A. Cusamano, "How Companies Become Platform Leaders," *Sloan School of Management Review* (Winter, 2008): 28–35.

17  T. Chi, "Option to Acquire or Divest a Joint Venture," *Strategic Management Journal* 21 (2000): 665–87.

18  B. Kogut and N. Kulatilaka, "Capabilities as Real Options," *Organization Science* 12 (2001): 744–58; R. G. McGrath, W. Furrier and A. Mendel, "Real Options as Engines of Choice and Heterogeneity," *Academy of Management Review* 29 (2004): 86–101.

19  Koller, Goedhart, and Wessels, *Valuation* op. cit.: Chapter 13.

20  J. A. Kay and C. Meyer, "On the Application of Accounting Rates of Return," *Economic Journal* 96 (1986): 199–207; J. A. Kay, *Foundations of Corporate Success: How Business Strategies Create Value* (Oxford: Oxford University Press, 1993): 207.

21  R. S. Kaplan and D. P. Norton. "The Balanced Scorecard: Measures that Drive Performance," *Harvard Business Review* (January–February, 1992) 71–79; R. S Kaplan and D. P. Norton: "Using the Balanced Scorecard as a Strategic Management System," *Harvard Business Review* (January-February, 1996): 75–85.

22  R. S. Kaplan and D. P. Norton, *The Strategy-focused Organization* (Boston: Harvard Business School Press, 2001): Chapter 2, "How Mobil Became a Strategy-focused Organization."

23  See www.abelard.org/ford.

24  J. Collins and J. Porras, "Building Your Company's Vision," *Harvard Business Review* (September–October, 1996): 65–77.

25  Author's interview.

26  Joseph Schumpeter, *The Theory of Economic Development* (Cambridge MA, Harvard University Press, 1934).

27  C. A. Montgomery, "Putting Leadership Back into Strategy" *Harvard Business Review* (January, 2008): 54–60.

28  T. Peters and R. Waterman *In Search of Excellence* (New York: HarperCollins, 1982).

29  Collins and Porras, "Building Your Company's Vision," op. cit.

30 M. Friedman, *Capitalism and Freedom* (Chicago: University of Chicago Press, 1963). See also: M. Friedman, "The Social Responsibility of Business is to Increase its Profits," *New York Times Magazine* (September 13, 1970).

31 W. T. Allen, "Our Schizophrenic Conception of the Business Corporation," *Cardozo Law Review* 14 (1992): 261–81.

32 C. Handy, "What's a Business For?" *Harvard Business Review* (December, 2002): 133–43.

33 A. De Geus, "The Living Company," *Harvard Business Review* (March–April, 1997): 51–9.

34 M. E. Porter and M. R. Kramer, "Strategy and Society: The Link Between Competitive Advantage and Corporate Social Responsibility," *Harvard Business Review* (December, 2006): 78–92.

35 C. K. Prahalad and A. Hammond, "Serving the World's Poor, Profitably," *Harvard Business Review* (September, 2002); C. K. Prahalad, *Fortune at the Bottom of the Pyramid, Eradicating Poverty Through Profits* (Philadelphia: Wharton Publishing, 2004).

# 3 Industry Analysis: The Fundamentals

*When a management with a reputation for brilliance tackles a business with a reputation for poor fundamental economics, it is the reputation of the business that remains intact.*

—WARREN BUFFETT, CHAIRMAN, BERKSHIRE HATHAWAY

*The reinsurance business has the defect of being too attractive-looking to new entrants for its own good and will therefore always tend to be the opposite of, say, the old business of gathering and rendering dead horses that always tended to contain few and prosperous participants.*

—CHARLES T. MUNGER, CHAIRMAN, WESCO FINANCIAL CORP.

## OUTLINE

# Introduction and Objectives

In this chapter and the next we explore the external environment of the firm. In Chapter 1 we observed that profound understanding of the competitive environment is a critical ingredient of a successful strategy. We further noted that business strategy is essentially a quest for profit. The primary task for this chapter is to identify the sources of profit in the external environment. The firm's proximate environment is its industry environment; hence the focus of our environmental analysis will be industry analysis.

   Industry analysis is relevant both to corporate-level and business-level strategy.

◆ Corporate strategy is concerned with deciding which industries the firm should be engaged in and how it should allocate its resources among them. Such decisions require assessment of the attractiveness of different industries in terms of their profit potential. The main objective of this chapter is to understand how the competitive structure of an industry determines its profitability.

◆ Business strategy is concerned with establishing competitive advantage. By analyzing customer needs and preferences and the ways in which firms compete to serve customers, we identify the general sources of competitive advantage in an industry—what we call *key success factors*.

By the time you have completed this chapter you will be able to:

◆ identify the main structural features of an industry that influence competition and profitability;

◆ use industry analysis to explain why in some industries competition is more intense and profitability lower than in other industries;

◆ use evidence on structural trends within industries to forecast changes in competition and profitability in the future;

◆ develop strategies that (a) position the firm most favorably in relation to competition and (b) influence industry structure in order to enhance industry attractiveness;

◆ analyze competition and customer requirements in order to identify opportunities for competitive advantage within an industry (*key success factors*).

# From Environmental Analysis to Industry Analysis

The business environment of the firm consists of all the external influences that affect its decisions and performance. Given the vast number and range of external influences, how can managers hope to monitor, let alone analyze, environmental conditions? The starting point is some kind of system or framework for organizing information. For example, environmental influences can be classified by *source*—for example, into political, economic, social, and technological factors ("PEST analysis")—or by *proximity*—the "micro-environment" or "task environment" can be distinguished from the wider influences that form the "macro-environment".[1] Systematic, continuous scanning of the whole range of external influences might seem desirable but such extensive environmental analysis incurs high costs and creates information overload.

The prerequisite for effective environmental analysis is to distinguish the vital from the merely important. To do this let us return to first principles. For the firm to make profit it must create value for customers. Hence, it must understand its customers. Second, in creating value, the firm acquires goods and services from suppliers. Hence, it must understand its suppliers and manage relationships with them. Third, the ability to generate profitability depends on the intensity of competition among firms that vie for the same value-creating opportunities. Hence, the firm must understand competition. Thus, the core of the firm's business environment is formed by its relationships with three sets of players: customers, suppliers and competitors. This is its industry environment.

This is not to say that macro-level factors such as general economic trends, changes in demographic structure, or social and political trends are unimportant to strategy analysis. These factors may be critical determinants of the threats and opportunities a company will face in the future. The key issue is how these more general environmental factors affect the firm's industry environment (Figure 3.1). Consider the threat of global warming. For most companies this is not an important strategic issue (at least, not for the next hundred years). However, for the producers of automobiles, global warming is a vital issue. But, to analyze the strategic implications of global warming, the automobile manufacturers need to trace its implications for their industry environment. For example, what will be the impact on consumers and their preferences? Will there be a switch from private to public

**FIGURE 3.1** From environmental analysis to industry analysis

transportation? With regard to competition, will there be new entry by manufacturers of electric vehicles into the car industry? Will increased R&D costs cause the industry to consolidate?

## The Determinants of Industry Profit: Demand and Competition

The starting point for industry analysis is a simple question: what determines the level of profit in an industry?

The prerequisite for profit is the creation of value for the customer. Value is created when the price the customer is willing to pay for a product exceeds the costs incurred by the firm. But value creation does not translate directly into profit. The surplus of value over cost is distributed between customers and producers by the forces of competition. The stronger competition is among producers, the more of the surplus is received by customers in *consumer surplus* (the difference between the price they actually pay and the maximum price they would have been willing to pay) and the less is the surplus received by producers (as *producer surplus* or *economic rent*). A single supplier of bottled water at an all-night rave can charge a price that fully exploits the dancers' thirst. If there are many suppliers of bottled water, then, in the absence of collusion, competition causes the price of bottled water to fall toward the cost of supplying it.

The surplus earned by producers over and above the minimum costs of production is not entirely captured in profits. Where an industry has powerful suppliers—monopolistic suppliers of components or employees united by a strong labor union—a substantial part of the surplus may be appropriated by these suppliers (the profits of suppliers or premium wages of union members).

The profits earned by the firms in an industry are thus determined by three factors:

- the value of the product to customers
- the intensity of competition
- the bargaining power of producers relative to their suppliers and buyers.

Industry analysis brings all three factors into a single analytic framework.

## Analyzing Industry Attractiveness

Table 3.1 shows the profitability of different U.S. industries. Some industries (such as tobacco and pharmaceuticals) consistently earn high rates of profit; others (airlines, paper, and food production) fail to cover their cost of capital. The basic premise that underlies industry analysis is that the level of industry profitability is neither random nor the result of entirely industry-specific influences—it is determined by the systematic influences of the industry's structure. The pharmaceutical industry and the personal computer industry not only supply very different products; they also have very different structures, which make one highly profitable and the other a nightmare of price competition and weak margins. The pharmaceutical industry produces highly differentiated products bought by price-insensitive consumers and new products receive monopoly privileges in the form of patents. The personal computer industry comprises many firms, produces commoditized products, and is squeezed by powerful suppliers (for example, Intel and Microsoft).

Small markets can often support much higher profitability that large markets for the simple reason that small markets can more easily be dominated by a single firm.

**TABLE 3.1** The profitability of U.S. industries, 1999–2007

| Industry | Median ROE 1999–2007 (%) | Leading companies |
| --- | --- | --- |
| Household and personal products | 26.0 | Procter & Gamble, Kimberley-Clark, Colgate-Palmolive |
| Pharmaceuticals | 21.0 | Pfizer, Johnson & Johnson, Merck |
| Petroleum | 20.1 | ExxonMobil, Chevron, ConocoPhillips |
| Tobacco | 19.7 | Altria, Reynolds American, Universal |
| Food consumer products | 19.5 | PepsiCo, Sara Lee, Conagra |
| Securities and investment banking | 18.4 | Morgan Stanley, Merrill Lynch, Goldman Sachs |
| Mining, crude oil production | 18.0 | Occidental Petroleum, Devon Energy |
| Medical products and equipment | 17.7 | Medtronic, Baxter International |
| Beverages | 17.2 | Coca-Cola, Anheuser-Busch |
| Food services | 16.6 | McDonald's, Yum Brands |
| Scientific, photographic, and control equipment | 15.6 | Eastman Kodak, Danaher, Aligent |
| Diversified financials | 15.5 | General Electric, American Express |
| Commercial banks | 14.8 | Citigroup, Bank of America |
| Apparel | 14.4 | Nike, VF, Jones Apparel |
| Electronics, electrical equipment | 14.3 | Emerson Electric, Whirlpool |
| Oil and gas equipment and services | 14.3 | Halliburton, Baker Hughes |
| Computer software | 14.0 | Microsoft, Oracle, CA |
| Aerospace and defense | 13.9 | Boeing, United Technologies, Lockheed Martin |
| Specialty retailers | 13.8 | Home Depot, Costco, Lowe's |
| Chemicals | 13.8 | Dow Chemical, DuPont |
| Computers, office equipment | 13.5 | IBM, Hewlett-Packard, Dell Computer |

**TABLE 3.1** (*Continued*)

| Industry | Median ROE 1999–2007 (%) | Leading companies |
|---|---|---|
| Healthcare | 13.1 | United Health Group, Wellpoint, HCA, Medco |
| Industrial and farm equipment | 13.1 | Caterpillar, Deere, Illinois Tool Works |
| Hotels, casinos, resorts | 12.7 | Marriott International, Harrah's Entertainment |
| Publishing, printing | 12.5 | R. R. Donnelley & Sons, Gannett |
| Engineering, construction | 12.4 | Flour, Jacobs Engineering |
| I.T. services | 12.4 | EDS, Computer Sciences, Science Applications Intl. |
| General merchandisers | 12.3 | Wal-Mart, Target, Sears Holdings |
| Trucking, truck leasing | 12.2 | YRC Worldwide, Ryder System |
| Metals | 11.8 | Alcoa, U.S. Steel, Nucor |
| Wholesalers: food and grocery | 11.3 | Sysco, Supervalu, CHS |
| Energy production | 11.2 | Constellation Energy, ONEOK |
| Pipelines | 11.2 | Plains All-American Pipeline, Enterprise Products |
| Packaging and containers | 10.9 | Smurfit-Stone Container, Owens-Illinois |
| Automotive retailing and services | 10.7 | AutoNation, United Auto Group |
| Utilities: gas and electric | 10.6 | DU.K.e Energy, Dominion Resources |
| Food and drug stores | 10.6 | Kroger, Walgreen, Albertson's |
| Furniture | 10.4 | Leggett & Platt, Steelcase |
| Real estate | 9.9 | Cendant, Host Marriott, Simon Property Group |
| Building materials, glass | 9.9 | Owens Corning, USG, Armstrong Holdings |
| Insurance: property and casualty | 9.5 | American Intl. Group, Berkshire Hathaway |
| Motor vehicles and parts | 9.3 | GM, Ford, Johnson Controls |
| Insurance: life and health | 9.1 | MetLife, New York Life |
| Forest and paper products | 7.3 | International Paper, Weyerhaeuser |
| Food production | 6.5 | Archer Daniels Midland, Tyson Foods |
| Semiconductors and electronic components | 6.2 | Intel, Texas Instruments, Sanmina-SCI |
| Network and communications equipment | 5.9 | Motorola, Cisco Systems, Lucent |
| Telecommunications | 5.8 | Verizon, AT&T, Sprint-Nextel |
| Entertainment | 2.7 | Time Warner, Walt Disney, News Corp. |
| Airlines | (12.6) | AMR, UAL, Delta Airlines |

*Note:*

Median ROE for each industry averaged across the seven years 1999–2007. Industries with five or fewer firms were excluded. Also omitted were industries that were substantially redefined during 1999–2007.

*Source:*

Data from Fortune 1000 by industry.

Strategy Capsule 3.1 offers examples of niche markets that are havens from the rigors of fierce competition.

The underlying theory of how industry structure drives competitive behavior and determines industry profitability is provided by industrial organization (IO) economics. The two reference points are the *theory of monopoly* and the *theory of*

## STRATEGY CAPSULE 3.1
# Chewing Tobacco, Sausage Skins, and Slot Machines: The Joys of Niche Markets

*UST Inc.* was the most profitable company in the S&P500 over the period 2003–8 (in 2008 it was acquired by Altria, the owner of Philip Morris) with an average annual ROIC (operating profit as percentage of total assets less current liabilities) of 63%. What's the secret of UST's profitability? It controls 78% of the U.S. market for "smokeless tobacco" (chewing tobacco and snuff), with brands such as Skoal, Copenhagen and Red Seal. Despite its association with a bygone era of cowboys and farm workers, chewing tobacco has been a growth market in the U.S. UST's long-established brands, its distribution through tens of thousands of small retail outlets, and restrictions on advertising tobacco products have created formidable barriers to entry into this market.

*Devro plc,* based in the Scottish village of Moodiesburn, is the world's leading supplier of collagen sausage skins ("casings"). "From the British 'Banger' to the Chinese Lap Cheong,

from the French Merguez to the South American Chourizo, Devro has a casing to suit all product types." Its overall world market share is around 60%, with about 80% of the U.K. and Australian markets. In recent years its ROIC has averaged 18% and its return on equity was 20%.

*International Game Technology* (IGT) based in Reno, Nevada, is the world's dominant manufacturer of slot machines for casinos. ITG maintains its 70% U.S. market share through close relations with casino operators and a continuous flow of new products. With heavy investment in R&D, new product saturation, tight control over distribution and servicing, and a policy of leasing rather than selling machines, IGT offers little opportunity to rivals. During 2004–7, IGT earned an average ROE of 31%.

*Sources:* www.ustinc.com, www.devro.com, www.igt.com.

*perfect competition,* which form end points of the spectrum of industry structures. *Monopoly* exists where an industry comprises a single firm protected by high barriers to entry. The monopolist can appropriate in profit the full amount of the value it creates. At the other extreme, *perfect competition* exists where there are many firms supplying an identical product with no restrictions on entry or exit. Here, the rate of profit falls to a level that just covers firms' cost of capital. In the real world, industries fall between these two extremes. The U.S. market for chewing tobacco is close to being a monopoly; the Chicago grain markets are close to being perfectly competitive. Most manufacturing industries and many service industries tend to be *oligopolies:* they are dominated by a small number of major companies. Table 3.2 identifies some key points on the spectrum. By examining the principal structural features and their interactions for any particular industry, it is possible to predict the type of competitive behavior likely to emerge and the resulting level of profitability.

**TABLE 3.2**  The spectrum of industry structures

|  | Perfect Competition | Oligopoly | Duopoly | Monopoly |
|---|---|---|---|---|
| *Concentration* | Many firms | A few firms | Two firms | One firm |
| *Entry and exit barriers* | No barriers | Significant barriers | | High barriers |
| *Product differentiation* | Homogeneous product (Commodity) | Potential for product differentiation | | |
| *Information availability* | No impediments to information flow | Imperfect availability of information | | |

## Porter's Five Forces of Competition Framework

Table 3.2 identifies four structural variables influencing competition and profitability. In practice there are many features of an industry that determine the intensity of competition and the level of profitability. A helpful, widely used framework for classifying and analyzing these factors was developed by Michael Porter of Harvard Business School.[2] Porter's five forces of competition framework views the profitability of an industry (as indicated by its rate of return on capital relative to its cost of capital) as determined by five sources of competitive pressure. These five forces of competition include three sources of "horizontal" competition: competition from substitutes, competition from entrants, and competition from established rivals; and two sources of "vertical" competition: the power of suppliers and power of buyers (see Figure 3.2).

**FIGURE 3.2**  Porter's five forces of competition framework

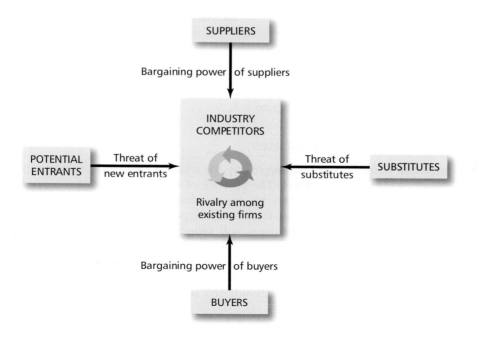

**FIGURE 3.3** The structural determinants of the five forces of competition

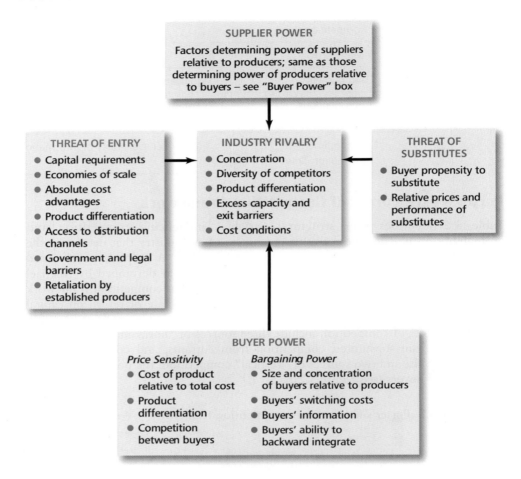

The strength of each of these competitive forces is determined by a number of key structural variables, as shown in Figure 3.3.

## Competition from Substitutes

The price that customers are willing to pay for a product depends, in part, on the availability of substitute products. The absence of close substitutes for a product, as in the case of gasoline or cigarettes, means that consumers are comparatively insensitive to price (demand is inelastic with respect to price). The existence of close substitutes means that customers will switch to substitutes in response to price increases for the product (demand is elastic with respect to price). The internet has provided a new source of substitute competition that has proved devastating for a number of established industries. Travel agencies, newspapers and telecommunication providers have all suffered severe competition from internet-based substitutes.

The extent to which substitutes depress prices and profits depends on the propensity of buyers to substitute between alternatives. This, in turn, depends on their price-performance characteristics. If city-center to city-center travel between Washington and New York is 50 minutes quicker by air than by train and the average traveler values time at $30 an hour, the implication is that the train will be competitive at fares of $25 below those charged by the airlines. The more complex the product and the more difficult it is to discern performance differences, the lower the extent of substitution by customers on the basis of price differences. The failure of low-priced imitations of leading perfumes to establish significant market share reflects consumers' difficulty in recognizing the performance characteristics of different fragrances.

## Threat of Entry

If an industry earns a return on capital in excess of its cost of capital, it will act as a magnet to firms outside the industry. If the entry of new firms is unrestricted, the rate of profit will fall toward its competitive level. The U.S. bagel industry faced a flood of new entrants in the late 1990s that caused a sharp decline in profitability.[3] Why is it that my wife, a psychotherapist, earns much less than our niece, a recently qualified medical doctor? Barriers to entry are one factor. In psychotherapy there are multiple accrediting bodies and limited state licensing, hence the entry barriers to psychotherapy are much lower than in medicine.

Threat of entry rather than actual entry may be sufficient to ensure that established firms constrain their prices to the competitive level. Only American Airlines offers a direct service between Dallas-Fort Worth and Santa Barbara, California, for example. Yet American may be unwilling to exploit its monopoly power to the full if Southwest or another airline can easily extend its routes to cover the same two cities. An industry where no barriers to entry or exit exist is *contestable*: prices and profits tend towards the competitive level, regardless of the number of firms within the industry.[4] Contestability depends on the absence of sunk costs—investments whose value cannot be recovered on exit. An absence of sunk costs makes an industry vulnerable to "hit-and-run" entry whenever established firms raise their prices above the competitive level.

In most industries, however, new entrants cannot enter on equal terms with those of established firms. A barrier to entry is any advantage that established firms have over entrants. The height of a barrier to entry is usually measured as the unit cost disadvantage faced by would-be entrants. The principal sources of barriers to entry are discussed below.

*Capital Requirements*  The capital costs of becoming established in an industry can be so large as to discourage all but the largest companies. The duopoly of Boeing and Airbus in large passenger jets is protected by the huge capital costs of establishing R&D, production and service facilities for supplying these planes. Likewise with the business of launching commercial satellites: the costs of developing rockets and launch facilities make new entry highly unlikely. In other industries, entry costs can be modest. One reason why the e-commerce boom of the late 1990s ended in financial disaster for most participants is that the initial setup costs of new internet-based ventures were typically very low. Across the service sector more generally, startup costs tend to be low. For example, startup costs for a franchised pizza outlet begin at $120 000 for a Domino's and $638 000 for a Pizza Hut.[5]

*Economies of Scale* In industries that are capital or research or advertising intensive, efficiency requires large-scale operation. The problem for new entrants is that they are faced with the choice of either entering on a small scale and accepting high unit costs, or entering on a large scale and bearing the costs of underutilized capacity. In automobiles, cost efficiency means producing at least three million vehicles a year. As a result, the only recent entrants into volume car production have been state-supported companies (for example, Proton of Malaysia and Maruti of India). The main source of scale economies is new product development costs. Thus, developing and launching a new model of car typically costs over $1.5 billion. Airbus's A380 superjumbo cost about $18 billion to develop and must sell about 400 planes to break even. Once Airbus had committed to the project, then Boeing was effectively excluded from the superjumbo segment of the market.

*Absolute Cost Advantages* Established firms may have a unit cost advantage over entrants irrespective of scale. Absolute cost advantages often result from the acquisition of low-cost sources of raw materials. Saudi Aramco's access to the world's biggest and most accessible oil reserves give it an unassailable cost advantage over Shell, Exxon Mobil, and BP, whose costs per barrel are at least four times those of Saudi Aramco. Absolute cost advantages may also result from economies of learning. Sharp's cost advantage in LCD flat screen TVs results from its early entry into LCDs and its speed in moving down the learning curve.

*Product Differentiation* In an industry where products are differentiated, established firms possess the advantages of brand recognition and customer loyalty. The percentage of U.S. consumers loyal to a single brand varies from under 30% in batteries, canned vegetables and garbage bags, up to 61% in toothpaste, 65% in mayonnaise and 71% in cigarettes.[6] New entrants to such markets must spend disproportionately heavily on advertising and promotion to gain levels of brand awareness and brand goodwill similar to those of established companies. One study found that, compared to early entrants, late entrants into consumer goods markets incurred additional advertising and promotional costs amounting to 2.12% of sales revenue.[7]

*Access to Channels of Distribution* For many new suppliers of consumer goods, the principal barrier to entry is likely to be gaining distribution. Limited capacity within distribution channels (for example, shelf space), risk aversion by retailers and the fixed costs associated with carrying an additional product result in retailers being reluctant to carry a new manufacturer's product. The battle for supermarket shelf space between the major food processors (typically involving "slotting fees" to reserve shelf space) further disadvantages new entrants. One of the most important competitive impacts of the internet has been allowing new businesses to circumvent barriers to distribution.

*Governmental and Legal Barriers* Economists from the Chicago School claim that the only effective barriers to entry are those created by government. In taxi cabs, banking, telecommunications and broadcasting, entry usually requires a license from a public authority. From medieval times to the present day, companies and favored individuals have benefitted from governments granting them an exclusive right to ply a particular trade or offer a particular service. In knowledge-intensive industries, patents, copyrights and other legally protected forms of intellectual property are major barriers to entry. In the pharmaceutical industry, the major players seek to delay entry by generic drug makers by extending their original patents through changes in dosage and delivery modes. Regulatory requirements and environmental and safety standards often put new entrants at a disadvantage in comparison with established firms because compliance costs tend to weigh more heavily on newcomers.

*Retaliation*  Barriers to entry also depend on the entrants' expectations as to possible retaliation by established firms. Retaliation against a new entrant may take the form of aggressive price cutting, increased advertising, sales promotion, or litigation. The major airlines have a long history of retaliation against low-cost entrants. Southwest and other budget airlines have alleged that selective price cuts by American and other major airlines amounted to predatory pricing designed to prevent its entry into new routes.[8] To avoid retaliation by incumbents, new entrants may seek initial small-scale entry into less visible market segments. When Toyota, Nissan and Honda first entered the U.S. auto market, they targeted the small car segments, partly because this was a segment that had been written off by the Detroit Big Three as inherently unprofitable.[9]

*The Effectiveness of Barriers to Entry*  Industries protected by high entry barriers tend to earn above average rates of profit.[10] Capital requirements and advertising appear to be particularly effective impediments to entry.[11]

The effectiveness of barriers to entry depends on the resources and capabilities that potential entrants possess. Barriers that are effective against new companies may be ineffective against established firms that are diversifying from other industries.[12] Google has used its massive web presence as a platform for entering a number of other markets—including Microsoft's seemingly impregnable position in browsers.

## Rivalry Between Established Competitors

For most industries, the major determinant of the overall state of competition and the general level of profitability is competition among the firms within the industry. In some industries, firms compete aggressively—sometimes to the extent that prices are pushed below the level of costs and industry-wide losses are incurred. In other industries, price competition is muted and rivalry focuses on advertising, innovation, and other nonprice dimensions. The intensity of competition between established firms is the result of interactions between six factors. Let us look at each of them.

*Concentration*  Seller concentration refers to the number and size distribution of firms competing within a market. It is most commonly measured by the *concentration ratio*: the combined market share of the leading producers. For example, the four-firm concentration ratio (*CR4*) is the market share of the four largest producers. In markets dominated by a single firm (for example, Microsoft in PC operating systems, or UST in the U.S. smokeless tobacco market), the dominant firm can exercise considerable discretion over the prices it charges. Where a market is dominated by a small group of leading companies (an oligopoly), price competition may also be restrained, either by outright collusion, or more commonly through "parallelism" of pricing decisions.[13] Thus, in markets dominated by two companies, such as alkaline batteries (Duracell and Energizer), color film (Kodak and Fuji) and soft drinks (Coke and Pepsi), prices tend to be similar and competition focuses on advertising, promotion and product development. As the number of firms supplying a market increases, coordination of prices becomes more difficult and the likelihood that one firm will initiate price cutting increases. However, despite the frequent observation that the exit of a competitor reduces price competition, while the entry of a new competitor stimulates it, there is little systematic evidence that seller concentration increases profitability. Richard Schmalensee concluded that: "The relation, if any, between seller concentration and profitability is weak statistically and the estimated effect is usually small."[14]

*Diversity of Competitors*   The extent to which a group of firms can avoid price competition in favor of collusive pricing practices depends on how similar they are in their origins, objectives, costs and strategies. The cozy atmosphere of the U.S. auto industry prior to the advent of import competition was greatly assisted by the similarities of the companies in terms of cost structures, strategies, and top management mindsets. The intense competition that affects the car markets of Europe and North America today is partly due to the different national origins, costs, strategies, and management styles of the competing firms. Similarly, the key challenge faced by OPEC is agreeing and enforcing output quotas among member countries that are sharply different in terms of objectives, production costs, politics and religion.

*Product Differentiation*   The more similar the offerings among rival firms, the more willing are customers to switch between them and the greater is the inducement for firms to cut prices to boost sales. Where the products of rival firms are virtually indistinguishable, the product is a *commodity* and price is the sole basis for competition. Commodity industries such as agriculture, mining and petrochemicals tend to be plagued by price wars and low profits. By contrast, in industries where products are highly differentiated (perfumes, pharmaceuticals, restaurants, management consulting services), price competition tends to be weak, even though there may be many firms competing.

*Excess Capacity and Exit Barriers*   Why does industry profitability tend to fall so drastically during periods of recession? The key is the balance between demand and capacity. Unused capacity encourages firms to offer price cuts to attract new business. Excess capacity may be cyclical (for example, the boom-bust cycle in the semiconductor industry); it may also be part of a structural problem resulting from overinvestment and declining demand. In these latter situations, the key issue is whether excess capacity will leave the industry. *Barriers to exit* are costs associated with capacity leaving an industry. Where resources are durable and specialized, and where employees are entitled to job protection, barriers to exit may be substantial.[15] In the European and North American auto industry, excess capacity together with high exit barriers have devastated industry profitability. Conversely, rapid demand growth creates capacity shortages that boost margins. Expanding world trade, fueled by the growth of China, pushed up charter rates of large bulk carriers ("Capesizes") from under $18 000 a day at the beginning of 2003 to a peak of $233 988 per day on June 5, 2008. With the onset of global recession and fleet expansion by ship owners, rates declined precipitously to a mere $2773 a day by November 26, 2008.[16]

**FIGURE 3.4** The impact of growth on profitability

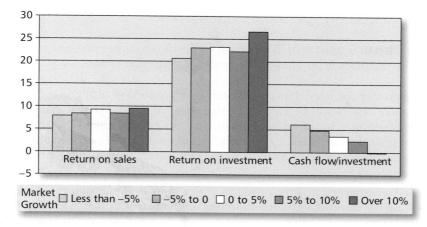

*Source:*

R. D. Buzzell and B. T. Gale, *The PIMS Principles* (New York: Free Press, 1987): 56–7. © 1987 The Free Press. Reproduced by permission of Simon & Schuster.

On average, companies in growing industries earn higher profits than companies in slow growing or declining industries (see Figure 3.4).

*Cost Conditions: Scale Economies and the Ratio of Fixed to Variable Costs* When excess capacity causes price competition, how low will prices go? The key factor is cost structure. Where fixed costs are high relative to variable costs, firms will take on marginal business at any price that covers variable costs. The consequences for profitability can be disastrous. In the airline industry, the emergence of excess capacity almost invariably leads to price wars and industry-wide losses. The willingness of airlines to offer heavily discounted tickets on flights with low bookings reflects the very low variable costs of filling empty seats. During the 2009 recession, the industries that have suffered the most drastic falls in profitability (autos, mining, hotels) tended to be those where fixed costs are high and firms are willing to accept additional business at any price that covers variable costs.

Scale economies may also encourage companies to compete aggressively on price in order to gain the cost benefits of greater volume. If scale efficiency in the auto industry means producing four million cars a year, a level that is currently achieved by only five companies, the outcome is a battle for market share as each firm tries to achieve critical mass.

## Bargaining Power of Buyers

The firms in an industry compete in two types of markets: in the markets for inputs and the markets for outputs. In input markets firms purchase raw materials, components and financial and labor services. In the markets for outputs, firms sell their goods and services to customers (who may be distributors, consumers or other manufacturers). In both markets the transactions create value for both buyers and sellers. How this value is shared between them in terms of profitability depends on their relative economic power. Let us deal first with output markets. The strength of buying power that firms face from their customers depends on two sets of factors: buyers' price sensitivity and relative bargaining power.

*Buyers' Price Sensitivity*  The extent to which buyers are sensitive to the prices charged by the firms in an industry depends on four main factors:

- The greater the importance of an item as a proportion of total cost, the more sensitive buyers will be about the price they pay. Beverage manufacturers are highly sensitive to the costs of aluminum cans because this is one of their largest single cost items. Conversely, most companies are not sensitive to the fees charged by their auditors, since auditing costs are a tiny fraction of total company expenses.
- The less differentiated the products of the supplying industry, the more willing the buyer is to switch suppliers on the basis of price. The manufacturers of T-shirts and light bulbs have much more to fear from Wal-Mart's buying power than have the suppliers of perfumes.
- The more intense the competition among buyers, the greater their eagerness for price reductions from their sellers. As competition in the world automobile industry has intensified, so component suppliers face greater pressures for lower prices.
- The more critical an industry's product to the quality of the buyer's product or service, the less sensitive are buyers to the prices they are charged. The buying power of personal computer manufacturers relative to the manufacturers of microprocessors (Intel and AMD) is limited by the vital importance of these components to the functionality of PCs.

*Relative Bargaining Power*  Bargaining power rests, ultimately, on refusal to deal with the other party. The balance of power between the two parties to a transaction depends on the credibility and effectiveness with which each makes this threat. The key issue is the relative cost that each party sustains as a result of the transaction not being consummated. A second issue is each party's expertise in managing its position. Several factors influence the bargaining power of buyers relative to that of sellers:

- *Size and concentration of buyers relative to suppliers.* The smaller the number of buyers and the bigger their purchases, the greater the cost of losing one. Because of their size, health maintenance organizations (HMOs) can purchase healthcare from hospitals and doctors at much lower cost than can individual patients. Empirical studies show that buyer concentration lowers prices and profits in the supplying industry.[17]
- *Buyers' information.* The better informed buyers are about suppliers and their prices and costs, the better they are able to bargain. Doctors and lawyers do not normally display the prices they charge, nor do traders in the bazaars of Tangier and Istanbul. Keeping customers ignorant of relative prices is an effective constraint on their buying power. But knowing prices is of little value if the quality of the product is unknown. In the markets for haircuts, interior design, and management consulting, the ability of buyers

to bargain over price is limited by uncertainty over the precise attributes of the product they are buying.

- *Ability to integrate vertically.* In refusing to deal with the other party, the alternative to finding another supplier or buyer is to do it yourself. Large food-processing companies such as Heinz and Campbell Soup have reduced their dependence on the manufacturers of metal cans by manufacturing their own. The leading retail chains have increasingly displaced their suppliers' brands with their own-brand products. Backward integration need not necessarily occur—a credible threat may suffice.

## Bargaining Power of Suppliers

Analysis of the determinants of relative power between the producers in an industry and their suppliers is precisely analogous to analysis of the relationship between producers and their buyers. The only difference is that it is now the firms in the industry that are the buyers and the producers of inputs that are the suppliers. The key issues are the ease with which the firms in the industry can switch between different input suppliers and the relative bargaining power of each party.

Because raw materials, semi-finished products and components are often commodities supplied by small companies to large manufacturing companies, their suppliers usually lack bargaining power. Hence, commodity suppliers often seek to boost their bargaining power through cartelization (for example, OPEC, the International Coffee Organization, and farmers' marketing cooperatives). A similar logic explains labor unions. Conversely, the suppliers of complex, technically sophisticated components may be able to exert considerable bargaining power. The dismal profitability of the personal computer industry may be attributed to the power exercised by the suppliers of key components (processors, disk drives, LCD screens) and the dominant supplier of operating systems (Microsoft).

Labor unions are important sources of supplier power. Where an industry has a high percentage of its employees unionized—as in steel, airlines, and automobiles—profitability is reduced (see Figure 3.5).

**FIGURE 3.5** The impact of unionization on profitability

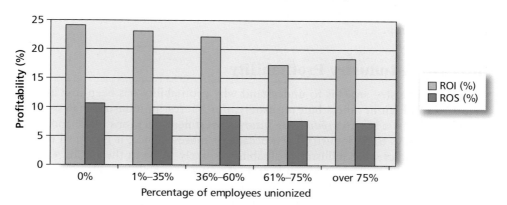

*Source:*

R. D. Buzzell and B. T. Gale, *The PIMS Principles* (New York: Free Press, 1987): 56–7. © 1987 The Free Press. Reproduced by permission of Simon & Schuster.

## Applying Industry Analysis

Once we understand how industry structure drives competition, which, in turn, determines industry profitability, we can apply this analysis, first to forecast industry profitability in the future, second, to position the firm in relation it the competitive forces it faces and, third, to find ways of changing industry structure for the better.

## Describing Industry Structure

The first stage of industry analysis is to identify the key elements of the industry's structure. In principle, this is a simple task. It requires identifying who are the main players—the producers, the customers, the input suppliers, and the producers of substitute goods—then examining some of the key structural characteristics of each of these groups that will determine competition and bargaining power.

In most manufacturing industries the identity of the different groups of players is usually straightforward, in other industries—particularly in service industries—building a picture of the industry may be more difficult. Consider the supply of television programming. There are a number of different types of player and establishing which are buyers, which are sellers, and where the industry boundaries lie is not simple. In terms of industry definition, do we consider all forms of TV distribution or identify separate industries for broadcast TV, cable TV and satellite TV? In terms of identifying buyers and sellers we see that there the industry has quite a complex value chain with the producers of the individual shows, networks that put together program schedules, and local broadcasting and cable companies that undertake final distribution. For the distribution companies there are two buyers—viewers and advertisers. Some companies are vertically integrated across several stages of the value chain—thus, networks such as Fox and NBC not only create and distribute program schedules, they are also backward integrated into producing some TV shows and they are forward integrated into local distribution through ownership of local TV stations.

Sorting out the different players and their relationships therefore involves some critical issues of industry definition. Which activities within the value chain do we include in the industry? What are the horizontal boundaries of the industry in terms of both products and geographical scope? We shall return to some of these issues of industry definition.

## Forecasting Industry Profitability

We can use industry analysis to understand why profitability has been low in some industries and high in others but, ultimately, our interest in industry analysis is not to explain the past but to *predict the future*. Investment decisions made today will commit resources to an industry for a decade or more—hence, it is critical that we are able to predict what industry profitability is likely to be in the future. Current profitability tends to be a poor indicator of future profitability. However, if an industry's profitability is determined by the structure of that industry then we can use observations of the structural trends in an industry to forecast the likely changes in competition and profitability. Changes in industry structure tend to be the result of fundamental shifts in customer buying behavior, technology and firm strategies.

Hence we can use our current observations of the developments to identify emerging trends in industry structure.

To predict the future profitability of an industry, our analysis proceeds in three stages:

**1** Examine how the industry's current and recent levels of competition and profitability are a consequence of its present structure.

**2** Identify the trends that are changing the industry's structure. Is the industry consolidating? Are new players seeking to enter? Are the industry's products becoming more differentiated or more commoditized? Will additions to industry capacity will outstrip growth of demand?

**3** Identify how these structural changes will affect the five forces of competition and resulting profitability of the industry. Will the changes in industry structure cause competition to intensify or to weaken? Rarely do all the structural changes move competition in a consistent direction—typically, some factors will cause competition to increase; others will cause competition to moderate. Hence, determining the overall impact on profitability is likely to be a matter of judgment.

Strategy Capsule 3.2 discusses the outlook for profitability in the wireless handset industry while Strategy Capsule 3.3 takes a retrospective look at the dotcom boom of 1998–2001. Could industry analysis have alerted us to the fact that that most e-commerce markets had limited scope for profitability?

---

**STRATEGY CAPSULE 3.2**

# The Future of the Wireless Handset Industry

Wireless telephony has been one of the greatest growth industries of the past two decades—and almost as lucrative for the handset makers as for the service providers. During the 1990s, growth of handset sales in North America, Europe and Japan averaged close to 50% each year and generating massive profits and shareholder value for the early leaders, Motorola and Nokia.

The current decade has witnessed a profound change in competition and margins. Despite continued demand growth (especially in emerging markets), profitability has fallen. During 2000–5, the industry leaders—Nokia, Motorola, Sony-Ericsson, and Samsung—earned an average pretax margin of 20.2% on their sales of mobile devices; by 2006–8 this had fallen to 8.9% (with Motorola incurring substantial losses). Departures from the industry included Philips, Siemens, Mitsubishi and Sanyo.

The structural changes undermining industry profitability are not hard to find. Low entry barriers have resulted in a large number and a wide variety of companies competing. In addition to established telecom equipment manufacturers (Ericsson, Lucent, Alcatel) and consumer electronics companies (Sony, Sharp, LG, Samsung, Hitachi, Toshiba and Matsushita), a number of new players have emerged onto the international stage. These include a number of manufacturers from Taiwan (HTC, BenQ) and mainland China (Huawei, ZTE, Lenovo)—many of these recent entrants were former contract manufacturers now supplying under their own brands. During 2007/8, the world handset market was further shaken up with the entry of Apple's iPhone and Google's introduction of its Android mobile operating system.

The handset manufacturers also face strong vertical bargaining power on both sides. Not only are the service providers the biggest distributors of mobile handsets—they are in a continuous struggle with the handset manufacturers for preeminence in consumer brand loyalty. Thus, Vodafone, Orange and Verizon seek to strengthen their bargaining power by ordering specially-designed handsets manufactured under their own brands.

At the other end, the manufacturers deal with powerful suppliers including the suppliers of digital signaling chips and operating systems (Microsoft, Symbian, and Palm).

Over the period 2010–14, the structural trends that have eroded profitability over the past decade seem likely to continue. Market saturation will spread from the mature to the emerging markets. The global recession will further dampen demand growth. Yet despite the prospect of excess manufacturing capability, there is a continuous risk that new entry will continue to boost the already excessive number of mobile phone suppliers. Widespread outsourcing by the leading suppliers to contract manufacturers in Asia and elsewhere means that there are many firms with the manufacturing capability and know-how ready to enter the market with their own brands of handset.

Two major uncertainties are, first, the future of product differentiation and, second, the balance of bargaining power between handset manufacturers and service providers. In terms of product differentiation there are two conflicting forces: the growing demand for low-cost, technologically unsophisticated handsets in emerging markets, which suggests increasing commoditization, and the technological opportunities provided by 3G and 4G technologies, mobile internet, and convergence of handheld digital devices. While advancing technologies and multifunctionality (for example, mobile phone as a device for internet access, GPS, TV and music) increases the potential for product differentiation, it also appears that most forms of differentiation are easily imitated. The distinction between "smartphones", such as RIM's Blackberry and Apple's iPhone, and mainstream wireless handsets has been disappearing. During 2009, it seemed that, as a result of market power and control over distribution, the service producers would continue to hold the balance of vertical power. Much would depend upon which side had greater control over technology.

## STRATEGY CAPSULE 3.3

# The Internet: Value Creator or Value Destroyer?

The diffusion of the internet during the late 1990s and the wave of e-business startups that sought to exploit it contributed to one of the most spectacular stock market booms in history. Webvan, Pets.com, Kozmo, eToys.com, and Boo.com burned through hundreds of millions of dollars of venture capital and achieved stock market values that reached $1.2 billion (in the case of Webvan) before descending into oblivion.

Could the application of strategic analysis to e-business have revealed the dubious profit potential of dotcoms? Applying five forces analysis to the sectors offers some simple yet startling insights:

- *Substitutes.* Most new e-commerce startups were not fundamentally new businesses; they used a new distribution channel for existing goods and services: books (Amazon), airline tickets (Expedia), groceries (Peapod) and securities (E-trade). As such, they faced strong substitute competition from traditional retailers

- *Threat of entry.* Most e-commerce businesses are characterized by low costs of entry and ease of market access (setting up a web site costs little). Most markets suffered many more entrants than the level of demand could support.

- *Rivalry.* Ease of entry implied many competitors, the ubiquity of internet technology made differentiation difficult, while the internet's global span meant the absence of geographical niches.

- *Supplier power.* The suppliers of web software and owners of major portals possessed significant bargaining power.

- *Buyer power.* The transparency of prices and low switching costs resulted in high price sensitivity of customers.

The implication is that most "e-tailing" markets—whether for books, securities, household goods or hotel accommodation, will tend to be highly competitive and, on average, will generate low margins. Will any e-businesses offer high profitability? The key is the potential to reduce rivalry and raise barriers to entry through strategies that exploit network effects, economies of scale or product differentiation. For example, E-bay exploits network effects to dominate the person-to-person auction business. In books Amazon relies on scale economies and product differentiation through its range of customer services. Google exploits scale economies and differentiation based upon rapid innovation to dominate web search.

**Sources**: M. E. Porter, "Strategy and the Internet," *Harvard Business Review* (March 2001): 63–77; "The E-Commerce Winners," *Business Week* (August 3, 2001)

## Positioning the Company

Recognizing and understanding the competitive forces that a firm faces within its industry allows managers to position the firm where competitive forces are weakest. The record industry, once reliance on sales of CDs, has been devastated by the substitute competition in the form of digital downloads, piracy and file sharing. Yet not all segments of the recorded music business have been equally affected. The old are less inclined to turn to digital downloading than younger listeners with the result that classical music, country and golden oldies have become comparatively more attractive than pop and hip-hop genres.

Porter describes the success of U.S. truck-maker, Paccar, in sheltering itself from the bargaining power of fleet buyers. By focusing on the preferences of independent owner-operators—for example by providing superior sleeping cabins, higher specification seats, a roadside assistance program—Paccar has consistently been able to earn the higher rate of return in the industry.[18]

Effective positioning requires the firm to anticipate changes in the competitive forces likely to affect the industry. Between 2006 and 2008, the pornographic video industry suffered a massive revenue decline as customers turned to free web sites that featured user-generated content. A leading survivor in the industry is Vivid Entertainment, which invested in its brand and in high-quality production in an effort to differentiate its DVDs from content available on free websites. Vivid has also initiated legal moves—suing AEBN, owner of PornTube—for copyright infringement.[19]

## Strategies to Alter Industry Structure

Understanding how the structural characteristics of an industry determine the intensity of competition and the level of profitability provides a basis for identifying opportunities for changing industry structure to alleviate competitive pressures. The first issue is to identify the key structural features of an industry that are responsible for depressing profitability. The second is to consider which of these structural features are amenable to change through appropriate strategic initiatives. For example:

- The remarkable profit revival in the world steel industry between 2002 and 2008 was mainly the result of rising demand, however it was also supported by the rapid consolidation of the industry, led by Mittal Steel.[20]

- Excess capacity was a major problem in the European petrochemicals industry. Through a series of bilateral plant exchanges, each company built a leading position within a particular product area.[21]

- In the U.S. airline industry, the major airlines have struggled to change an unfavorable industry structure. In the absence of significant product differentiation, the airlines have used frequent-flier schemes to build customer loyalty. Through hub-and-spoke route systems, the companies have achieved dominance of particular airports: American at Dallas-Fort Worth, U.S. Airways at Charlotte NC, and Northwest at Detroit and Memphis. Mergers and alliances have reduced the numbers of competitors on many routes.[22]

- Building entry barriers is a vital strategy for preserving high profitability in the long run. A primary goal of the American Medical Association has been to maintain the incomes of its members by controlling the numbers of doctors trained in the U.S. and imposing barriers to the entry of doctors from overseas.

It is often assumed that dominant firms or firms acting in concert can change their industry structure. Michael Jacobides notion of *architectural advantage* begins with the premise that firms are in a continual state of evolution and all firms—even quite small ones—have the potential to influence the development of industry structure to suit their own interests.[23] Apple has profoundly influenced both the recorded music and audio hardware industries, positioning itself as an intermediary between the two. Google is seeking to influence the development of wireless communications through its Android operating system for mobile phones with a view to extending its dominance of Web search to a wireless internet environment. Achieving "architectural advantage" is all about identifying and then controlling actual and "bottlenecks" within industries. Alleviating bottlenecks that are barriers to oneself (as IKEA did when it transferred furniture assembly from furniture manufacturers to furniture consumers) and creating new ones that protect one's own position (as Microsoft did when it became the supplier of the operating system for the IBM PC) can create massive profit for a firm. To identify opportunities for architectural advantage requires looking beyond the existing boundaries of an industry to consider interacting clusters of industries. Digital imaging comprises suppliers of cameras, printers, software, consumables, and memory. The key to making money in this fiercely competitive sector is to identify potential bottlenecks—activities and technologies where economic power can be established. These might include image editing software (such as Adobe's Photoshop) and sensors.

# Defining Industries: Where to Draw the Boundaries

In our earlier discussion of the structure of the television broadcasting industry, I noted that a key challenge in industry analysis is defining the relevant industry. The Standard Industrial Classification (SIC) offers an official guide but this provides limited practical assistance. Suppose Jaguar, now part of the Tata Group, is assessing its future prospects. In forecasting the profitability of its industry, should Jaguar consider itself part of the "motor vehicles and equipment" industry (SIC 371), the automobile industry (SIC 3712), or the luxury car industry? Should it view its industry as national (U.K.), regional (Europe), or global?

## Industries and Markets

The first issue is clarifying what we mean by the term "industry." Economists define an industry as a group of firms that supplies a market. Hence, a close correspondence exists between markets and industries. So, what's the difference between analyzing industry structure and analyzing market structure? The principal difference is that industry analysis—notably five forces analysis—looks at industry profitability being determined by competition in two markets: product markets and input markets.

Everyday usage makes a bigger distinction between industries and markets. Typically, industries are identified with relatively broad sectors, whereas markets refer to specific products. Thus, the firms within the packaging industry compete in many distinct product markets—glass containers, steel cans, aluminum cans, paper cartons, plastic containers and so on.

Similar issues arise in relation to geographical boundaries. From an economist's viewpoint, the U.S. automobile industry would denote all companies supplying the U.S. auto market—irrespective of their location. In everyday usage, the term "U.S. auto industry" typically refers to auto manufacturers located within the U.S., and is often restricted to U.S.-owned automakers (which now includes primarily Ford and General Motors).

For the purposes of industry analysis, I suggest we adopt the economist's approach to identifying and defining industries. Thus, our starting point is the market: which are the firms that compete to supply a particular product or service? This approach may lead us to discard conventional concepts of industry boundaries. For example, if we are examining competition within the banking industry, it is likely that we would want to regard banking as comprising a number of industries—banks supply a number of distinct services and competition in each product market comprises different sets of firms. Most basic is the distinction between retail banking, corporate (or "wholesale") banking and investment banking. Even retail banking we might want to disaggregate into several different product markets. Thus, deposit taking, transaction services, credit cards and mortgage lending are distinct product offerings with different groups of competing firms. We can disaggregate even further, Strategy Capsule 3.4 outlines a micro-level approach to competitive analysis that focuses on consumers' choices between rival offerings.

## STRATEGY CAPSULE 3.4

# Analyzing Competition in Markets for Offerings

Mathur and Kenyon argue that our conventional concept of industry is fundamentally flawed. To analyze competition, we must begin with customer choice. Customers do not choose a product or a company; their unit of choice is the single *offering*. To analyze competition, it makes no sense to talk about the "watch market" or the "watch industry"—the Patek Philippe 10-day Tourbillon (list price $335 000) does not compete with the $35 Timex Sport Watch. Similarly, a $1400 Swatch Lustrous Bliss Sapphire Watch is not a close competitor to Swatch's $39.95 Pampas Rider. Each model by each watch maker is a separate offering where competitors can be ranked according to their proximity to the focal offering in the mind of the customer.

This micro approach to analyzing competition focuses on customer choices and contrasts sharply with Porter's industry analysis, which examines competition at a much higher level of aggregation.

Should we abandon our more aggregated industry analysis in favor of the meticulously micro analysis advocated by Mathur and Kenyon? The critical consideration is the type of question that we want our competitive analysis to answer. For decisions relating to marketing strategy—including product design, pricing, advertising, distribution, and entry into specific market segments—analysis of competition between narrowly defined offerings in relation to specific customers and customer groups is likely to be particularly revealing.

For understanding and predicting medium-term profit trends, the conventional five forces analysis of broadly defined industries has two virtues. First, it allows us to consider competition in two markets simultaneously—the market for outputs and markets for inputs. Second, it takes account of supply-side substitution. Thus, the Swatch Group can easily switch production capacity between models. Given that it owns 16 brands—including Swatch, Omega, Longines, and Tissot—there is scope for reallocating resources between brands. Hence, for analyzing broad questions of profitability and competitive advantage, it can be useful to consider the watch industry in broad terms.

*Source*: Based on Shiv Mathur and Alfred Kenyon, *Winning Business Strategies* (Oxford: Butterworth-Heinemann, 2007).

# Defining Markets: Substitution in Demand and Supply

I have argued that the key to defining industry boundaries is identifying the relevant market. By focusing on the relevant market, we do not lose sight of the critical relationship among firms within an industry: competition. But how do we define markets?

A market's boundaries are defined by *substitutability*. There are two dimensions to this—substitutability on the demand side and the supply side. Let us consider once more the market within which Jaguar competes. Starting with the demand side, if customers are unwilling to substitute trucks for cars on the basis of price differences, Jaguar's market should be viewed as automobiles rather than all motor vehicles. Again, if customers are only willing to substitute between Jaguars and other makes of luxury cars, then Jaguar's relevant market is luxury cars rather than the automobile market as a whole.

But this fails to take account of substitutability on the supply side. If manufacturers find it easy to switch their production from luxury cars to family sedans to sports cars and the like, such supply-side substitutability would suggest that Jaguar is competing within the broader automobile market. The ability of Toyota, Nissan and Honda to penetrate the luxury car market suggests that supply-side substitutability between mass-market autos and specialty autos is moderately high. Similarly, the automobile industry is frequently defined to include vans and light trucks, since these can be manufactured at the same plants as automobiles (often using the same platforms and engines). So too with "major appliance" manufacturers. They tend to be classified as a single industry, not because consumers are willing to substitute between refrigerators and dishwashers, but because the manufacturers can use the same manufacturing plants and distribution channels for different appliances.

The same considerations apply to the geographical boundaries of markets. Should Jaguar view itself as competing in a single global market or in a series of separate national or regional markets? The criterion here again is substitutability. If customers are willing and able to substitute cars available on different national markets, or if manufacturers are willing and able to divert their output among different countries to take account of differences in margins, then a market is global. The key test of the geographical boundaries of a market is price: if price differences for the same product between different locations tend to be eroded by demand-side and supply-side substitution, then these locations lie within a single market.

In practice, drawing the boundaries of markets and industries is a matter of judgment that depends on the purposes and context of the analysis. If Tata is considering the pricing and market positioning of its Jaguar cars, it must take a micro-level approach that defines markets around each model, in each country, and in relation to different categories of customer (for example, distinguishing between sales to car rental companies and sales to individual consumers). In considering decisions over investments in technology, component plants, and new products, Tata will view Jaguar as one part of its Tata Motor business and will define its market as global and extending across its full range of models. The longer term the decisions are that it is considering, the more broadly it will wish to consider its markets, since substitutability is higher in the long run than in the short term.

Second, the precise delineation of the boundaries of a market or industry is seldom critical to the outcome of our analysis so long as we remain wary of external influences. The market in which an offering competes is a continuum rather than a bounded space. Thus, we may view the competitive market of Disneyland, Anaheim as a set of concentric circles. Closest is Universal Studios Tour. Slightly more distant competitors are Sea World and Six Flags. Further still might be a trip to Las Vegas, or a skiing weekend. Beyond these would be the broader entertainment market that might include cinemas, the beach, or playing video games.

For the purposes of applying the five forces framework, industry definition is not critical. We define an industry "box" within which industry rivals compete, but because we include competitive forces outside the industry box—notably entrants and substitutes—the precise boundaries of the industry box are not greatly important. If we define Disneyland as competing within the broad entertainment industry, then beach and ski resorts are rivals; if we define Disneyland as competing in the theme park industry, then beach and ski resorts are substitutes.[24]

## From Industry Attractiveness to Competitive Advantage: Identifying Key Success Factors

The five forces framework allows us to determine an industry's potential for profit. But how is industry profit shared between the different firms competing in that industry? Let us look explicitly at the sources of competitive advantage within an industry. In subsequent chapters we develop a more comprehensive analysis of competitive advantage. Our goal here is to identify those factors within the firm's market environment that determine the firm's ability to survive and prosper—its *key success factors*.[25] In Strategy Capsule 3.5, Kenichi Ohmae of McKinsey's Tokyo office discusses key success factors in forestry and their link with strategy.

### STRATEGY CAPSULE 3.5

## Probing for Key Success Factors

As a consultant faced with an unfamiliar business or industry, I make a point of first asking the specialists in the business, "What is the secret of success in this industry?" Needless to say, I seldom get an immediate answer and so I pursue the inquiry by asking other questions from a variety of angles in order to establish as quickly as possible some reasonable hypotheses as to key factors for success. In the course of these interviews it usually becomes quite obvious what analyses will be required in order to prove or disprove these hypotheses. By first identifying the probable key factors for success and then screening them by proof or disproof, it is often possible for the strategist to penetrate very quickly to the core of a problem.

Traveling in the U.S. last year, I found myself on one occasion sitting in a plane next to a director of one of the biggest lumber companies in the country. Thinking I might learn something useful in the course of the five-hour flight, I asked him, "What are the key factors for success in the lumber industry?" To my surprise, his reply was immediate: "Owning large forests and maximizing the yield from them." The first of these key factors is a relatively simple matter: purchase of forest land. But his second point required further explanation. Accordingly, my next question was: "What variable or variables do you control in order to maximize the yield from a given tract?"

He replied: "The rate of tree growth is the key variable. As a rule, two factors promote growth: the amount of sunshine and the amount of water. Our company doesn't have many forests with enough of both. In Arizona and Utah, for example, we get more than enough sunshine but too little water and so tree growth is very low. Now, if we could give the trees in those states enough water, they'd be ready in less than 15 years instead of the 30 it takes now. The most important project we have in hand at the moment is aimed at finding out how to do this."

Impressed that this director knew how to work out a key factor strategy for his business, I offered my own contribution: "Then under the opposite conditions, where there is plenty of water but too little sunshine—for example, around the lower reaches of the Columbia River—the key factors should be fertilizers to speed up the growth and the choice of tree varieties that don't need so much sunshine."

Having established in a few minutes the general framework of what we were going to talk about, I spent the rest of the long flight very profitably hearing from him in detail how each of these factors was being applied.

*Source*: Kenichi Ohmae, *The Mind of the Strategist* (New York: McGraw-Hill, 1982): 85. Reproduced by permission of McGraw-Hill.

Like Ohmae, our approach to identifying key success factors is straightforward and commonsense. To survive and prosper in an industry, a firm must meet two criteria: first, it must supply what customers want to buy; second, it must survive competition. Hence, we may start by asking two questions:

- What do our customers want?
- What does the firm need to do to survive competition?

To answer the first question we need to look more closely at customers of the industry and to view them, not as a threat to profitability because of their buying power but as *raison d'être* of the industry and its underlying source of profit. This requires that we inquire: Who are our customers? What are their needs? How do they choose between competing offerings? Once we recognize the basis of customers' preferences we can then identify the factors that confer success upon the individual firm. For example, if consumers choose supermarkets

**FIGURE 3.6** Identifying key success factors

on the basis of price then cost efficiency is the primary basis for competitive advantage and the key success factors are the determinants of inter-firm cost differentials.

The second question requires that we examine the nature of competition in the industry. How intense is competition and what are its key dimensions? Thus, in airlines, it is not enough to offer low fares, convenience and safety. Survival requires sufficient financial strength to weather the intense price competition that accompanies cyclical downturns.

A basic framework for identifying key success factors is presented in Figure 3.6. Application of the framework to identify key success factors in three industries is outlined in Table 3.3.

Key success factors can also be identified through the direct modeling of profitability. In the same way that the five forces analysis models the determinants of industry-level profitability, we can also model firm-level profitability by identifying the drivers of a firm's relative profitability within an industry. Using the same approach as in Chapter 2 (see Figure 2.2), we can disaggregate return on capital employed into component ratios which then point to the main drivers of superior profitability. Figure 3.7 applies this analysis to identifying success factors in retailing.

In some industries, the key drivers of firm-level profitability are well known. Strategy Capsule 3.6 draws upon a well-known profitability formula used in the airline industry to identify key success factors.

The value of success factors in formulating strategy has been scorned by some strategy scholars. Pankaj Ghemawat observes that the "whole idea of identifying a success factor and then chasing it seems to have something in common with the ill-considered medieval hunt for the philosopher's stone, a substance that would

**TABLE 3.3**  Identifying key success factors: steel, fashion clothing, and supermarkets

| | What do customers want? (Analysis of demand) | How do firms survive competition? (Analysis of competition) | Key success factors |
|---|---|---|---|
| **Steel** | Low price<br>Product consistency<br>Reliability of supply Specific technical specifications for special steels | Commodity products, excess capacity, high fixed costs, excess capacity, exit barriers, and substitute competition mean intense price competition and cyclical profitability<br><br>Cost efficiency and financial strength essential | Cost efficiency requires: large-scale plants, low-cost location, rapid capacity adjustment<br><br>Alternatively, high technology, small-scale plants can achieve low costs through flexibility and high productivity<br><br>Differentiation through technical specifications and service quality |
| Fashion clothing | Diversity of customer preferences in terms of garment type, style, quality, color<br>Customers willing to pay premium for brand, style, exclusivity, and quality<br>Mass market highly price sensitive | Low barriers to entry and exit, low seller concentration, and buying power of retail chains imply intense competition<br><br>Differentiation can yield substantial price premium, but imitation is rapid | Combining differentiation with low costs<br>Differentiation requires speed of response to changing fashions, style, reputation, and quality<br>Cost efficiency requires manufacture in low wage countries |
| Supermarkets | Low prices<br>Convenient location<br>Wide range of products adapted to local preferences<br>Fresh/quality produce; good service; ease of parking; pleasant ambience | Intensity of price competition depends on number and proximity of competitors<br>Bargaining power a critical determinant of cost of bought-in goods | Low costs require operational efficiency, scale-efficient stores, large aggregate purchases, low wage costs<br>Differentiation requires large stores (to allow wide product range), convenient location, familiarity with local customer preferences |

transmute everything it touched into gold."[26] Our goal is not to identify "generic strategies" that can guarantee success, simply to recognize commonalities in customer motivation and the nature of competition. In the fashion clothing business we identified key success factors (see Table 3.3). However, if we compare the strategies of Zara, H&M, Diesel, and Benetton, we can see that unique resources and capabilities applied to common success factors results in the adoption of very different strategies.

**FIGURE 3.7** Identifying key success factors through analyzing profit drivers: the case of retailing

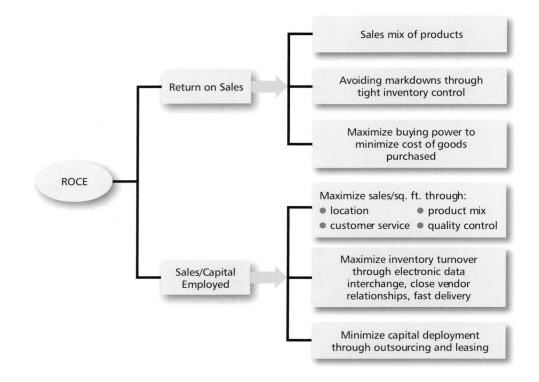

---

## Identifying Key Success Factors by Modeling Profitability: Airlines

Profitability, as measured by operating income per available seat-mile (ASM), is determined by three factors: yield, which is total operating revenues divided by the number of revenue passenger miles (RPMs); load factor, which is the ratio between RPMs and ASMs; and unit cost, which is total operating expenses divided by ASMs. Thus:

$$\frac{income}{ASMs} = \frac{revenue}{RPMs} \times \frac{RPMs}{ASMs} - \frac{expenses}{ASMs}$$

Some of the primary determinants of each of these measures are the following:

- Revenue/RPMs
  - intensity of competition on routes flown
  - effective yield management to permit quick price adjustment to changing market conditions
  - ability to attract business customers
  - superior customer service.

- Load factors
  - competitiveness of prices
  - efficiency of route planning (for example, through hub-and-spoke systems)
  - building customer loyalty through quality of service, frequent-flier programs
  - matching airplane size to demand for individual flights.
- Expenses/ASMs
  - wage rates and benefit levels
  - fuel efficiency of aircraft
  - productivity of employees (determined partly by their job flexibility)
  - load factors
  - level of administrative cost.

In their battle for survival, the airlines have sought to optimize as many of these factors as possible in order to improve their profitability. To enhance revenue, several airlines have withdrawn from their most intensely competitive routes; others have sought to achieve a fare premium over the cut-price airlines through superior punctuality, convenience, comfort, and services. To improve load factors, companies have become more flexible in their pricing and in allocating different planes to different routes. Most notably, companies have sought to cut costs by increasing employee productivity, reducing overhead, sharing services with other airlines and reducing salaries and benefits.

## Summary

In Chapter 1 we established that profound understanding of the competitive environment is a critical ingredient of a successful strategy. In this chapter we have developed a systematic approach to analyzing a firm's industry environment in order to evaluate the industry's profit potential and to identify the sources of competitive advantage. The centerpiece of our approach is Porter's *five forces of competition* framework, which links the structure of an industry to the competitive intensity within it and to the profitability that it realizes. Although every industry is unique, competition and profitability are the result of the systematic influences of a common set of structural variables. The Porter framework provides a simple yet powerful organizing framework for identifying the relevant features of an industry's structure and predicting their implications for competitive behavior. The framework is particularly useful for predicting industry profitability, positioning the firm in relation to these forces, and identifying how the firm can improve industry attractiveness.

As with most of the tools for strategy analysis that we shall consider in this book, the Porter five forces framework is easy to comprehend. Its basis is a substantial body of microeconomic theory but the relationships it posits are straightforward and consistent with common sense. However, real learning about industry analysis and about the Porter framework in particular derives from its *application*. It is only when we apply the Porter framework to analyzing competition and diagnosing the causes of high or low profitability in an industry that we are forced to confront the complexities and subtleties of the model. What industry (or industries) does a company compete in? Where do the industry's boundaries lie? How wide a range of substitutes do we consider? How do the structural features of an industry interact with one another?

I urge you to put the tools of industry analysis to work—not just in your strategic management coursework, but also in your interpretation of everyday business events. What will be the impact of Google's *Android* software platform on the wireless handset industry? How will the financial crisis of 2008–9 affect the structure of U.S. and European banking and what will this mean for competition and profitability?

Through practical applications of the Porter framework, we shall also become aware of its limitations. In the next chapter we look to ways in which we can extend and augment our analysis with additional concepts, tools, and frameworks.

## Self-Study Questions

1   The major forces shaping the business environment of the fixed-line telecom industry are technology and government policy. The industry has been influenced by fiber-optics (greatly increasing transmission capacity), new modes of telecommunication (wireless and internet telephony), deregulation, and privatization. Using the five forces of competition framework, show how each of these developments has influenced competition in the fixed-line telecom industry.

2   From Table 3.1, select a high-profit industry and a low-profit industry. From what you know of the structure of your selected industry, use the five forces framework to explain why profitability has been either high or low.

3   With reference to Strategy Capsule 3.1, use the five forces framework to explain why the U.S. smokeless tobacco industry is so profitable (as indicated by the profitability of its dominant firm).

4   The leading companies in the online travel agency industry are Expedia, Travelocity (which owns Lastminute.com), Orbitz, Priceline, Cheaptickets and a host of others. The online agents compete both with traditional travel agents (American Express, Thomas Cook, Carlson) and direct online sales by airlines, cruise lines and car rental companies. Their biggest business is selling airline tickets, where they employ the services of computerized airline reservation systems such as Sabre, Amadeus, Worldspan and Galileo. Use Porter's five forces framework to predict the likely profitability of the online travel agency industry over the next ten years.

5   Wal-Mart (like Carrefour, Ahold and Metro) competes in several countries of the world, yet most shoppers choose between retailers within a radius of a few miles. For the purposes of analyzing profitability and competitive strategy, should Wal-Mart consider the discount retailing industry to be global, national, or local?

6   What do you think are key success factors in:

(a)  The pizza delivery industry?
(b)  The investment banking industry?

# Notes

1   "Pest Analysis," mindtools.
    www.mindtools.com/pages/article/newTMC_09.htm.

2   M. E. Porter, "The Five Competitive Forces that Shape
    Strategy," *Harvard Business Review* 57 (January 2008):
    57–71.

3   "For Bagel Chains, Investment May Be Money in the
    Hole," *Wall Street Journal* (December 30, 1997): B8.

4   W. J. Baumol, J. C. Panzar and R. D. Willig,
    *Contestable Markets and the Theory of Industry
    Structure* (New York: Harcourt Brace Jovanovich,
    1982). See also Michael Spence, "Contestable Markets
    and the Theory of Industry Structure: A Review
    Article," *Journal of Economic Literature* 21
    (September 1983): 981–90.

5   "Annual Franchise 500," *Entrepreneur* (January 2009).

6   "Brand Loyalty is Rarely Blind Loyalty," *Wall Street
    Journal* (October 19, 1989): B1.

7   R. D. Buzzell and P. W. Farris, "Marketing Costs in
    Consumer Goods Industries," in H. Thorelli (ed.),
    *Strategy + Structure = Performance* (Bloomington, IN:
    Indiana University Press, 1977): 128–9.

8   In October 1999, the Department of Justice alleged that
    American Airlines was using unfair means in attempting
    to monopolize air traffic out of Dallas-Fort Worth
    (http://www.aeroworldnet.com/1tw05179.htm, accessed
    July 2, 2009).

9   M. Lieberman , "Excess Capacity as a Barrier to Entry,"
    *Journal of Industrial Economics* 35, June 1987: 607–27
    argues that, to be credible, the threat of retaliation
    needs to be supported by incumbents holding excess
    capacity giving them the potential to flood the market.

10  See for example: J. S. Bain, *Barriers to New
    Competition* (Cambridge, MA: Harvard University
    Press, 1956) and H. M. Mann, "Seller Concentration,
    Entry Barriers, and Rates of Return in Thirty
    Industries," *Review of Economics and Statistics* 48
    (1966): 296–307.

11  W. S. Comanor and T. A. Wilson, *Advertising and
    Market Power* (Cambridge: Harvard University Press,
    1974); J. L. Siegfried and L. B. Evans, "Empirical
    Studies of Entry and Exit: A Survey of the Evidence,"
    *Review of Industrial Organization* 9 (1994): 121–55.

12  G. S. Yip, "Gateways to Entry," *Harvard Business
    Review* 60 (September-October 1982): 85–93.

13  F. M. Scherer and D. R. Ross, *Industrial Market
    Structure and Economic Performance*, 3rd edn (Boston:
    Houghton Mifflin, 1990); R. M. Grant, "Pricing
    Behavior in the U.K. Wholesale Market for Petrol.

A 'Structure-Conduct Analysis'," *Journal of Industrial
    Economics* 30 (March 1982) 271–292.

14  R. Schmalensee, "Inter-Industry Studies of Structure and
    Performance," in R. Schmalensee and R. D. Willig,
    *Handbook of Industrial Organization*, 2nd edn
    (Amsterdam: North Holland, 1988): 976; M. A. Salinger,
    "The Concentration-Margins Relationship Reconsidered,"
    *Brookings Papers: Microeconomics* (1990): 287–335.

15  The problems caused by excess capacity and exit
    barriers are discussed in C. Baden-Fuller (ed.), *Strategic
    Management of Excess Capacity* (Oxford: Basil
    Blackwell, 1990).

16  "Dry bulk shipping rates approach all-time low,"
    *Financial Times* (November 27, 2008).

17  S. H. Lustgarten, "The Impact of Buyer Concentration
    in Manufacturing Industries," *Review of Economics and
    Statistics* 57 (1975): 125–32; T. Kelly and M. L.
    Gosman, "Increased Buyer Concentration and its Effects
    on Profitability in the Manufacturing Sector," *Review of
    Industrial Organization* 17 (2000): 41–59.

18  M. E. Porter, "The Five Competitive Forces that Shape
    Strategy" op. cit.

19  "Rude Awakening" *FT Weekend*, Financial Times
    (October 4/5, 2008): 16–23.

20  "Globalization or Concentration?" *Business Week*
    (November 8, 2004): 54; "Mittal: Blood, Steel and
    Empire Building," *Business Week* (February 13, 2006).

21  J. Bower, *When Markets Quake* (Boston: Harvard
    Business School Press, 1986).

22  M. Carnall, S. Berry and P. Spiller, "Airline Hubbing,
    Costs and Demand," in D. Lee (ed.), *Advances in
    Airline Economics,* vol. 1 (Amsterdam: Elsevier, 2006).

23  M. G. Jacobides, "Building Architectural Advantage:
    Don't just compete *in* your sector. Shape your sector
    and win!" AIM White Paper, London Business School
    (May 2008).

24  For a concise discussion of market definition see Office
    of Fair Trading, *Market Definition* (London: December
    2004), especially pp. 7–17.

25  The term was coined by Chuck Hofer and Dan
    Schendel, *Strategy Formulation: Analytical Concepts*
    (St Paul: West Publishing, 1977): 77. They defined key
    success factors as "those variables that management can
    influence through its decisions and that can affect
    significantly the overall competitive positions of the
    firms in an industry."

26  P. Ghemawat, *Commitment: The Dynamic of Strategy*
    (New York: Free Press, 1991): 11.

# 4 Further Topics in Industry and Competitive Analysis

# Introduction and Objectives

The Porter five forces model offers a systematic approach to analyzing competition. At the same time, it offers a highly simplified view of industry and competition. Consider the following:

◆ The only relationships between products that we have considered are substitute relations. Many products—both goods and services—have *complementary* relationships with one another. What do complements imply for competition and the potential for profit?

◆ In many sectors industry structure may be much less stable than envisaged by the Porter model. Rather than structure determining competition in some predictable way, competition—particularly when it involves innovation—may reshape industry structure very rapidly. How do we analyze industries where structure is continually being recreated by firms' strategies?

◆ We have not explored the dynamic rivalry that characterizes business competition in the real world. Pepsi-Cola's competitive environment is determined more by the strategy and marketing tactics of Coca-Cola than by the structure of the world soft drinks industry—similarly with Reuters and Bloomberg and with Boeing and Airbus. To understand competition as a dynamic process we shall draw upon the tools of game theory and competitor analysis.

◆ In discussing the problems of drawing industry boundaries, we noted the advantages of analyzing competition at different levels. American Airlines competes in the world airline industry. However, each route comprises a different market with a different set of competitors. To take account of the internal heterogeneity of industries we shall disaggregate industries into segments and analyze each segment as a separate market.

This chapter will extend the analysis of industry and competition to address the above topics. In doing so, you will acquire the ability to:

◆ analyze relationships of *complementarity* between products and recognize the potential for the firm to make profit through managing these relationships;

◆ recognize the implications of *game theory* for competitive analysis—in particular, the potential gains from cooperative strategies and the use of threats, commitments, signaling, deterrence and preemption to gain and sustain competitive advantage;

◆ utilize *competitor analysis* to predict the competitive moves by rivals;

◆ *segment* an industry into its constituent markets, to appraise the relative attractiveness of different segments, and identify differences in key success factors among them;

◆ classify the firms within an industry into *strategic groups* based on similarities in their strategies.

# Extending the Five Forces Framework

## Does Industry Matter?

Porter's five forces of competition framework has been subject to two main attacks. Some have criticized its theoretical foundations, arguing that the structure-conduct-performance approach to industrial organization that underlies it lacks rigor (especially when compared with the logical robustness of game theory).

Others have noted its empirical weaknesses. It appears that industry environment is a relatively minor determinant of a firm's profitability. Studies of the sources of interfirm differences in profitability have produced very different results (see Table 4.1)—but all acknowledge that industry factors account for a minor part (less than 20%) of variation in return on assets among firms.

My defense of industry analysis in general, and the Porter framework in particular, is that it is very useful for understanding competition, for predicting profitability changes and for guiding strategy formulation. Nevertheless, these criticisms also point to the need to go further in our industry analysis. First, we must understand more deeply the determinants of competitive behavior between companies and how competition influences industry-level profitability. We need to reconsider the relationship between industry structure and competition and explore more rigorous and sophisticated approaches to analyzing competition—game theory in particular. Second, we need to disaggregate broad industry groupings and examine competition at the level of particular segments and strategic groupings of firms. Let us begin by considering the possibilities of extending the Porter framework.

## Complements: A Missing Force in the Porter Model?

The Porter framework identifies the suppliers of substitute goods and services as one of the forces of competition that reduces the profit available to the firms within an industry. However, economic theory identifies two types of relationship between different products: *substitutes* and *complements*. While the presence of substitutes

**TABLE 4.1**  What determines interfirm differences in profitability? The role of industry

| | Percentage of variance in firms' return on assets explained by: | | |
|---|---|---|---|
| | Industry effects (%) | Firm effects (%) | Unexplained variance (%) |
| Schmalensee (1985) | 19.6 | 0.6 | 79.9 |
| Rumelt (1991) | 4.0 | 44.2 | 44.8 |
| McGahan & Porter (1997) | 18.7 | 31.7 | 48.4 |
| Hawawini et al. (2003) | 8.1 | 35.8 | 52.0 |
| Roquebert et al. (1996) | 10.2 | 55.0 | 32.0 |
| Misangyi et al. (2006) | 7.6 | 43.8 | n.a. |

**Notes:**
"Firm effects" combine business unit and corporate effects. The rows do not sum to 100% because other sources of variance are not reported.

**Sources:**
R. Schmalensee, "Do markets differ much?" *American Economic Review* 75 (1985): 341–51;
R. P. Rumelt, "How much does industry matter?" *Strategic Management Journal* 12 (1991): 167–85;
A. M. McGahan and M. E. Porter, "How much does industry matter, really?" *Strategic Management Journal* 18 (1997): 15–30; G. Hawawini, V. Subramanian, and P. Verdin, "Is Performance Driven by Industry or Firm-Specific Factors? A New Look at the Evidence," *Strategic Management Journal* 24 (2003): 1–16; J. A. Roquebert, R. L. Phillips, and P. A. Westfall, "Markets vs. Management: What 'Drives' Profitability?" *Strategic Management Journal* 17 (1996): 653–64; V. F. Misangyi, H. Elms, T. Greckhamer and J. A. Lepine, "A New Perspective on a Fundamental Debate: A Multilevel Approach to Industry, Corporate and Business Unit Effects," *Strategic Management Journal* 27 (2006): 571–90.

reduces the value of a product, complements increase value. The availability of ink cartridges for my printer transforms its value to me.

Given the importance of complements to most products—the value of my car depends on the availability of gasoline, insurance, and repair services—our analysis of the competitive environment needs to take them into account. The simplest way is to add a sixth force to Porter's framework (see Figure 4.1).[1]

Complements have the opposite effect to substitutes. While substitutes reduce the value of an industry's product, complements increase it. Indeed, where products are close complements, they have little value to customers individually—customers value the whole system. But how is the value shared between the producers of the different complementary products? Bargaining power and its deployment are the key. During the early 1990s, Nintendo earned huge profits from its video game consoles. Although most of the revenue and consumer value was in the software—mostly supplied by independent developers—Nintendo was able to appropriate most of the profit potential of the entire system through establishing dominance over the games developers. Nintendo used its leadership in the console market and ownership of the console operating system to enforce restrictive developer licenses to software producers of games, and maintain tight control over the manufacture and distribution of games cartridges (from which Nintendo earned a hefty royalty).[2]

**FIGURE 4.1** Five forces, or six?

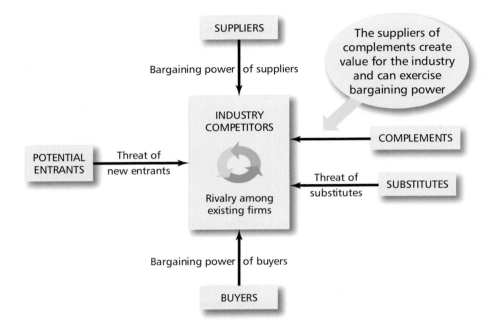

In PCs, by contrast, power has been on the side of the software suppliers—Microsoft in particular. IBM's adoption of open architecture meant that Microsoft Windows became a proprietary standard, while PCs were gradually reduced to commodity status. This is a very different situation from video games, where hardware suppliers keep proprietary control over their operating systems.

Where two products are complements to one another, profit will accrue to the supplier that builds the stronger market position and reduces the value contributed by the other. How is this done? The key is to achieve monopolization, differentiation and shortage of supply in one's own product, while encouraging competition, commoditization and excess capacity in the production of the complementary product. IBM is attempting to shift the balance of power between hardware and software producers through its promotion of Linux and other open-source software programs. By pressing to differentiate its hardware products while commoditizing software, it can reduce the power of Microsoft and garner a bigger share of the profit returns from systems of hardware and software.[3]

## Dynamic Competition: Creative Destruction and Hypercompetition

The notion that industry structure is relatively stable and determines competitive behavior in a predictable way ignores the dynamic forces of innovation and entrepreneurship that transform industry structure. Joseph Schumpeter viewed competition as a "perennial gale of creative destruction" through which favorable industry structures—monopoly in particular—contain the seeds of their own destruction by attracting incursions from new and established firms deploying innovatory strategies and innovatory products to unseat incumbents.[4]

This view of Schumpeter (and the "Austrian school" of economics) that competition is a dynamic process that continually reformulates industry structure suggests that it may be more appropriate to view structure as the outcome of competitive behavior rather than vice versa.[5] The key consideration is the speed of structural change in the industry—if structural transformation is rapid, the five forces model has limited predictive value.

In practice, Schumpeter's process of "creative destruction" tends to be more of a breeze than a gale. In established industries entry occurs so slowly that profits are undermined only gradually,[6] while changes in industrial concentration tend to be slow.[7] One survey observed: "the picture of the competitive process . . . is, to say the least, sluggish in the extreme."[8] As a result, both at the firm and the industry level, profits tend to be highly persistent in the long run.[9]

What about recent decades? Has accelerating technological change and intensifying international competition reinforced the processes of "creative destruction"? Rich D'Aveni argues that a general feature of industries today is *hypercompetition*: "intense and rapid competitive moves, in which competitors must move quickly to build [new] advantages and erode the advantages of their rivals."[10] If industries are hypercompetitive, their structures are likely to be less stable than in the past, superior profitability will tend to be transitory and the only route to sustained superior performance is through continually recreating and renewing competitive advantage.

Despite the plausibility of this thesis and everyday observations that markets are becoming more volatile and market leadership more tenuous, systematic evidence of this trend is ambiguous. One large-scale statistical study concluded: "The heterogeneity and volatility of competitive advantage in U.S. manufacturing industries has steadily and astonishingly increased since 1950. Industry structures are destabilizing. These results suggest that a shift towards hypercompetition has indeed occurred."[11] This volatility is observed not just in technology-intensive industries and not just in manufacturing industries.[12] However, another study found a "lack of widespread evidence . . . that markets are more unstable now than in the recent past."[13]

## The Contribution of Game Theory

Central to the criticisms of Porter's five forces as a static framework is its failure to take full account of competitive interactions among firms. In Chapter 1, we noted that the essence of strategic competition is the interaction among players, such that the decisions made by any one player are dependent on the actual and anticipated decisions of the other players. By relegating competition to a mediating variable that links industry structure with profitability, the five forces analysis offers little insight into competition as a process of interactive decision making by rival firms. Game theory allows us to model this competitive interaction. In particular, it offers two especially valuable contributions to strategic management:

- *It permits the framing of strategic decisions.* Apart from any theoretical value of the theory of games, game theory provides a structure, a set of concepts, and a terminology that allows us to describe a competitive situation in terms of:

- identity of the players;
- specification of each player's options;
- specification of the payoffs from every combination of options;
- the sequencing of decisions using game trees.

This permits us to understand the structure of the competitive situation and facilitates a systematic, rational approach to decision making.

- *It can predict the outcome of competitive situations and identify optimal strategic choices.* Through the insight that it offers into situations of competition and bargaining, game theory can predict the equilibrium outcomes of competitive situations and the consequences of strategic moves by any one player. Game theory provides penetrating insights into central issues of strategy that go well beyond pure intuition. Simple game models (for example, "prisoners' dilemma") predict cooperative versus competitive outcomes, whereas more complex games permit analysis of the effects of reputation,[14] deterrence,[15] information[16] and commitment[17]—especially within the context of multiperiod games. Particularly important for practicing managers, game theory can indicate strategies for improving the structure and outcome of the game through manipulating the payoffs to the different players.[18]

During the past two decades, game theory has provided illuminating insights into a wide variety of competitive situations, including the Cuban missile crisis of 1962,[19] rivalry between Boeing and Airbus,[20] NASCAR race tactics,[21] auctions of airwave spectrum,[22] and the reasons why evolution has conferred such magnificent tails upon male peacocks.[23]

## Cooperation

One of the key merits of game theory is its ability to encompass both competition and cooperation. A key deficiency of the five forces framework is in viewing interfirm relations as exclusively competitive in nature. The central message of Adam Brandenburger and Barry Nalebuff's book *Co-opetition* is recognizing the competitive/cooperative duality of business relationships.[24] While some relationships are predominantly competitive (Coca-Cola and Pepsi-Cola) and others are predominantly cooperative (Intel and Microsoft), there is no simple dichotomy between competition and cooperation: all business relationships combine elements of both. For all their intense rivalry, Coca-Cola and PepsiCo cooperate on multiple fronts, including common policies on sales of soda drinks within schools, environmental issues and health concerns. There is also some evidence of coordination in pricing and product introductions.[25] Exxon and Shell have battled for over a century for leadership of the world petroleum industry. At the same time, Exxon and Shell cooperate in a number of joint ventures. The desire of competitors to cluster together—antique dealers in London's Bermondsey

Market and movie studios in Hollywood—points to the common interests of competing firms in growing the size of their market and developing its infrastructure.

In many business relationships, competition results in an inferior outcome for the players compared with cooperation. The prisoners' dilemma game analyzes this predicament (see Strategy Capsule 4.1).

---

**STRATEGY CAPSULE 4.1**
# The Prisoners' Dilemma

The classic prisoners' dilemma game involves a pair of crime suspects who are arrested and interrogated separately. The dilemma is that each will "rat" on the other with the result that both end up in jail despite the fact that, if both had remained silent, both would have been released for lack of evidence.

The dilemma arises in almost all competitive situations—everyone could be better off with collusion. Consider competition between Coca-Cola and Pepsi-Cola in Ukraine where each has the choice of spending big or small on advertising. The matrix below shows the payoffs to each firm.

COCA-COLA (Payoffs in $ millions)

| PEPSI | Small Advertising Budget | Big Advertising Budget |
|---|---|---|
| Small Advertising Budget | 10 / 10 | 15 / −2 |
| Big Advertising Budget | −2 / 15 | 4 / 4 |

In each cell, the lower-left number is the payoff to Pepsi; the upper-right the payoff to Coke.

Clearly, the best solution for both firms is for them to each restrain their advertising expenditure (the upper left cell). However, in the absence of cooperation, the outcome for both firms is to adopt big budgets (the lower right cell)—the reason being that each will fear that any restraint will be countered by the rival seeking advantage by shifting to a big advertising budget. The resulting maxi-min choice of strategies (each company chooses the strategy that maximizes the minimum payoff) is a Nash equilibrium: no player can increase his/her payoff by a unilateral change in strategy. Even if collusion can be achieved, it will be unstable because of the incentives for cheating—a constant problem for OPEC, where the member countries agree quotas but then cheat on them.

How can a firm escape from such prisoners' dilemmas? One answer is to change a one-period game (single transaction) into a repeated game.

In the case of the supplier–buyer relationship, moving from a spot transaction to a long-term vendor relationship gives the supplier the incentive to offer a better quality product and the buyer to offer a price that offers the seller a satisfactory return. In the case of price competition, markets dominated by two or three suppliers tend to converge toward patterns of price leadership where price competition is avoided.

A second solution is to change the payoffs through deterrence. In the classic prisoners' dilemma, the Mafia shifts the equilibrium from the suspects confessing to their not talking by using draconian reprisals to enforce its "code of silence". Similarly, if both Coca-Cola and Pepsi were to threaten one another with an aggressive price cuts should the other seek advantage through a big advertising budget, this could shift the equilibrium to the top left cell.

*Sources:* A. Dixit and B. Nalebuff, "Prisoners' Dilemma," *The Concise Encyclopedia of Economics* (www.econlib.org/library/Enc/PrisonersDilemma.html); "Prisoners' Dilemma," *Stanford Encyclopedia of Philosophy* (http://plato.stanford.edu/entries/prisoner-dilemma/).

## Deterrence

As we saw in Strategy Capsule 4.1, one way of changing a game's equilibrium is through *deterrence*. The principle behind deterrence is to impose costs on the other players for actions deemed to be undesirable. By establishing the certainty that deserters would be shot, the British army provided a strong incentive to its troops to participate in advances on heavily fortified German trenches during the First World War.

The key to the effectiveness of any deterrent is that it must be credible. The problem here is that if administering the deterrent is costly or unpleasant for the threatening party, the deterrent is not credible. When King of Shaves (owned by KMI Ltd; annual sales $90 million) entered the U.K. razor market, Gillette might have threatened it with a price cut. But would such a threat have been credible? Once King of Shaves had entered, Gillette's dominant market share meant that a price cut would inflict more damage on itself than on rivals.[26] Investing in excess capacity can be an effective means of discouraging entry. Prior to the expiration of its NutraSweet patents, Monsanto invested heavily in unneeded plant capacity to deter manufacturers of generic aspartame.[27] Conversely, in compact disks, the reluctance of the dominant firm (Philips) to invest heavily in new capacity to meet growing demand encouraged a wave of new entrants.[28]

Deterrence has provided a central theme in international relations. The nuclear arms race between the U.S. and the then Soviet Union was based on the logic of "mutual assured destruction." However, the ability for deterrence to produce a stable, peaceful equilibrium depends on the willingness of the adversaries to be deterred. A central weakness of George W. Bush's "war on terror" was that ideologically motivated terrorists are not susceptible to deterrence.[29]

## Commitment

For deterrence to be effective it must be credible, which means being backed by commitment. Commitment involves the elimination of strategic options: "binding an organization to a future course of action."[30] When Hernan Cortes destroyed his ships on arrival in Mexico in 1519, he communicated, both to Montezuma and his men, that there was no alternative to conquest of the Aztec empire. Once Airbus had decided to build its A380 superjumbo, it was critical to signal its commitment to the project. During 2000–2 Airbus spent heavily on advertising the plane, even before completing the design phase, in order encourage airlines to place orders and discourage Boeing from developing a rival plane.

These commitments to aggressive competition have been described as "hard commitments." A company may also make commitments that moderate competition; these are called "soft commitments."[31] The airlines' frequent-flier programs commit the airlines to redeem miles flown with free tickets. They also signal to other airlines a willingness to avoid price competition and indicate less vulnerability to a rival's price cuts. How these different types of commitment affect the profitability of the firm making the commitment depends on the type of game being played. Where companies compete on price, game theory shows that they tend to match one another's price changes.[32] Hence, under price adjustments, hard commitments (such as a commitment to cut price) tend to have a negative profit impact and soft commitments (such as a commitment to raise prices) have a positive impact. Conversely, where companies compete on output, game theory shows that increases in output by one firm results in output reductions by the other.[33] Hence, under quantity adjustments, a hard commitment (for example, a commitment to build new plants) will tend to have a positive effect on the committing firm's profitability because it will tend to be met by other firms reducing their output.[34]

## Changing the Structure of the Game

Creative strategies can change the structure of the competitive game. A company may seek to change the structure of the industry within which it is competing in order to increase the profit potential of the industry or to appropriate a greater share of the available profit. Thus, establishing alliances and agreements with competitors can increase the value of the game by increasing the size of the market and building joint strength against possible entrants. There may be many opportunities for converting win-lose (or even lose-lose) games into win-win games. A cooperative solution was found to the 1997 bidding war between Norfolk Southern and CSX for control of Conrail, for example. The bidding war was terminated when the two firms agreed to cooperate in acquiring and dismembering Conrail. [35]

In some cases, it may be advantageous for a firm to create competition for itself. By offering second-sourcing licenses to AMD, Intel gave up its potential monopoly over its x86 microprocessors. Although Intel was creating competition for itself, it was also encouraging the adoption of the x86 chip by computer manufacturers (including IBM) who were concerned about overdependence on Intel. As we shall see in Chapter 11, standards battles often involve the deliberate sacrificing of potential monopoly positions by the main contestants.

## Signaling

Competitive reactions depend on how the competitor perceives its rival's initiative. The term *signaling* is used to describe the selective communication of information to competitors (or customers) designed to influence their perception and hence to provoke or avoid certain types of reaction.[36] The use of misinformation is well developed in military intelligence. In 1944, Allied deception was so good that even during the D-Day landings in Normandy, the Germans believed that the main invasion would occur near Calais. But, as noted in discussing deterrence, information on its own is not enough: signals need to be credible. Thus, Allied misinformation concerning the invasion of Europe included the marshaling of a phantom army designed to convince the German military that the Normandy invasion was merely a diversionary mission.

The credibility of threats is critically dependent on reputation.[37] Even though carrying out threats against rivals is costly and depresses short-term profitability, exercising such threats can build a reputation for aggressiveness that deters competitors in the future. The benefits of building a reputation for aggressiveness may be particularly great for diversified companies where reputation can be transferred from one market to another.[38] Hence, Procter & Gamble's protracted market share wars in disposable diapers and household detergents have established a reputation for toughness that protects it from competitive attacks in other markets.

Signaling may also be used to communicate a desire to cooperate. Price announcements can facilitate collusive pricing among firms.[39]

## Is Game Theory Useful?

The value of game theory to strategic management has generated lively debate. For economists this seems paradoxical because to them game theory *is* the theory of strategy. The great virtue of game theory is its rigor. In microeconomics, the game theory revolution of the past quarter-century has established the analysis of markets and firm behavior on a much more secure theoretical foundation.

However, the price of mathematical rigor has been limited applicability to real world situations. Game theory provides clear prediction in highly stylized situations involving few external variables and highly restrictive assumptions. The result is a mathematically sophisticated body of theory that suffers from unrealistic assumptions, lack of generality, and an analysis of dynamic situations through a sequence of static equilibriums. When applied to more complex (and more realistic) situations, game theory frequently results in either no equilibrium or multiple equilibriums, and outcomes that are highly sensitive to small changes in initial assumptions. In general, game theory has not developed to the point where it permits us to model real business situations in a level of detail that can generate precise predictions.[40]

In its empirical applications, game theory has done a much better job of explaining the past than of predicting the future. In diagnosing Nintendo's domination of the video games industry in the 1980s, Monsanto's efforts to prolong NutraSweet's market leadership beyond the expiration of its patents, or Airbus's wresting of market leadership from Boeing, game theory provides penetrating insight into the competitive situation and deep understanding of the rationale behind the strategies deployed. However, in predicting outcomes and designing strategies, game theory has been much less impressive—the use of game theory by U.S. and European governments to auction wireless spectrum has produced mixed results.[41]

So, where can game theory assist us in designing successful strategies? As with all our theories and frameworks, game theory is useful not because it gives us answers but because it can help us understand business situations. Game theory provides a set of tools that allows us to structure our view of competitive interaction. By identifying the players in a game, the decision choices available to each, and the implications of each combination of decisions, we have a systematic framework for exploring the dynamics of competition. Most importantly, by describing the structure of the game we are playing, we have a basis for suggesting ways of changing the game and thinking through the likely outcomes of such changes.

Game theory continues its rapid development and, although it is still a long way from providing the central theoretical foundation for strategic management, we draw upon it in several places in this book—especially in exploring competitive dynamics in highly concentrated markets. However, our emphasis in strategy formulation will be less on achieving advantage through influencing the behavior of competitors and much more on transforming competitive games through building positions of unilateral competitive advantage. The competitive market situations with which we shall be dealing will, for the most part, be different from those considered by game theory. Game theory typically deals with competitive situations with closely matched players where each has a similar range of strategic options (typically relating to price changes, advertising budgets, capacity decisions, and new product introductions). The outcome of these games is highly dependent on order of moves, signals, bluffs, and threats. Our emphasis will be less on managing competitive interactions and more on establishing competitive advantage through exploiting uniqueness.

# Competitor Analysis

In highly concentrated industries, the dominant feature of a company's competitive environment is likely to be the behavior of its closest rivals. In household detergents, Unilever's industry environment is dominated by the strategy of Procter & Gamble. The same is true in soft drinks (Coca-Cola and Pepsi), jet engines (GE, United Technologies, and Rolls-Royce), and business news periodicals (*Business Week*, *Fortune*, and *Forbes*). Similar circumstances exist in more local markets. The competitive environment of my local Costa coffee shop is dominated by the presence of Starbucks across the road. Game theory provides a theoretical apparatus for analyzing competitive interaction between small numbers of rivals but, for everyday business situations, a less formal and more empirically based approach to predicting competitors' behavior may be more useful. Let us examine how information about competitors can help us to predict their behavior.

## Competitive Intelligence

Competitive intelligence involves the systematic collection and analysis of public information about rivals for informing decision making. It has three main purposes:

- to forecast competitors' future strategies and decisions;
- to predict competitors' likely reactions to a firm's strategic initiatives;
- to determine how competitors' behavior can be influenced to make it more favorable.

For all three purposes, the key requirement is to understand competitors in order to predict their responses to environmental changes and our own competitive moves. To understand competitors, it is important to be informed about them. Competitive intelligence is a growth field, with a flood of recent books,[42] a dedicated journal,[43] specialist consulting firms, and professional associations.[44] About one-quarter of large U.S. corporations have set up competitive intelligence units.

The boundary between legitimate competitive intelligence and illegal industrial espionage is not always clear. The distinction between public and private information can be uncertain. Trade secrets law does not offer clear guidance. Well publicized cases of information theft include Procter & Gamble's acquisition of documents concerning Unilever's hair care business that had been removed from Unilever dumpsters[45] and the $100 million fine levied on the McLaren-Mercedes Formula One team for possessing confidential technical information belonging to Ferrari.[46]

## A Framework for Predicting Competitor Behavior

Competitive intelligence is not simply about collecting information. The problem is likely to be too much rather than too little information. The key is a systematic approach that makes it clear what information is required and for what purposes it will be used. The objective is to *understand* one's rival. A characteristic of great generals from Hannibal to Patton has been their ability to go beyond military intelligence and to "get inside the heads" of their opposing commanders. Michael Porter proposes a four-part framework for predicting competitor behavior (see Figure 4.2).

- *Competitor's current strategy.* To predict how a rival will behave in the future, we must understand how that rival is competing at present. As we noted in Chapter 1, identifying a firm's strategy requires looking at what the

**FIGURE 4.2** A framework for competitor analysis

company says and what it does. (See "Identifying a Company's Strategy" in Chapter 1). The key is to link the content of top management communication (with investors, the media, and financial analysts) with the evidence of strategic actions—particularly those that involve commitment of resources. For both sources of information, company web sites are invaluable.

● *Competitor's objectives.* To forecast how a competitor might change its strategy, we must identify its goals. A key issue is whether a company is driven by financial goals or market goals. A company whose primary goal is attaining market share is likely to be much more aggressive a competitor than one that is mainly interested in profitability. The willingness of the U.S. automobile and consumer electronics producers to cede market share to Japanese competitors was partly a result of their preoccupation with short-term profitability. By comparison, companies like Procter & Gamble and Coca-Cola are obsessed with market share and tend to react aggressively when rivals step on their turf. The most difficult competitors can be those that are not subject to profit disciplines at all—state-owned enterprises in particular. The level of current performance in relation to the competitor's objectives determines the likelihood of strategy change. The more a company is satisfied with present performance, the more likely it is to continue with its present strategy. But if performance is falling well short of target, radical strategic change, possibly accompanied by a change in top management, is likely.

● *Competitor's assumptions about the industry.* A competitor's strategic decisions are conditioned by its perceptions of itself and its environment. These perceptions are guided by the beliefs that senior managers hold about their industry and the success factors within it. Evidence suggests that not only do these systems of belief tend to be stable over time, they also tend to converge among the firms within an industry: what J. C. Spender refers to as *industry recipes.*"[47] Industry recipes may engender "blindspots" that limit the capacity of a firm—even an entire industry—to respond to an external threat. During the 1960s, the Big Three U.S. automobile manufacturers firmly believed that small cars were unprofitable. This belief was partly a product of their own overhead allocation procedures. The result was a willingness to yield the fastest-growing segment of the U.S. automobile market to imports. The complacency of British and U.S. motorcycle manufacturers in the face of Japanese competition reflected similar beliefs (see Strategy Capsule 4.2).

● *Competitor's resources and capabilities.* Evaluating the likelihood and seriousness of a competitor's potential challenge requires assessing the strength of that competitor's resources and capabilities. If our rival has a massive cash pile, it would be unwise for our company to unleash a price war by initiating price cuts. Conversely, if we direct our competitive initiative towards our rivals' weaknesses, it may be difficult for them to respond. Richard Branson's Virgin Group has launched a host of entrepreneurial new ventures, typically in markets dominated by a powerful incumbent—British Airways in airlines, EMI in music, Vodafone in wireless telecommunications. Branson's strategy has been to adopt innovative forms of differentiation that are difficult for established incumbents to respond to.

---

**STRATEGY CAPSULE 4.2**

## Motorcycle Myopia

During the 1960s, BSA was the leading motorcycle manufacturer in Britain, while Harley-Davidson was the leader in the U.S. During the 1960s, both markets experienced increased import penetration from Japan, but given the emphasis by Honda, Suzuki, and Yamaha on smaller motorcycles, the Japanese challenge was largely discounted.

Eric Turner, chairman of BSA Ltd (manufacturer of Triumph and BSA motorcycles), commented in 1965:

> The success of Honda, Suzuki, and Yamaha has been jolly good for us. People start out by buying one of the low-priced Japanese jobs. They get to enjoy the fun and exhilaration of the open road and they frequently end up buying one of our more powerful and expensive machines.

Similar complacency was expressed by William Davidson, president of Harley-Davidson:

> Basically, we do not believe in the lightweight market. We believe that motorcycles are sports vehicles, not transportation vehicles. Even if a man says he bought a motorcycle for transportation, it's generally for leisure time use. The lightweight motorcycle is only supplemental. Back around World War I, a number of companies came out with lightweight bikes. We came out with one ourselves. We came out with another in 1947 and it just didn't go anywhere. We have seen what happens to these small sizes.

By the end of the 1970s, BSA and Triumph had ceased production and Harley-Davidson was barely surviving. The world motorcycle industry, including the large bike segments, was dominated by the Japanese.

**Sources:** *Advertising Age* (December 27, 1965); *Forbes* (September 15, 1966); Richard T. Pascale, *Honda A* (Harvard Business School Case No. 9-384-049, 1983).

---

# Segmentation Analysis[48]

## The Uses of Segmentation

In Chapter 3 we noted the difficulty of drawing industry boundaries and the need to define industries both broadly and narrowly according to the types of question we are seeking to answer. Initially it may be convenient to define industries broadly, but for a more detailed analysis of competition we need to focus on markets that are drawn more narrowly in terms of both products and geography. This process of disaggregating industries into specific markets we call *segmentation*.

Segmentation is particularly important if competition varies across the different submarkets within an industry such that some are more attractive than others. A company can avoid some of the problems of an unattractive industry by judicious segment selection. In the intensely competitive personal computer industry, Dell has used its highly flexible direct distribution system to target products, geographical areas, and customers that offer the best margins: "We cut the market and then cut it again, looking for the most profitable customers to serve," says CEO Kevin Rollins.[49] In the cut-throat tire industry, Pirelli has achieved superior margins by investing heavily in technology and focusing on high-performance tires for sports and luxury cars. [50]

## Stages in Segmentation Analysis

The purpose of segmentation analysis is to identify attractive segments, to select strategies for different segments, and to determine how many segments to serve. The analysis proceeds in five stages (see Strategy Capsule 4.3 for a summary and application).

*1 Identify Key Segmentation Variables* The first stage of segmentation analysis is to determine the basis of segmentation. Segmentation decisions are essentially choices about which customers to serve and what to offer them: hence

---

**STRATEGY CAPSULE 4.3**

# Segmenting the European Metal Can Industry

1  Identify key segmentation variables and categories.

- Identify possible segmentation variables. Raw material, can design, can size, customer size, customer's industry, location.

- Reduce the number of segmentation variables. Which are most significant? Which are closely correlated and can be combined? Type of can, customer industry, customer location.

- Identify discrete categories for each segmentation variable. Type of can: steel three-piece, steel two-piece, aluminum two-piece, general cans, composite cans, aerosols. Type of customer: food processing, fruit juice, pet food, soft drink, toiletries, beer, oil.

Location: France, Germany, Spain/Portugal, Italy, U.K., Benelux.

2  Construct a segmentation matrix.

3  Analyze segment attractiveness. Apply five forces analysis to individual segments.

4  Identify key success factors in each segment. Within each segment, how do customers choose, and what is needed to survive competition?

5  Analyze attractions of broad versus narrow segment scope.

- What is the potential to share costs and transfer skills across segments?

- How similar are key success factors between segments?

- Are there benefits of segment specialization?

**FIGURE 4.3** The basis for segmentation: the characteristics of buyers and products

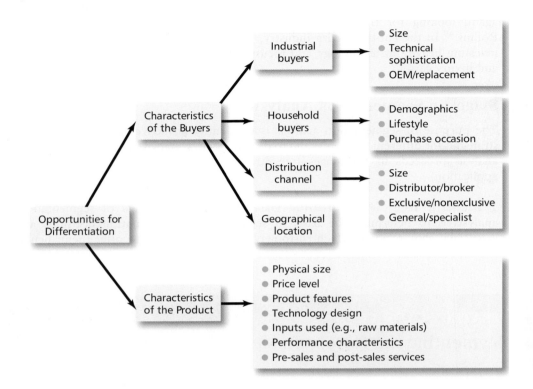

segmentation variables relate to the characteristics of customers and the product (see Figure 4.3). The most appropriate segmentation variables are those that partition the market most distinctly in terms of limits to substitution by customers (demand-side substitutability) and producers (supply-side substitutability). Price differentials are a good guide to market segments. Thus, in the auto industry, color is probably not a good segmentation variable (white and red Honda Civics sell at much the same price); size is a better segmentation variable (full-size cars sell at a price premium over subcompact cars). Typically, segmentation analysis generates far too many segmentation variables. For our analysis to be manageable, we need to reduce these to two or three. To do this we need to:

- Identify the most *strategically significant* segmentation variables. Which variables are most important in creating meaningful divisions in a market?
- Combine segmentation variables that are closely correlated. Thus, in the restaurant industry, price level, service level (waiter service/self-service), cuisine (fast-food/full meals), and alcohol license (wine served/soft drinks only) are likely to be closely related. We could use a single variable, restaurant type, with three categories—full-service restaurants, cafés, and fast-food outlets—as a proxy for all of these variables.

*2  Construct a Segmentation Matrix*  Once the segmentation variables have been selected and discrete categories determined for each, the individual segments may be identified using a two- or three-dimensional matrix. Thus, the European metal container industry might be analyzed in a three-dimensional segmentation matrix (see Strategy Capsule 4.3), whereas the world automobile industry might be segmented simply by vehicle type and geographical region (see Strategy Capsule 4.4).

---

**STRATEGY CAPSULE 4.4**

# Segmenting the World Automobile Market

A global automobile producer such as Ford or Toyota might segment the world auto market by product type and geography. A first-cut segmentation might be along the following lines:

To identify segments with the best profit prospects for the future, we need to understand why, in the past, some segments have been more profitable than others. For example, during the 1990s:

● The North American market for small cars was unprofitable due to many competitors (all the world's major auto producers were

| | | REGIONS | | | | | |
|---|---|---|---|---|---|---|---|
| | North America | Western Europe | Eastern Europe | Asia | Latin America | Australia & N.Z. | Africa |
| **P R O D U C T S**   Luxury cars | | | | | | | |
| Full-size cars | | | | | | | |
| Mid-size cars | | | | | | | |
| Small cars | | | | | | | |
| Station wagons | | | | | | | |
| Minivans | | | | | | | |
| Sports cars | | | | | | | |
| Sport utility | | | | | | | |
| Pickup trucks | | | | | | | |
| Hybrids | | | | | | | |

represented), lack of clear product differentiation, and customers' price sensitivity.

- Sport utility vehicles and passenger minivans
were highly profitable segments due to
strong demand relative to capacity, and
comparatively few participants. However,
the influx of companies into these segments
has eroded margins.

- The luxury car segment is traditionally a high-
margin segment due to few players, high

product differentiation, and price insensitivity
of buyers. However, new entry and excess
capacity has increased competition.

- Hybrids have earned big margins due to
few players and shortage of capacity relative
to demand.

Once we understand the factors that
determined segment profitability in the past, we
can predict segment profitability in the future.

*3 Analyze Segment Attractiveness* Profitability within an industry segment is
determined by the same structural forces that determine profitability within an
industry as a whole. As a result, Porter's five forces of competition framework is
equally effective in relation to a segment as to an entire industry. Strategy Capsule
4.4 points to some implications of a five forces analysis for certain segments of the
world automobile industry.

There are, however, a few differences. First, when analyzing the pressure of
competition from substitute products, we are concerned not only with substitutes
from other industries but, more importantly, substitutes from other segments within
the same industry. Second, when considering entry into the segment, the main source
of entrants is likely to be producers established in other segments within the same
industry. The barriers that protect a segment from firms located in other segments are
called *barriers to mobility* to distinguish them from the *barriers to entry,* which
protect the industry as a whole.[51] When barriers to mobility are low, then the
superior returns of high-profit segments tend to be quickly eroded. Thus, the high
margins earned on sport utility vehicles during the mid-1990s were competed away
once most of the world's main auto producers had entered the segment.

Segmentation analysis can also be useful in identifying unexploited opportunities
in an industry. For example, a segmentation matrix of the restaurant industry in a
town or locality might reveal a number of empty segments. Companies that have
built successful strategies by concentrating on unoccupied segments include Wal-
Mart (discount stores in small towns), Enterprise Rent-A-Car (suburban locations),
and Edward Jones (full-service brokerage for small investors in smaller cities). This
can be an intermediate step in the quest for "blue oceans"—new markets untainted
by competition.[52]

*4 Identify the Segment's Key Success Factors (KSFs)* Differences in competitive structure and in customer preferences between segments result in different key
success factors. By analyzing buyers' purchase criteria and the basis of competition
within individual segments, we can identify key success factors for individual segments.
For example, we can segment the U.S. bicycle market into high-price enthusiasts' bikes
sold through specialist bike stores. Key success factors in the enthusiast segment are
technology, reputation and dealer relations. In the economy segment, KSFs are low-cost
manufacture (most likely in China) and a supply contract with a leading retail chain.

**5 *Select Segment Scope*** Finally, a firm needs to decide whether it wishes to be a segment specialist, or compete across multiple segments. The advantages of a broad over a narrow segment focus depend on two main factors: similarity of key success factors and the presence of shared costs. If key success factors are different across segments, a firm will need to deploy distinct strategies and may have difficulties in drawing upon the same capabilities. Harley-Davidson's attempt to compete in sports motorcycles through its Buell brand has met limited success.

The ability to share costs across different segments has been a major factor in automobiles where very few specialist manufacturers survive and most of the world's main automakers offer a full range of vehicles allowing cost economies from common platforms and components.

## Vertical Segmentation: Profit Pools

Segmentation is usually horizontal—markets are disaggregated according to products, geography and customer groups. An industry can also be segmented vertically by identifying different value chain activities. Bain & Company show that profitability varies greatly between different vertical activities and proposes *profit pool mapping* as a technique for analyzing the vertical structure of profitability.[53] For example, in the U.S. automobile industry, downstream activities such as finance, leasing, insurance, and service and repair are much more profitable than manufacturing (see Figure 4.4). During 2003-8, Ford and GM's sole source of profits were financial services to dealers and customers.

**FIGURE 4.4**  The U.S. auto industry profit pool

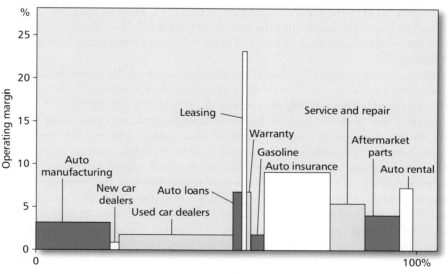

***Source:***
O. Gadiesh and J. L. Gilbert, "Profit Pools: A Fresh Look at Strategy," ***Harvard Business Review*** (May-June 1998): 142. © 1998 by the Harvard Business School Publishing Corporation, all rights reserved. Reproduced with permission.

To map an industry's profit pool, Bain & Company identifies four steps:

1 *Define the pool's boundaries.* What is the range of value-adding activities that your business sector encompasses? It may be useful to look upstream and downstream beyond conventional industry boundaries.

2 *Estimate the pool's overall size.* Total industry profit may be estimated by applying the average margin earned by a sample of companies to an estimate of industry total revenues.

3 *Estimate profit for each value chain activity in the pool.* Here is the key challenge. It requires gathering data from companies that are "pure players"—specialized in the single value chain activity—and disaggregating data for "mixed players"—those performing multiple activities.

4 *Check and reconcile the calculations.* Compare the aggregation of profits in each activity (stage 3) with the total for the industry (stage 2).

## Strategic Groups

Whereas segmentation analysis concentrates on the characteristics of markets as the basis for disaggregating industries, strategic group analysis segments an industry on the basis of the strategies of the member firms. A strategic group is "the group of firms in an industry following the same or a similar strategy along the strategic dimensions."[54] These strategic dimensions might include product range, geographical breadth, choice of distribution channels, level of product quality, degree of vertical integration, choice of technology and so on. By selecting the most important strategic dimensions and locating each firm in the industry along them, it is possible to identify groups of companies that have adopted more or less similar approaches to competing within the industry. Figure 4.5 identifies strategic groups within the world automobile industry; Figure 4.6 shows strategic groups within the oil industry.[55]

Strategic group analysis developed out of initial work on the domestic appliance[56] and brewing industries.[57] Most of the empirical research into strategic groups has been concerned with analyzing differences in profitability among firms.[58] The basic argument is that mobility barriers between strategic groups permit some groups of firms to be persistently more profitable than other groups. In general, the proposition that profitability differences *within* strategic groups are less than differences *between* strategic groups has not received robust empirical support.[59] The inconsistency of empirical findings may reflect the fact that the members of a strategic group, although pursuing similar strategies, are not necessarily in competition with one another. For example, within the European airline industry, budget airlines such as EasyJet, BalticAir, SkyEurope, Volare, and Ryanair pursue similar strategies, but do not, for the most part, compete on the same routes. Strategic group analysis is very useful in identifying strategic niches within an industry and the strategic positioning of different firms; it is less useful as a tool for analyzing interfirm profitability differences.[60]

**FIGURE 4.5** Strategic groups within the world automobile industry

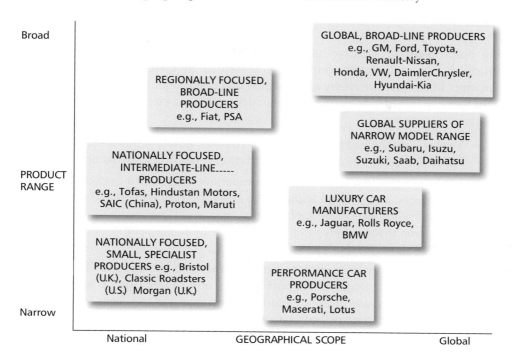

**FIGURE 4.6** Strategic groups within the world petroleum industry

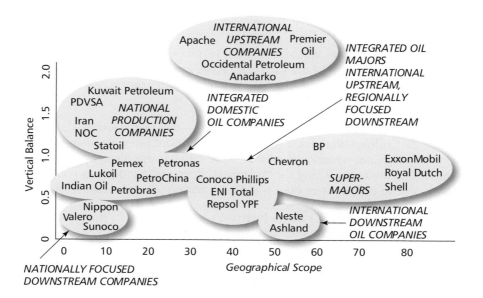

## Summary

The purpose of this chapter has been to go beyond the basic analysis of industry structure, competition and profitability presented in Chapter 3, and consider the dynamics of competitive rivalry and the internal complexities of industries.

In terms of industry and competitive analysis, we have extended our strategy tool kit in several directions:

● We have recognized the potential for complementary products to add value and noted the importance of strategies that can exploit this source of value.

● We have noted the importance of competitive interactions between close rivals and learned a structured approach to analyzing competitors and predicting their behavior. At a more sophisticated theoretical level, we have recognized how game theory offers insight into competition, bargaining, and the design of winning strategies.

● We examined the microstructure of industries and markets and the value of segmentation analysis, profit pool analysis, and strategic group analysis in understanding industries at a more detailed level and in selecting an advantageous strategic position within an industry.

## Self-Study Questions

1    HP, Canon, Lexmark, and other manufacturers of inkjet printers make most of their profits on the sales of ink cartridges. Why are cartridges more profitable than printers? If cartridges were manufactured by different firms from those which make printers, would the situation be different?

2    In November 2005, six of Paris's most luxurious hotels—including George V, Le Bristol, the Ritz, and Hotel de Crillon—were fined for colluding on room rates. Regular guests showed little concern—noting that, whatever the listed "rack rate," it was always possible to negotiate substantial discounts. Using the "prisoners' dilemma" model, can you explain why the hotels were able to collude over their listed rates but not over discounts?

3    In August 2006, Rupert Murdoch's News International announced its intention of launching a free evening newspaper, *The London Paper*, to challenge Associated Newspapers' London *Evening Standard* (daily sales 390 000). Given that the *Evening Standard* was already believed to be loss making, the new competition could be fatal for the paper. What steps might Associated Newspapers take to deter News International from launching its new paper, and if it goes ahead with the launch, what would Associated Newspapers' best response be?

**4** During 2007–9, the Nintendo Wii established leadership over the Sony PS3 and Microsoft Xbox360 in the market for video game consoles. Unlike Sony and Microsoft, Nintendo is completely dependent upon the video games industry for its revenues. How might Nintendo use the competitor analysis framework outlined in Figure 4.2 to predict the likely reactions of Sony and Microsoft to its market success?

**5** How would you segment the restaurant market in your home town? How would you advise someone thinking of starting a new restaurant which segments might be most attractive in terms of profit potential?

# Notes

1 A. Brandenburger and B. Nalebuff, *Co-opetition* (New York: Doubleday, 1996) propose an alternative framework, the *value net*, for analyzing the impact of complements.

2 See A. Brandenburger and B. Nalebuff, "The Right Game: Use Game Theory to Shape Strategy," *Harvard Business Review* (July–August, 1995): 63-4 and A. Brandenburger, J. Kou and M. Burnett, *Power Play (A): Nintendo in 8-bit Video Games* (Harvard Business School Case No. 9-795-103, 1995).

3 C. Baldwin, S. O'Mahony and J. Quinn, *IBM and Linux (A)* (Harvard Business School Case No. 903-083, 2003).

4 J. A. Schumpeter, *The Theory of Economic Development* (Cambridge, MA: Harvard University Press, 1934).

5 See R. Jacobson, "The Austrian School of Strategy," *Academy of Management Review* 17 (1992): 782–807; and G. Young, K. Smith and C. Grimm, "Austrian and Industrial Organization Perspectives on Firm-Level Competitive Activity and Performance," *Organization Science* 7 (May-June 1996): 243–54.

6 R. T. Masson and J. Shaanan, "Stochastic Dynamic Limit Pricing: An Empirical Test," *Review of Economics and Statistics* 64 (1982): 413–22; R. T. Masson and J. Shaanan, "Optimal Pricing and Threat of Entry: Canadian Evidence," *International Journal of Industrial Organization* 5 (1987): 520–535.

7 R. Caves and M. E. Porter, "The Dynamics of Changing Seller Concentration," *Journal of Industrial Economics* 19 (1980): 1–15; P. Hart and R. Clarke, *Concentration in British Industry* (Cambridge: Cambridge University Press, 1980).

8 P. A. Geroski and R. T. Masson, "Dynamic Market Models in Industrial Organization," *International Journal of Industrial Organization* 5 (1987): 1–13.

9 D. C. Mueller, *Profits in the Long Run* (Cambridge: Cambridge University Press, 1986).

10 R. D'Aveni, *Hypercompetition: Managing the Dynamics of Strategic Maneuvering* (New York: Free Press, 1994): 217–18.

11 L. G. Thomas and R. D'Aveni, "The Rise of Hypercompetition in the U.S. Manufacturing Sector, 1950-2002." Tuck School of Business, Dartmouth College, Working Paper #2004-11 (2004).

12 R. R. Wiggins and T. W. Ruefli, "Schumpeter's Ghost: Is Hypercompetition Making the Best of Times Shorter?" *Strategic Management Journal* 26 (2005): 887–911.

13 G. McNamara, P. M. Vaaler, and C. Devers, "Same As It Ever Was: The Search for Evidence of Increasing Hypercompetition," *Strategic Management Journal* 24 (2003): 261–78.

14 K. Weigelt and C. F. Camerer, "Reputation and Corporate Strategy: A Review of Recent Theory and Applications," *Strategic Management Journal* 9 (1988): 137–42.

15 A. K. Dixit, "The Role of Investment in Entry Deterrence," *Economic Journal* 90 (1980): 95–106.

16 P. Milgrom and J. Roberts, "Informational Asymmetries, Strategic Behavior and Industrial Organization," *American Economic Review* 77, no. 2 (May 1987): 184–9; J. Tirole, *The Theory of Industrial Organization* (Cambridge, MA: MIT Press, 1988).

17 P. Ghemawat, *Commitment: The Dynamic of Strategy* (New York: Free Press, 1991).

18 See, for example: A. K. Dixit and B. J. Nalebuff, *Thinking Strategically: The Competitive Edge in Business, Politics, and Everyday Life* (New York: W. W. Norton, 1991) and J. McMillan, *Games, Strategies, and Managers* (New York: Oxford University Press, 1992).

19 G. T. Allison and P. Zelikow, *Essence of Decision: Explaining the Cuban Missile Crisis*, 2nd edn (Boston: Little Brown, 1999).

20 B. C. Esty and P. Ghemawat, "Airbus vs. Boeing in Superjumbos: A Case of Failed Preemption," Harvard Business School Working Paper No. 02-061 (2002).

21 D. Ronfelt, "Social Science at 190 mph on NASCAR's Biggest Superspeedways," *First Monday* 5 (February 7, 2000).

22 "Game Theory in Action: Designing the U.S. Airwaves Auction," *Financial Times* Mastering Strategy Supplement (October 11, 1999): 4.

23 J. Maynard Smith, "Sexual Selection and the Handicap Principle," *Journal of Theoretical Biology* 57 (1976): 239–42.

24 A. Brandenburger and B. Nalebuff (1996), op. cit.

25 T. Dhar, J.-P. Chatas, R. W. Collerill, and B. W. Gould, Strategic Pricing Between Coca-Cola Company and PepsiCo, *Journal of Economics and Management Strategy* 14 (2005): 905–31.

26 "A Sharp Act Gets an Edge" *Financial Times* (September 10, 2008).

27 *Bitter Competition: Holland Sweetener vs. NutraSweet (A)* (Harvard Business School Case No. 9-794-079, 1994).

28 A. M. McGahan, "The Incentive not to Invest: Capacity Commitments in the Compact Disk Introduction," in R. A. Burgelman and R. S. Rosenbloom (eds), *Research on Technological Innovation Management and Policy*, vol. 5 (Greenwich, CT: JAI Press, 1994).

29 D. K. Levine and R. A. Levine, "Deterrence in the Cold War and the War on Terror," working paper, UCLA Department of Economics (2006).

30 D. N. Sull, "Managing by Commitments," *Harvard Business Review* (June 2003): 82–91.

31 J. Chevalier, "When It Can Be Good to Burn Your Boats," *Financial Times* Mastering Strategy Supplement (October 25, 1999): 2–3.

32 Games where price is the primary decision variable are called Bertrand models after the 19th century French economist Joseph Bertrand.

33 Games where quantity is the primary decision variable are called Cournot models after the 19th century French economist Augustin Cournot.

34 F. Scott Morton, "Strategic Complements and Substitutes," *Financial Times* Mastering Strategy Supplement (November 8, 1999): 10–13.

35 R. Loving, *The Men who Loved Trains* (Bloomington, IA: Indiana University Press, 2006).

36 For a review of research on competitive signaling, see O. Heil and T. S. Robertson, "Toward a Theory of Competitive Market Signaling: A Research Agenda," *Strategic Management Journal* 12 (1991): 403–18.

37 For a survey of the strategic role of reputation, see K. Weigelt and C. Camerer, "Reputation and Corporate Strategy: A Review of Recent Theory and Applications," *Strategic Management Journal* 9 (1988): 443–54.

38 P. Milgrom and J. Roberts, "Predation, Reputation, and Entry Deterrence," *Journal of Economic Theory* 27 (1982): 280–312.

39 R. M. Grant, "Pricing Behavior in the U.K. Wholesale Market for Petrol," *Journal of Industrial Economics* 30 (1982): 271–92; L. Miller, "The Provocative Practice of Price Signaling: Collusion versus Cooperation," *Business Horizons* (July–August, 1993).

40 On the ability of game theory to predict almost any equilibrium solution (the "Pandora's Box Problem")

see C. F. Camerer, "Does Strategy Research Need Game Theory?" *Strategic Management Journal*, Special Issue, 12 (Winter 1991): 137–52; and F. M. Fisher, "The Games Economists Play: A Noncooperative View," *Rand Journal of Economics* 20 (Spring 1989): 113–24. Steve Postrel illustrates the point with a game theory model to explain the rationality of bank presidents setting fire to their trousers. See S. Postrel, "Burning Your Britches Behind You: Can Policy Scholars Bank on Game Theory?" *Strategic Management Journal*, Special Issue, 12 (Winter 1991): 153–5.

41 P. Milgrom, *Putting Auction Theory to Work* (Cambridge: Cambridge University Press, 2004); J. McMillan, *Reinventing the Bazaar* (New York: Norton, 2002).

42 L. Field, *The Secret Language of Competitive Intelligence* (New York: Random House, 2006); J. E. Prescott and S. H. Miller, *Proven Strategies in Competitive Intelligence: Lessons from the Trenches* (Wiley: New York, 2001).

43 *Competitive Intelligence Review* (New York: John Wiley & Sons, Inc.).

44 The Society of Competitive Intelligence Professionals (www.scip.org).

45 "P&G's Covert Operation," *Fortune* (September 17, 2001).

46 "McLaren Docked F1 Points for Spying" *Financial Times* (September 14, 2007).

47 J.-C. Spender, *Industry Recipes: The Nature and Sources of Managerial Judgement* (Oxford: Basil Blackwell, 1989). How social interaction promotes convergence of perceptions and beliefs is discussed by Anne Huff in "Industry Influences on Strategy Reformulation," *Strategic Management Journal* 3 (1982): 119–31.

48 This section draws heavily on M. E. Porter, *Competitive Advantage* (New York: Free Press, 1985): Chapter 7.

49 O. Gadiesh and J. L. Gilbert, "Profit Pools: A Fresh Look at Strategy," *Harvard Business Review* (May–June 1998): 146.

50 "Pirelli's Bet on High-performance Tires," *International Herald Tribune* (April 2, 2005).

51 R. E. Caves and M. E. Porter, "From Entry Barriers to Mobility Barriers: Conjectural Decisions and Contrived Deterrence to New Competition," *Quarterly Journal of Economics* 91 (1977): 241–62.

52 W. C. Kim and R. Mauborgne, "Blue Ocean Strategy: From Theory to Practice," *California Management Review* 47 (Spring 2005): 105–21.

53 O. Gadiesh and J. L. Gilbert, "How to Map Your Industry's Profit Pools," *Harvard Business Review* (May-June 1998): 149–62.

54 M. E. Porter, *Competitive Strategy* (New York: Free Press, 1980): 129.

55 For more on strategic groups, see John McGee and Howard Thomas's "Strategic Groups: Theory, Research, and Taxonomy," *Strategic Management Journal* 7 (1986): 141–60.

56 M. Hunt, "Competition in the Major Home Appliance Industry," doctoral dissertation (Harvard University, 1973).

57 K. Hatten, D. Schendel and A. Cooper, "A Strategic Model of the U.S. Brewing Industry," *Academy of Management Journal* 21 (1978): 592–610.

58 K. Cool and D. Schendel, "Strategic Group Formation and Performance: The Case of the U.S. Pharmaceutical Industry," *Management Science* 33 (1987): 1102–24; A. Feigenbaum and H. Thomas, "Strategic Groups and Performance: The U.S. Insurance Industry," *Strategic Management Journal* 11 (1990): 197–215.

59 K. Cool and I. Dierickx, "Rivalry, Strategic Groups, and Firm Profitability," *Strategic Management Journal* 14 (1993): 47–59.

60 K. Smith, C. Grimm and S. Wally, "Strategic Groups and Rivalrous Firm Behavior: Toward a Reconciliation," *Strategic Management Journal* 18 (1997): 149–57.

# 5 Analyzing Resources and Capabilities

Analysts have tended to define assets too narrowly, identifying only those that can be measured, such as plant and equipment. Yet the intangible assets, such as a particular technology, accumulated consumer information, brand name, reputation, and corporate culture, are invaluable to the firm's competitive power. In fact, these invisible assets are often the only real source of competitive edge that can be sustained over time.

—HIROYUKI ITAMI, *MOBILIZING INVISIBLE ASSETS*

*You've gotta do what you do well.*

—LUCINO NOTO, FORMER VICE CHAIRMAN, EXXON MOBIL

# Introduction and Objectives

In Chapter 1 I noted that the focus of strategy thinking has been shifted from the external environment towards its internal environment. In this chapter, we will make the same transition. Looking within the firm, we will concentrate our attention on the resources and capabilities that firms possess. In doing so, we shall build the foundations for our analysis of competitive advantage (which began in Chapter 3 with the discussion of key success factors).

By the time you have completed this chapter you will be able to:

◆ appreciate the role of a firm's resources and capabilities as a basis for formulating strategy;

◆ identify and appraise the resources and capabilities of a firm;

◆ evaluate the potential for a firm's resources and capabilities to confer sustainable competitive advantage;

◆ use the results of resource and capability analysis to formulate strategies that exploit internal strengths while defending against internal weaknesses.

We begin by explaining why a company's resources and capabilities are so important to its strategy.

# The Role of Resources and Capabilities in Strategy Formulation

Strategy is concerned with matching a firm's resources and capabilities to the opportunities that arise in the external environment. So far, the emphasis of the book has been on the identification of profit opportunities in the external environment of the firm. In this chapter, our emphasis shifts from the interface between strategy and the external environment towards the interface between strategy and the internal environment of the firm—more specifically, with the resources and capabilities of the firm (see Figure 5.1).

Increasing emphasis on the role of resources and capabilities as the basis for strategy is the result of two factors. First, as firms' industry environments have become more unstable, so internal resources and capabilities rather than external market focus has been viewed as a more secure base for formulating strategy. Second, it has become increasingly apparent that competitive advantage rather than industry attractiveness is the primary source of superior profitability. Let us consider each of these factors.

## Basing Strategy on Resources and Capabilities

During the 1990s, ideas concerning the role of resources and capabilities as the principal basis for firm strategy and the primary source of profitability coalesced into what has become known as the *resource-based view of the firm*.[1]

To understand why the resource-based view has had a major impact on strategy thinking, let us go back to the starting point for strategy formulation: typically some statement of the firm's identity and purpose (often expressed in a mission statement). Conventionally, firms have answered the question "what is our business?" in terms of the market they serve: "who are our customers?" and "which of their needs are we seeking to serve?" However, in a world where customer preferences are volatile and the identity of customers and the technologies for serving them are changing, a market-focused strategy may not provide the stability and constancy of direction needed to guide strategy over the long term.[2] When the external environment is in

**FIGURE 5.1** Analyzing resources and capabilities: the interface between strategy and the firm

**FIGURE 5.2** Honda Motor Company: product development milestones

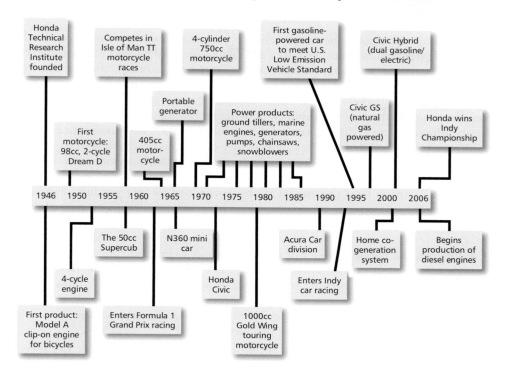

a state of flux, the firm itself, in terms of its bundle of resources and capabilities, may be a much more stable basis on which to define its identity.

In their 1990 landmark paper, "The Core Competence of the Corporation," C. K. Prahalad and Gary Hamel pointed to the potential for capabilities to be the "roots of competitiveness," source of new products and foundation for strategy.[3] For example:

- Honda Motor Company is the world's biggest motorcycle producer and a leading supplier of automobiles but it has never defined itself either as a motorcycle company or a motor vehicle company. Since its founding in 1948, its strategy has been built around its expertise in the development and manufacture of engines; this capability has successfully carried it from motorcycles to a wide range of gasoline-engined products (see Figure 5.2).

- Canon Inc. had its first success producing 35 mm cameras. Since then it has gone on to develop fax machines, calculators, copy machines, printers, video cameras, camcorders, semiconductor manufacturing equipment and many other products. Almost all of Canon's products involve the application of three areas of technological capability: precision mechanics, microelectronics and fine optics.

- 3M Corporation expanded from sandpaper into adhesive tapes, audio and videotapes, road signs, medical products and floppy disks. Its product list now comprises over 30 000 products. Is it a conglomerate? Certainly not, claims 3M. Its vast product range rests on a foundation of key technologies relating to adhesives, thin-film coatings, and materials sciences supported by outstanding capability in the development and launching of new products.

In general, the greater the rate of change in a firm's external environment, the more likely it is that internal resources and capabilities rather than external market focus will provide a secure foundation for long-term strategy. In fast-moving, technology-based industries, new companies are built around specific technological capabilities. The markets where these capabilities are applied are a secondary consideration. Motorola, the supplier of wireless telecommunications equipment, semiconductors, and direct satellite communications, has undergone many transformations, from being a leading provider of TVs and car radios to its current focus on telecom equipment. Yet, underlying these transformations has been a consistent focus on wireless electronics.

When a company faces the imminent obsolescence of its core product, should its strategy focus on continuing to serve the same basic customer needs or on deploying its resources and capabilities in other markets?

- Olivetti, the Italian supplier of typewriters and adding machines, was a pioneer in electronic computers during the 1960s, but was unable to establish long-term viability in either mainframes or personal computers.[4] Rather than maintain its focus on serving the word processing needs of business, should Olivetti have sought to exploit its electro-mechanical and precision engineering capabilities in other product markets?

- Eastman Kodak's dominance of the world market for photographic products based on chemical imaging has been threatened by digital imaging. Since 1990, Kodak has invested billions of dollars developing digital technologies and digital imaging products. Yet profits and market leadership in digital imaging remain elusive for Kodak. Might Kodak have been better off sticking with its chemical know-how and developing its interests in specialty chemicals, pharmaceuticals and healthcare?[5]

The difficulties experienced by established firms in adjusting to technological change within their own markets are well documented—in typesetting and in disk-drive manufacturing, successive technological waves have caused market leaders to falter and have allowed new entrants to prosper.[6]

## Resources and Capabilities as Sources of Profit

In Chapter 1, we identified two major sources of superior profitability: industry attractiveness and competitive advantage. Of these, competitive advantage is the more important. Internationalization and deregulation have increased competitive pressure within most sectors; as a result, few industries (or segments) offer cozy refuges from vigorous competition. As we observed in the previous chapter (see Table 4.1), industry factors account for only a small proportion of interfirm profit differentials. Hence, establishing competitive advantage through the development and deployment of resources and capabilities, rather than seeking shelter from the storm of competition, has become the primary goal for strategy.

The distinction between industry attractiveness and competitive advantage (based on superior resources) as sources of a firm's profitability corresponds to economists' distinction between different types of profit (or *rent*). The profits arising from market power are referred to as *monopoly rents*; those arising from superior resources are *Ricardian rents*, after the nineteenth-century British economist David Ricardo. Ricardo showed that, in a competitive wheat market, when land at the margin of cultivation earned a negligible return, fertile land would yield high returns. Ricardian rent is the return earned by a scarce resource over and above the cost of bringing it into production.[7]

Distinguishing between profit arising from market power and profit arising from resource superiority is less clear in practice than in principle. A closer look at Porter's five forces framework suggests that industry attractiveness derives ultimately from the ownership of resources. Barriers to entry, for example, are the result of patents, brands, distribution channels, learning, or some other resource possessed by incumbent firms. Monopoly is usually based on the ownership of a key resource such as a technical standard or government license.

The resource-based approach has profound implications for companies' strategy formulation. When the primary concern of strategy was industry selection and positioning, companies tended to adopt similar strategies. The resource-based view, by contrast, emphasizes the uniqueness of each company and suggests that the key to profitability is not through doing the *same* as other firms but rather through exploiting *differences*. Establishing competitive advantage involves formulating and implementing a strategy that exploit a firm's unique strengths.

The remainder of this chapter outlines a resource-based approach to strategy formulation. Fundamental to this approach is a thorough and profound understanding of the resources and capabilities of a firm. Such understanding provides a basis for selecting a strategy that exploits key resource and capability strengths of an organization—or an individual (see Strategy Capsule 5.1). Walt Disney's turnaround under Michael Eisner is a classic example of the benefits of exploiting underutilized resources (see Strategy Capsule 5.2).

Analyzing resources and capabilities is also concerned with filling resource gaps and building capability for the future. We shall consider the development of resources and capabilities in the next chapter.

Our starting point is to identify and assess the resources and capabilities available to the firm.

---

**STRATEGY CAPSULE 5.1**

## Focusing Strategy around Core Capabilities: Lyor Cohen on Mariah Carey

2001 was a disastrous year for Mariah Carey. Her first movie, *Glitter*, was a flop, the soundtrack was Carey's most poorly received album in a decade, her $80 million recording contract was dropped by EMI, and she suffered a nervous breakdown.

Lyor Cohen, the aggressive, workaholic chief executive of Island Def Jam records was quick to spot an opportunity: *"I cold-called her on the day of her release from EMI and I said, I think you are an unbelievable artist and you should hold your head up high. What*

*I said stuck on her and she ended up signing with us."*

His strategic analysis of Carey's situation was concise: *"I said to her, what's your competitive advantage? A great voice, of course. And what else? You write every one of your songs—you're a great writer. So why did you stray from your competitive advantage? If you have this magnificent voice and you write such compelling songs, why are you dressing like that, why are you using all these collaborations [with other artists and other songwriters]? Why? It's like*

*driving a Ferrari in first—you won't see what that Ferrari will do until you get into sixth gear."*

Cohen signed Carey in May 2002. Under Universal Music's Island Def Jam Records, Carey returned to her core strengths: her versatile voice, song-writing talents, and ballad style. Her next album, *The Emancipation of Mimi*, was the biggest-selling album of 2005, and in 2006 she won a Grammy award.

*Source*: "Rap's Unlikely Mogul," *Financial Times* (August 5, 2002).

---

## STRATEGY CAPSULE 5.2

# Resource Utilization: Revival at Walt Disney

In 1984, Michael Eisner became CEO of the Walt Disney Company. Between 1984 and 1988, Disney's sales revenue increased from $1.66 billion to $3.75 billion, net income from $98 million to $570 million, and the stock market's valuation of the company from $1.8 billion to $10.3 billion.

The key to the Disney turnaround was the mobilization of Disney's considerable resource base. Prominent among Disney's underutilized resources were 28 000 acres of land in Florida. With the help of the Arvida Corporation, a land development company acquired in 1984, Disney began hotel, resort, and residential development of these land-holdings. New attractions were added to the Epcot Center, and a new theme park, the Disney-MGM Studio Tour, was built. Disney World expanded beyond theme parks into resort vacations, the convention business, and residential housing.

To exploit its huge film library, Disney introduced videocassette sales of Disney movies and licensed packages of movies to TV networks. The huge investments in the Disney theme parks were more effectively exploited through heavier marketing effort and increased admission charges. Encouraged by the success of Tokyo Disneyland, Disney embarked on further international duplication of its U.S. theme parks with Euro Disneyland just outside Paris, France. A chain of Disney Stores was established to push sales of Disney merchandise.

The most ambitious feature of the turnaround was Disney's regeneration as a movie studio. Eisner began a massive expansion of its Touchstone label, which had been established in 1983 with the objectives of putting Disney's film studios to fuller use and establishing the company in the teenage and adult markets. Disney Studios doubled the number of movies in production. In 1988, it became America's leading studio in terms of box office receipts. Studio production was further boosted by Disney's increasing TV presence, both through the Disney Channel and programs for network TV.

Above all, the new management team was exploiting Disney's most powerful and enduring asset: the affection of millions of people of different nations and different generations for the Disney name and the Disney characters.

# The Resources of the Firm

It is important to distinguish between the resources and the capabilities of the firm: resources are the productive assets owned by the firm; capabilities are what the firm can do. Individual resources do not confer competitive advantage; they must work together to create *organizational capability*. It is capability that is the essence of superior performance. Figure 5.3 shows the relationships among resources, capabilities and competitive advantage.

Drawing up an inventory of a firm's resources can be surprisingly difficult. No such document exists within the accounting or management information systems of most corporations. The corporate balance sheet provides a limited view of a firm's resources—it comprises mainly financial and physical resources. To take a wider view of a firm's resources it is helpful to identify three principal types of resource: tangible, intangible, and human resources.

**FIGURE 5.3**  The links among resources, capabilities and competitive advantage

## Tangible Resources

Tangible resources are the easiest to identify and evaluate: financial resources and physical assets are identified and valued in the firm's financial statements. Yet balance sheets are renowned for their propensity to obscure strategically relevant information and to distort asset values. Historic cost valuation can provide little indication of an asset's market value. Disney's movie library had a balance sheet value of only $5.4 billion in 2008, based on production cost less amortization. Its land assets (including its 28 000 acres in Florida) were valued at a paltry $1.2 billion.

However, the primary goal of resource analysis is not to value a company's assets but to understand their potential for creating competitive advantage. Information that British Airways possessed fixed assets valued at £8 billion in 2008 is of little use in assessing their strategic value. To assess British Airways' ability to compete effectively in the world airline industry we need to know about the composition of these assets: the location of land and buildings, the types of plane, the landing slots and gate facilities at airports, and so on.

Once we have fuller information on a company's tangible resources we explore how we can create additional value from them. This requires that we address two key questions:

- *What opportunities exist for economizing on their use?* It may be possible to use fewer resources to support the same level of business, or to use the existing resources to support a larger volume of business. In the case of British Airways there may be opportunities for consolidating administrative offices and engineering and service facilities. Improved inventory control may allow economies in inventories of parts and fuel. Better control of cash and receivables permits a business to operate with lower levels of cash and liquid financial resources.

- *What are the possibilities for employing existing assets more profitably?* Could British Airways generate better returns on some of its planes by redeploying them into cargo carrying? Should BA seek to redeploy its assets from Europe and the North Atlantic to the Asia-Pacific region? Might it reduce costs in its European network by reassigning routes to small franchised airlines (as it does with GB Airways and Loganair)?

## Intangible Resources

For most companies, intangible resources are more valuable than tangible resources. Yet, in company financial statements, intangible resources remain largely invisible—particularly in the U.S. where R&D is expensed.[8] The exclusion or undervaluation of intangible resources is a major reason for the large and growing divergence between companies' balance-sheet valuations ("book values") and their stock-market valuations (see Table 5.1). Among the most important of these undervalued or unvalued intangible resources are brand names. Table 5.2 shows companies owning brands valued at $15 billion or more.

Brand names and other trademarks are a form of *reputational asset*: their value is in the confidence they instill in customers. Different approaches can be used to estimate brand value (or "brand equity"). One method takes the price premium attributable to a brand, multiplies it by the brand's annual sales volume, then calculates the present

**TABLE 5.1** Major companies with the highest market-to-book ratios, December 2006

| Company | Valuation Ratio | Country | Company | Valuation Ratio | Country |
|---|---|---|---|---|---|
| Yahoo! Japan | 72.0 | Japan | Coca-Cola | 7.8 | U.S. |
| Colgate-Palmolive | 20.8 | U.S. | Diageo | 7.4 | U.K. |
| GlaxoSmithKline | 13.4 | U.K. | 3M | 7.3 | U.S. |
| Anheuser-Busch | 12.6 | U.S. | Nokia | 6.7 | Finland |
| eBay | 11.2 | U.S. | Sanofi-Aventis | 6.3 | France |
| SAP | 10.8 | Germany | AstraZeneca | 5.9 | U.K. |
| Yahoo! | 10.7 | U.S. | Johnson & Johnson | 5.7 | U.S. |
| Dell Computer | 10.0 | U.S. | Boeing | 5.7 | U.S. |
| Sumitomo Mitsui Financial | 8.8 | Japan | Eli Lily | 5.6 | U.S. |
| Procter & Gamble | 8.4 | U.S. | Cisco Systems | 5.5 | U.S. |
| Qualcomm | 8.3 | U.S. | Roche Holding | 5.5 | Switz. |
| Schlumberger | 8.2 | U.S. | L'Oréal | 5.3 | France |
| Unilever | 8.1 | Neth./U.K. | Altria | 5.2 | U.S. |
| PepsiCo | 8.0 | U.S. | Novartis | 5.1 | Switz. |

**Note:** The table includes companies with the highest market capitalization as a proportion of balance-sheet net asset value among the top 200 companies of the world with the largest market capitalization at the end of 2006.

**TABLE 5.2** The world's most valuable brands, 2008

| Rank | Brand | Brand value in 2008, $ billion | Change from 2007 | Country of origin |
|---|---|---|---|---|
| 1 | Coca-Cola | 66.7 | −1% | U.S. |
| 2 | IBM | 59.0 | +11% | U.S. |
| 3 | Microsoft | 59.0 | −2% | U.S. |
| 4 | GE | 53.1 | +14% | U.S. |
| 5 | Nokia | 35.9 | +35% | Finland |
| 6 | Toyota | 34.1 | +37% | Japan |
| 7 | Intel | 31.3 | 6% | U.S. |
| 8 | McDonald's | 31.0 | 0% | U.S. |
| 9 | Disney | 29.3 | +11% | U.S. |
| 10 | Google | 25.6 | +96% | U.S. |
| 11 | Mercedes Benz | 25.6 | +28% | Germany |
| 12 | Hewlett-Packard | 23.9 | +26% | U.S. |
| 13 | BMW | 23.3 | +36% | Germany |
| 14 | Gillette | 22.1 | +5% | U.S. |
| 15 | American Express | 21.9 | +18% | U.S. |
| 16 | Louis Vuitton | 21.6 | +34% | France |
| 17 | Cisco | 21.3 | +22% | U.S. |
| 18 | Marlboro | 21.3 | 0% | U.S. |
| 19 | Citi | 20.2 | +1% | U.S. |
| 20 | Honda | 19.1 | +21% | Japan |

**Note:** Brand values are calculated as the net present value of future earnings generated by the brand.
**Source:** Interbrand.

value of this revenue stream. The brand valuations in Table 5.2 are based upon the operating profits for each company (after taxation and a capital charge), estimating the proportion attributable to the brand, then capitalizing these returns.

The value of a company's brands can be increased by extending the range of products over which a company markets its brands. Johnson & Johnson, Samsung and General Electric derive considerable economies from applying a single brand to a wide range of products. As a result, companies that succeed in building strong consumer brands have a powerful incentive to diversify—for example, Nike's diversification from athletic shoes into apparel and sports equipment.[9]

Like reputation, technology is an intangible asset whose value is not evident from most companies' balance sheets. Intellectual property—patents, copyrights, trade secrets, and trademarks—comprise technological and artistic resources where ownership is defined in law. Since the 1980s, companies have become more attentive to the value of their intellectual property. For IBM (with the world's biggest patent portfolio) and Qualcomm (with its patents relating to CDMA digital wireless telephony), intellectual property is the most valuable resource that they own.

## Human Resources

The firm's human resources comprise the expertise and effort offered by employees. Like intangible resources, human resources do not appear on the firm's balance sheet—for the simple reason that the firm does not own its employees; it purchases their services under employment contacts. The reason for including human resources as part of the resources of the firm is their stability—although employees are free to move from one firm to another (most employment contracts require no more than a month's notice on the part of the employee)—in practice most employment contracts are long term. In the U.S. the average length of time an employee stays with an employer is four years, in Europe it is longer—ranging from eight years in Britain to 13 in Greece.[10]

Most firms devote considerable effort to appraising their human resources. This appraisal occurs at the hiring stage when potential employees are evaluated in relation to the requirements of their job and as part of an ongoing appraisal process of which annual employee reviews form the centerpiece. The purposes of appraisal are to assess past performance for the purposes of compensation and promotion, set future performance goals and establish employee development plans. Trends in appraisal include greater emphasis on assessing results in relation to performance targets (for example, *management by objectives*) and broadening the basis of evaluation (for example, 360-degree appraisal).

Since the 1990s human resource appraisal has become far more systematic and sophisticated. Many organizations have established assessment centers specifically for the purpose of providing comprehensive, quantitative assessments of the skills and attributes of individual employees and appraisal criteria are increasingly based upon empirical research into the components and correlated of superior job performance. *Competency modeling* involves identifying the set of skills, content knowledge, attitudes, and values associated with superior performers within a particular job category, then assessing each employee against that profile.[11] An important finding of research into HR competencies is the critical role of psychological and social aptitudes in determining superior performance: typically these factors outweigh technical skills and educational and professional qualifications. Recent interest in *emotional intelligence* reflects growing recognition of these psychological and social attributes.[12] Overall, these finding explain the growing trend among companies to "hire for attitude; train for skills."

The ability of employees to harmonize their efforts and integrate their separate skills depends not only on their interpersonal skills but also the organizational context. This organizational context as it affects internal collaboration is determined by a key intangible resource: the *culture* of the organization. The term *organizational culture* is notoriously ill defined. It relates to an organization's values, traditions, and social norms. Building on the observations of Peters and Waterman that "firms with sustained superior financial performance typically are characterized by a strong set of core managerial values that define the ways they conduct business," Jay Barney identifies organizational culture as a firm resource of great strategic importance that is potentially very valuable.[13]

## Organizational Capabilities

Resources are not productive on their own. A brain surgeon is close to useless without a radiologist, anesthetist, nurses, surgical instruments, imaging equipment and a host of other resources. To perform a task, a team of resources must work together. An *organizational capability* is a "firm's capacity to deploy resources for a desired end result."[14] Just as an individual may be capable of playing the violin, ice skating, and speaking Mandarin, so an organization may possess the capabilities needed to manufacture widgets, distribute them globally and hedge the resulting foreign exchange exposure. We use the terms *capability* and *competence* interchangeably.[15]

Our primary interest is in those capabilities that can provide a basis for competitive advantage. Selznick used *distinctive competence* to describe those things that an organization does particularly well relative to its competitors.[16] Prahalad and Hamel coined the term *core competences* to distinguish those capabilities fundamental to a firm's strategy and performance.[17] Core competences, according to Hamel and Prahalad, are those that:

- make a disproportionate contribution to ultimate customer value, or to the efficiency with which that value is delivered and
- provide a basis for entering new markets.[18]

Prahalad and Hamel criticize U.S. companies for emphasizing product management over competence management. They compare the strategic development of Sony and RCA in consumer electronics. Both companies were failures in the home video market. RCA introduced its videodisk system, Sony its Betamax videotape system. For RCA, the failure of its first product marked the end of its venture into home video systems and heralded a progressive retreat from the consumer electronics industry. RCA was acquired by GE and later sold to Thomson of France. Sony, on the other hand, acknowledged the failure of Betamax but continued to develop its capabilities in video technology and produced a string of successful video products including camcorders, digital cameras, and the PlayStation game console.

## Classifying Capabilities

Before focusing upon "distinctive" or "core" capabilities, it is helpful to take a comprehensive look at the full range of an organization's capabilities. To identify a firm's capabilities, we need to have some basis for classifying and disaggregating its activities. Two approaches are commonly used:

- A *functional analysis* identifies organizational capabilities in relation to each of the principal functional areas of the firm. Table 5.3 classifies the principal functions of the firm and identifies organizational capabilities located within each function.
- A *value-chain analysis* separates the activities of the firm into a sequential chain. Michael Porter's representation of the value chain distinguishes between *primary activities* (those involved with the transformation of inputs and interface with the customer) and *support activities* (see Figure 5.4). Porter's generic value chain identifies a few broadly defined activities that can be disaggregated to provide a more detailed identification of the firm's activities (and the capabilities that correspond to each activity). Thus, marketing might include market research, test marketing, advertising, promotion, pricing and dealer relations.[19]

**TABLE 5.3** A functional classification of organizational capabilities

| Functional area | Capability | Exemplars |
|---|---|---|
| CORPORATE FUNCTIONS | Financial control | ExxonMobil, PepsiCo |
| | Management development | General Electric, Shell |
| | Strategic innovation | Google, Haier |
| | Multidivisional coordination | Unilever, Shell |
| | Acquisition management | Cisco Systems, Luxottica |
| | International management | Shell, Banco Santander |
| MANAGEMENT INFORMATION | Comprehensive, integrated MIS network linked to managerial decision making | Wal-Mart, Capital One, Dell Computer |
| RESEARCH AND DEVELOPMENT | Research | IBM, Merck |
| | Innovative new product development | 3M, Apple |
| | Fast-cycle new product development | Canon, Inditex (Zara) |
| OPERATIONS | Efficiency in volume manufacturing | Briggs & Stratton, YKK |
| | Continuous improvements in operations | Toyota, Harley-Davidson |
| | Flexibility and speed of response | Four Seasons Hotels |
| PRODUCT DESIGN | Design capability | Nokia, Apple |
| MARKETING | Brand management | Procter & Gamble, Altria |
| | Building reputation for quality | Johnson & Johnson |
| | Responsiveness to market trends | MTV, L'Oréal |
| SALES AND DISTRIBUTION | Effective sales promotion and execution | PepsiCo, Pfizer |
| | Efficiency and speed of order processing | L. L. Bean, Dell Computer |
| | Speed of distribution | Amazon.com |
| | Customer service | Singapore Airlines, Caterpillar |

**FIGURE 5.4** Porter's value chain

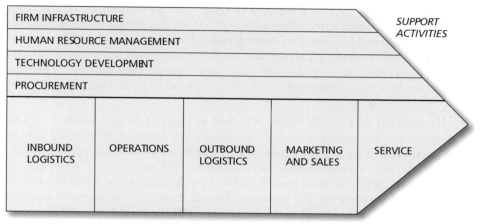

PRIMARY ACTIVITIES

## The Nature of Capability

Identifying and drawing up an inventory of a firm's resources is fairly straightforward. Organizational capabilities pose greater problems—they are much more elusive. Apple's distinctive capability in the design of consumer electronic products that combine pleasing aesthetics with a superior user interface is evident from its iMac, iPod, and iPhone products—but where within Apple is this capability located? To better understand organizational capabilities, let us take a look at their structure.

*Capability as Process and Routine*  Organizational capability requires the efforts of various individuals to be integrated with one another and with capital equipment, technology and other resources. But how does this integration occur? Productive activity within an organization involves coordinated actions undertaken by teams of people engaged in a series of productive tasks. We refer to the sequence of actions through which a specific task is performed as an *organizational process*. The sequences that comprise organizational processes can be mapped using a flowchart.[20] For example, the process of fixing bugs in the operating system developed by a large computer company involved a sequence of 30 distinct activities that began with problem recognition and ended with changes in software documentation.[21]

A key feature of most processes performed by an organization is their routinized nature. Routinization is an essential step in translating directions and operating practices into capabilities—only by becoming routine do processes become efficient and reliable. In every McDonald's hamburger restaurant, operating manuals provide precise directions for a comprehensive range of tasks, from the placing of the pickle on the burger to the maintenance of the milkshake machine. In practice, the operating manuals are seldom consulted—tasks become routinized through continuous repetition.

These *organizational routines*—"regular and predictable behavioral patterns [comprising] repetitive patterns of activity"[22]—are viewed by evolutionary economists as the fundamental building blocks of what firms do and who they are. It is through the adaptation and replication of routines that firms develop. Like individual skills, organizational routines develop through learning by doing. Just as individual skills become rusty when not exercised, so it is difficult for organizations to retain coordinated responses to contingencies that arise only rarely. Hence, there may be a tradeoff between efficiency and flexibility. A limited repertoire of routines can be performed highly efficiently with near-perfect coordination. The same organization may find it extremely difficult to respond to novel situations.[23]

*The Hierarchy of Capabilities*   Whether we start from a functional or value chain approach, the capabilities that we identify are likely to be broadly defined: operational capability, marketing capability, supply chain management capability. However, having recognized that capabilities are the outcome of processes and routines, it is evident that these broadly defined capabilities can be disaggregated into more specialist capabilities. For example, human resource management capability can be disaggregated recruitment capability, HR appraisal capability, career development capability,—and others too. We can also recognize that even broadly defined functional capabilities integrate to form wider cross-functional capabilities: new product development, business development, the provision of customer solutions. What we observe is a hierarchy of capabilities where more general,

**FIGURE 5.5**  The hierarchical nature of capabilities: a manufacturer of PBXs

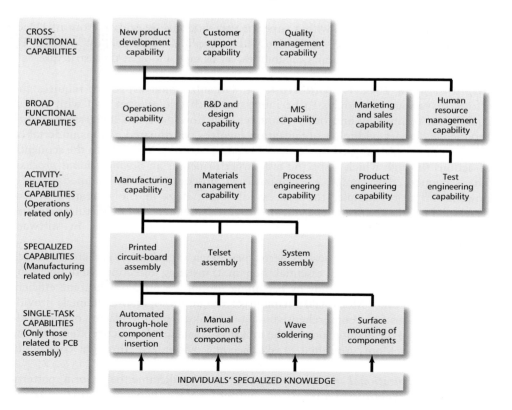

broadly defined capabilities are formed from the integration of more specialized capabilities. For example:

- A hospital's capability in treating heart disease depends on its integration of capabilities relating to patient diagnosis, physical medicine, cardiovascular surgery, preoperative and postoperative care, as well as capabilities relating to training, information technology and various administrative and support functions.

- Toyota's manufacturing capability—its system of "lean production"— integrates capabilities relating to the manufacture of components and subassemblies, supply-chain management, production scheduling, assembly, quality-control procedures, systems for managing innovation and continuous improvement, and inventory control.

Figure 5.5 offers a partial view of the hierarchy of capabilities of a telecom equipment maker. The capabilities at the highest level of integration—typically those that involve cross-functional and cross-divisional integration—are most difficult to develop, for the simple reason that they require integration across many individuals and across a broad spectrum of specialist knowledge. As a result, achieving excellence in new product development capabilities represents one of the greatest challenges that companies face in capability management—we will return to the topic of new product development in subsequent chapters.[24]

## Appraising Resources and Capabilities

So far, we have established what resources and capabilities are, how they can provide a long-term focus for a company's strategy and how we can go about identifying them. However, given our emphasis on strategy as a quest for profit, the next stage of our analysis is to appraise the potential for resources and capabilities to earn profits for the company.

The profits that a firm obtains from its resources and capabilities depend on three factors: their abilities to *establish* a competitive advantage, to *sustain* that competitive advantage and to *appropriate* the returns to that competitive advantage. Each of these depends on a number of resource characteristics. Figure 5.6 shows the key relationships.

### Establishing Competitive Advantage

For a resource or capability to establish a competitive advantage, two conditions must be present:

- *Scarcity*. If a resource or capability is widely available within the industry, then it may be essential to possess it in order to compete, but it will not be a sufficient basis for competitive advantage. In oil and gas exploration, new technologies such as directional drilling and 3-D seismic analysis are critical to reducing the costs of finding new reserves. However, these technologies are widely available from oilfield service and IT companies. As a result, such technologies are "needed to play," but they are not sufficient to win.

**FIGURE 5.6** Appraising the strategic importance of resources and capabilities

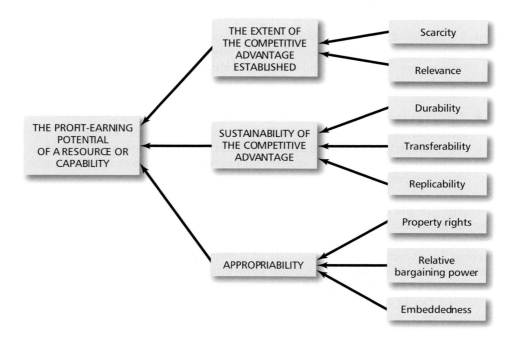

- *Relevance*. A resource or capability must be relevant to the key success factors in the market. British coal mines produced some wonderful brass bands. Unfortunately, musical capabilities did little to assist the mines in meeting competition from cheap imported coal and North Sea gas. As retail banking shifts toward automated teller machines and online transactions, so the retail branch networks of the banks have become less relevant for customer service.

## Sustaining Competitive Advantage

The profits earned from resources and capabilities depend not just on their ability to *establish* competitive advantage but also on how long that advantage can be *sustained*. This depends on whether resources and capabilities are *durable* and whether rivals can *imitate* the competitive advantage they offer. Resources and capabilities are imitable if they are *transferable* or *replicable*.

*Durability*  Some resources are more durable than others and, hence, are a more secure basis for competitive advantage. The increasing pace of technological change is shortening the useful life span of most resources including capital equipment and proprietary technologies. Brands, on the other hand, can show remarkable resilience to time. Heinz sauces, Kellogg's cereals, Guinness stout, Burberry raincoats and Coca-Cola have been market leaders for over a century.

*Transferability*  The simplest means of acquiring the resources and capabilities necessary for imitating another firm's strategy is to buy them. The ability to buy a resource or capability depends on its *transferability*—the extent to which it is mobile between companies. Some resources, such as finance, raw materials, components, machines produced by equipment suppliers and employees with standardized skills (such as short-order cooks and auditors) are transferable and can be bought and sold with little difficulty. Some resources are not easily transferred—either they are entirely firm specific or their value depreciates on transfer.[25]

Sources of immobility include:

- Geographical immobility of natural resources, large items of capital equipment and some types of employees may make it difficult for firms to acquire these resources without relocating themselves. The competitive advantage of the Laphroaig distillery and its 10-year-old, single-malt whiskey is its water spring on the Isle of Islay, which supplies water flavored by peat and sea spray.

- Imperfect information regarding the quality and productivity of resources creates risks for buyers. Such imperfections are especially important in relation to human resources—hiring decisions are typically based on very little knowledge of how the new employee will perform. Sellers of resources have better information about the characteristics of the resources on offer than potential buyers—this creates a "lemons problem" for firms seeking to acquire resources.[26] Jay Barney has shown that different valuations of resources by firms can result in their being either underpriced or overpriced, giving rise to differences in profitability between firms.[27]

- Complementarity between resources means that the detachment of a resource from its "home team" causes it to lose productivity and value. Thus, if brand reputation is associated with the company that created it, a change in ownership of the brand erodes its value. The sale of Jaguar Cars, first to Ford and then to Tata Motors of India has almost certainly eroded its brand value.[28]

- Organizational capabilities, because they are based on teams of resources, are less mobile than individual resources. Even if the whole team can be transferred (in investment banking it has been commonplace for whole teams of analysts or mergers and acquisitions specialists to defect from one bank to another), the dependence of the team on a wider network of relationships and corporate culture may pose difficulties for recreating the capability in the new company.

*Replicability* If a firm cannot buy a resource or capability, it must build it. In financial services, most innovations in new derivative products can be imitated easily by competitors. In retailing, too, competitive advantages that derive from store layout, point-of-sale technology, charge cards and extended opening hours can be copied easily by competitors.

Capabilities based on complex organizational routines are less easily replicable. Federal Express's national, next-day delivery service and Nucor's system for steel manufacturing, which combines efficiency with flexibility, are complex capabilities based on unique corporate cultures. Some capabilities appear simple but prove difficult to replicate. Throughout the 1980s and 1990s, General Motors struggled to understand and replicate the Toyota lean production system. The NUMMI joint venture between the two companies gave GM a birds-eye view of Toyota's system in operation. Yet, after two decades of benchmarking, capital investment and employee training, GM was still lagging in efficiency, quality, and flexibility.[29]

Even where replication is possible, incumbent firms benefit from the fact that resources and capabilities that have been accumulated over a long period can only be replicated at disproportionate cost by would-be imitators. Dierickx and Cool identify two major sources of incumbency advantage:

- *Asset mass efficiencies* occur where a strong initial position in technology, distribution channels, or reputation facilitates the subsequent accumulation of these resources.
- *Time compression diseconomies* are the additional costs incurred by imitators when attempting to accumulate rapidly a resource or capability. Thus, "crash programs" of R&D and "blitz" advertising campaigns tend to be less productive than similar expenditures made over a longer period.[30]

## Appropriating the Returns to Competitive Advantage

Who gains the returns generated by superior capabilities? We should normally expect that such returns accrue to the owner of that capability. However, ownership is not always clear-cut: capabilities depend heavily on the skills and efforts of employees—who are not owned by the firm. For companies dependent on human ingenuity and know-how, the mobility of key employees represents a constant threat to their competitive advantage (see Strategy Capsule 5.3). In investment banks and other human capital-intensive firms, the struggle between employees and shareholders to appropriate rents is reminiscent of the war for surplus value between labor and capital that Marx analyzed. It is notable that in 2006, average employee pay among Goldman Sachs' 27 000 staff (including secretaries and janitors) was $622 000.[31] The prevalence of partnerships (rather than joint-stock companies) in professional service industries (lawyers, accountants, and management consultants) reflects the desire to avoid conflict between its owners and its human resources.

### STRATEGY CAPSULE 5.3

# When Your Competitive Advantage Walks Out the Door: Gucci

On September 10, 2001, French retailer Pinault Printemps Redoute (PPR) agreed to acquire Gucci Group—the Italian-based fashion house and luxury goods maker. On November 4, 2003, the managers and shareholders of the two companies were stunned to learn that Chairman Domenico De Sole and Vice Chairman Tom Ford would be leaving Gucci in April, 2004.

The duo had masterminded Gucci's transformation from a near-bankrupt family firm with an over-extended brand into one of the world's hottest fashion houses. As creative director, Tom

Ford had established Gucci as a style leader and hired young designers such as Stella McCartney and Alexander McQueen. De Sole's astute leadership had instituted careful planning and financial discipline, and built Gucci's global presence—especially in Asia.

How great a blow was De Sole and Ford's departure to the parent PPR? In principle, a new CEO and new head of design could be hired. In practice, talent of the ilk of De Sole and Ford was rare—especially a combination of designer and CEO who could collaborate around a shared vision.

The stock market's reaction was ominous. On November 3, 2003, Gucci's share price was $86.10; on November 6 it had fallen to $84.60. However, in the absence of PPR's guarantee to acquire Gucci's shares at $85.52, analysts estimated that Gucci would be trading at around $74. The implication was that Gucci was worth $1.2 billion less without De Sole and Ford than with them.

*Source:* Adapted from articles in the *Financial Times* during November 5–8, 2003.

The less clearly defined are property rights in resources and capabilities, the greater the importance of relative bargaining power in determining the division of returns between the firm and its individual members. In the case of team-based organizational capabilities, this balance of power between the firm and an individual employee depends crucially on the relationship between individuals' skills and organizational routines. The more deeply embedded are individual skills and knowledge within organizational routines, and the more they depend on corporate systems and reputation, the weaker the employee is relative to the firm.

Conversely, the closer an organizational capability is identified with the expertise of individual employees, and the more effective those employees are at deploying their bargaining power, the better able employees are to appropriate rents. If the individual employee's contribution to productivity is clearly identifiable, if the employee is mobile, and if the employee's skills offer similar productivity to other firms, the employee is in a strong position to appropriate most of his or her contribution to the firm's value added. Does the $29 million annual salary paid to Alex Rodriguez fully exploit his value to the New York Yankees? In most professional sports, it appears that strategies based exclusively on signing superstar players result in the players appropriating most of the rents, with little surplus available for the clubs—this was certainly the fate of Real Madrid, Chelsea, and Manchester City soccer clubs in recent years. The emphasis by investment banks and consulting companies upon the capabilities of their teams, rather than upon the role of star employees, is a strategy for improving the bargaining power of the firm relative to that of its key employees.

## Putting Resource and Capability Analysis to Work: A Practical Guide

We have covered the principal concepts and frameworks for analyzing resources and capabilities. How do we put this analysis into practice? Let me offer a simple, step-by-step approach to how a company can appraise its resources and capabilities and then use the appraisal to guide strategy formulation.

## Step 1 Identify the Key Resources and Capabilities

To draw up a list of the firm's resources and capabilities we can begin from outside or inside the firm. From an external focus, we begin with key success factors (see Chapter 3). Which factors determine why some firms in an industry are more successful than others and on what resources and capabilities these success factors are based? Suppose we are evaluating the resources and capabilities of Volkswagen AG, the German-based automobile manufacturer. We can start with key success factors in the world automobile industry: low-cost production, attractively designed new models embodying the latest technologies, the financial strength to weather the heavy investment requirements and cyclical nature of the industry. What capabilities and resources do these key success factors imply? They would include manufacturing capabilities, new product development capability, effective supply-chain management, global distribution, brand strength, scale-efficient plants with up-to-date capital equipment, a strong balance sheet, and so on.

To organize these various resources and capabilities, it is useful to take an inside view of VW and examine the company's value chain, identifying the sequence of activities from new product development to purchasing, to supply chain management, to component manufacture, assembly, and right the way through to dealership support and after-sales service. We can then look at the resources that underpin the capabilities at each stage of the value chain. Table 5.4 lists VW's principal resources and capabilities.

## Step 2 Appraising Resources and Capabilities

Resources and capabilities need to be appraised against two key criteria. First, their *importance*: which resources and capabilities are most important in conferring sustainable competitive advantage? Second, where are strengths and weaknesses as compared with competitors?

*Assessing Importance* The temptation in assessing which resources and capabilities are most important is to concentrate on customer choice criteria. What we must bear in mind, however, is that our ultimate objective is not to attract customers but to make superior profit through establishing a sustainable competitive advantage. For this purpose we need to look beyond customer choice to the underlying strategic characteristics of resources and capabilities. To do this we need to apply the set of appraisal criteria outlined in the previous section on "Appraising Resources and Capabilities." In the case of VW, many resources and capabilities are essential to compete in the business but several of them are not scarce (for example, total quality management capability and technologically advanced assembly plants have become widely diffused within the industry), while others (such as IT capability and design capability) are outsourced to external providers—either way, they are "needed to play" but not "needed to win." On the other hand, resources such as brand strength and a global distribution network and capabilities such as fast-cycle new product development and global logistics capability, cannot be easily acquired or internally developed—they are critical to establishing and sustaining advantage.

*Assessing Relative Strengths* It is difficult to appraise objectively the comparative strengths and weaknesses of a company's resources and capabilities relative to competitors. In assessing their own competencies, organizations

**TABLE 5.4** Appraising VW's resources and capabilities

| | Importance[a] | VW's relative strength[b] | Comments |
|---|---|---|---|
| RESOURCES | | | |
| R1. Finance | 6 | 6 | Credit rating is above average for the industry but free cash flow remains negative |
| R2. Technology | 7 | 5 | Despite technical strengths, VW is not a leader in automotive technology |
| R3. Plant and equipment | 8 | 8 | Has invested heavily in upgrading plants |
| R4. Location | 4 | 4 | Plants in key low-cost, growth markets (China, Mexico, Brazil) but German manufacturing base is very expensive |
| R5. Distribution (dealership network) | 8 | 5 | Geographically extensive distribution with special strength in emerging markets. Historically weak position within the U.S. |
| R6. Brands | 6 | 5 | VW, Audi, Bentley and Bugatti are strong brands but, together with Skoda and Seat, VW's brand portfolio lacks coherence and clear market positioning |
| CAPABILITIES | | | |
| C1. Product development | 9 | 4 | Traditionally weak at VW. Despite a few big hits: Beetle (introduced 1938), Golf (1974), Passat (1974), Vanagon (1979), VW still not an industry leader in new product development |
| C2. Purchasing | 7 | 5 | Traditionally weak—strengthened by senior hires from Opel and elsewhere |
| C3. Engineering | 7 | 9 | The core technical strength of VW |
| C4. Manufacturing | 8 | 4 | VW is a high-cost producer, but struggles to attain above average quality |
| C5. Financial management | 6 | 4 | Has traditionally lacked a strong financial orientation |
| C6. R&D | 5 | 4 | Despite several technical strengths, VW is not a leader in automotive innovation |
| C7. Marketing and sales | 9 | 4 | Despite traditional weakness in recognizing and meeting customer needs in different national markets, VW has increased its sensitivity to the market, improved brand management, and managed its advertising and promotion with increasing dexterity |
| C8. Government relations | 4 | 8 | Important in emerging markets |
| C9. Strategic management | 7 | 4 | Effective restructuring and cost cutting, but lack of consistency and consensus at top management level |

[a]Both scales range from 1 to 10 (1 = very low, 10 = very high).

[b]Volkswagen's resources and capabilities are compared with those of GM, Ford, Toyota, DaimlerChrysler, Nissan, Honda, Fiat, and PSA, where 5 represents parity. The ratings are based on the author's subjective judgment.

frequently fall victim to past glories, hopes for the future and their own wishful thinking. The tendency toward hubris among companies—and their senior managers—means that business success often sows the seeds of its own destruction.[32] Among the failed industrial companies in America and Europe are many whose former success blinded them to their stagnating capabilities and declining competitiveness: examples include the cutlery producers of Sheffield, England, and the integrated steel giants of the U.S.

To identify and appraise a company's capabilities, managers must look both inside and outside. Internal discussion can be valuable in sharing insights and evidence and building consensus regarding the organization's resource and capability profile. The evidence of history can be particularly revealing in reviewing instances where the company has performed well and those where it has performed poorly: do any patterns appear?

Finally, to move the analysis from the subjective to the objective level, *benchmarking* is a powerful tool for quantitative assessment of performance relative to that of competitors. Benchmarking is "the process of identifying, understanding, and adapting outstanding practices from organizations anywhere in the world to help your organization improve its performance."[33] Benchmarking offers a systematic framework and methodology for identifying particular functions and processes and then for comparing their performance with other companies. Strategy Capsule 5.4 offers some examples. As McKinsey & Co. has shown, performance differentials between top-performing and average-performing companies in most activities tends to be wide.[34]

## STRATEGY CAPSULE 5.4
# Using Benchmarking to Assess Capabilities

By systematically comparing processes and activities with those of other firms, benchmarking allows a company to make an objective appraisal of its capabilities. The key stages in the benchmarking process are

1   Deciding what to benchmark.
2   Identifying partners.
3   Establishing benchmarking metrics.
4   Gathering data.
5   Analysis.

This then forms the foundation for programs to imitate the superior capabilities of other firms.

Xerox Corporation was the pioneer of benchmarking. Losing market share during the 1980s, logistics engineer Robert Camp performed detailed comparisons that showed the massive superiority of Japanese competitors in cost efficiency, quality and new product development. Every department at Xerox was encouraged to look beyond competitors to identify best-in-class companies against which to benchmark. For inventory control and customer responsiveness, Xerox benchmarked against L. L. Bean, the direct-mail clothing company.

During the early 1990s, Chrysler benchmarked its new product development against Honda. The result was a total reorganization of Chrysler's product development organization, which resulted in greatly reduced cycle time for new models and enhanced launch quality.

Bank of America (B of A) engaged in a series of benchmarking studies with Royal Bank of Canada which was similar in size and philosophy but was not a direct competitor. These allowed B of A first to highlight anomalies and then carry out more detailed comparisons of processes.

However, benchmarking carries risks. Jeff Pfeffer laments the propensity for benchmarking to encourage uniformity: "Take an airplane flight. With very few exceptions, can you tell them apart?" Dan Levinthal points to the danger of looking at specific practices without taking account of interdependencies with other processes and the organizational context more broadly: "Companies should be cautious about benchmarking or imitating certain policies and practices of other firms . . . the implicit assumption in this thinking is that the policy that is benchmarked and adopted is independent of what my firm is already doing. The best human resource management practice for Nordstrom may not be the best for McDonald's. It may actually be dysfunctional."

*Sources*: Robert C. Camp, *Benchmarking: The Search for Industry Best Practices that Lead to Superior Performance* (Florence, KY: Productivity Press, 2006). J. Pfeffer, *What Were They Thinking?* (Boston: Harvard Business School Press, 2007, Chapter 23 "Dare to be Different"). "A New Tool for Resurrecting an Old Theory of the Firm," Knowledge@Wharton, May 17, 2006 (http://knowledge.wharton.upenn.edu/article/1480.cfm, accessed 16 June, 2009).

Ultimately, appraising resources and capabilities is not about data—it is about insight and understanding. Every organization has some activity where it excels or has the potential to excel. For Federal Express, it is a system that guarantees next-day delivery anywhere within the U.S. For BMW it is the ability to integrate world-class engineering with design excellence and highly effective marketing. For McDonald's, it is the ability to supply millions of hamburgers from thousands of outlets throughout the world, with remarkable uniformity of quality, customer service and hygiene. For General Electric, it is a system of corporate management that reconciles coordination, innovation, flexibility and financial discipline in one of the world's largest and most diversified corporations. All these companies are examples of highly successful enterprises. One reason why they are successful is that they have recognized what they can do well and have based their strategies on their strengths. For poor-performing companies the problem is not necessarily an absence of distinctive capabilities but a failure to recognize what they are and to deploy them effectively.

*Bringing Together Importance and Relative Strength* Putting the two criteria—importance and relative strength—together allows us to highlight a company's key strengths and key weaknesses. Consider, for example, Volkswagen AG. Table 5.4 provides a partial (and hypothetical) identification and appraisal of VW's resources and capabilities at the beginning of the 21st century in relation to the two criteria of importance and relative strength outlined above. Figure 5.7 then brings the two criteria together into a single display. Dividing this display into four quadrants allows us to identify those resources and capabilities that we may regard

**FIGURE 5.7**  Appraising VW's resources and capabilities (hypothetical)

**Note:** Figure 5.7  is based on the ratings of resources and capabilities in Table 5.4.

as key strengths and those that we may identify as key weaknesses. For example, our assessment suggests that plant and equipment, engineering capability and supply chain management are key strengths of VW, whereas distribution (a relatively weak presence in the U.S. and Japan), new product development (no consistent record of fast-cycle development of market-winning new models) and financial management are key weaknesses.

## Step 3 Developing Strategy Implications

Our key focus is on the two right-hand quadrants of Figure 5.7. How do we exploit our key strengths most effectively? How can we address our key weaknesses in terms of both reducing our vulnerability to them and correcting them? Finally, what about our "inconsequential" strengths? Are these really superfluous or are there ways in which we can deploy them to greater effect?

*Exploiting Key Strengths*  Having identified resources and capabilities that are important and where our company is strong relative to competitors, the key task is to formulate our strategy to ensure that these resources are deployed to the greatest effect. If engineering is a key strength of VW, then it may wish to seek differentiation advantage through technical sophistication and safety features. If VW is effective in managing government relations and is well positioned in the potential growth markets of China, Eastern Europe, and Latin America, exploiting this strength may require developing models that will appeal to these markets.

To the extent that different companies within an industry have different capability profiles, this implies differentiation of strategies within the industry. Thus, Toyota's outstanding manufacturing capabilities and fast-cycle new product development, Hyundai's low-cost manufacturing capability that derives from its South Korean location, and Peugeot's design flair suggest that each company should be pursuing a distinctively different strategy.

*Managing Key Weaknesses* What does a company do about its key weaknesses? It is tempting to think of how companies can upgrade existing resources and capabilities to correct such weaknesses. However, converting weakness into strength is likely to be a long-term task for most companies. In the short to medium term, a company is likely to be stuck with the resources and capabilities that it inherits from the previous period.

The most decisive—and often most successful—solution to weaknesses in key functions is to outsource. Thus, in the automobile industry, companies have become increasingly selective in the activities they perform internally. During the 1930s, Ford was almost completely vertically integrated. At its massive River Rouge plant, which once employed over 100 000 people, coal and iron ore entered at one end, completed cars exited at the other. In 2004, Ford opened its Dearborn Truck Plant on the old River Rouge site. The new plant employed 3 200 Ford workers and an equal number of suppliers' employees. Almost all component production was outsourced along with a major part of design, engineering, assembly, IT and security. In athletic shoes and clothing, Nike undertakes product design, marketing, and overall "systems integration," but manufacturing, logistics, and many other functions are contracted out. We shall consider the vertical scope of the firm at greater depth in Chapter 14.

Through clever strategy formulation a firm may be able to negate the impact of its key weaknesses. Consider Harley-Davidson: in competition with Honda, Yamaha, and BMW and with sales of 300 000 bikes a year (compared with 10 million at Honda), Harley is unable to compete on technology. How has it dealt with this problem? It has made a virtue out of its outmoded technology and traditional designs. Harley-Davidson's obsolete push-rod engines and recycled designs have become central to the retro-look appeal of the "hog."

*What about Superfluous Strengths?* What about those resources and capabilities where a company has particular strengths, but these don't appear to be important sources of sustainable competitive advantage? One response may be to lower the level of investment from these resources and capabilities. If a retail bank has a strong but increasingly underutilized branch network, this may be an opportunity to prune its real estate assets and invest in web-based customer services.

However, in the same way that companies can turn apparent weaknesses into competitive strengths, so it is possible to develop innovative strategies that turn apparently inconsequential strengths into key strategy differentiators. Edward Jones' network of brokerage offices and 8 000-strong sales force looked increasingly irrelevant in an era when brokerage transactions were going online. However, by emphasizing personal service, trustworthiness, and its traditional, conservative investment virtues, Edward Jones has built a successful contrarian strategy based on its network of local offices.[35]

In the fiercely competitive MBA market, business schools should also seek to differentiate on the basis of idiosyncratic resources and capabilities. Georgetown's Jesuit heritage is not an obvious source of competitive advantage for its MBA programs. Yet, the Jesuit approach to education is about developing the whole person; this fits well with an emphasis on developing the values, integrity and emotional intelligence necessary to be a successful business leader. Similarly, Dartmouth College's location in woods of New Hampshire far from any major business center is not an obvious benefit to its business programs. However, Dartmouth's Tuck Business School has used the isolation and natural beauty of its locale to create an MBA program that features unparalleled community and social involvement that fosters personal development and close network ties.

## Summary

We have shifted the focus of our attention from the external environment of the firm to its internal environment. This internal environment comprises many features of the firm but, for the purposes of strategy analysis, the key issue is what the firm *can do*. This means looking at the resources of the firm and the way resources combine to create organizational capabilities. Our interest is the potential for resources and capabilities to establish sustainable competitive advantage. Systematic appraisal of a company's resources and capabilities provides the basis for formulating (or reformulating) strategy. How can the firm deploy its strengths to maximum advantage? How can it minimize its vulnerability to its weaknesses? Figure 5.8 provides a simplified view of the approach to resource analysis developed in this chapter.

**FIGURE 5.8** Summary: a framework for analyzing resources and capabilities

Although much of the discussion has been heavy on concepts and theory, the issues are practical. The management systems of most firms devote meticulous attention to the physical and financial assets that are valued on their balance sheets; much less attention has been paid to the critical intangible and human resources of the firm, and even less to the identification and appraisal of organizational capability. Most senior managers are now aware of the importance of their resources and capabilities but the techniques of identifying, assessing and developing them are woefully underdeveloped.

Because the resources and capabilities of the firm form the foundation for building competitive advantage, we shall return again and again to the concepts of this chapter. At the same time, I have deliberately limited the scope of this chapter. My emphasis has been on identifying, appraising and deploying firms' existing resources and capabilities. What about developing resources and capabilities for the future? In particular, can firms develop entirely new capabilities or are they restricted to playing the hand that the past has dealt them? This is our next port of call.

## Self-Study Questions

1   In recent years Google has expanded from internet search across a broad range of internet services, including email, photo management, satellite maps, digital book libraries, blogger services, and telephony. To what extent has Google's strategy been built upon a common set of resources and capabilities rather than specific customer needs? What are Google's principal resources and capabilities?

2   Microsoft's main capabilities relate to the development and marketing of complex computer software and its greatest resource is its huge installed base of its Windows operating system. Does Microsoft's entry into video game consoles indicate that its strategy is becoming divorced from its principal resources and capabilities?

3   During 1984–8, Michael Eisner, the newly installed CEO of Walt Disney Company, successfully exploited Disney's existing resources to boost profitability (see Strategy Capsule 5.2). During the last eight years of Eisner's tenure (1998–2005), however, profitability stagnated and share price declined. To what extent did Eisner focus too much on exploiting existing resources and not enough on developing Disney's capabilities to meet the entertainment needs of a changing world?

4   Many companies announce in their corporate communications: "Our people are our most important resource." In terms of the criteria listed in Figure 5.6, can employees be considered to be of the utmost strategic importance?

5   Given the profile of VW's resources and capabilities outlined in Table 5.4 and Figure 5.7, what strategy recommendations would you offer VW?

**6**   Apply the approach outlined in the section "Putting Resource and Capability Analysis to Work" to your own business school. Begin by identifying the resources and capabilities relevant to success in the market for business education, appraise the resources and capabilities of your school, then make strategy recommendations regarding such matters as the programs to be offered and the overall positioning and differentiation of the school and its offerings.

# Notes

1  The "resource-based view" is described in J. B. Barney, "Firm Resources and Sustained Competitive Advantage," *Journal of Management* 17 (1991): 99–120; J. Mahoney and J. R. Pandian, "The Resource-Based View within the Conversation of Strategic Management," *Strategic Management Journal* 13 (1992): 363–80; M. A. Peterlaf, "The Cornerstones of Competitive Advantage: A Resource-Based View," *Strategic Management Journal* 14 (1993): 179–92; and R. M. Grant, "The Resource-based Theory of Competitive Advantage," *California Management Review* 33 (1991): 114–35.

2  Ted Levitt, "Marketing Myopia," *Harvard Business Review* (July–August 1960): 24–47 proposed that firms should define their strategies on the basis of customer needs rather than products, for example, railroad companies should view themselves as in the transportation business. However, this fails to address the resource implications of serving these broad customer needs.

3  C. K. Prahalad and G. Hamel, "The Core Competence of the Corporation," *Harvard Business Review* (May–June 1990): 79–91.

4  E. Danneels, B. Provera and G. Verona, "Legitimizing Exploration: Olivetti's Transition from Mechanical to Electronic Technology" Management Department, Bocconi University, 2008; also "Olivetti Reinvents Itself Once More," *Wall Street Journal* (February 22, 1999): A.1.

5  "Eastman Kodak: Meeting the Digital Challenge," in R. M. Grant, *Cases to Accompany Contemporary Strategy Analysis* 6th edn (Oxford: Blackwell, 2008).

6  M. Tripsas, "Unraveling the Process of Creative Destruction: Complementary Assets and Incumbent Survival in the Typesetter Industry," *Strategic Management Journal* 18, Summer Special Issue (1997): 119–42; J. Bower and C. M. Christensen, "Disruptive Technologies: Catching the Wave," *Harvard Business Review* (January-February 1995): 43–53.

7  A. Madhok and S. Li, "Ricardo Revisited: The Resource Based View, Comparative Advantage and Competitive Heterogeneity" (September 28, 2004). Available at SSRN: http://ssrn.com/abstract=611182, accessed 16 June, 2009.

8  "Why It Is So Hard to Value a Mystery," *Financial Times* Special Report (January 7, 2008): 2.

9  Economies of scope in brands can also be exploited by licensing. Harley-Davidson licenses its brands to the manufacturers of apparel, toys, autos, and toiletries.

10  *Economic Survey of the European Union, 2007* (Paris: OECD, 2007).

11  E. Lawler, "From Job-Based to Competency-Based Organizations," *Journal of Organizational Behavior* 15 (1994): 3–15; L. Spencer, D. McClelland, and S. Spencer, *Competency Assessment Methods: History and State of the Art* (Hay/McBer Research Group, 1994); L. Spencer and S. Spencer, *Competence At Work: Models for Superior Performance* (New York: John Wiley & Sons, Inc., 1993).

12  D. Goleman, *Emotional Intelligence* (New York: Bantam, 1995).

13  J. Barney, "Organizational Culture: Can It Be a Source of Sustained Competitive Advantage?" *Academy of Management Review* 11 (1986): 656–65.

14  C. E. Helfat and M. Lieberman, "The Birth of Capabilities: Market Entry and the Importance of Prehistory," *Industrial and Corporate Change* 12 (2002): 725–60.

15  G. Hamel and C. K. Prahalad argue (*Harvard Business Review*, May-June 1992: 164–5) that "the distinction between competencies and capabilities is purely semantic."

16  P. Selznick, *Leadership in Administration: A Sociological Interpretation* (New York: Harper & Row, 1957).

17  C. K. Prahalad and G. Hamel, "The Core Competence of the Corporation," op. cit.

18  G. Hamel and C. K. Prahalad, letter, *Harvard Business Review* (May-June 1992): 164–5.

19  Porter's value chain is the main framework of his *Competitive Advantage* (New York: Free Press, 1984). McKinsey & Company refers to the firm's value chain as its "business system." See: C. F. Bates, P. Chatterjee, F. W. Gluck, D. Gogel, A. Puri, "The Business System: A New Tool for Strategy Formulation and Cost Analysis," in *McKinsey on Strategy* (Boston: McKinsey & Company, 2000).

20  T. W. Malone, K. Crowston, J. Lee and B. Pentland, "Tools for Inventing Organizations: Toward a Handbook of Organizational Processes" *Management Science* 45 (1999): 425–43.

21  K. Crowston, "A Coordination Theory Approach to Organization Design" *Organization Science* 8 (1997): 157–75.

22  R. R. Nelson and S. G. Winter, *An Evolutionary Theory of Economic Change* (Cambridge, MA: Belknap, 1982).

23  As a result, specialists perform well in stable environments while generalists do well in variable conditions. See J. Freeman and M. Hannan, "Niche Width and the Dynamics of Organizational Populations," *American Journal of Sociology* 88 (1984): 1116–45.

24  K. B. Clark and T. Fujimoto, *Product Development Performance* (New York: Free Press, 1991).

25  See Richard Caves' discussion of "specific assets" in "International Corporations: The Industrial Economics of Foreign Investment," *Economica* 38 (1971): 1–27.

26  G. Akerlof, "The Market for Lemons: Qualitative Uncertainty and the Market Mechanism," *Quarterly Journal of Economics* 84 (1970): 488–500.

27  J. B. Barney, "Strategic Factor Markets: Expectations, Luck and Business Strategy," *Management Science* 32 (October 1986): 1231–41.

28  "Is India Bad for Jaguar," *Time* (December 14, 2007).

29  K. Ichijo and I. Nonaka, *Knowledge Creation and Management* (New York: Oxford University Press, 2006): 127–8; "The Open Secret of Success," *The New Yorker* (May 12, 2008).

30  I. Dierickx and K. Cool, "Asset Stock Accumulation and Sustainability of Competitive Advantage," *Management Science* 35 (1989): 1504–13.

31  "Good deal," *Boston Globe* (December 12, 2006).

32  D. Miller, *The Icarus Paradox: How Exceptional Companies Bring About Their Own Downfall* (New York: Harper-Business, 1990).

33  Benchnet: The Benchmarking Exchange (www.benchnet.com, accessed 16 June, 2009).

34  S. Walleck, D. O'Halloran, and C. Leader, "Benchmarking World-Class Performance," *McKinsey Quarterly* (1991): 3–24; "The Link Between Management and Productivity," *McKinsey Quarterly* (February, 2006). http://www.mckinseyquarterly .com/The_link_between_management_and_productivity_ 1725

35  C. Markides, *All the Right Moves* (Boston: Harvard Business School Press, 1999).

# 6 Developing Resources and Capabilities

*An organization's ability to learn, and translate that learning into action rapidly is the ultimate competitive advantage.*

— JACK WELCH, CHAIRMAN AND CEO, GENERAL ELECTRIC 1980–2001

## Introduction and Objectives

Our analysis of resources and capabilities has focused upon appraising and then deploying the firm's existing stock of resources and capabilities. Ultimately, however, sustaining and renewing competitive advantage in a changing world requires the continuous development and extension of existing resources and capabilities, and the nurturing of new ones. So what's the big deal? How difficult can this be? The short answer is "very difficult". In this chapter we shall address the challenge of developing and creating resources and capabilities. Our emphasis will be on organizational capabilities as this is where the critical challenges lie.

By the time you have completed this chapter, it is my intention that you will have achieved the following:

◆ recognition of the difficulties that managers face in developing the resources and capabilities of the organization—capabilities in particular;

◆ familiarity with the different approaches that firms have taken in developing organizational capabilities—and the merits and pitfalls of each;

◆ appreciation of the role of knowledge as the most important resource of the firm and the contribution knowledge management can play in developing organizational capability.

## Developing Resources

Resources are comparatively simple—we know what they are and we have a formidable arsenal of concepts and techniques that we can deploy in developing them. In the case of brands, marketing has developed sophisticated approaches to understanding the nature of brand loyalty and the dynamics through which it can be built. In the case of technology, a substantial body of research and practical knowledge informs us about the sources of invention, the nurturing of innovation and the management of intellectual capital (which we shall encounter in Chapter 12). Human resource management has been one of the most active and rich areas of management where the principles of job design, motivation, training, and appraisal have developed enormously since the early days of scientific management 100 years ago.

There is still scope for improvement. As the 2007–8 credit crisis revealed, many financial institutions lacked good understanding of the risk characteristics of some of their financial assets—mortgage-backed securities in particular. Indeed, a major outcome of the credit crisis was recognition of the strategic importance of the liquidity characteristics of financial resources once financial markets had become frozen by risk aversion.[1] Nevertheless, for most categories of resource—whether tangible or intangible, human or nonhuman—we are aware both of the problems of limited information that is the primary risk of acquiring resources from the market and of the challenges involved in developing resources internally. Organizational capabilities are a different matter altogether.

## The Challenge of Capability Development

Possibly the most difficult problem in developing capabilities is that we know little about the linkage between resources and capabilities. One observation that is confirmed repeatedly across very different fields of competitive endeavor is that capabilities are not simply an outcome of the resources upon which they are based.

In sport it is common to see resource-rich teams failing to match the achievements of teams that create strong capabilities from modest resources. In European soccer, teams built with modest finances and without the acquisition of top-class players (Arsenal, Bayern Munich, PSV Eindhoven and Valencia) frequently outplay star-studded teams built from massive finance outlays (Chelsea, Real Madrid, Manchester City and Inter Milan). In my former home town, Washington DC, the Redskins (NFL), Wizards (NBA), and Capitols (NHL) were among the most financially well-endowed teams in their leagues but succeeded in consistently disappointing their long-suffering fans. International competition tells a similar story; it is small, resource-poor countries that regularly outperform the pre-eminent national teams. Despite dominating the ranks of the world's best basketball players, the U.S. has won the World Basketball Championship just once since 1986. At the Beijing Olympics, the U.S. sprint relay teams—despite having some of the world's fastest runners—failed to win a single medal.

It is the same in business: the firms that demonstrate the most outstanding capabilities are not necessarily those with the greatest resource endowments:

- In automobiles, GM has four times the output of Honda and four times the R&D expenditure, yet, since 1980, it is Honda, not GM, that has been the world leader in power train technology.
- In animated movies, the most successful productions in recent years were by newcomers Pixar (Toy Story, The Incredibles) and Aardman Animations (Wallace and Gromit) rather than by industry giant, Walt Disney.
- In telecom equipment it was the upstart Cisco rather than established incumbents Alcatel-Lucent, Ericsson and Siemens that led the new era of package switching.

That said, there is one resource that does seem to be critical to the development of capabilities: the managers with the requisite knowledge for capability building. There is a great deal that we do not know about why some companies have developed certain capabilities to higher levels than other firms but one thing is clear—managers play a critical role in nurturing and shaping those capabilities. Among the founders of new companies, a substantial number have prior managerial experience within the same sector.[2] In new industries, the best-performing firms are often those whose founders had prior experience in closely related sector.[3] It is reasonable to suppose that the key knowledge that these entrepreneurs carry with them is an understanding of what it takes to build key organizational capabilities.

## Path Dependency and the Role of Early Experiences

If organizational capability is not simply the result of the application of resources, what determines the capabilities in which a firm achieves distinctiveness? If we examine the types of capability that make different firms distinctive in their particular industries (the companies listed in Table 5.3 for example), one obvious feature is that these capabilities have developed over significant periods of time. In many cases we can trace the origins of a distinctive capability (or "core competence") to the circumstances which prevailed during the founding and early development of the company. In other words, organizational capability is *path dependent*—a company's capabilities today are the result of its history.[4]

Consider Wal-Mart Inc., the world's biggest retailer. How did it develop its outstanding capability in supply chain logistics? This superefficient system of warehousing, distribution and vendor relationships was not the result of careful planning and design; it evolved from the circumstances that Wal-Mart faced during its early years of existence. Its small-town locations in Arkansas and Oklahoma resulted in unreliable delivery from its suppliers, consequently Wal-Mart established its own distribution system. Similarly with its remarkable commitment to cost efficiency. Its management systems are undoubtedly important but ultimately it is Wal-Mart's origins in the rural South and the values and personality of its founder, Sam Walton, that sustain its obsession with cutting cost and eliminating waste.

Consider too the world's largest oil and gas majors (see Table 6.1). Despite long histories of competing together in the same markets, with near-identical products and similar strategies, the majors display very different capability profiles. Industry

**TABLE 6.1** Distinctive capabilities as a consequence of childhood experiences: the oil majors

| Company | Distinctive capability | Early history |
|---|---|---|
| Exxon | Financial management | Exxon's predecessor, Standard Oil (NJ), was the holding company for Rockefeller's Standard Oil Trust |
| Royal Dutch Shell | Coordinating a decentralized global network of 200 operating companies | Shell Transport & Trading headquartered in London and founded to sell Russian oil in China and the Far East. Royal Dutch Petroleum headquartered in The Hague; founded to exploit Indonesian reserves |
| BP | "Elephant hunting" | Discovered huge Persian reserves, went on to find Forties field (North Sea) and Prudhoe Bay (Alaska) |
| ENI | Deal making in politicized environments | The Enrico Mattei legacy; the challenge of managing government relations in postwar Italy |
| Mobil | Lubricants | Vacuum Oil Co. founded in 1866 to supply patented petroleum lubricants |

leaders Exxon and Royal Dutch Shell exemplify these differences. Exxon (now ExxonMobil) is known for its outstanding financial management capabilities exercised through rigorous investment controls and unrelenting cost efficiency. Shell is known for its decentralized, international management capability, which allows it to adapt to different national environments and to become an "insider" wherever it does business. These differences can be traced back to the companies' nineteenth-century origins. Exxon (then Standard Oil New Jersey) acted as holding company for Rockefeller's Standard Oil Trust, exercising responsibility for overall financial management. Shell was established to sell Russian oil in China and the Far East, while Royal Dutch was established to exploit Indonesian oil reserves. With head offices thousands of miles away in Europe, both parts of the group developed a decentralized, adaptable management style.

## The Linkage between Resources and Capabilities

These observations are troubling for ambitious executives anxious to adapt and regenerate their companies: if a firm's capabilities are determined during the early stages of its life, is it really possible to develop the new capabilities needed to meet the challenges of tomorrow?

To explore this question let us look more closely at the structure of organizational capability—a topic we addressed briefly in Chapter 5. Capabilities, we observed, involve coordination between organizational members such that they integrate their skills with one another and with a variety of other resources. We will explore coordination more fully in the next chapter. Here let us focus on the primary means through which multiple resources become integrated and organizational members coordinate their activities. Figure 6.1 provides the framework for the discussion that follows.

As we shall explore further in the next chapter, coordination is the essence of what organizations do. We can distinguish formal and informal dimensions of this coordination. The literature on organizational routines emphasizes the informal

**FIGURE 6.1** Integrating resources to create organizational capabilities

dimension. Routinization involves "repetitive patterns of activity," which are "ordinarily accomplished without conscious awareness."[5] Two factors contribute to the efficiency and effectiveness with which teams of individuals perform these repetitive patterns of activity. The first is *organizational learning*. Coordination is perfected through repetition. The more complex the task, the greater the gains from learning-by-doing.

The second is *culture*. Recall that in Chapter 5, I included culture as one of the intangible resources of the firm. In relation to capabilities, culture plays a pivotal role. The capacity for organizational members to comprehend one another and collaborate together without continual managerial direction depends upon shared perceptions, common values, and behavioral norms—all elements of the complex phenomenon that we refer to as *organizational culture*.

There is also an important formal dimension to the organizational aspects of capability. At the most basic level, coordination requires that the individuals required to perform a particular capabilities need to be located within a defined organizational unit. This seems obvious—yet organizations often disregard it. The major reason for the superior product development performance of Japanese car companies relative to their U.S. and European competitors was their creation of crossfunctional product development teams. Until the end of the 1980s, most U.S. auto companies operated a sequential "over-the-wall" product development system where new product development involved first marketing, then design, then engineering, then manufacturing, and finally finance.[6]

At several of the business schools I have worked, a common complaint among students has been lack of integration across courses while a common aspiration of several MBA course directors has been to introduce multidisciplinary courses that involve students in cross-functional problem solving. However, little can be achieved if faculty members are located within specialist, discipline-defined departments and coordination across courses is limited to a single "teachers' meeting" held each semester.

The coordination needed for organizational capability also requires appropriate management systems. These include information systems to allow each organizational member to identify changing circumstances and the actions of co-workers, and incentive systems to promote cooperation and effort. The weaknesses in teaching capabilities that I detect at several of the universities that I visit may reflect, first, the fact that the career-advancement incentives available to professors are heavily weighted towards research and, second, teaching incentives are almost wholly linked to individual performance—there is little inducement to collaboration.

Ultimately, however, key drivers for capability development are not the penalties and rewards built into the system of human resource appraisal but the overall drive and direction of the organization and the effectiveness with which it is communicated by the leadership. Behind most examples of outstanding organizational capability is an ambitious strategic intent that is instilled among organizational members by the leadership. Consider Honda's leadership in engine technology. The driving force for innovation and continuous improvement in engine design and manufacture was the obsession of founder Soichiro Honda for world leadership in this field, an obsession most clearly revealed in Mr. Honda's passion for racing (see Strategy Capsule 6.1).

## STRATEGY CAPSULE 6.1
# Siochiro Honda and the Isle of Man TT

The Isle of Man TT, which takes place on a rocky, rainswept island between England and Ireland, is one of the world's oldest—and most dangerous—motorcycle races. On March 20, 1954, when Honda Motor Company was still a tiny company less than six years old, company president, Soichiro Honda, made the following declaration to employees:

> . . . Since I was a small child, one of my dreams has been to compete in motor vehicle races all over the world . . . I have reached the firm decision to enter the TT Races next year.
>
> I will fabricate a 250 cc (medium class) racer for this race, and as the representative of our Honda Motor Co., I will send it out into the spotlight of the world. I am confident that this vehicle can reach speeds

exceeding 180 km/h . . . I address all employees!

> Let us bring together the full strength of Honda Motor Co. to win through to this glorious achievement. The future of Honda Motor Co. depends on this, and the burden rests on your shoulders. I want you to turn your surging enthusiasm to this task, endure every trial, and press through with all the minute demands of work and research, making this your own chosen path. The advances made by Honda Motor Co. are the growth you achieve as human beings, and your growth is what assures our Honda Motor Co. its future.
>
> With this, I announce my determination, and pledge with you that I will put my entire heart and soul, and turn all my creativity and skills to the task of entering

*the TT Races and winning them.*
*This I affirm.*

A series of impediments (including opposition by the Japanese government and difficulties in conforming to the TT rules and regulations) delayed Honda's entry until 1958. In that year Honda won the manufacturer's prize.

*Source*: Honda Motor Company

We have examined the role of strategic intent and "big, hairy, ambitious goals" in discussing the drivers of firm success and in observing how such ambition is articulated in statements of corporate vision and mission. However, closer examination reveals that it is through its impact on the development of organizational capabilities that strategic intent impacts performance. In case after case, a similar story emerges: a business leader (very often the company founder) communicates a sincere and passionate commitment to a vision of the company. This communication typically takes the form of words and example, and inspires organizational members not only to substitute organizational goals for their own personal goals, but—equally importantly—to subordinate their personal preferences, principles and prejudices to team collaboration. This spirit of community and achievement is apparent at Samsung Electronics under the leadership of Jong-Yong Yun, at Swatch under Nicolas Hayek, and Southwest Airlines under Herb Kelleher. One of the roles of these leaders was to motivate capability upgrading by raising performance aspirations above levels of actual and expected performance levels.[7]

## Are Organizational Capabilities Rigid or Dynamic?

If capabilities develop over long time periods, are embodied within organizational structure and are embedded within organizational culture, they act as barriers to a firm's ability to change. The more highly developed a firm's organizational capabilities are, the narrower its repertoire, and the more difficult it is for the firm to adapt them to new circumstances. Because Dell Computer's direct sales model was so highly developed, Dell found it difficult to adapt to selling though retail outlets as well. Thus, Dorothy Leonard-Barton argues that core capabilities are simultaneously *core rigidities*—they inhibit firms' ability to access and develop new capabilities.[8]

The idea that capabilities impose rigidities on firms has been challenged from two directions:

- *Flexibility in organizational routines.* The notion that routines are fixed patterns of interaction that function through automatic stimulus-response mechanisms has been undermined by studies that demonstrate that even basic operations display variation and the capacity to adapt.[9]

- *Dynamic capability.* Many companies are able to adapt to changing circumstances. The capacity to change may itself be regarded as an organizational capability. David Teece and his colleagues introduced the term *dynamic capabilities* to refer to a "firm's ability to integrate, build, and reconfigure internal and external competences to address rapidly changing environments."[10] The precise definition of a dynamic capability has proven contentious. Eisenhardt and Martin consider dynamic capabilities to be any capabilities that allow an organization to reconfigure its resources in order to adapt and change.[11] Winter and Zollo are more precise: a dynamic capability is a "higher level" process through which the firm modifies its operating routines.[12]

What is agreed is that dynamic capabilities are far from common. For most companies, highly developed capabilities in existing products and technologies create barriers to developing capabilities in new products and new technologies. When adapting to radical change within an industry, or in exploiting entirely new business opportunities, are new firms at an advantage or disadvantage compared with established firms? It depends on whether the change or the innovation is competence enhancing or competence destroying. In TV manufacturing, the most successful new entrants were existing producers of radios—the new technology was compatible with their capabilities. However, in most new industries, the most successful firms tend to be startups rather than established firms. In personal computers, it was newcomers such as Dell, Acer, Compaq and Gateway that emerged as most successful during the 1990s. Among established firms, relatively few (IBM, Hewlett-Packard, and Toshiba) went on to significant success. Many others (such as, Xerox, GE, Texas Instruments, AT&T and Olivetti) exited. In wireless telephony, too, startups—Vodafone, McCaw Cellular, Orange—were more successful than established telephone companies.[13]

## Approaches to Capability Development

So, how do companies go about developing new capabilities? Our focus here is on the internal development of capabilities. However, we need to acknowledge that firms can also import capabilities from outside—either by acquisition or alliance. Let us begin with a brief review of the issues involved in acquiring and accessing other firms' capabilities (we shall deal with mergers and, acquisitions more fully in Chapter 17), before considering different approaches to the internal development of organizational capability.

### Acquiring Capabilities: Mergers, Acquisitions and Alliances

Acquiring a company that has already developed the desired capability can short-circuit the tortuous process of capability development. Among the many motives for corporate acquisition, obtaining another company's capabilities is common—especially in technologically fast-moving environments where established firms target specific technical capabilities. Microsoft's adaptation to the internet and its entry into video games was facilitated by multiple acquisitions. Each year, Microsoft hosts its VC Summit, where venture capitalists from all over the world are invited to market their companies. In building digital imaging capabilities, Eastman Kodak has made a host of acquisitions since 1994. Acquisitions are also used for obtaining other types of capability: Procter & Gamble's takeover of Gillette was motivated by P&G's desire to acquire Gillette's new product development capability.

However, using acquisitions to extend a company's capability base involves major risks. To begin with, acquisitions are expensive. In addition to the acquisition premium that must be paid, the targeted capability comes with a mass of additional resources and capabilities that are most likely surplus to requirements for the acquiring firm. Most important, once the acquisition has been made, the acquiring company must find a way to integrate the acquiree's capabilities with its own. All too often, culture clashes, personality clashes between senior managers, or incompatibility of management systems can result in the degradation or destruction of the very capabilities that the acquiring company was seeking. Selecting and integrating company acquisitions is itself an organizational capability. Cisco Systems' 136 acquisitions between 1996 and 2004 were critical to its expanding its base of technological and product development capabilities.[14]

These costs and risks add to the attractions of strategic alliances as a targeted and cost-effective means to access another company's capabilities. A *strategic alliance* is a cooperative relationship between firms involving the sharing of resources in pursuit of common goals. Long-running technical collaboration between HP and Canon has allowed both firms to enhance their printer technology. Prior to acquisition in 2005, Pixar's alliance with Disney allowed it to access Disney's marketing and distribution capabilities.

A key issue that arises in the formation and management of strategic alliances is whether their purpose is to gain *access* to the capabilities of the partner firm or to *acquire* those capabilities through one partner learning from the other.[15] The strategic alliance between Intel and DreamWorks Animation allows each company to access the other's capabilities in order to jointly develop next-generation stereoscopic 3D films.[16] Conversely, General Motors' NUMMI joint venture with Toyota to make cars at the former GM Fremont, California plant was primarily motivated by GM's desire to learn about the Toyota Production System.[17] Where both alliance partners are trying to acquire one another's capabilities, the result may well be a "competition for competence" that ultimately destabilizes the relationship.[18]

It is tempting to view strategic alliances as a quick and low-cost means of extending the capabilities available to a firm. However, managing alliance relationships is itself a critically important organizational capability. "Relational capability" comprises building trust, developing interfirm knowledge sharing routines, and establishing mechanisms for coordination.[19] The more a company outsources its value chain activities to a network of alliance partners, the more it needs to develop the "systems integration capability" to coordinate and integrate the dispersed activities.[20]

## Internal Development: Focus and Sequencing

We have observed that, to build organizational capability, obtaining the necessary resources is the easy part. The challenge is in integrating these resources in order to do something. Indeed, achieving excellence in resources may militate against achieving high levels of integration. At London's Arsenal Football Club, manager Arsene Wenger sold his star players, Patrick Viera and Thierry Henry, on the basis that their presence inhibited coordinated effort from his young team.

Integrating resources into capabilities, we have seen, requires *organization* and *management systems* and is facilitated by culture and strategic intent. The implication is that capability development needs to be *systematic*. It needs to bring together the requisite human and nonhuman resources, locate these resources within a suitable organizational unit, establish the processes that perform the capability, allow these processes to develop through routinization, design management systems that support the capability and lead the entire effort through appropriate strategic intent.[21]

Achieving this complex task is likely to mean that an organization must limit the number and scope of the capabilities that it is attempting to create at any point in time. Hamel and Prahalad argue that the key to developing superior capabilities is "resource leveraging." Two key components of this leveraging are, first, "concentrating resources" by *focusing* the efforts of each group, department, and business unit on specific priorities and, second, "accumulating resources" through "mining experience" in order to accelerate learning.[22]

Focusing implies developing capabilities *sequentially*. Thus, complex capabilities can be developed incrementally through several stages and, in order to develop multiple capabilities, it is advisable to target no more than a few capabilities in each time period.

Given our limited knowledge about how capabilities are created and developed, companies often find it helpful to focus their capability development efforts not on the organizational capabilities themselves but on developing and supplying the products that use those capabilities. A trajectory through time of related, increasingly sophisticated products allows a firm to develop the "integrative knowledge" that is at the heart of organizational capability.[23] Matsushita utilizes this approach in developing operational capabilities in countries where it is establishing plants for the first time:

> In every country batteries are a necessity, so they sell well. As long as we bring a few advanced automated pieces of equipment for the processes vital to final product quality, even unskilled labor can produce good products. As they work on this rather simple product, the workers get trained, and this increased skill level then permits us to gradually expand production to items with increasingly higher technology levels, first radios, then televisions.[24]

Where a company is developing an entirely new area of business, such an approach can allow the sequential upgrading of products to be linked to targeting specific capabilities. Strategy Capsule 6.2 considers the development of Hyundai Motor.

Where a new capability requires structure, systems and culture that are different from those that support the firm's existing capabilities it may be helpful to develop the new capability within a new unit that is organizationally—and, preferably, geographically—separated from the main organization. Strategy Capsule 6.3 discusses examples of this approach.

## STRATEGY CAPSULE 6.2

# Hyundai Motor: Developing Capabilities through Product Sequencing

Hyundai's emergence as a world-class automobile producer is a remarkable example of capability development over a sequence of compressed phases. Each phase of the development process was characterized by a clear objective in terms of product outcome, a tight time deadline, an empowered development team, a clear recognition of the capabilities that needed to be developed in each phase, and an atmosphere of impending crisis should the project not succeed. The first phase was the construction of an assembly plant in the unprecedented time of 18 months in order to build Hyundai's first car—a Ford Cortina imported in semi-knocked down (SKD) form. Subsequent phases involved products of increasing sophistication and the development of more advanced capabilities.

*Source*: L. Kim, "Crisis construction and organizational learning: Capability building and catching up at Hyundai Motor," *Organizational Science* 9 (1998): 506–21.

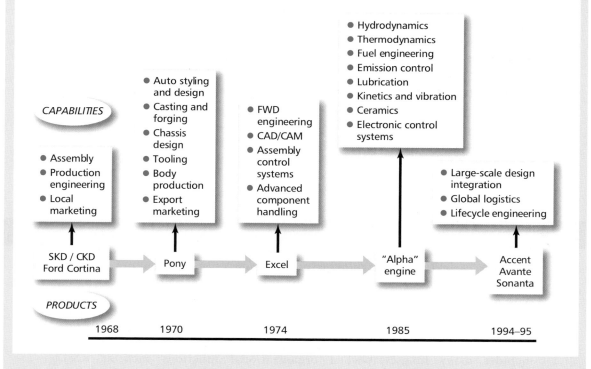

**STRATEGY CAPSULE 6.3**

## Incubating Capabilities in Separate Organizational Units

The model for organizationally separate development units was Lockheed's "skunk works"—a product development team established in Burbank, California during the Second World War to develop innovative new military aircraft. Since then, a number of companies have used satellite units to develop new organizational capabilities:

- IBM developed its PC at a new unit led by veteran executive Bill Lowe and located in Florida—a thousand miles from IBM's corporate headquarters in New York. Lowe claimed that isolation from IBM's main organization was critical to the team's creation of a product design and business system that were radically different from those of IBM's mainframe business. In particular, the PC unit relied heavily on outsourcing in contrast to IBM's traditional emphasis on vertical integration.[25]
- The pioneering online financial services company Egg was established by its London-

based parent, Prudential Insurance, in the Midlands towns of Dudley and Derby—well away from the London headquarters.

These separate incubator units combine the flexibility and autonomy of a startup, while drawing on the resources and capabilities of the parent. However, the critical challenge is in reintegrating the new capabilities back into the parent company. Xerox's Palo Alto Research Center (PARC) pioneered many of the technologies that formed the basis of the microcomputer revolution of the 1980s. However, it was much easier for these technologies to flow to nearby competitors— Hewlett-Packard, Apple, Microsoft, and Sun Microsystems—than it was for them to be absorbed by Xerox's east coast establishment.[26] GM's Saturn has had a similar experience. The Tennessee-based subsidiary achieved its objective of developing new manufacturing and marketing capabilities, but the Saturn experiment did little to revitalize the parent organization.[27]

## Knowledge Management and the Knowledge-based View

Since the early 1990s, our thinking about resources and capabilities and their management has been extended greatly by a set of concepts and practices referred to as *knowledge management*. Knowledge management is an umbrella term that comprises a range of organizational processes and practices whose common feature is their concern with generating value from knowledge. The term "knowledge management" is of recent vintage but much of its content is not: it includes many long-established organizational functions such as R&D, management information systems, employee training, and managing intellectual property—even strategic planning could be regarded as a knowledge management activity. Initially, knowledge management was primarily concerned with information technology—especially the use of databases, intranets, expert systems and groupware for storing, analyzing and disseminating information. Subsequent developments in knowledge management have been concerned less with data and more with organizational learning—especially the transfer of best practices and the derivation of "lessons learned" from ongoing activities. Knowledge management has attracted its share of skepticism and ridicule. Lucy Kellaway of the *Financial Times* observes that it has "attracted more needless obfuscation and wooly thinking by academics and consultants than any other [area]."[28] *The Wall Street Journal* reports Saatchi & Saatchi's director of knowledge management as "absorbing everything under the sun" including an interest in Japanese pantyhose "embedded with millions of microcapsules of vitamin C and seaweed extract that burst when worn to provide extra nourishment for the limbs."[29]

The real value of knowledge management is, first, in providing a single overall view of the multiplicity of knowledge development, knowledge transfer and knowledge utilization activities that occur within the firm and, second, in explicitly recognizing their commonalities and differences. In terms of resources, almost all the resources of the firm can be viewed as a form of knowledge. While information and technology may be the only "pure" knowledge resources, the value of people derives almost entirely from the knowledge they can deploy. Similarly capital equipment may be viewed as the physical embodiment of knowledge. Capabilities represent knowledge at the organizational level resulting from the integration of the knowledge of multiple individuals.[30]

At the foundation of knowledge management is recognition of knowledge as the most important resource of the firm and the essence of organizational capability. What has become known as the *knowledge-based view of the firm* is a conception of the firm as an assemblage of knowledge assets where value is created by deploying this knowledge. The knowledge-based view offers a revealing perspective on the existence of the firm, the determination of its boundaries and its design and management.[31]

To appreciate how the knowledge-based view and knowledge management can further our understanding of how resources and capabilities can be developed within the firm, let us consider, first, the characteristics of knowledge and, second, the processes through which knowledge is created and applied.

## Types of Knowledge

The single most important insight that knowledge management offers to the strategic management of resources and capabilities is recognizing that different types of knowledge have different characteristics. A key distinction is between *knowing how* and *knowing about*:

- *Know-how* is primarily *tacit* in nature—it involves skills that are expressed through their performance (riding a bicycle, playing the piano).
- *Knowing about* is primarily *explicit*—it comprises facts, theories, and sets of instructions.

The principal implication of this distinction between tacit and explicit knowledge relates to transferability:

- Explicit knowledge can be communicated at negligible marginal cost between individuals and across space and time. This ability to disseminate knowledge such that any one person's use does not limit any one else's access to the same knowledge means that explicit knowledge has the characteristic of a *public good*: once created, it can be replicated among innumerable users at low cost. The digital revolution and the internet have further reduced the costs of disseminating explicit knowledge.

- Tacit knowledge, on the other hand, cannot be directly articulated or codified. It can only be observed through its application and acquired through practice. Hence, its transfer between people is slow, costly, and uncertain.

This distinction has major implications for strategy. If explicit knowledge can be transferred so easily, it is seldom the foundation of sustainable competitive advantage. It is only secure from rivals when it is protected, either by intellectual property rights (patents, copyrights, trade secrets) or by secrecy ("The formula for Coca-Cola will be kept in a safe in the vault of our Atlanta headquarters guarded by heavily-armed Coca-Cola personnel."). The challenge of tacit knowledge is the opposite. If the culinary skills of award-winning chef Daniel Boulud have been acquired through intuition and learning-by-doing, how does he transfer this knowhow to the chefs and managers of his six restaurants in New York, Las Vegas, and Palm Beach, Florida? For consulting companies, the distinction between tacit ("personalized") and explicit ("systematized") knowledge defines their business model and is a central determinant of their strategy.[32]

The result is a "paradox of replication". In order to utilize knowledge—whether it is in the form of technology, human capital, or organizational capability— we need to replicate it; and replication is much easier if the knowledge is in explicit form. Yet, in doing so, we also make it easier for rivals to imitate our knowledge. Facilitating internal replication, while limiting external replication, is a key challenge for firms.[33]

## Knowledge Processes that Promote Capability Development

A key distinction is between those knowledge processes that focus on the acquisition of new knowledge and those which exploit existing knowledge—James March refers to this as the tradeoff between *exploration* and *exploitation*.[34] Figure 6.2 categorizes the main knowledge processes that are relevant to developing organizational capabilities.

In the context of our previous discussion of types of capability, exploration activities are associated most closely with *dynamic capabilities*—they are processes through which the firm changes itself. Exploration activities that build the organization's stock of knowledge include both the internal creation of knowledge (*knowledge creation*) and the identification and absorption of existing knowledge from outside the organization (*knowledge acquisition*). The mechanisms for acquiring outside knowledge include: hiring skilled employees, acquiring companies or their knowledge resources, benchmarking "best-in-class" companies, and learning through alliances. We shall return to the themes creativity and innovation in Chapter 12.

**FIGURE 6.2** Types of knowledge process within an organization

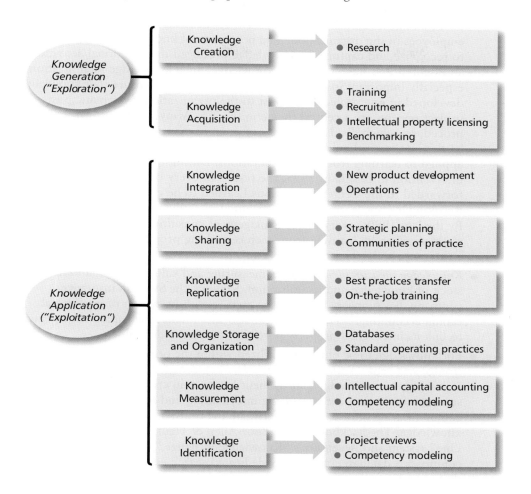

The exploration-exploitation distinction is less clear in practice than in principle—exploitation involves not only the use of existing knowledge but also its development.[35] These development processes are critical to the ungrading and improvement of existing operational and functional capabilities. Some of the most important contributions of knowledge management to capability building are in improving the utilization of existing knowledge and capturing knowledge generated by the firm's ongoing operations.

The best-developed and most widely applied techniques of knowledge management have focused on some of the most basic aspects of knowledge application and exploitation. For example:

- In the area of *knowledge identification*, the basic challenge is to recognize the knowledge assets that are available within the firm. This includes identifying and assessing the intellectual property of the firm (the patent portfolio in particular) and identifying the skills and know-how of employees. BP's *Connect* is a corporate yellow pages comprising personnel data that allows each employee to identify the skills and experience of other employees in the organization. The next stage of knowledge identification is to recognize and capture the knowledge produced in operational activities—an essential first stage in reusing knowledge. Such knowledge identification is especially important in project-based organizations to ensure that knowledge developed in one project is not lost to the organization. Systematic post-project reviews are a central theme in the U.S. Army's "lessons learned" procedure, which distils the results of practice maneuvers and simulated battles into tactical guidelines and recommended procedures. A process is applied to learning from actual operations. During the NATO military intervention in Bosnia in 1995, the results of every operation were forwarded to the Center for Lessons Learned to be collected and codified. Resulting lessons learned were distributed to active units every 72 hours.[36] By the late 1990s, every major management consulting firm had introduced a system whereby learning from each consulting project was identified, written up, and submitted to the firm's database.

- *Knowledge measurement* involves measuring and valuing the organization's stock of knowledge and its utilization. Skandia, the Swedish insurance company, has pioneered knowledge metrics with its system of intellectual capital accounting.[37] Dow Chemical also uses intellectual capital management to link its intellectual property portfolio to shareholder value.

- For knowledge to be efficiently utilized within the organization, *knowledge storage and organization* are critical. The key contribution of information technology to knowledge management has been in creating databases for storing information, for organizing information, and for accessing and communicating information, to facilitate the transfer of and access to knowledge. The backbone of the Booz-Allen & Hamilton's "Knowledge-On-Line" system and Accenture's "Knowledge Xchange," is an IT system that comprises a database, groupware, dedicated search engine, and an intranet that permits employees to input and access information.[38]

- *Knowledge sharing and replication* involves the transfer of knowledge from one part of the organization (or from one person) to be replicated in another part (or by another individual). A central function of IT-based knowledge management systems is to facilitate such transfer. However, tacit knowledge is not amenable to codification within an IT system. The traditional answer to the problem of replicating tacit knowledge is to use apprenticeships and other forms of on-the-job training. Recently, organizations have discovered the important role played by informal networks in transferring experiential knowledge. These self-organizing *communities of practice* are increasingly being deliberately established and managed as a means of facilitating knowledge sharing and group learning.[39] Replicating capabilities poses an even greater challenge. Transferring best practices within companies is not simply about creating appropriate incentives; complexity and credibility of the knowledge involved are key impediments.[40]

- *Knowledge integration* represents one of the greatest challenges to any company. Ultimately, organizational capability is about integrating knowledge across a broad range of expertise for the purposes of supplying goods and services. While knowledge management provides few specific tools or techniques for integrating knowledge, appreciating the conditions under which knowledge is transferred and combined can offer profound insight into the role of rules, structure, information systems, leadership, and interpersonal relations on the ability to integrate knowledge effectively and efficiently.[41] For certain corporate functions knowledge integration plays a critical role. A strategic planning system is a vehicle for integrating the different knowledge bases of managers at different levels of the organization and from different functions in order to design the possible strategy for a company. New product development teams are systems for integrating the knowledge of many experts and across a range of functions and technical areas.[42]

## Knowledge Conversion and the Challenge of Replication

The close linkage between the use of knowledge and its generation is evident from the key role of learning-by-doing in upgrading the firm's capability. Nonaka goes further: his theory of knowledge creation distinguishes types of knowledge (tacit and explicit) and levels of knowledge (individual and organizational). He argues that knowledge *conversion* between tacit and explicit forms and between individual and organizational levels produce a "knowledge spiral" in which the organization's stock of knowledge broadens and deepens (see Figure 6.3). For example, explicit knowledge is *internalized* into tacit knowledge in the form of intuition, know-how, and routines, while tacit knowledge is *externalized* into explicit knowledge through articulation and codification.[43]

In business schools, education is concerned primarily with the acquisition of explicit knowledge; however, it is often argued that the real learning takes place

**FIGURE 6.3** Knowledge conversion

**Source:**
Based upon I. Nonaka, "A Dynamic Theory of Organizational Knowledge Creation," *Organization Science* 5 (1994): 14–37.

when the concepts, frameworks and theories of business become internalized through repeated application. The result is the development of tacit managerial knowledge in the form of judgment, intuition, and the ability to assess business situations.

Knowledge conversion is also critical to the development of companies—and societies as well. The transition from the *craft enterprise*, based upon individual tacit knowledge, to the industrial enterprise based upon explicit knowledge owned by the organization is a stage in firm development and marks the emergence of the industrial society. This transition is depicted in Figure 6.3 and is illustrated by the following examples:

- Henry Ford's Model T was initially produced on a small scale by skilled metal workers one car at a time. Ford's assembly line mass-production technology systematized that tacit knowledge and built it into machines and processes. The Ford industrial system was no longer dependent upon skilled craftsmen—the assembly lines could be operated by former farm workers and immigrants straight off the boat.

- When Ray Kroc discovered the McDonald brothers' hamburger stand in Riversdale, California, he quickly recognized the potential for systematizing and replicating their process. The result was a global fast-food empire in which the McDonald's business model was replicated through operating manuals and training programs and now serves 47 million customers using some 400 000 employees—few of whom possess significant culinary skills.

This systematization of knowledge offers massive potential for value creation. The craft enterprise is typically small scale and skilled employees appropriate a major share of the value that is created. Systematization allows replication and deskilling. Ford built his assembly-line plants not only in Detroit but also in Canada, the U.K., France, Denmark, Germany, Austria, Argentina, South Africa, Australia, and the Soviet Union. The industrialization of craft industries has been a key feature of the evolution of service industries led by Hilton in hotels, Hertz in car rental, Andersen Consulting (now Accenture) in IT consulting, and Starbucks in coffee shops.[44]

The replication of knowledge—and of the business systems within which it is embedded—offers one of the most powerful and lucrative sources of scale economy. Its power is well recognized by venture capitalists, and one of the key criteria for evaluating new business proposals is: "Is it scalable?" The replication we have discussed so far has been built upon systematization: the translation of a business system into a set of rules and procedures that provide programmed instructions for the creation of new business units. But supposing the knowledge upon which the business is based cannot be fully articulated, is replication possible? Even if the knowledge of a business cannot be articulated into operating procedures and training videos, replication can still occur through imitation. In the case of microprocessors, fabrication processes are so complex and the knowhow involved so deeply embedded that the only way that Intel can replicate its production capabilities is by replicating its lead plant in every detail—a process called "Copy Exactly."[45] However, firms may also seek a middle way between full systematization and pure imitation by basing their replication on a set of fundamental principles that act as guidelines in setting up new business units.[46]

## Designing Knowledge Management Systems

Knowledge management covers a wide range of practices—indeed, there are few management activities that do not involve managing knowledge in one form or another. A focus on capability development can provide focus and direction for an organization's knowledge management practices. The starting point is to identify the capabilities needed to ensure continuing success in the face of a changing external environment. This allows identification of the knowledge required to develop the required capabilities and the knowledge processes through which that knowledge can be acquired and deployed. The implication is that knowledge management systems are likely to vary greatly between companies. Consider the following examples:

- For Dow Chemical, the core of its value creation is in developing new chemical products and exploiting globally the intellectual property that is created. Enhancing Dow's capabilities in research, product development, and intellectual property protection are the core goals of Dow's knowledge management practices. Dow's "Intellectual Capital Management" places its central emphasis on the company's patent portfolio and links its intellectual property to a broad range of intellectual capital variables and processes and ultimately to the company's total value.[47]

- For McKinsey & Co., creating value for clients requires continually building on the knowledge it generates from client assignments, and conceptualizing and sharing that knowledge base. This is achieved through a system that ensures the knowledge generated from each project is captured and made available for subsequent client projects; a matrix structure of industry and functional practices that permits specialized knowledge to be created and stored; and an R&D function in the form of the McKinsey Global Institute.[48]

- For McDonald's Corporation, knowledge management has traditionally involved the global replication of the McDonald's system. This has required the development of a standardized set of operating practices that are disseminated through meticulously managed training practices, which include formal training programs at Hamburger University, and on-the-job training at individual establishments. However, competition and changing consumer preferences have required adaptation and innovation from McDonald's. Developing decentralized capabilities in market research, new product development, restaurant design and the internal transfer of product and process innovations has required major changes in the processes through which McDonald's collects information, stimulated creativity among middle managers and disseminated knowledge internally. The result has been the introduction of new products into national markets (see Chapter 15, Strategy Capsule 15.3, McDonalds Goes Glocal), new restaurant designs and new concepts (McCafes, Ronald Gym Clubs).[49]

The design of every knowledge process must take account of the characteristics of the knowledge being deployed. The fundamental distinction here is between explicit and tacit knowledge. Take a simple example of the transfer of best practice between the different fabrication plants of a multinational semiconductor plant. If the knowledge is explicit, then such knowledge can be disseminated in the form of reports, or directives requiring every plant to adopt a new standard operating procedure. If the knowledge is tacit—it is the result of the experience or intuition of a single plant manager—the task is more difficult. Transferring the best practice is likely to require either visits by other plant managers to the innovating plant, or for the innovating plant manager to adopt a consulting role and visit other plants in the group for the purpose of teaching employees there.

It is in the area of managing tacit knowledge (which includes, typically, the major part of the knowledge relevant to organizational capability) where the major challenges and opportunities in knowledge management lie. Information technology has made huge strides in the storage, analysis and systematization of explicit knowledge. However, the greater part of organizational learning is experience based and intuitive. Identifying this knowledge, and transferring it to other parts of the organization in order to utilize it more effectively, remains a fundamental management challenge.

## Summary

For a company to be successful—even to survive—over the long-term requires that it upgrades it resource and capability base. The critical management challenges are in developing existing capabilities and acquiring or creating new ones.

Some of the most important developments in strategic management research in recent years are in deepening our understanding of what organizational capabilities are and how they develop. A number of key themes, principles and tools are emerging. These include: the role of top management leadership through establishing strategic intent, the role of organizational structure and corporate culture in facilitating coordination and critical contributions that knowledge management can offer. At the same time we have much to learn. The reasons why some companies are able to reinvent themselves through the development of new capabilities (and whole new areas of business) such as Nokia and SMH/Swatch, while others, such as Eastman Kodak and General Motors struggle to develop the new capabilities needed to thrive under changed market circumstances remain poorly understood. In the subsequent chapters we shall return repeatedly to the challenge of adaptation to a changing business environment. In the next chapter we will focus attention upon the structures and systems through which companies deploy their resources and build and exercise organizational capability.

## Self-Study Questions

1   Identify two sports teams: one that is rich in resources (such as talented players) but whose capabilities (as indicated by performance) have been poor; one that is resource-poor but has displayed strong team capabilities. What clues can you offer as to the determinants of capabilities among sports teams?

**2**   In 2006, Disney completed its acquisition of the film animation company Pixar for $7.4 billion. The high purchase price reflected Disney's eagerness to gain Pixar's animation capabilities, its talent (animators, technologists and storytellers) and its culture of creativity. What risks does Disney face in achieving the goals of this acquisition?

**3**   The dean of your business school wishes to upgrade the effectiveness with which the school designs and delivers its educational programs and increase the effectiveness of its graduates in their subsequent careers. Advise your dean on what tools and systems of knowledge management might be deployed in order to support these goals.

# Notes

1   "Modern Management: All You Need is Cash," *Economist* (November 20, 2008): 78–80.
2   C. B. Schoonhoven and E. Romanelli, "The Local Origins of New Firms" in C. B. Schoonhoven and E. Romanelli (eds), *The Entrepreneurship Dynamic* (Stanford: Stanford University Press, 2001): 40–67.
3   S. Klepper, "The Capabilities of New Firms and the Evolution of the U.S. Automobile Industry" *Industrial and Corporate Change* 11, 4 (2001): 645–6.
4   B. Wernerfelt, "Why do Firms Tend to Become Different?" in Constance Helfat (ed.) *Handbook of Organizational Capabilities* (Oxford: Blackwell, 2006): 121–33.
5   R. R. Nelson and S. G. Winter, *An Evolutionary Theory of Economic Change* (Cambridge, MA: Belknap, 1982): 15, 97.
6   K. B. Clark and T. Fujimoto, *Product Development Performance* (New York: Free Press, 1991).
7   S. G. Winter, "The Satisficing Principle in Capability Learning," *Strategic Management Journal* 21 (2000): 981–96; G. Gavetti and D. Levinthal, "Looking Forward and Looking Backward: Cognitive and Experiential Search," *Administrative Science Quarterly* 45 (2000): 113–37.
8   D. Leonard-Barton, "Core Capabilities and Core Rigidities," *Strategic Management Journal*, Summer Special Issue (1992): 111–26.
9   M. S. Feldman and B. T. Pentland, "Reconceptualizing Organizational Routines as a Source of Flexibility and Change," *Administrative Science Quarterly*, 48 (2003): 94–118.
10   D. J. Teece, G. Pisano, and A. Shuen, "Dynamic Capabilities and Strategic Management," *Strategic Management Journal* 18 (1997): 509–33.
11   K. M. Eisenhardt and J. A. Martin, "Dynamic Capabilities: What Are They?" *Strategic Management Journal* 21 (2000): 1105–21 and H. Volberda, *Building the Flexible Firm* (Oxford: Oxford University Press, 1998).
12   M. Zollo and S. G. Winter, "Deliberate Learning and the Evolution of Dynamic Capabilities," *Organization Science* 13 (2002): 339–51; S. G. Winter, "Understanding Dynamic Capabilities" *Strategic Management Journal* 24 (2003): 991–5.
13   Established firms typically fail to survive radical innovation. See, for example, R. M. Henderson and K. B. Clark, "Architectural Innovation: The Reconfiguration of Existing Product Technologies and Failure of Established Firms," *Administrative Science Quarterly* 35 (1990): 9–30; C. Christensen, "The Rigid Disk Drive Industry: A History of Commercial and Technological Turbulence," *Business History Review* 67 (1993): 531–88; M. Tripsas, "Unravelling the Process of Creative Destruction: Complementary Assets and Incumbent Survival in the Typesetter Industry," *Strategic Management Journal* 18 (Summer Special Issue, 1997): 119–42; A. Henderson, "Firm Strategy and Age Dependence: A Contingent View of the Liabilities of Newness, Adolescence and Obsolescence," *Administrative Science Quarterly* 44 (1999): 281–314.
14   C. E. Helfat, S. Finkelstein, W. Mitchell, M. A. Peteraf, H. Singh, D. J. Teece, S. G. Winter, *Dynamic Capabilities: Understanding Strategic Change in Organizations* (Malden, MA: Blackwell Publishing, 2007): Chapter 6.
15   See, for example, A. Mody, "Learning Through Alliances," *Journal of Economic Behavior and Organization* 20 (1993): 151–70; D. C. Mowery, J. E. Oxley and B. S. Silverman, "Strategic Alliances and Interfirm Knowledge Transfer," *Strategic Management Journal* 17, Winter Special Issue (1996): 77–93; A. C. Inkpen and M. M. Crossan, "Believing Is Seeing: Joint Ventures and Organizational Learning," *Journal of Management Studies* 32 (1995): 595–618.
16   Intel News Release, "*Intel, Dreamworks Animation Form Strategic Alliance to Revolutionize 3-D Filmmaking Technology*" (July 8, 2008), http://www.intel.com/pressroom/archive/releases/20080708corp.htm, accessed July 3, 2009.

17  J. A. Badaracco, *The Knowledge Link: How Firms Compete Through Strategic Alliances* (Boston: Harvard Business School Press, 1991).

18  G. Hamel, "Competition for Competence and Inter-partner Learning within International Strategic Alliances," *Strategic Management Journal* 12, Summer Special Issue (1991): 83–103.

19  P. Kale, J. H. Dyer and H. Singh. "Alliance Capability, Stock Market Response and Long Term Alliance Success" *Strategic Management Journal* 23 (2002): 747–67; C. E. Helfat et al. *Dynamic Capabilities* op. cit.: Chapter 5.

20  A. Prencipe, "Corporate Strategy and Systems Integration Capabilities" in A. Prencipe, A. Davies and M. Hobday, *The Business of Systems Integration* (Oxford University Press, 2003): 114–32.

21  A. Bakhru and R. M. Grant, "A Managerial Process Model of Organizational Capability Development: Evidence from New E-commerce Businesses", CROMA Discussion Paper, Bocconi University, Milan, 2008.

22  G. Hamel and C. K. Prahalad, *Competing for the Future* (Boston: Harvard Business School Press, 1994).

23  C. E. Helfat and Ruth S. Raubitschek, "Product Sequencing: Co-evolution of Knowledge, Capabilities and Products," *Strategic Management Journal* 21 (2000): 961–79. The parallel development of capabilities and products has also been referred to as "dynamic resource fit". See: H. Itami, *Mobilizing Invisible Assets* (Boston: Harvard University Press, 1987): 125.

24  A. Takahashi, *What I Learned from Konosuke Matsushita* (Tokyo: Jitsugyo no Nihonsha, 1980); in Japanese, quoted by Itami, op. cit.: 25.

25  T. Elder, "Lessons from Xerox and IBM," *Harvard Business Review* (July–August 1989): 66–71.

26  *Xerox PARC: Innovation without Profit?* ICMR Case Study, 2004.

27  J. O'Toole, *Forming the Future: Lessons from the Saturn Corporation* (New York: Harper, 1996).

28  Lucy Kellaway column, *Financial Times* (June 23, 1999): 13.

29  "Saatchi's 'Manager of Knowledge' Keeps Track of What's Trendy," *Wall Street Journal* (February 28, 1997): B.16.

30  R. M. Grant, "Prospering in Dynamically-competitive Environments: Organizational Capability as Knowledge Integration", *Organization Science* 7 (1996): 375–87.

31  "The knowledge-based view" offers a rationale for the firm that is based on its effectiveness as an institution for creating, assembling, and transforming knowledge into goods and services. See: B. Kogut and U. Zander, "Knowledge of the Firm, Combinative Capabilities and the Replication of Technology", *Organization Science* 3 (1992): 387–99; R. M. Grant, "Toward a Knowledge-based Theory of the Firm," *Strategic Management Journal* 17, Winter Special Issue (1996): 109–22.

32  M. Hansen, N. Nohria and T. Tierney, "What's Your Strategy for Managing Knowledge?" *Harvard Business Review* (March 1999): 106–16.

33  See: B. Kogut and U. Zander, "Knowledge of the Firm, Combinative Capabilities, and the Replication of Knowledge" *Organization Science* 3 (1992): 383–97. However, at moderate levels of complexity, internal replication can be achieved while avoiding imitation by rivals: J. Rivkin, "Reproducing Knowledge: Replication without Imitation at Moderate Complexity" *Organization Science* 12 (2001): 274–93.

34  J. G. March, "Exploration and Exploitation in Organizational Learning," *Organization Science* 2 (1991): 71–87. J.-C. Spender makes a similar distinction between *knowledge generation* and *knowledge application* ("Limits to Learning from the West," *The International Executive* 34 (September/October 1992): 389–410.

35  This distinction between use and development within knowledge exploitation is made by P. McNamara and C. Baden-Fuller, "Shareholder returns and the exploration–exploitation dilemma: R&D announcements by biotechnology firms" *Research Policy* 36 (2007): 548–65.

36  "Lessons Learned: Army Devises System to Decide What Does and What Does Not Work," *Wall Street Journal* (May 23, 1997): A1 and A10.

37  L. Edvinsson and S. Malone, *Intellectual Capital: Realizing Your Company's True Value by Finding its Hidden Brainpower* (New York: Harper Business, 1997); D. Marchand and J. Roos, *Skandia AFS: Measuring and Visualizing Intellectual Capital*, Case No. GM 624 (Lausanne: IMD, 1996).

38  *Cultivating Capabilities to Innovate: Booz-Allen & Hamilton*, Case No. 9-698-027 (Boston: Harvard Business School, 1997); "Recycling Internal Know-How: Knowledge Management at Accenture", *Corporate Universities International* 8, No. 2 (March 2002).

39  E. C. Wenger and W. M. Snyder, "Communities of Practice: The Organizational Frontier," *Harvard Business Review* (January–February 2000).

40  G. Szulanski, "Exploring Internal Stickiness: Impediments to the Transfer of Best Practices within the Firm," *Strategic Management Journal* 17, Winter Special Issue (1996): 27–44.

41  S. Brusoni and L. Cassi, "Re-Inventing the Wheel: Knowledge Integration in Fact-Changing Environments" CESPRI WP no. 209, Bocconi University (Milan: December 2007); C. Schmickl and A. Kieser "How much do specialists have to learn from each other when they jointly develop radical product innovations?" *Research Policy* 37 (2008): 473–91.

42  See, for example, M. C. Becker and F. Zirpoli, "Organizing New Product Development: Knowledge Hollowing-out and Knowledge Integration: The Fiat Auto Case." DRUID Working Paper No 03-05 (2003).

43  I. Nonaka and H. Takeuchi, *The Knowledge-Creating Company* (Oxford: Oxford University Press, 1995).

44  S. Segal-Horn, "Strategy in Service Organizations," in D. O. Faulkner and A. Campbell (eds) *The Oxford Handbook of Strategy* (Oxford University Press, 2006): 472–508.

45  "Copy Exactly Factory Strategy" (www.intel.com/design/quality/mq_ce.htm). See also: G. Szulanski and S. Winter, "Getting it Right the Second Time," *Harvard Business Review* (January 2002): 62–9.

46  C. Baden-Fuller and S. G. Winter, "Replicating Organizational Knowledge: Principles or Templates?" Papers on Economics and Evolution, Max Planck Institute, 2005.

47  D. Near, "Intellectual Capital Management," Dow Chemical Company (April 15, 2002), http://www.km-iptask.org/ICM_Overview_4_15.ppt#371,1.

48  *McKinsey & Company: Managing Knowledge and Learning*, Case No. 9-396-357 (Boston: Harvard Business School, 1996).

49  "A Golden Recipe for McDonald's Europe," *Business Week* (July 17, 2008).

# 7 Organization Structure and Management Systems: The Fundamentals of Strategy Implementation

*Ultimately, there may be no long-term sustainable advantage other than the ability to organize and manage.*

—JAY GALBRAITH AND ED LAWLER

*I'd rather have first-rate execution and second-rate strategy anytime than brilliant ideas and mediocre management.*

—JAMIE DIMON, CEO, JP MORGAN CHASE & CO.

## OUTLINE

## Introduction and Objectives

"Great strategy; lousy implementation," is an epithet that has been applied to organizational failures from Philip II of Spain's attempted invasion of England with the Spanish Armada in 1588[1] to the dismal outcome of the 2006 merger between Alcatel and Lucent that created "a new global leader in telecommunication equipment".[2] The idea that the formulation of strategy can be separated from its implementation has become institutionalized by the numerous strategic management texts that devote separate sections to strategy formulation and strategy implementation.

This supposed division between formulation and implementation is fiction. At the most obvious level, formulating a strategy without taking into account the conditions under which it will be implemented will result in a poorly designed strategy. A fundamental flaw in the corporate planning systems of 25 years ago was separating strategy formulation—the task of corporate executives and strategic planners—from its implementation by divisional heads and middle managers.

The design of organization structure and management form key components of strategy implementation. Hence, the view of strategy formulation and strategy implementation as a sequential process is summed up in the adage "structure follows strategy." Yet, management guru Tom Peters argues the reverse: if capabilities are the primary basis of strategy, and if capabilities are a product of organizational structure, then *strategy follows structure*.[3] The key point, however, is not whether strategy or structure takes precedence but the recognition that the two are closely interdependent.[4] For Domino's Pizza with its global network of 8000 franchised outlets, or Amway, with its pyramid of commission-based, independent distributors, the structure is the strategy.

Having established that the way in which a company organizes itself is fundamental to its strategy and performance, the goal of this chapter is to introduce the key concepts and ideas necessary to understand and design companies' structures and systems. The approach is concise and selective. I do not intend to offer a potted overview of organizational theory. My aim is to introduce some basic principles of organizational design and to apply these to key aspects of firm structure. The principles outlined here will be further developed in later chapters when we consider strategies within particular business contexts. For example, Chapter 12 considers the organizational conditions conducive to innovation; Chapter 13 considers organization and organizational change within mature industries; Chapter 14 discusses vertical structures and outsourcing; Chapter 15 examines the structure and systems of the multinational corporation; and Chapter 16 deals with organizing the multibusiness company.

By the time you have completed this chapter you will be able to:

◆ recognize the key organizational innovations that have shaped the evolution of the modern corporation;

◆ understand the basic principles that determine the structural characteristics of complex human organizations;

◆ apply the principles of organizational design to recommend the types of organizational structure suited to particular tasks and particular business environments;

◆ understand the role of information systems, strategic planning, financial control, and human resource management in the coordination and control of corporations;

◆ appreciate the forces that are causing companies to seek new organizational structures and management systems.

## The Evolution of the Corporation

### Firms and Markets

This book is concerned with the strategy of business organizations—entities that I have referred to, more or less synonymously, as *firms*, *companies* or *enterprises*. Firms are the dominant feature of the capitalist economy—it is through them that we obtain our food, clothing and shelter and they provide us with the income to enjoy this consumption. Yet despite their central role, economists have paid them limited attention. Their focus has been upon the role of markets. In practice, firms and markets are twin institutions that organize the capitalist economy. Markets are organized by the "invisible hand" of the price mechanism; firms are organized by the "visible hand" of management.[5]

One reason for economists' neglect of firms is that they are of recent origin. At the beginning of the nineteenth century, most production—even in Britain, the most industrially advanced economy of the time—was undertaken by individuals and by families. Woolen textile production—upon which much British prosperity was based—involved networks of self-employed workers producing in their own homes. Mechanization and the rise of the factory system changed all this; however, most of the new factories were owner-proprietorships employing small numbers of workers. In the United States, the biggest business organizations in the mid-nineteenth century, in terms of numbers of employees, were family-owned farms—especially some of the large plantations of the South.[6]

The modern firm—the business corporation—is one of the greatest innovations of modern society. Its emergence is the result of two developments: legal and organizational.

### Legal Development

A *corporation* is an organization that has a legal identity—it can own property, enter contacts, sue and be sued. Such a legal identity is essential to the operation of a business enterprise that involves more than a few people. Corporations were originally created by royal decree of acts of legislation. Some of the first business corporations were the colonial trading companies—the British East India Company (1600), the Dutch East India Company (1602), the Virginia Company of London (1606) and Hudson's Bay Company (1670) which were given monopoly rights over development and trade with specific colonies. Because corporations were legally distinct from their owners, this means that they could have large numbers of owners (shareholders) and ownership could be transferred.

Britain's Joint Stock Companies Act of 1844 allowed corporations to be established without the need for a royal decree or act of parliament. The Limited Liability Act of 1844 established that shareholders of corporations were not liable for the debts of a corporation beyond the share capital they owned—this opened up the potential for large-scale financing of industry.[7]

### Organizational Development

Until the late nineteenth century, the world's only large-scale organizations—apart from colonial trading companies the aforementioned were the Roman

Catholic Church and national armies. Most ideas about organizing large companies derived from the organizational structure of armies. Indeed, prior to the development of business education, the role of the military as the training ground for most business leaders meant that a large proportion of management principles derived from the military. General Von Moltke's reorganization of the Prussian army into divisions and a functionally specialized general staff during the 1860s provided the basic model for large industrial corporations until well into the twentieth century.[8]

The emergence of the modern corporation occurred in the U.S. in what has been termed "the Second Industrial Revolution." Business historian, Alfred Chandler, identifies the modern corporation as a result of two "critical organizational transformations."[9]

*Line-and-Staff Structure*  Until the mid-nineteenth century, companies were located in just one place—lack of transportation placed limits on firms' market reach; lack of communication prevented firms from operating in multiple locations. The railroad and the telegraph changed all that. In the U.S., the railroad companies were the first to create geographically separate operating units managed by an administrative headquarters. This *line-and-staff* structure divided employees into those allocated to operational tasks within operating units (*line*) and administrators and functional specialists located at head office (*staff*).

By the end of the late nineteenth century, simple line-and-staff structures had developed into more complex *functional structures*—companies such as DuPont, Sears Roebuck & Co. and Shell Transport and Trading managed a number of separate operating units with large functional departments that conducted sales, finance, R&D, legal affairs and other specialist activities.

The other organizational form for large business enterprises was the *holding company*. Standard Oil (of the U.S.), Mitsui (of Japan), and the British South Africa Company were financial enterprises created by a series of acquisitions in which the parent bought controlling equity stakes in a number of subsidiary companies. The management structure of these holding companies was primitive: the parent appointed the board of directors of the subsidiaries and received dividends, but otherwise there was little integration or overall managerial control.

*The Multidivisional Corporation*  The second critical transformation was the emergence during the 1920s of the divisionalized corporation, which, over time, replaced both the centralized, functional structures that characterized most industrial corporations and the loose-knit holding companies created in the merger wave of the early twentieth century. The pioneers were DuPont and General Motors.

At DuPont, increasing size and a widening product range strained the functional structure and overloaded top management:

> . . . the operations of the enterprise became too complex and the problems of coordination, appraisal and policy formulation too intricate for a small number of top officers to handle both long-run, entrepreneurial and short-run, operational administrative activities.[10]

The solution devised by Pierre Du Pont was to decentralize: ten product divisions were created, each with their own sales, R&D, and support activities. The corporate

**FIGURE 7.1** General Motors Corporation: organizational structure, 1921

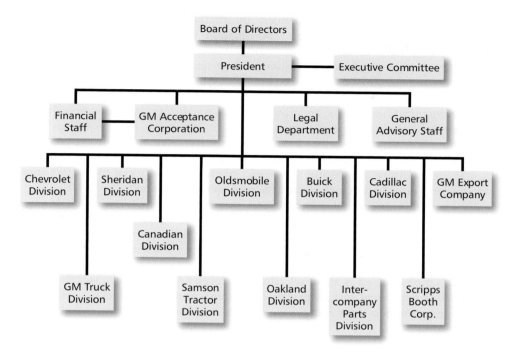

*Source*:

A. P. Sloan, *My Years with General Motors* (Orbit Publishing, 1972): 57. © 1963 by Alfred P. Sloan. © renewed 1991, Alfred P. Sloan Foundation. Reproduced with permission.

head office headed by an Executive Committee took responsibility for coordination, strategy, and resource allocation.[11]

General Motors, which had grown by acquisition into a loose holding company, adopted a similar structure as a solution to the problems of weak financial control and a confused product line. The new structure (shown in Figure 7.1) divided decision making responsibility between the chief executives of the divisions who were responsible for their divisions' operation and performance and the president who headed the general office and was responsible for the development and control of the corporation as a whole.[12]

## Organizational Change since the 1950s

The rise of the public (i.e. stock market listed), divisionalized corporation as the dominant organizational form in large-scale American business was followed by its diffusion internationally. This diffusion was accelerated, first, by the success of American multinationals overseas and, second, by international political developments—including the U.S. occupation of Japan after the Second World War, the collapse of the Soviet Union and China's transition to capitalism.

At the same time, the organizational forms of business enterprise have continued to evolve. If the divisionalized corporation represented a fundamental breakthough in the problem of how to reconcile overall coordination with flexibility and responsiveness, subsequent developments have addressed the same problem. As companies have diversified, expanded internationally and developed greater functional sophistication, so their coordination challenges have increased. In response, they have developed *matrix organizations*—where separate hierarchies coordinate within products, functions and geographical areas. Simultaneously, increased need for flexibility and responsiveness has resulted in the *delayering* of hierarchies, the shift from functionally organized headquarters staff to *shared services organizations* and the creation of porous organizational boundaries through alliances and outsourcing partnerships.

Within these structures considerable progress has been made in designing the systems through which companies are managed. These include operational and capital expenditure budgeting, strategic planning, performance management systems, and information and knowledge management systems.

Despite the existence of some general trends in the ways in which business enterprises organize themselves, the critical challenge is for companies to design structures and systems that match the particular circumstances of their own business situations. In the same way that strategic management is a quest for unique solutions to the matching of internal resources and capabilities to external business opportunity, so organizational design is about selecting structures, systems and management styles that can best implement such strategies. To establish principles, guidelines and criteria for designing business organizations we need to consider the fundamental challenges of organizing.

## The Organizational Problem: Reconciling Specialization with Coordination and Cooperation

To design a firm we must first recognize what it is supposed to do. According to Henry Mintzberg:

> Every organized human activity—from making pots to placing a man on the moon—gives rise to two fundamental and opposing requirements: the division of labor into various tasks, and the coordination of these tasks to accomplish the activity. The structure of the organization can be defined simply as the ways in which labor is divided into distinct tasks and coordination is achieved among these tasks.[13]

### Specialization and Division of Labor

Firms exist because they are efficient institutions for the organization of economic activities, particularly the production of goods and services. The fundamental source of efficiency in production is *specialization* through the *division of labor* into separate tasks. The classic statement on the gains due to specialization is Adam Smith's description of pin manufacture:

> One man draws out the wire, another straightens it, a third cuts it, a fourth points it, a fifth grinds it at the top for receiving the head; to make the head

requires two or three distinct operations; to put it on is a peculiar business, to whiten the pins is another; it is even a trade by itself to put them into the papers.[14]

Smith's pin makers produced about 4 800 pins per person each day. "But if they had all wrought separately and independently, and without any of them having been educated to this peculiar business, they certainly could not each have made 20, perhaps not one pin, in a day." Similarly, Henry Ford achieved huge productivity gains by his assembly-line system, which assigned individuals to highly specific tasks. Between the end of 1912 and early 1914 the time taken to assemble a Model T fell from 106 hours to six hours.

But specialization comes at a cost. The more a production process is divided between different specialists, the more complex is the challenge of integrating the efforts of individual specialists. The more volatile and unstable the external environment, the greater the number of decisions that need to be made and the greater are these coordination costs. Hence, the more stable is the environment, the greater is the optimal division of labor. This is true both for firms and for entire societies. Civilizations are built on increased division of labor, which is only possible through stability. As the strife-torn parts of Somalia, Haiti, and the Congo have demonstrated so tragically, once chaos reigns, societies regress toward subsistence mode where each family unit must be self-sufficient.

## The Cooperation Problem

Integrating the efforts of specialist individuals involves two organizational problems: there is the *cooperation problem*—that of aligning the interests of individuals who have divergent goals—and *coordination problem*—even in the absence of goal conflict, how do individuals harmonize their different activities?

The economics literature analyzes cooperation problems arising from goal misalignment as the *problem of agency*.[15] An *agency relationship* exists when one party (the principal) contracts with another party (the agent) to act on behalf of the principal. The problem is ensuring that the agent acts in the principal's interest. Within the firm, the major agency problem is between owners (shareholders) and managers. The problem of ensuring that managers operate companies to maximize shareholder wealth is at the center of the corporate governance debate. During the 1990s, changes in top management remuneration—in particular the increasing emphasis given to stock options—were intended to align the interests of managers with those of shareholders.[16] However, at Enron, WorldCom, and other companies, these incentives induced managers to manipulate reported earnings rather than to work for long-term profitability.

Agency problems exist throughout the hierarchy. For individual employees, systems of incentives, monitoring and appraisal are designed to encourage pursuit of organizational objectives and overcome employees' tendency to do their own thing or simply shirk. The organization structure may create its own problems. Organizational departments create their own subgoals that do not align with one another. The classic conflicts are between different functions: sales wishes to please customers, production wishes to maximize output, R&D wants to introduce mind-blowing new products, while finance worries about profit and loss.

Several mechanisms are available to management for achieving goal alignment within organizations:

- *Control mechanisms* typically operate through hierarchical supervision. Managers supervise the behavior and performance of subordinates who must seek approval for actions that lie outside their defined area of discretion. Control is enforced through positive and negative incentives: the primary positive incentive is the opportunity for promotion up the hierarchy; negative incentives are dismissal and demotion.

- *Performance incentives* link rewards to output: they include piece-rates for production workers and profit bonuses for executives. Such performance-related incentives have two main benefits: first, they are *high powered*—they relate rewards directly to output—and second, they economize on the need for costly monitoring and supervision of employees. Pay-for-performance becomes more difficult where employees work in teams or on activities where output is difficult to measure.

- *Shared values.* Some organizations are able to achieve high levels of cooperation and low levels of goal conflict without extensive control mechanisms or performance-related incentives. Churches, charities, clubs and voluntary organizations typically display a commonality of purpose and values among members. Similarly with firms: the presence of shared core values appears to be a key influence on sustained success.[17] The role of culture as a control mechanism that is an alternative to bureaucratic control or the price mechanism is central to Bill Ouchi's concept of *clan control*.[18] The role of shared values and behavioral norms among organizational members is a powerful force aligning individual actions with company strategy. The key advantages of culture as a control device are, first, it is cheap: it saves on costs of monitoring and providing financial incentives; second, it permits flexibility: when individuals internalize the goals and principles of the organization, they can be allowed to use their initiative and creativity in their work. However, to view corporate culture as a tool of management control fails to recognize that culture is a property of the organization as a whole, which is not amenable to top management manipulation. At the British bank NatWest during the 1990s, John Weeks identified a "culture of complaining", which was resistant to top-down cultural change initiatives.[19]

## The Coordination Problem

The desire to cooperate is not enough to ensure that organizational members integrate their efforts—it is not lack of a common goal that causes Olympic relay teams to drop the baton. Unless individuals can find ways of coordinate their efforts, production doesn't happen. As we have already seen in our discussion of organizational capabilities, the exceptional performance of Wal-Mart, the Cirque du Soleil, and the U.S. Marine Corp Band derives less from the skills of the individual members as from superb coordination between them. Among the mechanism for coordination, the following can be found in all firms:

- *Rules and directives.* A basic feature of the firm is the existence of general employment contracts under which individual agree to perform a range of duties as required by their employer. This allows managers to exercise authority by means of *general rules* ("Secret agents on overseas missions will have essential expenses reimbursed only on production of original receipts") and *specific directives* ("Miss Moneypenny, show Mr. Bond his new cigarette case with 4G communication and a concealed death ray").

- *Routines.* Where activities are performed recurrently, coordination based on mutual adjustment and rules becomes institutionalized within organizational routines. As we noted in the previous chapter, these "regular and predictable sequences of coordinated actions by individuals" are the foundation of organizational capability. If organizations are to perform complex activities at extreme levels of efficiency and reliability, coordination by rules, directives, or mutual adjustment is not enough—coordination must become embedded in routines.

- *Mutual adjustment.* The simplest form of coordination involves the mutual adjustment of individuals engaged in related tasks. In soccer or doubles tennis, each player coordinates with fellow team members without any authority relationship among them. Such mutual adjustment occurs in leaderless teams and is especially suited to novel tasks where routinization is not feasible.

The relative roles of these different coordination devices depend on the types of activity being performed and the intensity of collaboration required. Rules tend to work well for activities where standardized outcomes are required and the decision-making abilities of the operatives involved may be limited—most quality control procedures involve the application of simple rules. Routines form the basis for coordination in most activities where close interdependence exists between individuals, whether a basic production task (supplying customers at Starbucks) or a more complex activity (performing a heart bypass operation or implementing a systems integration project for a multinational corporation). Mutual adjustment works best where the individuals involved are well-informed of the actions of their co-workers, either because they are in close visual contact (a chef de cuisine and her sous-chefs), or through information exchange (designers using interactive CAD software).

## Hierarchy in Organizational Design

Hierarchy is the fundamental feature of organizational structure. It is the primary means by which companies achieve specialization, coordination, and cooperation. Despite the negative images that hierarchy often stimulates, I shall argue that hierarchical structures are essential for efficiency and flexibility in firms. The critical issue is not whether or not to organize by hierarchy—there is little alternative—but how the hierarchy should be structured and how the various parts should be linked.

### Hierarchy as Coordination: Modularity

Hierarchy is a feature, not only of human organizations but of almost all complex systems:[20]

- The human body which is hierarchy of cells, organs and subsystems such as the respiratory system, nervous system, digestive system and so on.

**FIGURE 7.2** How hierarchy economizes on coordination

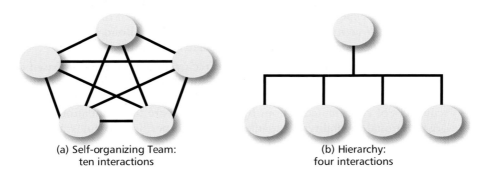

(a) Self-organizing Team:
ten interactions

(b) Hierarchy:
four interactions

- Physical systems are composed at the macro level of planets, stars, and galaxies and at the micro level of subatomic particles, atoms and molecules.
- Social systems comprises of individuals, families, communities, and nations.
- A book consists of letters, words, sentences, paragraphs, and chapters.

This systems view of hierarchy (in contrast to the concept of an *administrative hierarchy*) points to two key advantages of hierarchical structures:

- *Economizing on coordination*. As we have noted, the gains from specialization come at the cost of coordination. Suppose there are five programmers designing a piece of customized computer software. If they are structured as a "self-organized team," where coordination is by mutual adjustment (see Figure 7.2a), ten bilateral interactions must be managed. Alternatively, suppose the programmer with the biggest feet is selected to be supervisor. In this simple hierarchy (Figure 7.2b), there are only four relationships to be managed. Of course, this says nothing about the *quality* of the coordination: if the programmers' work is highly interdependent, hierarchical relationships may not allow for rich collaboration among team members.

  However, even if individual units are organized as self-managed teams, hierarchy can still be an effective structure for linking the teams in a modular structure. By breaking up a complex system into discrete pieces—which can then communicate with one another through standard interfaces within a standardized architecture—one can eliminate what would otherwise be an unmanageable spaghetti tangle of interconnections.[21]

- *Adaptability*. Hierarchical, modular systems are able to evolve more rapidly than unitary systems that are not partitioned into subsystems. Such adaptability requires some degree of *decomposability*: the ability of each component subsystem to operate with some measure of independence from the other subsystems. Modular systems that allow significant independence for each module are referred to as *loosely coupled*.[22] The modular structure of an automobile allows the gearbox to be replaced without the need to scrap the whole car. Organizing the development of a new car is similar: if separate teams work on different subassemblies (power train, brakes, steering, electricals and so forth), so long as there is agreement on how the different subassemblies fit together, each team can get on with its design without the need for constant communication and coordination with every other team.[23] The multidivisional firm is a modular structure. At Procter & Gamble, decisions about developing new shampoos can be made by the Global Hair Care division without involving the Global Fabric Care, Global Health Care or the Duracell divisions. A divisional structure also makes it easier for P&G to add new businesses (Gillette; Wella) and to divest them (Folgers Coffee; paper products).[24]

The merits of hierarchical structures in economizing on efficiency in communication and permitting decentralized flexibility are evident in Nelson Mandela's restructuring of the ANC (see Strategy Capsule 7.1). But what about the role of hierarchies as a vehicle for top-down control through *bureaucracy*?

**STRATEGY CAPSULE 7.1**

## Hierarchical Structures: The 1952 Mandela Plan for the ANC

Along with many others, I had become convinced that the government intended to declare the ANC (African National Congress) and the SAIC (South African Indian Congress) illegal organizations, just as it had done with the Communist Party. It seemed inevitable that the state would attempt to put us out of business as a legal organization. With this in mind, I approached the National Executive with the idea that we must come up with a contingency plan . . . They instructed me to draw up a plan that would enable the organization to operate from underground. This strategy came to be known as the Mandela-Plan, or simply, M-Plan.

The idea was to set up organizational machinery that would allow the ANC to take decisions at the highest level, which could then be swiftly transmitted to the organization as a whole without calling a meeting. In other words, it would allow the organization to continue to function and enable leaders who were banned to continue to lead. The M-Plan was designed to allow the organization to recruit new members, respond to local and national problems and maintain regular contact between the membership and the underground leadership.

I worked on it for a number of months and came up with a system that was broad enough to adapt itself to local conditions and not fetter individual initiative, but detailed enough to facilitate order. The smallest unit was the cell, which in urban townships consisted of roughly ten houses on a street. A cell steward would be in charge of each of these units. If a street had more than ten houses, a street steward would take charge and the cell stewards would report to him. A group of streets formed a zone directed by a chief steward, who was in turn responsible to the secretariat of the local branch of the ANC. The secretariat was a subcommittee of the branch executive, which reported to the provincial secretary. My notion was that every cell and street steward would know every person and family in his area, so that he would be trusted by his people and know whom to trust. The cell steward arranged meetings, organized political classes, and collected dues. He was the linchpin of the plan.

The plan was accepted and was implemented immediately. Word went out to the branches to begin to prepare for this covert restructuring . . . As part of the M-Plan, the ANC introduced an elementary course of political lectures for its members throughout the country. These lectures were meant not only to educate but to hold the organization together. They were given in secret by branch leaders. Those members in attendance would in turn give the same lectures to others in their homes and communities.

*Source:* Nelson Mandela, *Long Walk to Freedom* (London: Little Brown, 1994): 134-5. © 1994, 1995 by Nelson Rolihlahla Mandela. Reproduced by permission of Little Brown.

## Hierarchy as Control: Bureaucracy

Hierarchy, I have argued, is an efficient solution to the problem of *coordination* in organizing complex tasks. However, what hierarchies are best known for is their ability to resolve the problem of *cooperation* in organizations through the imposition of top-down control.

The notion of the hierarchy as an administrative mechanism through which centralized power can be exercised can be traced back to the government system of the Ch'in dynasty of China around 220 BC. For Max Weber, "the father of organizational theory," hierarchy was the central feature of his system of *bureaucracy* which involved: "each lower office under the control and supervision of a higher one"; a "systematic division of labor"; formalization in writing of "administrative acts, decisions, and rules", and work governed by standardized rules and operating procedures, where authority is based on "belief in the legality of enacted rules and the right of those elevated to authority under such rules to issue commands."[25]

Weber's obsession with rationality, efficiency, and controlling against the personal use of hierarchical authority resulted in organizational designs that sought safeguards against human traits such as emotion, creativity, fellowship, and idiosyncrasies of personality. As a result bureaucratic organizations have been described as *mechanistic*[26] or as *machine bureaucracies*.[27]

## Contingency Approaches to Organization Design

Led by the military and the civil service, the bureaucratic model dominated thinking about organizational structure during the first half of the twentieth century. However, it soon became clear that bureaucratic systems also nurtured inertia, alienation and a lack of initiative and innovation.

During the 1950s and 1960s, the *human relations school* recognized that cooperation and coordination within organizations was about social relationships, which bureaucracy stifled. Studying Scottish engineering companies, Burns and

**TABLE 7.1** Mechanistic versus organic organizational forms

| Feature | Mechanistic forms | Organic forms |
|---|---|---|
| Task definition | Rigid and highly specialized | Flexible and broadly defined |
| Coordination and control | Rules and directives vertically imposed | Mutual adjustment, common culture |
| Communication | Vertical | Vertical and horizontal |
| Knowledge | Centralized | Dispersed |
| Commitment and loyalty | To immediate superior | To the organization and its goals |
| Environmental context | Stable with low technological uncertainty | Dynamic with significant technological uncertainty and ambiguity |

*Source:*

Adapted from Richard Butler, *Designing Organizations: A Decision-Making Perspective* (London: Routledge, 1991): 76.

Stalker found that firms in stable environment had *mechanistic* forms, characterized by bureaucracy; those in less stable market had *organic* forms that were less formal and more flexible. Table 7.1 contrasts key characteristics of the two forms.

These findings fueled *contingency approaches* to organizational design—the idea that a firm's optimal structure and systems depended upon the strategy it pursued, the technology it employed and the environment it inhabited. [28] Although Google and McDonald's are of similar sizes in terms of revenue, their structures and systems are very different. McDonald's is highly bureaucratized: high levels of job specialization, formal systems, a strong emphasis on rules and procedures. Google's freewheeling informality with low job specialization, emphasis on horizontal communication and emphasis of principles over rules reflects its emphasis on innovation, rapid growth, and its fast changing business environment. The more standardized goods or services are (beverage cans, blood tests, or haircuts for army inductees) and the more stable the environment is, the greater the efficiency advantages of the bureaucratic model with its standard operating procedures and high levels of specialization. But as soon as market turbulence arrives, innovation becomes a priority, or heterogeneous outputs are required from heterogeneous inputs—then the bureaucratic model breaks down.

These contingency factors also cause functions within companies to be organized differently. Stable, standardized activities such as payroll, treasury, taxation, customer support and purchasing activities tend to operate well when organized along bureaucratic principles; research, new product development, marketing, and strategic planning require more organic modes of organization.

## Rethinking Hierarchy

Increasing turbulence of the business environment over time has created difficulties for large companies run on bureaucratic lines. Since the mid-1980s almost all large companies have made strenuous efforts to restructure and reorganize in order to achieve greater flexibility and responsiveness. Giant corporations such as BP and General Electric have retained their basic multidivisional structures, but have decentralized decision making, reduced their number of hierarchical layers, shrunk headquarters staffs, emphasized horizontal rather than vertical communication, and shifted the emphasis of control from *supervision* to *accountability*.[29]

The trend towards decentralization has not been one way. The need to build capabilities that integrate across products, across countries and across technologies has encouraged many large companies—including GE and BP—to recentralize many aspects of their strategy and operation. These cycles of centralization and decentralization may be a means by which companies are able to balance the tradeoff between integration and flexible responsiveness.[30]

Achieving effective integration while avoiding the cost and rigidities associated with centralized coordination has encouraged organizations to explore informal approaches to coordination—including many of the features of coordination associated with "organic" organizational forms. Here, companies have been assisted by developments in information and communication technology (ICT), the huge leaps in the availability of information available to organizational members and the ease with which they can communicate with one another has increased vastly the capacity for mutual adjustment without the need for intensive hierarchical guidance and leadership.

## Applying the Principles of Organizational Design

We have established that the fundamental problem of organization is reconciling specialization with coordination and cooperation. The basic design for complex organizations—whether they are business enterprises, religious orders, political associations, or criminal organizations—is hierarchy. The essence of hierarchy is creating specialized units coordinated and controlled by a superior unit. But this does not take us very far. On what basis should specialized units be defined? How should decision-making authority be allocated? And what kind of relationships should there be between different organizational units?

In this section we will tackle the first two of these questions: the basis of grouping and the allocation of decision-making power. In the next section, we identify some typical organizational structures found in business enterprises. Then, in the following section we shall look at structuring relations between units—the operation and design of management systems.

### Defining Organizational Units

In creating a hierarchical structure, on what basis are individuals assigned to organizational units within the firm? This issue is fundamental and complex. Multinational, multiproduct companies are continually grappling with the issue of whether they should be structured around product divisions, country subsidiaries, or functional departments, and periodically they undergo the disruption of changing from one to another. Some of the principal bases for grouping employees are common tasks, products, geography, and process:

- *Tasks*. Organizational units can be created around common tasks. This usually means grouping together employees who do the same job—thus, a firm might create a machine shop, a maintenance department, a secretarial pool, and a sales office.

- *Products*. Where a company offers multiple products, these can provide a basis for structure. In a department store, departments are defined by products: kitchen goods, bedding, lingerie, and so on. PepsiCo comprises three main product groups: PepsiCo Beverages, Frito-Lay (snack foods), and Quaker Foods (cereals and processed foods).

- *Geography*. Where a company serves multiple local markets, organizational units can be defined around these localities. Wal-Mart is organized by individual stores, groups of stores within an area, and groups of areas within a region. The Roman Catholic church is organized into parishes, dioceses, and archdioceses.

- *Process*. A process is a sequence of interlinked activities. An organization may be viewed as a set of processes: the product development process, the manufacturing process, the sales and distribution process, and so on. A process may correspond closely with an individual product, or a process may be dominated by a single task. Functional organizations tend to combine task-based and process-based grouping.

## Organizing on the Basis of Coordination Intensity

How do we decide whether to use task, product, geography, or process to define organizational units? The fundamental issue is achieving the coordination necessary to integrate the efforts of different individuals. This implies grouping individuals according to the intensity of their coordination needs. Those individuals whose tasks require the most intensive coordination should work within the same organizational unit.

- In a geographically dispersed organization where coordination across distance is difficult, the organization must be built on local units. The ANC is an example (see Strategy Capsule 7.1), as are most large service companies.

- Where an organization has a narrow product range and does not need to be differentiated by location, but possesses strong functional specializations, then a grouping around functional tasks is appropriate. For example, British Airways is organized primarily around functions: flight operations, engineering, marketing, sales, customer service, human resources, information, and finance.

- Where a company is diversified over many products and these products are substantially different in terms of technology and markets, it is vital that individuals who work on the same product should interact closely—a product-based organization is the appropriate structure. Virtually all diversified companies—General Electric, 3M, Sony, Siemens, and Unilever— are organized by product divisions.

Having created organizational units that bring together individuals whose coordination needs are most intense, the next challenge is to create hierarchical control that permits effective coordination while giving as much operational autonomy as possible to the subordinate units. Oliver Williamson refers to this as the *principle of hierarchical decomposition*. At the operating level (where decision making is high frequency), organization units are created where the interactions are strong. At the strategic level (where decision making is low frequency), a separate organization unit is created to exercise coordination and direction. Hence:

> The hierarchical decomposition principle can be stated as follows: Internal organization should be designated in such a way as to effect quasi-independence between the parts, the high frequency dynamics (operating activities) and low frequency dynamics (strategic planning) should be clearly distinguished, and incentives should be aligned within and between components so as to promote both local and global effectiveness.[31]

To organize according to intensity of coordination needs requires understanding the nature of interdependence within an organization. James Thompson distinguished three levels of interdependence: *pooled interdependence* (the loosest), where individuals operate independently but depend on one another's performance; *sequential interdependence*, where the output of one individual is the input of the other; and *reciprocal interdependence* (the most intense), where individuals are mutually dependent. Thompson argued that organizational design needed to begin with creating organizational units where interdependence was the most intense.[32]

Over time, the relative importance of these different dependencies changes. Hence, companies need to change the basis on which they define their structure. For example, as trade and communication between countries has become easier and consumer preferences between countries have become more homogeneous, multinational corporations have shifted from geographically based structures to worldwide product divisions.

## Other Factors Influencing the Definition of Organizational Units

Coordination requirements are not the only consideration in deciding how to group together employees and activities within the firm. Additional factors that influence the efficiency of different organizational arrangements include:

- *Economies of scale.* There may be advantages in grouping together activities where scale economies are present. Thus, it may be desirable to group together research activities even if there is little coordination among different research projects, simply to exploit scale economies in specialized facilities and technical personnel.
- *Economies of utilization.* It may also be possible to exploit efficiencies from grouping together similar activities that result from fuller utilization of employees. Even though there may be little need for individual maintenance engineers to coordinate with one another, establishing a single maintenance department permits maintenance personnel to be utilized more fully than assigning a maintenance engineer to each manufacturing cell.
- *Learning.* If establishing competitive advantage requires building distinctive capabilities, firms must be structured to maximize learning. Typically, it was

assumed that learning was best achieved by grouping together individuals doing similar jobs—creating a manufacturing engineering department, a quality control department, and a finance function. More recently, it has been observed that the specialized functional and discipline-based knowledge may be less important than *architectural knowledge*—knowing how to link together specialized knowledge from different fields. This implies the creation of multifunctional work groups comprising experts from different knowledge bases.

- *Standardization of control systems.* Tasks may be grouped together to achieve economies in standardized control mechanisms. An advantage of the typing pool and the sales department was that employees doing near-identical jobs could be subject to the same system of monitoring, performance measurement, training, and behavioral norms. Creative activities such as research and new product development need to be managed in a different way from routine activities such as manufacturing and accounting—hence they should be located in different organizational units.[33]

## Alternative Structural Forms

On the basis of these alternative approaches to grouping tasks and activities we can identify three basic organizational forms: the functional structure, the multidivisional structure and the matrix structure.

### The Functional Structure

Single-business firms tend to be organized along functional lines. Grouping together functionally similar tasks is conducive to exploiting scale economies, promoting learning and capability building, and deploying standardized control systems. Since cross-functional integration occurs at the top of the organization, functional structures are conducive to a high degree of centralized control by the CEO and top management team.

However, even for single-product firms, functional structures are subject to the problems of cooperation and coordination. Different functional departments develop their own goals, values, vocabularies and behavioral norms that make cross-functional integration difficult. As the size of the firm increases, the pressure on top management to achieve effective integration increases. Because the different functions of the firm tend to be *tightly coupled* rather than *loosely coupled*, there is limited scope for decentralization. In particular, it is very difficult to operate individual functions as semi-autonomous profit centers.

The real problems arise when the firm grows its range of products and businesses. As we noted with DuPont during the early twentieth century, once a functionally organized company expands its product range, coordination within each product area becomes difficult.

Although the long-term trend among very large companies has been for product-based, divisionalized companies to replace functionally organized companies, the trend is not entirely one way. As companies mature, the need for strong centralized control and well-developed functional capabilities has caused some companies to revert to functional structures. For example:

- When John Scully became CEO of Apple in 1984, the company was organized by product: Apple II, Apple III, Lisa, and Macintosh. Despite strong cross-functional coordination within each product group, there was little integration across products. Each product was completely incompatible with the others, and the structure failed to exploit scale economies within functions. Scully's response was to reorganize Apple along functional lines to gain control, reduce costs, and achieve a more coherent product strategy.

- General Motors, pioneer of the multidivisional structure, has adopted a more functional structure. As its strategic priorities have shifted from differentiation and segmentation toward cost efficiency, it has maintained its brand names (Cadillac, Chevrolet, Buick) but merged the separate divisions into a more functionally based structure to exploit scale economies and faster technical transfer (see Figure 7.3 and compare it with Figure 7.1).

## The Multidivisional Structure

We have seen how the product-based, multidivisional structure emerged during the twentieth century in response to the coordination problems caused by diversification. The key advantage of divisionalized structures (whether product based or geographically based) is the potential for decentralized decision making. The

**FIGURE 7.3** General Motors Corporation: organizational structure, 1997

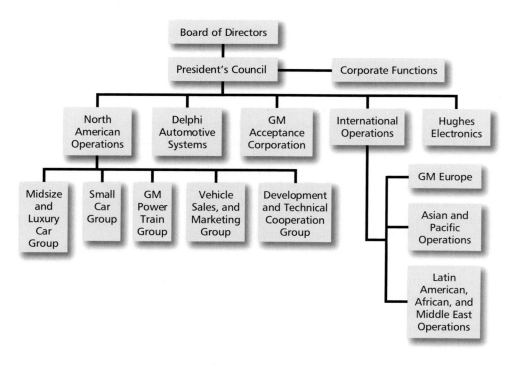

multidivisional structure is the classic example of a loose-coupled, modular organization where business-level strategies and operating decisions can be made at the divisional level, while the corporate headquarters concentrates on corporate planning, budgeting, and providing common services.

Central to the efficiency advantages of the multidivisional corporation is the ability to apply a common set of corporate management tools to a range of different businesses. At ITT, Harold Geneen's system of "managing by the numbers" allowed him to cope with over 50 divisional heads reporting directly to him. At British Petroleum, John Browne's system of "performance contracts" allowed direct reporting by over 20 "strategic performance units." Divisional autonomy also fosters the development of top management leadership capability among divisional heads—an important factor in CEO succession.

The large, divisionalized corporation is typically organized into three levels: the corporate center, the divisions, and individual business units, each representing a distinct business for which financial accounts can be drawn up and strategies formulated. Figure 7.4 shows General Electric's organizational structure at the corporate and divisional levels.

In Chapter 17, we shall look in greater detail at the organization of the multibusiness corporation.

## Matrix Structures

Whatever the primary basis for grouping, all companies that embrace multiple products, multiple functions, and multiple locations must coordinate across all three dimensions. Organizational structures that formalize coordination and control across multiple dimensions are called *matrix structures*.

**FIGURE 7.4**  General Electric: organizational structure, 2009

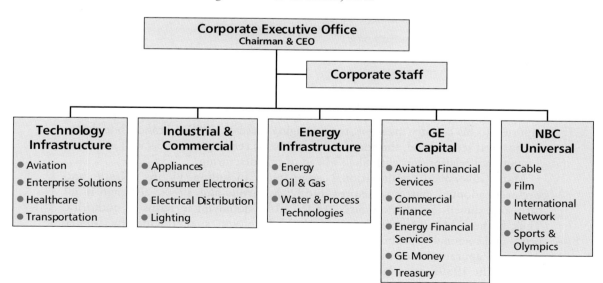

*Source*:
Based on information in General Electric Annual Report, 2008.

**FIGURE 7.5** Royal Dutch Shell Group: pre-1996 matrix structure

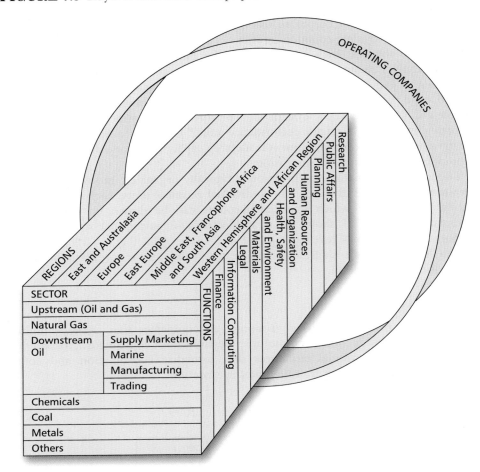

Figure 7.5 shows the Shell management matrix (prior to reorganization in 1996). Within this structure, the general manager of Shell's Berre refinery in France reported to his country manager, the managing director of Shell France, but also to his business sector head, the coordinator of Shell's refining sector, as well as having a functional relationship with Shell's head of manufacturing.

Many diversified, multinational companies, including Philips, Nestlé and Unilever, adopted matrix structures during the 1960s and 1970s, although in all cases one dimension of the matrix tended to be dominant in terms of authority. Thus, in the old Shell matrix the geographical dimension, as represented by country heads and regional coordinators, had primary responsibility for budgetary control, personnel appraisal, and strategy formulation.

Since the 1980s, most large corporations have dismantled or reorganized their matrix structures. Shell abandoned its matrix during 1995–6 in favor of a structure based on four business sectors: upstream, downstream, chemicals, and gas and power. During 2001–2, the Swiss-Swedish engineering giant ABB abandoned its much-lauded matrix structure in the face of plunging profitability and mounting debt. In fast-moving business environments companies have found that the benefits from formally coordinating across multiple dimensions have been outweighed by excessive complexity, larger head-office staffs, slower decision making, and diffused authority. Bartlett and Ghoshal observed that matrix structures "led to conflict and confusion; the proliferation of channels created informational logjams as a proliferation of committees and reports bogged down the organization; and overlapping responsibilities produced turf battles and a loss of accountability."[34]

Yet, all complex organizations that comprise multiple products, multiple functions, and multiple geographical markets need to coordinate within each of these dimensions. The problem of the matrix organization is not that it attempts to coordinate across multiple dimensions—in complex organizations such coordination is essential—but that this multiple coordination is overformalized, resulting in excessive corporate staffs and overcomplex systems that slow decision making and dull entrepreneurial initiative. The trend has been for companies to focus formal systems of coordination and control on one dimension, then allowing the other dimensions of coordination to be mainly informal.[35] Thus, while Shell is organized primarily around four business sectors and these sectors exercise financial and strategic control over the individual operating companies, Shell still has country heads, responsible for coordinating all Shell activities in relation to legal, taxation and government relations within each country, and functional heads, responsible for technical matters and best-practice transfer within their particular function, whether it is manufacturing, marketing, or HR.

## Beyond Hierarchy?

For several decades consultants and management scholars have proclaimed the death of hierarchical structures in business firms. In 1993, two of America's most prominent scholars of organization announced: ". . . the new organizational revolution is sweeping one industry after another . . . quantum changes in manufacturing and computer-mediated communication technologies have given managers radical new options for designing organizations." The new organizations featured ". . . flatter hierarchies, decentralized decision making, greater tolerance for ambiguity, permeable internal and external boundaries, empowerment of employees, capacity for renewal, self-organizing units, self-integrating coordination mechanisms."[36]

As I noted in the earlier section on "Rethinking Hierarchy," there have been substantial changes in the way in which corporate hierarchies have been organized. Layers have been removed; mechanistic formality has been replaced by organic informality. Yet, hierarchy remains as the basic structural form of almost all companies. Are there alternative modes of organization?

Several organizational forms have been identified which, although they comprise some hierarchical elements, are sufficiently distinctive to be regarded as alternative organizational forms:

- *Adhocracies.* In some organizations, the presence of shared values, motivation and willingness to participate, mutual respect and communication effectiveness may allow a high level of coordination with little need for hierarchy, authority, or tools of control. These organizations, which Henry

Mintzberg calls *adhocracies*,[37] feature flexible, spontaneous coordination and collaboration around problem solving and other nonroutine activities. Adhocracies tend to exist among organizations where expertise is prized. In research organizations, new product development groups, jazz bands, and consulting firms, each specialist is valued for his or her expertise and there is little exercise of authority.

- *Team-based and project-based organizations.* Adhocracies are one example of an organizational form based on informal structure with flexible patterns of coordination. Flexibility and adaptability can also be achieved in project-based organizations—common in sectors such as construction, consulting, oil exploration, and engineering services—where business takes the form of projects of limited duration. Because every project is different, and every project goes through a changing sequence of activities, each project needs to be undertaken by a closely interacting team that relies on problem solving and mutual adjustment as well as rules and routines. Increasingly, companies are introducing elements of team- and project-based organizations into their conventional divisional and functional structures. For example, in most divisionalized corporations, new product development, change management, knowledge management, and research is organized in projects and undertaken by teams.

- *Networks.* Localized networks of small, closely interdependent firms have been a feature of manufacturing for many hundreds of years. In Italy such networks are prominent in the clothing industry of Prato, near Florence, and in packaging equipment.[38] Hollywood movie making[39] and microelectronics in Silicon Valley have similar structures—highly specialized firms that coordinate to design and produce complex products. Often these networks feature a central firm that acts as a "systems integrator,"[40] as in the case of Benetton and Toyota.[41] In fast-moving industries, the ability of highly specialized, knowhow-intensive firms to reconfigure their relationships can be conducive to innovation, product differentiation, and rapid new product development. In the developing world, such networks can be a viable alternative to industrial development where large enterprises are lacking.[42]

These different organizational forms share several common characteristics:

- *A focus on coordination rather than control.* In contrast to the "command-and-control" hierarchy, these structures focus almost wholly upon achieving coordination. Financial incentives, culture, and social controls take the place of hierarchical control.

- *Reliance on coordination by mutual adjustment.* Central to all nonhierarchical structures is their dependence on voluntaristic coordination through bilateral and multilateral adjustment. The capacity for coordination through mutual adjustment has been greatly enhanced by information technology.

- *Individuals in multiple organizational roles.* Reconciling complex patterns of coordination with high levels of flexibility and responsiveness is difficult if job designs and organizational structures are rigidly defined. Adhocracies and team-based organizations feature individuals switching their organizational roles and occupying multiple roles simultaneously. For example, for most of the 1990s AES had no finance function, no HR function, no safety or environmental affairs functions, and no public relations department. These functions were performed by teams of operatives and line managers.

## Management Systems for Coordination and Control

The relationship between management systems and organizational structure is similar to that between the skeleton and bodily systems in the human body. The skeleton provides the framework; the respiratory system, digestive system, and nervous system are the means by which the body operates. Computer networks offer another analogy: the hardware provides the structure and the software provides the systems that make the network operational.

Management systems provide the mechanisms of communication, decision making, and control that allow companies to solve the problems of achieving both coordination and cooperation. Four management systems are of primary importance: the information systems, the strategic planning systems, the financial systems, and the human resource management systems.

### Information Systems

Information is fundamental to the operation of all management systems. Communication technology—the telephone and telegraphy—were essential for the companies to span multiple locations. The computer has had an equally dramatic impact during the past half century. Accounting systems are key components of firms' information systems. They collect, organize, and communicate financial information to top management facilitating hierarchical control.

Administrative hierarchies are founded on vertical information flows: the upward flow of information to the manager and the downward flow of instructions. The trend towards decentralization and informality in organizations rests on two key aspects of increased information availability: *information feedback* to the individual on job performance, which has made self-monitoring possible, and *information networking*, which has allowed individuals to coordinate their activities voluntarily without hierarchical supervision. For example, a central element of total quality management has been recognition that regular, real-time, performance feedback to employees permits them to take responsibility for quality control, reducing or eliminating the need for supervisors and quality controllers. During the past decade, corporate intranets, web-based information systems, and groupware have transformed organizations' capacity for decentralized coordination.

### Strategic Planning Systems

Small enterprises can operate successfully without an explicit strategy. The firm's strategy may exist only in the head of the founder and, unless the founder needs to write a business plan in order to attract outside financing, the strategy may never be articulated. Most large companies have a regular (normally annual) strategic planning process. For a multibusiness company, the strategic planning process creates business plans for the individual divisions that are then integrated into a corporate plan.

Whether formal or informal, systematic or *ad hoc,* documented or not, the strategy formulation process is an important vehicle for achieving coordination within a company. As discussed in Chapter 1, the strategy process brings together knowledge from different parts of the company, ensures consistency between the decisions being made at different levels and in different parts of the company, and commits managers to ambitious performance targets.

The system through which strategy is formulated varies considerably from company to company. Even after the entrepreneurial startup has grown into a large company, strategy making may remain the preserve of the chief executive. Functional managers may provide key inputs such as financial projections and market analysis, but the key elements of strategy—goals, new business developments, capital investment, and key competitive initiatives—are often decided by the chief executive.[43] At MCI Communications former CEO Orville Wright observed: "We do it strictly top-down at MCI."[44] The first director of strategic planning was warned: "If you ever write a strategic plan, you will be fired!"

As companies mature, their strategic planning processes become more systematized and typically follow an annual cycle. Strategic plans tend to be for three to five years and combine top-down initiatives (indications of performance expectations and identification of key strategic initiatives) and bottom-up business plans (proposed strategies and financial forecasts for individual divisions and business units). After discussion between the corporate level and the individual businesses, the business plans are amended and agreed and integrated into an overall corporate plan that is presented to and agreed by the board of directors. Figure 7.6 shows a typical strategic planning cycle.

The resulting strategic plan typically comprises the following elements:

- A *statement of the goals* the company seeks to achieve over the planning period with regard to both financial targets (for example, targets for revenue growth, cost reduction, operating profit, return on capital employed, return to shareholders) and strategic goals (such as market share, new products,

**FIGURE 7.6** The generic strategic planning cycle

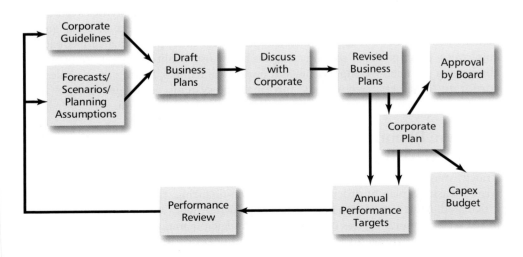

overseas market penetration and new business development). For example, in BP's February 2006 strategy statement, the company established that its "primary objective is to deliver sustainable growth in free cash flow," which it would achieve through "growing production by about 4% a year to 2010" and "delivering further improvements in return on average capital employed relative to our peer group."[45]

- *A set of assumptions or forecasts* about key developments in the external environment to which the company must respond. For example, BP's 2006–10 strategic plan assumed an oil price of $40 a barrel.

- A *qualitative statement* of how the shape of the business will be changing in relation to geographical and segment emphasis, and the basis on which the company will be establishing and extending its competitive advantage. For example, BP's 2006–10 strategy emphasized capital discipline (capex to increase by $0.5 billion per year) and upgrading BP's asset portfolio by selective divestments of about $3 billion per year.

- *Specific action steps* with regard to decisions and projects, supported by a set of mileposts stating what is to be achieved by specific dates. For example, BP's strategic commitments included 24 start-ups of upstream projects during 2006-8, $6 billion capital expenditure on its Russian joint venture, and growth in wind power to 450 MW.

- A set of *financial projections*, including a capital expenditure budget and outline operating budgets. For example, BP's 2006 strategy statement set a capital expenditure budget of $15–16 billion per year, shareholder distribution of $50 billion during 2006–8, and operating costs to increase at less than the rate of inflation.

Although strategic planning tends to emphasize the specific commitments and decisions that are documented in written strategic plans, the most important aspect of strategic planning is the *strategy process*: the dialog through which knowledge is shared and ideas communicated, the consensus that is established, and the commitment to action and results that is built.

Increasing turbulence in the business environment has caused strategic planning processes to become less formalized and more flexible. For example, among the world's largest petroleum majors, the key changes have been as follows:

- Strategic plans have become less concerned with specific actions and became more heavily focused on performance targets, especially on financial goals such as profitability and shareholder return. Planning horizons have also shortened (two to five years is the typical planning period).

- Companies recognized the impossibility of forecasting the future and based their strategies less on medium- and long-term economic and market forecasts of the future and more on more general issues of strategic direction (in the form of vision, mission, and strategic intent) and alternative views of the future (for example, using scenario analysis).

- Strategic planning shifted from a *control perspective*, in which senior management used the strategic planning mechanisms as a means of controlling decisions and resource deployments by divisions and business units and departments, toward more of a *coordination perspective*, in which the strategy process emphasized dialog involving knowledge sharing and consensus building. As a result, the process became increasingly informal and put less emphasis on written documents.

- A diminishing role for strategic planning staff as responsibility for strategic decisions and the strategy-making process become located among senior managers.[46]

## Financial Planning and Control Systems

Financial flows form the life blood of the enterprise. Revenues from customers provide the funds to pay suppliers and employees and any surplus remunerates owners. If inflows are insufficient to cover outflows, the firm becomes insolvent. Hence, financial systems are inevitably the primary mechanism through which top management seeks to control the enterprise. At the center of financial planning is the *budgetary process*. This involves setting and monitoring financial estimates with regard to income and expenditure over a specified time period, both for the firm as a whole and for divisions and departments. Budgets are in part an estimate of incomes and expenditures for the future, in part a target of required financial performance in terms of revenues and profits, and in part a set of authorizations for expenditure up to specified budgetary limits. Two types of budget are set: the capital expenditure budget and the operating budget.

*The Capital Expenditure Budget Capital expenditure budgets* are established through both top-down and bottom-up processes. From the top down, strategic plans establish annual capital expenditure budgets for the planning period both for the company as a whole and for individual divisions. From the bottom up, capital expenditures are determined by the approval of individual capital expenditure projects. Companies have standardized processes for evaluating and approving projects. Requests for funding are prepared according to a standardized methodology, typically based on a forecast of cash flows discounted at the relevant cost of capital (adjusted for project risk). The extent to which the project's returns are sensitive to key environmental uncertainties is also estimated. Capital expenditure approvals take place at different levels of a company according to their size. Projects up to $5 million might be approved by a business unit head; projects up to $25 million might be approved by divisional top management; larger projects might need to be approved by the top management committee, while the biggest projects require approval by the board of directors.

*The Operating Budget* The *operating budget* is a pro forma profit and loss statement for the company as a whole and for individual divisions and business units for the upcoming year. It is usually divided into quarters and months to permit continual monitoring and the early identification of variances. The operating budget is part forecast and part target. It is set within the context of the performance targets established by the strategic plan. Each business typically prepares an operating budget for the following year that is then discussed with the top management committee and, if acceptable, approved. At the end of the financial year, business-level divisional managers are called upon to account for the performance over the past year.

# Human Resource Management Systems

Strategies may arise from principles, formulae, or divine inspiration, but their implementation depends on people. Ultimately, strategic and financial plans come to nothing unless they influence the ways in which people within the organization behave. To support strategic and financial plans, companies need systems for setting goals, creating incentives and monitoring performance at the level of the individual employee. Human resource management has the task of establishing an incentive system that supports the implementation of strategic plans and performance targets through aligning employee and company goals, and ensuring that each employee has the skills necessary to perform his or her job. The general problem, we have noted, is one of agency: how can a company induce employees to do what it wants?

The problem is exacerbated by the imprecision of employment contracts. Unlike most contracts, employment contracts are vague about employee performance expectations. The employer has the right to assign the employee to a particular category of tasks for a certain number of hours per week but the amount of work to be performed and the quality of that work are unspecified. Employment contracts give the right to the employer to terminate the contract for unsatisfactory performance by the employee, but the threat of termination is an inadequate incentive: it imposes costs on the employer and only requires the employee to perform better than a new hire would. Moreover, the employer has imperfect information as to employees' work performance—in team production individual output is not separately observable.[47]

The firm can ensure the employee's compliance with organizational goals using direct supervision of the type that administrative hierarchies are designed to do. The weaknesses of such administrative supervision are, first, there is little incentive for performance in excess of minimum requirements, second, supervision imposes costs, and third, the system presupposes that the supervisor has the knowledge required to direct the employee effectively.

The key to promoting more effective cooperation is for more sophisticated incentives than the threat of dismissal. The principal incentives available to the firm for promoting cooperation are compensation and promotion. The key to designing compensation systems is to link pay either to the inputs required for effective job performance (hours of work, punctuality, effort, numbers of customers visited) or to outputs. The simplest form of output-linked pay is piecework (paying for each unit of output produced) or commission (paying a percentage of the revenue generated).

Relating pay to individual performance is suitable for tasks performed individually. However, firms exist primarily to permit complex coordination among individuals; encouraging such collaboration requires linking pay to team or departmental performance. Where broad-based, enterprise-wide collaboration is required, there may be little alternative to linking pay to company performance through some form of profit sharing.

## Corporate Culture as a Control Mechanism

We have already noted how shared values can align the goals of different stakeholders within the organization. More generally, we can view the culture of the organization as a mechanism for achieving coordination and control. *Corporate culture* comprises the beliefs, values and behavioral norms of the company, which influence how employees think and behave.[48] It is manifest in symbols, ceremonies, social practices, rites, vocabulary, and dress. It is embedded within national cultures, and incorporates elements of social and professional cultures. As a result, a corporate culture may be far from homogeneous: very different cultures may be evident in the research lab, on the factory floor, and within the accounting department. To this extent, culture is not necessarily an integrating device—it can contribute to divisiveness.

Culture can play an important role in facilitating both cooperation and coordination. In companies such as Starbucks, Shell, Nintendo, and Google, strong corporate cultures create a sense of identity among employees that facilitates communication and the building of organizational routines, even across national boundaries. The unifying influence of corporate culture is likely to be especially helpful in assisting coordination through mutual adjustment in large cross-functional teams of the type required for new product development. One of the advantages of culture as a coordinating device is that it permits substantial flexibility in the types of interactions it can support.

The extent to which corporate culture assists coordination depends on the characteristics of the culture. Salomon Brothers (now part of Citigroup) was renowned for its individualistic, internally competitive culture; this was effective in motivating drive and individual effort, but did little to facilitate cooperation. The British Broadcasting Corporation has a strong culture that reflects internal politicization, professional values, internal suspicion and a dedication to the public good, but without a strong sense of customer focus.[49] However, culture is far from being a flexible management tool. Cultures take a long time to develop and cannot easily be changed. As the external environment changes, a highly effective culture may become dysfunctional. The Los Angeles Police Department's culture of professionalism and militarism, which made it one of the most admired and effective police forces in America, later contributed to problems of isolation and unresponsiveness to community needs.[50]

While recognizing the importance of corporate culture—according to Merck's CEO, "Culture eats strategy for lunch!"—chief executives have limited power to change the culture that they inherit. The key issue is to recognize the culture of the organization and to ensure that structure and systems work with the culture and not against it.[51]

## Integrating Different Control Mechanisms

The past ten years have seen substantial progress in integrating different control systems. As strategy has become more and more focused on creating shareholder value, so financial planning has become more closely integrated with strategic planning. Performance management systems have also done much to link strategic and financial planning with human resource management—especially in terms of goal setting and performance appraisal. The central aspect of the "metrics" movement within management is the ability not just to establish quantitative goals for individual employees and groups, but to create mechanisms for measuring and reporting the attainment of these targets. The balanced scorecard system outlined in Chapter 2 is but one approach to this linking of employee goals to company-wide goals.

## Summary

The internal structure and systems of the firm are not simply a matter of "strategy implementation," which can be separated from the hard analytics of strategy formulation. Not only is strategy implementation inseparable from strategy formulation, but issues of structure and systems are central to the fundamental issues of competitive advantage and strategy choice—the existence of organizational capability in particular.

Despite the importance of these issues, this chapter provides only a brief introduction to some of the key issues in organization design. Subsequent chapters develop many of the themes more fully in relation to particular areas of strategy and particular business contexts. Nevertheless, our progress is limited by the weakness of theory in this area. Organization theory is an exceptionally rich field that still lacks adequate integration of its component disciplines: sociology, psychology, organizational economics, systems theory, population ecology, and organizational evolution. While business enterprises continue to experiment with new organizational forms, we business school academics are still struggling to articulate general principles of organizational design.

The chapters that follow will have more to say on the organizational structures and management systems appropriate to different strategies and different business contexts. In the final chapter (Chapter 18) we shall explore some of the new trends and new ideas that are reshaping our thinking about organizational design.

## Self-Study Questions

1  As DuPont expanded its product range (from explosives into paints, dyes, plastics, and synthetic fibers) why do you think that the functional structure (organized around manufacturing plants and other functions such as sales, finance and R&D) became unwieldy? Why did the multidivisional structure based on product groups improve management effectiveness?

2  Within your own organization (whether a university, company, or not-for-profit organization), which departments or activities are organized mechanistically and which organically? To what extent does the mode of organization fit the different environmental contexts and technologies of the different departments or activities?

3  In 2008, Citigroup announced that its Consumer business would be split into Consumer Banking, which would continue to operate through individual national banks, and Global Cards, which would form a single global business (similar to Citi's Global Wealth Management division). On the basis of the arguments relating to *Organizing on the Basis of Coordination Intensity,* why should credit cards be organized as a global unit and all other consumer banking services as national units?

**4**   The examples of Apple Computer and General Motors (see section on "Functional Structure") point to the evolution of organizational structures over the industry life cycle. During the growth phase many companies adopt multidivisional structures, during maturity and decline many companies revert to functional structures. Why might this be? (*Note*: you may wish to refer to Chapter 11, which outlines the main features of the life-cycle model.)

**5**   Draw an organizational chart for a business school that you are familiar with. Does the school operate with a matrix structure (for instance, are there functional/discipline-based departments together with units managing individual programs)? Which dimension of the matrix is more powerful, and how effectively do the two dimensions coordinate? How would you reorganize the structure to make the school more efficient and effective?

# Notes

1  G. Parker, *The Grand Strategy of Philip II* (New Haven: Yale University Press, 1998).

2  "Alcatel-Lucent: Goodbye and Adieu," *Economist* (July 13, 2008).

3  T. Peters, "Strategy Follows Structure," *California Management Review*, 26 (Spring, 1984): 114–28.

4  R. Whittington, A. Pettigrew, S. Peck, E. Fenton, and M. Conyon, "Change and Complementarities in the New Competitive Landscape," *Organization Science* 10 (1999): 583–96.

5  A. D. Chandler, *The Visible Hand: The Managerial Revolution in American Business* (Cambridge, MA: MIT Press, 1977): Chapter 2.

6  Ibid.

7  J. Micklethwait and A. Wooldridge, *The Company: a Short History of a Revolutionary Idea* (New York: Modern Library, 2005).

8  R. Stark, *Sociology*, 10th edn (Belmont, CA: Wadsworth, 2006).

9  A. D. Chandler, *Strategy and Structure* (Cambridge: MIT Press, 1962); Chandler, *The Visible Hand*, op. cit.

10  Chandler, *Strategy and Structure*, op. cit.: 382–3.

11  See http://heritage.dupont.com/floater/fl_management/floater.shtml.

12  A. P. Sloan, *My Years at General Motors* (London: Sidgwick & Jackson, 1963): 42–56.

13  H. Mintzberg, *Structure in Fives: Designing Effective Organizations* (Englewood Cliffs: Prentice Hall, 1993): 2.

14  A. Smith, *The Wealth of Nations* (London: Dent, 1910): 5.

15  S. Ross, "The Economic Theory of Agency," *American Economic Review*, 63 (1973): 134–9; K. Eisenhardt, "Agency Theory: An Assessment and Reviews," *Academy of Management Review*, 14 (1989): 57–74.

16  I. T. Kay and S. Van Ritten, *Myths and Realities of Executive Pay* (Cambridge University Press, 2007): Chapter 6.

17  T. Peters and R. Waterman, *In Search of Excellence* (New York: Harper & Row, 1982).

18  W. G. Ouchi, *Theory Z* (Reading, MA: Addison-Wesley, 1981).

19  J. Weeks, *Unpopular Culture: The Ritual of Complaint in a British Bank* (Chicago: University of Chicago Press, 2004).

20  H. A. Simon, "The Architecture of Complexity," *Proceedings of the American Philosophical Society* 106 (1962): 467–82.

21  R. N. Langlois, "Modularity in Technology and Organization," *Journal of Economic Behavior and Organization* 49 (September 2002): 19–37.

22  J. D. Orton and K. E. Weick, "Loosely Coupled Systems: A Reconceptualization," *Academy of Management Review* 15 (1990): 203–23.

23  M. Sako and F. Murray, "Modular Strategies in Car and Computers," *Financial Times*, Mastering Strategy Part 11 (December 6, 1999): 4–7.

24  Modularity in organizations is explored in: R. Sanchez and J. T. Mahoney, "Modularity, Flexibility, and Knowledge Management in Product and Organizational Design," *Strategic Management Journal* 17, Winter Special Issue (1996): 63–76; M. A. Schilling, "Toward a General Modular Systems Theory and its Application to Interfirm Product Modularity," *Academy of Management Review* 25 (2000): 312–34; and C. Baldwin and K. Clark, "Managing in an Age of Modularity," *Harvard Business Review* (September-October 1997): 84–93.

25  M. Weber, *Economy and Society: An Outline of Interpretive Sociology* (Berkeley: University of California Press, 1968).

26   T. Burns and G. M. Stalker, *The Management of Innovation* (London: Tavistock Institute, 1961).

27   H. Mintzberg, op. cit.: Chapter 9.

28   "The Contingency Theory of Organizational Design: Challenges and Opportunities" in R. M. Burton, B. Eriksen, D. D. Hakenssen and C. C. Snow, *Organization Design: The Evolving State of the Art* (New York: Springer-Verlag, 2006): 19–42.

29   H. J. Leavitt, "Why Hierarchies Thrive," *Harvard Business Review* (March 2003): 97–102.

30   J. Nickerson and T. Zenger refer to this as "structural modulation": "Being Efficiently Fickle: A Dynamic Theory of Organizational Choice," *Organization Science* 13 (September–October 2002): 547–67.

31   O. E. Williamson, "The Modern Corporation: Origins, Evolution, Attributes," *Journal of Economic Literature* 19 (1981): 1537–68.

32   J. D. Thompson, *Organizations in Action* (New York: McGraw-Hill, 1967). The nature of interdependence in organizational processes is revisited in T. W. Malone, K. Crowston, J. Lee, and B. Pentland, "Tools for Inventing Organizations: Toward a Handbook of Organizational Processes," *Management Science* 45 (March 1999): 489–504.

33   The need for organizations to differentiate management and organization between different functional departments and product units is discussed in P. R. Lawrence and J. W. Lorsch, *Organization and Environment* (Boston: Harvard Business School Press, 1986).

34   C. A. Bartlett and S. Ghoshal, "Matrix Management: Not a Structure, a Frame of Mind," *Harvard Business Review* (July–August 1990): 138–45.

35   "A Survey of the Company: The New Organization," *Economist* (January 21, 2006).

36   R. Daft and A. Lewin, "Where are the theories for the new organizational forms?" *Organization Science* 3 (1993): 1–6.

37   H. Mintzberg, op. cit.: Chapter 12.

38   M. H. Lazerson and G. Lorenzoni, "The Firms that Feed Industrial Districts: A Return to the Italian Source," *Industrial and Corporate Change* 8 (1999): 235–66; G. Lorenzoni and A. Lipparini, "The leveraging of interfirm relationships as a distinctive organizational capability: a longitudinal study," *Strategic Management Journal* 20 (1999): 317–38; A. Grandori, *Interfirm Networks* (London: Routledge, 1999).

39   R. J. DeFilippi and M. B. Arthur, "Paradox in Project-based Enterprise: The Case of Film Making," *California Management Review* 42 (1998): 186–91.

40   G. Lorenzoni and C. Baden-Fuller, "Creating a Strategic Center to Manage a web of Partners," *California Management Review* 37, no. 3 (1995): 146–63.

41   J. H. Dyer and K. Nobeoka, "Creating and managing a high-performance knowledge-sharing network: the Toyota case," *Strategic Management Journal* 21 (2000): 345–67; A. Camuffo, P. Romano, and A. Vinelli, "Back to the Future: Benetton Transforms Its Global Network," *Sloan Management Review* 43 (Fall 2001): 46–52.

42   D. Wheeler, K. McKague, J. Thomson, R. Davies, J. Medalye, and M. Prada, "Sustainable Local Enterprise Networks," *Sloan Management Review* (Fall 2005): 33–40.

43   W. C. Finnie, *Hands-On Strategy: The Guide to Crafting Your Company's Strategy* (New York: John Wiley & Sons, Inc., 1994).

44   *MCI Communications: Planning for the 1990s*, Case No. 9-190-136 (Boston: Harvard Business School, 1990): 1.

45   BP Strategy and Fourth Quarter 2005 Results Presentation, February 7, 2006 (www.bp.com).

46   R. M. Grant, "Strategic Planning in a Turbulent Environment: Evidence from the Oil Majors," *Strategic Management Journal* 24 (2003): 491–518. Similar findings have been reported by the American Productivity and Quality Center among "best practice companies" (*Strategic Planning: Final Report*, Houston: APQC, 1996).

47   A. Alchian and H. Demsetz, "Production, Information Costs, and Economic Organization," *American Economic Review* 62 (1972): 777–97.

48   E. H. Schein, "Organizational Culture," *American Psychologist* 45 (1990): 109–19.

49   T. Burns, *The BBC: Public Institution and Private World* (London: Macmillan, 1977).

50   "LAPD: Storming the Rampart," *Economist* (December 2, 2000): 72.

51   J. Weeks, "On Management: Culture Eats Strategy" *Management Today* (June 2006).

# III

# THE ANALYSIS OF COMPETITIVE ADVANTAGE

# 8 The Nature and Sources of Competitive Advantage

One Saturday afternoon in downtown Chicago, Milton Friedman, the famous free-market economist, was shopping with his wife.

"Look, Milton!" exclaimed Mrs. Friedman. "There's a $20 bill on the sidewalk!"
"Don't be foolish, my dear," replied the Nobel laureate. "If that was a $20 bill, someone would have picked it up by now."

—ECONOMIST'S ANECDOTE OF DOUBTFUL AUTHENTICITY

## OUTLINE

## Introduction and Objectives

In this chapter, we integrate and develop the elements of competitive advantage that we have analyzed in prior chapters. Chapter 1 noted that a firm can earn superior profitability either by locating in an attractive industry or by establishing a competitive advantage over its rivals. Of these two, competitive advantage is the more important. As competition has intensified across almost all industries, very few industry environments can guarantee secure returns; hence, the primary goal of a strategy is to establish a position of competitive advantage for the firm.

Chapters 3 and 5 provided the two primary components of our analysis of competitive advantage. The last part of Chapter 3 analyzed the external sources of competitive advantage: customer requirements and the nature of competition determine the *key success factors* within a market. Chapter 5 analyzed the internal sources of competitive advantage: the potential for the firm's resources and capabilities to establish and sustain competitive advantage.

This chapter looks more deeply at competitive advantage. We focus on the dynamic relationship between competitive advantage and the competitive process. Competition provides the incentive for establishing advantage and is the means by which advantage is eroded. By understanding the characteristics of competition in a market we can identify the opportunities for competitive advantage.

By the time you have completed this chapter you will be able to:

◆ identify the circumstances in which a firm can create a competitive advantage over a rival;

◆ predict the potential for competition to erode competitive advantage through imitation;

◆ recognize how resource conditions create imperfections in the competitive process which offer opportunities for competitive advantage;

◆ distinguish the two primary types of competitive advantage: cost advantage and differentiation advantage;

◆ apply this analysis to assess the potential for a business strategy to establish and sustain competitive advantage given the characteristics of the industry setting.

# The Emergence of Competitive Advantage

To understand how competitive advantage emerges, we must first understand what competitive advantage is. Most of us can recognize competitive advantage when we see it: Wal-Mart has a competitive advantage in discount retailing within the U.S.; Toyota has a competitive advantage in making mass-produced cars; SAP has a competitive advantage in enterprise resource planning (ERP) software. Yet, defining competitive advantage is troublesome. At a basic level we can define it as follows: "When two or more firms compete within the same market, one firm possesses a competitive advantage over its rivals when it earns (or has the potential to earn) a persistently higher rate of profit."

The problem here is that if we identify competitive advantage with superior profitability, why do we need the concept of competitive advantage at all? The key difference is that competitive advantage may not be revealed in higher profitability—a firm may forgo current profit in favor of investment in market share, technology, customer loyalty, or executive perks.[1]

## External Sources of Change

In the long run, competition eliminates differences in profitability between competing firms—hence, competitive advantage is a disequilibrium phenomenon that is a consequence of change. The source of the change may be external or internal to the industry (see Figure 8.1). For an external change to create competitive advantage, the change must have differential effects on companies because of their different resources and capabilities or strategic positioning. For example, during 2000–4, General Motors' return on assets (ROA) was 14.0%; Toyota's was 8.1%. During 2004–7, General Motors' ROA was −5.2%; Toyota's was 7.6%. Over the period oil prices had tripled and demand had shifted away from the advanced industrialized countries. Toyota, with its fuel-efficient product range and superior distribution in emerging market countries, was the advantaged competitor.

**FIGURE 8.1** The emergence of competitive advantage

The extent to which external change creates competitive advantage and disadvantage depends on the magnitude of the change and the extent of firms' strategic differences. The more turbulent an industry's environment, the greater the number of sources of change and the greater the differences in firms' resources and capabilities, the greater the dispersion of profitability within the industry. In the world tobacco industry, the external environment is fairly stable and the leading firms pursue similar strategies with similar resources and capabilities. Hence, competitive advantages, as reflected in interfirm profit differentials, tend to be small. The toy industry, on the other hand, comprises a heterogeneous group of firms that experience unpredictable shifts in consumer preferences and technology. As a result, profitability differences are wide and variable.

## Competitive Advantage from Responsiveness to Change

The competitive advantage that arises from external change also depends on firms' ability to respond to change. Any external change creates opportunities for profit, including opportunities for new business initiatives (what is known as *entrepreneurship*).

Responsiveness involves one of two key capabilities. The first is the ability to anticipate changes in the external environment. Thus, Nokia's ability to maintain market leadership in wireless handsets owes much to its anticipation of the shift in demand from advanced to emerging economies. The second is speed. An unexpected rain shower creates an upsurge in the demand for umbrellas. Those street vendors who are quickest to position themselves outside a busy railroad station will benefit most.

As markets become more turbulent and unpredictable, so speed of response through greater flexibility has become increasingly important as a source of competitive advantage. The first requirement for quick response capability is information. As conventional economic and market forecasting has become less effective, so companies rely increasingly on "early warning systems" through direct relationships with customers, suppliers and even competitors. The second requirement is short cycle times that allow information on emerging market developments to be acted upon speedily. In fashion retailing, fast response to emerging fashion trends is critical to success. Zara, the chain of retail clothing stores owned by the Spanish company Inditex, has pioneered leading-edge fashion clothes for budget-minded young adults through a tightly-integrated vertical structure that cuts the time between a garment's design and retail delivery to under three weeks (against an industry norm of three to six months.[2]

The notion of speed as a source of competitive advantage was pioneered by the Boston Consulting Group with its concept of *time-based competition*.[3] However, it was the advent of the internet, real-time electronic data exchange and wireless communication that facilitated radical improvements in response capability across the business sector as a whole.

## Competitive Advantage from Innovation: "New Game" Strategies

The changes that create competitive advantage may also be generated internally through innovation. Innovation not only creates competitive advantage; it provides a basis for overturning the competitive advantage of other firms—Schumpeter's view of competition as "a gale of creative destruction." Although innovation is typically thought of as new products or processes that embody new technology, a key source of competitive advantage is *strategic innovation*— new approaches to doing business including new business models.

Strategic innovation typically involves creating value for customers from novel products, experiences, or modes of product delivery. Thus, in the retail sector competition is driven by a constant quest for new retail concepts and formats. This may take the form of: big-box stores with greater variety (Toys-R-Us, Home Depot); augmented customer service (Nordstrom) and novel approaches to display and store layout (Sephora in cosmetics).

Strategic innovation may also be based on redesigned processes and novel organizational designs:

- In the U.S. steel industry, Nucor achieved unrivaled productivity and flexibility by combining new process technologies, flat and flexible organizational structures and innovative management systems. Since 1997, it has been the biggest steel producer in the U.S.

- Southwest Airlines' point-to-point, no-frills airline service using a single type of plane and flexible, nonunion employees has made it the only consistently profitable airline in North America and the model for budget airlines throughout the world.

- Nike built its large and successful businesses on a business system that totally reconfigured the shoe industry's traditional value chain—notably by outsourcing manufacturing and concentrating upon design and marketing, and orchestrating a vast global network of producers, logistics providers and retailers.

- Apple Computer's resurgence during 2003-6 was the result of its reinvention of the recorded music business by combining an iconic MP3 player with its iTunes music download service.

How do we go about formulating innovative strategies? Strategic innovations tend to involve pioneering along one or more dimensions of strategy:

- New industries. Some companies launch products which create a whole new market. Xerox created the plain-paper copier industry; Freddie Laker pioneered budget air travel; Craig McCaw and McCaw Communications launched the mass market for wireless telephony. For Kim and Mauborgne, creating new markets is the purest form of blue ocean strategy—the creation of "uncontested market space."[4]

- New customer segments. Creating new customer segments for existing product concepts can also open up vast new market spaces. Apple did not invent the personal computer, but it launched the market for computers in the home. The video cassette recorder was developed by Ampex for use in television studios; Sony and Matsushita's innovation was in designing VCRs for domestic use. The success of the Nintendo Wii video games console has been based upon extending video gaming into new customer segments.

- New sources of competitive advantage. As Kim and Mauborgne acknowledge, most successful blue-ocean strategies do not launch whole new industries but introduce novel approaches to creating customer value. Thus, Dell's strategic innovation was an integrated system for ordering, assembling and distributing PCs, which permitted unprecedented customer choice and speedy fulfillment of orders. Cirque de Soleil has reinvented the circus business as a multimedia entertainment spectacle that meshes technology with highly developed acrobatic and choreographic capabilities.[5] McKinsey & Company show that a key element of strategic innovation—what they call new game strategy—involves reconfiguring the industry value chain in order to change the "rules of the game" within a market.[6] For example, Canon's successful penetration of the plain-paper copier market during 1973–6, was based upon a strategy that was radically different from that of the incumbent, Xerox. While Xerox's dominance was based upon large machines, which used dry toner and were leased to customers, Canon introduced small machines that used liquid toner and were sold outright to customers.[7] In their study of rejuvenation among mature firms, Charles Baden-Fuller and John Stopford observe that strategic innovation often involves combining performance dimensions that were previously viewed as conflicting. For example, Richardson, a U.K. kitchen knife producer, used an innovative design, process innovation, and a lean, entrepreneurial management to supply kitchen knives that combined price competitiveness, durability, sharpness, and responsive customer service.[8] However, according to Gary Hamel, even innovative strategies are subject to imitation. He argues that the most durable forms of competitive advantage are those that derive from management innovation such as Procter & Gamble's invention of modern brand management and Toyota's lean production system.[9]

## Sustaining Competitive Advantage

Once established, competitive advantage is subject to erosion by competition. The speed with which competitive advantage is undermined depends on the ability of competitors to challenge either by imitation or innovation. Imitation is the most direct form of competition; thus, for competitive advantage to be sustained over time, barriers to imitation must exist. Rumelt uses the term *isolating mechanisms* to describe "barriers that limit the *ex post* equilibration of rents among individual firms."[10] The more effective these isolating mechanisms are, the longer competitive advantage can be sustained against the onslaught of rivals. In most industries the erosion of the competitive advantage of industry leaders is a slow process: interfirm profit differentials often persist for period of a decade or more.[11] However, as we discussed in Chapter 4 (see the section on "Dynamic Competition"), the advent of hypercompetition has accelerated the erosion of profit differentials.

To identify the sources of isolating mechanisms, we need to examine the process of competitive imitation. For one firm successfully to imitate the strategy of another, it must meet four conditions:

- *Identification*. The firm must be able to identify that a rival possesses a competitive advantage.
- *Incentive*. Having identified that a rival possesses a competitive advantage (as shown by above-average profitability), the firm must believe that by investing in imitation, it too can earn superior returns.

**FIGURE 8.2** Sustaining competitive advantage: types of isolating mechanism

| REQUIREMENT FOR IMITATION | ISOLATING MECHANISM |
| --- | --- |
| Identification | —*Obscure* superior performance |
| Incentives for imitation | —*Deterrence*: signal aggressive intentions to imitators<br>—*Preemption*: exploit all available investment opportunities |
| Diagnosis | —Rely on multiple sources of competitive advantage to create *"causal ambiguity"* |
| Resource acquisition | —Base competitive advantage on resources and capabilities that are *immobile* and *difficult to replicate* |

- *Diagnosis*. The firm must be able to diagnose the features of its rival's strategy that give rise to the competitive advantage.
- *Resource acquisition*. The firm must be able to acquire through transfer or replication the resources and capabilities necessary for imitating the strategy of the advantaged firm.

Figure 8.2 illustrates these stages and the types of isolating mechanism that exist at each stage.

## Identification: Obscuring Superior Performance

A simple barrier to imitation is to obscure the firm's superior profitability. According to George Stalk of the Boston Consulting Group: "One way to throw competitors off balance is to mask high performance so rivals fail to see your success until it's too late."[12] In the 1948 movie classic *The Treasure of the Sierra Madre*, Humphrey Bogart and his partners went to great lengths to obscure their find from other gold prospectors.[13] The Mongolian gold rush of 2002–3 also featured secretive behavior as miners with positive test results sought to acquire exploration rights on nearby properties.[14]

For firms that dominate a niche market, one of the attractions of remaining a private company is to avoid disclosing financial performance. Few food processors realized just how profitable cat and dog food could be until the U.K. Monopolies Commission revealed that the leading firm, Pedigree Petfoods (a subsidiary of Mars Inc.) earned a return on capital employed of 47%.[15]

Avoiding competition through avoiding disclosure of a firm's profits is much easier for a private than a public company. For Mars Inc., the nondisclosure of financial results assited the firm in protecting the profitably of its pet food and confectionery businesses.

The desire to avoid competition may be so strong as to cause companies to forgo short-run profits. The *theory of limit pricing*, in its simplest form, postulates that a firm in a strong market position sets prices at a level that just fails to attract entrants.[16]

## Deterrence and Preemption

A firm may avoid competition by undermining the incentives for imitation. If a firm can persuade rivals that imitation will be unprofitable, it may be able to avoid competitive challenges. In Chapter 4 we discussed strategies of deterrence and the role of signaling and commitment in supporting them.[17]

As we have seen, reputation is critically important in making threats credible. Brandenburger and Nalebuff argue that in the aspartame market, NutraSweet's aggressive price war against the Holland Sweetener Company deterred other would-be entrants.[18]

A firm can also deter imitation by preemption—occupying existing and potential strategic niches to reduce the range of investment opportunities open to the challenger. Preemption can take many forms:

- Proliferation of product varieties by a market leader can leave new entrants and smaller rivals with few opportunities for establishing a market niche. Between 1950 and 1972, for example, the six leading suppliers of breakfast cereals introduced 80 new brands into the U.S. market.[19]

- Large investments in production capacity ahead of the growth of market demand also preempt market opportunities for rivals. Monsanto's heavy investment in plants for producing NutraSweet ahead of its patent expiration was a clear threat to would-be producers of generic aspartame.

- Patent proliferation can protect technology-based advantage by limiting competitors' technical opportunities. In 1974, Xerox's dominant market position was protected by a wall of over 2000 patents, most of which were not used. When IBM introduced its first copier in 1970, Xerox sued it for infringing 22 of these patents.[20]

The ability to sustain competitive advantage through preemption depends on the presence of two imperfections of the competitive process. First, the market must be small relative to the minimum efficient scale of production, such that only a very small number of competitors is viable. Second, there must be first-mover advantage that gives an incumbent preferential access to information and other resources, putting rivals at a disadvantage.

## Diagnosing Competitive Advantage: "Causal Ambiguity" and "Uncertain Imitability"

If a firm is to imitate the competitive advantage of another, it must understand the basis of its rival's success. In most industries there is a serious identification problem in linking superior performance to the strategic decisions that generate that performance. Consider the remarkable success of Wal-Mart in discount retailing.

For Wal-Mart's struggling competitor, Sears Holdings (owner of the Kmart chain of discount stores), it is easy to point to the differences between Wal-Mart and itself. As one Wal-Mart executive commented: "Retailing is an open book. There are no secrets. Our competitors can walk into our stores and see what we sell, how we sell it, and for how much." The difficult task is to identify which differences are the critical determinants of superior profitability. Is it Wal-Mart's store locations (typically in small towns with little direct competition)? Its tightly integrated supply chain? Its unique management system? The information system that supports Wal-Mart's logistics and decision-making practices? Or is it a culture built on traditional rural American values of thrift and hard work?

The problem for Kmart/Sears and other wannabe Wal-Marts is what Lippman and Rumelt refer to as *causal ambiguity*.[21] The more multidimensional a firm's competitive advantage and the more it is based on complex bundles of organizational capabilities, the more difficult it is for a competitor to diagnose the determinants of success. The outcome of causal ambiguity is *uncertain imitability*: where there is ambiguity associated with the causes of a competitor's success, any attempt to imitate that strategy is subject to uncertain success.

Recent research suggests that the problems of strategy imitation may run even deeper. We observed in Chapter 5 that capabilities are the outcome of complex combinations of resources and that different capabilities interact to confer competitive advantage. However, work in complementarity among firms' activities suggests that these interactions extend across the whole range of management practices.[22] Where these linkages are tight, complexity theory—NK modeling in particular—predicts that within a particular competitive environment a number of "fitness peaks" will appear, each associated with a unique combination of strategic variables.[23] Michael Porter and Nicolaj Siggelkow quote Urban Outfitters as an example of a unique "activity system" (see Strategy Capsule 8.1).[24] If company success is the outcome of a complex configuration of strategy, structure, management systems, personal leadership, and host of business processes, the implication is that imitation may well be impossible.

## STRATEGY CAPSULE 8.1
# Urban Outfitters

During the three years to January 2009, Urban Outfitters Inc., which comprises 130 Urban Outfitters stores (together with Anthropologie and Free People chains), has grown at an average of 20% annually and earned a return on equity of 21%. The company describes itself as

> targeting well-educated, urban-minded, young adults aged 18 to 30 through its

unique merchandise mix and compelling store environment . . . We create a unified environment in our stores that establishes an emotional bond with the customer. Every element of the environment is tailored to the aesthetic preferences of our target customers. Through creative design, much of the existing retail space is modified to incorporate a mosaic of fixtures, finishes *and revealed architectural details. In our stores, merchandise is integrated into a variety of creative vignettes and displays designed to offer our customers an entire look at a distinct lifestyle.*

According to Michael Porter and Nicolaj Siggelkow, Urban Outfitters offers a set of management practices that is both distinctive and highly interdependent. The urban-bohemian-styled product mix, which includes clothing, furnishings and gift items are displayed within bazaar-like stores each of which have a unique design. To encourage frequent customer visits, the layout of each store is changed every two weeks, creating a new shopping experience whenever customers return. Emphasizing community with its customers, it foregoes traditional forms of advertising in favor of blogs and word-of-mouth transmission. Each practice makes little sense on its own, but together they represent a distinctive, integrated strategy. Attempts to imitate Urban Outfitters' competitive advantage would most likely fail because of the difficulty of replicating every aspect of the strategy then integrating them in the right manner.

*Sources:* Urban Outfitters Inc. 10-K Report to January 31, 2009 (Washington: SEC, 2008); M.E. Porter and N. Siggelkow, "Contextuality Within Activity Systems and Sustainable Competitive Advantage," *Academy of Management Perspectives* 22 (May 2008): 34–56.

One of the challenges for the would-be imitator is deciding which management practices are generic best practices and which are "contextual"—complementary with other management practices. For example, if we consider Sears Holdings' deliberation of which of Wal-Mart's management practices to imitate in its Kmart stores, some practices (for example, employees required to smile at customers, point-of-sale data transferred direct into the corporate database) are likely to be generically beneficial. Others, such as Wal-Mart's "everyday low prices" pricing policy, low advertising sales ratio, and hub-and-spoke distribution are likely to be beneficial only when combined with other practices.[25]

## Acquiring Resources and Capabilities

Having diagnosed the sources of an incumbent's competitive advantage, the imitator can mount a competitive challenge only by assembling the resources and capabilities necessary for imitation. As we saw in Chapter 5, a firm can acquire resources and capabilities in two ways: it can buy them or it can build them. The period over which a competitive advantage can be sustained depends critically on the time it takes to acquire and mobilize the resources and capabilities needed to mount a competitive challenge.

There is little to add here to the discussion of transferability and replicability in Chapter 5. The ability to buy resources and capabilities from outside factor markets depends on their transferability between firms. Even if resources are mobile, the market for a resource may be subject to *transaction costs* including search costs, negotiation costs, and contract enforcement costs. Transaction costs are greater for highly differentiated (or "idiosyncratic") resources.[26]

The alternative to buying a resource or capability is to create it through internal investment. As we noted in Chapter 5, where capabilities are based on organizational routines, accumulating the coordination and learning required for their efficient operation can take considerable time.

Businesses that require the integration of a number of complex, team-based routines may take years to reach the standards set by industry leaders. General Motors' attempt to transfer team-based, lean production from its NUMMI joint venture with Toyota at Fremont, California, to the GM Van Nuys plant 400 miles to the south involved complex management problems that remained unsolved two years later.[27]

Conversely, where a competitive advantage does not require the application of complex, firm-specific resources, imitation is often fast. In financial services, most new products are copied quickly by competitors. *Collateralized debt obligations*, the derivative securities that played a central role in the financial crisis of 2008 were developed first by Drexel Burnham Lambert. During the late 1990s, several leading investment banks began issuing CDOs and by 2005 the annual volume of new CDOs exceeded $500 billion.[28]

A key issue for would-be imitators is the extent to which first-mover advantage exists within the market. The idea of first-mover advantage is that the initial occupant of a strategic position or niche gains access to resources and capabilities that a follower cannot match. This is either because the first-mover is able to preempt the best resources, or can use early entry to build superior resources and capabilities.[29] We shall return to the issue of first-mover advantage when we consider competitive advantage in emerging and technology-based industries (Chapter 12).

## Competitive Advantage in Different Market Settings

To identify opportunities for establishing and sustaining competitive advantage requires that we understand the competitive process in the specific market. For competitive advantage to exist, there must be some imperfection of competition. To understand these imperfections in the competitive process, we need to identify the types of resources and capabilities necessary to compete and the circumstances of their availability.

Our initial discussion of the nature of business in Chapter 1 identified two types of value-creating activity: trading and production. Trading involves arbitrage across space (trade) and time (speculation). Production involves the physical transformation of inputs into outputs. These different types of business activity correspond to different market types: trading markets and production markets (see Figure 8.3). We begin with a discussion of a special type of trading market: an efficient market.

### Efficient Markets: The Absence of Competitive Advantage

In Chapter 3, we introduced the concept of perfect competition. Perfect competition exists where there are many buyers and sellers, no product differentiation, no barriers to entry or exit, and free flow of information. In equilibrium, all firms earn the competitive rate of profit, which equals the cost of capital. The closest real-world examples of perfect competition are financial and commodity markets (for example, the markets for securities, foreign exchange and

**FIGURE 8.3** Competitive advantage in different industry settings: trading and production

grain futures). These markets are sometimes described as *efficient*. An *efficient market* is one in which prices reflect all available information. Because prices adjust instantaneously to newly available information, no market trader can expect to earn more than any other. Any differences in *ex post* returns reflect either different levels of risk selected by different traders or purely random factors (luck). Because all available information is reflected in current prices, no trading rules based on historical price data or any other available information can offer excess returns: it is not possible to "beat the market" on any consistent basis. In other words, competitive advantage is absent.

The absence of competitive advantage in efficient markets can be linked to resource availability. If financial markets are efficient, it is because only two types of resource are required to participate—finance and information. If both are equally available to all traders, there is no basis for one to gain competitive advantage over another.

## Competitive Advantage in Trading Markets

For competitive advantage to exist, imperfections (or "inefficiencies") must be introduced into the competitive process. In trading markets, several types of imperfection to the competitive process create opportunities for competitive advantage.

*Imperfect Availability of Information* Financial markets (and most other trading markets) are subject to imperfect availability of information. This provides opportunities for competitive advantage through superior access to information. Trading on the basis of privileged private information is a key source of advantage in markets for traded goods and securities—although such trading is affected by legal restrictions on "insider trading." Insider information creates advantage but the advantage is often short lived: once detected insider trading tends to be imitated by other market participants.

*Transaction Costs*   If markets are efficient except for the presence of transaction costs, then competitive advantage accrues to the traders with the lowest transaction costs. In stock markets, low transaction costs are attained by traders who economize on research and market analysis and achieve efficient portfolio diversification. John Bogle estimated that actively managed U.S. mutual funds underperformed the market index by about 2.5% annually—roughly equal to the funds' costs of transactions and administration.[30] Bogle's Vanguard S&P 500 Index fund with transaction and operating costs of 0.5% annually has outperformed 90% of U.S. equity mutual funds.

*Systematic Behavioral Trends*   If the current prices in a market fully reflect all available information, then price movements are caused by the arrival of new information and follow a random walk.[31] If, however, other factors influence price movements, there is scope for a strategy that uses insight into how prices really do move. Some stock market anomalies are well documented, notably the "small firm effect," the "January effect," and "weekend effects." More generally, there is evidence that prices in financial markets follow systematic patterns that result from "market psychology", allowing trends and turning points to be deduced from past data. Chart analysis uses patterns of price movements—such as "support and resistance levels," "head and shoulders," "double tops," "flags," and "candlesticks"—as prediction tools. Despite mixed evidence on the success of chart analysis in financial markets,[32] systematic behavior among market participants offers opportunity for competitive advantage by traders with superior skill in diagnosing such behavior.

*Overshooting*   One well-documented behavioral aberration is the propensity towards "herd behavior" where imitative trading and converging expectations cause prices to overshoot.[33] The implication is that competitive advantage can be gained, in the short term, by following the herd—"momentum trading." In the long run, overshooting is corrected by an opposite corrective movement, offering opportunity for a *contrarian* strategy. The world's richest man, Warren Buffett, is a prominent contrarian who is "fearful when others are greedy, and greedy when others are fearful."

## Competitive Advantage in Production Markets

The transitory nature of competitive advantage in trading markets is a result of the characteristics of the resources required to compete: finance and information. Finance is a relatively homogeneous resource that is widely available. Information, although highly differentiated, is transferable easily and at very low cost; hence, the competitive advantage it offers tends to be fleeting.

Production markets are quite different. Production activities require complex combinations of resources and capabilities and these resources and capabilities are highly differentiated. The result, as we have noted, is that each producer possesses a unique combination of resources and capabilities. The greater the heterogeneity of firms' endowments of resources and capabilities, the greater the potential for competitive advantage. In the European electricity generating industry, the growing diversity of players—utilities (GdF, ENEL, Iberdrola), oil and gas majors (Shell, Eni), independent power producers (AES, Powergen), and wind power generators—has expanded opportunities for competitive advantage and widened the profit differentials between them.

Differences in resource endowments among firms also influence the erosion of competitive advantage. Where firms possess very similar bundles of resources and capabilities, imitation of the competitive advantage of the incumbent firm is most likely. Where resource bundles are highly differentiated, competition is more likely to be through distinctive strategies that substitute the incumbent's competitive advantage.[34] For example:

- In video game consoles, Nintendo, with a very different resource base from Sony and Microsoft, gained market leadership with a distinctive strategy for its *Wii* console.
- In the U.S. airline industry, newcomer Virgin America has drawn upon its distinctive resources and capabilities to position itself differently from either the "legacy airlines" (American, United) and the low-cost carriers (Southwest, AirTran).

Since substitute competition can come from many directions its deterrence requires building defenses on multiple fronts—including commitments to key stakeholders.[35]

## Types of Competitive Advantage: Cost and Differentiation

A firm can achieve a higher rate of profit (or potential profit) over a rival in one of two ways: either it can supply an identical product or service at a lower cost, or it can supply a product or service that is differentiated in such a way that the customer is willing to pay a price premium that exceeds the additional cost of the differentiation. In the former case, the firm possesses a cost advantage; in the latter, a differentiation advantage. In pursuing cost advantage, the goal of the firm is to become the cost leader in its industry or industry segment. Cost leadership requires that the firm "must find and exploit all sources of cost advantage . . . [and] . . . sell a standard, no-frills product."[36] Differentiation by a firm from its competitors is achieved "when it provides something unique that is valuable to buyers beyond simply offering a low price."[37] Figure 8.4 illustrates these two types of advantage.

The two sources of competitive advantage define two fundamentally different approaches to business strategy. A firm that is competing on low cost is distinguishable from a firm that competes through differentiation in terms of market positioning, resources and capabilities, and organizational characteristics. Table 8.1 outlines some of the principal features of cost and differentiation strategies.

**FIGURE 8.4** Sources of competitive advantage

**TABLE 8.1** Features of cost leadership and differentiation strategies

| Generic strategy | Key strategy elements | Resource and organizational requirements |
|---|---|---|
| Cost leadership | Scale-efficient plants<br>Design for manufacture<br>Control of overheads and R&D<br>Process innovation<br>Outsourcing (especially overseas)<br>Avoidance of marginal customer accounts | Access to capital<br>Process engineering skills<br>Frequent reports<br>Tight cost control<br>Specialization of jobs and functions<br>Incentives linked to quantitative targets |
| Differentiation | Emphasis on branding advertising, design, service, quality, and new product development | Marketing abilities<br>Product engineering skills<br>Cross-functional coordination<br>Creativity<br>Research capability<br>Incentives linked to qualitative performance targets |

By combining the two types of competitive advantage with the firm's choice of scope—broad market versus narrow segment—Michael Porter has defined three generic strategies: cost leadership, differentiation, and focus (see Figure 8.5). Porter views cost leadership and differentiation as mutually exclusive strategies. A firm that attempts to pursue both is "stuck in the middle":

The firm stuck in the middle is almost guaranteed low profitability. It either loses the high-volume customers who demand low prices or must bid away its profits to get this business from the low-cost firms. Yet it also loses high-margin business—the cream—to the firms who are focused on high-margin targets or have achieved differentiation overall. The firm that is stuck in the middle also probably suffers from a blurred corporate culture and a conflicting set of organizational arrangements and motivation system.[38]

**FIGURE 8.5** Porter's generic strategies

In practice, few firms are faced with such stark alternatives. Differentiation is not simply an issue of "to differentiate or not to differentiate." All firms must make decisions as to which customer requirements to focus on and where to position their product or service in the market. A cost leadership strategy typically implies a narrow-line, limited-feature, standardized offering. However, such a positioning does not necessarily imply that the product or service is an undifferentiated commodity. In the case of IKEA furniture and Southwest Airlines, a low-price, no-frills offering is also associated with clear market positioning and a unique brand image. The VW Beetle shows that a low-cost, utilitarian, mass-market product can achieve cult status. At the same time, firms that pursue differentiation strategies cannot be oblivious to cost.

In most industries, market leadership is held by a firm that maximizes customer appeal by reconciling effective differentiation with low cost—Toyota in cars, McDonald's in fast food, Nike in athletic shoes. In many industries, the cost leader is not the market leader but is a smaller competitor with minimal overheads, nonunion labor and cheaply acquired assets. In oil refining, the cost leaders tend to be independent refining companies rather than integrated giants such as ExxonMobil or Shell. In car rental, the cost leader is more likely to be Rent-A-Wreck (a division of Bundy American Corporation) rather than Hertz or Avis. Simultaneously pursuing differentiation, cost efficiency and innovation was a key element in the global success of Japanese companies in cars, motorcycles, consumer electronics and musical instruments. Reconciling different performance dimensions has been facilitated by new management techniques. For example, total quality management has refuted the perceived tradeoff between quality and cost.

# Summary

Making money in business requires establishing and sustaining competitive advantage. Both these conditions for profitability demand profound insight into the nature and process of competition within a market. Competitive advantage depends critically on the presence of some imperfection in the competitive process—under perfect competition, profits are transitory. Our analysis of the imperfections of the competitive process has drawn us back to the resources and capabilities that are required to compete in different markets and to pursue different strategies. Sustaining competitive advantage depends on the existence of *isolating mechanisms*: barriers to rivals' imitation of successful strategies. The greater the difficulty that rivals face in accessing the resources and capabilities needed to imitate or substitute the competitive advantage of the incumbent firm, the greater the sustainability of that firm's competitive advantage. Hence, one outcome of our analysis is to reinforce the argument made in Chapter 5: the characteristics of a firm's resources and capability are fundamental to its strategy and its performance in decision making and long-term success.

In the next two chapters, we analyze the two primary dimensions of competitive advantage: cost advantage and differentiation advantage. In both of these areas we emphasize the importance of a deep understanding of both the firm and its industry environment. To this end, it is useful to disaggregate the firm into a series of separate but interlinked activities. A useful and versatile framework for this purpose is the value chain, which is an insightful tool for understanding the sources of competitive advantage in an industry, for assessing the competitive position of a particular firm, and for suggesting opportunities to enhance a firm's competitiveness.

# Self-Study Questions

1  Figure 8.1 implies that stable industries, where firms have similar resources and capabilities, offer less opportunity for competitive advantage than industries where change is rapid and firms are heterogeneous. Think of an example of each of these two types of industry. Is there any evidence that interfirm profit differences are wider in the more dynamic, heterogeneous industry than in the more stable, homogeneous industry?

2  Apple has been successful in dominating the market for both MP3 players with its iPod and for music downloads with its iTunes service. Can Apple sustain its leadership in these markets? How?

3  Illy, the Italian-based supplier of quality coffee and coffee-making equipment, is launching an international chain of gourmet coffee shops. What advice would you offer Illy for how it can best build competitive advantage in the face of Starbucks' market leadership?

4  Do you believe that some mutual funds ("unit trusts" in British parlance) can deliver consistently superior returns (once adjusted for risk)? If so, what is the basis for such superior performance and what can fund managers do to achieve superior performance?

5  Target (the U.S. discount retailer), H&M (the Swedish fashion clothing chain) and Primark (the U.K. discount clothing chain) have pioneered "cheap chic"—combining discount store prices with fashion appeal. What are the principal challenges of designing and implementing a "cheap chic" strategy? Design a "cheap chic" strategy for a company entering another market, e.g. restaurants, sports shoes, cosmetics, or office furniture.

## Notes

1  Richard Rumelt argues that competitive advantage lacks a clear and consistent definition ("What in the World is Competitive Advantage," Policy Working Paper 2003-105, Anderson School, UCLA, August, 2003).

2  K. Ferdows, M. A. Lewis, and J. Machuca, "Rapid-Fire Fulfillment," *Harvard Business Review* (November 2004): 104–10.

3  G. Stalk Jr., "Time—The Next Source of Competitive Advantage," *Harvard Business Review* (July–August, 1988): 41–51.

4  C. Kim and R. Mauborgne, "Blue Ocean Strategy," *Harvard Business Review* (October 2004).

5  Ibid.

6  R. Buaron, "New Game Strategies," *McKinsey Quarterly Anthology* (2000): 34–6.

7  "Canon Inc.: Worldwide Copier Strategy," Harvard Business School Case 9-384-151 (1988).

8  C. Baden-Fuller and J. M. Stopford, *Rejuvenating the Mature Business* (London and New York: Routledge, 1992).

9  G. Hamel, "The Why, What, and How of Management Innovation," *Harvard Business Review* (February 2006).

10  R. P. Rumelt, "Toward a Strategic Theory of the Firm," in R. Lamb (ed.), *Competitive Strategic Management* (Englewood Cliffs, NJ: Prentice Hall, 1984): 556–70.

11  See J. Cubbin and P. Geroski, "The Convergence of Profits in the Long Run: Interfirm and Interindustry Comparisons," *Journal of Industrial Economics* 35 (1987): 427–42; R. Jacobsen, "The Persistence of Abnormal Returns," *Strategic Management Journal* 9 (1988): 415–30; and R. R. Wiggins and T. W. Ruefli, "Schumpeter's Ghost: Is Hypercompetition Making the Best of Times Shorter?" *Strategic Management Journal* 26 (2005): 887–911.

12  G. Stalk, "Curveball: Strategies to Fool the Competition," *Harvard Business Review* (September 2006): 114–22.

13  The film was based on the book, by B. Traven, *The Treasure of the Sierra Madre* (New York: Knopf, 1947).

14  "The Great Mongolian Gold Rush," *Fortune Investors Guide 2004* (December, 2003).

15  Monopolies and Mergers Commission, *Cat and Dog Foods* (London: Her Majesty's Stationery Office, 1977).

16  S. Martin, *Advanced Industrial Economics*, 2nd edn. (Oxford: Blackwell Publishers, 2001): Chapter 8.

17  T. C. Schelling, *The Strategy of Conflict*, 2nd edn. (Cambridge: Harvard University Press, 1980): 35–41.

18  A. Brandenburger and B. Nalebuff, *Co-opetition* (New York: Doubleday, 1996): 72–80.

19  R. Schmalensee, "Entry Deterrence in the Ready-to-Eat Breakfast Cereal Industry," *Bell Journal of Economics* 9 (1978): 305–27.

20  Monopolies and Mergers Commission, *Indirect Electrostatic Reprographic Equipment* (London: Her Majesty's Stationery Office, 1976): 37, 56.

21  S. A. Lippman and R. P. Rumelt, "Uncertain Imitability: An Analysis of Interfirm Differences in Efficiency under Competition," *Bell Journal of Economics* 13 (1982): 418–38. See also: R. Reed and R. DeFillippi, "Causal Ambiguity, Barriers to Imitation, and Sustainable Competitive Advantage," *Academy of Management Review* 15 (1990): 88–102.

22  P. R. Milgrom and J. Roberts, "Complementarities and Fit: Strategy, Structure and Organizational Change in Manufacturing," *Journal of Accounting and Economics* 19 (1995): 179–208.

23  J. W. Rivkin, "Imitation of Complex Strategies," *Management Science* 46 (2000): 824–44.

24  M. E. Porter and N. Siggelkow, "Contextuality Within Activity Systems and Sustainable Competitive Advantage," *Academy of Management Perspectives* 22 (May 2008): 34–56.

25  Ibid.

26  See O. E. Williamson, "Transaction Cost Economics: The Governance of Contractual Relations," *Journal of Law and Economics* 19 (1979): 153–6.

27  C. Brown and M. Reich, "When Does Union-Management Cooperation Work? A Look at NUMMI and GM-Van Nuys," *California Management Review* 31 (Summer 1989): 26–44.

28  "CDOs May Bring Subprime-like Bust for LBOs, Junk Debt," www.bloomberg.com (March 13, 2007).

29  For an analysis of first-mover advantage, see M. Lieberman and D. Montgomery, "First-Mover Advantages," *Strategic Management Journal* 9 (1988): 41–58; M. Lieberman and D. Montgomery, "First-Mover (Dis)Advantages: Retrospective and Link with the Resource-based View," *Strategic Management Journal* 19 (1998): 1111–25.

30  J. C. Bogle, *Common Sense on Mutual Funds* (Chichester: John Wiley & Sons, Ltd, 2000).

31  E. F. Fama, "Efficient Capital Markets: A Review of Theory and Empirical Work," *Journal of Business* 35 (1970): 383–417.

32  A. W. Lo, H. Mamaysty and J. Wang, "Foundations of Technical Analysis," *Journal of Finance* 55 (2000): 1705–70.

33  W. De Bondt and R. Thaler, "Does the Stock Market Overreact?" *Journal of Finance* 42 (1985): 793–805.

34  J. B. Barney, "Firm Resources and Sustained Competitive Advantage," *Journal of Management* 17 (1991): 99–120.

35  S. K. McEvily, S. Das and K. McCabe, "Avoiding Competence Substitution through Knowledge Sharing," *Academy of Management Review* 25 (2000): 294–311.

36  M. E. Porter, *Competitive Advantage* (New York: Free Press, 1985): 13.

37  Ibid.: 120.

38  M. E. Porter, *Competitive Strategy* (New York: Free Press, 1980): 42.

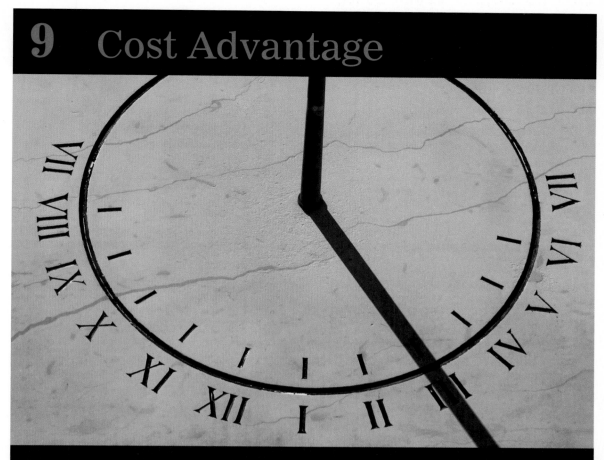

*SEARS MOTOR BUGGY: $395*

*For car complete with rubber tires, Timken roller bearing axles, top, storm front, three oil-burning lamps, horn, and one gallon of lubricating oil. Nothing to buy but gasoline.*

*. . . We found there was a maker of automobile frames that was making 75 percent of all the frames used in automobile construction in the United States. We found on account of the volume of business that this concern could make frames cheaper for automobile manufacturers than the manufacturers could make them themselves. We went to this frame maker and asked him to make frames for the Sears Motor Buggy and then to name us prices for those frames in large quantities. And so on throughout the whole construction of the Sears Motor Buggy. You will find every piece and every part has been given the most careful study; you will find that the Sears Motor Buggy is made of the best possible material; it is constructed to take the place of the top buggy; it is built in our own factory, under the direct supervision of our own expert, a man who has had fifteen years of automobile experience, a man who has for the past three years worked with us to develop exactly the right car for the people at a price within the reach of all.*

—EXTRACT FROM AN ADVERTISEMENT IN THE SEARS ROEBUCK & CO. CATALOG, 1909: 1150

# Introduction and Objectives

In the last chapter, we identified cost and differentiation as the two principal forms of competitive advantage. Here we consider cost advantage. For some industries, particularly those that supply commodity products, cost advantage is the predominant basis for competitive advantage. But even where competition focuses on product differentiation, intensifying competition means that cost efficiency is a prerequisite for profitability. During recessionary periods the pressure for cost efficiency becomes intense. During 2008-9, lack of cost effectiveness led to the demise of many thousands of firms.

By the time you have completed this chapter, you will be able to:

- Identify the determinants of relative cost within the industry or activity ("cost drivers").

- Assess a firm's cost position relative to its competitors and identify the factors responsible for cost differentials.

- Recommend cost-reduction measures.

The analysis in this chapter is oriented around these objectives. In pursuing these objectives, we shall examine techniques for:

- Identifying the primary sources of cost advantage in an industry.

- Appraising the cost position of a firm within its industry by disaggregating the firm into its separate activities.

- Using the analysis of costs and relative cost position as a basis for recommending strategies for enhancing cost competitiveness.

## Strategy and Cost Advantage

Historically, strategic management has emphasized cost advantage as the primary basis for competitive advantage in an industry. This focus on cost reflected the traditional emphasis by economists on price as the principal medium of competition—price competitiveness requires cost efficiency. It also reflected the strategy preoccupations of large industrial corporations. For much of the twentieth century, the development of large corporations was dominated by the quest for economies of scale and scope through investments in mass production and mass distribution. During the 1970s and 1980s, the analysis of cost advantage became focused around the *experience curve*—the relationship between unit cost and cumulative output identified by the Boston Consulting Group (see Strategy Capsule 9.1).

### STRATEGY CAPSULE 9.1

# BCG and the Experience Curve

The experience curve has its basis in the systematic reduction in the time taken to build airplanes and Liberty ships during the Second World War.[1] In a series of studies, ranging from bottle caps and refrigerators to long-distance calls and insurance policies, the Boston Consulting Group (BCG) observed a remarkable regularity in the reductions in unit costs with increased cumulative output, which it called the "Law of Experience": *the unit cost of value added to a standard product declines by a constant percentage (typically between 20 and 30%) each time cumulative output doubles.* ("Unit cost of value added" is total cost per unit of production less the cost per unit of production of bought-in components and materials.) The figure below shows examples of experience curves.

The relationship between unit cost and production volume may be expressed as follows:

$$C_n = C_1 \cdot n^{-a}$$

where   $C_1$ is the cost of the first unit of production
$C_n$ is the cost of the $n$th unit of production

$n$ is the cumulative volume of production
$a$ is the elasticity of cost with regard to output.

The experience curve has important implications for strategy. If a firm can expand its output faster than its competitors, it can move down the experience curve more rapidly and open up a widening cost differential. The inference drawn by BCG was that a firm's primary strategic goal should be maximizing market share.[2]

To achieve this, firms should price not on the basis of current costs, but on the basis of anticipated costs—using *penetration pricing* rather than *full-cost pricing*. In the British motorcycle market, BCG observed that local manufacturers adopted cost-plus pricing, whereas Honda priced to meet market share objectives.[3] The quest for experience-based economies also points to the advantages of increasing volume by broadening product range and expanding internationally.[4]

The quest for market share was supported by numerous studies confirming a positive relationship between profitability and market share.[5] However, *association* does not imply *causation*—it seems likely that market share and profitability are both outcomes of some other source of competitive advantage— product innovation or superior marketing.[6]

The experience curve lost favor as a strategy tool, first, because it combines several sources of cost reduction (learning, scale, process innovation) that can be better understood individually; second, because of the realization that cost reductions from experience are not automatic—they must be managed.

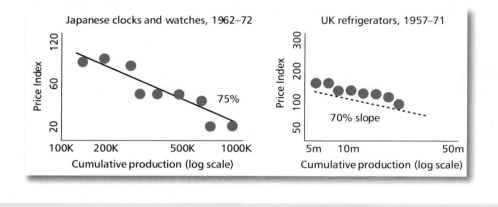

In recent decades, companies have been forced to think more broadly and radically about cost efficiency. The most dramatic shifts in cost advantage have been the result of international differences in labor costs (e.g. the declining competitiveness of Western manufactures to Chinese firms manufacturing), exchange rate shifts (e.g. the rising costs of Euro zone and Japanese firms during 2007–9) and new technologies (e.g. internet telephony). The response has been novel approaches to cost reduction involving outsourcing, process re-engineering and organizational delayering.

Cost analysis requires taking account of multiple factors, the importance of each depending on industry context. In the clothing industry, wage rates are the critical factor; in petrochemicals, it is feedstock costs; in semiconductors, it is yield rates. Some industries offer alternative routes to low cost—in the steel industry, Severstal of Russia with its low input costs and Nucor of the U.S. with its advanced ninimill technologies are both low-cost producers. Our approach to analyzing cost advantage will be to identify the basic determinants of a firm's cost position within its particular industry.

# The Sources of Cost Advantage

There are seven principal determinants of a firm's unit costs (cost per unit of output) relative to its competitors; we refer to these as *cost drivers* (see Figure 9.1).

The relative importance of these different cost drivers varies across industries, across firms within an industry and across the different activities within a firm. By examining each of these different cost drivers in relation to a particular firm we can do the following:

- Analyze a firm's cost position relative to its competitors and diagnose the sources of inefficiency.
- Make recommendations as to how a firm can improve its cost efficiency.

Let's examine the nature and the role of each of these cost drivers.

**FIGURE 9.1**  The drivers of cost advantage

**FIGURE 9.2** The long-run average cost curve for a plant

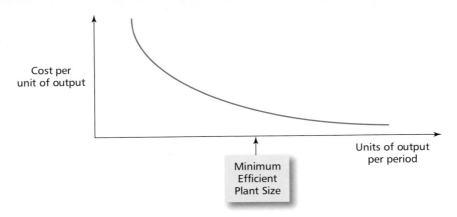

## Economies of Scale

The predominance of large corporations in most manufacturing and service industries is a consequence of economies of scale. Economies of scale exist wherever proportionate increases in the amounts of inputs employed in a production process result in lower unit costs. Economies of scale have been conventionally associated with manufacturing. Figure 9.2 shows a typical relationship between unit cost and plant capacity. The point at which most scale economies are exploited is the Minimum Efficient Plant Size (MEPS). Scale economies are also important in nonmanufacturing operations such as purchasing, R&D, distribution, and advertising.

Scale economies arise from three principal sources:

- *Technical input-output relationships*. In many activities, increases in output do not require proportionate increases in input. A 10 000-barrel oil storage tank does not cost five times as much as a 2000-barrel tank. Similar volume-related economies exist in ships, trucks, and steel and petrochemical plants.

- *Indivisibilities*. Many resources and activities are "lumpy"—they are unavailable in small sizes. Hence, they offer economies of scale as firms are able to spread the costs of these items over larger volumes of output. A national TV advertising campaign or a research program into fuel cell technology will cost much the same whether it is being undertaken by Toyota or Mazda. However, the costs as a percentage of sales will be much lower for Toyota because it has almost eight times the sales of Mazda.

- *Specialization*. Increased scale permits greater task specialization that is manifest in greater *division of labor*. Mass production—whether in Adam Smith's pin factory or Henry Ford's auto plants (see Chapter 7)—involves breaking down the production process into separate tasks performed by specialized workers using specialized equipment. Specialization promotes learning, avoids time loss from switching activities, and assists mechanization and automation. Similar economies are important in knowledge-intensive industries such as investment banking, management consulting, and design engineering, where large firms are able to offer specialized expertise across a broad range of knowhow.

**FIGURE 9.3** Economies of scale in advertising: U.S. soft drinks

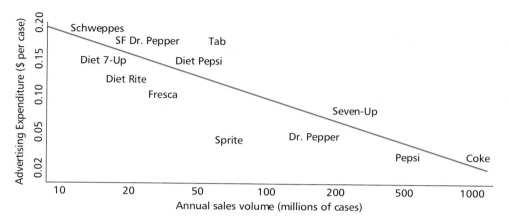

*Scale Economies and Industry Concentration* Scale economies are a key determinant of an industry's level of concentration (the proportion of industry output accounted for by the largest firms). However, the critical scale advantages of large companies are seldom in production. In packaged consumer goods—cigarettes, household detergents, beer, and soft drinks—economies of scale in marketing are the key factor causing world markets to be dominated by a few giant companies. Advertising is a key indivisibility: a 60-second TV commercial can cost over $5 million to produce but the real cost is in showing it—Sony's launch of its PlayStation 3 incurred advertising costs of over half a billion dollars. Figure 9.3 shows the relationship between sales volume and average advertising costs for different brands of soft drinks.

Consolidation in the world car industry has been driven by the escalating huge costs associated with new model development. Most small and medium-sized auto companies have been acquired by larger rivals because they lacked the volume necessary to amortize new model development costs. Volkswagen acquired Skoda, Seat and Rolls-Royce; Ford acquired Jaguar, Mazda, Land Rover, Aston Martin and Volvo (before subsequently divesting many of them).[7] Table 9.1 gives examples of some of the world's most costly new product development programs.

The huge development costs of new aircraft models mean that global market leadership within a product segment is critical to profitability. The Boeing 747 was a hugely profitable project because 1415 were built. Concorde, with only 20 planes built, was a financial disaster.

*Limits to Scale Economies* Despite the prevalence of scale economies, small and medium-sized companies continue to survive and prosper in competition with much bigger rivals. In the automobile industry, the most profitable companies in recent years have been medium-sized producers such as Peugeot, Renault, and BMW. In U.S. and European banking, there is no evidence that big players outperform smaller banks either on profitability or costs.[8] How do small and medium-sized firms offset the disadvantages of small scale? First, by exploiting the

**TABLE 9.1** Some of the world's most expensive new product development projects

| Product | Lead company | Estimated development cost | Launch date |
|---|---|---|---|
| F-35 Lightening II joint strike fighter | Lockheed Martin | $40 billion[a] | 2012[b] |
| B-2 Spirit "stealth bomber" | Northrup Grumman | $23 billion | December 1993[b] |
| A380 "super-jumbo" | Airbus Industrie | $19 billion | October 2007[b] |
| 787 Dreamliner | Boeing | $16–18 billion | 3rd Quarter 2010[b] |
| Windows Vista | Microsoft | $7 billion | January 2007 |
| Playstation 3 | Sony | $7 billion[c] | November 2006 |
| Iridium wireless satellite communication system | Motorola/Iridium Satellite LLC | $6 billion | July 1999 |
| Ford Contour/Modeo | Ford Motor Company | $6 billion[d] | October 1992 |

**Notes:**
[a] Total program cost estimated at $300 billion; [b] Date of entering service; [c] Including development of Blu-ray DVD; [d] Including costs of tooling.

flexibility advantages of smaller size; second, by avoiding the difficulties of motivation and coordination that accompanies large scale.[9]

## Economies of Learning

The experience curve is based primarily on learning-by-doing on the part of individuals and organizations. Repetition develops both individual skills and organizational routines. In 1943 it took 40 000 labor-hours to build a B-24 Liberator bomber. By 1945 it took only 8000 hours.[10] The more complex a process or product, the greater the potential for learning. Learning curves are exceptionally steep in semiconductor fabrication. When IBM introduced 0.18 micron, copper-interconnector chips, yields increased from zero to over 50% within the first two months. LCD flat screens are notoriously difficult to manufacture—a single defective chip may render an entire screen useless. The dominant position of Sharp and Samsung in flat screens is primarily a result of volume-based learning resulting in exceptionally high yields.[11] Learning occurs both at the individual level through improvements in dexterity and problem solving, and at the group level through the development and refinement of organizational routines.[12]

## Process Technology and Process Design

For most goods and services, alternative process technologies exist. A process is technically superior to another when, for each unit of output, it uses less of one input without using more of any other input. Where a production method uses more of some inputs but less of others, then cost efficiency depends on the relative prices of the inputs. Hence, in the assembly of desktop PCs, Dell's Palmer North 2 plant in Austin, Texas is highly automated, while its two plants in Xiamen, China (where wages are about 90% lower) are much more labor intensive.

New process technology may radically reduce costs. Pilkington's float glass process gave it (and its licensees) an unassailable cost advantage in producing flat glass. Ford's moving assembly line reduced the time taken to assemble a Model T from 106 hours to six hours between 1912 and 1914.

When process innovation is embodied in new capital equipment, diffusion is likely to be rapid. However, the full benefits of new processes typically require system-wide changes in job design, employee incentives, product design, organizational structure and management controls.[13] Between 1979 and 1986, General Motors spent $40 billion on new process technology with the goal of becoming the world's most efficient manufacturer of automobiles. Yet, in the absence of fundamental changes in organization and management, the productivity gains were meager. After a tour of Cadillac's state-of-the-art Hamtramck plant in Detroit, Toyota chairman Eiji Toyoda told a colleague, "It would have been embarrassing to comment on it."[14] By contrast, the cost leadership established by Toyota, Nucor, Dell Computer, McDonald's, and Wal-Mart is the result of matching their structures, decision processes and human resource management to the requirements of their process technologies.

Indeed, the greatest productivity gains from process innovation are typically the result of organizational improvements rather than technological innovation and new hardware. The central components of Toyota's system of lean production are just-in-time scheduling, total quality management, continuous improvement (*kaisan*), teamworking, job flexibility, and supplier partnerships rather than robotics or IT.[15] Harley-Davidson's gains in productivity during the 1984-94 resulted from reorganizing around team-based production and commitment to continuous improvement, but with limited investment in advanced automation.[16]

*Business Process Re-engineering* During the 1990s, recognition that the redesign of operational processes could achieve substantial efficiency gains stimulated a surge of interest in a new management tool called *business process re-engineering* (BPR). "Re-engineering gurus" Michael Hammer and James Champy defined BPR as: "the fundamental rethinking and radical redesign of business processes to achieve dramatic improvements in critical contemporary measures of performance, such as cost, quality, service, and speed."[17]

Business process re-engineering recognizes that operational and commercial processes involve evolve over time without consistent direction or systematic appraisal of their efficiency or effectiveness. With information technology, the temptation is to automate existing processes—"paving over cowpaths," as Michael Hammer calls it.[18] The key is to detach from the way in which a process is currently organized and to begin with the question: "If we were starting afresh, how would we design this process?" Hammer and Champy point to the existence of a set of "commonalities, recurring themes, or characteristics" that can guide BPR. These include:

- Combining several jobs into one.
- Allowing workers to make decisions.
- Performing the steps of a process in a natural order.
- Recognizing that processes have multiple versions and designing processes to take account of different situations.

- Performing processes where it makes the most sense, for example, if the accounting department needs pencils, it is probably cheaper for such a small order to be purchased directly from the office equipment store along the block than to be ordered via the firm's purchasing department.
- Reducing checks and controls to the point where they make economic sense.
- Minimizing reconciliation.
- Appointing a case manager to provide a single point of contact at the interface between processes.
- Reconciling centralization with decentralization in process design—for example, via a shared database, decentralized decisions can be made while permitting overall coordination simply through information sharing.

Despite major gains in efficiency, quality and speed from BPR projects (see Strategy Capsule 9.2), there are also many disappointing outcomes. One of the major realizations to emerge from BPR is that most business processes are complex. To redesign a process one must first understand it. Process mapping exercises reveal that even seemingly simple business processes, such as the procurement of office supplies, involve complex and sophisticated systems of interactions among multiple organizational members. In Chapter 5 we saw that a process is often embodied within an organizational routine that is not fully comprehended by any single person. To this extent, Hammer and Champy's recommendation to "obliterate" existing processes and start with a "clean sheet of paper" runs the risk of destroying organizational capabilities that have been nurtured over a long period of time.

While BPR may be a "faded fad," it is still true that businesses processes are the fundamental productive activities of the firm and their design and development is critical to cost efficiency. Over the past decade, BPR has evolved into *business process management*, where the emphasis has shifted form workflow management to the broader application of information technology (web-based applications in particular) to the redesign and enhancement of organizational processes.[19]

IBM Credit offers credit to IBM customers purchasing IBM hardware and software. Under the old system, five stages were involved: first, an IBM salesperson telephoned a request for financing, which was logged on a piece of paper; second, the request was sent to the Credit Department where it was logged onto a computer and the customer's creditworthiness was checked; third, the request and credit check were sent to the Business Practices Department where a loan covenant was drawn up; fourth, the paperwork was passed to a pricer who determined the interest rate; finally, the clerical group prepared a quote letter that was sent to the salesperson.

The process took an average of six days, resulting in many lost sales. After many efforts to improve the process, two managers undertook an experiment. They took a financing request and walked it around through all five steps. The process took 90 minutes!

On this basis, the credit approval process was redesigned by replacing the specialists (credit checkers, pricers, and so on) with generalists who undertook all five processes. Only where the request was nonstandard or unusually complex were specialists called in. The basic problem was that the system had been designed for the most complex credit requests that IBM received, whereas in the vast majority of cases no specialist judgment was called for—simply looking up credit ratings, plugging numbers into standard formulae, and so on.

The result was that credit requests were processed in four hours compared to six days, total employees were reduced, while the total number of deals increased one hundred times.

*Source:* Adapted from M. Hammer and J. Champy, *Reengineering the Corporation: A Manifesto for Business Revolution* (New York: HarperBusiness, 1993): 36–9.

## Product Design

Design-for-manufacture—designing products for ease of production rather than simply for functionality and esthetics—can offer substantial cost savings, especially when linked to the introduction of new process technology.

- Volkswagen cut product development and component costs by redesigning its 30 different models around just four separate platforms. The VW Beetle, Audi TT, Golf, and Audi A3, together with several Seat and Skoda models, all share a single platform.

- The IBM "Proprinter," one of the most successful computer printers of the 1980s, owed its low costs (and reliability) to an innovative design that:
  - reduced the number of parts from 150, found in the typical PC printer, to 60;
  - designed the printer in layers so that robots could build it from the bottom up;
  - eliminated all screws, springs, and other fasteners that required human insertion and adjustment and replaced them with molded plastic components that clipped together.[20]

- Service offerings too can be designed for ease and efficiency of production. Motel 6, cost leader in U.S. budget motels, carefully designs its product to keep operating costs low. Its motels occupy low-cost, out-of-town locations, it uses standard motel designs, it avoids facilities such as pools and restaurants and it designs rooms to facilitate easy cleaning and low maintenance. However, efficiency in service design is compromised by the tendency for customers to "interfere" in service delivery. This requires a clear strategy to manage variability either through accommodation or restriction.[21]

## Capacity Utilization

Over the short and medium term, plant capacity is more-or-less fixed and variations in output cause capacity utilization to rise or fall. Underutilization raises unit costs because fixed costs must be spread over fewer units of production. In businesses where virtually all costs are fixed (for example, airlines, theme parks), profitability is highly sensitive to shortfalls in demand. Conversely, pushing output beyond normal full-capacity operation also creates inefficiencies. As Boeing discovered in 1997 and then in 2006, operating above normal capacity increased unit costs due to overtime pay, premiums for night and weekend shifts, increased defects and higher maintenance.

In cyclical industries, the ability to speedily adjust capacity to downturns in demand can be a major source of cost advantage. During the 2008–9 recession, survival in hard-hit sectors such as housebuilding, construction equipment and retailing required moving early to cut capacity through shedding jobs and closing units. The key is to make adjustments in advance of downturns in demand: Caterpillar announced it was cutting 20 000 jobs on January 28, 2008, the same day it revealed that its sales in the previous quarter had increased from the previous year.[22] A critical challenge to effective capacity adjustment is distinguishing *cyclical* overcapacity which is short-term from *structural* overcapacity that is long-term.[23]

## Input Costs

The firms in an industry do not necessarily pay the same price for identical inputs. There are several sources of lower input costs:

- *Locational differences in input prices.* The prices of inputs may vary between locations, the most important being differences in wage rates from one country to another. In the U.S., software engineers earned an average of $89 000 in 2007. In India the average was $29 000. In less-skilled occupations, differentials are much wider: in auto assembly the hourly rate in Chinese plants was about $2 an hour in 2008 compared with $60–$70 in the U.S. (inclusive of benefits).[24]

- *Ownership of low-cost sources of supply.* In raw material-intensive industries, ownership or access to low-cost sources can offer crucial cost advantage. In oil and gas, lifting costs for the three "supermajors" (ExxonMobil, Royal Dutch Shell, and BP) were over $11 per barrel in 2007; for Saudi Aramco they were about $4.

- *Nonunion labor.* Labor unions result in higher levels of pay and benefits and work restrictions that lower productivity. In the U.S. airline industry, nonunion AirTran had average salary and benefit cost per employee of $60 863 in 2007 compared with $87 245 for United (80% unionized).

- *Bargaining power.* Where bought-in products are a major cost item, differences in buying power among the firms in an industry can be an important source of cost advantage.[25] Wal-Mart's U.K. entry (with its acquisition of Asda) was greeted with dismay by other British supermarket chains—they recognized that Wal-Mart would be able to use its massive bargaining power to extract additional discounts from Asda's suppliers, which it could use to fuel aggressive price competition.

## Residual Efficiency

In many industries, the basic cost drivers—scale, technology, product and process design, input costs, and capacity utilization—fail to provide a complete explanation for why one firm in an industry has lower unit costs than a competitor. Even after taking all these cost drivers into account, unit cost differences between firms remain. These residual efficiencies relate to the extent to which the firm approaches its efficiency frontier of optimal operation. Residual efficiency depends on the firm's ability to eliminate "organizational slack"[26] or "X-inefficiency"[27]—surplus costs that keep the firm from maximum-efficiency operation. These costs are often referred to as "organizational fat" and build up unconsciously as a result of employees—both in management and on the shop floor—maintaining some margin of slack in preference to the rigors of operating at maximum efficiency.

Eliminating excess costs is difficult. It may take a shock to a company's very survival to provide the impetus for rooting out institutionalized inefficiencies. When faced with bankruptcy or a precipitous fall in profitability, companies can demonstrate a remarkable capacity for paring costs. In his first year as CEO of Nissan Motor, Carlos Ghosn cut operating costs by 20%.[28]

In the absence of a threat to survival, high levels of residual efficiency are typically the result of management system and company values that are intolerant toward unnecessary costs and glorify frugality.[29] At companies such as Wal-Mart, Ryanair, IKEA, and Air Asia, relentless cost efficiency is embodied in management systems and embedded in the corporate culture.

## Using the Value Chain to Analyze Costs

To analyze costs and make recommendations for building cost advantage, the company or even the business unit is too big a level for us to work at. As we saw in Chapter 5, every business may be viewed as a chain of activities. In most value chains each activity has a distinct cost structure determined by different cost drivers. Analyzing costs requires disaggregating the firm's value chain to identify:

- the relative importance of each activity with respect to total cost;
- the cost drivers for each activity and the comparative efficiency with which the firm performs each activity;
- how costs in one activity influence costs in another;
- which activities should be undertaken within the firm and which activities should be outsourced.

## The Principal Stages of Value Chain Analysis

A value chain analysis of a firm's cost position comprises the following stages:

1 *Disaggregate the firm into separate activities.* Determining the appropriate value chain activities is a matter of judgment. It requires understanding the chain of processes involved in the transformation of inputs into output and its delivery to the customer. Very often, the firm's own divisional and departmental structure is a useful guide. Key considerations are:

  • the separateness of one activity from another;
  • the importance of an activity;
  • the dissimilarity of activities in terms of cost drivers;
  • the extent to which there are differences in the way competitors perform the particular activity.

2 *Establish the relative importance of different activities in the total cost of the product.* Our analysis needs to focus on the activities that are the major sources of cost. In disaggregating costs, Michael Porter suggests the detailed assignment of operating costs and assets to each value activity. Though the adoption of activity-based costing has made such cost data more available, detailed cost allocation can be a major exercise.[30] Even without such detailed cost breakdown it is usually possible to identify which activities are the principal sources of total cost and establish which activities are performed relatively efficiently or inefficiently.

3 *Identify cost drivers.* For each activity, what factors determine the level of cost relative to other firms? For some activities, cost drivers can be deduced simply from the nature of the activity and the types of cost incurred. For capital-intensive activities such as the operation of a body press in an auto plant, the principal factors are likely to be capital equipment costs, weekly production volume, and downtime between changes of dies. For labor-intensive assembly activities, critical issues are wage rates, speed of work, and defect rates.

4 *Identify linkages.* The costs of one activity may be determined, in part, by the way in which other activities are performed. Xerox discovered that its high service costs relative to competitors reflected the complexity of design of its copiers, which required 30 different interrelated adjustments.

5 *Identify opportunities for reducing costs.* By identifying areas of comparative inefficiency and the cost drivers for each, opportunities for cost reduction become evident. For example:

  • If scale economies are a key cost driver, can volume be increased? One feature of Caterpillar's cost-reduction strategy was to broaden its model range and begin selling diesel engines to other vehicle manufacturers in order to expand its sales base.
  • Where wage costs are the issue, can wages be reduced either directly or by relocating production?
  • If a certain activity cannot be performed efficiently within the firm, can it be outsourced?

Figure 9.4 shows how the application of the value chain to automobile manufacture can yield suggestions for possible cost reductions.

**FIGURE 9.4**  Using the value chain in cost analysis: an automobile manufacturer

| SEQUENCE OF ANALYSIS | VALUE CHAIN | COST DRIVERS |
|---|---|---|

**SEQUENCE OF ANALYSIS**

**1. IDENTIFY ACTIVITIES**
Establish the basic framework of the value chain by identifying the principal activities of the firm.

**2. ALLOCATE TOTAL COSTS**
For a first-stage analysis, a rough estimate of the breakdown of total cost by activity is sufficient to indicate which activities offer the greatest scope for cost reductions.

**3. IDENTIFY COST DRIVERS**
(See diagram)

**4. IDENTIFY LINKAGES**
Examples include:
1. Consolidating purchase orders to increase discounts increases inventories.
2. High-quality parts and materials reduce costs of defects at later stages.
3. Reducing manufacturing defects cuts warranty costs.
4. Designing different models around common components and platforms reduces manufacturing costs.

**5. IDENTIFY OPPORTUNITIES**
**COST REDUCTION**
For example:
*Purchasing*: Concentrate purchases on fewer suppliers to maximize purchasing economies. Institute just-in-time component supply to reduce inventories.

*R&D/Design/Engineering*: Reduce frequency of model changes. Reduce number of different models (e.g., single range of global models). Design for commonality of components and platforms.

*Component manufacture*: Exploit economies of scale through concentrating production of each component on fewer plants. Outsource wherever scale of production or run lengths are suboptimal or where outside suppliers have technology advantages. For labor-intensive components (e.g., seats, dashboards, trim), relocate production in low-wage countries. Improve capacity utilization through plant rationalization or supplying components to other manufacturers.

**VALUE CHAIN**

**PURCHASING COMPONENTS AND MATERIALS**

**COST DRIVERS**
Prices of bought-in components depend upon:
• Order sizes
• Average value of purchases per supplier
• Location of suppliers

**R&D, DESIGN AND ENGINEERING**
Size of R&D commitment
Productivity of R&D
Number and frequency of new models
Sales per model

**COMPONENT MANUFACTURE**
Scale of plants
Run length per component
Capacity utilization
Location of plants

**ASSEMBLY**
Scale of plants
Number of models per plant
Degree of automation
Level of wages
Location of plants

**TESTING AND QUALITY CONTROL**
Level of quality targets
Frequency of defects

**INVENTORIES OF FINISHED PRODUCTS**
Predicatability of sales
Flexibility of production
Customers' willingness to wait

**SALES AND MARKETING**
Size of advertising budget
Strength of existing reputation
Sales volume

**DISTRIBUTION AND DEALER SUPPORT**
Number of dealers
Sales per dealer
Desired level of dealer support
Frequency of defects requiring repair under warranty of recalls

## Summary

Cost efficiency may no longer be a guarantee of profitability in today's hypercompetitive markets but in almost all industries it is a prerequisite for success. In industries where competition has always been primarily price based—steel, textiles, and mortgage banking—increased intensity of competition requires relentless cost-reduction efforts. In industries where price competition was once muted—airlines, retail banking, and electrical power—firms have been forced to reconcile the pursuit of reliability, differentiation and service quality with vigorous cost reduction.

The foundation for a cost-reduction strategy must be an understanding of the determinants of a company's costs. The principal message of this chapter is the need to look behind cost accounting data and beyond simplistic approaches to the determinants of cost efficiency, and to analyze the factors that drive relative unit costs in each of the firm's activities in a systematic and comprehensive manner.

Increasingly, approaches to cost efficiency are less about incremental efficiencies, and more about fundamentally rethinking the activities undertaken by the firm and the ways in which it organizes them. By focusing on those activities in which the firm possesses a cost advantage and outsourcing others, and by extensively re-engineering operating and administrative processes, firms can achieve dramatic reductions in operating costs.

Given multiple drivers of relative cost, cost management implies multiple initiatives at different organizational levels. Careful analysis of existing activities relative to competitors can pinpoint cost-reduction opportunities through lowering input costs, accessing scale economies and better utilizing capacity. At the same time the firm must seek opportunities for innovation and process redesign to exploit new sources of dynamic efficiency.

## Self-Study Questions

1   A number of industries have experienced rapidly increasing global concentration in recent years: commercial aircraft (led by Boeing and Airbus), steel (led by Mittal Steel), beer (led by SAB-Miller, Anheuser-Busch-Inbev, and Heineken), commercial banking (led by Citigroup, HSBC, Bank of America, Royal Bank of Scotland, and Banco Santander), defense equipment (led by Lockheed Martin, Northrop Grumman and EADS), and delivery services (led by UPS, Federal Express, and Deutsche Post/DHL). For each industry, are economies of scale the major reason for increasing concentration? If so, identify the sources of economies of scale. If not, how can increasing global concentration be explained?

2   In Strategy Capsule 2.3 (Chapter 2), we observed that Ford's profitability was low primarily because its costs were high. Using the value chain shown in Figure 9.4 and what you know

about Ford (including the information in Strategy Capsule 2.3), what suggestions would you offer as to how Ford might lower its costs of producing cars?

**3**   To what extent are the seven cost drivers shown in Figure 9.1 relevant in analyzing the costs per student at your business school? What recommendations would you make to your dean for improving the cost efficiency of the school?

# Notes

1  Louis E. Yelle, "The Learning Curve: Historical Review and Comprehensive Survey," *Decision Sciences* 10 (1979): 302–28.

2  See D. Ross, "Learning to Dominate," *Journal of Industrial Economics* 34 (1986): 337–53.

3  Boston Consulting Group, *Strategy Alternatives for the British Motorcycle Industry* (London: Her Majesty's Stationery Office, 1975).

4  C. Baden-Fuller, "The Implications of the Learning Curve for Firm Strategy and Public Policy," *Applied Economics* 15 (1983): 541–51.

5  R. Jacobsen and D. Aaker, "Is Market Share All That It's Cracked up to Be?" *Journal of Marketing* 49 (Fall 1985): 11–22.

6  R. Wensley, "PIMS and BCG: New Horizons or False Dawn?" *Strategic Management Journal* 3 (1982): 147–58.

7  To be more precise, the economies of amortizing product development costs are *economies of volume* rather than *economies of scale*. The product development cost per unit depends on the total volume of production over the life of the model.

8  M. Venzin, *Building an International Financial Services Firm: How Successful Firms Design and Execute Cross-border Strategies* (Oxford: Oxford University Press, 2009)

9  R. P. McAfee and J. McMillan, "Organizational Diseconomies of Scale," *Journal of Economics and Management Strategy* 4 (1996): 399–426.

10  L. Rapping, "Learning and World War II Production Functions," *Review of Economics and Statistics* (February 1965): 81–6.

11  G. Linden, J. Hart, S. A. Lenway, and T. P. Murtha, "Flying Geese as Moving Targets," *Industry and Innovation* 5 (June 1998): 11–34.

12  L. Argote, S. L. Beckman, and D. Epple, "The Persistence and Transfer of Learning in Industrial Settings," *Management Science* 36 (1990): 140–54; M. Zollo and S. G. Winter, "Deliberate Learning and the Evolution of Dynamic Capabilities," *Organization Science* 13 (2002): 339–51.

13  R. H. Hayes and R. Jaikumar, "Manufacturing's Crisis: New Technologies, Obsolete Organizations," *Harvard Business Review* (September-October 1988): 85; and R. M. Grant, A. B. Shani, R. Krishnan, and R. Baer, "Appropriate Manufacturing Technology: A Strategic Approach," *Sloan Management Review* 33, no. 1 (Fall 1991): 43–54.

14  M. Keller, *Collision* (New York: Doubleday, 1993): 169–71.

15  J. Womack and D. T. Jones, "From Lean Production to Lean Enterprise," *Harvard Business Review* (March-April 1994); J. Womack and D. T. Jones, "Beyond Toyota: How to Root Out Waste and Pursue Perfection," *Harvard Business Review* (September–October, 1996).

16  R. Teerlink and L. Ozley, *More than a Motorcycle* (Cambridge, MA: Harvard Business School Press, 2000).

17  M. Hammer and J. Champy, *Re-engineering the Corporation: A Manifesto for Business Revolution* (New York: HarperBusiness, 1993): 32.

18  M. Hammer, "Re-engineering Work: Don't Automate, Obliterate," *Harvard Business Review* (July–August, 1990).

19  V. Glover and M. L. Marcus, "Business Process Transformation," *Advances in Management Information Systems* 9 (M.E. Sharpe, March 2008); R. Merrifield, J. Calhoun, and D. Stevens, "The Next Revolution in Productivity," *Harvard Business Review* (November 2006): 72–9.

20  R. E. Gomory, "From the Ladder of Science to the Product Development Cycle," *Harvard Business Review* (November–December 1989): 103.

21  F. X. Frei, "Breaking the Tradeoff between Efficiency and Service," *Harvard Business Review* (November 2006): 92–103.

22  "Caterpillar to Cut 20 000 Jobs as Downturn Worsens," *Wall Street Journal* (January 28, 2009).

23  J. Billington, "Listening to Overcapacity—Lessons from the Auto and Health Care Industries," *Harvard Management Update* (Boston: Harvard Business School, 1998, Reprint # U98068).

24  *Plunkett's Automotive Almanac 2008.*

25  "Buying Power of Multiproduct Retailers," *OECD Journal of Competition Law and Policy* 2 (March, 2000).

26 R. Cyert and J. March, *A Behavioral Theory of the Firm* (Englewood Cliffs, NJ: Prentice Hall, 1963).

27 H. Leibenstein, "Allocative Efficiency Versus X-Efficiency," *American Economic Review* 54 (June, 1966): 392-415.

28 K. Kase, F. J. Saez and H. Riquelme, *The New Samurais of Japanese Industry* (Cheltenham: Edward Elgar, 2006).

29 At the head office of Amazon.com, employees' desks built from doors became symbols of frugality. See "Jeff Bezos," in J. Middleton, *Gurus on E-business* (Abingdon: Thorogood Publishing, 2006): 37–9.

30 On activity-based costing, see R. S. Kaplan and S. R. Anderson, "Time-Driven Activity-based Costing," *Harvard Business Review* (November 2004): 131–8; J. Billington, "The ABCs of ABC: Activity-based Costing and Management," *Harvard Management Update* (Boston: Harvard Business School Publishing, May 1999).

# 10 Differentiation Advantage

> *If the three keys to selling real estate are location, location, location, then the three keys of selling consumer products are differentiation, differentiation, differentiation.*
>
> —ROBERT GOIZUETA, FORMER CHAIRMAN, COCA-COLA COMPANY

> *If you gave me $100 billion and said, "Take away the soft drink leadership of Coca-Cola in the world," I'd give it back to you and say, "It can't be done."*
>
> —WARREN BUFFETT, CHAIRMAN, BERKSHIRE HATHAWAY, AND COCA-COLA'S BIGGEST SHAREHOLDER

## OUTLINE

## Introduction and Objectives

A firm differentiates itself from its competitors "when it provides something unique that is valuable to buyers beyond simply offering a low price."[1] Differentiation advantage occurs when a firm is able to obtain from its differentiation a price premium in the market that exceeds the cost of providing the differentiation.

Every firm has opportunities for differentiating its offering to customers, although the range of differentiation opportunities depends on the characteristics of the product. An automobile or a restaurant offers greater potential for differentiation than cement, wheat or memory chips. These latter products are called "commodities" precisely because they lack physical differentiation. Yet, even commodity products can be differentiated in ways that create customer value: "Anything can be turned into a value-added product or service for a well-defined or newly created market," claims Tom Peters.[2] Consider the following:

◆ Cement is the ultimate commodity product, yet Cemex, the Mexican-based supplier of cement and ready-mix concrete, has established itself as the world's biggest supplier using a strategy that emphasizes "building solutions." One component of this strategy is ensuring that 98% of its deliveries are on time (compared to 34% for the industry as a whole).[3]

◆ Online bookselling is inherently a commodity business—any online bookseller has access to the same titles and same modes of distribution. Yet Amazon has exploited the information generated by the business to offer a range of value-adding services: best-seller lists, reviews and customized recommendations.

The lesson is this: differentiation is not simply about offering different product features; it is about identifying and understanding every possible interaction between the firm and its customers and asking how these interactions can be enhanced or changed in order to deliver additional value to the customer.

Analyzing differentiation requires looking at both the firm (the supply side) and its customers (the demand side). While supply-side analysis identifies the firm's potential to create uniqueness, the critical issue is whether such differentiation creates value for customers and whether the value created exceeds the cost of the differentiation. Hence, in this chapter we shall be concerned especially with the demand side of the market. By understanding what customers want, how they choose, and what motivates them, we can identify opportunities for profitable differentiation.

Differentiation strategies are not about pursuing uniqueness for the sake of being different. Differentiation is about understanding customers and how our product can meet their needs. To this extent, the quest for differentiation advantage takes us to the heart of business strategy. The fundamental issues of differentiation are also the fundamental issues of business strategy: Who are our customers? How do we create value for them? And how do we do it more effectively and efficiently than anyone else?

Because differentiation is about uniqueness, establishing differentiation advantage requires creativity—it cannot be achieved simply through applying standardized frameworks and techniques. This is not to say that differentiation advantage is not amenable to systematic analysis. As we have observed, there are two requirements for creating profitable differentiation. On the supply side, the firm must be aware of the resources and capabilities through which it can create uniqueness (and do it better than competitors). On the demand side, the key is insight into customers and their needs and preferences. These two sides form the major components of our analysis of differentiation.

By the time you have completed this chapter you will be able to:

◆ understand what differentiation is, recognize its different forms and appreciate its potential for creating competitive advantage;

◆ analyze the sources of differentiation in terms of customers' preferences and characteristics, and of the firm's capacity for supplying differentiation;

◆ formulate strategies that create differentiation advantage by linking the firm's differentiation capability to customers' demand for differentiation.

## The Nature of Differentiation and Differentiation Advantage

Let us begin by exploring what differentiation is and why it is such an important basis for competitive advantage.

### Differentiation Variables

The potential for differentiating a product or service is partly determined by its physical characteristics. For products that are technically simple (a pair of socks, a brick), that satisfy uncomplicated needs (a corkscrew, a nail) or must meet rigorous technical standards (a spark plug, a thermometer), differentiation opportunities are constrained by technical and market factors. Products that are technically complex (an airplane), that satisfy complex needs (an automobile, a vacation) or that do not need to conform to particular technical standards (wine, toys) offer much greater scope for differentiation.

Beyond these constraints, the potential in any product or service for differentiation is limited only by the boundaries of the human imagination. For seemingly simple products such as shampoo, toilet paper, and bottled water, the proliferation of brands on any supermarket's shelves is testimony both to the ingenuity of firms and the complexity of customer preferences. Differentiation extends beyond the physical characteristics of the product or service to encompass everything about the product or service that influences the value that customers derive from it. This means that differentiation includes every aspect of the way in which a company relates to its customers. Starbucks' ability to charge up to $4 for a cup of coffee rests not just on the characteristics of the coffee but also on the overall "Starbucks Experience," which encompasses the retail environment, the values the company projects and a sense of community in which customers participate. Differentiation is not an activity specific to particular functions such as design and marketing; it infuses all activities through which an organization relates to its customers and is built into the identity and culture of a company.

In analyzing differentiation opportunities, we can distinguish *tangible* and *intangible* dimensions of differentiation. Tangible differentiation is concerned with the observable characteristics of a product or service that are relevant to customers' preferences and choice processes. These include size, shape, color, weight, design, material and technology. Tangible differentiation also includes the performance of the product or service in terms of reliability, consistency, taste, speed, durability, and safety.

Tangible differentiation extends to products and services that complement the product in question. There is little that is distinctive about Dell's computers. The differentiation lies in the speed with which they are delivered, the flexibility with which customers can configure their own systems, and after-sales services including technical support, online training courses, repair service, upgrading service, and customer discussion forum—to mention but a few.

Opportunities for intangible differentiation arise because the value that customers perceive in a product or service does not depend exclusively on the tangible aspects of the offering. There are few products where customer choice is determined solely by observable product features or objective performance criteria. Social, emotional, psychological and esthetic considerations are present in choices over all products and services. The desires for status, exclusivity, individuality, and security are powerful motivational forces in choices relating to most consumer goods. Where a product or service is meeting complex customer needs, differentiation choices involve the overall image of the firm and its offering. Image differentiation is especially important for those products and services whose qualities and performance are difficult to ascertain at the time of purchase ("experience goods"). These include cosmetics, medical services, and education.

## Differentiation and Segmentation

Differentiation is different from segmentation. Differentiation is concerned with *how* a firm competes—the ways in which it can offer uniqueness to customers. Such uniqueness might relate to consistency (McDonald's), reliability (Federal Express), status (American Express), quality (BMW), and innovation (Apple). Segmentation is concerned with *where* a firm competes in terms of customer groups, localities and product types.

Whereas segmentation is a feature of market structure, differentiation is a strategic choice by a firm. A segmented market is one that can be partitioned according to the characteristics of customers and their demand. Differentiation is concerned with a firm's positioning within a market (or market segment) in relation to the product, service and image characteristics that influence customer choice.[4] By locating within a segment, a firm does not necessarily differentiate itself from its competitors within the same segment. Ameritrade, E-Trade, and Scottrade are all located within the online segment of the brokerage industry, yet are not significantly differentiated from one another. Conversely, IKEA, Honda, Amazon and Starbucks pursue differentiation, but position themselves within the mass market and span multiple demographic and socioeconomic segments.

Nevertheless, differentiation decisions tend to be closely linked to choices over the segments in which a firm competes. By offering uniqueness in its offerings, a firm may inevitably target certain market niches. By selecting performance, engineering and style as the basis on which BMW competes in the automobile industry, it inevitably appeals to different market segments than does VW. To the extent that differentiation is imitated by other companies, the result can be the creation of new market segments. In the beer industry innovative differentiation to offer light beer, high-alcohol beer, microbrews, and brewpubs has resulted in the emergence of new market segments.[5]

## The Sustainability of Differentiation Advantage

Differentiation offers a more secure basis for competitive advantage than low cost. The growth of international competition has revealed the fragility of seemingly well-established positions of domestic cost leadership. The cost advantages of Ford in autos, Honda in motorcycles, Indesit in domestic appliances, and Matsushita in consumer electronics have all been overturned by the emergence of new competitors from countries with low labor costs.

In addition, cost advantage is highly vulnerable to unpredictable external forces. During 2008, the Japanese yen appreciated by 19% against the U.S. dollar and 68% against the Korean won. During 2009, Japanese manufacturers were facing reduced demand and massive losses in export markets.

Cost advantage is also vulnerable to new technology and strategic innovation. United States' integrated iron and steel producers lost ground to the minimill producers—Nucor, Chaparral Steel, and Steel Dynamics. Discount brokers such as Quick & Reilly, Brown & Company, Olde, and Siebert were undercut by online brokers such as Ameritrade and E-Trade. Internet telephony (VoIP) offered by Skype, Vonage, and other upstarts has devastated the profitability of fixed-line, long-distance telecom providers.

Hence, sustained high profitability is associated more with differentiation than cost leadership. Large companies that consistently earn above average return on equity—such as Colgate-Palmolive, Diageo, Nokia, Johnson & Johnson, Kellogg's, Procter & Gamble, 3M, and Wyeth—tend to be those that have pursued differentiation through quality, branding and innovation.

# Analyzing Differentiation: The Demand Side

Successful differentiation involves matching customers' demand for differentiation with the firm's capacity to supply differentiation. Let's begin with the demand side. Analyzing customer demand enables us to determine which product characteristics have the potential to create value for customers, customers' willingness to pay for differentiation, and a company's optimal competitive positioning in terms of differentiation variables.

Analyzing demand begins with understanding why customers buy a product or service. What are the needs and requirements of a person who is purchasing a personal computer? What is motivating a company when it hires management consultants? Market research systematically explores customer preferences and customer perceptions of existing products. However, the key to successful differentiation is to *understand* customers. To gain insight into customer requirements and preferences, simple, direct inquiry into the purpose of a product and the needs of its customers can often be far more illuminating than statistically validated market research (see Strategy Capsule 10.1).

## STRATEGY CAPSULE 10.1

# Understanding What a Product is About

Getting back to strategy means getting back to a deep understanding of what a product is about. Some time ago, for example, a Japanese home appliance company was trying to develop a coffee percolator. Should it be a General Electric-type percolator, executives wondered? Should it be the same drip type that Philips makes? Larger? Smaller? I urged them to ask a different kind of question: Why do people drink coffee? What are they looking for when they do? If your objective is to serve the customer better, then shouldn't you understand why that customer drinks coffee in the first place? Then you would know what kind of percolator to make.

The answer came back: good taste. Then I asked the company's engineers what they were doing to help the consumer enjoy good taste in a cup of coffee. They said they were trying to design a good percolator. I asked them what influences the taste in a cup of coffee. No one

knew. That became the next question we had to answer. It turns out that lots of things can affect taste—the beans, the temperature, the water. We did our homework and discovered all the things that affect taste . . .

Of all the factors, water quality, we learned, made the greatest difference. The percolator in design at the time, however, didn't take water quality into account at all . . . We discovered next the grain distribution and the time between grinding the beans and pouring in the water were crucial. As a result we began to think about the product and its necessary features in a new way. It had to have a built-in dechlorinating function. It had to have a built-in grinder. All the customer should have to do is pour in water and beans . . .

To start you have to ask the right questions and set the right kinds of strategic goals. If your only concern is that General Electric has just brought out a percolator that brews coffee in ten minutes, you will get your engineers to design one that brews it in seven minutes. And if you stick to that logic, market research will tell you that instant coffee is the way to go . . . Conventional marketing approaches won't solve the problem. If you ask people whether they want their coffee in ten minutes or seven, they will say seven, of course. But it's still the wrong question. And you end up back where you started, trying to beat the competition at its own game. If your primary focus is on the competition, you will never step back and ask what the customers' inherent needs are, and what the product really is about.

*Source:* Kenichi Ohmae, "Getting Back to Strategy," *Harvard Business Review* (November–December 1988): 154. Copyright © 1988 by the Harvard Business School Publishing; all rights reserved. Reprinted by permission of Harvard Business School Publishing.

## Product Attributes and Positioning

Virtually all products and services serve multiple customer needs. As a result, understanding customer needs requires the analysis of multiple attributes. Market research has developed several techniques for analyzing customer preferences in relation to product attributes. These can guide decisions concerning the positioning of new products, repositioning of existing products, and pricing.

*Multidimensional Scaling*   Multidimensional scaling (MDS) permits customers' perceptions of competing products' similarities and dissimilarities to be represented graphically and for the dimensions to be interpreted in terms of key product attributes.[6] For example, a survey of consumer ratings of competing pain relievers resulted in the mapping shown in Figure 10.1. Multidimensional scaling has also been

**FIGURE 10.1** Consumer perceptions of competing pain relievers: a multidimensional scaling mapping

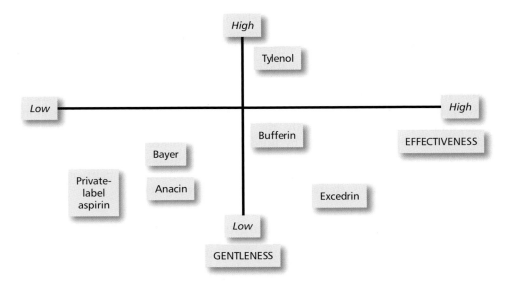

used to classify 109 single-malt Scotch whiskies according to the characteristics of their color, nose, palate, body and finish.[7]

*Conjoint Analysis* Conjoint analysis measures the strength of customer preferences for different product attributes. The technique requires, first, an identification of the underlying attributes of a product and, second, market research to rank hypothetical products that contain alternative bundles of attributes. The results can then be used to estimate the proportion of customers who would prefer a hypothetical new product to competing products already available in the market.[8] Conjoint analysis has been used to predict market shares of forthcoming new models of personal computer, to analyze windsurfer preferences, and to design new products, including Marriott's Courtyard hotel chain and nature tourism in the Amazon basin.

*Hedonic Price Analysis* The demand for a product may be viewed as the demand for the underlying attributes that the product provides.[9] The price at which a product can sell in the market is the aggregate of the values derived from each of these individual attributes. Hedonic price analysis uses regression to relate price differences for competing products to the levels of different attributes offered by each, thereby allowing the implicit market price for each attribute to be calculated. For example:

- For European automatic washing machines, price differences were related to differences in capacity, spin speed, energy consumption, number of programs, and reliability. For example, a machine that spins at 1000 rpm sold at about a $200 price premium to one that spins at 800 r.p.m.[10]
- Price differences between models of personal computer reflected differences in processor speed, memory and hard drive capacity.[11]

*Value Curve Analysis* Selecting the optimal combination of attributes depends not only on which attributes are valued by customers but also on where competitors' offerings are positioned in relation to different attributes. By mapping the performance characteristics of competing products on to a *value curve*, Chan Kim and Renee Mauborgne identify how superior combinations of product characteristics or a whole new market space can be created.[12] Thus, in book retailing, key value metrics include price, knowledge levels of staff, selection of books, store ambiance, store hours and facilities such as cafés and reading areas. By viewing the positioning of independent book stores and chain bookstores along these dimensions we can identify the opportunity for new combinations of attributes—such as those offered by Borders and Barnes & Noble. Deploying the value curve to create differentiation advantage requires looking beyond the conventionally defined boundaries of competition to consider competitive offerings from different industries, strategic groups, and buyer segments.

## The Role of Social and Psychological Factors

The problem with analyzing product differentiation in terms of measurable performance attributes is that it does not delve very far into customers' underlying motivations. Very few goods or services are acquired to satisfy basic physical needs: most buying is motivated by social and psychological needs such as the desire to find community with others and to reinforce one's own identity. Psychologist Abraham Maslow proposed a hierarchy of human needs. Once basic needs for survival are established, there is a progression from security needs, to belonging needs, to esteem needs, to self-actualization needs.[13] For most goods, brand equity has more to do with status and identity than with tangible product performance. The disastrous introduction of "New Coke" in 1985 was the result of Coca-Cola giving precedence to tangible differentiation (taste preferences) over intangible differentiation (authenticity).[14] Harley-Davidson harbors no such illusions: it recognizes quite clearly that it is in the business of selling lifestyle, not transportation.

If the key customer needs that a product satisfies are identity and social affiliation, the implications for differentiation are far reaching. In particular, to understand customer demand and identify profitable differentiation opportunities requires that we analyze the product and its characteristics, but also customers, their lifestyles and aspirations, and the relationship of the product to these lifestyles and aspirations. Market research that explores the demographic (age, sex, race, location), socioeconomic (income, education), and psychographic (lifestyle, personality type) characteristics of potential customers may be less useful than deep understanding of consumers' relationship with a product. According to Tom Peters, the answer is simple: business people need to "get out from behind their desks to where the customers are . . . [and] construct settings so as to maximize 'naive' listening."[15]

In practice, understanding customer needs and preferences is likely to require more than listening. Typically, consumers cannot clearly articulate the motives that drive them and the emotions that different products trigger. Companies must observe carefully their customers to understand how a product relates to their lifestyles. Before opening its *Fresh and Easy* chain of foodstores in the western U.S., British supermarket giant, Tesco, sent a team of executives to live with local families.[16] Going beyond functionality to explore the emotional and esthetic aspects of consumers' relationships with products is central to Japanese approaches to marketing.[17]

Figure 10.2 summarizes the key points of this discussion by posing some basic questions that explore the potential for demand-side differentiation.

## Analyzing Differentiation: The Supply Side

Demand analysis identifies customers' demands for differentiation and their willingness to pay for it, but creating differentiation advantage also depends on a firm's ability to offer differentiation. To identify the firm's potential to supply differentiation, we need to examine the activities that the firm performs and the resources it has access to.

### The Drivers of Uniqueness

Differentiation is concerned with the provision of uniqueness. A firm's opportunities for creating uniqueness in its offerings to customers are not located within a particular function or activity, but can arise in virtually everything that it does.

**FIGURE 10.2** Identifying differentiation potential: the demand side

Michael Porter identifies a number of drivers of uniqueness that are decision variables for the firm:

- product features and product performance;
- complementary services (such as credit, delivery, repair);
- intensity of marketing activities (such as rate of advertising spending);
- technology embodied in design and manufacture;
- the quality of purchased inputs;
- procedures influencing the conduct of each of the activities (for example, rigor of quality control, service procedures, frequency of sales visits to a customer);
- the skill and experience of employees;
- location (for example, with retail stores);
- The degree of vertical integration (which influences a firm's ability to control inputs and intermediate processes).[18]

Most offerings do not involve a single product or a single service, but are a combination of products and services. In analyzing the potential for differentiation, we can distinguish between differentiation of the product ("hardware") and ancillary services ("software"). On this basis, four transaction categories can be identified (see Figure 10.3).[19]

As markets mature, so systems comprising both hardware and software tend to "unbundle." Products become commoditized while complementary services become provided by specialized suppliers. However, as customer preferences become

**FIGURE 10.3** Differentiation of merchandise (hardware) and support (software)

Source: Shiv Mathur and Alfred Kenyon, *Creating Value* (Oxford: Butterworth-Heinemann, 1997). Reproduced by permission of Elsevier.

increasingly sophisticated and companies seek new opportunities for differentiation advantage, so hardware and software is repackaged into new systems. Service stations once offered a comprehensive array of services to motorists—gasoline, oil changes, car repair, tires, car washing and so on. As more and more of these services have become commodities provided by specialist suppliers, so the oil companies have sought differentiation through creating new bundles of retail services at their service stations.

A critical issue is whether such bundling really creates customer value. Thus, "one-stop shopping" by financial service companies diversified across retail banking, brokerage, fund management and insurance has had limited appeal to customers. Electronic commerce allows customers to assemble their own bundles of goods and services at low cost with little inconvenience. This trend explains the declining fortunes of European tour operators: most vacationers enjoy the flexibility of online information and reservations systems to create their own customized vacations.[20] The result, according to McKinsey consultants Hagel and Singer, is not just unbundling of products, but the unbundling of the corporation itself.[21]

## Product Integrity

All companies face a range of differentiation opportunities. The primary issue is likely to be determining which forms of differentiation may be most successful in distinguishing the firm in the market and which are most valued by customers. Such choices cannot be made on a piecemeal basis. Establishing a coherent and effective differentiation position requires that the firm assembles a complementary package of differentiation attributes. If Beck's beer wishes to differentiate itself on the basis of the quality of its ingredients then it must adopt production methods that are consistent with quality ingredients, and packaging, advertising, and distribution appropriate to a quality, premium-priced product.

Product integrity refers to the consistency of a firm's differentiation; it is the extent to which a product achieves:

. . . total balance of numerous product characteristics, including basic functions, esthetics, semantics, reliability, and economy . . . Product integrity has both internal and external dimensions. Internal integrity refers to consistency between the function and structure of the product—e.g., the parts fit well, components match and work well together, layout achieves maximum space efficiency. External integrity is a measure of how well a product's function, structure, and semantics fit the customer's objectives, values, production system, lifestyle, use pattern, and self-identity.[22]

In their study of product development in the auto industry, Clark and Fujimoto argue that simultaneously achieving internal and external integrity is the most complex organizational challenge facing automakers because it requires linking close cross-functional collaboration with intimate customer contact. The organizational changes among U.S. and European automakers, including the growing role of product managers, have attempted to imitate the success of Toyota and Honda in achieving internal-external integration.[23]

Combining internal and external product integrity is especially important to those supplying "lifestyle" products whose differentiation is based on customers' social and psychological needs. Here, the credibility of the image depends critically on the consistency of the image presented. A critical factor in such differentiation is the ability of employees and customers to identify with one another. Thus:

- Harley-Davidson's ability to develop its image of ruggedness, independence, and individuality is supported by a top management team that dons biking leathers and rides its "hogs" to owners' group rallies, and a management system that empowers shop-floor workers and fosters quality, initiative, and responsibility.
- MTV's capacity to stay at the leading edge of popular culture and embody "coolness" for new generations of young people owes much to its internal culture and human resource management, which rely heavily on the ideas and enthusiasm of its youngest employees.[24]

Maintaining integrity of differentiation is ultimately dependent on a company's ability to live the values embodied in the images with which its products are associated.

## Signaling and Reputation

Differentiation is only effective if it is communicated to customers. But information about the qualities and characteristics of products is not always readily available to potential customers. The economics literature distinguishes between *search goods*, whose qualities and characteristics can be ascertained by inspection, and *experience goods*, whose qualities and characteristics are only recognized after consumption. This latter class of goods includes medical services, baldness treatments, frozen TV dinners, and wine. Even after purchase, performance attributes may be slow in revealing themselves. Bernie Madoff established Bernard L. Madoff Investment Securities LLC in 1960—it took almost half a century before the renowned investment house was revealed as a "giant Ponzi scheme."[25]

In the terminology of game theory (see Chapter 4), the market for experience goods corresponds to a classic "prisoners' dilemma." A firm can offer a high-quality or a low-quality product. The customer can pay either a high or a low price. If quality cannot be detected, then equilibrium is established, with the customer offering a low price and the supplier offering a low-quality product, even though both would be better off with a high-quality product sold at a high price (see Figure 10.4).

**FIGURE 10.4** The problem of quality in experience goods: a "prisoners' dilemma"

**Note:** In each cell, the lower-left number is the payoff to the consumer and the upper-right number the payoff to the producer.

The resolution of this dilemma is for producers to find some credible means of signaling quality to the customer. The most effective signals are those that change the payoffs in the prisoners' dilemma. Thus, an extended warranty is effective because providing such a warranty would be more expensive for a low-quality producer than a high-quality producer. Brand names, warranties, expensive packaging, money-back guarantees, sponsorship of sports and cultural events and a carefully designed retail environment in which the product is sold are all signals of quality. Their effectiveness stems from the fact that they represent significant investments by the manufacturer that will be devalued if the product proves unsatisfactory to customers.

The need for signaling variables to complement performance variables in differentiation depends on the ease with which performance can be assessed by the potential buyer. The more difficult it is to ascertain performance prior to purchase, the more important signaling is.

- A perfume can be sampled prior to purchase and its fragrance assessed, but its ability to augment the identity of the wearer and attract attention remains uncertain. Hence, the key role of branding, packaging, advertising, and lavish promotional events in establishing an identity for the perfume in terms of the implied personality, lifestyle and aspirations of the user.
- In financial services, the customer cannot easily assess the honesty, financial security, or competence of the supplier. Hence, financial service companies emphasize symbols of security and stability: imposing head offices, conservative office decor, smartly dressed employees, and trademarks such as Prudential's rock and Travelers' red umbrella. Bernie Madoff's multi-billion investment swindle was sustained by his close association with leading figures among New York's Jewish community, his prominent role in cultural and charitable organizations, and the aura of exclusivity around his investment club.[26]

Strategies for reputation building have been subjected to extensive theoretical analysis.[27] Some of the propositions that arise from this research include the following:

- Quality signaling is primarily important for products whose quality can only be ascertained after purchase ("experience goods").

- Expenditure on advertising is an effective means of signaling superior quality, since suppliers of low-quality products will not expect repeat buying and hence it is not profitable for them to spend money on advertising.
- A combination of premium pricing and advertising is likely to be superior in signaling quality than either price or advertising alone.
- The higher the sunk costs required for entry into a market and the greater the total investment of the firm, the greater the incentives for the firm not to cheat customers through providing low quality at high prices.

## Brands

Brand names and the advertising that supports them are especially important as signals of quality and consistency—because a brand is a valuable asset, it acts as a disincentive to provide poor quality. For many consumer goods (and some producer goods) companies, their brand is their most important asset.

Brands fulfill multiple roles. Most importantly, a brand provides a guarantee by the producer to the consumer of the quality of the product. It does so in several ways. At its most basic, a brand identifies the producer of a product. This ensures that the producer is legally and morally accountable for the products supplied to market. Further, the brand represents an investment that provides an incentive to maintain quality and customer satisfaction. Hence, the brand represents a guarantee to the customer that reduces uncertainty and search costs. The more difficult it is to discern quality on inspection, and the greater the cost to the customer of purchasing a defective product, the greater the value of a brand. Thus, a well-known brand name is likely to be more important to us when we purchase mountaineering equipment than when we buy a pair of socks.

The traditional role of the brand as a guarantor of reliability is particularly significant in e-commerce. Internet transactions are characterized by the anonymity of buyers and sellers and lack of government regulation. As a result, well-established players in e-commerce—Amazon, Microsoft, eBay, and Yahoo!—can use their brand to reduce consumers' perceived risk.

By contrast, the value conferred by consumer brands such as Red Bull, Harley-Davidson, Mercedes-Benz, Gucci, Virgin, and American Express is less a guarantee of reliability and more an embodiment of identity and lifestyle. Traditionally, advertising has been the primary means of influencing and reinforcing customer perceptions. Increasingly, however, consumer goods companies are seeking new approaches to brand development that focus less on product characteristics and more on "brand experience," "tribal identity," "shared values," and "emotional dialogue." Traditional mass-market advertising is less effective for promoting this type of brand identity as word-of-mouth promotion deploying web-based social networks—what has been referred to as *viral marketing* or *stealth marketing*.[28]

## The Costs of Differentiation

Differentiation adds cost. The direct costs of differentiation include higher quality inputs, better trained employees, higher advertising costs and better after-sales service. The indirect costs of differentiation arise through the interaction of differentiation variables with cost variables. If differentiation narrows a firm's segment scope, it also limits the potential for exploiting scale economies. If differentiation requires continual product redesign, it hampers the exploitation of learning economies.

One means of reconciling differentiation with cost efficiency is to postpone differentiation to later stages of the firm's value chain. Economies of scale and the cost advantages of standardization are frequently greatest in the manufacturing of basic components. Modular design with common components permits scale economies while maintaining considerable product variety. All the major automakers have reduced the number of platforms and engine types and increased the commonality of components across their model ranges, while offering customers a greater variety of colors, trim and accessory options.

New manufacturing technology and the internet have redefined traditional tradeoffs between efficiency and variety. Flexible manufacturing systems and just-in-time scheduling have increased the versatility of many plants, made model changeovers less costly and made the goal of an "economic order quantity of one" increasingly realistic. Automobile and domestic appliance plants increasingly produce multiple models on a single assembly line.[29] Internet communication allows consumers to design their own products and quickly communicate their requirements to manufacturers. Pioneers of mass-customization include Capital One, which offers a unique package of credit facilities and interest rate charges to its credit card customers,[30] and Adidas, whose *mi adidas* program offers individually customized sports shoes through foot scanners installed in its retail stores.[31]

## Bringing It All Together: The Value Chain in Differentiation Analysis

There is little point in identifying the product attributes that customers value most if the firm is incapable of supplying those attributes. Similarly, there is little purpose in identifying a firm's ability to supply certain elements of uniqueness if these are not valued by customers. The key to successful differentiation is matching the firm's capacity for creating differentiation to the attributes that customers value most. For this purpose, the value chain provides a particularly useful framework. Let's begin with the case of a producer good, i.e., one that is supplied by one firm to another.

### Value Chain Analysis of Producer Goods

Using the value chain to identify opportunities for differentiation advantage involves four principal stages:

1 *Construct a value chain for the firm and the customer*. It may be useful to consider not just the immediate customer but also firms further downstream in the value chain. If the firm supplies different types of customers—for example, a steel company may supply steel strip to automobile manufacturers and white goods producers—draw separate value chains for each major category of customer.

2 *Identify the drivers of uniqueness in each activity*. Assess the firm's potential for differentiating its product by examining each activity in the firm's value chain and identifying the variables and actions through which the firm can

**FIGURE 10.5** Using the value chain to identify differentiation potential on the supply side

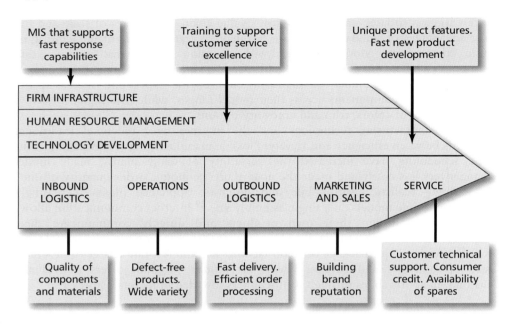

achieve uniqueness in relation to competitors' offerings. Figure 10.5 identifies sources of differentiation within Porter's generic value chain.

3 *Select the most promising differentiation variables for the firm.* Among the numerous drivers of uniqueness that we can identify within the firm, which one should be selected as the primary basis for the firm's differentiation strategy? On the supply side, there are three important considerations.

- First, we must establish where the firm has greater potential for differentiating from, or can differentiate at lower cost than, rivals. This requires some analysis of the firm's internal strengths in terms of resources and capabilities.

- Second, to identify the most promising aspects of differentiation, we also need to identify linkages among activities, since some differentiation variables may involve interaction among several activities. Thus, product reliability is likely to be the outcome of several linked activities: monitoring purchases of inputs from suppliers, the skill and motivation of production workers, and quality control and product testing.

- Third, the ease with which different types of uniqueness can be sustained must be considered. The more differentiation is based on resources specific to the firm or skills that involve the complex coordination of a large number of individuals, the more difficult it will be for a competitor to imitate the particular source of differentiation. Thus, offering business-class passengers wider seats and more leg room is an easily imitated source of differentiation. Achieving high levels of punctuality represents a more sustainable source of differentiation.

4 *Locate linkages between the value chain of the firm and that of the buyer.*
The objective of differentiation is to yield a price premium for the firm. This
requires that the firm's differentiation creates value for the customer.
Creating value for customers requires either that the firm lowers customers'
costs, or that customers' own product differentiation is facilitated. Thus, by
reorganizing its product distribution around quick-response technologies,
Procter & Gamble has radically reduced distribution time and increased
delivery reliability. This permits retailers to reduce costs of inventory while
simultaneously increasing their reliability to shoppers through lowering the
risk of stockouts. To identify the means by which a firm can create value for
its customers it must locate the linkages between differentiation of its own
activities and cost reduction and differentiation within the customer's
activities. Analysis of these linkages can also evaluate the potential
profitability of differentiation. The value differentiation created for the
customer represents the maximum price premium the customer will pay. If
the provision of just-in-time delivery by a component supplier costs an
additional $1000 a month but saves an automobile company $6000 a month
in reduced inventory, warehousing, and handling costs, then it should be
possible for the component manufacturer to obtain a price premium that
easily exceeds the costs of the differentiation.

Strategy Capsule 10.2 demonstrates the use of value chain analysis in identifying
differentiation opportunities available to a manufacturer of metal containers.

## STRATEGY CAPSULE 10.2
# Analyzing Differentiation Opportunities for a Manufacturer of Metal Containers

The metal container industry is a highly competitive, low-growth, low-profit industry. Cans lack much potential for differentiation and buyers (especially beverage and food canning companies) are very powerful. Clearly, cost efficiency is essential but are there also opportunities for differentiation advantage? A value chain analysis can help a metal can manufacturer identify profitable opportunities for differentiation.

STAGE 1.   Construct a value chain for firm and customers. The principal activities of the can manufacturer and its customers are shown in the diagram below.

STAGE 2.   Identify the drivers of uniqueness. For each of the canmaking activities it is possible to suggest several possible differentiation variables. Examples are shown in the diagram.

STAGE 3.   Select key variables. To select the most promising differentiation variables, the company's internal strengths must be considered. If the firm has strong technical capabilities, then it might design and manufacture products to meet difficult technical and design specifications, and provide sophisticated technical services to customers. If its logistics capabilities are strong it might offer fast and reliable delivery, possibly extended to electronic data interchange with customers.

STAGE 4.          Identify linkages. To determine differentiation likely to create value for the customer, identify linkages between the canmaker's potential for differentiation and the potential for reducing cost or enhancing differentiation within the customer's value chain. The diagram identifies five such linkages.

**Identifying differentiation opportunities through linking the value chains of the firm and its customers: can manufacture**

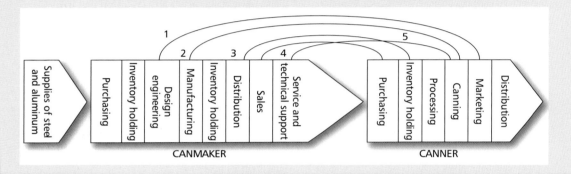

1.  Distinctive can designs support canners' own marketing activities.
2.  High manufacturing tolerances minimize breakdowns on customers' canning lines.
3.  Frequent, punctual deliveries enable canners to minimize inventories.
4.  Efficient order processing system reduces canners' ordering costs.
5.  Speedy, competent technical support increases capacity utilization of canning lines.

## Value Chain Analysis of Consumer Goods

Value chain analysis of differentiation opportunities can also be applied to consumer goods. Few consumer goods are consumed directly; in most cases consumers are involved in a chain of activities involving the acquisition and purchase of the product. Hence, even when the customer is a consumer, it is still feasible to draw a value chain showing the activities that the consumer engages in when purchasing and consuming a product.

In the case of consumer durables, customers are involved in a long chain of activities from search, purchase, financing, acquiring accessories, operation, service and repair to eventual disposal. Complex consumer value chains offer many potential linkages with the manufacturer's value chain, with considerable opportunity for innovative differentiation. Japanese producers of automobiles, consumer electronics and domestic appliances have a long tradition of observing their customers' behavior in selecting and utilizing products, then using the information of customer usage and selection processes in planning product design and marketing. Harley-Davidson has been particularly effective at achieving differentiation advantage through careful examination of the activities that customers undertake in selecting, purchasing, using, and maintaining their motorcycles. Harley creates value for its customers through providing test ride facilities at its dealerships, financing, driving instruction, insurance, service and repair facilities, owners' club activities, and various sponsored events for Harley riders. Even nondurables involve the consumer in a chain of activities. Consider a frozen TV dinner: it must be purchased, taken home, removed from the package, heated and served before it is consumed. After eating, the consumer must clean any used dishes, cutlery, or other utensils. A value chain analysis by a frozen foods producer would identify ways in which the product could be formulated, packaged, and distributed to assist the consumer in performing this chain of activities.

## Summary

The attraction of differentiation over low cost as a basis for competitive advantage is its potential for sustainability. It is less vulnerable to being overturned by changes in the external environment, and it is more difficult to replicate.

The potential for differentiation in any business is vast. It may involve physical differentiation of the product, it may be through complementary services, it may be intangible. Differentiation extends beyond technology, design, and marketing to include all aspects of a firm's interactions with its customers.

The essence of differentiation advantage is to increase the perceived value of the offering to the customer either more effectively or at lower cost than do competitors. This requires that the firm matches the requirements and preferences of customers with its own capacity for creating uniqueness.

The value chain provides a useful framework for analyzing differentiation advantage. By analyzing how value is created for customers and by systematically appraising the scope of each of the firm's activities for achieving differentiation, the value chain permits matching demand-side and supply-side sources of differentiation.

Successful differentiation requires a combination of astute analysis and creative imagination. The two are not antithetical. A systematic framework for the analysis of differentiation can act as a stimulus to creative ideas.

## Self-Study Questions

1   Bottled water sells at least 200 times the price of tap water, with substantial price differentials between different brands. What are the key differentiation variables that determine the price premium that can be obtained for bottled water?

**2** The section on "Differentiation and Segmentation" notes that IKEA furnishings, Honda cars, Amazon, and Starbucks have achieved differentiation while maintaining a broad market appeal. How do companies achieve differentiate their products without limiting their appeal to certain market segments? If The Gap wishes to develop differentiation advantage while still appealing to customers across a broad demographic and socioeconomic range, what advice would you offer it?

**3** Sony, which once dominated the market for portable music players with its Walkman products, has been the big loser to Apple in the market for MP3 music players. Using the framework shown in Figure 10.2, suggest opportunities for how Sony might differentiate its MP3 Walkman to increase its customer appeal.

**4** Advise a chain of movie theaters on a differentiation strategy to restore its flagging profitability. Use the value chain framework outlined in Strategy Capsule 10.2 to identify potential linkages between the company's value chain and that of its customers in order to identify differentiation opportunities.

# Notes

1 M. E. Porter, *Competitive Advantage* (New York: Free Press, 1985): 120.

2 T. Peters, *Thriving on Chaos* (New York: Knopf, 1987): 56.

3 "Cemex: Cementing a Global Strategy," Insead Case No. 307-233-1 (2007).

4 These distinctions are developed in more detail by P. R. Dickson and J. L. Ginter, "Market Segmentation, Product Differentiation and Marketing Strategy," *Journal of Marketing* 51 (April 1987): 1–10.

5 G. R. Carroll and A. Swaminathan, "Why the Microbrewery Movement?" *American Journal of Sociology* 106 (2000): 715–62.

6 S. Schiffman, M. Reynolds and F. Young, *Introduction to Multidimensional Scaling: Theory, Methods, and Applications* (Cambridge, MA: Academic Press, 1981).

7 F.-J. Lapointe and P. Legendre, "A Classification of Pure Malt Scotch Whiskies," *Applied Statistics* 43 (1994): 237–57. On principles of MDS, see I. Borg and P. Groenen, *Modern Multidimensional Scaling: Theory and Application* (Springer Verlag, 1997).

8 See P. Cattin and D. R. Wittink, "Commercial Use of Conjoint Analysis: A Survey," *Journal of Marketing* (Summer 1982): 44–53.

9 K. Lancaster, *Consumer Demand: A New Approach* (New York: Columbia University Press, 1971).

10 P. Nicolaides and C. Baden-Fuller, "Price Discrimination and Product Differentiation in the European Domestic Appliance Market," discussion paper (London: Center for Business Strategy, London Business School, 1987).

11 A. Pates, "A Reconsideration of Hedonic Price Indexes with an Application to PCs," *American Economic Review* 93 (2003): 1578–96.

12 C. Kim and R. Mauborgne, "Creating New Market Space," *Harvard Business Review* (January–February 1999): 83–93.

13 A. Maslow, "A Theory of Human Motivation," *Psychological Review* 50 (1943): 370–96.

14 M. Bastedo and A. Davis, "God, What a Blunder: The New Coke Story," December 17, 1993 (http://www.reference.com/browser/wiki.New_Coke).

15 T. Peters, op. cit.: 149.

16 "Fresh, but far from Easy," *Economist* (June 21, 2007).

17 J. K. Johansson and I. Nonaka, *Relentless: The Japanese Way of Marketing* (New York: HarperBusiness, 1996).

18 M. E. Porter, op. cit.: 124–5.

19 S. Mathur, "Competitive Industrial Marketing Strategies," *Long Range Planning* 17, no. 4 (1984): 102–9.

20 "Turbulent times for air charters," *Financial Times* (October 21, 2003): 21.

21 J. Hagel and M. Singer, "Unbundling the Corporation," *McKinsey Quarterly* no. 3 (2000).

22 K. Clark and T. Fujimoto, *Product Development Performance* (Boston: Harvard Business School Press, 1991): 29–30.

23 Ibid.: 247–85; K. B. Clark and T. Fujimoto, "The Power of Product Integrity," *Harvard Business Review* (November–December, 1990): 107–18.

24 J. Seabrook, "Rocking in Shangri-La," *The New Yorker* (October 10, 1994): 64–78.

25 "The Madoff Affair: Going Down Quietly," *Economist* (March 14, 2009).

26 "The Madoff Affair: Con of the Century," *Economist* (December 20, 2008): 119–20.

27 For a survey, see K. Weigelt and C. Camerer, "Reputation and Corporate Strategy: A Review of Recent Theory and Applications," *Strategic Management Journal* 9 (1988): 443–54.

28 D. J. Watts and J. Peretti, "Viral Marketing for the Real World," *Harvard Business Review* (May 2007): 22–3.

29 J. Pine, B. Victor, A. Boynton, "Making Mass-customization Work," *Harvard Business Review* (September–October 1993): 108–16; "Flexible Manufacturing Strategy lets Chrysler add New Model to Plant," *Industry Week* (June 6, 2007).

30 *Capital One Financial Corporation*, Harvard Business School Case No. 7-900-124 (2000).

31 "Adidas' High Tech Footwear," *Business Week* (November 3, 2006).

# IV

# BUSINESS STRATEGIES IN DIFFERENT INDUSTRY CONTEXTS

# 11 Industry Evolution and Strategic Change

*No company ever stops changing . . . Each new generation must meet changes—in the automotive market, in the general administration of the enterprise, and in the involvement of the corporation in a changing world. The work of creating goes on.*

—ALFRED P. SLOAN JR., PRESIDENT OF GENERAL MOTORS 1923–37, CHAIRMAN 1937–56

## OUTLINE

# Introduction and Objectives

Everything is in a state of constant change—the business environment especially. Management's greatest challenge is to ensure that the enterprise adapts to the changes occurring within its environment.

Change in the industry environment is driven by the forces of technology, consumer need, politics, economic growth and a host of other influences. In some industries, these forces for change combine to create massive, unpredictable changes. For example, in telecommunications new digital and wireless technologies combined with regulatory changes have resulted in the telecom industry of 2009 being almost unrecognizable from that which existed 20 years previously. In other industries—food processing, aircraft production, and funeral services—change is more gradual and more predictable. Change is the result both of external forces and the competitive strategies of the firms within the industry. As we have seen, competition is a dynamic process in which firms vie for competitive advantage, only to see it eroded through imitation and innovation by rivals. The outcome is an industry environment that is being continually recreated by competition.

The purpose of this chapter is to help us to understand, predict, and manage change. To do this we shall explore the forces that drive change and look for patterns of change that can help us to predict how industries are likely to evolve over time. While recognizing that every industry follows a unique development path, we shall look for common drivers of change that produce similar patterns. Recognizing such patterns can help us to identify and exploit opportunities for competitive advantage.

However, understanding and predicting changes in the industry environment is only one aspect of the management challenge. By far the greater challenge is ensuring the adaptation of the firm to these changes. Change is disruptive, costly, and uncomfortable for individuals; for organizations the forces of inertia are even stronger. As a result, the life cycles of firms tend to be much shorter than the life cycles of industries: changes at the industry level tend to occur through the death of existing firms and birth of new firms rather than through continuous adaptation by a constant population of firms.

Our starting point is the *industry life cycle*. We shall consider the extent to which industries follow a common development pattern, examine the changes in industry structure over the cycle, and explore the implications for business strategy. We will then study the challenges of managing organizational change, including threats posed by technological change. While our main emphasis will be on the problems of adaptation to changing external circumstances, we shall also investigate the potential for firms to become agents of change—using strategy as a means of transforming their business environments.

By the time you have completed this chapter, you will be able to:

◆ recognize the different stages of industry development and understand the factors that drive the process of industry evolution;

◆ identify the key success factors associated with industries at different stages of their development;

◆ identify the strategies, organizational structures, and management systems appropriate to different stages of industry development;

◆ use scenarios to explore industry futures;

◆ appreciate the challenges of managing organizational change and be familiar with alternative approaches to strategic change.

# The Industry Life Cycle

One of the best known and most enduring marketing concepts is the *product life cycle*.[1] Products are born, their sales grow, they reach maturity, they go into decline, and they ultimately die. If products have life cycles, so too do the industries that produce them. The *industry life cycle* is the supply-side equivalent of the product life cycle. To the extent that an industry produces multiple generations of a product, the industry life cycle is likely to be of longer duration than that of a single product.

The life cycle comprises four phases: *introduction* (or *emergence*), *growth*, *maturity*, and *decline* (see Figure 11.1). Before we examine the features of each of these stages, let us examine the forces that are driving industry evolution. Two factors are fundamental: demand growth and the production and diffusion of knowledge.

**FIGURE 11.1**  The industry life cycle

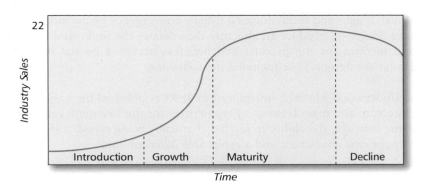

## Demand Growth

The life cycle and the stages within it are defined primarily by changes in an industry's growth rate over time. The characteristic profile is an S-shaped growth curve.

1   In the *introduction stage*, sales are small and the rate of market penetration is low because the industry's products are little known and customers are few. The novelty of the technology, small scale of production, and lack of experience means high costs and low quality. Customers for new products tend to be affluent, innovation-oriented, and risk-tolerant.

2   The *growth stage* is characterized by accelerating market penetration as technical improvements and increased efficiency open up the mass market.

3   Increasing market saturation causes the onset of the *maturity stage*. Once saturation is reached, demand is wholly for replacement.

4   Finally, as the industry becomes challenged by new industries that produce technologically superior substitute products, the industry enters its *decline stage*.

## Creation and Diffusion of Knowledge

The second driver of the industry life cycle is knowledge. New knowledge in the form of product innovation is responsible for an industry's birth, and the dual processes of knowledge creation and knowledge diffusion exert a major influence on industry evolution.

In the introduction stage, product technology advances rapidly. There is no dominant product technology, and rival technologies compete for attention. Competition is primarily between alternative technologies and design configurations:

- The first 30 years of steam ships featured competition between paddles and propellers, wooden hulls and iron hulls and, eventually, between coal and oil.
- The beginnings of the home computer industry during 1978–82 saw competition between different data storage systems (audio tapes versus floppy disks), visual displays (TV receivers versus dedicated monitors), operating systems (CPM versus DOS versus Apple II) and microprocessors.

*Dominant Designs and Technical Standards*   The outcome of competition between rival designs and technologies is usually convergence by the industry around a *dominant design*—a product architecture that defines the look, functionality and production method for the product and becomes accepted by the industry as a whole. Dominant designs have included the following:

- The Underwood Model 5 introduced in 1899 established the basic architecture and main features of typewriters for the twentieth century: a moving carriage, the ability to see the characters being typed, a shift function for upper case characters, and a replacable inked ribbon.[2]
- Leica's Ur-Leica camera developed by Oskar Barnack and launched in Germany in 1924 established key features of the 35 mm camera, though it

was not until Canon began mass-producing cameras based on the Leica original that this design of 35 mm camera came to dominate still photography.

- When Ray Kroc opened his first McDonald's hamburger restaurant in Illinois in 1955, he established what would soon become a dominant design for the fast-food restaurant industry: a limited menu, no waiter service, eat-in and take-out options, roadside locations for motorized customers and a franchising model of business system licensing.

The concepts of *dominant design* and *technical standard* are closely related. Dominant design refers to the overall configuration of a product or system. A technical standard is a technology or specification that is important for compatibility. A dominant design may or may not embody a technical standard. IBM's PC established the MS-DOS operating system and Intel x86 series of microprocessor as technical standards for personal computing. Conversely, the Boeing 707 was a dominant design for large passenger jets but did not set industry standards in aerospace technology that would dominate subsequent generations of airplanes. Technical standards emerge where there are *network effects*—the need for users to connect in some way with one another. Network effects cause each customer to choose the same technology as everyone else to avoid being stranded. Unlike a proprietary technical standard, which is typically embodied in patents or copyrights, a firm that sets a dominant design does not normally own intellectual property in that design. Hence, except for some early mover advantage, there is not necessarily any profit advantage from setting a dominant design.

Dominant designs also exist in processes. In the flat glass industry there has been a succession of dominant process designs from glass cylinder blowing to continuous ribbon drawing to float glass.[3] Dominant designs are present, too, in business models. In many new markets, competition is between rival *business models*. In home grocery delivery, dotcom startups such as Webvan and Peapod soon succumbed to competition from "bricks 'n' clicks" retailers such as Giant, Safeway, and Wal-mart.

*From Product to Process Innovation*   The emergence of a dominant design marks a critical juncture in an industry's evolution. Once the industry coalesces around a leading design, there's a shift from radical to incremental product innovation. This transition may be necessary to inaugurate the industry's growth phase: greater standardization reduces risks to customers and encourages firms to invest in production capacity. The shift in emphasis from design to manufacture typically involves increased attention to process innovation as firms seek to reduce costs and increase product reliability through large-scale production methods (see Figure 11.2). The combination of process improvements, design modifications, and scale economies results in falling costs and greater availability that drives rapidly increasing market penetration. Strategy Capsule 11.1 uses the history of the automobile industry to illustrate these patterns of development.

Knowledge diffusion is also important on the customer side. Over the course of the life cycle, customers become increasingly informed. As they become more knowledgeable about the performance attributes of rival manufacturers' products, so they are better able to judge value for money and become more price sensitive.

**FIGURE 11.2** Product and process innovation over time

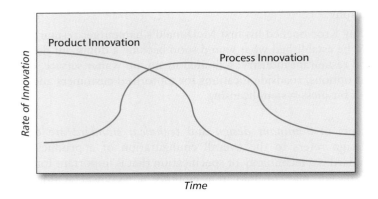

## STRATEGY CAPSULE 11.1
# Evolution of the Automobile Industry

The period 1890–1912 was one of rapid product innovation in the auto industry. After 1886, when Karl Benz received a patent on his three-wheel motor carriage, a flurry of technical advances occurred in Germany, France, the U.S. and Britain. Developments included:

- the first four-cylinder four-stroke engine (by Karl Benz in 1890);
- the honeycomb radiator (by Daimler in 1890);
- the speedometer (by Oldsmobile in 1901);
- automatic transmission (by Packard in 1904);
- electric headlamps (by General Motors in 1908);
- the all-steel body (adopted by General Motors in 1912).

Ford's Model T, introduced in 1908, with its front-mounted, water-cooled engine and transmission with a gearbox, wet clutch, and rear-wheel drive, acted as a dominant design for the industry. During the remainder of the twentieth century, automotive technology and design converged. A key indicator of this was the gradual elimination of alternative technologies and designs. Volkswagen's Beetle was the last mass-produced car with a rear-mounted, air-cooled engine. Citroën abandoned its distinctive suspension and braking systems. Four-stroke engines with four or six inline cylinders became dominant. Distinctive national differences eroded as American cars became smaller and Japanese and Italian cars became bigger. The fall of the Iron Curtain extinguished the last outposts of nonconformity: by the mid-1990s, East German two-stroke Wartburgs and Trabants were collectors' items.

As product innovation slowed, so process innovation took off. In October 1913, Ford opened its Highland Park Assembly Plant, with its revolutionary production methods based on interchangeable parts and a moving assembly line. In the space of one year, chassis assembly time was cut from 12 hours and 8 minutes to 1 hour and 33 minutes. The price of the Model T fell from $628 in 1908 to $260 in 1924.

Between 1908 and 1927 over 15 million Model Ts had been produced.

The second revolutionary process innovation in automobile manufacturing was Toyota's system of "lean production," involving a tightly integrated "pull" system of production embodying just-in-time scheduling, team-based production, flexible manufacturing and total quality management. During the 1970s and 1980s, lean production diffused throughout the world vehicle industry in the same way that Ford's mass-production system had transformed the industry half a century before.

*Sources:* www.ford.com; http://en.wikipedia.org/wiki/History_of_the_automobile

## How General is the Life-Cycle Pattern?

To what extent do industries conform to this life-cycle pattern? To begin with, the duration of the life cycle varies greatly from industry to industry:

- The introduction phase of the U.S. railroad industry extended from the building of the first railroad, the Baltimore and Ohio in 1827, to the growth phase of the 1870s. With the growth of road transport, the industry entered its decline phase during the late 1950s.

- The introduction stage of the U.S. automobile industry lasted about 25 years, from the 1890s until growth took off in 1913–15. Maturity set in during the mid-1950s followed by decline during the past decade.

- In personal computers, the introduction phase lasted only about four years before growth took off in 1978. Between 1978 and 1983 a flood of new and established firms entered the industry. Toward the end of 1984, the first signs of maturity appeared: growth stalled, excess capacity emerged, and the industry began to consolidate around fewer companies; however, growth remained strong until the end of the 1990s.

- Digital audio players (MP3 players) were first introduced by Seehan Information Systems and Diamond Multimedia during 1997–8. With the launch of Apple's iPod in 2001 the industry entered its growth phase. By 2008–9, slackening growth indicated entry into the mature phase.

The tendency over time has been for life cycles to become compressed. This is especially evident in e-commerce. Businesses such as online gambling, business-to-business online auctions, and online travel services have gone from initial introduction to apparent maturity within a few years. "Competing on internet time" requires a radical rethink of strategies and management processes.[4]

Patterns of evolution also differ. Industries supplying basic necessities such as residential construction, food processing and clothing may never enter a decline phase because obsolescence is unlikely for such needs. Some industries may experience a rejuvenation of their life cycle. In the 1960s, the world motorcycle industry, in decline in the U.S. and Europe, re-entered its growth phase as Japanese manufacturers pioneered the recreational use of motorcycles. The market for TV

**FIGURE 11.3** Innovation and renewal in the industry life cycle: retailing

receivers has experienced multiple revivals: color TVs, computer monitors, flat-screen TVs and, most recently, HDTVs. Similar waves of innovation have revitalized retailing (see Figure 11.3). These rejuvenations of the product life cycle are not natural phenomena—they are typically the result of companies resisting the forces of maturity through breakthrough product innovations or developing new markets.

An industry is likely to be at different stages of its life cycle in different countries. Although the automobile markets of the E.U., Japanese, and U.S. have entered their decline phase, those of China, India, and Russia are in their growth phases. Multinational companies can exploit such differences: developing new products and introducing them into the advanced industrial countries, then shifting attention to other growth markets once maturity sets in.

A more fundamental critique of the life-cycle model is posed by recent work on industrial dynamics by Michael Jacobides. A key feature industrial evolution, he argues, is the shifting boundaries of industries. As a result industrial evolution needs to explore changes in "industry architecture" at the sectoral level—focusing in particular on the shifting vertical structure of clusters of related industries. In the computer sector and mortgage banking sector the major trend has been towards vertical deintegration.[5]

## Structure, Competition and Success Factors over the Life Cycle

Changes in demand growth and technology over the cycle have implications for industry structure, competition, and the sources of competitive advantage (key success factors). Table 11.1 summarizes the principal features of each stage of the industry life cycle.

### Product Differentiation

The introduction stage typically features a wide variety of product types that reflect the diversity of technologies and designs—and the lack of consensus over customer

**TABLE 11.1**   The evolution of industry structure and competition over the life cycle

|  | Introduction | Growth | Maturity | Decline |
|---|---|---|---|---|
| *Demand* | Limited to early adopters: high-income, avant-garde | Rapidly increasing market penetration | Mass market, replacement/repeat buying. Customers knowledgeable and price sensitive | Obsolescence |
| *Technology* | Competing technologies, rapid product innovation | Standardization around dominant technology, rapid process innovation | Well-diffused technical knowhow: quest for technological improvements. | Little product or process innovation |
| *Products* | Poor quality, wide variety of features and technologies, frequent design changes. | Design and quality improve, emergence of dominant design | Trend to commoditization. Attempts to differentiate by branding, quality, bundling | Commodities the norm: differentiation difficult and unprofitable |
| *Manufacturing and distribution* | Short production runs, high-skilled labor content, specialized distribution channels | Capacity shortages, mass production, competition for distribution. | Emergence of overcapacity, deskilling of production, long production runs, distributors carry fewer lines | Chronic overcapacity, reemergence of specialty channels |
| *Trade* | Producers and consumers in advanced countries | Exports from advanced countries to rest of world | Production shifts to newly industrializing then developing countries. | Exports from countries with lowest labor costs |
| *Competition* | Few companies | Entry, mergers and exits | Shakeout, price competition increases | Price wars, exits |
| *Key success factors* | Product innovation, establishing credible image of firm and product | Design for manufacture, access to distribution, brand building, fast product development, process innovation | Cost efficiency through capital intensity, scale efficiency, and low input costs | Low overheads, buyer selection, signaling commitment, rationalizing capacity |

requirements. Convergence around a dominant design is often followed by commoditization during the mature phase unless producers develop new dimensions for differentiation. Personal computers, credit cards, online financial services, wireless communication services, and internet access have all become commodity items which buyers select primarily on price.

## Organizational Demographics and Industry Structure

The number of firms in an industry changes substantially over the life cycle. The field of *organizational ecology*, founded by Michael Hannan, John Freeman and Glen Carroll, analyzes the population of industries and the processes of founding and selection that determine entry and exit.[6] Some of the main findings of the organizational ecologists in relation to industry evolution are:

- The number of firms in an industry increases rapidly during the early stages of an industry's life. Initially an industry may be pioneered by a few firms. However, as the industry gains legitimacy, failure rates decline and the rate of new firm foundings increases. New entrants have very different origins. Some are startup companies (*de novo* entrants); others are established firms diversifying from related industries (*de alio* entrants). The U.S. automobile industry comprised 272 manufacturers in 1909,[7] while in TV receivers there were 92 companies in 1951.[8]

- With the onset of maturity, the number of firms begins to fall. Very often, industries go through one or more "shakeout" phases during which the rate of firm failure increases sharply. After this point, rates of entry and exit decline and the survival rate for incumbents increases substantially.[9] The shakeout phase of intensive acquisition, merger, and exit occurs, on average, 29 years into the life cycle and results in the number of producers being halved.[10] In the U.S. tire industry, the number of firms grew from one (Goodrich) in 1896 to 274 in 1922 before shakeout reduced the industry to 49 firms in 1936.[11]

- As industries become increasingly concentrated and the leading firms focus on the mass market, so a new phase of entry may take place as new firms create niche positions in the market. An example of this "resource partitioning" is the U.S. brewing industry: as the mass market became dominated by a handful of national brewers, so opportunities arose for new types of brewing companies— microbreweries and brew pubs—to establish themselves in specialist niches.[12]

However, in different industries structural change follows very different evolutionary paths. In most industries maturity is associated with increasing concentration but in industries where scale economies are unimportant and entry barriers are low, maturity and commoditization may cause concentration to decline (as in credit cards, television broadcasting, and frozen foods). Some industries, especially where the first mover achieves substantial patent protection, may start out as near-monopolies, then become increasingly competitive. Plain-paper copiers were initially monopolized by the Xerox Corporation and it was not until the early 1980s that the industry was transformed by a wave of new entry. Seemingly stable mature industries can be transformed within a few years by a wave of mergers. The world petroleum industry consolidated considerably during 1998–2001, as did the world steel industry during 2001–7.

## Location and International Trade

Industries move internationally during their life cycles as a result of shifts in demand decreasing dependence on advanced knowledge. New industries begin in the advanced industrial countries because of the presence of affluent consumers and the availability of technical and scientific resources. As demand grows in other countries, they are serviced initially by exports, but reduced need for sophisticated labor skills makes production attractive in newly industrialized countries. The advanced industrialized countries begin to import. With maturity, commoditization, and deskilling of production processes, production eventually shifts to developing countries where labor costs are lowest.

At the beginning of the 1990s, the production of wireless handsets was concentrated in the U.S., Japan, Finland and Germany. By the end of the 1990s, South Korea had joined this leading group. During 2009, production in North America, western Europe and Japan was in rapid decline as manufacturers shifted output to China, India, Brazil, Vietnam, Hungary and Romania.

## The Nature and Intensity of Competition

The changes in industry structure that we have identified over the life cycle—commoditization, new entry, and international diffusion of production—have implications for competition. First, there is a shift from nonprice competition to price competition. Second, the intensity of competition grows, causing margins to narrow. During the introduction stage, competitors battle for technological leadership and competition focuses on technology and design. Gross margins can be high, but heavy investments in innovation and market development tend to depress return on capital. The growth phase is more conducive to profitability as market demand outstrips industry capacity—especially if incumbents are protected by barriers to entry. With the onset of maturity, increased product standardization and excess capacity stimulates price competition—especially during shakeout. How intense this is depends a great deal on the capacity/demand balance and the extent of international competition. In food retailing, airlines, motor vehicles, metals and insurance, maturity was associated with strong price competition and slender profitability. In household detergents, breakfast cereals, cosmetics and cigarettes, high seller concentration and successful maintenance of product differentiation has limited price rivalry and supported high margins. The decline phase is almost always associated with strong price competition (often degenerating into destructive price wars) and dismal profit performance.

## Key Success Factors and Industry Evolution

These same changes in structure together with changes in demand and technology over the industry life cycle also have important implications for the sources of competitive advantage at each stage of industry evolution:

1 During the introductory stage, product innovation is the basis for initial entry and for subsequent success. Soon, however, other requirements for success emerge. In moving from the first generation of products to subsequent generations, investment requirements grow and financial resources become increasingly important. Capabilities in product development also need to be supported by capabilities in manufacturing, marketing, and distribution.

2 Once the growth stage is reached, the key challenge is scaling up. As the market expands, the firm needs to adapt its product design and its manufacturing capability to large-scale production. As Figure 11.4 shows,

investment in R&D, plant and equipment and sales tends to be high during the growth phase. To utilize increased manufacturing capability, access to distribution becomes critical. At the same time, the tensions that organizational growth impose create the need for internal administrative and strategic skills. We consider these issues in Chapter 12.

**3** With the maturity stage, competitive advantage is increasingly a quest for efficiency—particularly in industries that tend toward commoditization. Cost efficiency through scale economies, low wages and low overheads become the key success factors. Figure 11.4 shows that R&D, capital investment, and marketing are lower in maturity than during the growth phase.

**4** The transition to decline intensifies pressures for cost cutting. It also requires maintaining stability by encouraging the orderly exit of industry capacity and capturing residual market demand. We consider the strategic issues presented by mature and declining industries more fully in Chapter 13.

**FIGURE 11.4** Differences in strategy and performance between businesses at different stages of the industry life cycle

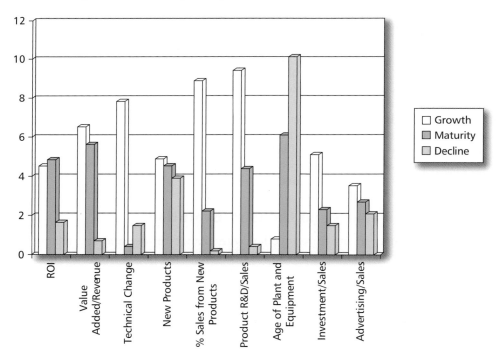

**Note:** The figure shows standardized means for each variable for businesses at each stage of the life cycle.

**Source:** C. Anderson and C. Zeithaml, "Stage of the Product Life Cycle, Business Strategy and Business Performance," *Academy of Management Journal* 27 (1984): 5–24. Reproduced with permission.

# Organizational Adaptation and Change

The problem of change is that it is difficult. It is stressful and painful for individuals; it is even more difficult for companies—they comprise multiple individuals who must change in a coordinated way. Hence, our starting point for the analysis of organizational change is to understand why change is so problematic for companies.

## The Sources of Organizational Inertia

Different theories of organizational and industrial change emphasize different barriers to change:

- *Organizational routines.* Evolutionary economists emphasize the fact that capabilities are based on organizational routines—patterns of coordinated interaction among organizational members that develop through continual repetition. The more highly developed are an organization's routines, the more difficult it is to develop new routines. Hence, organizations get caught in *competency traps*[13] where "core capabilities become core rigidities."[14]

- *Social and political structures.* Organizations develop social patterns of interaction that make organizational change stressful and disruptive.[15] Similarly, organizations create stable systems of political power. To the extent that change disrupts social patterns and threatens the power of those in positions of authority, organizations tend to resist change.

- *Conformity.* Institutional sociologists emphasize the propensity of firms to imitate one another to gain legitimacy.[16] The process of *institutional isomorphism* locks organizations into common structures and strategies that make it difficult for them to adapt to change. External pressures for conformity arise from governments, investment analysts, banks and other sources of resources and legitimacy but also through voluntary imitation— risk aversion encourages companies to adopt similar strategies and structures to their peers.[17]

- *Limited search.* The Carnegie School of organizational theory (associated with Herbert Simon, Jim March and Richard Cyert) views organizations' capacity for major changes as limited by a combination of cognitive and behavioral factors. Organizations tend to limit search to areas close to their existing activities—they prefer *exploitation* of existing knowledge over *exploration* for new opportunities. This is reinforced, first, by *bounded rationality*—human beings limited information processing capacity which constrains the set of choices that managers are capable of considering and, second, *satisficing*—the propensity for individuals (and organizations) to terminate the search for better solutions when they reach a satisfactory level of performance rather than to pursue optimal performance. The implication is that organizational change is triggered by declining performance.[18]

- *Complementarities between strategy, structure, and systems.* Organizational economics,[19] sociotechnical systems[20] and complexity theory[21] have all emphasized the importance of *fit* between an organization's strategy, structure, management systems, culture, employee skills—indeed, all the characteristics of an organization. Organizations struggle to establish complex, idiosyncratic combinations of multiple characteristics during their early phases of development in order to match the conditions of their business environment. However, once established, this complex configuration becomes a barrier to change. To respond to a change in its external environment, it is not enough to make incremental changes in few dimensions of strategy—it is likely that the firm will need to find a new configuration that involves a comprehensive set of changes.[22] The implication is that organizations tend to evolve through a process of *punctuated equilibrium*, involving long periods of stability during which the widening misalignment between the organization and its environment ultimately forces radical and comprehensive change on the company.[23] Systematic changes that involve establishing a new configuration of activities that better matches the requirements of the external environment may require the appointment of a CEO from outside who is not wedded to the previous configuration.

## Evolutionary Theory and Organizational Change

Different theories of organizational change are distinguished, not only by their focus on different sources of inertia, but also by their emphasis on different processes of change. The two major approaches to industry evolution—the organizational ecology school and the evolutionary economics school—both draw upon biological theories of evolution which view organizations adapting to external change through *variation*, *selection*, and *retention*.[24] However, they differ according to the level at which these evolutionary processes occur:

- *Organizational ecology*—at least in its initial formulation, views organizational change as restricted by powerful forces of inertia, hence, evolutionary processes work at the level of the industry through changes in the population of firms. Industries develop and grow through new entry which is spurred by the imitation of initial successful entrants. The competitive process is a *selection mechanism*, in which organizations whose characteristics match the requirements of their environment can attract resources, those that do not are eliminated. Thus, industry evolution occurs through changes in the *population of firms* rather than through changes in the firms themselves.[25]

- *Evolutionary economics* focuses upon individual organizations as the primary agents of evolution. The process of variation, selection, and retention takes place at the level of the *organizational routine*—unsuccessful routines are abandoned; successful routines are replicated within the organization.[26] As we discussed in Chapter 5, these patterns of coordinated activity are the basis for organizational capability. While evolutionary theorists view firms as adapting to external change through the search for new routines, replication of successful routines, and abandonment of unsuccessful routines, such adaptation is neither fast nor costless.

## Empirical Evidence on Organizational Adaptation

The ability of some companies to adapt is indicated by the fact that many have been leaders in their industries for a century or more—BASF, the world's largest

**TABLE 11.2** World's biggest companies in terms of market capitalization, 1912 and 2009

| 1912 | $ bn | 2009 | $ bn |
|---|---|---|---|
| U.S. Steel | 0.74 | ExxonMobil | 395 |
| Exxon | 0.39 | PetroChina | 241 |
| J&P Coates | 0.29 | Wal-Mart Stores | 202 |
| Pullman | 0.20 | ChinaMobile | 197 |
| Royal Dutch Shell | 0.19 | Procter & Gamble | 179 |
| Anaconda | 0.18 | Microsoft | 174 |
| General Electric | 0.17 | General Electric | 168 |
| Singer | 0.17 | AT&T | 157 |
| American Brands | 0.17 | Chevron | 148 |
| Navistar | 0.16 | BP | 148 |
| BAT | 0.16 | Nestlé | 139 |
| De Beers | 0.16 | BHP Billiton | 135 |

**Sources:** *Financial Times, Economist.*

chemical company, has been a leader in chemicals since it was founded in 1865 as a producer of synthetic dyes. ExxonMobil and Royal Dutch Shell have led the world's petroleum industry for over a century.[27] Budweiser Budvar, the Czech beer company that has been involved in a trademark dispute with Anheuser Busch for several decades, traces its origins to 1785. Mitsui Group, the Japanese conglomerate is even older—its first business, a retail store, was established in 1673. Yet these companies are exceptions. Among the companies forming the original Dow Jones Industrial Average in 1896, only General Electric remains in the index today. Of the world's 12 biggest companies in 1912, just three were in the top 12 in 2006 (see Table 11.2).

A firm's ability to adapt to external change depends on the nature of that change. Generally, evolutionary change is less threatening than radical change—major technological shifts in particular. Let us look at some of the evidence.

*Adapting to Changes over the Life Cycle* Even though the industry life cycle involves changes that are largely predictable, the changes in key success factors that we have already identified imply that the different stages of the life cycle require different resources and capabilities. Markides and Geroski show that the "innovators" that pioneer the creation of a new industry are typically different companies from the "consolidators" that develop it:

> The fact that the firms that create new product and service markets are rarely the ones that scale them into mass markets has serious implications for the modern corporation. Our research points to a simple reason for this phenomenon: the skills, mind-sets, and competences needed for discovery and invention are not only different from those needed for commercialization; they conflict with the needed characteristics. This means that the firms good at invention are unlikely to be good at commercialization and vice versa.[28]

In plant biotechnology, the pioneers were research-based start-ups such as Calgene, Cetus Corporation, DNA Plant Technologies and Mycogen. By 2008, the leading suppliers of genetically modified seeds were DuPont, Monsanto, Syngenta, and Dow Chemical. In U.S. wireless telephony the pioneer was McCaw Communications; the current market leaders are AT&T and Verizon.

*Adapting to Technological Change: Architectural Innovation*   The ability of firms to adapt to technological change depends to a great extent on the implications of the new technology. Some new technologies may enhance a company's existing capabilities, others may be "competence destroying."[29] This depends, in part, on whether the technology's impact is at the "component" or the "architectural" level—whether it involves a single process or product feature or whether it necessitates a new configuration of the product.[30] In many sectors of e-commerce—online grocery purchases and online banking—the internet involved innovation at the component level (it provided a new channel of distribution for existing products). Hence, existing supermarket chains and established retail banks with their "clicks-and-bricks" business models have dominated online groceries and online financial services. Conversely, the transistor radio involved an architectural innovation that required established radio producers to radically change their approaches to product design, manufacturing and marketing:

> In the mid-1950s engineers at RCA's corporate R&D center developed a prototype of a portable, transistorized radio receiver. The new product used technology in which RCA was accomplished (transistors, radio circuits, speakers, tuning devices), but RCA saw little reason to pursue such an apparently inferior technology. In contrast, Sony, a small, relatively new company, used the small transistorized radio to gain entry into the U.S. market. Even after Sony's success was apparent, RCA remained a follower in the market as Sony introduced successive models with improved sound quality and FM capability. The irony of the situation was not lost on the R&D engineers: for many years Sony's radios were produced with technology licensed from RCA, yet RCA had great difficulty matching Sony's product in the marketplace.[31]

*Disruptive Technologies*   Clay Christiansen argues that the ability of established firms to successfully adopt new technology depends upon whether the new technology is *sustaining*, i.e., it augments existing performance attributes, or whether it is *disruptive*, incorporating different performance attributes than the existing technology.[32] In the disk drive industry, some technological innovations—such as thin-film heads and more finely-dispersed ferrous oxide disk coatings—have enhanced the dominant performance criterion: recording density. Such innovation has typically been led by established industry leaders.

Other disk-drive technologies—notably new product generations with smaller diameters—were disruptive in their impact: established companies were, on average, two years behind newcomers in launching the new disk sizes and typically lost their industry leadership.[33] Incumbents' resistance to the new disk sizes reflected inferior initial performance and customer resistance. In 1987 Connor Peripherals began shipping a 3.5 inch disk drive. Industry leader Seagate had developed a 3.5 inch drive but recognized that in terms of capacity and cost per megabyte of memory, it was inferior to the existing 5.25 inch disk. However, the key reason that Seagate abandoned development of the 3.5 inch disks was lack of interest among its major customers—the manufacturers of desktop PCs. The 3.5 inch disks were adopted initially by Compaq for its compact PCs and makers of laptop computers who appreciated its small size and robustness. However, within a year the rapid development of 3.5 inch disks resulted in their closing the gap with 5.25 inch disks in terms of cost and capacity. By 1990 even desktop computers were being fitted with 3.5 inch drives.[34]

Similarly with other technologies. Steam-powered ships were initially slower, more expensive and less reliable than sailing ships. However, they were used for use on inland waters, which lacked constant winds. The leading shipbuilders failed to make the transition to steam power because their leading customers—the transocean shipping companies—remained loyal to sail until after the turn of the twentieth century.

However, the evidence is not wholly one way—in some industries, established firms have successfully adjusted to technological changes that were both architectural and disruptive. Since the late 19th century, the typesetting industry has undergone three waves of wrenching technological change. Yet, although new entrants had advantages in technology and new product development, incumbent firms have been able to use their strengths in certain key resources that newcomers were unable to replicate—notably customer relationships, sales and service networks, and font libraries—to survive and prosper.[35]

*Established Firms in New Industries* If established companies have difficulties adapting to evolutionary and technological changes within their own industries, it seems reasonable to expect that they would experience difficulties entering into entirely new industries. In most new industries we find both new startup companies ("*de novo* entrants") competing with established companies that have diversified from other sectors ("*de alio* entrants"). The issue is the same as within an existing industry that is undergoing change: do the flexibility advantages of new firms outweigh the superior resources and capabilities of established firms? It depends upon the extent to which the resources and capabilities required in the new industry are similar to those present in an existing industry. Where linkages are close, then diversifying entrants are likely to have an advantage over new startups. Thus:

- In the U.S. automobile industry, former bicycle, carriage, and engine manufacturers tended to be the best performers.[36]
- The U.S. television manufacturing industry was dominated by former producers of radios.[37]

However, some of the best performing firms in a new industry are often spinoffs from existing companies within that industry—i.e. new ventures established by former employees of existing companies. This was evident in the Akron tire industry[38] and the Silicon Valley semiconductor industry—where most of the leading players, including Intel, trace their origins to Shockley Semiconductor Laboratories, the pioneering producer of integrated circuits.[39]

## Managing Organizational Change

Given the many barriers to organizational change, how can companies adapt to changes in their environment? Traditionally the management of organizational change has been viewed as a distinct area of management: *organizational development* (OD) comprises a set of methodologies through which an internal or external consultant acts as a catalyst for systemic change within a team or organizational unit.[40] In recent years the management of organizational change has been viewed as a continuous activity that forms the central component of a manager's responsibilities. The starting point for managing ongoing change is to recognize the sources of inertia: by identifying the barriers to change it becomes possible to identify opportunities for alleviating and circumventing them.

*Dual Strategies and Separate Organizational Units* Given the tendency for strategies and structures to be founded upon routinized behavior patterns and locked into complex patterns of interdependency, it may be easier to effect change by creating new organizational units rather than trying to change the existing organization. For example, faced with the challenge of disruptive technologies, Christensen and Overdorf suggest that established companies develop products and businesses that embody the new technologies in organizationally separate units.[41]

The broader issue is the challenge of *dual strategies*: how a company manages its existing activities while also nurturing new initiatives will form the basis for its business in the future. Most of the evidence points to the difficulties of reconciling strategies that require different capabilities and management systems within the same company: attempts by Continental, United and British Airways to establish budget airline subsidiaries were costly failures; attempts by the oil and gas majors to set up business development units that would create new businesses out of their technological innovations made little progress. Nevertheless, some companies have been able to reconcile the launch of new businesses with the effective management of established businesses (e.g. 3M, Google). Other companies have achieved coexistence of cost leadership and differentiation strategies (HSBC in full-service and internet banking; Merck in patented and generic drugs). Costas Markides argues that the successful pursuit of dual strategies requires either organizational separation (e.g. the allocation of new strategic initiatives to a separate organizational unit) or the development of "ambidexterity" such that the different strategy can access and deploy the same resources and capabilities.[42]

Given the general challenge of competing for today and developing the resources, capabilities and business initiatives needed to compete for tomorrow (see the discussion on strategic and dynamic notions of strategy in Chapter 1), all companies must—to some extent—pursue dual strategies. According to Derek Abell, such dual strategies require dual planning systems: short-term planning that focuses on strategic fit and performance over a one- or two-year period; and longer term planning to develop vision, reshape the corporate portfolio, redefine and reposition individual businesses, develop new capabilities and redesign organizational structures over periods of five years or more.[43] Given companies' bias towards the exploitation of current resources and capabilities in relation to known opportunities, the challenge for top management is to shift the emphasis towards building opportunities and new capabilities for the future.

*Bottom-up Processes of Decentralized Organizational Change* In Chapter 6, we noted that the appeal of modular, loosely coupled organizational structures was the potential for decentralized adaptation that avoided disrupting the whole organization. Yet, typically, simply decentralizing decision making is not enough to speed the processes of organizational adaptation. The strategy literature points to the need for top management to manage the conditions that foster and extend the processes of change. For example:

- If search for new strategies and new opportunities is limited by satisficing behavior, then top management needs to stimulate performance by raising performance expectations—establishing "stretch targets" for example.

- Corporate top management can challenge divisional and business unit managers to seek new opportunities by issuing specific company-wide initiatives. General Electric's former CEO, Jack Welch, would issue a new corporate challenge every two or three years: "Be number 1 or number 2 in your industry," "six-sigma quality," "destroy-your-business.com."

- Andy Grove of Intel has pointed to the necessity for top management to be alert to the emergence of "strategic dissonance" created by divergent strategic directions within the company. Such dissonance is likely to signal a "strategic inflection point"—a fundamental change in industry dynamics—at which point the company must be willing to make a radical strategic shift. For Intel, such an inflection point occurred when it recognized that its future lay in microprocessors rather than its initial business of DRAM chips.[44]

- By periodically changing organizational structure, a company can stimulate decentralized search and local initiatives while encouraging more effective exploitation of the outcomes of such search.[45] A typical pattern is to oscillate from periods of decentralization to periods of centralization.[46]

*Imposing Top-down Organizational Change* If organizational change occurs periodically through a punctuated equilibrium process, the implication is that these instances of concentrated organizational change must be orchestrated from the top. Most large companies exhibit periodic restructuring involving simultaneous changes in strategy, structure, management systems, and top management personnel. Such restructuring typically follows declining performance. For example, the oil and gas majors all experienced far-reaching restructuring during 1986–92 following depressed profitability that accompanied the oil price decline of 1986.[47] The challenge for top management is to undertake large-scale change before the company is pressured by declining performance. This may require that the CEO manufactures a perception of impending crisis within the company.

*Using Scenarios to Prepare for the Future* A company's ability to adapt to changes in its environment depends on its capacity to anticipate such changes. Yet predicting the future is hazardous, if not impossible. "Only a fool would make predictions—especially about the future," remarked movie mogul Samuel Goldwyn. But the inability to predict does not mean that it is not useful to think about what might happen in the future. *Scenario analysis* is a systematic way of thinking about how the future might unfold that builds on what we know about current trends and signals. Scenario analysis is not a forecasting technique, but a process for thinking and communicating about the future.

Herman Kahn, who pioneered their use first at the Rand Corporation and subsequently at the Hudson Institute, defined scenarios as "hypothetical sequences of events constructed for the purpose of focusing attention on causal process and decision points."[48] The multiple scenario approach constructs several distinct, internally consistent views of how the future may look five to 25 years ahead (shorter in the case of fast-moving sectors). Its key value is in combining the interrelated impacts of a wide range of economic, technological, demographic and political factors into a few distinct alternative stories of how the future might unfold. Scenario analysis can be either qualitative or quantitative or involve some combination of the two. Quantitative scenario analysis models events and runs simulations to identify likely outcomes. Qualitative scenarios typically take the form of narratives and can be particularly useful in engaging the insight and imagination of decision makers.

For the purposes of strategy making, scenario analysis is used to explore likely paths of industry evolution, to examine developments in particular country markets, to think about the impact of new technologies, and to analyze prospects for specific investment projects. Applied to industry evolution, scenarios can clarify and develop alternative views of how changing customer requirements, emerging technologies, government policies and competitor strategies might have an impact on industry structure and what the implications for competition and competitive advantage might be.

However, as with most strategy techniques, the value of scenario analysis is not in the results but in the process. Scenario analysis is a powerful tool for bringing together different ideas and insights, for surfacing deeply held beliefs and assumptions, for identifying possible threats and opportunities, for generating and evaluating alternative strategies, for encouraging more flexible thinking by managers and for building consensus. Evaluating the likely performance of different strategies under different scenarios can help identify which strategies are most robust and can assist in contingency planning by forcing managers to address "what if?" questions. Strategy Capsule 11.2 outlines the use of scenarios at Shell.

## STRATEGY CAPSULE 11.2
# Multiple Scenario Development at Shell

Royal Dutch Shell has pioneered the use of scenarios as a basis for long-term strategic planning in an industry where the life of investment projects (up to 50 years) far exceeds the time horizon for forecasting (two or three years). In 1967, a "Year 2000" study was inaugurated and scenario development soon became fundamental to Shell's planning process. Mike Pocock, Shell's former chairman, observed: "We believe in basing planning not on single forecasts, but on deep thought that identifies a coherent pattern of economic, political, and social development."

Shell views its scenarios as critical to its transition from planning toward strategic management, in which the role of the planning function is not so much to produce a plan, but to manage a process, the outcome of which is improved decision making by managers. This involves continually challenging current thinking within the group, encouraging a wider look at external influences on the business, promoting learning, and forging coordination among Shell's 200-odd subsidiaries.

Shell's global scenarios are prepared about every four years by a team comprising corporate planning staff, executives, and outside experts. Economic, political, technological, and demographic trends are analyzed 20 years into the future. Shell's 2005–25 scenarios were based on three sets of forces—market incentives, community, and coercion and regulation; and three objectives—efficiency, social cohesion, and security. Their interactions produced three scenarios each embodying different social, political, and economic conditions:

- *Low Trust Globalization*. A legalistic world where emphasis is on security and efficiency at the expense of social cohesion.

- *Open Doors*. A pragmatic world emphasizing social cohesion and efficiency with the market providing built-in solutions to crises of security and trust.

- *Flags*. A dogmatic world where community and security values are emphasized at the expense of efficiency.

Once approved by top management, the scenarios are disseminated by reports, presentations, and workshops, where they form the basis for long-term strategy discussion by business sectors and operating companies.

Shell is adamant that its scenarios are not forecasts. They represent carefully thought-out stories of how the various forces shaping the global energy environment of the future might play out. Their value is in stimulating the social and cognitive processes through which managers envisage the future. CEO Van Der Veer commented: ". . . the imperative is to use this tool to gain deeper in sights into our global business environment and to achieve the cultural change that is at the heart of our group strategy . . . I know that they broaden one's mindset and stimulate discussions."

*Sources:* Pierre Wack, "Scenarios: Uncharted Waters Ahead," *Harvard Business Review* (September–October, 1985): 72 and "Scenarios: Shooting the Rapids," *Harvard Business Review* (November–December 1985): 139; Arie De Geus, "Planning as Learning," *Harvard Business Review* (March–April 1988): 70–4; Paul Schoemacher, "Multiple Scenario Development: Its Conceptual and Behavioral Foundation," *Strategic Management Journal* 14 (1993): 193–214; *Shell Global Scenarios to 2025* (Shell International, 2005).

## Shaping the Future

A succession of management gurus from Tom Peters to Gary Hamel have argued that the key to organizational change is not to adapt to external change but to create the future. Companies that adapt to change are doomed to playing catch-up; competitive advantages accrue to those companies that act as leaders and initiate change. Hamel and Prahalad's "new strategy paradigm" emphasizes the role of strategy as a systematic and concerted approach to redefining both the company and its industry environment in the future.[49]

According to Gary Hamel, in an age of revolution, "the company that is evolving slowly is already on its way to extinction."[50] The only option is to give up incremental improvement and adapt to a nonlinear world—revolution must be met by revolution. Achieving internal revolution requires changing the psychological and sociological norms of an organization that restrict innovation (see Figure 11.5).

Hamel's challenge for managers to cast off their bureaucratic chains and become revolutionaries is invigorating and inspiring. But is revolution among established

**FIGURE 11.5** Shaking the foundations

| OLD BRICK | NEW BRICK |
|---|---|
| Top management is responsible for setting strategy | Everyone is responsible for setting strategy |
| Getting better, getting faster is the way to win | Rule-busting innovation is the way to win |
| IT creates competitive advantage | Unconventional business concepts create competitive advantage |
| Being revolutionary is high risk | More of the same is high risk |
| We can merge our way to competitiveness | There's no correlation between size and competitiveness |
| Innovation equals new products and new technology | Innovation equals entirely new business concepts |
| Strategy is the easy part; implementation the hard part | Strategy is the easy part only if you're content to be an imitator |
| Change starts at the top | Change starts with activists |
| Our real problem is execution | Our real problem is incrementalism |
| Big companies can't innovate | Big companies can become gray-haired revolutionaries |

*Source:* adapted from G. Hamel, *Leading the Revolution* (Boston: Harvard Business School Press, 2000): 280–1. Reproduced with permission.

companies either feasible or desirable? Some established companies have achieved radical change:

- Nokia underwent a metamorphosis from a manufacturer of paper and rubber goods into the world's leading supplier of mobile phones;
- BP transformed itself from a bureaucratic state-owned oil company to one of the most flexible and innovative of the supermajors;
- Microsoft has successfully ridden a series of disruptive changes in the world's computer industry, including the transition to object-oriented computing and the networking revolution of the late 1990s, and is currently positioning itself for the conversion of computing, telecommunications, and home entertainment.

However, for most established companies, efforts at radical change have resulted in disaster:

- Enron's transformation from a utility and pipeline company to a trader and market-maker in energy futures and derivatives ended in its demise in 2001;
- Vivendi's multimedia empire built on the base of French water and waste utility fell apart in 2002;
- GEC's reincarnation as Marconi, a telecom equipment supplier, was swiftly followed by bankruptcy in 2002;

- ICI, the former British chemical giant, has yet to recover from its attempt to reinvent itself as a specialty chemical company;

- Skandia's quest to become one of the world's most innovative insurance companies ended in top management scandal and the sale of most of the company's businesses outside of Sweden.

The perils of radical strategic change are not difficult to understand. We have noted that competitive advantage depends on the deployment of superior organizational capabilities and these capabilities develop slowly. Strategic changes that take a company beyond its competence domain involve massive risks.

## Summary

Strategy is about establishing an identity and a direction for the development of a business into the future. How can we formulate a strategy for the future if the future is unknown and difficult to predict?

In this chapter we have learned that some regularities are evident in the evolutionary paths that industries follow. The life cycle model is a useful approach to exploring the impact of temporal processes of market saturation and technology development and dissemination, and their impact on industry structure and the basis of competitive advantage. Classifying industries according to their stage of development can in itself be an insightful exercise:

- It acts as a shortcut in strategy analysis. Categorizing an industry according to its stage of development can alert us to the type of competition likely to emerge and the kinds of strategy likely to be effective.

- Classifying an industry encourages comparison with other industries. By highlighting similarities and differences with other industries, such comparisons can help us gain a deeper understanding of the strategic characteristics of an industry.

- It directs attention to the forces of change and direction of industry evolution, thereby helping us to anticipate and manage change.

Even if we can identify certain regularities in the pattern of industry evolution, adapting to change presents a huge challenge to companies. Organizational theories that emphasize inertia and conformity among organizations suggest that industry adjustment may occur more through the birth of new firms and death of old ones than through adaptation by established firms. This analysis is supported by empirical evidence that points to the limited success of established firms in dealing with industry evolution and disruptive technologies.

While various management consultants and commentators advocate radical and continuous change among established companies, there is little evidence that most companies have the capacity to manage such change. Certain tools and techniques—scenario analysis in particular—may help managers understand and cope with change in the external environment; nevertheless, the fundamental truth is that, so long as developing new capabilities is slow and risky, a firm's capacity to undergo radical change successfully is inherently uncertain.

In the next two chapters, we discuss strategy formulation and strategy implementation in industries at different stages of their development: emerging industries, those characterized by technology-based competition, and mature industries.

# Self-Study Questions

1   Consider the changes that have occurred in a comparatively new industry (for example, wireless communication services, wireless handsets, video game consoles, online auctions, bottled water, online book retailing). To what extent has the evolution of the industry followed the pattern predicted by the industry life-cycle model? What particular features does the industry have that have influenced its pattern of evolution? At what stage of development is the industry today? How is the industry likely to evolve in the future?

2   Select a product that has become a *dominant design* for its industry (for example, the IBM PC in personal computers, McDonald's in fast food, Harvard in MBA education, Southwest in budget airlines). What factors caused one firm's product architecture to become dominant? Why did other firms imitate this dominant design? To what extent has the dominant design evolved or been displaced?

3   The "resource partitioning" model argues that as industries become dominated by a few major companies whose strategies and products converge, so opportunities open for new entrants to build specialist niches. Identify an opportunity for establishing a specialist new business in an industry dominated by mass market giants.

4   Consider an industry facing fundamental technology change (e.g. the recorded music Industry and digital technology, computer software and open-source, newspapers and the internet, automobiles and alternative fuels, corporate IT services and cloud computing). Develop two alternative scenarios for the future evolution of your chosen industry. In relation to one leading player in the industry, identify the problems posed by the new technology and develop a strategy for how the company might adapt to and exploit the changes you envisage.

# Notes

1 T. Levitt, "Exploit the Product Life Cycle," *Harvard Business Review* (November–December 1965): 81–94; G. Day, "The Product Life Cycle: Analysis and Applications," *Journal of Marketing* 45 (Autumn 1981): 60–7.

2 J. M. Utterback and F. F. Suarez, "Patterns of Industrial Evolution, Dominant designs, and Firms' Survival," Sloan working paper #3600-93 (MIT, 1993).

3 P. Anderson and M. L. Tushman, "Technological Discontinuities and Dominant Designs," *Administrative Science Quarterly* 35 (1990): 604–33.

4 M. A. Cusumano and D. B. Yoffie, *Competing on Internet Time: Lessons From Netscape and Its Battle with Microsoft* (New York: Free Press, 1998).

5 In Shiv Mathur and Alfred Kenyon's "transaction cycle," differentiation re-emerges as products and service are bundled into new systems. See "Competitive System Dynamics," in *Creating Wealth: Shaping Tomorrow's Business* (Oxford: Butterworth-Heinemann, 1997): Chapter 9.

6 M. G. Jacobides, "Industry Change through Vertical Disintegration: How and why Markets Emerged in Mortgage Banking," *Academy of Management Journal* 48, no. 3: 465–98; M. G. Jacobides, C. Y. Baldwin and R. Dizaji, "From the Structure of the Value Chain to the Strategic Dynamics of Industry Sectors," Academy of Management Presentation (Philadelphia, August 7, 2007).

7 G. Carroll and M. Hannan, *The Demography of Corporations and Industries* (Princeton: Princeton University Press, 2000). For a survey see: J. Baum, "Organizational Ecology," in S. R. Clegg, C. Hardy and W. R. Nord, *Handbook of Organizational Studies* (Thousand Oaks: Sage, 1996); D. Barron, "Evolutionary Theory," in D. O. Faulkner and A. Campbell (eds), *The Oxford Handbook of Strategy* (Oxford: Oxford University Press, 2003), vol. 1: 74–97.

8 G. R. Carroll, L. S. Bigelow, M.-D. Seidel and B. Tsai, "The Fates of de novo and de alio Producers in the American Automobile Industry, 1885–1981," *Strategic Management Journal* 17, Summer Special Issue (1996): 117–37.

9 S. Klepper and K. L. Simons, "Dominance by Birthright: Entry of Prior Radio Producers and Competitive Ramifications in the U.S. Television Receiver Industry," *Strategic Management Journal* 17 (2000): 997–1016.

10 High rates of entry and exit may continue well into maturity. In U.S. manufacturing industries in any given year, it was found that 39% of larger companies were not industry participants five years earlier and 40% would not be participants five years later. See T. Dunne, M. J. Roberts, and L. Samuelson, "Patterns of Firm Entry and Exit in U.S. Manufacturing Industries," *Rand Journal of Economics* 19 (1988): 495–515.

11 S. Klepper and E. Grady, "The Evolution of New Industries and the Determinants of Industry Structure," *Rand Journal of Economics* (1990): 27–44.

12 S. Klepper and K. Simons, "The Making of an Oligopoly: Firm Survival and Technological Change in the Evolution of the U.S. Tire Industry," *Journal of Political Economy* 108 (2000): 728-760.

13 G. Carroll and A. Swaminathan, "Why the Microbrewery Movement? Organizational Dynamics of Resource Partitioning in the American Brewing Industry," *American Journal of Sociology* 106 (2000): 715–62.

14 J. G. March, "Exploration and Exploitation in Organizational Learning," *Organizational Science* 2 (1991): 71–87.

15 D. Leonard-Barton, "Core Capabilities and Core Rigidities: A Paradox in Managing New Product Development," *Strategic Management Journal*, Summer Special Issue (1992): 111–25.

16 M. T. Hannan, L. Polos, and G. R. Carroll, "Structural Inertia and Organizational Change Revisited III: The Evolution of Organizational Inertia," Stanford GSB Research Paper 1734 (April 2002).

17 P. J. DiMaggio and W. Powell, "'The Iron Cage Revisited': Institutional Isomorphism and Collective Rationality in Organizational Fields," *American Sociological Review* 48 (1983): 147–60.

18 J.-C. Spender, *Industry Recipes* (Oxford: Blackwell, 1989).

19 J. G. March and H. A. Simon, *Organizations* (New York: John Wiley & Sons, Inc., 1958); J. G. March, "Exploration and Exploitation . . ." op. cit.

20 P. R. Milgrom and J. Roberts, "Complementarities and Fit: Strategy, Structure, and Organizational Change in Manufacturing," *Journal of Accounting and Economics* 19 (1995): 179–208; M. E. Porter and N. Siggelkow, "Contextual Interactions within Activity Systems and Sustainable Competitive Advantage," Working Paper, Harvard Business School, Boston, 2002.

21 E. Trist, "The Sociotechnical Perspective." In Van de Ven and Joyce (eds) *Perspectives on Organization Design and Behavior* (New York: John Wiley & Sons, Inc., 1984).

22 J. W. Rivkin, "Imitation of Complex Strategies," *Management Science* 46 (2000): 824–44.

23 M. E. Porter and N. Siggelkow, "Contextual Interactions within Activity Systems," *Academy of Management Perspectives* 22 (May 2008): 34–56.

24 M. L. Tushman and E. Romanelli, "Organizational Evolution: A Metamorphosis Model of Convergence and Reorientation," in L. L. Cummins and B. M. Staw (eds), *Research in Organizational Behavior* 7 (1985): 171–26; E. Romanelli and M. L. Tushman, "Organizational Transformation as Punctuated Equilibrium: An Empirical Test," *Academy of Management Journal* 37 (1994): 1141–66.

25 H. E. Aldrich, *Organizations and Environments* (Stanford University Press, 2007).

26 For an introduction to organizational ecology, see: M. T. Hannan and G. R. Carroll, "An introduction to organizational ecology," in *Organizations in Industry* (Oxford: Oxford University Press, 1995): 17–31.

27 For a survey of evolutionary approaches, see R. R. Nelson, "Recent Evolutionary Theorizing About Economic Change," *Journal of Economic Literature* 33 (March 1995): 48–90.

28 ExxonMobil Corporation is a descendent of Standard Oil; Royal Dutch Shell was created in 1907 by Royal Dutch Petroleum Co. and Shell Transport and Trading Co.

29 C. Markides and P. Geroski, "Colonizers and Consolidators: The Two Cultures of Corporate Strategy," *Strategy and Business* 32 (Fall, 2003). http://www.strategy-business.com/press/16635507/03306.

30 M. L. Tushman and P. Anderson, "Technological Discontinuities and Organizational Environments," *Administrative Science Quarterly* 31 (1986): 439–65.

31 R. M. Henderson and K. B. Clark, "Architectural Innovation: The Reconfiguration of Existing Systems and the Failure of Established Firms," *Administrative Science Quarterly* (1990): 9–30.

32 Ibid.

33 J. Bower and C. M. Christensen, "Disruptive Technologies: Catching the Wave," *Harvard Business Review* (January–February 1995): 43–53.

34 C. M. Christensen, *The Innovator's Dilemma* (Harvard Business School Press, 1997).

35 M. Tripsas, "Unravelling the Process of Creative Destruction: Complementary Assets and Incumbent Survival in the Typesetter Industry," *Strategic Management Journal* 18, Summer Special Issue (July 1997): 119–42.

36 S. Klepper, "The Capabilities of New Firms and the Evolution of the U.S. Automobile Industry," *Industrial and Corporate Change* 11 (2002): 645–66.

37 S. Klepper and K. L. Simons, "Dominance by Birthright: Entry of Prior Radio Producers and Competitive Ramifications in the U.S. Television Receiver Industry," *Strategic Management Journal* 21 (2000): 997–1016.

38 G. Buenstorf and S. Klepper, "Heritage and Agglomeration: The Akron Tire Cluster Revisited," Department of Social and Decision Sciences Working Paper, Carnegie Mellon University, March 2005.

39 D. A. Kaplan, *The Silicon Boys and Their Valley of Dreams* (New York: Morrow, 1999).

40 T. G. Cummins and C. G. Worley, *Organization Development and Change,* 8th edn. (Cincinatti, Ohio: Southwestern College Publishing: 2005).

41 C. M. Christensen and M. Overdorf, "Meeting the Challenge of Disruptive Change," *Harvard Business Review* (March–April 2000): 66–76.

42 C. Markides and C. D. Charitou, "Competing with Dual Strategies," *Academy of Management Executive* 18 (2004): 22–36.

43 D. F. Abell, *Managing with Dual Strategies* (New York: Free Press, 1993).

44 A. Grove, *Only the Paranoid Survive* (New York: Doubleday, 1996).

45 N. Siggelkow and D. A. Levinthal, "Escaping Real (Non-benign) Competency Traps: Linking the Dynamics of Organizational Structure to the Dynamics of Search," *Strategic Organization* 3 (2005): 85–115.

46 J. Nickerson and T. Zenger, "Being Efficiently Fickle: A Dynamic Theory of Organizational Choice," *Organization Science* 13 (September–October 2002): 547–67.

47 R. Cibin and R. M. Grant, "Restructuring among the World's Leading Oil Companies," *British Journal of Management* 7 (1996): 283–308.

48 H. Kahn, *The Next 200 Years: A Scenario for America and the World* (New York: William Morrow, 1976). For a guide to the use of scenarios in strategy making, see K. van der Heijden, *Scenarios: The Art of Strategic Conversation* (Chichester: John Wiley & Sons, Ltd, 2005).

49 G. Hamel and C. K. Prahalad, *Competing for the Future* (Boston: Harvard Business School Press, 1995).

50 G. Hamel, *Leading the Revolution* (Boston: Harvard Business School Press, 2000): 5.

# 12 Technology-based Industries and the Management of Innovation

*Whereas a calculator on the ENIAC is equipped with 18 000 vacuum tubes and weighs 30 tons, computers in the future may have only 1000 vacuum tubes and perhaps weigh only 1.5 tons.*

—POPULAR MECHANICS, *MARCH 1949*

*I can think of no conceivable reason why an individual should wish to have a computer in his own home.*

—KENNETH OLSEN, CHAIRMAN, DIGITAL EQUIPMENT CORPORATION, 1977

# Introduction and Objectives

In the previous chapter we saw that technology is the primary force that creates new industries and transforms existing ones. In the past quarter century, new technology-based industries include wireless telephony, biotechnology, photovoltaic power, fiber optics, online financial services, nanotechnology and laser printing. Industries transformed by technology include the telecom sector, which has been turned upside-down by wireless technology and the internet. The new global leaders are companies that pioneered the new technologies: on the service side Vodafone, China Mobile, and Skype (owned by eBay); on the hardware side Cisco Systems, Nokia, and Qualcomm.

The impact of technology has not been limited to science-based industries such as chemicals, healthcare, and electronics. A key feature of the past decade has been the pervasive influence of digital technologies—including communication technologies and the internet.

Our focus in this chapter is on business environments where technology is a key driver of change and an important source of competitive advantage. These technology-intensive industries include both emerging industries (those in the introductory and growth phases of their life cycle) and established industries where technology continues to be the major driver of competition (such as pharmaceuticals, chemicals, telecommunications and electronics). The issues we examine, however, are also relevant to a much broader range of industries where technology has the potential to create competitive advantage.

In the last chapter, we viewed technology as an external force that drove industrial change. In this chapter our primary concern will be the use of technology as a tool of competitive strategy. How does the firm use technology to establish competitive advantage?

---

By the time you have completed this chapter, you will be able to:

♦ analyze how technology affects industry structure and competition;

♦ identify the factors that determine the returns to innovation, and evaluate the potential for an innovation to establish competitive advantage;

♦ formulate strategies for exploiting innovation and managing technology, focusing in particular on:

   ♦ the relative advantages of being a leader or a follower in innovation;

   ♦ identifying and evaluating strategic options for exploiting innovation;

   ♦ how to win standards battles;

   ♦ how to manage risk;

♦ design the organizational conditions needed to implement such strategies successfully.

---

This chapter is organized as follows. First, we examine the links between technology and competition in technology-intensive industries. Second, we explore the potential for innovation to establish sustainable competitive advantage. Third, we deal with key issues in designing technology strategies, including timing (to lead or to follow), alternative strategies for exploiting an innovation, setting industry standards, and managing risk. Finally, we examine the organizational conditions for the successful implementation of technology-based strategies.

## Competitive Advantage in Technology-intensive Industries

The principal link between technology and competitive advantage is *innovation*. It is the quest for competitive advantage that causes firms to invest in innovation; it is innovation that is responsible for new industries coning into being; and it is innovation that allows some firms to dominate their industries. Let us begin by exploring the conditions under which innovation generates profit.

## The Innovation Process

*Invention* is the creation of new products and processes through the development of new knowledge or from new combinations of existing knowledge. Most inventions are the result of novel applications of existing knowledge. Samuel Morse's telegraph, patented in 1840, was based on several decades of research into electromagnetism from Ben Franklin to Orsted, Ampere and Sturgion. The compact disk embodies knowledge about lasers developed several decades previously.

*Innovation* is the initial commercialization of invention by producing and marketing a new good or service or by using a new method of production. Once introduced, innovation diffuses: on the demand side, through customers purchasing the good or service; on the supply side, through imitation by competitors. An innovation may be the result of a single invention (most product innovations in chemicals and pharmaceuticals involve discoveries of new chemical compounds) or it may combine many inventions. The first automobile, introduced by Benz in 1885, embodied a multitude of inventions, from the wheel, invented some 5000 years previously, to the internal combustion engine, invented nine years earlier. Not all invention progresses into innovation: among the patent portfolios of most technology-intensive firms are inventions that have yet to find a viable commercial application. Many innovations may involve little or no new technology: the personal computer brought together existing components and technologies; most new types of packaging—including the vast array of tamper-proof packages—involve novel design but no new technology.

Figure 12.1 shows the pattern of development from knowledge creation to invention and innovation. Historically, the lags between knowledge creation and innovation have been long:

- Chester F. Carlson invented xerography in 1938 by combining established knowledge about electrostatics and printing. The first patents were awarded in 1940. Xerox purchased the patent rights and launched its first office copier in 1958. By 1974, the first competitive machines were introduced by IBM, Kodak, Ricoh, and Canon.

**FIGURE 12.1** The development of technology: from knowledge creation to diffusion

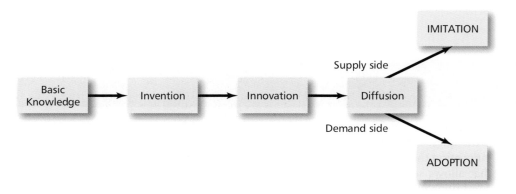

- The jet engine, employing Newtonian principles, was patented by Frank Whittle in 1930. The first commercial jet airliner, the DeHavilland Comet, flew in 1957. Two years later, the Boeing 707 was introduced.

Recently, the innovation cycle has speeded up:

- The mathematics of *fuzzy logic* were developed by Lofti Zadeh at Berkeley during the 1960s. By the early 1980s, Dr. Takeshi Yamakawa of the Kyushu Institute of Technology had registered patents for integrated circuits embodying fuzzy logic and in 1987 a series of fuzzy logic controllers for industrial machines was launched by Omron of Kyoto. By 1991, the world market for fuzzy logic controllers was estimated at $2 billion.[1]
- MP3, the audio file compression software, was developed at the Fraunhofer Institute in Germany in 1987; by the mid-1990s, the swapping of MP3 music files had taken off in U.S. college campuses and in 1998 the first MP3 player, Diamond Multimedia's *Rio*, was launched. Apple's iPod was introduced in 2001.

## The Profitability of Innovation

"If a man can . . . make a better mousetrap than his neighbor, though he build his house in the woods, the world will make a beaten path to his door," claimed Emerson. Yet the inventors of new mousetraps, and other gadgets too, are more likely to be found at the bankruptcy courts than in the millionaires' playgrounds of the Caribbean. Certainly, innovation is no guarantor of fame and fortune, either for individuals or for companies. There is no consistent evidence that either R&D intensity or frequency of new product introductions are positively associated with profitability.[2]

The profitability of an innovation to the innovator depends on the value created by the innovation and the share of that value that the innovator is able to appropriate. The value created by an innovation is distributed among a number of different parties (see Figure 12.2). In the case of the personal computer, the innovators—MITS, Tandy, Apple, and Xerox—earned modest profits from their innovation. The imitators—IBM, Dell, Compaq, Acer, Toshiba and a host of other

**FIGURE 12.2** Appropriation of value: who gets the benefits from innovation?

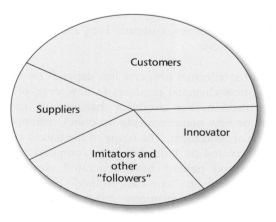

later entrants did somewhat better but their returns were overshadowed by the huge profits earned by the suppliers to the industry: Intel in microprocessors, Seagate in disk drives, Sharp in flat-panel displays and Microsoft in operating systems. However, because of strong competition in the industry, the greatest part of the value created by the personal computer was appropriated by customers, who typically paid prices for their PCs that were far below the value that they derived.[3]

The term *regime of appropriability* is used to describe the conditions that influence the distribution of returns to innovation. In a strong regime of appropriability, the innovator is able to capture a substantial share of the value created: NutraSweet artificial sweetener (developed by Searle, subsequently acquired by Monsanto), Pfizer's Viagra, and Pilkington's float glass process generated huge profits for their owners. In a weak regime of appropriability, other parties derive most of the value. In internet telephony (VoIP), ownership of technologies is diffused and standards are public, with the result that no players are likely to earn massive profits. Four factors are critical in determining the extent to which innovators are able to appropriate the value of their innovation: property rights, the tacitness and complexity of the technology, lead time and complementary resources.

*Property Rights in Innovation* Appropriating the returns on innovation depends, to a great extent, on the ability to establish property rights in the innovation. It was the desire to protect the returns to inventors that prompted the English Parliament to pass the 1623 Statute of Monopolies, which established the basis of patent law. Since then, the law has been extended to several areas of *intellectual property*, including:

- *Patents*—exclusive rights to a new and useful product, process, substance, or design. Obtaining a patent requires that the invention is novel, useful, and not excessively obvious. Patent law varies from country to country. In the U.S., a patent is valid for 17 years (14 for a design).
- *Copyrights*—exclusive production, publication, or sales rights to the creators of artistic, literary, dramatic, or musical works. Examples include articles, books, drawings, maps, photographs, and musical compositions.
- *Trademarks*—words, symbols, or other marks used to distinguish the goods or services supplied by a firm. In the U.S. and U.K., they are registered with the Patent Office. Trademarks provide the basis for brand identification.
- *Trade secrets*—offer a modest degree of legal protection for recipes, formulae, industrial processes, customer lists, and other knowledge acquired in the course of business.

The effectiveness of intellectual property law depends on the type of innovation being protected. For new chemical products (a new drug or plastic), patents can provide effective protection. For products that involve new configurations of existing components or new manufacturing processes, patents may fail to prevent rivals from innovating around them. The scope of the patent law has been extended to include life forms created by biotechnology, computer software, and business methods. Business method patents have generated considerable controversy— especially Amazon's patent on "one-click-to-buy" internet purchasing.[4] While patents and copyright establish property rights, their disadvantage (from the inventor's viewpoint) is that they make information public. Hence, companies may prefer secrecy to patenting as a means of protecting innovations.

In recent decades, companies have devoted increased attention to protecting and exploiting the economic value of their intellectual property. When Texas Instruments began exploiting its patent portfolio as a revenue source during the 1980s, the technology sector as a whole woke up to the value of its knowledge assets. During the 1990s, TI's royalty income exceeded its operating income from other sources. One outcome has been an upsurge in patenting. An average of 180 000 patents were granted by the U.S. Patent Office in each year between 2000 and 2008—well over double the annual rate during the 1980s.

*Tacitness and Complexity of the Technology* In the absence of effective legal protection the extent to which an innovation can be imitated by a competitor depends on the ease with which the technology can be comprehended and replicated. This depends, first, on the extent to which the technical knowledge is codifiable. *Codifiable knowledge*, by definition, is that which can be written down. Hence, if it is not effectively protected by patents or copyright, diffusion is likely to be rapid and the competitive advantage not sustainable. Financial innovations such as mortgage-backed securities and credit default swaps embody readily codifiable knowledge that can be copied very quickly. Similarly, Coca-Cola's recipe is codifiable and, in the absence of trade secret protection, is easily copied. Intel's designs for advanced microprocessors are codified and copyable; however, the processes for manufacturing these integrated circuits are based on deeply tacit knowledge.

The second key factor is *complexity*. Every new fashion, from the Mary Quant miniskirt of 1962 to Frida Giannini's "folkboho" look of 2009, involves simple, easy-to-copy ideas. Airbus's A380 and Nvidia's GT212 graphics chip represent entirely different challenges for the would-be imitator.

*Lead Time* Tacitness and complexity do not provide lasting barriers to imitation, but they do offer the innovator *time*. Innovation creates a *temporary* competitive advantage that offers a window of opportunity for the innovator to build on the initial advantage.

The innovator's *lead time* is the time it will take followers to catch up. The challenge for the innovator is to use initial lead time advantages to build the capabilities and market position to entrench industry leadership. Microsoft, Intel, and Cisco Systems were brilliant at exploiting lead time to build advantages in efficient manufacture, quality, and market presence. Conversely, British companies are notorious for having squandered their lead-time advantage in jet planes, radars, CT scanners, and genomics.

Lead time allows a firm to move down its learning curve ahead of followers. In new generations of microprocessors, Intel has traditionally been first to market, allowing it to move quickly down its experience curve, cut prices and so pressure the profit margins of its rival, AMD.

*Complementary Resources* Bringing new products and processes to market requires not just invention—it also requires the diverse resources and capabilities needed to finance, produce, and market the innovation. These are referred to as *complementary resources* (see Figure 12.3). Chester Carlson invented xerography but was unable for many years to bring his product to market because he lacked the complementary resources needed to develop, manufacture, market, distribute and service his invention. Conversely, Searle (and its later parent, Monsanto) was able to provide almost all the development, manufacturing, marketing and distribution resources needed to exploit its NutraSweet innovation. As a result, Carlson was able to appropriate only a tiny part of the value created by his invention of the plain-paper

**FIGURE 12.3** Complementary resources

Xerox copier, whereas Searle/Monsanto was successful in appropriating a major part of the value created by its new artificial sweetener.

Complementary resources may be accessed through alliances with other firms—for example, biotech firms ally with large pharmaceutical companies for clinical trials, manufacture and marketing.[5] When an innovation and the complementary resources that support it are supplied by different firms, the division of value between them depends on their relative power. A key determinant of this is whether the complementary resources are *specialized* or *unspecialized*. Fuel cells may eventually displace internal combustion engines in many of the world's automobiles. However, the problem for the developers of fuel cells is that their success depends on automobile manufacturers making specialized investments in designing a whole new range of cars, service station owners providing specialized refueling facilities, and repair firms investing in training and new equipment. For fuel cells to be widely adopted will require that the benefits of the innovation are shared widely with the different providers of these complementary resources. Where complementary resources are generic, the innovator is in a much stronger position to capture value. Because Adobe Systems' Acrobat Portable Document Format (pdf) works with files created in almost any software application, Adobe is well positioned to capture most of the value created by its innovatory software product. However, one advantage of co-specialized complementary resources is that they raise barriers to imitation. Consider the threat that Linux presents to Microsoft Window's dominance of PC operating systems. Intel has adapted its microprocessors to the needs of Windows and most applications software is written to run on Windows, so the challenge for the Linux community is not just to develop a workable operating system but also to encourage the development of applications software and hardware that are compatible with the Linux operating system.

## Which Mechanisms are Effective at Protecting Innovation?

How effective are these different mechanisms in protecting innovations? Table 12.1 shows that, despite considerable variation across industries, patent protection is of limited effectiveness as compared with lead-time, secrecy, and complementary

**TABLE 12.1** The effectiveness of mechanisms for protecting innovation: percentage of innovations for which different mechanisms were considered effective

| | Product innovations | | | | | Process innovations | | | | |
|---|---|---|---|---|---|---|---|---|---|---|
| | Secrecy (%) | Patents (%) | Lead-time (%) | Sales/service (%) | Manufacturing (%) | Secrecy (%) | Patents (%) | Lead-time (%) | Sales/service[1] (%) | Manufacturing[1] (%) |
| Food | 59 | 18 | 53 | 40 | 51 | 56 | 16 | 42 | 30 | 47 |
| Chemicals | 53 | 37 | 49 | 45 | 41 | 54 | 20 | 27 | 28 | 42 |
| Drugs | 54 | 50 | 50 | 33 | 49 | 68 | 36 | 36 | 25 | 44 |
| Computers | 44 | 41 | 61 | 35 | 42 | 43 | 30 | 40 | 24 | 36 |
| Electronic components | 34 | 21 | 46 | 50 | 51 | 47 | 15 | 43 | 42 | 56 |
| Telecom equipment | 47 | 26 | 66 | 42 | 41 | 35 | 15 | 43 | 34 | 41 |
| Medical equipment | 51 | 55 | 58 | 52 | 49 | 49 | 34 | 45 | 32 | 50 |
| All industries | 51 | 35 | 53 | 43 | 46 | 51 | 23 | 38 | 31 | 43 |

[1]Shows the percentage of companies that reported that complementary capabilities in sales and service, and in manufacturing, were effective in protecting their innovations.

**Source:**

W. M. Cohen, R. R. Nelson, And J. P. Walsh, "Protecting their Intellectual Assets: Appropriability Conditions and Why us Manufacturing Firms Patent (or not)," NBER Working Paper No. W7552 (February 2000). © 2000. Reprinted by Permission of the Authors.

**TABLE 12.2** Why do companies patent? (Responses by 674 US manufacturers)

|  | Product Innovations (%) | Process Innovations (%) |
|---|---|---|
| To prevent copying | 95 | 77 |
| For licensing revenue | 28 | 23 |
| To prevent law suits | 59 | 47 |
| To block others | 82 | 64 |
| For use in negotiations | 47 | 43 |
| To enhance reputation | 48 | 34 |
| To measure performance | 6 | 5 |

*Source:* W. M. Cohen, R. R. Nelson, and J. P. Walsh, "Protecting their Intellectual Assets: Appropriability Conditions and Why us Manufacturing Firms Patent (Or Not)," NBER Working Paper No. W7552 (February 2000). Reproduced with permission.

manufacturing and sales/service resources. Indeed, since the late 1980s, the effectiveness of patents appeared to have declined despite the strengthening of patent law. Although patents are effective in increasing the lead time before competitors are able to bring imitative products to market, these gains tend to be small. The great majority of patented products and processes are duplicated within three years.[6]

Given the limited effectiveness of patents, why do firms continue to engage in patenting? As shown in Table 12.2, although protection from imitation is the principal motive, several others are also very important. In particular, much patenting activity appears to be strategic—it is directed towards blocking the innovation efforts of other companies and establishing property rights in technologies that can then be used in bargaining with other companies for access to their proprietary technologies. In semiconductors and electronics, cross-licensing arrangements—where one company gives access to its patents across a field of technology in exchange for access to another company's patents—are critical in permitting "freedom to design": the ability to design products that draw on technologies owned by different companies.[7]

## Strategies to Exploit Innovation: How and When to Enter

Having established some of the key factors that determine the returns to innovation, let us consider some of the main questions concerning the formulation of strategies to manage technology and exploit innovation.

### Alternative Strategies to Exploit Innovation

How should a firm maximize the returns to its innovation? A number of alternative strategies are available. Figure 12.4 orders them according to the size of the commitment of resources and capabilities that each requires. Thus, licensing requires little involvement by the innovator in subsequent commercialization; hence a limited

**FIGURE 12.4** Alternative strategies for exploiting innovation

| | Licensing | Outsourcing certain functions | Strategic alliance | Joint venture | Internal commercialization |
|---|---|---|---|---|---|
| **Risk and return** | Little investment risk but returns also limited. Risk that the licensee either lacks motivation or steals the innovation | Limits capital investment, but may create dependence on suppliers/partners | Benefits of flexibility. Risks of informal structure | Shares investment and risk. Risk of partner disagreement and culture clash | Biggest investment requirement and corresponding risks. Benefits of control |
| **Resource requirements** | Few | Permits external resources and capabilities to be accessed | Permits pooling of the resources and capabilities of more than one firm | | Substantial requirements in terms of finance, production capability, marketing capability, distribution, etc. |
| **Examples** | Ericsson with its Bluetooth wireless technology; Dolby Labs with its sound reduction technology; Qualcomm and CDMA | Microsoft's XBox was largely designed by other companies and Flextronics does the manufacturing | Ballard's strategic alliance with DaimlerChrysler to develop fuel cells | Psion created Symbian as a joint venture with Ericsson, Nokia, and Motorola to develop the Symbian mobile phone operating system | Larry Page and Sergey Brin established Google Inc. to develop and market their Internet search technology |

investment. Internal commercialization—possibly through creating a new enterprise or business unit—involves a much greater investment of resources and capabilities. In between there are various opportunities for collaboration with other companies. Joint ventures and strategic alliances typically involve substantial resource sharing between companies. On a more limited scale, specific activities may be outsourced to other companies.

The choice of strategy mode depends on two main sets of factors: the characteristics of the innovation, and the resources and capabilities of the firm.

*Characteristics of the Innovation* The extent to which a firm can establish clear property rights in an innovation critically determines the choice of strategy options. Licensing is only viable where ownership in an innovation is clearly defined by patent or copyrights. Thus, in pharmaceuticals, licensing is widespread because patents are clear and defensible. Many biotech companies engage only in R&D and license their drug discoveries to large pharmaceutical companies that possess the necessary complementary resources. Royalties from licensing its sound-reduction technologies accounted for 76% of Dolby Laboratories' 2006 revenues. Conversely, Steve Jobs and Steve Wozniak, developers of the Apple I and Apple II computers, had little option other than to go into business themselves—the absence of proprietary technology ruled out licensing as an option.

The advantages of licensing are, first, that it relieves the company of the need to develop the full range of complementary resources and capabilities needed for commercialization and, second, that it can allow the innovation to be commercialized quickly. If the lead time offered by the innovation is short, multiple licensing can allow for a fast global rollout. The problem, however, is that the success of the innovation in the market is totally dependent on the commitment and effectiveness of the licensees. James Dyson, the British inventor of the bagless vacuum cleaner, created his own company to manufacture and market his "dual cyclone" vacuum cleaners after failing to interest any major appliance company in a licensing deal for his technology.

*Resources and Capabilities of the Firm* As Figure 12.4 shows, different strategies require very different resources and capabilities. Hence, the choice of how to exploit an innovation depends critically upon the resources and capabilities that the innovator brings to the party. Startup firms possess few of the complementary resources and capabilities needed to commercialize their innovations. Inevitably they will be attracted to licensing or to accessing the resources of larger firms through outsourcing, alliances, or joint ventures. In several industries we observe a sequential process of innovation where different stages are conducted by different types of firm. In biotechnology and electronics, technology is typically developed initially by a small, technology-intensive startup, which then licenses to, or is acquired by, a larger established firm. (See Adapting to Changes over the Life Cycle, pp. 283–4.)

Conversely, large, established corporations, which can draw on their wealth of resources and capabilities, are better placed for internal commercialization. Companies such as Sony, DuPont, Siemens, Hitachi, and IBM have traditionally developed innovations internally—yet, as technologies evolve, converge and splinter, even these companies have increasingly resorted to joint ventures, strategic alliances, and outsourcing arrangements to access technical capabilities outside their corporate boundaries.

Ron Adner observes that innovation increasingly requires coordinated responses by multiple companies. Innovating firms need to identify and map their *innovation ecosystem,* then manage the interdependencies within it. The failed introduction of HDTV can be attributed to inadequate coordination among TV manufacturers, production studios and broadcasters.[8]

## Timing Innovation: To Lead or to Follow?

To gain competitive advantage in emerging and technologically intensive industries, is it best to be a leader or a follower in innovation? As Table 12.3 shows, the evidence is mixed: in some products the leader has been the first to grab the prize, in others the leader has succumbed to the risks and costs of pioneering. Optimal timing of entry into an emerging industry and the introduction of new technology are complex issues. The advantage of being an early mover depends on the following factors:

- *The extent to which innovation can be protected by property rights or lead-time advantages.* If an innovation is appropriable through a patent, copyright, or lead-time advantage, there is advantage in being an early mover. This is especially the case where patent protection is important, as in pharmaceuticals. Notable patent races include that between Alexander Bell and Elisha Gray to patent the telephone (Bell got to the Patent Office a few hours before Gray),[9] and between Celera Inc. and the National Institutes of Health to patent the sequence of the human genome.[10]

**TABLE 12.3**  Leaders, followers, and success in emerging industries

| Product | Innovator | Follower | The winner |
|---|---|---|---|
| Jet airliner | De Havilland (Comet) | Boeing (707) | Follower |
| Float glass | Pilkington | Corning | Leader |
| X-ray scanner | EMI | General Electric | Follower |
| Office PC | Xerox | IBM | Follower |
| VCRs | Ampex/Sony | Matsushita | Follower |
| Instant camera | Polaroid | Kodak | Leader |
| Pocket calculator | Bowmar | Texas Instruments | Follower |
| Microwave oven | Raytheon | Samsung | Follower |
| Fiber-optic cable | Corning | Many companies | Leader |
| Video games player | Atari | Nintendo/Sony | Followers |
| Disposable diaper | Procter & Gamble | Kimberley-Clark | Leader |
| Ink jet printer | IBM and Siemens | Hewlett Packard | Follower |
| Web browser | Netscape | Microsoft | Follower |
| MP3 music players | Diamond Multimedia | Apple (iPod) | Follower |
| Operating systems for mobile phones | Symbian | Microsoft | Leader |
| Laser printer | Xerox, IBM | Canon | Follower |
| Flash memory | Toshiba | Samsung, Intel | Followers |
| E-book reader | Sony (Digital Reader) | Amazon (Kindle) | Follower |

*Source:* Based in Part on D. Teece, *the Competitive Challenge: Strategies for Industrial Innovation and Renewal* (Cambridge: Ballinger, 1987): 186–8.

- *The importance of complementary resources.* The more important complementary resources are in exploiting an innovation, the greater the costs and risks of pioneering. Several firms—from Clive Sinclair with a battery-driven car to General Motors with a fuel-cell car—have already failed in their attempts to develop and market an electric automobile. The problem for the pioneer is that the development costs are huge because of the need to orchestrate multiple technologies and establish self-sufficiency across a range of business functions. Followers are also favored by the fact that, as an industry develops, specialist firms emerge as suppliers of complementary resources. Thus, in pioneering the development of the British frozen foods industry, Unilever's Bird's Eye subsidiary had to set up an entire chain of cold stores and frozen distribution facilities. Later entrants were able to rely on the services of public cold stores and refrigerated trucking companies.

- *The potential to establish a standard.* As we shall see later in this chapter, some markets converge toward a technical standard. The greater the importance of technical standards, the greater the advantages of being an early mover in order to influence those standards and gain the market momentum needed to establish leadership. Once a standard has been set, displacing it becomes exceptionally difficult. IBM had little success with its OS/2 operating system against the entrenched position of Microsoft Windows. Linux has succeeded in taking market share from Windows. However, the main reason is that Linux is free!

Optimal timing depends also on the resources and capabilities that the individual firm has at its disposal. Different companies have different *strategic windows*—periods in time when their resources and capabilities are aligned with the opportunities available in the market. A small, technology-based firm may have no choice but to pioneer innovation: its opportunity is to grab first-mover advantage and then develop the necessary complementary resources before more powerful rivals appear. For the large, established firm with financial resources and strong production, marketing, and distribution capabilities, the strategic window is likely to be both longer and later. The risks of pioneering are greater for an established firm with a reputation and brands to protect, while to exploit its complementary resources effectively typically requires a more developed market. Consider the following examples:

- In personal computers, Apple was a pioneer, IBM a follower. The timing of entry was probably optimal for each. Apple's resources were its vision and its technology: only by pioneering could it hope to become a leading player. IBM had enormous strengths in manufacturing, distribution, and reputation. It could build competitive advantage even without a clear technological advantage. The key for IBM was to delay its entry until the time when the market had developed to the point where IBM's strengths could have their maximum impact.
- In the browser war between Netscape and Microsoft, Microsoft had the luxury of being able to follow the pioneer, Netscape. Microsoft's huge product development, marketing, and distribution capabilities, and—most important—its vast installed base of the Windows operating system allowed it to overhaul Netscape's initial lead.
- Although General Electric entered the market for CT scanners some four years after EMI, GE was able to overtake EMI within a few years because of its ability to apply vast technological, manufacturing, sales, and customer service capabilities within the field of medical electronics.

The most effective follower strategies are those that initiate a new product's transition from niche market to mass market. According to Markides and Geroski, successful first movers pioneer new products that embody new technologies and new functionality.[11] The opportunity for the fast-second entrant is to grow the niche market into a mass market by lowering cost and increasing quality. Timing is critical. Don Sull argues that a successful follower strategy requires "active waiting": a company needs to monitor market developments and assemble resources and capabilities while it prepares for large scale market entry.[12]

## Managing Risks

Emerging industries are risky. There are two main sources of uncertainty:

- *Technological uncertainty* arises from the unpredictability of technological evolution and the complex dynamics through which technical standards and dominant designs are selected. Hindsight is always 20/20, but *ex ante* it is difficult to predict how technologies and the industries that deploy them will evolve.

- *Market uncertainty* relates to the size and growth rates of the markets for new products. When Xerox introduced its first plain-paper copier in 1959, Apple its first personal computer in 1977, or Sony its Walkman in 1979, none had any idea of the size of the potential market. Forecasting demand for new products is hazardous since all forecasting is based on some form of extrapolation or modeling based on past data. One approach is to use analogies.[13] Another is to draw on the combined insight and experience of experts through the *Delphi technique*.[14]

If reliable forecasting is impossible, the keys to managing risk are alertness and responsiveness to emerging trends together with limiting vulnerability to mistakes through avoiding large-scale commitments. Useful strategies for limiting risk include:

- *Cooperating with lead users.* During the early phases of industry development, careful monitoring of and response to market trends and customer requirements is essential to avoid major errors in technology and design. Von Hippel argues that lead users provide a source of leading market indicators, they can assist in developing new products and processes, and offer an early cash flow to fund development expenditures.[15] In computer software, "beta versions" are released to computer enthusiasts for testing. Nike has two sets of lead users: professional athletes who are trendsetters for athletic footwear and gang members and hip-hop artists who are at the leading edge of urban fashion trends. In communications and aerospace, government defense contracts play a crucial role in developing new technologies.[16]

- *Limiting risk exposure.* The financial risks of emerging industries can be mitigated by financial and operational practices that minimize a firm's exposure to adversity. By avoiding debt and keeping fixed costs low, a firm can lower its financial and operational gearing. Outsourcing and strategic alliance can also hold down capital investment and fixed costs.

- *Flexibility.* Uncertainty necessitates rapid responses to unpredicted events. Achieving such flexibility means keeping options open and delaying commitment to a specific technology until its potential becomes clear. Large, well-resourced companies have the luxury of pursuing multiple strategic options (see Strategy Capsule 12.1).

## STRATEGY CAPSULE 12.1
# Keeping your Options Open: Microsoft in Operating Systems

In 1988, as I wandered about the floor of Comdex, the computer industry's vast annual trade show, I could feel the anxiety among the participants. Since the birth of the IBM PC, six years earlier, Microsoft's Disk Operating System (DOS) had been the de facto standard for PCs. But DOS was now starting to age. Everyone wanted to know what would replace it.

Apple Computer, at the peak of its powers, had one of the largest booths showcasing the brilliantly graphical Macintosh operating system . . . Two different alliances of major companies, including AT&T, HP, and Sun Microsystems, offered graphical versions of Unix . . . And IBM was touting its new OS/2.

Amid the uncertainty, there was something very curious about the Microsoft booth . . . [which] resembled a Middle Eastern bazaar. In one corner, the company was previewing its highly criticized Windows system . . . In another, Microsoft touted its latest release of DOS. Elsewhere it was displaying OS/2, which it had developed with IBM. In addition, Microsoft was demonstrating new releases of Word and Excel

that ran on Apple's Mac. Finally, in a distant corner, Microsoft displayed SCO Unix . . .

"What am I supposed to make of this?" grumbled a corporate buyer standing next to me. Columnists wrote that Microsoft was adrift, that its chairman and COO, Bill Gates, had no strategy.

Although the outcome of this story is now well known, to anyone standing on the Comdex floor in 1988 it wasn't obvious which operating system would win. In the face of this uncertainty, Microsoft followed the only robust strategy: betting on every horse.

*Source:* E. D. Beinhocker, "Robust Adaptive Strategies," *Sloan Management Review* (Spring 1999): 95–106. © 1999 Massachusetts Institute of Technology.

## Competing for Standards

In the previous chapter, I noted that the establishment of standards is a key event in industry evolution. The emergence of the digital, networked economy has made standards increasingly important, and companies that own and influence industry standards are capable of earning returns that are unmatched by any other type of competitive advantage. The shareholder value generated by Microsoft and Intel from the "Wintel" PC standard, by Qualcomm from its CDMA digital wireless communications technology, and Cisco from its leadership role in setting internet protocol standards are examples of this potential. Table 12.4 lists several companies whose success is closely associated with their control of standards within a particular product category.

### Types of Standard

A standard is a format, an interface, or a system that allows interoperability. It is adherence to standards that allows us to browse millions of different web pages, that ensures the light bulbs made by any manufacturer will fit any manufacturer's lamps, and that keeps the traffic moving in Los Angeles (most of the time). Standards can be *public* or *private*.

- Public (or *open*) standards are those that are available to all either free or for a nominal charge. Typically they do not involve any privately owned intellectual property, or the IP owners make access free (such as Linux). Public standards are set by public bodies and industry associations. Thus, the GSM mobile phone standard was set by the European Telecom Standards Institute. Internet protocols—standards governing internet addressing and

**TABLE 12.4**  Examples of companies that own de facto industry standards

| Company | Product category | Standard |
|---------|-----------------|----------|
| Microsoft | PC operating systems | Windows |
| Intel | PC microprocessors | x86 series |
| Matsushita | Videocassette recorders | VHS system |
| Sony/Philips | Compact disks | CD-ROM format |
| ARM (Holdings) | Microprocessors for mobile devices | ARM architecture |
| Sun Microsystems | Programming language for web apps | Java |
| Rockwell and 3Com | 56K modems | V90 |
| Qualcomm | Digital cellular wireless communication | CDMA |
| Adobe Systems | Common file format for creating and viewing documents | Acrobat Portable Document Format |
| Bosch | Antilock braking systems | ABS and TCS (Traction Control System) |
| Symbian | Operating systems for mobile phones | Symbian OS |
| Sony | High definition DVD | Blu-ray |

routing—are mostly public. They are governed by several international bodies, including the internet Engineering Task Force.

- Private (*proprietary*) standards are those where the technologies and designs are owned by companies or individuals. If I own the technology that becomes a standard, I can embody the technology in a product that others buy (Microsoft Windows) or license the technology to others who wish to use it (Qualcomm's CDMA).

Standards can also be classified according to who sets them. *Mandatory standards* are set by government and have the force of law behind them. They include standards relating to automobile safety and construction specifications and to TV broadcasting. *De facto standards* emerge through voluntary adoption by producers and users. Table 12.4 gives examples.

A problem with *de facto* standards is that they may take a long time to emerge, resulting in duplication of investments and delayed development of the market. It was 40 years before a standard railroad gauge was agreed in the U.S.[17] One reason for the slow transition of wireless telecoms in the U.S. from analog to digital technology was continuing competition between TDMA and CDMA standards. By contrast, Europe officially adopted GSM (a close relative of TDMA) in 1992.[18] Delayed emergence of a standard may kill the technology altogether. The failure of quadraphonic sound to displace stereophonic sound during the 1970s resulted from incompatible technical standards, which inhibited audio manufacturers, record companies and consumers from investing in the technology.[19]

## Why Standards Appear: Network Externalities

Standards emerge in markets that are subject to *network externalities*. A network externality exists whenever the value of a product to an individual customer depends on the number of other users of that product. The classic example of network externality is the telephone. Since there is little satisfaction to be gained from talking to oneself on the telephone, the value of a telephone to each user depends on the number of other users connected to the same telephone system. This is different from most products. When I pour myself a glass of Glenlivet after a couple of exhausting MBA classes, my enjoyment is independent of how many other people in the world are also drinking Glenlivet. Indeed, some products may have *negative* network externalities—the value of the product is less if many other people purchase the same product. If I spend $3000 on an Armani silver lamé tuxedo and find that half my colleagues at the faculty Christmas party are wearing the same jacket, my satisfaction is lessened.

Network externalities do not require everyone to use the same product or even the same technology, but rather that the different products are *compatible* with one another through some form of common interface. In the case of wireless telephone service, it doesn't matter (as far as network access is concerned) whether I purchase service from AT&T, Nextel, or T-Mobile because compatibility between each network allows connectivity. Similarly with railroads; if I am transporting coal from Wyoming to Boston, my choice of railroad company is not critical. Unlike in the 1870s, every railroad company now uses a standard gauge and is required to give "common carrier" access to other companies' rolling stock.

Network externalities arise from several sources:

- *Products where users are linked to a network.* Telephones, railroad systems, and email instant messaging groups are networks where users are linked together. Applications software, whether spreadsheet programs or video games, also link users—they can share files and play games interactively. User-level externalities may also arise through social identification. I watch *American Idol* and the Hollywood Oscar presentations on TV not because I enjoy them, but so that I have something to talk to my colleagues about in the faculty common room.[20]

- *Availability of complementary products and services.* Where products are consumed as systems, the availability of complementary products and services depends on the number of customers for that system. Apple's key problem in the computer market is that, because the Macintosh accounts for only 9% of the installed base of personal computers, few leading software firms are writing Mac-based applications. I choose to drive a Ford Focus rather than a Ferrari Testarossa because I know that, should I break down 200 miles from Bismarck, North Dakota, spare parts and a repair service will be more readily available.

- *Economizing on switching costs.* By purchasing the product or system that is most widely used, there is less chance that I shall have to bear the costs of switching. By using Microsoft Office rather than Lotus SmartSuite, it is more likely that I will avoid the costs of retraining and file conversion when I become a visiting professor at another university.

The implication of network externalities is that they create *positive feedback*. Once a technology or system gains market leadership, it attracts a growing proportion of new buyers. Conversely, once market leadership is lost, a downward spiral is likely. This process is called *tipping*: once a certain threshold is reached, cumulative forces become unstoppable.[21] The result is a tendency toward a *winner-takes-all* market. The markets subject to significant network externalities tend to be dominated by a single supplier (Microsoft in PC operating systems and office applications, eBay in internet auctions).

Once established, technical and design standards tend to be highly resilient. Standards are difficult to displace due to learning effects and collective lock-in. Learning effects cause the dominant technology and design to be continually improved and refined. Even where the existing standard is inherently inferior, switching to a superior technology may not occur because of collective lock in. The classic case is the QWERTY typewriter layout. Its 1873 design was based on the need to *slow* the speed of typing to prevent typewriter keys from jamming. Although the jamming problem was soon solved, the QWERTY layout has persisted, despite the patenting in 1932 of the more ergonomic Dvorak Simplified Keyboard (DSK).[22]

## Winning Standards Wars

In markets subject to network externalities, control over standards is the primary basis for competitive advantage. Sony and Apple are unusual in that they lost their standards wars (in VCRs and personal computers, respectively) but returned as winners in other markets. Most of losers in standards wars—Lotus in spreadsheet software, Netscape in browsers, WordPerfect in word processing software—become mere footnotes in the history of technology. What can we learn from these and other standards wars about designing a winning strategy in markets subject to network externalities?

The first key issue is to determine whether we are competing in a market that will converge around a single technical standard. This requires a careful analysis of the presence and sources of network externalities.

The second strategic issue in standards setting is recognizing the role of positive feedback: the technology that can establish early leadership will rapidly gain momentum. Building a "bigger bandwagon," according to Shapiro and Varian,[23] requires the following:

- *Before you go to war, assemble allies.* You'll need the support of consumers, suppliers of complements, even your competitors. Not even the strongest companies can afford to go it alone in a standards war.

- *Preempt the market*—enter early, achieve fast-cycle product development, make early deals with key customers and adopt penetration pricing.

- *Manage expectations.* The key to managing positive feedback is to convince customers, suppliers and the producers of complementary goods that you will emerge as the victor. These expectations become a self-fulfilling prophecy. The massive pre-launch promotion and publicity built up by Sony prior to the American and European launch of PlayStation 2 in October 2000 was an effort to convince consumers, retailers and game developers that the product would be the blockbuster consumer electronics product of the new decade, thereby stymieing Sega and Nintendo's efforts to establish their rival systems.

The lesson that has emerged from the classic standards battles of the past is that in order to create initial leadership and maximize positive feedback effects, a company must share the value created by the technology with other parties (customers, competitors, complementors, and suppliers). If a company attempts to appropriate too great a share of the value created, it may well fail to build a big enough bandwagon to gain market leadership (see Strategy Capsule 12.2). Thus, recent standards battles involve broad alliances, where the owner enlists the support of complementors and would-be competitors. In the 2006–8 struggle between Sony (Blu-ray) and Toshiba (HD-DVD) each camp recruited movie studios, software firms and producers of computers and consumer electronics using various inducements— including direct cash payments. The defection of Warner Brothers to the Sony camp was critical to the market tipping suddenly in Sony's favor. However, it appears that all the financial gains from owning the winning DVD standard were dissipated by the costs of the war.[24]

Achieving compatibility with existing products is a critical issue in standards battles. Advantage typically goes to the competitor that adopts an *evolutionary strategy* (i.e., offers backward compatibility) rather than one that adopts a *revolutionary strategy*.[25] Microsoft Windows won the PC war against the Apple Macintosh for many reasons. Both companies offered an operating system with a graphical user interface. However, while Windows was designed for compatibility with the DOS operating system, the Apple Mac was incompatible both with DOS and the Apple II. Similarly, a key advantage of the Sony PlayStation 2 over the Sega Dreamcast and Nintendo Cube was its compatibility with the PlayStation 1.

What are the key resources needed to win a standards war? Shapiro and Varian emphasize the following:

- control over an installed base of customers;
- owning intellectual property rights in the new technology;
- the ability to innovate in order to extend and adapt the initial technological advance;
- first-mover advantage;
- strength in complements (e.g., Intel has preserved its standard in microprocessors by promoting standards in buses, chipsets, graphics controllers, and interfaces between motherboards and CPUs);
- reputation and brand name.[26]

As companies become more familiar with the dynamics of standards competition, they are launching their strategic initiatives earlier—long before product release dates. As a result, standards wars are increasingly about the management of expectations. Companies are also more alert to the emergence of tipping points. As a result, standards wars are being resolved quicker: in high definition DVDs a mere 19 months elapsed between Toshiba's launch of its HD-DVD and its withdrawal announcement.

## STRATEGY CAPSULE 12.2

# Building a Bandwagon by Sharing Value: Lessons from VCRs and PCs

Profiting from standards requires, first, setting the standard; second, retaining a proprietary interest in the standard in order to appropriate part of its value. There is a tradeoff between the two—the more value a company tries to appropriate, the greater the difficulty in building early support for its technology. Consider the standards wars in VCRs and PCs:

- In VCRs, Matsushita's VHS format won against Sony's Betamax format not because of the technical superiority of VHS, but—in contrast to Sony's tight proprietary control of Betamax—Masushita licensed its VHS system to Sharp, Philips, GE, RCA, and others, allowing it to gain market leadership.

- In personal computers, IBM was highly successful in setting the standard, partly because it did not restrict access to its technology. Its product specifications were openly available to "clone makers," and its suppliers (including Microsoft and Intel) were free to supply them with microprocessors and the MS-DOS operating system. IBM was remarkably successful at setting the standard, but failed to appropriate much value because it retained no significant proprietary interest

in the standard—it was Intel and Microsoft that owned the key intellectual property. For Apple, the situation was the reverse. It kept tight control over its Macintosh operating system and product architecture, it earned high margins, but it forfeited the opportunity to set the industry standard.

The tradeoff between market acceptance of a technology and appropriating the returns to a technology is shown above. Realizing the lessons of these two epic contests, the owners of technical standards have forfeited more and more value to complementors, competitors, and customers in order to establish market leadership. In the browser war of 1995–8, both Netscape (Navigator) and Microsoft (Explorer) ended up giving away their products.

Companies are now seeking ways to reconcile market acceptance with value appropriation. Adobe gives away its Acrobat Reader to broaden the user base, but charges for the software needed to create pdf documents.

*Sources: The World VCR Industry,* Case No. 9-387-098 (Boston: Harvard Business School, 1990); *Apple Computer— 1992,* Case No. 9-792-081 (Boston: Harvard Business School, 1994); *The Browser Wars, 1994-1998,* Case No. 9-798-094 (Boston: Harvard Business School, 1998).

# Implementing Technology Strategies: Creating the Conditions for Innovation

As we have noted previously, strategy formulation cannot be separated from its implementation. Nowhere is this more evident than in technology-intensive businesses.

Our analysis so far has taught us about the potential for generating competitive advantage from innovation and about the design of technology-based strategies but has said little about the conditions under which innovation is achieved. The danger is that strategic analysis can tell us a great deal about making money out of innovation, but this isn't much use if we cannot generate innovation in the first place. While innovation requires certain resources—people, facilities, information, and time— there is no predetermined relationship between R&D input and innovation output.[27] Clearly the productivity of R&D depends heavily on the organizational conditions that foster innovation. Hence, the crucial challenge facing firms in emerging and technology-based industries is to create the conditions conducive to innovation.

To address this issue, we must return to the critical distinction between invention and innovation. While these activities are complementary, they require different resources and different organizational conditions. While invention depends on creativity, innovation requires collaboration and cross-functional integration.

## Managing Creativity

*The Conditions for Creativity* Invention is an act of creativity requiring knowledge and imagination. The creativity that drives invention is typically an individual act that establishes a meaningful relationship between concepts or objects that had not previously been related. This reconceptualizing can be triggered by accidents: an apple falling on Isaac Newton's head or James Watt observing a kettle boiling. Creativity is associated with particular personality traits. Creative people tend to be curious, imaginative, adventurous, assertive, playful, self-confident, risk taking, reflective, and uninhibited.[28]

Individual creativity also depends on the organizational environment in which they work—this is as true for the researchers and engineers at Amgen and Google as it was for the painters and sculptors of the Florentine and Venetian schools. Few great works of art or outstanding inventions are the products of solitary geniuses. Creativity is stimulated by human interaction: the productivity of R&D laboratories depends critically on the communication networks that the engineers and scientists establish.[29] An important catalyst of interaction is *play*, which creates an environment of inquiry, liberates thought from conventional constraints, and provides the opportunity to establish new relationships by rearranging ideas and structures at a safe distance from reality. The essence of play is that it permits unconstrained forms of experimentation.[30] The potential for low-cost experimentation has expanded vastly thanks to advances in computer modeling and simulation that permit prototyping and market research to be undertaken speedily and virtually.[31]

*Organizing for Creativity* Creativity requires management systems that are quite different from those appropriate for efficiency. In particular, creatively oriented people tend to be responsive to distinctive types of incentive. They desire to work in an egalitarian culture with enough space and resources to provide the opportunity to be spontaneous, experience freedom, and have fun in the performance of a task that, they feel, makes a difference to the strategic performance of the firm. Praise, recognition and opportunities for education and professional growth are also more important than assuming managerial responsibilities.[32] Nurturing the drive to create may require a degree of freedom and flexibility that conflicts with conventional HR practices. At Google engineers have considerable discretion as to which project they join.

Organizational environments conducive to creativity tend to be both nurturing and competitive. Creativity requires a work context that is secure but not cozy. Dorothy Leonard points to the merits of *creative abrasion* within innovative teams—fostering innovation through the interaction of different personalities and perspectives. Managers must resist the temptation to clone in favor of embracing diversity of cognitive and behavioral characteristics within work groups—creating *"whole brain teams."*[33] Exploiting diversity may require constructive conflict. Microsoft's development team meetings are renowned for open criticism and intense disagreement. Such conflict can spur progress towards better solutions.

Table 12.5 contrasts some characteristics of innovative organizations compared with those designed for operational efficiency.

## From Invention to Innovation: The Challenge of Integration

*Balancing Creativity and Commercial Direction* For creativity to create value—both for the company and for society—it must be directed and harnessed. Balancing creative freedom with discipline and integration is a key issue to companies such as Apple and Google which position themselves on the leading edge of

**TABLE 12.5** The characteristics of "operating" and "innovating" organizations

|  | Operating organization | Innovating organization |
|---|---|---|
| *Structure* | Bureaucratic. Specialization and division of labor. Hierarchical control. Defined organizational boundaries. | Flat organization without hierarchical control. Task-oriented project teams. Fuzzy organizational boundaries. |
| *Processes* | Emphasis on eliminating variation (e.g. six-sigma). Top-down control. Tight financial controls. | Emphasis on enhancing variation. Loose controls to foster idea generation. Flexible strategic planning and financial control. |
| *Reward systems* | Financial compensation, promotion up the hierarchy, power, and status symbols. | Autonomy, recognition, equity participation in new ventures |
| *People* | Recruitment and selection based on the needs of the organization structure for specific skills: functional and staff specialists, general managers, and operatives. | Key need is for idea generators that combine required technical knowledge with creative personality traits. Managers must act as sponsors and orchestrators. |

***Source:*** Based on J. K. Galbraith and R. K. Kazanjian, *Strategy Implementation: Structure, Systems and Processes,* 2nd Edn (St. Paul, Mn: West, 1986).

innovation. The problem is especially acute in media companies: "The two cultures—of the ponytail and the suit—are a world apart, and combustible together."[34] Many creative companies have been formed by frustrated innovators leaving established companies. Disney's 2006 acquisition of Pixar was motivated by its desire to reinvigorate its animated movies. Yet Pixar's John Lasseter, who was appointed creative head of Disney's animation studio had been fired from Disney 20 years earlier for his advocacy of computer animation![35] Conversely, HBO's remarkable run of successful TV series between 1999 and 2007 (*The Sopranos*, *Sex in the City*, *The Wire* and *Six Feet Under*) reveals a remarkable ability to mesh creativity with commercial acuity.

The critical linkage between creative flair and commercial success is *market need*. Few important inventions have been the result of spontaneous creation by technologists; almost all have resulted from grappling with practical problems. The invention of the Xerox copying process (xerography) by Chester Carlson, a patent attorney, was inspired by his frustration with the tedious task of making multiple copies of patent applications for submission to the U.S. Patent Office. The old adage that "necessity is the mother of invention" explains why customers are such fertile sources of innovation—they are most acutely involved with matching existing products and services to their needs.[36] Involving customers in the innovation process is an initial stage in the move towards *open innovation* (which I will say more about below).

*Organizational Approaches to the Management of Innovation*   The key organizational challenge is the one that we explored back in Chapter 7—that of reconciling *differentiation* and *integration*. As we have already noted, creative activities require different organizational structures and management systems than operational activities. Yet, the commercialization of new technology—developing and introducing new products and implementing new processes—requires the integration of creativity and technological expertise with capabilities in production, marketing, finance, distribution, and customer support. Achieving such integration is difficult. Tension between the operating and the innovating parts of organizations is inevitable. Innovation upsets established routines and threatens the status quo. The more stable the operating and administrative side of the organization, the greater the resistance to innovation. A classic example was the opposition by the U.S. naval establishment to continuous-aim firing, a process that offered huge improvements in gunnery accuracy.[37]

As innovation has become an increasing priority for established corporations, so chief executives have sought to emulate the flexibility, creativity, and entrepreneurial spirit of technology-based startups. Organizational initiatives aimed at stimulating new product development and the exploitation of new technologies include the following:

- *Cross-functional product development teams*. Cross-functional product development teams have proven to be highly effective mechanisms for integrating creativity with functional effectiveness. Conventional approaches to new product development involved a sequential process that began in the corporate research lab then went "over the wall" to engineering, manufacturing, finance, and so on. Japanese companies pioneered autonomous product development teams staffed by specialists seconded from different departments with leadership from a "heavyweight" team manager who was able to protect the team from undue corporate influence.[38] Such teams have proven effective in deploying a broad range of specialist knowledge and, most importantly, integrating that knowledge flexibility and quickly—for example, through rapid prototyping and concurrent engineering.[39]

● *Product champions* provide a means, first, for incorporating individual creativity within organizational processes and, second, for linking invention to subsequent commercialization. The key is to permit the individuals who are sources of creative ideas to lead the teams which develop those ideas—but also to allow this leadership to continue through into the commercialization phases. Companies that are consistently successful in innovation have the ability to design organizational processes that capture, direct and exploit individuals' drive for achievement and success and their commitment to their innovations. The rationale for creating product champions is that these committed individuals can overcome resistance to change within the organization and generate the enthusiasm that attracts the involvement of others and forges cross-functional integration. Schön's study of 15 major innovations concluded that: "the new idea either finds a champion or dies."[40] A British study of 43 matched pairs of successful and unsuccessful innovations similarly concluded that a key factor distinguishing successful innovation was the presence of a "business innovator" to exert entrepreneurial leadership.[41] 3M Corporation has a long tradition of using product champions to develop new product ideas and grow them into new businesses (see Strategy Capsule 12.3).

---

## STRATEGY CAPSULE 12.3
# Innovation at 3M: The Role of the Product Champion

### START LITTLE AND BUILD

We don't look to the president or the vice-president for R&D to say, all right, on Monday morning 3M is going to get into such-and-such a business. Rather, we prefer to see someone in one of our laboratories, or marketing, or manufacturing units bring forward a new idea that he's been thinking about. Then, when he can convince people around him, including his supervisor, that he's got something interesting, we'll make him what we call a "project manager" with a small budget of money and talent, and let him run with it. Throughout all our 60 years of history here, that has been the mark of success. Did you develop a new business? The incentive? Money, of course. But that's not the key. The key . . . is becoming the general manager of a new business . . . having such a hot project that management just has to become involved whether it wants to or not. (Bob Adams, Vice-President for R&D, 3M Corporation)

### SCOTCHLITE

Someone asked the question, "Why didn't 3M make glass beads, because glass beads were going to find increasing use on the highways?"

. . . I had done a little working in the mineral department on trying to color glass beads and had learned a little about their reflecting properties. And, as a little extra-curricular activity, I'd been trying to make luminous house numbers.

Well, this question and my free-time lab project combined to stimulate me to search out where glass beads were being used on the highway. We found a place where beads had been sprinkled on the highway and we saw that they did provide a more visible line at night . . . From there, it was only natural for us to conclude that, since we were a coating company, and probably knew more than anyone else about putting particles onto a web, we ought to be able to coat glass beads very accurately on a piece of paper.

So, that's what we did. The first reflective tape we made was simply a double-coated tape—glass beads sprinkled on one side and an adhesive on the other. We took some out here in St. Paul and, with the cooperation of the highway department, put some down. After the first frost came, and then a thaw, we found we didn't know as much about adhesives under all weather conditions as we thought . . .

We looked around inside the company for skills in related areas. We tapped knowledge that existed in our sandpaper business on how to make waterproof sandpaper. We drew on the expertise of our roofing people who knew something about exposure. We reached into our adhesive and tape division to see how we could make the tape stick to the highway better.

The resulting product became known as "Scotchlite." Its principal application was in reflective signs; only later did 3M develop the market for highway marking. The originator of the product, Harry Heltzer, interested the head of the New Products Division in the product, and he encouraged Heltzer to go out and sell it. Scotchlite was a success and Heltzer became the general manager of the division set up to produce and market it.

*Source:* "The Technical Strategy of 3M: Start More Little Businesses and More Little Businesses," *Innovation* 5 (1969).

- *Buying innovation.* Recognition that small, technology-intensive startups have advantages in the early stages of the innovation process, while large corporations have superior capabilities, has encouraged large companies to enhance their technological performance by acquiring innovation from other firms. Such acquisition may involve licensing, outright purchase of patents, or acquiring the whole company. In biotechnology, pharmaceutical companies have pioneered this outsourcing of innovation. In addition to licensing drug patents, signing marketing agreements, and acquiring specialist biotech firms (these include Genentech by Roche in 2009, ICOS by Eli Lily in 2007, Chiron by Novartis in 2006, Scious by Johnson & Johnson in 2003), pharmaceutical companies have formed research alliances with biotech specialists.[42] In telecom equipment, Cisco Systems built its leading position in internet protocol switching technologies through acquiring small technology intensive firms—55 of them between 1993 and 2000 alone.[43]

- *Open innovation.* The shift from vertically integrated systems of innovation, where companies develop their own technologies in house then exploit them internally, to more market-based systems, where companies buy in technology while also licensing out their own technologies, has given way to ideas of *open innovation.* As innovation increasingly requires the integration of multiple technologies often from traditionally separate scientific areas, so firms have been forced to look wider in their sourcing technology and in sharing knowhow and ideas. Evidence that external linkages promote innovation has reinforced firms' desire to seek technological knowledge from beyond their own borders.[44] Open innovation requires creating a network of collaborative relationships that comprises licensing deals, component outsourcing, joint research, collaborative product development, and informal problem solving and exchanges of ideas. Strategy Capsule 12.4 outlines Procter & Gamble's approach to open innovation.

---

### STRATEGY CAPSULE 12.4
## Procter & Gamble's Open Innovation Initiative

In 2000 it became clear that P&G's internally focused approach to innovation and new product development was incapable of delivering the growth targets that the company had set itself. Despite a research staff numbering 7500, P&G estimated that for every one of its on research scientists there were probably 200 outside the company with the potential to contribute to P&G's development efforts. When CEO A. G. Laffey challenged the company to obtain 50% of its innovations from outside the company, the quest for a new innovation model began.

P&G's *Connect and Develop* innovation model seeks to "identify promising ideas throughout the world and apply our own R&D, manufacturing, marketing and purchasing capabilities to them to create better and cheaper products, faster."

The starting point is to identify what P&G is looking for. The approach was to avoid "blue sky" innovation and seek ideas that had already been successfully embodied in a product, a prototype or a technology. To focus the search each business was asked to identify its top ten customer needs. These included: "reduce wrinkles, improve skin texture and tone . . . softer paper products with higher wet strength." These

needs were then translated into specific technical requirements: for example, biotechnology solutions that permit detergents to perform well at low temperatures. Priorities are then reordered by identifying initiatives which fit with existing areas of brand strength ("adjacencies") and those which have permit strengthening of P&G's strategically important areas of technology ("technology game boards").

P&G's innovation network comprises a number of organizations:

- Within P&G, 70 *technology entrepreneurs* are responsible for developing external contacts and exploring for innovation in particular localities and with a focus around particular product or technology area.

- *Suppliers.* P&G has an IT platform that allows it to share technology briefs with its suppliers. This is complemented by regular meetings between senior P&G executives and senior executives at individual suppliers which explore mutual development opportunities.

- *Technology brokers.* P&G is a member (in some cases a founder member) of several prominent technology brokering networks. These include *NineSigma* which links companies with universities, private labs, government bodies, consultants and other potential solutions providers; *Innocentive,* which brokers solutions to science-based problems; *YourEncore,* a network of retired scientists and engineers; and *Yet2.com,* an online marketplace for intellectual capital.

These networks generate an enormous flow of suggestions and proposals that are initially screened and disseminated through P&G's *Eureka* online catalog. It is then up to executives within the business groups to identify interesting proposals, to pursue these with the

external provider through P&G's External Business Development group, and to then to take move the initiative into their own product development process.

By 2005, 35% of P&G's new product launches had their origins outside the company. Some of P&G's most successful new products—including Swiffer cleaning cloths, Olay Regeneration, and Crest Spinbrush—had been initiated by outsiders.

*Source:* L. Huston and N. Sakkab, "Connect and Develop: Inside Procter & Gamble's New Model for Innovation" *Harvard Business Review* (March 2006): 58–66. Reproduced with permission.

- *Corporate incubators* are business developments established to fund and nurture new businesses based upon technologies that have been developed internally but have limited applications within a company's established businesses. Corporate incubators became very popular during the IT boom at the end of the 1990s when companies saw the potential to generate substantial value from establishing then spinning off new tech-based ventures.[45] Despite a sound strategic and organizational logic, few major companies have achieved sustained success from the incubator units that they established and among the successful ones, many have been sold to venture capital firms. A key problem, according to Gary Hamel, is that: "Many corporate incubators became orphanages for unloved ideas that had no internal support or in-house sponsorship."[46] Despite their uneven track record, several leading companies have experienced considerable success in introducing company-wide processes for developing new businesses based upon internally generated innovations. Strategy Capsule 12.5 outlines the approaches of IBM and Cisco Systems.

### STRATEGY CAPSULE 12.5

## Incubating innovation at IBM and Cisco Systems

IBM uses *Innovation Jam*—a massive online brainstorming process—to generate, select, and develop new business ideas. The 2006 Jam was based upon an initial identification of 25

technology clusters grouped into six broad categories. Web sites were built for each technology cluster and, for a 72-hour period, IBM employees, their families and friends, suppliers and customers from all around the world were invited to contribute ideas for innovations based on these technologies. The 150 000 participants generated vast and diverse sets of suggestions that were subject to text mining software and review by 50 senior executives and technical specialists who worked in nine separate teams to identify promising ideas. The next phase of the Jam subjected the selected innovation ideas to comments and review by the online community. This was followed by a further review process in which the 10 best proposals were selected and a budget of $100 million was allocated to their development. The selected business ideas included a real-time foreign language translation service, smart healthcare payment systems, IT applications to environmental projects, and 3-D internet. The new businesses were begun as incubator projects and were then transferred to one or other of IBM's business groups. As well as divisional links, the new ventures were also subject to monthly review by IBM's corporate top management.

Cisco Systems created its *Emerging Technology Business Group* with the goal of creating 20 new ventures by 2012. Within 18 months, 400 ideas for new businesses had been posted on the Cisco wiki and the Emerging Technology Business Group had begun developing several of these suggestions including *TelePresence*, a video surveillance security system and an IP interoperability and collaboration systems server for emergency services. By 2008 *TelePresence* was established as a regular business group. Like IBM's *Innovation Jam* a key feature of Cisco's incubator model is its close linkage with the rest of the company: the Emerging Technology Group is part of Cisco's R&D organization and is subject to close involvement by Cisco's senior management—including CEO John Chambers.

**Sources:** O. M. Bjelland and R. C. Wood, "An Inside View of IBM's Innovation Jam" MIT Sloan Management Review (Fall 2008): 32–43. Tom Sanders "Cisco Reinvents the Corporate Incubator" (July 27, 2007): http://www.vnunet.com/vnunet /news/2194961/ cisco-reinvents-corporate, accessed 6 July, 2009.

# Summary

In emerging and technology-based industries, nurturing and exploiting innovation is the fundamental source of competitive advantage and the focus of strategy formulation. Yet the basic tools of strategy analysis are the same as those that we have already encountered in this book. The fundamental strategic issues we are concerned with include the drivers of competition in these markets, the resources and capabilities through which a firm can establish competitive advantage, and the design of structures and systems to implement strategy.

Yet, the unpredictability and instability of these industries mean that strategic decisions in technology-driven industries have a very special character. The remarkable dynamics of these industries mean that difference between massive value creation and ignominious failure may be the result of small errors of timing or technological choices.

In technology-based industries, traditional approaches to strategy based upon forecasting and detailed planning are inadequate. The combination of speed and unpredictability of change means that effective strategies are those which combine clarity of vision with flexibility and responsiveness. The companies that have succeeded in emerging and technology based industries are those that recognized most clearly the strategic characteristics of their industries and adapted most effectively to them. In industries that have been turned upside-down by technological change—whether telecommunications equipment, medical imaging, information storage, or sports equipment—it is companies that have understood the sources of competitive advantage and assembled the resources and capabilities needed to exploit them that have emerged as winners.

I hope to have persuaded you that, despite the turbulence and uncertainty of these industries, there are analytic principles that can guide us towards strategies which do not guarantee success but certainly improve the odds. For example, our learning has included:

- evaluating an innovation's potential to generate profit;
- assessing the relative merits of licensing, alliances, joint ventures and internal development as alternative strategies for exploiting an innovation;
- identifying the factors that determine the comparative advantages of being a leader or a follower in innovation.

This chapter also pointed to the central importance of strategy implementation in determining success. The key to successful innovation is not resource allocation decisions, but creating the structure, integration mechanisms, and organizational climate conducive to innovation. No other type of industry environment reveals so clearly the inseparability of strategy formulation and strategy implementation. Strategies aimed at the exploitation of innovation, choices of whether to be a leader or a follower, and the management of risk must take careful account of organizational characteristics.

Technology-based industries also reveal some of the dilemmas that are a critical feature of strategic management in complex organizations and complex business environments. For example, technology-based industries are unpredictable, yet some investments in technology have time horizons of a decade or more. Successful strategies must be responsive to changing market conditions, but successful strategies also require long-term commitment. The fundamental dilemma is that innovation is an unpredictable process that requires creating a nurturing organizational context, whereas strategy is about resource-allocation decisions. How can a company create the conditions for nurturing innovation while planning the course of its development? John Scully, a former CEO of Apple, observed: *"Management and creativity might even be considered antithetical states. While management demands consensus, control, certainty, and the status quo, creativity thrives on the opposite: instinct, uncertainty, freedom, and iconoclasm."*[47]

Fortunately, the experiences of companies such as 3M, Cisco Systems, Amgen and Nintendo offer solutions to these dilemmas. The need for innovation to reconcile individual creativity with coordination points toward the advantages of cross-functional team-based approaches over the isolation of R&D in a separate "creative" environment. Moreover, the need to reconcile innovation with efficiency points toward the advantage of parallel organizational structures where, in addition to the "formal" structure geared to the needs of existing businesses and products, an informal structure exists, which is the source of new products and businesses. The role of top management in balancing creativity with order and innovation with efficiency becomes critical—such reconciliation requires senior executives who are not necessarily experts in technology but who, at minimum appreciate its strategic implications.

The increasing pace of technological change and intensifying international competition suggests that the advanced, industrialized countries will be forced to rely increasingly on their technological capabilities as the basis for international competitiveness. Strategies for promoting innovation and managing technology will become more important in the future.

# Self-Study Questions

1   Trevor Bayliss, a British inventor, submitted a patent application in November 1992 for a wind-up radio for use in Africa in areas where there was no electricity supply and people were too poor to afford batteries. He was excited by the prospects for radio broadcasts as a means of disseminating health education in areas of Africa devastated by AIDS. After appearances on British and South African TV, Bayliss attracted a number of entrepreneurs and companies interested in manufacturing and marketing his clockwork radio. However, Bayliss was concerned by the fact that his patent provided only limited protection for his invention: most of the main components—a clockwork generator and transistor radio—were long-established technologies. What advice would you offer Baylis as to how he can best protect and exploit his invention?

2   Table 12.1 shows that:

   (a)  Patents have been more effective in protecting product innovations in drugs and medical equipment than in food or electronic components;
   (b)  Patents are more effective in protecting product innovations than process innovations.

   Can you suggest reasons why?

3   Page 306 refers to James Dyson's difficulties in licensing his innovative vacuum cleaner (see http://www.cdf.org/issue_journal/dyson_fills_a_vacuum.html for further information). What lessons would you draw from Dyson's experience concerning the use of licensing by small firms to exploit innovation?

4   From the evidence presented in Table 12.3, what conclusions can you draw regarding the factors that determine whether leaders or followers win out in the markets for new products?

5   In the battle for dominance of the ebook reader market, Amazon with Kindle 2 was ahead of Sony with its Reader Digital Book. Kindle 2 had the biggest number of recent titles available, but thanks to a deal with Google, Sony had a huge number of out-of-copyright titles. What are the sources of network externalities in this market? Will ebook readers become a winner-take-all market? Why has Amazon been able to gain a lead over Sony (and Samsung)? What can Sony do to fight back?

## Notes

1   "The Logic that Dares Not Speak its Name," *Economist* (April 16, 1994): 89–91.

2   In the U.S., the return to R&D spending was estimated at between 3.7% and 5.5%. See M. Warusawitharana, "Research and Development, Profits and Firm Value: A Structural Estimation," Discussion Paper (Washington, DC: Federal Reserve Board, September, 2008).

3   The excess of the benefit received by the consumer over the price they paid is called *consumer surplus*. See: D. Besanko, D. Dranove and M. Shanley, *Economics of Strategy* (New York: John Wiley & Sons, Inc., 1996): 442–3.

4   "Knowledge Monopolies: Patent Wars," *Economist* (April 8, 2000): 95–9.

5   F. T. Rothermael, "Incumbent Advantage Through Exploiting Complementary Assets via Interfirm Cooperation," *Strategic Management Journal* 22 (2001): 687–99.

6   R. C. Levin, A. K. Klevorick, R. R. Nelson and S. G. Winter, "Appropriating the Returns from Industrial Research and Development," *Brookings Papers on Economic Activity* 18, no. 3(1987):783–832.

7   P. Grindley and D. J. Teece, "Managing Intellectual Capital: Licensing and Cross-Licensing in Semiconductors and Electronics," *California Management Review* 39 (Winter 1997): 8-41.

8   R. Adner, "Match your Innovation Strategy to your Innovation Ecosystem," *Harvard Business Review* (April 2006): 17–37.

9   S. Shulman, *The Telephone Gambit* (New York: Norton, 2008).

10  "The Human Genome Race," *Scientific American* (April 24, 2000).

11  C. Markides and P. A. Geroski, *Fast Second* (San Francisco: Jossey-Bass, 2005).

12  D. Sull, "Strategy as Active Waiting," *Harvard Business Review* (September 2005): 120–9.

13  For example, data on penetration rates for electric toothbrushes and CD players were used to forecast the

market demand for HD TVs in the United States (B. L. Bayus, "High-Definition Television: Assessing Demand Forecasts for the Next Generation Consumer Durable," *Management Science* 39 (1993): 1319–33).

14  See B. C. Twiss, *Managing Technological Innovation*, 2nd edn (New York: Longman, 1980).

15  E. Von Hippel, "Lead Users: A Source of Novel Product Concepts," *Management Science* 32 (July, 1986).

16  In electronic instruments, customers' ideas initiated most of the successful new products introduced by manufacturers. See E. Von Hippel, "Users as Innovators," *Technology Review* 5 (1976): 212–39.

17  A. Friedlander, *The Growth of Railroads* (Arlington, VA: CNRI, 1995).

18  C. Shapiro and H. R. Varian, *Information Rules: A Strategic Guide to the Network Economy* (Boston: Harvard Business School Press, 1999): 264–7.

19  S. Postrel, "Competing Networks and Proprietary Standards: The Case of Quadraphonic Sound," *Journal of Industrial Economics* 24 (December 1990): 169–86.

20  S. J. Liebowitz and S. E. Margolis ("Network Externality: An Uncommon Tragedy," *Journal of Economic Perspectives* 8, Spring 1994: 133–50) refer to these user-to-user externalities as *direct externalities*.

21  M. Gladwell, *The Tipping Point* (Boston: Little Brown, 2000).

22  P. David, "Clio and the Economics of QWERTY," *American Economic Review* 75 (May 1985): 332–7; S. J. Gould, "The Panda's Thumb of Technology," *Natural History* 96, no. 1 (1986): 14-23. For an alternative view see S. J. Liebowitz and S. Margolis, "The Fable of the Keys," *Journal of Law and Economics* 33 (1990): 1–26.

23  C. Shapiro and H. R. Varian, "The Art of Standards Wars," *California Management Review* 41 (Winter 1999): 8–32.

24  R. M. Grant "The DVD War of 2006-8: Blu-Ray vs. HD-DVD" (2010) John Wiley & Sons, Chichester Cases to Accompany Contemporary Strategy Analysis, 7th edn.

25 C. Shapiro and H. R. Varian, "The Art of Standards Wars," op cit: 15–16.

26 Ibid.: 16–18.

27 S. Ahn, "Firm Dynamics and Productivity Growth: A Review of Micro Evidence from OECD Countries," Economics Department Working Paper 297 (OECD, 2001).

28 J. M. George, "Creativity in Organizations," *Academy of Management Annals* 1 (2007): 439–77.

29 M. L. Tushman, "Managing Communication Networks in R&D Laboratories," *Sloan Management Review* (Winter 1979): 37–49.

30 D. Dougherty and C. H. Takacs, "Team Play: Heedful Interrelating as the Boundary for Innovation," *Long Range Planning* 37 (December 2004): 569–90.

31 S. Thomke, "Enlightened Experimentation: The New Imperative for Innovation," *Harvard Business Review* (February, 2001): 66–75.

31 L. Grundy, J. Kickel and C. Prather, "Building the Creative Organization," *Organizational Dynamics* (Spring 1994): 22–37.

32 R. Florida and J. Goodnight, "Managing for Creativity," *Harvard Business Review* (July–August 2005): 124–131.

33 D. Leonard and S. Straus, "Putting Your Company's Whole Brain to Work," *Harvard Business Review* (July–August 1997): 111–21; D. Leonard and P. Swap, *When Sparks Fly: Igniting Creativity in Groups* (Boston: Harvard Business School Press, 1999).

34 "How to Manage a Dream Factory," *Economist* (January 16, 2003).

35 "Lunch with the FT: John Lasseter," *Financial Times* (January 17, 2009).

36 E. Von Hippel, *The Sources of Innovation* (New York: Oxford University Press, 1988), provides strong evidence of the dominant role of users in the innovation process.

37 E. Morrison, "Gunfire at Sea: A Case Study of Innovation," in M. Tushman and W. L. Moore (eds), *Readings in the Management of Innovation* (Cambridge, MA: Ballinger, 1988): 165–78.

38 K. Clark and T. Fujimoto, *Product Development Performance: Strategy, Organization, and Management in the World Auto Industry* (Boston: Harvard Business School Press, 1991).

39 K. Imai, I. Nonaka and H. Takeuchi, "Managing the New Product Development Process: How Japanese Companies Learn and Unlearn," in K. Clark, R. Hayes and C. Lorenz (eds), *The Uneasy Alliance* (Boston: Harvard Business School Press, 1985).

40 D. A. Schön, "Champions for Radical New Inventions," *Harvard Business Review* (March–April, 1963): 84.

41 R. Rothwell, C. Freeman, A. Horlsey, V. T. Jervis, A. B. Robertson and J. Townsend, "SAPPHO Updated—Project SAPPHO Phase II," *Research Policy* 3 (1974): 258–91.

42 G. P. Pisano, *Science Business: The Promise, the Reality, and the Future of Biotech* (Boston: Harvard Business School Press, 2006).

43 "Cisco's Chambers: The Route Ahead," ICFASI Case Study No. 306-172-1 (Chennai, 2006),

44 A. Arora, A, Fosfur and A. Gambardella, *Markets for Technology* (Cambridge: MIT Press, 2001); S. Breschi and F. Malerba, *Clusters, Networks and Innovation* (Oxford: Oxford University Press, 2005).

45 M. T. Hansen, H. W. Chesborough, N. Nohria and D. N. Sull, "Networked Incubators: Hothouse of the New Economy," *Harvard Business Review* (September–October, 2000): 74–88; "How to Make the Most of a Brilliant Idea," *Financial Times* (December 6, 2000): 21.

46 "Nurturing Creativity: Putting Passions to Work" *Shell World* (Royal Dutch Shell, 14 September, 2007): 1–12.

47 J. Scully, *Odyssey* (Toronto: Fitzhenry and Whiteside, 1987): 18.

# 13 Competitive Advantages in Mature Industries

*We are a true "penny profit" business. That means that it takes hard work and attention to detail to be financially successful—it is far from being a sure thing. Our store managers must do two things well: control costs and increase sales. Cost control cannot be done by compromising product quality, customer service, or restaurant cleanliness, but rather by consistent monitoring of the "vital signs" of the business through observation, reports, and analysis. Portion control is a critical part of our business. For example, each Filet-O-Fish sandwich receives 1 fluid ounce of tartar sauce and 0.5 ounces of cheese. Our raw materials are fabricated to exacting tolerances, and our managers check them on an ongoing basis. Our written specification for lettuce is over two typewritten pages long. Our French fries must meet standards for potato type, solid and moisture content, and distribution of strand lengths.*

—EDWARD H. RENSI, PRESIDENT AND CHIEF OPERATING OFFICER, MCDONALD'S U.S.A.[1]

# Introduction and Objectives

Although technology-based industries grab the attention of both business journalists and strategy researchers, if importance is measured by share of GDP rather than share of media output, mature industries—food, energy, construction, vehicles, financial services, and restaurants—retain their preeminence, even in the advanced industrialized nations.

Despite their heterogeneity—they range from massage parlors to steel—mature industries present several similarities from a strategic perspective. The purpose of this chapter is to explore these characteristics of mature industries, identify strategies through which competitive advantage can be established within them, and recognize the implications of these strategies for structure, systems, and leadership style. As we shall see, maturity does not imply lack of opportunity. Companies such as Hennes & Mauritz (fashion clothing), Ryanair (airlines), Starbucks (coffee shops) and Nucor (steel) have successfully deployed novel strategies in mature sectors. Mature sectors are typically inhabited by mature companies—Coca-Cola, ExxonMobil, and HSBC Holdings were founded in the nineteenth century, yet, over the past two decades, have achieved combinations of profitability and growth that would make most high-tech companies envious. Nor does maturity mean lack of innovation: as we shall see, many mature industries have been transformed by new technologies and new strategies.

By the time you have completed this chapter, you will be able to:

◆ recognize the principal strategic characteristics of mature industries;

◆ identify key success factors within mature industries and formulate strategies directed toward their exploitation;

◆ locate and analyze opportunities for strategic innovation in mature industries to establish competitive advantage;

◆ design organizational structures and management systems that can effectively implement such strategies.

## Competitive Advantage in Mature Industries

Our analysis of the industry life cycle (Chapter 11) suggests that maturity has two principal implications for competitive advantage: first, it tends to reduce the number of opportunities for establishing competitive advantage; second, it shifts these opportunities from differentiation-based factors to cost-based factors.

Diminishing opportunities for sustainable competitive advantage in mature industries stem from:

● Less scope for differentiation advantage resulting from increased buyer knowledge, product standardization, and less product innovation.

● Diffusion of process technology means that cost advantages based on superior processes or more advanced capital equipment methods are difficult to obtain and sustain. Once a cost advantage is established, it is vulnerable to exchange rate movements and the emergence of low-cost overseas competitors.

● A highly developed industry infrastructure together with the presence of powerful distributors makes it easier to attack established firms that occupy particular strategic niches.

Using different terminology, Warren Buffett—"The Sage of Omaha"—views the process of maturity as one of value destruction during which enterprises make the transition from "franchises" into "businesses":

An economic franchise arises from a product or service that (1) is needed or desired; (2) is thought by customers to have no close substitute; and (3) is not subject to price regulation. Franchises earn high rates of return on capital . . . [and] can tolerate mismanagement . . . In contrast, "a business" earns exceptional profits only if it is a low-cost operator or if supply of its product or service is tight. And a business, unlike a franchise, can be killed by poor management.[2]

This trend toward deteriorating industry profitability is a constant threat in mature industries. The propensity towards overinvestment in capacity, internationalization and commoditization exacerbate price competition and make competitive advantage difficult to attain and even harder to sustain.

## Cost Advantage

If cost is the overwhelmingly important key success factor in most mature industries, what are the primary sources of low cost? Three cost drivers tend to be especially important:

- *Economies of scale.* In capital-intensive industries, or where advertising, distribution, or new product development is an important element of total cost, economies of scale are important sources of interfirm cost differences. The increased standardization that accompanies maturity greatly assists the exploitation of such scale economies. The significance of scale economies in mature industries is indicated by the fact that the association between return on investment and market share is stronger in mature industries than in emerging industries.[3]

- *Low-cost inputs.* Where small competitors are successful in undercutting the prices of market leaders in mature industries, it is frequently through their access to low-cost inputs. Established firms can become locked into high salaries and benefits, inefficient working practices and bloated overheads inherited from more prosperous times. New entrants into mature industries may gain cost advantages by acquiring plant and equipment at bargain-basement levels and by cutting labor costs. Valero Energy Corporation is the largest oil refiner in the U.S.: it acquired loss-making refineries from the majors at below book prices then operated them with rigorous cost efficiency. A lower cost of capital can also be a key source of cost advantage. Prior to the 2008 credit crunch, the acquisition of retailers, hotels, hospital groups, and chemical firms by private equity funds was motivated by the attractions of substituting low-cost debt for high-cost equity.[4]

- *Low overheads.* During the early 1990s, some of the most profitable companies in mature industries tended to be those that had achieved the most substantial reductions in overhead costs. In discount retailing, Wal-Mart is famous for its parsimonious approach to costs. Among the oil majors, Exxon is known for its rigorous control of overhead costs. Exxon's headquarters cost (relative to net worth) was estimated at less than one-quarter that of Mobil's.[5] When Exxon merged with Mobil, it was able to extract huge cost savings from Mobil. In newspaper and magazine publishing, newcomers such as EMAP in the U.K. and Media News Group in the U.S. (run by "Lean" Dean Singleton) have acquired multiple titles then slashed overhead costs.

As cost inefficiencies tend to become institutionalized within mature enterprises, cost reduction may require drastic interventions. *Corporate restructuring*—intensive periods of structural and strategic change—typically involves cost reduction through outsourcing, headcount reduction and downsizing—especially at corporate headquarters.[6] Successful turnaround strategies typically involve aggressive cost cutting. Empirical research among mature U.S. businesses has identified three successful approaches:

- *Asset and cost surgery*—aggressive cost reduction through reduction of excess capacity; halting of new investment in plant and equipment; and cutbacks in R&D, marketing expenditures, receivables, and inventories.

● *Selective product and market pruning*—refocusing on segments that were most profitable or where the firm possessed distinctive strength.

● *Piecemeal productivity moves*—adjustments to current market position rather than comprehensive refocusing or reorganizing, including reductions in marketing and R&D expenditures, higher capacity utilization, and increased employee productivity.[7]

## Segment and Customer Selection

Sluggish demand growth, lack of product differentiation, and international competition tend to depress the profitability of mature industries. Yet, even unattractive industries may offer attractive niche markets with strong growth of demand, few competitors, and abundant potential for differentiation. As a result, segment selection can be a key determinant of differences in the performance of companies within the same industry. Wal-Mart's profitability was boosted by locating its stores in small and medium-sized towns where it faced little competition. In the auto industry, there is a constant quest to escape competition by creating new market segments with "crossover" vehicles that span existing segments. Opportunities for establishing new segments can arise from the strategies of market leaders. The more that incumbents focus on the mass market, the more likely it is that new entrants can carve out new market niches by supplying underserved customer needs.[8]

The logic of segment focus implies further disaggregation of markets—down to the level of the individual customer. Information technology permits new approaches to *customer relationship management* (CRM), making it possible to analyze individual characteristics and preferences, identify individual customers' profit contribution to the firm, and organize marketing around individualized, integrated approaches to customers. In the same way that Las Vegas casinos have long recognized that the major part of their profits derives from a tiny minority of customers—the "high rollers"—so banks, supermarkets, credit card companies, and hotels increasingly use transactions data to identify their most attractive customers, and those that are a drag on profitability.

The next stage in this process is to go beyond customer selection to actively target more attractive customers and transform less valuable customers into more valuable customers. Alan Grant and Leonard Schlesinger point to the need for companies to optimize their *value exchange*—the relationship between the investment a company makes in a customer relationship and the return that investment generates.[9] For example:

● Credit card issuer Capital One has long been a leader in using data warehousing, experimentation, simulation, and sophisticated statistical modeling to adjust the terms and features of its credit card offers to the preferences and characteristics of individual customers. Capital One estimates the lifetime profitability of each customer and analyzes the four key events in the credit card life cycle: acquiring the customer, stimulating the customer's card use, retaining the customer, and managing default.[10]

● Amazon.com uses information on customers' prior transactions and comparisons with other customers making similar purchases to generate individualized purchase suggestions.

## The Quest for Differentiation

Cost leadership, we noted in Chapter 10, is difficult to sustain, particularly in the face of international competition. Hence, differentiating to attain some insulation from the rigors of price competition is particularly attractive in mature industries. The problem is that the trend toward commoditization narrows the scope for differentiation and reduces customer willingness to pay a premium for differentiation:

- In tires and domestic appliances, companies' investments in differentiation through product innovation, quality and brand advertising reputation have generated disappointing returns. Vigorous competition, price-sensitive customers and strong, aggressive retailers have limited the price premium that differentiation will support.
- Attempts by airlines to gain competitive advantage through offering more legroom, providing superior in-flight entertainment, and achieving superior punctuality have met little market response from consumers. The only effective differentiators appear to be frequent flier programs and services offered to first- and business-class travelers.

Standardization of the physical attributes of a product and convergence of consumer preferences constrains, but does not eliminate, opportunities for meaningful and profitable differentiation. Product standardization is frequently accompanied by increased differentiation of complementary services—financing terms, leasing arrangements, warranties, after-sales services and the like. In consumer goods, maturity often means a shift from physical differentiation to image differentiation. Entrenched consumer loyalties to specific brands of cola or cigarettes are a tribute to the capacity of brand promotion over long periods of time to create distinct images among near-identical products.

The intensely competitive retail sector produces particularly interesting examples of differentiation strategies. The dismal profitability earned by many retail chains (Toys-R-Us, J. C. Penney, and Circuit City in the U.S.; J. Sainsbury, Mothercare, and Kingfisher in the U.K.; Royal Ahold in the Netherlands) contrasts sharply with the sales growth and profitability of stores that have established clear differentiation through variety, style, and ambiance (Target, Lowe's, TJX, Bed, Bath and Beyond, and Wholefoods in the U.S.; Zara-Inditex from Spain; Hennes & Mauritz and IKEA from Sweden). A further lesson from highly competitive mature sectors such as retailing is that competitive advantage is difficult to sustain. Most of the outstandingly successful retailers of the previous decade—Toys-R-Us, Body Shop, and Marks & Spencer—have been displaced in the affections of consumers and investors by the rising stars of retail.

## Innovation

We have characterized mature industries as industries where the pace of technical change is low. In many mature industries—steel, textiles, food processing, insurance, and hotels—R&D expenditure is below 1% of sales revenue, while in U.S. manufacturing as a whole just three sectors—computers and electronics, pharmaceuticals, and aerospace—account for 65% of R&D spending.[11] Nevertheless, measured by patenting activity, there is evidence that many mature industries are as innovative as emerging industries.[12] Even in mature low-tech products such as tires, brassieres and fishing rods, continuing inventiveness is indicated by a steady flow of new patents (see Strategy Capsule 13.1).

Despite an increased pace of technological change in many mature industries, the most opportunities for establishing competitive advantage are likely to arise from *strategic innovation*—including "new game strategies" and "blue ocean strategies" that we discussed in Chapter 8. Indeed, as identified in Chapter 11, it may be that strategic innovation constitutes a third phase of innovation that becomes prominent once product and process innovation slacken. In addition to the "value chain reconfiguration" approach discussed in Chapter 8, firms can seek strategic innovation by redefining markets and market segments. This may involve:

- *Embracing new customer groups.* Harley-Davidson has created a market for expensive motorcycles among the middle-aged, while in the maturing market

---

### STRATEGY CAPSULE 13.1

# Innovation in Mature Industries: Brassiere Technology

The first patent for a "breast-supporting device" was issued in the U.S. in 1864. However, the first patent relating to an undergarment named "brassiere" was issued to Mary Phelps Jacob in 1913. By 1940 over 550 U.S. patents for brassieres and related breast supporters had been issued.

The technological quest for a better bra continued into the twenty-first century—the U.S. Patent Office has issued over 200 patents relating to brassieres since January 2000. The design innovations of recent years include:

- Wonderbra (owned by Sara Lee) introduced a "variable cleavage" bra equipped with a system of pulleys;
- the Airotic bra designed by Gossard (also owned by Sara Lee) features "twin air bags as standard"—these are inflatable by a "unique G-pump system";
- Charnos's Bioform bra replaces underwiring with soft molded polypropylene around a

rigid ring—a design inspired by the Frisbee and engineered by Ove Arup, who also engineered London's Millennium Bridge (which had to be closed because of excessive wobbling);

- The Ultimo bra, designed by Scottish model Michelle Mone assisted by a team of German scientists, is equipped with silicone gel pads;
- A number of new brassieres use "spacer fabric" which comprises "two outer textile layers separated by a ventilated inner layer of spacer yarns, to allow heat and moisture to escape. Various properties can be added to the fabrics, including anti-microbial, anti-mildew, anti-static, flame-retardant, absorptive, water-repellent, and abrasion-resistant attributes . . ."

*Sources:* "Bra Wars," *Economist* (December 2, 2000): 112; salon.com (August 28, 2000); U.S. Patent Database.

for video game consoles, Nintendo achieved remarkable success with its *Wii* by appealing to consumers outside the core market of teenage and preteenage boys. The most rapidly growing churches—for example Jehovah's Witnesses in Russia and Amway Christian Fellowship in America—tend to be those that recruit among non-church going social and demographic groups.

- *Augmenting products and services.* Some of the most successful approaches to differentiation in mature industries involve bundling additional products or services with the core offering. In book retailing, Barnes & Noble offer, not only a wide range of titles, but also include Starbucks coffee shops within its stores. Neighborhood bookstores that have survived competition from the megastores and Amazon.com are often those that have added poetry readings, live music and other recreational services. The adoption of themes by retail stores and restaurants—Virgin Megastores, Hard Rock Café and Planet Hollywood—reflect the desire to involve customers in an experience that goes beyond the product being sold. In the *experience economy*, companies go beyond providing a product or service that meets a clearly defined customer need and involve their customers in a process that engages them at the emotional, intellectual, even spiritual level.[13]

- The ability to create competitive advantage requires that managers free themselves from the cognitive limits associated with notions of maturity. Baden-Fuller and Stopford argue that maturity is a state of mind, not a state of the business—every enterprise has the potential for rejuvenation. The key to strategic innovation is for managers to prevent industry conventions from imprisoning their companies into conventional thinking about strategy. This is likely to cultivate an entrepreneurial organization where middle managers are encouraged to experiment and learn.[14]

Costas Markides identifies several firms that have successfully broken away from conventional wisdom to establish a unique positioning within mature industries:

- Edward Jones, with 2000 offices, mostly in the U.S. but also in Canada and the U.K., has rejected the conventional wisdom that successful brokerage firms require scale economies, product diversification, e-commerce and integration with investment banks. Edward Jones' office has just one investment adviser who is motivated to grow local business through face-to-face relationships; there are no proprietary investment products and no online investing.

- Enterprise Rent-A-Car has adopted a location strategy that is quite different from its major competitors, Hertz and Avis. Rather than concentrate on serving the business traveler through locating at airports and downtown, Enterprise concentrates on suburban locations, where it caters primarily to the consumer market.[15]

How do companies break away from the pack and achieve strategic innovation? The problem is that breaking with industry conventions requires confronting industry-wide systems of belief—what J.-C. Spender refers to as "industry recipes."[16] This is likely to require that managers find ways of altering their *cognitive maps*— the mental frameworks through which they perceive and understand their industry environments.[17] This may explain why strategic innovation in mature industries is so often associated with firms that are either outsiders or peripheral players.

According to Gary Hamel, the role of strategy should be to foster revolution through reorganizing the strategy-making process. This means breaking top management's monopoly over strategy formulation, bringing in younger people from further down the organization, and gaining involvement from those on the periphery of the organization.[18] Ultimately, strategic innovation is likely to require a process of organization-wide change—a "journey of strategic renewal."[19]

## Strategy Implementation in Mature Industries: Structure, Systems and Style

Across most mature industries, the primary basis for competitive advantage is operational efficiency, however, as we have seen, cost efficiency must be reconciled with innovation and customer responsiveness. What kinds of organizational structures, management systems, and leadership styles do mature businesses need to adopt in order to achieve these multiple performance goals?

### Efficiency through Bureaucracy

As we observed in Chapter 6, the conventional prescription for stable environments was "mechanistic" organizations characterized by centralization, precisely-defined roles, and predominantly vertical communication.[20] Henry Mintzberg describes this formalized type of organization dedicated to the pursuit of efficiency as the *machine bureaucracy*.[21] Efficiency is achieved through standardized routines, division of labor and close management control based on bureaucratic principles. Division of labor extends to management as well as operatives—high levels of vertical and horizontal specialization are typical among managers. Vertical specialization is evident in the concentration of strategy formulation at the apex of the hierarchy, while middle and junior management supervise and administer through the application of standardized rules and procedures. Horizontal specialization takes the form of functional structures.

The machine bureaucracy as described by Mintzberg is a caricature of actual organizations—probably the closest approximations are found in government departments performing highly routine administrative duties (for example, the Internal Revenue Service or departments of motor vehicle licensing). However, in most mature industries, the features of mechanistic organizations are evident in highly routinized operations controlled by detailed rules and procedures. McDonald's is far from being a typical bureaucracy—in particular, the majority of outlets are franchises operated by independent companies—however, the cost efficiency and consistency that characterizes its performance is the highly standardized and detailed operating procedures that govern virtually every aspect of how it does business (see the quotation that introduces this chapter). Similarly, in Marriott Hotels, HSBC, Toyota Motor Company, and Wal-Mart—the ability of these huge organizations to achieve efficiency and consistent high quality is the result of management systems that draw heavily upon the principles of bureaucracy. The key features of these mature organizations are summarized in Table 13.1.

**Table 13.1** Strategy implementation in mature industries: the conventional model

| | |
|---|---|
| STRATEGY | Primary goal is cost advantage through economies of scale and capital-intensive production of standardized products/services. Strategy formulation primarily the realm of top managers; middle managers responsible for strategy implementation. |
| STRUCTURE | Functional departments (e.g., production, marketing, customer service, distribution). Distinction between line and staff. Clearly defined job roles with strong vertical reporting/delegation relationships. |
| CONTROLS | Performance targets are primarily quantitative and short term and are specified for all members of the organization. Performance is closely monitored by well-established, centralized management information systems and formalized reporting requirements. Financial controls through budgets and profit targets particularly important. |
| INCENTIVES | Incentives are based on achievement of individual targets and take the form of financial rewards and promotion up the hierarchy. Penalties exist for failure to attain quantitative targets, for failure to adhere to the rules, and for lack of conformity to company norms. |
| COMMUNICATION | Primarily vertical for the purposes of delegation and reporting. Lateral communication limited, often achieved through interdepartmental committees. |
| LEADERSHIP | Primary functions of top management: control and strategic direction. Typical CEO profiles include: the *administrator* who guides the organization through establishing and operating organizational systems and principles and building consensus (e.g., Alfred Sloan Jr. of General Motors); the *autocrat*, who uses top-down decision making and leads through centralization of power and force of personality (Lee Iacocca of Chrysler and Al Dunlap of Sunbeam); and the *strategic leader* who combines clear strategic direction with considerable decentralization of decision making (John Brown at BP, Carlos Ghosn at Nissan, Jack Welch at GE). |

## Trends in Strategy Implementation among Mature Businesses

When competitive advantage in mature industries was all about cost advantage through scale and division of labor, management practices based upon standardized processes, elaborately defined rules, hierarchical control, quantitative performance targets and incentives closely linked to individual performance work well. However, as we have discussed, the requirements for success in mature industries and the strategies needed to achieve success given these requirements have become much more complex. In terms of cost efficiency, scale advantages have become less important than the flexibility to exploit low cost inputs and to outsource to low-cost specialists, and an organizational environment that constantly strives to eliminate waste and discover new sources of efficiency.

The efficiency leaders in mature industries are not necessarily the biggest firms that are able to exploit scale benefits to the maximum: they are more likely to be companies that have dedicated themselves to efficiency through implementing performance-oriented management systems. Top performing companies in mature businesses—UPS in delivery services, Wal-Mart in discount retailing, Nucor in steel, ExxonMobil in petroleum—are characterized by management systems that comprise integrated systems where performance goals are the centerpiece of strategy and these goals are implemented through financial controls, human resource policies, and operating practices which are closely integrated with these goals.

Unifying an organization around the pursuit of efficiency requires management systems that allow disaggregation of company-wide goals into specific performance targets for departments and individuals—the *balanced scorecard* is one of the most widely used techniques for achieving this (see Chapter 2). Most important, however, is embedding performance goals within the company's organizational culture:

- Central to UPS's performance driven management style is a corporate culture that simultaneously embraces high levels of employee autonomy and the company's "obsessive-compulsive personality".[22]

- Wal-Mart's culture of frugality reflects the values of founder Sam Walton. According to Wal-Mart executive Ron Loveless: "Sam valued every penny. People say that Wal-Mart is making $10 billion a year, or whatever. But that's not how people within the company think of it. If you spent a dollar, the question was: 'How many dollars of merchandise would you need to sell to make that dollar?'"[23]

- Ryanair is master of the art of managing for cost efficiency. From a simple strategic goal of being Europe's lowest cost airline, Ryanair's route structure, choice of airports, fleet, ticketing system and human resource practices are meticulously aligned to cost minimization. Ryanair's obsession with cost cutting is reflected in the large proportion of employees that are on temporary contracts, the requirement that crews pay for their own uniforms and training, and a heavy emphasis on incentive pay (cabin crew receive a commission on all inflight sales).[24]

Reconciling differentiation and innovation with a relentless drive for cost efficiency creates difficult challenges for designing management systems that promote these goals without blunting the imperatives for cost minimization. The conventional model for reconciling efficiency with innovation in mature companies is internal differentiation: innovation and entrepreneurship are the responsibility of specialist R&D, new product development and business development units. However, some established companies in mature industries have embraced *open innovation*. In the intensely competitive world market for domestic appliances, Whirlpool committed itself to innovation as the primary basis on which it would seek competitive advantage. Its decade-long program for opening up the company to innovation has involved creating a company-wide system for generating new ideas, establishing criteria for assessing proposals and funding them, and training people in the different phases of innovation—including some 600 I-mentors to facilitate the process and some 240 consultants to develop innovation projects.[25]

## Strategies for Declining Industries

The transition from maturity to decline can be a result of technological substitution (typewriters, photographic film), changes in consumer preferences (canned food, men's suits), demographic shifts (children's toys in Europe), or foreign competition (textiles in the advanced industrialized countries). Shrinking market demand gives rise to acute strategic issues. Among the key features of declining industries are:

- excess capacity;
- lack of technical change (reflected in a lack of new product introduction and stability of process technology);
- a declining number of competitors, but some entry as new firms acquire the assets of exiting firms cheaply;
- high average age of both physical and human resources;
- aggressive price competition.

Despite the inhospitable environment offered by declining industries, research by Kathryn Harrigan has uncovered declining industries where at least some participants earned surprisingly high profits. These included electronic vacuum tubes, cigars, and leather tanning. However, elsewhere—notably in prepared baby foods, rayon, and meat processing—decline was accompanied by aggressive price competition, company failures, and instability.[26]

What determines whether or not a declining industry becomes a competitive blood-bath? Two factors are critical: the balance between capacity and output, and the nature of the demand for the product.

## Adjusting Capacity to Declining Demand

The smooth adjustment of industry capacity to declining demand is the key to stability and profitability during the decline phase. In industries where capacity exits from the industry in an orderly fashion, decline can occur without trauma. Where substantial excess capacity persists, as has occurred in the steel industries of America and Europe, in the bakery industry, in gold mining, and in long-haul bus transportation, the potential exists for destructive competition. The ease with which capacity adjusts to declining demand depends on the following factors:

- *The predictability of decline*. If decline can be forecast, it is more likely that firms can plan for it. The decline of traditional photography with the advent of digital imaging was anticipated and planned for. Conversely, the long-term decline of the U.S. and Western European steel industries has been obscured by periodic cyclical upswings—most notably that of 2004–7. The more cyclical and volatile the demand, the more difficult it is for firms to perceive the trend of demand even after the onset of decline.
- *Barriers to exit*. Barriers to exit impede the exit of capacity from an industry. The major barriers are:
  - Durable and specialized assets. Just as capital requirements impose a barrier to entry into an industry, those same investments also discourage exit. The longer they last and the fewer the opportunities for using those assets in another industry, the more companies are tied to that particular industry.
  - Costs incurred in plant closure. Apart from the accounting costs of writing off assets, substantial cash costs may be incurred in redundancy payments to employees, compensation for broken contacts with customers and suppliers, dismantling the plant, and environmental clean up.

- Managerial commitment. In addition to financial considerations, firms may be reluctant to close plants for a variety of emotional and moral reasons. Resistance to plant closure and divestment arises from pride in company traditions and reputation, managers' unwillingness to accept failure, and loyalties to employees and the local community.
- *The strategies of the surviving firms.* Smooth exit of capacity ultimately depends on the willingness of the industry players to close plants and divest assets. The sooner companies recognize and address the problem, the more likely it is that independent and collective action can achieve capacity reduction. In European gasoline retailing, for example, the problem of excess capacity was partially solved by bilateral exchanges of service stations among the major oil companies. Stronger firms in the industry can facilitate the exit of weaker firms by offering to acquire their plants and take over their after-sales service commitments. A key strategy among private equity firms has been initiating "roll-ups" in declining industries—consolidating multiple acquisitions.

## The Nature of Demand

Where a market is segmented, the general pattern of decline can obscure the existence of pockets of demand that are not only comparatively resilient, but also price inelastic. For example, despite the obsolescence of vacuum tubes after the adoption of transistors, GTE Sylvania and General Electric earned excellent profits supplying vacuum tubes to the replacement, high-end audio, and military markets.[27] In fountain pens, survivors in the quality pen segment such as Cross and Mont Blanc have achieved steady sales and high margins through appealing to high-income professionals and executives. Despite overall decline of the cigar market, quality cigars have benefitted from strong demand and attractive margins.

## Strategies for Declining Industries

Conventional strategy recommendations for declining industries are either to divest or to harvest, i.e., to generate the maximum cash flow from existing investments without reinvesting. However, these strategies assume that declining industries are inherently unprofitable. If profit potential exists, then other strategies may be attractive. Harrigan and Porter identify four strategies that can profitably be pursued either individually or sequentially in declining industries:[28]

- *Leadership.* By gaining leadership, a firm is well placed to outstay competitors and play a dominant role in the final stages of the industry's life cycle. Once leadership is attained, the firm is in a good position to switch to a harvest strategy and enjoy a strong profit stream from its market position. Establishing leadership can be done by acquiring competitors, but a cheaper way is to encourage competitors to exit (and then acquire their plants). Inducements to competitors to exit may include showing commitment to the industry, helping to lower their exit costs, releasing pessimistic forecasts of the industry's future, and raising the stakes—for example, by supporting more stringent environmental controls that make it costly for them to stay in business.

- *Niche*. Identify a segment that is likely to maintain a stable demand and that other firms are unlikely to invade, then pursue a leadership strategy to establish dominance within the segment. The most attractive niches are those that offer the greatest prospects for stability and where demand is most inelastic.

- *Harvest*. By harvesting, a firm maximizes its cash flow from existing assets, while avoiding further investment. A harvesting strategy seeks to boost margins wherever possible through raising prices and cutting costs by rationalizing the number of models, number of channels, and number of customers. Note, however, that a harvest strategy can be difficult to implement. In the face of strong competition, harvesting may accelerate decline, particularly if employee morale is adversely affected by a strategy that offers no long-term future for the business.

- *Divest*. If the future looks bleak, the best strategy may be to divest the business in the early stages of decline before a consensus has developed as to the inevitability of decline. Once industry decline is well established it may be extremely difficult to find buyers.

Choosing the most appropriate strategy requires a careful assessment both of the profit potential of the industry and the competitive position of the firm. Harrigan and Porter pose four key questions:

- Can the structure of the industry support a hospitable, potentially profitable decline phase?
- What are the exit barriers that each significant competitor faces?
- Do your company strengths fit the remaining pockets of demand?
- What are your competitors' strengths in these pockets? How can their exit barriers be overcome?

Selecting an appropriate strategy requires matching the opportunities remaining in the industries to the company's competitive position. Figure 13.1 shows a simple framework for strategy choice.

**FIGURE 13.1** Strategic alternatives for declining industries

|  | | COMPANY'S COMPETITIVE POSITION | |
|---|---|---|---|
|  | | Strengths in remaining demand pockets | Lacks strength in remaining demand pockets |
| INDUSTRY STRUCTURE | Favorable to decline | LEADERSHIP or NICHE | HARVEST or DIVEST |
|  | Unfavorable to decline | NICHE or HARVEST | DIVEST QUICKLY |

# Summary

Mature industries present challenging environments for the formulation and implementation of business strategies. Competition—price competition in particular—is usually strong and competitive advantage is often difficult to build and sustain: cost advantages are vulnerable to imitation, differentiation opportunities are limited by the trend to standardization. Stable positions of competitive advantage in mature industries are traditionally associated with cost advantage from economies of scale or experience, and differentiation advantage through brand loyalty. Such strategies are typically implemented through hierarchical organizations, with high levels of specialization and formalization, and centralized decision making directed toward maximizing static efficiency.

Increased dynamism of mature industries resulting from international competition, economic turbulence, and greater pressure for innovation has had two consequences. First, the conditions for cost efficiency have changed. In a dynamic environment, cost efficiency is less dependent on scale, specialization, and rigid control, and more on rapid adjustment to change. Second, as competition has become more intense, companies (especially those in the advanced industrialized countries) have been forced to seek new sources of competitive advantage through innovation and differentiation. Reconciling the pursuit of scale economies with the need for responsiveness and flexibility, and the requirements of cost efficiency with the growing need for innovation and differentiation, poses complex strategic and organizational challenges. Some of the most successful companies in mature industries—Wal-Mart in retailing, BP in oil and gas, Nike in shoes and sportswear, and Coca-Cola in beverages—are companies that have achieved flexibility through dismantling bureaucratic structures and procedures, exploiting new technology to combine variety and flexibility with efficiency, encouraging high levels of employee commitment, and relentlessly pursuing financial targets. We return to some of these challenges in Chapter 18.

# Self-Study Questions

1 The clothing manufacturers of northern Italy are facing rapid decline as retail chains and fashion houses increasingly outsource to China and other low-cost countries. What strategies would you recommend to small and medium-sized Italian garment manufacturers to assist them in surviving the onslaught of low-cost foreign competition?

2 Under Jacques Nasser, Ford's response to intensifying competition in the auto industry was to acquire a stable of luxury brands and forward integrate into car rental (Hertz), car repair (Kwik Fit), and financial services. The present CEO, Alan Mulally, has moved in the opposite

direction: divesting car rental, car repair and the luxury brands (including Aston Martin, Land Rover and Jaguar), while aggressively cutting costs and capacity. Given the characteristics of the industry and the company, which CEO has the better strategy?

**3**  In both Europe and North America, established airlines are desperately cutting costs to compete with the increasing number of budget airlines. However, it is highly unlikely that these airlines will ever match the cost efficiency of Southwest, Jet Blue, or Ryanair. What opportunities are there for established airlines to improve their competitive position through differentiation strategies? Make specific proposals for how established airlines can differentiate their customer offerings more effectively.

**4**  Department stores (for example, Federated Department Stores and Mays in the U.S., Selfridges and House of Fraser in the U.K.) face increasing competition from specialized chain retailers and discount stores. What innovative strategies might department stores adopt to revitalize their competitiveness?

**5**  In an era of budget airlines, online booking for travel, hotels, and car hire, the elimination of commissions paid by airlines, and declining demand for "package vacations" (air travel + hotel reservations + other services), is there a future for retail travel agents? What survival strategies can you recommend?

# Notes

1  E. H. Rensi, "Computers at McDonald's," in J. F. McLimore and L. Larwood (eds), *Strategies, Successes: Senior Executives Speak Out* (New York: Harper & Row, 1988): 159–60.

2  Letter to Shareholders, Annual Report of Berkshire Hathaway Inc., 1991.

3  R. D. Buzzell and B. T. Gale, *The PIMS Principles* (New York: Free Press, 1987): 279.

4  "European Leveraged Buy-outs," *Economist* (August 10, 2006).

5  T. Copeland, T. Koller and J. Murrin, *Valuation: Measuring and Managing the Value of Companies*, 3rd edn (New York: John Wiley & Sons, Inc. 2000): 305.

6  R. Cibin and R. M. Grant, "Restructuring among the World's Leading Oil Companies," *British Journal of Management* 7 (December 1996): 283–308.

7  D. C. Hambrick and S. M. Schecter, "Turnaround Strategies for Mature Industrial-Product Business Units," *Academy of Management Journal* 26, no. 2 (1983): 231–48.

8  G. R. Carroll and A. Swaminathan, "Why the Microbrewery Movement? Organizational Dynamics of Resource Partitioning in the American Brewing Industry," *American Journal of Sociology* 106 (2000): 715–62; C. Boone, G. R. Carroll and A. van

Witteloostuijn, "Resource Distributions and Market Partitioning: Dutch Daily Newspapers 1964–94," *American Sociological Review* 67 (2002): 408–31.

9  A. W. H. Grant and L. A. Schlesinger, "Realize Your Customer's Full Profit Potential," *Harvard Business Review* (September–October 1995): 59–72.

10  *Capital One Financial Corporation*, Harvard Business School Case No. 9-700-124 (2000).

11  National Science Foundation, *Research and Development in Industry: 2002* (www.nsf.gov/statistics/industry).

12  A. M. McGahan and B. S. Silverman, "How Does Innovative Activity Change as Industries Mature?" *International Journal of Industrial Organization* 19, no. 7 (2001): 1141–60.

13  B. J. Pine and J. Gilmore, "Welcome to the Experience Economy," *Harvard Business Review* (July–August 1998): 97–105.

14  C. Baden-Fuller and J. Stopford, *Rejuvenating the Mature Business* (Boston: HBS Press, 1994): especially Chapters 3 and 4.

15  C. C. Markides, *All the Right Moves* (Boston: Harvard Business School Press, 1999).

16  J.-C. Spender, *Industry Recipes: The Nature and Sources of Managerial Judgment* (Oxford: Blackwell,

1989). On a similar theme, see also A. S. Huff, "Industry Influences on Strategy Reformulation," *Strategic Management Journal* 3 (1982): 119–31.

17 P. S. Barr, J. L. Stimpert, and A. S. Huff, "Cognitive Change, Strategic Action, and Organizational Renewal," *Strategic Management Journal* 13, Summer Special Issue (1992): 15–36.

18 G. Hamel, "Strategy as Revolution," *Harvard Business Review* 96 (July–August 1996): 69–82.

19 H. Volberda, C. Baden-Fuller, and F. van den Bosch, "Mastering Strategic Renewal," *Long Range Planning* 34 (April, 2001): 159–78.

20 T. Burns and G. M. Stalker, *The Management of Innovation* (London: Tavistock Institute, 1961).

21 H. Mintzberg, *Structure in Fives: Designing Effective Organizations* (Englewood Cliffs, NJ: Prentice Hall, 1983): Chapter 9.

22 G. Nieman, *Big Brown: The Untold Story of UPS* (Chichester: John Wiley & Sons, Ltd, 2007): 70.

23 C. Fishman, *The Wal-Mart Effect: The High Cost of Everyday Low Prices* (Harmondsworth: Penguin, 2006).

24 "Ryanair: Defying Gravity," IMD Case No. 3-1633 (2007). Available from www.ecch.com.

25 "How Whirlpool Defines Innovation," *Business Week* (March 6, 2006).

26 K. R. Harrigan, *Strategies for Declining Businesses* (Lexington, MA: D. C. Heath, 1980).

27 K. R. Harrigan, "Strategic Planning for Endgame," *Long Range Planning* 15 (1982): 45–8.

28 K. R. Harrigan and M. E. Porter, "End-Game Strategies for Declining Industries," *Harvard Business Review* (July–August 1983): 111–20.

# V

# CORPORATE
# STRATEGY

# 14 Vertical Integration and the Scope of the Firm

*The idea of vertical integration is anathema to an increasing number of companies. Most of yesterday's highly integrated giants are working overtime at splitting into more manageable, more energetic units—i.e., de-integrating. Then they are turning around and re-integrating—not by acquisitions but via alliances with all sorts of partners of all shapes and sizes.*

—TOM PETERS, LIBERATION MANAGEMENT

# Introduction and Objectives

Chapter 2 introduced the distinction between *corporate strategy* and *business strategy*. Corporate strategy is concerned primarily with the decisions over the *scope* of the firm's activities, including:

◆ *Product scope*. How specialized should the firm be in terms of the range of products it supplies? Coca-Cola (soft drinks), SAB-Miller (beer), Gap (fashion retailing), and SAP (software) are specialized companies: each is engaged in a single industry sector. Sony Corporation, General Electric and Tata Group are diversified companies: each spans multiple industries.

◆ *Geographical scope*. What is the optimal geographical spread of activities for the firm? In the restaurant business, Clyde's Restaurant Group owns 13 restaurants in the Washington DC area, Popeye's Chicken and Biscuits operates throughout the U.S., McDonald's Corporation operates in 121 different countries.

◆ *Vertical scope*. What range of vertically linked activities should the firm encompass? Walt Disney is a vertically integrated company: it produces its own movies, distributes them to cinemas and through its own TV networks (ABC and Disney Channel) and uses the movies' characters in its retail stores and theme parks. Nike is much more vertically specialized: it design and markets footwear and apparel, but outsources most activities in its value chain, including manufacturing, distribution, and retailing.

The distinction between business and corporate strategy may be summarized as follows: *corporate strategy* is concerned with *where* a firm competes; *business strategy* is concerned with *how* a firm competes with a particular area of business.[1] The major part of this book has been concerned with issues of business strategy. For the next four chapters, the emphasis is on corporate strategy: decisions that define the *scope of the firm*. I devote separate chapters to the different dimensions of scope—vertical scope (*vertical integration*), geographical scope (*multinationality*) and product scope (*diversification*). However, as we shall discover, the key underlying concepts for analyzing these different dimensions—economies of scope in resources and capabilities, transaction costs, and costs of corporate complexity—are common to all three.

In this chapter we begin by considering the overall scope of the firm. We then focus specifically on vertical integration. This takes us to the heart of the determinants of firm boundaries—in particular, the role of *transaction costs*. As we shall discover, vertical integration has been a hot topic in corporate strategy during the past decade. Opportunities for outsourcing, alliances, and electronic commerce have caused companies to rethink which of their activities should remain within their organizational boundaries.

By the time you have completed this chapter, you will be able to:

◆ identify the relative efficiencies of firms and markets in organizing economic activity and apply the principles of *transaction cost economics* to explain why boundaries between firms and markets shift over time;

◆ assess the relative advantages of vertical integration and outsourcing in organizing vertically-related activities, understand the circumstances that influence these relative advantages, and advise a firm whether a particular activity should be undertaken internally or outsourced;

◆ identify alternative ways of organizing vertical transactions—including spot market transactions, long-term contracts, franchise agreements, and alliances—and advise a firm on the most advantageous transaction mode given the characteristics and circumstances of the transaction.

## Transaction Costs and the Scope of the Firm

In Chapter 7, we noted that firms came into existence because they were more efficient in organizing production than were market contracts between self-employed workers. Let us explore this issue and consider the determinants of firm boundaries.

### Firms, Markets, and Transaction Costs

Although the capitalist economy is frequently referred to as a "market economy," in fact, it comprises two forms of economic organization. One is the *market mechanism*, where individuals and firms, guided by market prices, make independent decisions to buy and sell goods and services. The other is the *administrative mechanism* of firms, where decisions concerning production and resource allocation are made by managers and imposed through hierarchies. The market mechanism was characterized by Adam Smith, the eighteenth-century Scottish economist, as the "invisible hand" because its coordinating role does not require conscious planning. Alfred Chandler has referred to the administrative mechanism of firms as the "visible hand" because coordination involves active planning.[2]

Firms and markets may be viewed as alternative institutions for organizing production. Firms are distinguished by the fact that they comprise a number of individuals bound by employment contracts with a central contracting authority. But firms are not essential for organizing production. When I remodeled my basement, I contracted with a self-employed builder to undertake the work. He in turn subcontracted parts of the work to a plumber, an electrician, a joiner, a drywall installer and a painter. Although the job involved the coordinated activity of several individuals, these self-employed specialists were not linked by employment relations but by market contracts ("$4000 to install wiring, lights and sockets").

Firms and markets coexist, but their relative roles vary. If we compare the mainframe computer industry with the personal computer industry, the administrative mechanisms of firms predominate in the former, markets are more important in the latter. Thus, in mainframes, the dominant supplier, IBM, remains highly vertically integrated. It produces many of its own components (such as microprocessors), develops its own operating and applications software, and undertakes distribution, marketing, and customer support. Personal computers, by contrast, involve a network of firms linked by market contracts: design and marketing is undertaken by firms such as HP, Acer and Lenovo. Components are produced by firms such as Intel, Seagate, and Samsung. Assembly is outsourced to contract manufactures such as Asustek and Quanta Computer. Customer support is also outsourced to specialist suppliers—often located in India or Eastern Europe.

What determines which particular activity is undertaken within a firm and which through the market? Ronald Coase's answer was *relative cost*.[3] Markets are not costless: making a purchase or sale involves search costs, the costs of negotiating and drawing up a contract, the costs of monitoring to ensure that the other party's side of the contract is being fulfilled and the enforcement costs of arbitration or litigation should a dispute arise. All these costs are types of *transaction costs*.[4] If the transaction costs associated with organizing across markets are greater than the *administrative costs* of organizing within firms, we can expect the coordination of productive activity will be internalized within firms.

This situation is illustrated in Figure 14.1. With regard to vertical scope, which is more efficient: three independent companies—one producing steel, the next rolling the steel into sheet, and the third producing steel cans—or having all three stages of production within a single company? In the case of geographical scope, which is

**FIGURE 14.1**  The scope of the firm: specialization versus integration

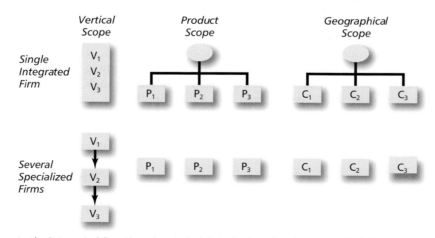

In the integrated firm there is an administrative interface between the different vertical units (V), product units (P), and country units (C). Where there is specialization, each unit is a separate firm linked by market interfaces.

more efficient: three independent companies producing cans in the U.S., U.K. and Italy, or a single multinational company owning and operating the can making plants in all three countries? In the case of product scope, should metal cans, plastic packaging, and domestic appliances be produced by three separate companies, or are there efficiencies to be gained by merging all three into a single company?

## The Shifting Boundary between Firms and Markets

The answers to these questions have changed over time. During the nineteenth and for most of the twentieth century, companies grew in size and scope, absorbing transactions that had previously taken place across markets. This was part of the evolutionary process we observed in Chapter 7: companies that were once small, specialized and localized became large, integrated, diversified and multinational. Using the Coase principle, can we attribute this trend to a fall in the administrative costs firms relative to the transaction costs of markets? Certainly there are two factors that have greatly increased the efficiency of firms in organizing economic activity:

- *Technology*. The telegraph, telephone, and computer have played an important role in facilitating communications within firms and expanding the decision-making capacity of managers.
- *Management techniques*. Developments in the principles and techniques of management have greatly expanded the organizational and decision-making effectiveness of managers. Beginning with the dissemination of double-entry bookkeeping in the nineteenth century,[5] and the introduction of scientific management in the early twentieth century,[6] the past six decades have seen rapid advances in all areas of management theory and methods.

By the late 1960s, the growth in large corporations and the impressive achievements of the new tools of management science and corporate planning encouraged a widespread view that the *market economy* had been replaced by a *corporate economy*. J. K. Galbraith predicted that the inherent advantages of firms over markets in planning and resource allocation would result in increasing dominance of capitalist economies by a small number of giant corporations.[7]

Yet, by the end of the 1990s, these predictions had been refuted by a sharp reversal of the trend toward increased corporate scope. Although large companies continued to expand internationally, the dominant trends of the past three decades have been "downsizing" and "refocusing," as large industrial companies reduced both their product scope through focusing on their core businesses, and their vertical scope through outsourcing. As a result, the Forbes 500's share of total U.S. private sector employment fell from 21.2% in 1980 to 14.9% in 1995.[8]

The contraction of corporate boundaries points to markets increasing their efficiency relative to firms' administrative processes. A key factor is greater turbulence of the business environment in recent decades. During periods of instability, the costs of administration within large, complex firms tend to rise as the need for flexibility and speed of response overwhelms traditional management systems. A second factor is the developments of information and communications technology (ICT). The advent of computers reinforced the advantages of the giant corporation—only large organizations could afford them. But with the PC, internet, and mobile communication revolution, the benefits of leading-edge ICT have diffused to small firms and individuals, and the creation of virtual digital markets and electronic data interchange have revolutionized market transactions.

Let us focus now on just one dimension of corporate scope: vertical integration. The question we will consider is this: is it better to be vertically integrated or vertically specialized? With regard to a specific activity, the simple question for the firm is: *to make, or to buy?* To answer this question, we shall draw in particular on Oliver Williamson's analysis of transaction costs, which forms the basis for a theory of economic organization that is particularly useful in designing vertical relationships.[9]

## The Costs and Benefits of Vertical Integration

Strategies towards vertical integration have been subject to shifting fashions. For most of the twentieth century the prevailing wisdom was that vertical integration was generally beneficial because it allowed superior coordination and reduced risk. During the past 25 years there has been a profound change of opinion: outsourcing, it is claimed, enhances flexibility and allows firms to concentrate on those activities where they possess superior capabilities. Moreover, many of the coordination benefits associated with vertical integration can be achieved through collaboration between vertically-related companies.

However, as in other areas of management, fashion is fickle. In the media sector, vertical integration between content and distribution has become viewed as a critical advantage in the face of rapid technological change. The resulting wave of mergers between content producers and distributors (TV broadcasters, cable companies, and internet portals) has transformed the industry (see Strategy Capsule 14.1).

Our task is to go beyond fads and fashions to uncover the factors that determine whether vertical integration enhances or weakens performance.

### STRATEGY CAPSULE 14.1

## Vertical Integration in the Media Sector: Value Creating or Value Destroying?

Considerable vertical integration has occurred between content companies (film studios, music publishing, newspapers) and distribution companies (TV broadcasting, cable, satellite TV, telecom providers). News Corp. has expanded from newspapers into movie production (Twentieth Century Fox), broadcast TV (Fox), satellite TV and other sectors of the media business; Disney acquired TV broadcaster ABC; Viacom, formerly a cable company, acquired Paramount and Dreamworks; GE's NBC Universal combines studio production with cable and broadcast TV distribution; and AOL merged with Time Warner, a leading magazine, film, and music company. In 2004, Comcast, America's biggest cable operator, made a $54 billion hostile bid for Walt Disney Company.

Does vertical integration between media content and media distribution create or destroy value? Here are two contrasting views:

## STEVE ROSENBUSH, BUSINESS WEEK, FEBRUARY 11, 2004

The economics of the TV-distribution business have been under siege for some time. That's why many of the business' smartest operators, like Liberty Media's John Malone and Viacom's Sumner Redstone, started shifting their investments into media years ago. Under Redstone, Viacom has been transformed from a cable operator into a media hothouse that includes everything from MTV to CBS. Buying Disney "shouldn't be a surprise. It's the logical next step," Comcast CEO Brian Roberts said at his February 11 press conference announcing his bid for the Mouse House.

It isn't enough to be just a media company, either. Most content providers benefit from having a certain amount of distribution, which helps lower their costs. That's why, in the future, media and communications will be dominated by hybrids such as News Corp. which recently acquired satellite-TV operator DirecTV.

Comcast's Roberts has embraced this future. The question now is whether Disney CEO Michael Eisner—who spurned an offer for a friendly deal—can accept the same future. For decades, Disney and other programmers have held the balance of power in distribution deals. That's changing. The cable-TV business isn't just a collection of small family companies running regional outfits anymore. Comcast, which began life in Tupelo, Mississippi, in 1963, now has national reach. It has a greater market cap than Disney.

And it's competing with satellite-distribution companies like DirecTV that are also national in scope. Now that DirecTV is under Rupert Murdoch's control, it would be folly for Disney to pretend that it can still compete without a distribution partner of comparable stature. Comcast fits the bill.

## JOHN KAY, FINANCIAL TIMES, MARCH 3, 2004

Media content needs delivery, and vice versa. And the same channels can often be used to disseminate text, images and music. This discovery was made at least 1000 years ago by people who developed religious services, still among the most moving and spectacular multimedia displays.

But this old idea is frequently rediscovered by visionary chief executives, excitable consultants, and greedy investment bankers: the people who proclaimed the AOL-Time Warner deal a marriage made in heaven. And it was revealed with Damascene force to Jean-Marie Messier, a humble French water carrier.

But activities can converge without requiring that the companies that undertake them converge. The erstwhile *maître du monde* might have drawn a useful lesson from his experience at Compagnie Générale des Eaux before his apotheosis as chief executive of Vivendi Universal: sewers and the stuff that goes down them do not need common ownership.

## Defining Vertical Integration

Vertical integration refers to a firm's ownership of vertically related activities. The greater a firm's ownership extends over successive stages of the value chain for its product, the greater its degree of vertical integration. The extent of vertical integration is indicated by the *ratio of a firm's value added to its sales revenue*: the more a firm makes rather than buys, the greater its value added relative to its sales revenue.

Vertical integration can be either *backward*, where the firm takes over ownership and control of producing its own components or other inputs, or *forward*, where the firm takes over ownership and control of activities previously undertaken by its customers.

Vertical integration may also be *full* or *partial*. Some California wineries are fully integrated: they produce wine only from the grapes they grow, and sell it all through direct distribution. Most are partially integrated: their home-grown grapes are supplemented with purchased grapes; they sell some wine through their own tasting rooms, but most through independent distributors.

## Technical Economies from the Physical Integration of Processes

Analysis of the benefits of vertical integration has traditionally emphasized the *technical economies* of vertical integration: cost savings that arise from the physical integration of processes. Thus, most steel sheet is produced by integrated producers in plants that first produce steel, then roll hot steel into sheet. Linking the two stages of production at a single location reduces transportation and energy costs. Similar technical economies arise in pulp and paper production and from linking oil refining with petrochemical production.

However, although these considerations explain the need for the co-location of plants, they do not explain why vertical integration in terms of *common ownership* is necessary. Why can't steel and steel strip production or pulp and paper production be undertaken by separate firms that own facilities which are physically integrated with one another? To answer this question, we must look beyond technical economies and consider the implications of linked processes for *transaction costs*.

## The Sources of Transaction Costs in Vertical Exchanges

Consider the value chain for steel cans, which extends from mining iron ore to delivering cans to food processing companies (see Figure 14.2). Between the production of steel and steel strip, most production is vertically integrated. Between the production of steel strip and steel cans, there is very little vertical integration: can producers such as Crown Holdings and Ball Corporation are specialist packaging companies that purchase steel strip from steel companies on contracts.[10]

The predominance of market contracts between steel strip production and can production is the result of low transaction costs in the market for steel strip: there are many buyers and sellers, information is readily available and the switching costs for buyers and suppliers are low. The same is true for many other commodity products: few jewelry companies own gold mines; few flour-milling companies own wheat farms.

**FIGURE 14.2** The value chain for steel cans

To understand why vertical integration predominates across steel production and steel strip production, let us see what would happen if the two stages were owned by separate companies. Because there are technical economies from hot-rolling steel as soon as it is poured from the furnace, steel makers and strip producers must invest in integrated facilities. A competitive market between the two stages is impossible; each steel strip producer is tied to its adjacent steel producer. In other words, the market becomes a series of *bilateral monopolies*.

Why are these relationships between steel producers and strip producers problematic? To begin with, where a single supplier negotiates with a single buyer, there is no market price: it all depends on relative bargaining power. Such bargaining is likely to be costly: the mutual dependency of the two parties is likely to give rise to *opportunism* and *strategic misrepresentation* as each company seeks to both enhance and exploit its bargaining power at the expense of the other. Hence, once we move from a competitive market situation to one where individual buyers and sellers are locked together in close bilateral relationships, the efficiencies of the market system are lost.

The culprits in this situation are *transaction-specific investments*. When a can maker buys steel strip, neither the steel strip producer nor the can maker needs to invest in equipment or technology that is specific to the needs of the other party. In the case of the steel producer and the steel roller, each company's plant is built to match the other party's plant. Once built, the plant's value depends upon the availability of the other party's complementary facilities—each seller is tied to a single buyer, which gives each the potential to *hold up* the other.

Thus, transaction-specific investments result in transaction costs arising from the difficulties of framing a comprehensive contract and the risks of disputes and opportunism that arise from contracts that do not cover every possible eventuality. Empirical research confirms the likelihood of vertical integration where transaction specific investments are required:[11]

- Among automakers, specialized components are more likely to be manufactured in-house than commodity items such as tires and spark plugs.[12] Similarly, in aerospace, company-specific components are more likely to be produced in house rather than purchased externally.[13]

- In the semiconductor industry, some companies specialize either in semiconductor design or in fabrication, while other companies are vertically integrated across both stages (for example, Intel, ST Microelectronics). The more technically complex the integrated circuit and, hence, the greater the need for the designer and fabricator to invest in technical collaboration and adapt processes to the needs of the other, the better the relative performance of integrated producers.[14]

The problem of hold-up could be eliminated by contracts that fully specify prices, quality, quantities, and other terms of supply under all possible circumstances. The problem is uncertainty about the future—it is impossible to anticipate all eventualities during the contract period—contracts are inevitably incomplete.

## Administrative Costs of Internalization

Just because there are transaction costs in intermediate markets does not mean that vertical integration is necessarily an efficient solution. Vertical integration avoids the costs of using the market, but internalizing a transaction imposes administrative cost. The size of this cost depends on several factors.

### *Differences in Optimal Scale between Different Stages of Production*
Suppose that Federal Express requires delivery vans that are designed and manufactured to meet its particular needs. To the extent that the van manufacturer must make transaction-specific investments, there is an incentive for Federal Express to avoid the ensuing transaction costs by building its own vehicles. Would this be an efficient solution? Almost certainly not: the transaction costs avoided by Federal Express are likely to be trivial compared with the inefficiencies incurred in manufacturing its own vans. Federal Express purchases over 40 000 trucks and vans each year, well below the 200 000 minimum efficient scale of an assembly plant. (Ford produced two million commercial vehicles in 2005.)

The same logic explains why specialist brewers such as Anchor Brewing of San Francisco or Adnams of Suffolk, England are not backward integrated into cans and bottles like Anheuser-Busch-InterBev or SAB-Miller. Dedicated can making plants involve specific investments, creating problems of opportunism that vertical integration can avoid. However, small brewers simply do not possess the scale needed for scale efficiency in can manufacture.

### *Developing Distinctive Capabilities*
A key advantage of a company that is specialized in a few activities is its ability to develop distinctive capabilities in those activities. Even large, technology-based companies such as Xerox, Kodak and Philips cannot maintain IT capabilities that match those of IT services specialists such as EDS, IBM, and Accenture. The ability of these IT specialists to work with many different customers stimulates learning and innovation. If General Motors' IT department only serves the in-house needs of GM, this does not encourage the rapid development of its IT capabilities.

However, this assumes that capabilities in different vertical activities are independent of one another. Where one capability builds on capabilities in adjacent activities, vertical integration may help develop distinctive capabilities. Thus, IBM's half-century of success in mainframe computers owes much to its technological leadership in semiconductors and software. The efficiency of Wal-Mart's retailing operations depends critically on specialized IT and logistics from its in-house departments.

*Managing Strategically Different Businesses*   These problems of differences in optimal scale and developing distinctive capabilities may be viewed as part of a wider set of problems—that of managing vertically related businesses that are strategically very different. A major disadvantage to FedEx of owning a truck-manufacturing company is that the management systems and organizational capabilities required for truck manufacturing are very different from those required for express delivery. These considerations may explain the lack of vertical integration between manufacturing and retailing. Firms that are integrated across design, manufacturing, and retailing, such as Zara and Gucci are rare. Most of the world's leading retailers—Wal-Mart, Gap, Carrefour—do not manufacture. Similarly, few manufacturing companies retail their own products. Not only do manufacturing and retailing require very different organizational capabilities, they also require different strategic planning systems, different approaches to control and human resource management, and different top management styles and skills.

These strategic dissimilarities are a key factor in the trend to vertical deintegration. Marriott's split into two separate companies, Marriott International and Host Marriott, was influenced by the belief that *owning* hotels is a strategically different business from *operating* hotels. Similarly, the Coca-Cola Company spun off its bottling activities as Coca-Cola Enterprises Inc. partly because managing local bottling and distribution operations is very different from managing the global Coca-Cola brand and the production and distribution of concentrates.

*The Incentive Problem*   Vertical integration changes the incentives between vertically related businesses. Where a market interface exists between a buyer and a seller, profit incentives ensure that the buyer is motivated to secure the best possible deal and the seller is motivated to pursue efficiency and service in order to attract and retain the buyer—these are termed *high-powered incentives*. With vertical integration, internal supplier-customer relationships are subject to *low-powered incentives*—if Shell's tanker fleet is inefficient, employees will lose their bonuses and the head of shipping may be fired. However, these consequences tend to be slow and undramatic. Most of us who have worked in large organizations have found that external contractors are often more responsive to our requests than internal service providers.

One approach to creating stronger performance incentives within vertically integrated companies is to open internal divisions to external competition. As we shall examine more fully in Chapter 17, many large corporations have created *shared service organizations* where internal suppliers of corporate services such as IT, training, and engineering compete with external suppliers of the same services to serve internal operating divisions.

*Competitive Effects of Vertical Integration*   Vertical integration can be used to extend a monopoly position at one stage of an industry's value chain to adjacent stages. The classic cases are Standard Oil, which used its dominance of transportation and refining to foreclose markets to independent oil producers; and Alcoa, which used its monopoly position in aluminum production to squeeze independent fabricators of aluminum products and favor its own fabrication subsidiaries. Such cases are rare. Economists have shown, once a company monopolizes one stage of the industry's value chain, there is no additional monopoly profit to be extracted by extending that monopoly to other stages.[15]

A more common situation is that a company which is strong at one vertical stage may disadvantage its market position by vertical integration. The firm's suppliers and customers are less willing to do business with the company if, through vertical integration, it becomes a competitor. Disney's acquisition of the ABC TV network adversely affected Disney's relationships with other TV networks and made other studios (for example, Dreamworks) more reluctant to collaborate with ABC in developing new TV productions.

*Flexibility*　Both vertical integration and market transactions can claim advantage with regard to different types of flexibility. Where the required flexibility is rapid responsiveness to uncertain demand, there may be advantages in market transactions. The lack of vertical integration in the construction industry reflects, in part, the need for flexibility in adjusting both to cyclical patterns of demand and to the different requirements of each project. Vertical integration may also be disadvantageous in responding quickly to new product development opportunities that require new combinations of technical capabilities. Some of the most successful new electronic products of recent years—Apple's iPod, Microsoft's Xbox, Dell's range of notebook computers—have been produced by contract manufacturers. Extensive outsourcing has been a key feature of fast-cycle product development throughout the electronics sector.

Yet, where system-wide flexibility is required, vertical integration may allow for speed and coordination in achieving simultaneous adjustment throughout the vertical chain. American Apparel is a rare example of a successful U.S. *manufacturer* of apparel. Its tightly coordinated vertical integration from its Los Angeles design and manufacturing base to its 160 retail stores across 10 countries allows a super-fast design-to-distribution cycle. Vertical integration is also a central theme of brand identity. Figure 14.3 shows one of its advertisements.

Zara is another fashion clothing business that has cut cycle times and maximized market responsiveness through a vertically integrated strategy that challenges the industry's dominant model of contract manufacture (see Strategy Capsule 14.2).

*Compounding Risk*　To the extent that vertical integration ties a company to its internal suppliers, vertical integration represents a compounding of risk insofar as problems at any one stage of production threaten production and profitability at all other stages. When union workers at a General Motors brake plant went on strike in 1998, GM's 24 U.S. assembly plants were quickly brought to a halt. If Disney animation studios fail to produce blockbuster animation movies with new characters, then the knock-on effects are felt through DVD sales, merchandise sales in Disney Stores, and lack of new attractions at Disney theme parks.

**FIGURE 14.3** An American Apparel advertisement

**Source:**
American Apparel Inc.

STRATEGY CAPSULE 14.2

## Making Vertical Integration Work: Zara

Zara is the main division and brand of the Spanish clothing company, Inditex (Industria de Diseño Textil, S.A). Zara contributes 68% of Inditex's sales. Between 2000 and 2006, Inditex achieved sales growth of 30% a year, a net margin of 11%, and a return on average equity of 29%—well ahead of Gap, H&M, or Mango. By the end of 2006, Zara operated over 1400 stores in 40 countries.

Zara's success is based on a business system that achieves a speed of response to market demand that is without precedent in the fast-moving fashion clothing sector. Zara's cycles of design, production, and distribution are substantially faster than any of its main competitors. For most fashion retailers there is a six-month lag between completing a new design and deliveries arriving at retail stores. Zara can take a new design from drawing board to retail store in as little as three weeks.

Products are designed at the Inditex headquarters in La Coruna on the northwest tip of Spain. Over 40 000 garments are designed annually with about one-quarter entering production. Designs are sketched, committed to the CAD system, then a sample is handmade by skilled workers located within the design facility. Working alongside the designers are "market specialists" who monitor sales and market trends in a particular country or region, and "buyers" who handle procurement and production planning. The three groups coordinate closely and jointly select which products go into production.

Close to half of Zara's products are manufactured within Zara's local network, which comprises Zara's own factories and subcontractors who undertake all sewing operations. The rest is outsourced to third-party manufacturers.

For its own production, 40% of fabric requirements are supplied by Comidex—a wholly owned subsidiary of Inditex. Most fabric is supplied undyed. Postponing dying until later in the production process allows colors to be changed at short notice.

Finished products are ironed, labeled (including tags with prices in local currencies), bagged in boxes or on hangers ready for retail display, then transferred by monorail to the La Coruna distribution center. Each retail store submits its orders twice a week and receives shipments twice a week. Orders are dispatched within eight hours of receipt and are delivered within 24 hours in Europe, 48 hours in the U.S., and 72 hours in Japan.

Zara owns and manages almost all its retail stores. This allows standardized layout and window displays and close communication and collaboration between store managers and headquarters.

Zara's tightly coordinated system allows quick response to market demand. At the beginning of each season only small numbers of each new item are produced and are placed in a few lead stores. According to market response, Zara then adjusts production. Typically, Zara's products spend no more than two weeks in a retail store. Product market specialists provide critical feedback that is used both to adjust production levels and to make design or color modifications to existing items.

The close, informal information networks within Zara are critical to product design. Although designers begin working on new designs some nine months before each new season, continuous adjustments to designs are made in response to new information on fashion trends and customer preferences. Designers and market specialists are encouraged to be alert to the new ranges released by the fashion houses of Milan, Paris, London, and New York; to the styles worn by trendsetters on TV, in popular music, and in the leading-edge clubs; and to feedback from store managers and other employees.

Zara's compressed product cycles have induced changes in customers' retail buying behavior. Zara customers make more frequent visits to their local stores than is typical for other fashion retailers. They also make faster purchase decisions in the knowledge that garments move quickly and are unlikely to be restocked.

*Sources:* Kasra Ferdows, Jose Machuca and Michael Lewis, *Zara*, ECCH Case Number 602-002-01, 2002; www.inditex.com.

**TABLE 14.1**  Vertical integration (VI) versus outsourcing: some key considerations

| Characteristics of the vertical relationship | Implication |
| --- | --- |
| How many firms are there in the vertically adjacent activity? | The fewer the number of firms, the greater are the transaction costs and bigger the advantages of VI |
| Do transaction-specific investments need to be made by either party? | Transaction-specific investments increase the advantages of VI |
| How evenly distributed is information between the vertical stages? | The greater are information asymmetries, the more likely is opportunistic behavior and the greater the advantages of VI |
| Are market transactions in intermediate products subject to taxes or regulations? | Taxes and regulations are a cost of market contracts that can be avoided by VI |
| How uncertain are the circumstances of the transactions over the period of the relationship? | The greater are uncertainties concerning costs, technologies, and demand, the greater the difficulty of writing contracts, and the greater the advantages of VI |
| Are two stages similar in terms of the optimal scale of operation? | The greater the dissimilarity, the greater the advantages of market contracts as compared with VI |
| Are the two stages strategically similar (e.g., similar key success factors, common resources/capabilities)? | The greater the strategic similarity, the greater the advantages of VI over outsourcing |
| How great is the need for continual investment in upgrading and extending capabilities within individual activities? | The greater the need to invest in capability development, the greater the advantages of outsourcing over VI |
| How great is the need for entrepreneurial flexibility and drive in the separate vertical activities? | The greater the need for entrepreneurship and flexibility, the greater the advantages of high-powered incentives provided by market contracts, and the greater the administrative disadvantages of VI |
| How uncertain is market demand? | The greater the unpredictability of demand, the greater the flexibility advantages of outsourcing |
| Does vertical integration compound risk, exposing the entire value chain risks affecting individual stages? | The heavier the investment requirements and the greater the independent risks at each stage, the more risky is VI |

## Assessing the Pros and Cons of Vertical Integration

We have seen that vertical integration is neither good nor bad. As with most questions of strategy: it all depends. The value of our analysis is that we are now able to identify the factors that determine the relative advantages of the market transactions *versus* internalization within the firm. Table 14.1 summarizes some of the key criteria. However, our analysis is not yet complete, we must consider some additional factors that influence the choice of vertical strategy—in particular, the fact that vertical relationships are not limited to the simple choice of make or buy.

## Designing Vertical Relationships

Our discussion so far has compared vertical integration with arm's-length market contracts. In practice buyers and sellers can interact and coordinate their interests through a variety of relationships. Figure 14.4 shows a number of different types of relationship between buyers and sellers. These relationships may be classified in relation to two characteristics. First, the extent to which the buyer and seller commit resources to the relationship: arm's-length, spot contracts involve no resource commitment beyond the single deal; vertical integration typically involves a substantial investment. Second, the formality of the relationship: long-term contracts and franchises are formalized by the complex written agreements they entail; spot contracts may involve little or no documentation, but are bound by the formalities of common law; collaborative agreements between buyers and sellers are usually informal, while the formality of vertical integration is at the discretion of the firm's management.

### Different Types of Vertical Relationship

These different types of vertical relationship offer different combinations of advantages and disadvantages. For example:

- *Long-term contracts.* Market transactions can be either *spot contracts*—buying a cargo of crude oil on the Rotterdam petroleum market—or *long-term contracts* that involve a series of transactions over a period of time and specify the terms of sales and the responsibilities of each party. Spot transactions work well under competitive conditions (many buyers and sellers and a standard product) where there is no need for transaction-specific investments by either party. Where closer supplier-customer ties are needed—particularly when one or both parties need to make transaction-specific

**FIGURE 14.4** Different types of vertical relationship

investments—then a longer term contract can help avoid opportunism and provide the security needed to make the necessary investment. However, long-term contracts face the problem of anticipating the circumstances that may arise during the life of the contract: either they are too restrictive, or so loose that they give rise to opportunism and conflicting interpretation. Long-term contracts often include provisions for the arbitration of contract disputes.

- *Vendor partnerships.* The greater the difficulties of specifying complete contracts for long-term supplier-customer deals, the greater the advantage of vertical relationships based on trust and mutual understanding will be. Such relationships can provide the security needed for transaction-specific investments, the flexibility to meet changing circumstances, and the incentives to avoid opportunism. Such arrangements may be entirely *relational contracts* with no written contract at all. The model for vendor partnerships has been the close collaborative relationships that many Japanese companies have with their suppliers. Japanese automakers have been much less backward integrated than their U.S. or European counterparts but have also achieved close collaboration with component makers in technology, design, quality, and production scheduling.[16]

- *Franchising.* A franchise is a contractual agreement between the owner of a business system and trademark (the franchiser) that permits the franchisee to produce and market the franchiser's product or service in a specified area. Franchising brings together the brand, marketing capabilities, and business systems of the large corporation with the entrepreneurship and local knowledge of small firms. The franchising systems of companies such as McDonald's, Century 21 Real Estate, Hilton Hotels and Seven-Eleven convenience stores facilitate the close coordination and investment in transaction-specific assets that vertical integration permits with the high-powered incentives, flexibility and cooperation between strategically dissimilar businesses that market contracts make possible.

## Choosing between Alternative Vertical Relationships

The criteria listed in Table 14.1 establish the basic features of the vertical relation that favor either market transactions or vertical integration. However, the availability of other types of vertical relationships, such as vendor partnerships and franchises mean that vertical integration is not the sole solution to problems of transaction costs. Moreover, many of these relational contracts and hybrid arrangements have the capacity to combine the advantages of both vertical integration and market contracts.

Choosing the optimal vertical relationships needs to take account of additional factors than those listed in Table 14.1. In particular:

- *Resources, capabilities, and strategy.* Within the same industry, different companies will choose different vertical arrangements according to their reactive resource and capability strengths and the strategies they pursue. Thus in fashion clothing, Zara's high level of vertical integration compared to Hennes & Mauritz or Gap reflects strategy based upon fast-cycle new product development and tight integration between its retail stores, designers, and manufacturers. While most fast food chains have expanded through franchising, California-based In-N-Out Burger seeks to maintain its unique culture and distinctive business practices by directly owning and managing its restaurants. While most banks have been outsourcing IT to companies such as IBM and EDS, U.S. credit card group Capital One sees IT as a key source of competitive advantage: "IT is our central nervous system . . . if we outsourced tomorrow we might save a dollar or two on each account, but we would lose flexibility and value and service levels."[17]

- *Allocation of risk.* Any arrangement beyond a spot contract must cope with uncertainties over the course of the contract. A key feature of any contract is that its terms involve, often implicitly, an allocation of risks between the parties. How risk is shared is dependent partly on bargaining power and partly on efficiency considerations. In franchise agreements, the franchisee (as the weaker partner) bears most of the risk—it is the franchisee's capital that is at risk and the franchisee pays the franchiser a flat royalty based on sales revenues. In oil exploration, outsourcing agreements between the oil majors (such as Chevron, ExxonMobil, and Eni) and drilling companies (such as Schlumberger and Halliburton) have moved from fixed-price contracts to risk-sharing agreements where the driller often takes an equity stake in the project.

- *Incentive structures.* Incentives are central to the design of vertical relationships: incentives for opportunistic behavior are the bugbear of market contacts, while weak ("low-powered") incentives for performance are the central problem of vertical integration. It seems possible that hybrid and intermediate governance modes offer some of the best solutions to the problems of appropriate incentives. Toyota, Benetton, Boeing, and Marks & Spencer have relationships with their vendors that may involve formal contracts, but their essence is that they are long-term and trust based. The key to these relationships is that the promise of a long-term, mutually beneficial relationship trumps short term opportunism.

## Recent Trends

The main feature of recent years has been a growing diversity of hybrid vertical relationships that have attempted to reconcile the flexibility and incentives of market transactions with the close collaboration provided by vertical integration. Although collaborative vertical relationships are viewed as a recent phenomenon— associated with microelectronics, biotechnology, and other hi-tech sectors—local clusters of vertically collaborating firms are a long-time feature of the craft industries of Europe. This is especially true of northern Italy—both in traditional sectors such as textiles[18] and newer sectors such as packaging equipment[19] and motorcycles.[20]

The supplier networks of Japanese manufacturers with their knowledge sharing and collaborative new product development have become models for many large American and European companies.[21] There has been a massive shift from arm's-length supplier relationships to long-term collaboration with fewer suppliers. In many instances, competitive tendering and multiple sourcing have been replaced by single-supplier arrangements. Vendor relationships frequently involve supplier certification and quality management programs and technical collaboration.

Enthusiasm for exploiting lower labor costs in emerging countries has intensified outsourcing among companies in North America, Europe, and Japan.[22] In the electronics sector, companies such as Nokia, Hewlett Packard, and Sony have outsourced manufacturing to China and services (including call centers and software development) to India. We shall return to these international dimensions of outsourcing in Chapter 15.

The mutual dependence that results from close, long-term supplier-buyer relationships creates vulnerability for both parties. While trust may alleviate some of the risks of opportunism, companies can also reinforce their vertical relationships and discourage opportunism through equity stakes and profit sharing arrangements. For example: Commonwealth Bank of Australia took an equity stake in its IT supplier, EDS Australia; pharmaceutical companies often acquire equity stakes in the biotech companies that undertake much of their R&D; and, as already noted, oilfield services companies are increasingly equity partners in upstream projects.

However, in this world of closer vertical relationships, some trends have been in the opposite direction. The internet has radically reduced the transaction costs of markets—particularly in pruning search costs and facilitating electronic payments. The result has been a revival in arm's-length competitive contracting through business-to-business e-commerce hubs such as Covisint (auto parts), Elemica (chemicals), and Rock and Dirt (construction equipment).[23]

The scope of outsourcing has extended from basic components to a wide range of business services including payroll, IT, training, and customer service and support. Increasingly, outsourcing involves not just individual components and services but whole chunks of the value chain. In electronics, the design and manufacture of entire products are often outsourced to contract manufacturers such as Hon Hai Precision Industry Co., which makes Apple iPods, Nokia phones, and Sony's PlayStation.

Extreme levels of outsourcing have given rise to the concept of the *virtual corporation*: a firm whose primary function is to coordinate the activities of a network of suppliers and downstream partners.[24] In this organizational form the hub company has the role of *systems integrator*. The critical issue is whether a company that outsources most functions can retain *architectural capabilities* needed to manage the *component capabilities* of the various partners and contractors. The risk is that the virtual corporation may degenerate into a "hollow corporation," where it loses the capability to evolve and adapt to changing circumstances.[25] If, as Prahalad and Hamel argue, core competences are embodied in "core products" then the more these core products are outsourced, the greater is the potential for the erosion of core competence.[26] Andrea Prencipe's research into aero engines points to the complementarity between architectural capabilities and component capabilities. Thus, even when the aero engine manufacturers outsource key components, they typically maintain R&D into those component technologies.[27] The problems experienced by Boeing in managing the outsourced network model it adopted for its 787 Dreamliner point to the complexity of the system integrator role.[28]

## Summary

Deciding which parts of the value chain to engage in presents companies with one of their most difficult strategic decisions. The conventional analysis of vertical integration has looked simply at the efficiency of markets as compared with the efficiency of firms: if the cost of transacting through the market is greater than the cost of administering within the firm, then the company should vertically integrate across the stages. Transaction cost analysis does not, however, provide the complete answer. In the first place, vertical strategies are not simply make-or-buy choices—there is a wide variety of ways in which a company can structure vertical relationships. Secondly, the most critical long-run consideration is the development of organizational capability. If a company is to sustain competitive advantage, it must restrict itself to those activities where it possesses the capabilities that are superior to those of the other companies that perform those activities. If my company's data-processing capabilities are inferior to those of IBM and its logistics capabilities are inferior to those of Federal Express, I should consider outsourcing these activities. The most difficult issues arise where there are linkages between value chain activities. Even though a contract manufacturer may be able to manufacture my remote-controlled lawnmower more efficiently than I can internally, what would be the implications for my new product development capability if I no longer have in-house manufacturing?

Ultimately, vertical integration decisions revolve around two key questions. First, which activities will we undertake internally and which will we outsource? Second, how do we design our vertical arrangements with both external and internal suppliers and buyers? In the case of external relations, these may be conducted through spot contracts, long-term contracts, or some form of strategic alliance. Similar ranges of alternatives face the vertically integrated firm—including the option of arm's-length negotiated contracts. Both types of decision are critically dependent on the firm's competitive strategy and the capabilities it possesses. As we have already noted, the critical issue for the individual business is not to follow conventional wisdom but to carefully evaluate its strategic needs, its resources and capabilities at different stages in the value chain, the characteristics of the transactions involved and the relative attractiveness of different stages of the value chain.

## Self-Study Questions

1   The discussion of "The Shifting Boundary between Firms and Markets" argues that the developments in information and communication technology (for example, telephone and computer) during most of the twentieth century tended to lower the costs of administration within the firm relative to the costs of market transactions, thereby increasing the size and scope of firms. What about the internet? How has this influenced the efficiency of large integrated firms relative to small, specialized firms coordinated by markets?

**2**  The discussion of "The Shifting Barrier between Firms and Markets" notes that the large U.S. companies account for a smaller percentage of total employment—a development that is attributed to a more turbulent business environment. Explain why external turbulence encourages outsourcing and increased focus on core business.

**3**  A large proportion of major corporations outsource their IT function to specialist suppliers of IT services such as IBM, EDS (now owned by Hewlett Packard), Accenture, and Cap Gemini. What transaction costs are incurred by these outsourcing arrangements and why do they arise? What are the offsetting benefits from IT outsourcing?

**4**  In Strategy Capsule 14.1, Steve Rosenbush argues that integration between media content and media distribution companies (and, specifically, between Disney and Comcast) is strategically advantageous. John Kay suggests that there is little need for common ownerships between distribution channels and the content they carry. Explain the arguments of each. Who do you agree with? As more content is being viewed via the internet and on mobile devices, how does this affect the arguments?

**5**  For its Zara brand, Inditex manufactures the majority of the garments sells and undertakes all of its own distribution from manufacturing plants to its directly managed retail outlets. Benetton outsources most of its production, and most of its retail outlets are owned and operated by franchisees. Which is a superior system?

# Notes

1  M. J. Piskorski ("A Note on Corporate Strategy," Harvard Business School 9-705-449, 2005) defines corporate strategy as: "a set of choices that a corporation makes to create value through configuration and coordination of its multimarket activities." In practice, determining the boundary between business strategy and corporate strategy depends on where we draw the boundaries of industries and markets.

2  A. Chandler Jr., *The Visible Hand: The Managerial Revolution in American Business* (Cambridge: MIT Press, 1977).

3  R. H. Coase, "The Nature of the Firm," *Economica* 4 (1937): 386–405.

4  The term *interaction costs* has also been used to describe "the time and money expended whenever people and companies exchange goods, services or ideas." See J. Hagel and M. Singer, "Unbundling the Corporation," *Harvard Business Review* (March–April 1999): 133–44.

5  Double-entry bookkeeping has its origins in fourteenth-century Italy and developed in Venice in the sixteenth century. See: L. Zan, "Accounting and Management Discourse in Preindustrial Settings: The Venice Arsenal at the Turn of the Sixteenth Century," *Accounting and Business Research* 32 (2004): 145–75.

6  F. W. Taylor, *The Principles of Scientific Management* (New York: Bulletin of the Taylor Society, 1916).

7  J. K. Galbraith, *The New Industrial State* (Harmondsworth: Penguin, 1969).

8  L. J. White, "Trends in Aggregate Concentration in the United States," *Journal of Economic Perspectives* 16 (Fall 2002): 137–60.

9  O. E. Williamson, *Markets and Hierarchies: Analysis and Antitrust Implications* (New York: Free Press, 1975); O. E. Williamson, *The Economic Institutions of Capitalism: Firms, Markets and Relational Contracting* (New York: Free Press, 1985).

10  The situation is different in aluminum cans, where aluminum producers such as Alcoa and Pechiney and users such as Coca-Cola and Anheuser-Busch are major producers of beverage cans.

11  For a review of empirical evidence on transaction costs and vertical integration see: J. T. Macher and B. D. Richman "Transaction Cost Economics: An Assessment of Empirical Research in the Social Sciences." *Business and Politics* 10 (2008): Article 1; M.D, Whinston, "On the Transaction Cost Determinants of Vertical Integration," *Journal of Law Economics and Organization* 19 (2003): 1–23.

12 K. Monteverde and J. J. Teece, "Supplier Switching Costs and Vertical Integration in the Automobile Industry," *Bell Journal of Economics* 13 (Spring 1982): 206–13.

13 S. Masten, "The Organization of Production: Evidence from the Aerospace Industry," *Journal of Law and Economics* 27 (October 1984): 403–17.

14 J. T. Macher, "Technological Development and the Boundaries of the Firm: A Knowledge-based Examination in Semiconductor Manufacturing," *Management Science* 52 (2006): 826–43; K. Monteverde, "Technical Dialogue as an Incentive for Vertical Integration in the Semiconductor Industry," *Management Science* 41 (1995): 1624–38.

15 R. Rey and J. Tirole, "A Primer on Foreclosure," Chapter 33 in R. Schmalensee, M. Armstrong, R. D. Willig and R.H. Porter, *Handbook of Industrial Organization* (Elsevier, 2007).

16 J. H. Dyer, "Effective Interfirm Collaboration: How Firms Minimize Transaction Costs and Maximize Transaction Value," *Strategic Management Journal* 18 (1997): 535–56; J. H. Dyer, "Specialized Supplier Networks as a Source of Competitive Advantage: Evidence from the Auto Industry," *Strategic Management Journal* 17 (1996): 271–92.

17 L. Willcocks and C. Sauer, "High Risks and Hidden Costs in IT Outsourcing," *Financial Times*, Mastering Risk (May 23, 2000): 3.

18 N. Owen and A. C. Jones, "A Comparative Study of the British and Italian Textile and Clothing Industries," Department of Trade and Industry (London: HMSO, 2003).

19 G. Lorenzoni and A. Lipparini, "The Leveraging of Interfirm Relationships as Distinctive Organizational Capabilities: A Longitudinal Study," *Strategic Management Journal* 20 (1999): 317–38.

20 G. Lorenzoni and A. Lipparini, "Organizing Around Strategic Relationships: Networks of Suppliers in the Italian Motorcycle Industry," in K. O. Cool, J. E. Henderson and R. Abate (eds), *Restructuring Strategy* (Oxford: Blackwell, 2005): 44–67.

21 J. H. Dyer and K. Nobeoka, "Creating and Managing a High-performance Knowledge-sharing Network: The Toyota Case," *Strategic Management Journal* 21 (2000): 345–68.

22 D. Farrell, "Smarter Offshoring," *Harvard Business Review* (June 2006): 85–92.

23 See www.covisint.com; www.elemica.com; www.rockanddirt.com.

24 "The Virtual Corporation," *Business Week* (February 8, 1993): 98–104; W. H. Davidow and M. S. Malone, *The Virtual Corporation* (New York: HarperCollins, 1992).

25 H. W. Chesborough and D. J. Teece, "When is Virtual Virtuous? Organizing for Innovation," *Harvard Business Review* (May–June 1996): 68–79.

26 C. K. Prahalad and G. Hamel, "The Core Competences of the Corporation," *Harvard Business Review* (May–June 1990): 79–91.

27 S. Brusoni, A. Prencipe, and K. Pavitt, "Knowledge Specialization, Organizational Coupling and the Boundaries of the Firm: Why Do Firms Know More Than They Make?" *Administrative Science Quarterly* 46 (2001): 597–621.

28 "Boeing's Dreamliner Delays Are a Nightmare" *SeekingAlpha*, http://seekingalpha.com/article/110735-boeing-s-dreamliner-delays-are-a-nightmare, accessed July 7, 2009.

# 15 Global Strategies and the Multinational Corporation

*The speed of light does not merely transform the world. It becomes the world. Globalization is the speed of light.*

—PAUL VIRILIO, PHILOSOPHER OF CULTURE AND SCIENCE

*Globalization has changed us into a company that searches the world, not just to sell or to source, but to find intellectual capital—the world's best talent and greatest ideas.*

—JACK WELCH, FORMER CHAIRMAN, GENERAL ELECTRIC

## OUTLINE

# Introduction and Objectives

In September 2007, Britain experienced its first bank run in 140 years as depositors queued to withdraw money from Northern Rock, a Newcastle-based mortgage bank. Despite having no direct exposure to the U.S. real estate market (only 0.24% of its assets were in U.S. collateralized debt obligations or U.S. home equity mortgage-backed securities), Northern Rock became the first non-U.S. casualty of the of the subprime mortgage crisis that began to unfold during spring 2007.

A year later the wave of bankruptcies precipitated by U.S. subprime mortgages claimed its first victim among sovereign nations: on October 9, 2008 Iceland's financial system collapsed and the government was forced to seek emergency support from the IMF. As with Northern Rock, the Icelandic banks that failed had almost no direct exposure to the U.S. real estate market or to securities based upon U.S. real estate loans.

The massive global fallout from the bursting of real estate bubbles in Miami, Las Vegas, Los Angeles, and other U.S. cities is a tribute to the power of internationalization to transmit and amplify local economic factors. Internationalization is the most important and pervasive force that has reshaped the competitive environment of business during the past half-century. While recent events have identified internationalization with global contagion, for most the past 60 years, internationalization has been a source of expanding opportunity for both firms and individuals. The opening of national markets has resulted in widening consumer choice, huge increases in efficiency, and growth options for both large and small firms.

Internationalization occurs through two mechanisms: trade and direct investment. The growth of world trade has consistently outstripped the growth of world output, increasing export/sales and import penetration ratios for all countries and all industries. For the OECD countries, total trade (imports and exports) rose from 11% of GDP in 1960 to 52% in 2007. The total stock of direct investment by OECD firms amounted to $13 trillion at the beginning of 2009—equivalent to 34% of OECD GDP.[1]

The forces driving both trade and direct investment are, first, the quest to exploit market opportunities in other countries, and, second, the desire to exploit resources and capabilities located in other countries. The resulting "globalization of business" has created vast flows of international transactions comprising payments for trade and services, flows of factor payments (interest, profits, and licensing fees) and flows of capital.

What does the internationalization of the world economy mean for our strategy analysis? As we shall see, internationalization is both a threat and an opportunity. Internationalization opens domestic markets to competitors from different countries— often with tragic consequences not just for individual firms but often for entire domestic industries. Internationalization also offers vast opportunity allowing firms with small domestic markets to become global leaders: Nokia (from Finland) in wireless handsets, Swatch (from Switzerland) in watches, A. P. Moller-Maersk (from Denmark) in shipping, Anheuser-Busch-InBev (from Belgium) in beer, BHP (from Australia) in metals mining, Research in Motion (from Canada) in smart phones. Most of all, the international dimension adds considerable complexity to our strategy analysis—not just in broadening the scope of markets (and competition) but also in complicating the analysis of competitive advantage.

By the time you have completed this chapter, you will be able to:

◆ use the tools of industry analysis to examine the impact of internationalization on industry structure and competition;

◆ analyze the implications of a firm's national environment for its competitive advantage;

◆ formulate strategies for exploiting overseas business opportunities, including overseas market entry strategies and overseas production strategies;

◆ shape international strategies that achieve an optimal balance between global integration and national differentiation;

◆ design organizational structures and management systems appropriate to the pursuit of international strategies.

We begin by exploring the implications of international competition, first for industry analysis, and then for the analysis of competitive advantage.

## Implications of International Competition for Industry Analysis

### Patterns of Internationalization

Internationalization occurs through *trade*—the sale and shipment of goods and services from one country to another—and *direct investment*—building or acquiring productive assets in another country. On this basis we can identify different types of industry according to the extent and mode of their internationalization (see Figure 15.1):

- *Sheltered industries* are served exclusively by indigenous firms. They are sheltered from both imports and inward direct investment by regulation, trade barriers, or because of the localized nature of the goods and services they offer. The forces of internationalization have made this category progressively smaller over time. Sheltered industries are primarily fragmented service industries (dry cleaning, hairdressing, auto repair, funeral services), some small-scale manufacturing (handicrafts, residential construction) and industries producing products that are nontradable because they are perishable (fresh milk, bread) or difficult to move (four-poster beds, garden sheds).

- *Trading industries* are those where internationalization occurs primarily through imports and exports. If a product is transportable, if it is not nationally differentiated and if it is subject to substantial scale economies, exporting from a single location is the most efficient means to exploit overseas markets. This is the case with commercial aircraft, shipbuilding, and defense

**FIGURE 15.1** Patterns of industry internationalization

equipment. Trading industries also include products whose inputs are available only in a few locations: diamonds from South Africa; caviar from Iran and Azerbaijan.

- *Multidomestic industries* are those that internationalize through direct investment—either because trade is not feasible (as in the case of service industries such as banking, consulting, or hotels) or because products are nationally differentiated (for example, frozen dinners, recorded music).

- *Global industries* are those in which both trade and direct investment are important. Most large-scale manufacturing industries tend to evolve towards global structures: in automobiles, consumer electronics, semiconductors, pharmaceuticals, and beer, levels of both trade and direct investment are high.

By which route does internationalization typically occur? In the case of manufacturing companies, internationalization normally begins with exports—typically to countries with the least "psychic distance" from the home country. Later a sales and distribution subsidiary is established in the overseas country. Eventually the company develops a more integrated overseas subsidiary that undertakes manufacturing and product development as well.[2] In service industries, internationalization may involve replication (McKinsey & Company), acquisition (HSBC), or franchising (McDonald's).[3]

## Implications for Competition

Internationalization usually means more competition and lower industry profitability. In 1976, the U.S. automobile market was dominated by GM, Ford, and Chrysler with 84% of the market. By 2009 there were 14 companies with auto plants within the U.S.; with the former "Big Three" accounting for just 43% of auto sales.

We can use Porter's five forces of competition framework to analyze the impact of internationalization on competition and industry profitability. If we define the industry in terms of the national market, internationalization directly influences three of the five forces of competition.

*Competition from Potential Entrants*   Barriers to entry into most national markets have fallen substantially. Tariff reductions, falling real costs of transportation, the removal of exchange controls, internationalization of standards, and convergence between customer preferences have made it much easier for producers in one country to supply customers in another. Many of the entry barriers that were effective against potential domestic entrants may be ineffective against potential entrants that are established producers in overseas countries.

*Rivalry Among Existing Firms*   Internationalization increases internal rivalry primarily because it increases the number of firms competing within each national market—it *lowers seller concentration*. In my youth, the European market for motor scooters was dominated by Piaggio (Vespa) and Innocenti (Lambretta). Apart from Piaggio, there are now over 25 manufacturers supplying scooters to the European market which include Japanese firms (Honda, Yamaha, Suzuki), Taiwanese (Kymco, Kwang Yang), Chinese (BenZhou/Yiying, Baotian, ZheJiang XingYue), Indian (Bajaj) and American (Baron, Vectrix).

Increasing global concentration is often accompanied by falling concentration in national markets. There has been massive consolidation of the global beer industry. Yet, in most countries I visit, I am struck by the widening range of beer available from more countries and more brewers. Moreover, even where global consolidation has been rapid (for example, paper, telecoms, oil, airlines, and aluminum), Ghemawat and Ghadar show that global concentration has declined as a result of national producers entering the global market.[4]

In addition, internationalization intensifies rivalry, first, by increasing the diversity of competitors in terms of goals, strategies and cost structures and, second, when internationalization occurs through direct investment in new plants, excess capacity increases. In the automobile industry, the massive overcapacity in the U.S. and China is primarily the result of direct investment by foreign auto producers.

***Increasing the Bargaining Power of Buyers***  A further implication of the internationalization of business is that large customers can exercise their buying power far more effectively. Global sourcing provides a key tool for cost reduction by manufacturers. The growth of internet-based markets for components and materials enhances the power of industrial buyers.

## Analyzing Competitive Advantage in an International Context

The growth of international competition over the past 20 years has been associated with some stunning reversals in the competitive positions of different companies. In 1989, U.S. Steel was the world's biggest steel company; in 2009 ArcelorMittal based in Luxemburg and India was the new global giant. In 1989, IBM, Compaq and Apple were world market leaders in PCs. By 2009, Hewlett-Packard and Acer were the new brand leaders, however, Asustek was the biggest manufacturer of PCs.

To understand how internationalization has shifted the basis of competition, we need to extend our framework for analyzing competitive advantage to include the influence of firms' national environments. Competitive advantage, we have noted, is achieved when a firm matches its internal strengths in resources and capabilities to the key success factors of the industry. In international industries, competitive advantage depends not just upon a firm's internal resources and capabilities, but also their national environments—in particular, the availability of resources within the countries where they do business. Figure 15.2 summarizes the implications of internationalization for our basic strategy model in terms of the impact both on industry conditions and firms' access to resources and capabilities.

## National Influences on Competitiveness: Comparative Advantage

The effect of national resource availability on international competitiveness is the subject of the *theory of comparative advantage*. The theory states that a country has a comparative advantage in those products that make intensive use of those resources available in abundance within that country. Thus, Bangladesh has an abundant supply of unskilled labor. The U.S. has an abundant supply of technological

**FIGURE 15.2** Competitive advantage in an international context

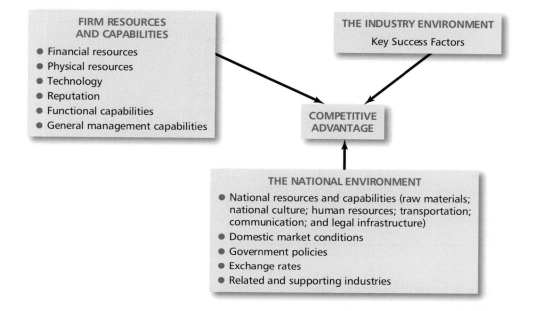

resources: trained scientists and engineers, research facilities, and universities. Bangladesh has a comparative advantage in products that make intensive use of unskilled labor, such as clothing, handicrafts, leather goods and assembly of consumer electronic products. The U.S. has a comparative advantage in technology-intensive products such as microprocessors, computer software, pharmaceuticals, medical diagnostic equipment and management consulting services.

The term "comparative advantage" refers to the *relative* efficiencies of producing different products. So long as exchange rates are well behaved (do not deviate far from their purchasing power parity levels), then comparative advantage translates into competitive advantage. Hence, comparative advantages are revealed in trade performance. Table 15.1 shows revealed comparative advantages for several product categories and several countries. Positive values show comparative advantage; negative values show comparative disadvantage.

Trade theory initially emphasized the role of natural resource endowments, labor supply and capital stock in determining comparative advantage. More recently emphasis has shifted to the central role of knowledge (including technology, human skills, and management capability) and the resources needed to commercialize knowledge (capital markets, communications facilities, and a legal system).[5] For industries where scale economies are important, a large home market is an additional source of comparative advantage (for example the U.S. in aerospace).[6]

## Porter's National Diamond

Michael Porter has extended our understanding of comparative advantage by examining the dynamics through which particular industries within a country develop the resources and capabilities that confer international competitive advantage.[7]

**TABLE 15.1** Indexes of revealed comparative advantage for certain broad product categories

|  | U.S. | U.K. | Japan | Switzerland | Canada | Australia | Taiwan |
|---|---|---|---|---|---|---|---|
| Cereals | +0.83 | −0.24 | −0.99 | −0.99 | +0.80 | +0.97 | −0.78 |
| Mineral fuels | −0.82 | −0.11 | −0.93 | −0.50 | 0.41 | +0.26 | −0.54 |
| Pharmaceuticals | −0.25 | +0.19 | −0.51 | +0.34 | −0.32 | −0.34 | −0.78 |
| Vehicles | −0.41 | −0.25 | +0.81 | −0.68 | +0.04 | −0.69 | +0.31 |
| Aerospace | +0.58 | −0.14 | −0.44 | −0.13 | +0.26 | −0.70 | −0.50 |
| Electrical and electronic equipment | −0.26 | +0.08 | +0.41 | −0.02 | −0.30 | −0.74 | +0.25 |
| Optical, photo, medical and scientific equipment | +0.09 | −0.02 | +0.21 | +0.37 | −0.36 | −0.46 | +0.20 |
| Apparel (woven) | −0.92 | −0.61 | −0.96 | −0.40 | −0.59 | −0.92 | −0.29 |
| Finance and insurance | −0.10 | +0.56 | +0.08 | +0.69 | −0.08 | +0.05 | −0.85 |

*Note:* Revealed comparative advantage for each product group is measured as: (exports less imports)/(exports + imports).
*Source:* OECD.

Porter's *national diamond* framework identifies four key factors that determine a country's competitive advantage within a particular sector (see Figure 15.3):[8]

*Factor Conditions* Whereas the conventional analysis of comparative advantage focuses on endowments of broad categories of resource, Porter emphasizes the role of highly specialized resources many of which are "home-grown" rather than "endowed." For example, in analyzing Hollywood's preeminence in film production, Porter points to the local concentration of highly skilled labor, including the roles of UCLA and USC schools of film. Also, resource constraints may encourage the development of substitute capabilities: in post-war Japan, raw material shortages spurred miniaturization and low-defect manufacturing; in Italy, restrictive labor laws have stimulated automation.

**FIGURE 15.3** Porter's national diamond framework

## Related and Supporting Industries

One of Porter's most striking empirical findings is that national competitive strengths tend to be associated with "clusters" of industries. Silicon Valley's cluster comprises semiconductor, computer, software and venture capital firms. For each industry, closely related industries are sources of critical resources and capabilities. Denmark's global leadership in wind power is based upon a cluster comprising wind turbine manufacturers, offshore wind farm developers and operators, and utilities.

*Demand Conditions*   Demand conditions in the domestic market provide the primary driver of innovation and quality improvement. For example:

- Switzerland's preeminence in watches is supported by the obsessive punctuality of the Swiss.
- Japanese dominant share of the world market for cameras by companies owes much to Japanese enthusiasm for amateur photography and their eager adoption of innovation in cameras.
- German dominance of the high-performance segment of the world automobile industry through Daimler, BMW, Porsche and VW-Audi reflects German motorists' love of quality engineering and their irrepressible urge to drive on autobahns at terrifying speeds.

*Strategy, Structure and Rivalry*   National competitive performance in particular sectors is inevitably related to the strategies and structures of firms in those industries. Porter puts particular emphasis on the role of intense domestic competition in driving innovation, efficiency, and the upgrading of competitive advantage. The international success of the Japanese in autos, cameras, consumer electronic and office equipment is based upon domestic industries that feature at least six major producers, all strongly competitive with one another. Conversely, European failure in many hi-tech industries may be a result of European governments' propensity to kill domestic competition by creating "national champions."

## Consistency Between Strategy and National Conditions

Establishing competitive advantage in global industries requires congruence between business strategy and the pattern of the country's comparative advantage. In audio equipment, it is sensible for Chinese producers, such as Skyworth and Desay, to concentrate on the low end of the market and to supply western mass retailers under their own brands. For Bose, international competitiveness requires exploiting U.S. strengths in basic research. For Danish consumer electronics maker Bang & Olufsen, international competitiveness requires exploiting European strengths in design and high-end marketing. Japanese producers such as Sony and Matsushita compete most effectively in the broad mid-market, exploiting national strengths in consumer electronic technology.

Achieving congruence between firm strategy and national conditions also extends to the embodiment of national culture within strategy and management systems. The success of U.S. companies in many areas of high technology, including computer software and biotechnology, owes much to a business system of entrepreneurial capitalism which exploits a national culture that emphasizes individuality, opportunity, and wealth acquisition. The global success of Korean corporate giants such as Samsung and LG reflects organizational structures and management systems that embody Korean cultural characteristics such as loyalty, respect for authority, conformity to group norms, commitment to organizational goals, and work ethic—what Professor Young-Ryeol Park refers to as "dynamic collectivism."[9]

## Applying the Framework: International Location of Production

To examine how national resource conditions influence international strategies, we look at two types of strategic decision in international business: first, where to locate production activities and, second, how to enter a foreign market. Let us begin with the first of these.

Firms move beyond their national borders not only to seek foreign markets, but also to access the resources and capabilities available in other countries. Traditionally, multinationals established plants to serve local markets. Increasingly, decisions concerning where to produce are being separated from decisions over where to sell. For example, ST Microelectronics, the world leader in application-specific integrated circuits (ASICs), is headquartered in Switzerland; production is mainly in France, Italy, and Singapore; R&D is conducted mainly in France, Italy, and the U.S.; and the biggest markets are Singapore, the Netherlands, the U.S., and Japan.

### Determinants of Geographical Location

The decision of where to manufacture requires consideration of three sets of factors:

- *National resource availability*. Where key resources differ between countries in their availability or cost, then firms should manufacture in countries where resource supplies are favorable. For the oil industry this means exploring in Kazakhstan, offshore Angola, and the Gulf of Mexico. In most areas of manufacturing, offshoring by companies from the advanced industrial nations has been driven primarily by the quest for lower wage costs. Table 15.2 shows differences in employment costs between countries. For many industries, gaining access to specialized knowhow is a critical consideration.

- *Firm-specific competitive advantages*. For firms whose competitive advantage is based on internal resources and capabilities, optimal location depends on where those resources and capabilities are situated and how mobile they are. Wal-Mart has experienced difficulty recreating its capabilities outside of the U.S. Conversely, Toyota and Goldman Sachs have successfully transferred their operational capabilities to their overseas subsidiaries.

- *Tradability*. The more difficult it is to transport a product and the more it is subject to trade barriers (such as tariffs and quotas), the more production will need to take place within the local market. Services—hairdressing, restaurant meals, and banking—typically need to be produced in close proximity to where they are consumed.

**TABLE 15.2** Hourly compensation costs in U.S. dollars for production workers in manufacturing

|  | 1975 | 2000 | 2006 |
| --- | --- | --- | --- |
| U.S. | 6.36 | 19.76 | 24.18 |
| Mexico | 1.47 | 2.08 | 2.75 |
| Australia | 5.62 | 14.47 | 26.00 |
| Japan | 3.00 | 22.27 | 19.99 |
| Korea | 0.32 | 8.19 | 14.72 |
| Taiwan | 0.40 | 5.85 | 6.56 |
| Sri Lanka | 0.28 | 0.48 | 0.56 |
| France | 4.52 | 15.70 | 24.90 |
| Germany | 6.31 | 24.42 | 34.21 |
| Italy | 4.67 | 14.01 | 25.07 |
| Spain | 2.53 | 10.78 | 18.83 |
| Switzerland | 6.09 | 21.24 | 30.67 |
| U.K. | 3.37 | 16.45 | 26.37 |

*Source:* U.S. Department of Labor, Bureau of Labor Statistics.

## Location and the Value Chain

The production of most goods and services comprises a vertical chain of activities where the input requirements of each stage vary considerably. Hence, different countries offer advantage at different stages of the value chain. Table 15.3 shows the pattern of international specialization within textiles and apparel. Similarly with consumer electronics: component production is research and capital intensive and is concentrated in the U.S., Japan, Korea, and Taiwan; assembly is labor intensive and is concentrated in China, Thailand, and Latin America.

A key feature of recent internationalization has been the international fragmentation of value chains as firms seek to locate countries whose resource availability and cost best matches each stage of the value chain.[10] Strategy Capsule 15.1 describes ECCO's globally dispersed value chain.

**TABLE 15.3** Comparative advantage in textiles and clothing by vertical stage

|  | Fiber production | Spun yarn | Textiles | Apparel |
| --- | --- | --- | --- | --- |
| Hong Kong | −0.96 | −0.81 | −0.41 | +0.75 |
| Italy | −0.54 | +0.18 | +0.14 | +0.72 |
| Japan | −0.36 | +0.48 | +0.78 | −0.48 |
| U.S. | +0.96 | +0.64 | +0.22 | −0.73 |

*Note:* Fiber production includes both natural and synthetic fibers. Revealed comparative advantage is measured as (exports − imports)/(exports + imports).
*Source:* United Nations.

## STRATEGY CAPSULE 15.1

# The Globally-dispersed Value Chain: ECCO A/S

ECCO is the world's second biggest supplier of "leisure casual branded footwear" behind Clarks and ahead of Rockport and Geoxx. ECCO was founded in Denmark in 1963 by Karl Toosbuy and is now owned and managed by his daughter Hanni and her husband. Its shoe making operations are characterized by their vertical integration ("from cow to consumer") and a proprietary process technology in which the shoe's sole and heel are molded directly on to the upper. Production was initially based in its home country, but its activities now span the globe:

- *Design* is based primarily at the company's headquarters in Bredebro, Denmark.

- *R&D* is centered in Portugal.

- *Leather production* takes place at three tanneries in the Netherlands, Indonesia and Thailand.

- *Production of shoe uppers* is a relatively labor-intensive activity and was concentrated in specialized factories in Thailand, Indonesia and China.

- *Shoe production* uses ECCO's direct injection technology and is fairly capital intensive. The main plants are in Thailand, China, Slovakia, Portugal and Indonesia. The Portuguese plant is the most technically advanced, deploying robotic production and laser technology.

- *Primary distribution centers* are in the Netherlands and Hong Kong.

- *Regional sales organizations* are based in the Netherlands (Western Europe), Denmark (Central Europe), Poland (Eastern Europe and Middle East), the U.S. (the Americas), and Hong Kong (Asia Pacific).

- *Retail distribution* is undertaken both by exclusive franchised retailers and independent retailers serviced by wholesalers.

**Sources:** www.ecco.com; B. B. Nielsen, T. Pedersen and J. Pyndt, *ECCO A/S—Global Value Chain Management* Ivey School of Business Case 908M14 (2008).

However, cost is just one factor in offshoring decisions. Cost advantages are vulnerable to exchange rate changes, so it is important to consider underlying issues concerning the availability and quality of resources and capabilities. For most Western and Japanese companies it is the potential for overall operational efficiency rather than local wage rates that is the key criterion influencing choice of location:

[W]estern companies are finding that offshoring locations such as China and India offer access to world-class skills. For example, Jim Breyer, managing partner of Accel Partners, a Silicon Valley venture capitalist, observed: "Taiwan and China have some of the world's best designers of wireless chips and wireless software." In certain types of precision manufacturing, including the processes that produce magnesium alloy casing for notebook computers, companies such as Waffer in Taiwan offer some of the most sophisticated technology in the world.

Most of the leading Indian IT outsourcing companies operate at level 5—the highest level of expertise—of the Capability Maturity Model (CMM), an international measure of technical skill, while most internal IT departments in western companies operate at level 2 or 3. Call centers, such as those operated by eTelecare—a Manila-based outsourcing provider—offer better average handling times and customer satisfaction relative to leading companies in the U.S.[11]

The modern laptop computer is the epitome of a globally dispersed value chain where every component and every process is located according the best combination of cost and technical knowhow (see Table 15.4).

The benefits from fragmenting the value chain must be traded off against the added costs of coordinating globally dispersed activities. Apart from costs of transportation costs and higher inventories, a key cost of dispersed activities is time. Just-in-time scheduling often necessitates that production activities are carried out in close proximity to one another. Companies that compete on speed and reliability of delivery (for example, Zara and Dell Computer) typically forsake the cost advantages of a globally dispersed value chain in favor of integrated operations with fast access to the final market. The financial crisis of 2008 created an additional cost of highly fragmented value chains—the need to ensure that distant suppliers have adequate access to credit.[12]

Figure 15.4 summarizes the relevant criteria in location decisions.

**TABLE 15.4**  Global production: the Hewlett Packard Pavilion 8000 laptop computer

| Component/Process | Provider and Location |
|---|---|
| Design | HP, California; also, HP design studios in Taiwan and China collaborate with third-party manufacturers |
| Assembly | Contracted to Quanta (Taiwan); assembled in China by Quanta and by third-party contractors |
| Microprocessor | Designed by Intel in California; manufactured at Intel plants in Oregon, New Mexico, and Israel |
| Graphics card | Designed by ATI Technologies in Canada; manufactured in Taiwan |
| Screen | Manufactured by LG Philips LCD Co. (a joint venture between LG of Korea and Philips of the Netherlands). Manufactured in South Korea |
| Hard disk drive | By Seagate. Designed in California; manufactured in Malaysia |
| Lithium ion battery | Manufactured by Sony in Japan |
| Logistics | Contracted to 40 third-party providers (some global, such as Federal Express, DHL, and TNT; others local) |
| Telephone sales and customer support | Contracted to third-party providers in Canada, U.K., Ireland and India |

*Sources:*
www.hp.com; "The Laptop Trail" *Wall Street Journal* (June 9, 2005).

**FIGURE 15.4** Determining the optimal location of value chain activities

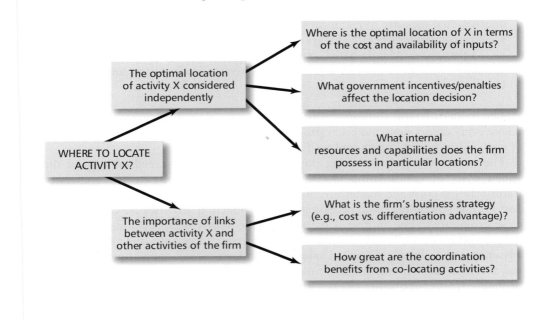

## Applying the Framework: Foreign Entry Strategies

Firms enter foreign markets in pursuit of profitability. The profitability of entering a foreign market depends upon the attractiveness of that market and whether the firm can establish a competitive advantage within it. While market attractiveness can be a magnet for foreign multinationals—the size and growth of the Chinese economy has been irresistible to many Western companies—over the longer term, the key determinant of profitability is likely to be ability to establish competitive advantage *vis-à-vis* local firms and other multinationals.

A firm's potential for establishing competitive advantage has important implications for the means by which it enters a foreign market. The basic distinction is between market entry by means of *transactions* and market entry by means of *direct investment*. Figure 15.5 shows a spectrum of market entry options arranged according to the degree of resource commitment by the firm. Thus, at one extreme there is exporting through individual spot-market transactions; at the other, there is the establishment of a wholly owned, fully integrated subsidiary.

How does a firm weigh the merits of different market entry modes? Five key factors are relevant:

**1** *Is the firm's competitive advantage based on firm-specific or country-specific resources?* If the firm's competitive advantage is country based, the firm must exploit an overseas market by exporting. Thus, to the extent that Tata Motor's competitive advantage in Western car markets is its low domestic cost base, it must produce in India and export to foreign markets. If Toyota's competitive advantage is its production and management capabilities, then as

**FIGURE 15.5**  Alternative modes of overseas market entry

long as it can transfer and replicate these capabilities, Toyota can exploit
foreign markets either by exports or by direct investment.[13]

**2**  *Is the product tradable and what are the barriers to trade?* If the product is
not tradable because of transportation constraints or import restrictions, then
accessing that market requires entry either by investing in overseas
production facilities or by licensing the use of key resources to local
companies within the overseas market.

**3**  *Does the firm possess the full range of resources and capabilities for
establishing a competitive advantage in the overseas market?* Competing in
an overseas market is likely to require that the firm acquires additional
resources and capabilities, particularly those related to marketing and
distributing in an unfamiliar market. Accessing such country-specific resources
is most easily achieved by collaborating with a firm in the overseas market.
The form of the collaboration depends, in part, on the resources and
capabilities required. If a firm needs marketing and distribution, it might
appoint a distributor or agent with exclusive territorial rights. If a wide range
of manufacturing and marketing capabilities is needed, the firm might license
its product and/or its technology to a local manufacturer. In technology-based
industries, licensing technology to local companies is common. In marketing-
intensive industries, firms with strong brands can license their trademarks to
local companies. Alternatively, a joint venture might be sought with a local
manufacturing company. United States' companies entered the Japanese
market by joint ventures with local companies (for example, Fuji-Xerox,
Caterpillar-Mitsubishi). These combined the technology and brand names of
the U.S. partner with the market knowledge and manufacturing and
distribution facilities of the Japanese firm.

**4**  *Can the firm directly appropriate the returns to its resources?* Whether a firm
licenses the use of its resources or chooses to exploit them directly (either
through exporting or direct investment) depends partly on appropriability
considerations. In chemicals and pharmaceuticals, the patents protecting

product innovations tend to offer strong legal protection, in which case patent licenses to local producers can be an effective means of appropriating their returns. In computer software and computer equipment the protection offered by patents and copyrights is looser, which encourages exporting rather than licensing as a means of exploiting overseas markets. With all licensing arrangements, key considerations are the capabilities and reliability of the local licensee. This is particularly important in licensing brand names, where the licenser must carefully protect the brand's reputation. Thus, Cadbury-Schweppes licenses to Hershey the trademarks and product recipes for its Cadbury's range of chocolate bars for sale in the United States. This arrangement reflects the fact that Hershey has production and distribution facilities in the U.S. that Cadbury cannot match, and that Cadbury views Hershey as a reliable business partner.

5 *What transaction costs are involved?* A key issue that arises in the licensing of a firm's trademarks or technology concerns the transaction costs of negotiating, monitoring and enforcing the terms of such agreements as compared with internationalization through a fully owned subsidiary. In expanding overseas, Starbucks owns and operates most of its coffee shops while McDonald's franchises its burger restaurants. McDonald's competitive advantage depends primarily upon the franchisee faithfully replicating the McDonald's system. This can be enforced effectively by means of franchise contracts. Starbucks believes that its success is achieved through creating the "Starbucks experience" which is as much about ambiance as it is about coffee. It is difficult to articulate the ingredients of this experience, let alone write it into a contract.

Issues of transaction costs are fundamental to the choices between alternative market entry modes. Barriers to exporting in the form of transport costs and tariffs are types of transaction costs; other costs include exchange rate risk and information costs. Transaction cost analysis has been central to theories of the existence of multinational corporations. In the absence of transaction costs in the markets either for goods or for resources, companies exploit overseas markets either by exporting their goods and services or by selling the use of their resources to local firms in the overseas markets.[14] Thus, multinationals tend to predominate in industries where:

- firm-specific intangible resources such as brands and technology are important (transaction costs in licensing the use of these resources favor direct investment);
- exporting is subject to transaction costs (for example, through tariffs or import restrictions);
- customer preferences are reasonably similar between countries.

## International Alliances and Joint Ventures

Strategic alliances—collaborative arrangements between firms—have become increasingly popular means of accessing foreign markets. International strategic alliances take many forms—some are informal collaborative arrangements, some involve one partner taking an equity stake in the other, others may involve equity cross-holdings. An international venture is where partners from different countries form a new company which they jointly own.

The traditional reason for cross-border alliances and joint ventures was the desire by multinational companies to access the market knowledge and distribution capabilities of a local company, together with the desire by local companies to access the technology, brands and product development of the multinationals. Western banks entering China's booming credit card market have usually formed marketing alliances with local banks, often reinforced with an equity stake.[15] Governments in emerging market countries often oblige foreign companies to take a local partner in order to encourage the flow of technology and management capabilities to the host country.

By sharing resources and capabilities between the partners, alliances not only economize on investment, they also allow access to more highly developed resources and capabilities than a firm could create for itself. Thus, the Freemove alliance formed by Telefonica Moviles (Spain), TIM (Italy), T-Mobile (Germany) and Orange (France) created a seamless third-generation, wireless communication network across Europe at a fraction of the cost incurred by Vodafone; it also allowed each firm access to the mobile network of the leading operator in at least five major European markets.[16] Fiat's joint venture with Tata motors gives Fiat access to the Indian market while allowing Tata to augment its product range by building and marketing Fiat-designed small cars.[17]

Some companies have based their international strategies almost entirely on alliances with foreign partners. For Gazprom, the Russian gas giant, alliances relate to shared pipeline projects with Eni (Italy), CNPC (China), EON (Germany), PDVSA (Venezuela) and MOL (Hungary); liquefied natural gas projects with PetroCanada and Sonotrach (Algeria) and long-term supply arrangements with Gaz de France.

While the strategic rationale is strong, the success of cross-border alliance (including joint ventures) has been mixed. The Fuji-Xerox copier joint venture, the Sony-Ericsson mobile phone joint venture, the Renault-Nissan alliance, and the collaboration between Hewlett Packard and Canon in printers have been very successful. Conversely, BT and AT&T's Concert alliance, the GM-Fiat alliance, and Swissair's network of airline alliances were all disasters. Disagreements over the sharing of the contributions to and returns from an alliance are a frequent source of friction, particularly in alliances between firms that are also competitors. When each partner seeks to access the other's capabilities, "competition for competence" results.[18] In several of the alliances between Japanese and Western firms, the Japanese partner was better at appropriating the benefits of the alliance.[19] We shall return to some of these issues of interfirm collaboration in the next chapter when we consider diversification.

## Multinational Strategies: Global Integration versus National Differentiation

So far, we have viewed international expansion, whether by export or by direct investment, as a means by which a company can exploit its competitive advantages not just in its home market but also in foreign markets. However, international scope may itself be a source of competitive advantage over geographically focused competitors. In this section, we explore whether, and under what conditions, firms that operate on an international basis are able to gain a competitive advantage over nationally focused firms. What is the potential for such "global strategies" to create competitive advantage? In what types of industry are they likely to be most effective? And how should they be designed and deployed in order to maximize their potential?

## The Benefits of a Global Strategy

A global strategy is one that views the world as a single, if segmented, market. The late Ted Levitt argued that companies that compete on a national basis are highly vulnerable to companies that compete on a global basis.[20] Global players win out over their national competitors for two reasons. First, supplying the world market allows access to scale economies in product development, manufacturing, and marketing. (Ghemawat refers to these as benefits from cross-border *aggregation*.[21]) Second, the key barriers to exploiting these scale economies, locally differentiated customer preferences, are fast disappearing in the face of the uniformity imposed by technology, communication and travel. "Everywhere everything gets more and more like everything else as the world's preference structure is relentlessly homogenized," observed Levitt. Subsequent contributions to the analysis of global strategy have elaborated Levitt's analysis of the potential for global strategies to create value.[22] Five major benefits have been proposed:

*Cost Benefits of Scale and Replication* As we noted in Chapter 9, the primary source of scale economy is product development—Boeing and Airbus in commercial aircraft and Microsoft and SAP in computer software have to operate on a global scale to amortize their huge investments in developing new products. In industries where internationalization occurs through direct investment rather than exporting, the major cost efficiencies from international operation derives from economies in the replication of knowledge-based assets—including organizational capabilities.[23] When a company has created a knowledge-based asset or product—whether a recipe, a piece of software, or an organizational system—subsequent replication costs a fraction of the original. With Disneyland theme parks in Tokyo, Paris, Hong Kong, and soon Shanghai, as well as Anaheim and Orlando, Disney can achieve significant economies in developing new rides. Similarly with McDonald's: it developed its business system within the U.S. and has subsequently replicated it across some 200 countries throughout the world.

*Serving Global Customers* In several industries—investment banking, audit services, advertising—the primary driver of globalization has been the need to service global customers.[24] Thus, the internationalization of auto parts manufacturers has tended to follow the internationalization patterns of the auto assemblers.

*Exploiting National Resources—Arbitrage Benefits* As we have already seen, global strategy does not necessarily involve production in one location and then distributing globally. Global strategies also involve exploiting the efficiencies from locating different activities in different places. As we have seen, companies internationalize not just in search of market opportunities but also in search of resource opportunities. Traditionally this has meant a quest for raw materials and low-cost labor. Increasingly it means a quest for knowledge. For example, among semiconductor firms, a critical factor determining the location of overseas subsidiaries is the desire to access knowledge within the host country.[25] Ghemawat refers to this exploitation of differences between countries as *arbitrage*.[26] While such arbitrage strategies are conventionally associated with exploiting wage differentials by offshoring production to low wage locations, increasingly arbitrage is about exploiting the distinctive knowledge available in different locations.

*Learning Benefits* The learning benefits of multinational operations refer not only to MNCs ability to access and transfer localized knowledge (*knowledge arbitrage*) but also integration of knowledge from different locations and the creation of new knowledge through interacting with different national environments. IKEA's expansion has required it to adjust to the Japanese style and design preferences, Japanese modes of living, and Japanese fanatical quality-consciousness. As a result, IKEA has developed its capabilities with regard to both quality and design that it believes will enhance its competitiveness worldwide. According to the CEO of IKEA Japan, "One reason for us to enter the Japanese market, apart from hopefully doing very good business, is to expose ourselves to the toughest competition in the world. By doing so, we feel that we are expanding the quality issues for IKEA all over the world." [27]

Recent contributions to the international business literature suggest that this ability of MNCs to develop knowledge in multiple locations, to synthesize that knowledge and transfer it across national borders may be their greatest advantage over nationally focused companies.[28] The critical requirement for exploiting these learning benefits is that the company possesses some form of global infrastructure for managing knowledge that permits new experiences, new ideas, and new practices to be diffused and integrated.

*Competing Strategically* A major advantage of the Romans over the Gauls, Goths, and other barbarian tribes, was the Romans' ability to draw upon the military and economic resources of the Roman Empire to fight local wars. Similarly, multinational companies possess a key strategic advantage over their nationally focused competitors: multinationals can fight aggressive competitive battles in individual national markets using their resources (cash flows in particular) from other national markets. At its most simple, this *cross-subsidization* of competitive initiatives in one market using profits from other markets involves *predatory pricing*—cutting prices to a level that drives competitors out of business. Such pricing practices are likely to contravene both the World Trade Organization's antidumping rules and national antitrust laws. More usually, cross-subsidization involves using cash flows from other markets to finance aggressive sales and marketing campaigns.[29] There is some evidence that Asian electronics firms use the profits from higher prices at home to subsidize expansion in Western markets.[30]

Strategic competition between MNCs presents more complex opportunities for attack, retaliation and containment.[31] The most effective response to competition in one's home market may be to retaliate in the foreign MNC's own home market. Fuji Film's incursion into Kodak's backyard was symbolized by Fuji's sponsorship of the 1984 Olympic Games in Los Angeles. Kodak responded by expanding its marketing efforts in Japan.[32] To effectively exploit such opportunities for national leveraging, some overall global coordination of competitive strategies in individual national markets is required.

Kenichi Ohmae has argued that to become effective global competitors, multinationals must become true insiders in all of the world's leading economic centers. This used to mean positioning within the "triad": North America, Europe, and Japan.[33] This doctrine has been weakened, first, by the rise of new industrial powers (notably China and India) and, second, the disappointing outcomes of several attempts to build "triad power"—for example, Daimler-Benz's acquisitions of Chrysler in the U.S. and Mitsubishi in Japan.

## The Need for National Differentiation

For all the advantages of global strategy, the evidence of the past decade is that national differences in customer preferences continue to exert a powerful influence in most markets: products designed to meet the needs of the "global customer" tend to be unappealing to most consumers. Moreover, costs of national differentiation can be surprisingly low if common basic designs and common major components are used. Most auto firms have abandoned attempts to create global car models in favor of common platforms.[34] Flexible manufacturing systems have reduced the costs of customizing products to meet the preferences of particular customer groups.

Domestic appliances provide an interesting refutation of the globalization hypothesis. In washing machines, national preferences have shown remarkable resilience: French and U.S. washing machines are primarily top loading, elsewhere in Europe they are mainly front loading; the Germans prefer higher spin speeds than the Italians; U.S. machines feature agitators rather than revolving drums; and Japanese machines are small. The pioneers of globalization in domestic appliances, such as Electrolux and Whirlpool, still struggle to outperform national and regional specialists.[35] Similarly in retail banking, despite some examples of successful internationalization (Banco Santander, HSBC), most of the evidence points to few economies from cross-border integration and the critical need to adapt to local market conditions.[36]

Every nation represents a unique combination of distinctive characteristics. How can we recognize and assess the extent of similarities and differences between countries? Pankaj Ghemawat proposes four key components: cultural distance, administrative and political distance, geographical distance, and economic distance—his "CAGE" framework (see Table 15.5).

Ghemawat's broad categories are only a starting point for exploring the national idiosyncrasies that make international expansion such a minefield. For consumer products firms, the structure of distribution channels are likely to be a critical barrier to global marketing and distribution. Procter & Gamble must adapt its marketing, promotion, and distribution of toiletries and household products to take account of the fact that, in the U.S., a few chains account for a major share of its U.S. sales; in southern Europe, most sales are through small, independent retailers; while in Japan, P&G must sell through a multitiered hierarchy of distributors. The closer an industry to the final consumer, the more important cultural factors are likely to be. Strategy Capsule 15.2 considers some dimensions of national culture. It is notable that so few retailers have become successful abroad. With the exception of IKEA, Hennes & Mauritz, and a handful of others, there are few international retailers that are truly global and few that have been as successful overseas as at home. For many, franchising has provided a lower risk internationalization strategy.

**TABLE 15.5**  Ghemawat's CAGE framework for assessing country differences

|  | Cultural distance | Administrative and political distance | Geographical distance | Economic differences |
|---|---|---|---|---|
| *Distance between two countries increases with* | • Different languages, ethnicities, religions, social norms<br>• Lack of connective ethnic or social networks | • Absence of shared political or monetary association<br>• Political hostility<br>• Weak legal and financial institutions | • Lack of common border, water way access, adequate transportation or communication links<br>• Physical remoteness | • Different consumer incomes<br>• Different costs and quality of natural, financial, and human resources<br>• Different information or knowledge |
| *Industries most affected by source of distance* | Industries with high linguistic content (TV, publishing) and cultural content (food, wine, music) | Industries viewed by government as strategically important (for example, energy, defense, telecommunications) | Products with low value-to-weight (cement), that are fragile or perishable (glass, milk) or dependent upon communications (financial services) | Products whose demand is sensitive to consumer income levels (luxury goods). Labor intensive products (clothing) |

*Source:*
Adapted from P. Ghemawat, "Distance Still Matters: The Hard Reality of Global Expansion," *Harvard Business Review* (September, 2001): 137–147. Used with permission.

## STRATEGY CAPSULE 15.2

# How do National Cultures Differ?

Do people differ between countries with regard to beliefs, norms, and value systems? The answer from a series of research studies is "yes."

The best known study of national cultural differences is by Geert Hofstede. The principal dimensions of national values he identified were:

- *Power distance*—the extent to which inequality, decision-making power in particular, is accepted within organizations

and within society. Power distance was high in Malaysia, and most Latin American and Arab countries; low in Austria and Scandinavia.

- *Uncertainty avoidance*. Preference for certainty and established norms was high in most southern European and Latin American countries; tolerance for uncertainty and ambiguity was high in Singapore, Sweden, the U.K., the U.S., and India.

- *Individualism*. Concern for individual over group interests was highest in the U.S., the U.K., Canada, and Australia. Identification with groups and the collective interest was strongest in Latin America and Asia (especially Indonesia, Pakistan, Taiwan and South Korea).

- *Masculinity/femininity*. Hofstede identifies emphasis on work and material goals and demarcation of gender roles as "masculine"; emphasis on personal relationships rather than efficiency and belief in gender equality was viewed as "feminine." Japan, Austria, Venezuela, and Italy scored high on masculinity; Scandinavia and the Netherlands scored very low.

Other studies have used different measures for characterizing national cultures. Fons Trompenaars (another Dutchman) emphasizes "universalism" versus "particularism" in outlook (the U.S. and Australia score highest on universalism); "neutral" versus "affective" relationships (Japan and the U.K. are highest in terms of neutrality; Mexico and the Netherlands the most affective); and achievement orientation (Australia and the U.S. very high; Venezuela, Indonesia, and China very low).

*Sources:* G. Hofstede, *Culture's Consequences: International Differences in Work-related Values* (Thousand Oaks, CA: Sage, 1984); F. Trompenaars, *Riding the Waves of Culture* (London: Economist Books, 1993).

## Reconciling Global Integration with National Differentiation

Choices about internationalization strategy have been viewed as a tradeoff between the benefits of global integration and those of national adaptation (see Figure 15.6).[37] Industries where scale economies are huge and customer preferences homogeneous call for a global strategy (for example, jet engines). Industries where national preferences are pronounced and where customization is not prohibitively expensive favor a "multidomestic" strategy (for example, retail banking). Indeed, if there are no significant benefits from global integration, then we may see these industries supplied almost entirely by locally specialized firms (as in funeral services and hairdressing). However, some industries may be low on most dimensions— cement and car repair services are fairly homogeneous worldwide, but also lack significant scale economies or other major benefits from global presence. Conversely, other industries offer substantial benefits from operating at global scale (telecommunications equipment, military hardware), but national preferences and standards may also necessitate considerable adaptation to the needs of specific national markets.

Reconciling conflicting forces for global efficiency and national differentiation represents one of the greatest strategic challenges facing MNCs. Achieving "global localization" involves standardizing product features and company activities where scale economies are substantial, and differentiating where national preferences are strongest and where achieving them is not over-costly. Thus, a global car such as the Honda Civic (introduced in 1972 and sold in 110 countries of the world) now embodies considerable local adaptations—not just to meet national safety and environmental standards, but also to meet local preferences for leg room, seat specifications, accessories, color, and trim. McDonald's too meshes global standardization with local adaptation (see Strategy Capsule 15.3).

**FIGURE 15.6** Benefits of global integration versus national differentiation

**STRATEGY CAPSULE 15.3**

## McDonald's Goes "Glocal"

For antiglobalization activists, McDonald's is a demon of globalization: it crushes national cuisines and small, traditional family businesses with the juggernaut of U.S. fast-food corporate imperialism. In reality, its global strategy is a careful blend of global standardization and local adaptation.

McDonald's menus include a number of globally standardized items—the Big Mac and potato fries are international features— however, in most countries McDonald's menus feature an increasing number of locally developed items. These include:

- Australia—a range of wraps including Seared Chicken, Tandoori Chicken and Crispy Sweet Chili Chicken;
- France—Croque McDo (a toasted ham and cheese sandwich);
- Hong Kong—Grilled Pork Twisty Pasta and Fresh Corn Cup;
- India—Shahi Paneer McCurry Pan, McAloo Tikki, Veg Pizza McPuff;
- Saudi Arabia—McArabia Kofta, McArabia Chicken;

- Switzerland—Shrimp Cocktail, Chickenburger Curry;
- U.K.—A range of deli sandwiches including "Spicy Veggie Deli" (chickpea patty with coriander and cumin) , and "Sweet Chili Chicken Deli";
- U.S.A.—Premium Grilled Chicken Ranch BLT Sandwich.

There are differences too in restaurant decor, service offerings (internet access in the U.K.; home delivery in India), and market positioning (McDonald's tends to have a more up-market positioning outside the U.S.). In Israel many McDonald's are kosher—they do not offer dairy products and are closed on Saturdays. In India neither beef nor pork is served. A key reason that almost all of McDonald's non-U.S. outlets are franchised is to facilitate adaptation to national environments and access to local knowhow.

Yet, the principal features of the McDonald's business system are identical throughout the world. McDonald's values and business principles are seen as universal and invariant. Its emphasis on families and children is intended to identify McDonald's with fun and family life wherever it does business. Community involvement and the Ronald McDonald children's charity are also worldwide. Corporate trademarks and brands are mostly globally uniform—including the golden arches logo and "I'm lovin' it" tag line. The business system itself—the franchising, the training of managers and franchisees through Hamburger University, restaurant operations, and supplier relations—is also highly standardized.

Traditionally, McDonald's international strategy was about adapting its U.S. model to local conditions. Increasingly McDonald's is using local differentiation as a basis for worldwide adaptation and innovation through transferring new menu items and business concepts from one country to another. For example, the McCafe gourmet coffeehouses within McDonald's restaurants were first developed in Australia. By 2003, McCafes had become established in 30 countries, including the U.S. In responding to the growing tide of concern over nutrition and obesity in the developed world, McDonald's has drawn upon country initiatives with regard to sandwiches, salads, and information labeling as a basis for global learning.

Whether or not McDonald's has the balance right between global standardization and local adaptation is open to debate. Simon Anholt, a British marketing expert, argues: "By putting local food on the menu, all you are doing is removing the logic of the brand, because this is an American brand. If McDonald's serves what you think is a poor imitation of your local cuisine, it's going to be an insult." But according to McDonald's C.E.O. Jim Skinner: "We don't run our business from Oak Brook. We are a local business with a local face in each country we operate in." His chief marketing manager, Mary Dillon, adds: "McDonald's is much more about local relevance than a global archetype. Globally we think of ourselves as the custodian of the brand, but it's all about local relevance."

*Sources:* www.mcdonalds.com; *McDonald's Localization Strategy: Brand Unification, Menu Diversification?* ICFAI Case Study 306-316–1 (2006).

Reconciling global efficiency with appealing to customer preferences in each country also means looking at the globalization/national differentiation tradeoff for individual products and individual functions. In retail banking, different products and services have different potential for globalization. Credit cards and basic savings products such as certificates of deposit tend to be globally standardized; checking accounts and mortgage lending are much more nationally differentiated. Similarly with business functions: R&D, purchasing, IT, and manufacturing have strong globalization potential; sales, marketing, customer service, and human resource management need to be much more nationally differentiated. These differences have important implications for how the MNC is organized.

## Strategy and Organization within the Multinational Corporation

These same factors—the benefits from global integration and need for national differentiation—that influence the design of international strategies also have critical implications for the design of organizational structures and management systems to implement these strategies. As we shall see, one of the greatest challenges facing the senior managers of MNCs is aligning organizational structures and management systems and their fit with the strategies being pursued.

### The Evolution of Multinational Strategies and Structures

Over the past hundred years, the forces driving the internationalization of companies have changed considerably; the tradeoff between the benefits of global integration and those of national differentiation has also shifted markedly. Hence, during different periods international firms have adopted different strategies and different structural configurations. Yet, these structural configurations have tended to persist. Although all companies are subject to organizational inertia, MNCs because of their complexity face particular difficulties in structural change. Hence, MNCs are captives of their history: their strategy-structure configurations today reflect choices they made at the time of their international expansion. Radical changes in strategy and structure are difficult: once an international distribution of functions, operations, and decision-making authority has been determined, reorganization is slow, difficult and costly—particularly when host governments become involved. Bartlett and Ghoshal argue that the "administrative heritage" of an MNC—its configuration of assets and capabilities, its distribution of managerial responsibilities, and its network of relationships—is a critical determinant of its current capabilities and a key constraint upon its ability to build new strategic capabilities.[38]

Bartlett and Ghoshal identify three eras in the development of the MNC (see Figure 15.7):

- *Early twentieth century: era of the European multinational.* European companies such as Unilever, Shell, ICI, and Philips were pioneers of multinational expansion. Because of the conditions at the time of internationalization—poor transportation and communications, highly differentiated national markets—the companies created "multinational federations": each national subsidiary was operationally autonomous and undertook the full range of functions, including product development, manufacturing, and marketing.

**FIGURE 15.7** The development of the multinational corporation: alternative parent-subsidiaries relations

The Europeans: Decentralized Federations

The Americans: Coordinated Federations

The Japanese: Centralized Hubs

*Note:* The density of shading indicates the concentration of decision making.

*Source:* C. A. Bartlett and S. Ghoshal, *Managing Across Borders: The Transnational Solution* (Boston: Harvard Business School Press, 1998). Copyright © 1989 by the Harvard Business School Publishing Corporation, all rights reserved. Reprinted by permission of Harvard Business School Publishing.

- *Post-Second World War: era of the American multinational.* United States economic dominance was the basis for the pre-eminence of U.S. multinationals such as GM, Ford, IBM, Coca-Cola, Caterpillar, and Procter & Gamble. While their overseas subsidiaries were allowed considerable autonomy, this was within the context of the dominant position of their U.S. parent in terms of capital, new product and process technology, management capabilities, and management systems. United States-based resources and capabilities were their primary competitive advantages in world markets.

- *The 1970s and 1980s: the Japanese challenge.* Japanese MNCs—Honda, Toyota, Matsushita, NEC, and YKK—pursued global strategies from centralized domestic bases. R&D and manufacturing were concentrated in Japan; overseas subsidiaries were responsible for sales and distribution. Globally standardized products manufactured in large-scale plants provided the basis for unrivalled cost and quality advantages. Over time, manufacturing and R&D were dispersed—initially because of trade protection by consumer countries and the rising value of the yen against other currencies.

The different administrative heritage of these different groups of MNCs continues to shape their organizational capabilities today. The strength of European multinationals is adaptation to the conditions and requirements of individual national markets. The strength of the U.S. multinationals is their ability to transfer technology and proven new products from their domestic strongholds to their national subsidiaries. That of the Japanese MNCs is the efficiency of global production and new product development. Yet, these core capabilities are also core rigidities. The challenge for European MNCs has been to achieve greater integration of their sprawling international empires—for Shell and Philips this has involved reorganizations over a period of more than two decades. For U.S. MNCs such as Ford and Procter & Gamble it has involved nurturing the ability to tap their foreign subsidiaries for technology, design, and new product ideas. For Japanese MNCs such as Nomura, Hitachi, and NEC the challenge is to become true insiders in the overseas countries where they do business.

## Reconfiguring the MNC: The Transnational Corporation

*Changing Organization Structure* For North American and European-based MNCs, the principal structural changes of recent decades have been a shift from organization around national subsidiaries and regional groupings to the creation of worldwide product divisions. For most MNCs, country and regional organizations are retained, but primarily for the purposes of national compliance and customer relationships. Thus, Hewlett-Packard conducts its business through global product groups: Technology Solutions Group (comprising Enterprise Storage and Servers, Services, and Software), Personal Systems Group (its personal computer and entertainment business), and Imaging and Printing Group (printers and cameras). At the same time, it maintains three regional headquarters: for the Americas (located in Houston), for Europe, Middle East and Africa (located in Geneva), and for Asia Pacific (located in Singapore).

*New Approaches to Reconciling Localization and Global Integration* However, the formal changes in structure are less important than the changes in responsibilities, decision powers, and modes of coordination within these structures. The fundamental challenge for MNCs has been reconciling the advantages of global integration with those of national differentiation. Escalating costs of research and new product development have made global strategies with global product platforms essential. At the same time, meeting consumer needs in each national market and responding swiftly to changing local circumstances requires greater decentralization. Accelerating technological change further exacerbates these contradictory forces: despite the cost and "critical mass" benefits of centralizing research and new product development, innovation occurs at multiple locations within the MNC and requires nurturing of creativity and initiative throughout the organization. "It's the corporate equivalent of being able to walk, chew gum, and whistle at the same time," notes Chris Bartlett.

According to Bartlett, the simultaneous pursuit of responsiveness to national markets and global coordination requires, "a very different kind of internal management process than existed in the relatively simple multinational or global organizations. This is the *transnational organization*."[39] The distinguishing characteristic of the transnational is that it becomes an integrated network of distributed and interdependent resources and capabilities (see Figure 15.8). This necessitates that:

- Each national unit is a source of ideas, skills and capabilities that can be harnessed for the benefit of the total organization.
- National units access global scale economies by designating them the company's world source for a particular product, component, or activity.
- The center must establish a new, highly complex managing role that coordinates relationships among units but in a highly flexible way. The key is to focus less on managing activities directly and more on creating an organizational context that is conducive to the coordination and resolution of differences. Creating the right organizational context involves "establishing clear corporate objectives, developing managers with broadly based perspectives and relationships, and fostering supportive organizational norms and values."[40]

**FIGURE 15.8** The transnational corporation

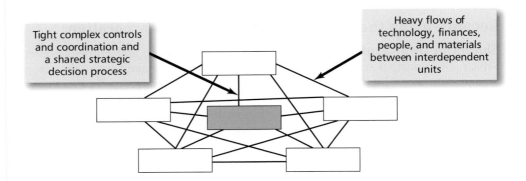

Tight complex controls and coordination and a shared strategic decision process

Heavy flows of technology, finances, people, and materials between interdependent units

Balancing global integration and national differentiation requires that a company adapts to the differential requirements of different products, different functions, and different countries. Procter & Gamble adopts global standardization for some of its products (Pringles potato chips and high-end perfumes, for example); for others (hair care products and laundry detergent, for example) it allows significant national differentiation. Across countries, P&G organizes global product divisions to serve most of the industrialized world because of the similarities between their markets, while for emerging market countries (such as China and India) it operates through country subsidiaries in order to adapt to the distinctive features of these markets. Among functions, R&D is globally integrated while sales are organized by national units that are differentiated to meet local market characteristics.

The transnational firm is a concept and direction of development rather than a distinct organizational archetype. It involves convergence of the different strategy configurations of MNCs. Thus, companies such as Philips, Unilever, and Siemens have reassigned roles and responsibilities to achieve greater integration within their traditional "decentralized federations" of national subsidiaries. Japanese global corporations such as Toyota and Matsushita have drastically reduced the roles of their Japanese headquarters. American multinationals such as Citigroup and IBM are moving in two directions: reducing the role of their U.S. bases while increasing integration among their different national subsidiaries.

Multinational corporations are increasingly locating management control of their global product divisions outside their home countries. When Philips adopted a product division structure, it located responsibility for medical electronics in its U.S. subsidiary and leadership in consumer electronics in Japan. Nexans, the world's biggest manufacturer of electric cables, has moved the head office of five of its 20 product divisions outside of France. For example, the head of ships' cables is based in South Korea—the world leader in shipbuilding.[41] Aligning structure, strategy, and national resources may even require shifting the corporate headquarters—HSBC moved from Hong Kong to London, Tetra Pak from Lund, Sweden to Lausanne, Switzerland.[42]

*Organizing R&D and New Product Development* Probably the greatest challenges facing the top managers of MNCs are organizing, fostering and exploiting innovation and new product development. Innovation is stimulated by diversity and autonomy, while its exploitation and diffusion require critical mass and coordination. The traditional European decentralized model is conducive to local initiatives—but not to their global exploitation. Philips has an outstanding record of innovation in consumer electronics. In its TV business, its Canadian subsidiary developed its first color TV; its Australian subsidiary developed its first stereo sound TV and its British subsidiary developed teletext TVs. However, lack of global integration constrained its success on a worldwide scale. Building a globally integrated approach to new product development has been a major priority of the past two decades.

Assigning national subsidiaries global mandates allows them to take advantage of local resources and develop distinctive capabilities while exploiting globally the results of their initiatives.[43] For example, P&G, recognizing Japanese obsessiveness over cleanliness, assigned increasing responsibility to its Japanese subsidiary for developing household cleaning products. Its "Swiffer" dust-collecting products were developed in Japan (using technology developed by other firms) then introduced into other markets. Where a local unit possesses unique capabilities, it can be designated a *center of excellence*.[44]

## Summary

Moving from a national to an international business environment represents a quantum leap in complexity. In an international environment, a firm's potential for competitive advantage is determined not just by its own resources and capabilities but also by the conditions of the national environment in which it operates, including input prices, exchange rates and a host of other factors. The extent to which a firm is positioned across multiple national markets also influences its economic power.

Our approach in this chapter has been to simplify the complexities of international strategy by applying the same basic tools of strategy analysis that we developed in earlier chapters. For example, to determine whether a firm should enter an overseas market, our focus has been the profit implications of such an entry. This requires an analysis of (a) the attractiveness of the overseas market using the familiar tools of industry analysis, and (b) the potential of the firm to establish competitive advantage in that overseas market, which depends on the firm's ability to transfer its resources and capabilities to the new location and their effectiveness in conferring competitive advantage.

However, establishing the potential for a firm to create value from internationalization is only a beginning. Subsequent analysis needs to design an international strategy: do we enter an overseas market by exporting, licensing, or direct investment? If the latter, should we set up a wholly owned subsidiary or a joint venture? Once the strategy has been established, then a suitable organizational structure needs to be designed.

The fact that so many companies that have been outstandingly successful in their home market have failed so miserably in their overseas expansion demonstrates the complexity of international management. In some cases, the companies have failed to recognize that the resources and capabilities that underpinned their competitive advantages in their home market could not be readily transferred or replicated in overseas markets. In others, the problems were in designing the structures and systems that could effectively implement the international strategy.

As the lessons of success and failure from international business become recognized and distilled into better theories and analytical frameworks, so we advance our understanding of how to design and implement strategies for competing globally. We are at the stage where we recognize the issues and the key determinants of competitive advantage in an international environment. However, there is much that we do not fully understand. Designing strategies and organizational structures that can reconcile critical tradeoffs between global scale economies versus local differentiation, decentralized learning and innovation versus worldwide diffusion and replication, and localized flexibilities versus international standardization remain key challenges for senior managers.

## Self-Study Questions

1   With reference to Figure 15.1, identify a "sheltered industry" (one that has been subject to little penetration either by imports or foreign direct investment). Explain why the industry has escaped internationalization. Explore whether there are opportunities for profitable internationalization within the industry and, if so, the strategy that would offer the best chance of success.

2   With reference to Table 15.1, what characteristics of national resources explain the different patterns of comparative advantage for the U.S. and Japan?

3   According to Michael Porter's *Competitive Advantage of Nations*, some of the industries where British companies have an international advantage are: advertising, auctioneering of antiques and artwork, distilled alcoholic beverages, hand tools, and chemical preparations for gardening and horticulture. Some of the industries where U.S. companies have an international competitive advantage are: photo film, aircraft and helicopters, computer hardware and software, oilfield services, management consulting, cinema films and TV programs, healthcare products and services, and financial services. For either the U.K. or the U.S., use Porter's national diamond framework (Figure 15.3) to explain the observed pattern of international competitive advantage.

4   When Porsche decided to enter the SUV market with its luxury Cayenne model, it surprised the auto industry by locating its new assembly plant in Leipzig in Eastern Germany. Many observers believed that Porsche should have located the plant either in Central or Eastern Europe where labor costs were very low, or (like Mercedes and BMW) in the U.S. where it would be close to its major market. Using the criteria outlined in Figure 15.4, can you explain Porsche's decision?

**5**   British expatriates living in the U.S. frequently ask friends and relatives visiting from the U.K. to bring with them bars of Cadbury's chocolate on the basis that the Cadbury's chocolate available in the U.S. (manufactured under license by Hershey's) is inferior to "the real thing." Should Cadbury-Schweppes plc maintain its licensing agreement with Hershey or should it seek to supply the U.S. market itself, either by export from the U.K. or by establishing manufacturing facilities in the U.S.?

**6**   Has McDonald's got the balance right between global standardization and national differentiation (see Strategy Capsule 15.3)? Should it offer its franchisees in overseas countries greater initiative in introducing products that meet national preferences? Should it also allow greater flexibility for its overseas franchisees to adapt store layout, operating practices, and marketing? What aspects of the McDonald's system should McDonald's top management insist on keeping globally standardized?

# Notes

1   *OECD in Figures 2008* (Organization for Economic Cooperation and Development, 2008). Note that the OECD members comprise the world's advanced industrialized countries.

2   This process was proposed by J. Johanson and J.-E. Vahlne, "The Internationalization Process of the Firm," *Journal of International Business Studies* 8 (1977): 23–32. See also L. Melin, "Internationalization as a Strategy Process," *Strategic Management Journal* 13 (1992 Special Issue): 99–118.

3   S. L. Segal-Horn, "Globalization of service industries," in J. McGee (ed.) *The Blackwell Encyclopedia of Management: Strategic Management* (Oxford: Blackwell Publishing, 2005): 147–54.

4   P. Ghemawat and F. Ghadar, "Global Integration— Global Concentration," *Industrial and Corporate Change* 15 (2006): 595–624.

5   A key finding was that *human capital* (knowledge and skills) was more important than *physical capital* in explaining U.S. comparative advantage. See W. W. Leontief, "Domestic Production and Foreign Trade," in R. Caves and H. Johnson (eds), *Readings in International Economics* (Homewood, IL: Irwin, 1968).

6   P. Krugman, "Increasing Returns, Monopolistic Competition, and International Trade," *Journal of International Economics* 9 (November, 1979): 469–79.

7   M. E. Porter, *The Competitive Advantage of Nations* (New York: Free Press, 1990).

8   For a review of the Porter analysis, see R. M. Grant, "Porter's *Competitive Advantage of Nations*: An Assessment," *Strategic Management Journal* 12 (1991): 535–48.

9   Y.-R. Park, "Korean Business Culture," Presentation, December 15, 2005, http://gc.sfc.keio.ac.jp/class/2005_14969/slides/10/, accessed July 7, 2009.

10   The linking of value-added chains to national comparative advantages is explained in B. Kogut, "Designing Global Strategies and Competitive Value-Added Chains," *Sloan Management Review* (Summer, 1985): 15–38.

11   J. Hagel and J. S. Brown, "Thinking Global, Acting Local," *Financial Times* (August 9, 2005).

12   "Sum of the Parts," *Financial Times* (November 17, 2008).

13   The role of firm-specific assets in explaining the multinational expansion is analyzed in R. Caves, "International Corporations: The Industrial Economics of Foreign Investment," *Economica* 38 (1971): 1–27.

14   D. J. Teece, "Transactions Cost Economics and Multinational Enterprise," *Journal of Economic Behavior and Organization* 7 (1986): 21–45. See also "Creatures of Imperfection," in "Multinationals: A Survey," *Economist* (March 27, 1993): 8–10.

15   D. von Emloh and Y. Wang, "Competing for China's Credit Card Market," *McKinsey Quarterly* (November, 2005): www.mckinseyquarterly.com.

16   "Freemove: Creating Value through Strategic Alliance in the Mobile Telecommunications Industry," IESE Case 0-305-013 (2004).

17   "Tata motors, Fiat to Halt competitive Launches," *Hindustan Times* (June 13, 2009).

18   G. Hamel, "Competition for Competence and Inter-partner Learning within International Strategic Alliances," *Strategic Management Journal* 12 (1991): 83–103.

19   See R. Reich and E. Mankin, "Joint Ventures with Japan Give Away our Future," *Harvard Business Review* (March–April 1986).

20   T. Levitt, "The Globalization of Markets," *Harvard Business Review* (May–June 1983): 92–102.

21   P. Ghemawat, *Redefining Global Strategy: Crossing Borders in a World Where Differences Still Matter* (Boston: Harvard Business School, 2007).

22 G. S. Yip, *Total Global Strategy II* (Upper Saddle River, NJ: Prentice Hall, 2003); C. Baden-Fuller and J. Stopford, "Globalization Frustrated," *Strategic Management Journal* 12 (1991): 493–507; "Rough and Tumble Industry," *Financial Times* (July 2, 1997): 13.

23 S. G. Winter and G. Szulanski, "Replication as Strategy," *Organization Science* 12 (2001): 730–43.

24 D. B. Montgomery, G. S. Yip, and B. Villalonga, "Explaining Supplier Behavior on Global Account Management," Stanford Research Paper No. 1767 (November, 2002). Abstract available at SSRN: http://ssrn.com/abstract=355240, accessed July 7, 2009.

25 P. Almeida, "Knowledge Sourcing by Foreign Multinationals: Patent Citation Analysis in the U.S. Semiconductor Industry," *Strategic Management Journal* 17, Winter Special Issue (1996): 155–65. See the McDonald's individual country web sites, such as www.mcdonalds.com (U.S.), www.mcdonalds.co.uk (U.K.), www.mcdonalds.fr (France).

26 P. Ghemawat, "The Forgotten Strategy," *Harvard Business Review* (November 2003): 76–84.

27 Comments by Tommy Kullberg (IKEA Japan) in "The Japan Paradox," Conference organized by the European Commission, Director General for External Affairs (December 2003): 62–3, available at http://www.deljpn.ec.europa.eu/data/current/japan-paradox.pdf, accessed July 7, 2009.

28 A. K. Gupta and P. Govindarajan, "Knowledge Flows within Multinational Corporations," *Strategic Management Journal* 21 (April 2000): 473–96; P. Almeida, J. Song and R. M. Grant, "Are Firms Superior to Alliances and Markets? An Empirical Test of Cross-Border Knowledge Building," *Organization Science* 13 (March–April 2002): 147–61.

29 G. Hamel and C. K. Prahalad, "Do You Really Have a Global Strategy?" *Harvard Business Review* (July–August 1985): 139–48.

30 H. Simon and Y. Eriguchi, "Pricing Challenges for Japanese Companies in the Twenty-first Century," *Journal of Professional Pricing* 14, no. 4 (2005), www.pricingsociety.com. B. Y. Aw, G. Batra, and M. J. Roberts, "Firm Heterogeneity and Export—Domestic Price Differentials: A Study of Taiwanese Electrical Products," *Journal of International Economics* 54 (2001): 149–69.

31 I. C. Macmillan, A. van Ritten and R. G. McGrath, "Global Gamesmanship," *Harvard Business Review* (May, 2003): 62–71.

32 R. C. Christopher, *Second to None: American Companies in Japan* (New York: Crown, 1986).

33 K. Ohmae, *Triad Power: The Coming Shape of Global Competition* (New York: Free Press, 1985).

34 The Ford Mondeo/Contour is a classic example of a global product that failed to appeal strongly to any national market. See M. J. Moi, "Ford Mondeo: A Model T World Car?" Working Paper, Rotterdam School of Management, Erasmus University (2001). C. Chandler, "Globalization: The Automotive Industry's Quest for a World Car": GlobalEdge working paper, Michigan State University (1997).

35 C. Baden-Fuller and J. Stopford, "Globalization Frustrated," *Strategic Management Journal* 12 (1991): 493–507.

36 M. Venzin, *Building an International Financial Services Firm: How Successful Firms Design and Execute Cross-border Strategies* (Oxford: Oxford University Press, 2009).

37 P. Ghemawat (*Redefining Global Strategy* op. cit.) proposes a three-way rather than a two-way analysis. In his Adaptation-Aggregation-Arbitrage ("AAA") framework he divides integration into aggregation and arbitrage.

38 C. A. Bartlett and S. Ghoshal, *Managing Across Borders: The Transnational Solution*, 2nd edn (Boston: Harvard Business School Press, 1998).

39 C. Bartlett, "Building and Managing the Transnational: The New Organizational Challenge," in Michael E. Porter (ed.) *Competition in Global Industries* (Boston: Harvard Business School Press, 1986): 377.

40 Ibid.: 388.

41 "The Country Prince Comes of Age," *Financial Times* (August 9, 2005).

42 J. Birkinshaw, P. Braunerhjelm, U. Holm and S. Terjesen, "Why do some Multinational Corporations Relocate their Headquarters Overseas?" *Strategic Management Journal* 27 (2006): 681–700.

43 J. Birkinshaw, N. Hood and S. Jonsson, "Building Firm-specific Advantages in Multinational Corporations: The Role of Subsidiary Initiative," *Strategic Management Journal* 19 (1998): 221–42.

44 T. S. Frost, J. M. Birkinshaw and P. C. Ensign, "Centers of Excellence in Multinational Corporations," *Strategic Management Journal* 23 (2002): 997–1018.

# 16 Diversification Strategy

*Telephones, hotels, insurance—it's all the same. If you know the numbers inside out, you know the company inside out.*

—HAROLD SYDNEY GENEEN, CHAIRMAN OF ITT, 1959–78, AND INSTIGATOR
OF 275 COMPANY TAKEOVERS

*For a company that has taken its original or main business as far as it can go, diversification as a means of channeling surplus resources should certainly be considered. For the company that has not yet developed its main business to the full potential, however, diversification is probably one of the riskiest strategic choices that can be made.*

—KENICHI OHMAE, FORMER HEAD OF MCKINSEY & CO.'S TOKYO OFFICE

## OUTLINE

# Introduction and Objectives

Deciding "What business are we in?" is the starting point of strategy and the basis for defining the firm's identity. In their statements of vision and mission, some companies define their businesses broadly. Shell's objective is "to engage efficiently, responsibly, and profitably in oil, oil products, gas, chemicals, and other selected businesses." Other companies define their businesses more narrowly: McDonald's vision is "to be the world's best quick-service restaurant chain"; Caterpillar will "be the leader in providing the best value in machines, engines, and support services for companies dedicated to building the world's infrastructure and developing and transporting its resources."

The business scope of firms changes over time. The dominant trend of the past two decades has been "refocusing on core businesses." Philip Morris Companies, Inc. (now renamed Altria Group, Inc.) sold off 7-Up, Miller Brewing and Kraft Foods and became a specialist tobacco company. Most diversified industrial groups—U.S. and European conglomerates such as ITT, Hanson, Gulf & Western, Cendant, Vivendi Universal, and Tyco—have broken up altogether.

Some companies have moved in the opposite direction. Microsoft, once a supplier of operating systems, expanded into application and networking software, information services, entertainment systems and video games consoles. Google is no longer simply a search engine company—it supplies a wide array of information products, advertising management services, an internet browser (Chrome), an operating system for mobile phones (Android), and a wide array of applications software.

Diversification is a conundrum. The quest to enter new fields of business has probably caused more value destruction than any other type of strategic decision. Yet, diversification also offers growth options and the potential for a firm to free itself of the restrictions of a single industry.

Our goal in this chapter is to establish the basis on which companies can make corporate strategy decisions that create rather than destroy value. Is it better to be specialized or diversified? Is there an optimal degree of diversification? What types of diversification are most likely to create value?

In practice, we make these types of decision every day in our personal lives. If my car doesn't start in the morning, should I try to fix it myself or have it towed directly to the garage? There are two considerations. First, is repairing a car an attractive activity to undertake? If the garage charges $85 an hour but I can earn $600 an hour consulting, then car repair is not attractive to me. Second, am I any good at car repair? If I am likely to take twice as long as a skilled mechanic then I possess no competitive advantage in car repair.

Diversification decisions by firms involve the same two issues:

◆ How attractive is the industry to be entered?

◆ Can the firm establish a competitive advantage within the new industry?

These are the very same factors we identified in Chapter 1 (see Figure 1.4) as determining a firm's profit potential. Hence, no new analytic framework is needed for appraising diversification decisions: diversification may be justified either by the superior profit potential of the industry to be entered, or by the ability of the firm to create competitive advantage in the new industry. The first issue draws on the industry analysis developed in Chapter 3; the second draws on the analysis of competitive advantage developed in Chapters 5 and 8.

Our primary focus will be the latter question: under what conditions does operating multiple businesses assist a firm in gaining a competitive advantage in each? This leads into exploring linkages between different businesses within the diversified firm—a phenomenon often referred to as "synergy." By the time you have completed this chapter, you will be able to:

◆ understand the factors that caused both the earlier trend of diversification and the recent trend toward refocusing;

◆ identify the conditions under which diversification creates value for shareholders and, in particular, to evaluate the potential for sharing and transferring resources and capabilities within the diversified firm;

◆ determine the relative merits of diversification and strategic alliances in exploiting the linkages between different businesses;

◆ recognize the organizational and managerial issues to which diversification gives rise and why diversification so often fails to realize its anticipated benefits.

# Trends in Diversification over Time

As a background to our analysis of diversification decisions, let's begin by examining the factors that have influenced diversification strategies in the past.

## The Era of Diversification, 1950–80

In Chapter 14, we identified diversification as a major component of the widening scope of the modern corporation during the twentieth century. Between 1950 and 1980, the expansion of companies into different product markets was a major source of corporate growth in all the advanced industrial nations.[1] The 1970s saw the peak of the diversification boom, with the emergence of a new corporate form—the *conglomerate*—represented in the U.S. by ITT, Textron, and Allied-Signal, and in the U.K. by Hanson, Slater-Walker, and BTR. These highly diversified enterprises were created from multiple, unrelated acquisitions. Their existence reflected the view that senior management no longer needed industry-specific experience; corporate management simply needed to deploy the new techniques of financial and strategic management.[2] Figure 16.1 shows changing patterns of diversification strategy during the latter part of the twentieth century.

## Refocusing, 1980–2009

After 1980, the diversification trend went into sharp reverse. Between 1980 and 1990, the average index of diversification for the Fortune 500 declined from 1.00 to

**FIGURE 16.1** Diversification strategies of large U.S. and U.K. companies during the late twentieth century

***Sources***: R. P. Rumelt, "Diversification Strategy and Profitability," *Strategic Management Journal* 3 (1982): 359–70; R. Whittington, M. Mayer, and F. Curto, "Chandlerism in Post-war Europe: Strategic and Structural Change in France, Germany and the UK, 1950–1993," *Industrial and Corporate Change* 8 (1999): 519–50; D. Channon, *The Strategy and Structure of British Enterprise* (Cambridge: Harvard University Press, 1973).

0.67.[3] Unprofitable "noncore" businesses were divested and many diversified companies fell prey to acquirers who promptly restructured them.[4] Acquisition activity was extremely heavy during the 1980s—some $1.3 trillion in assets were acquired, including 113 members of the Fortune 500—but, unlike the previous decade, only 4.5% of acquisitions represented unrelated diversification.[5] Moreover, acquisitions by the Fortune 500 were outnumbered by dispositions. The refocusing trend was strongest in the U.S., but was also evident in Canada and Europe and, to a lesser extent, in Japan.[6]

This trend towards specialization was the result of three principal factors.

*Emphasis on Shareholder Value* The primary driver of refocusing was the reordering of corporate goals from growth to profitability. Sluggish growth and high interest rates during the early 1980s and 1989–90 exposed the inadequate profitability of many large, diversified corporations. Institutional shareholders, including pension funds such as California's Public Employees Retirement system, became more active in pressuring top management for better shareholder returns—this led to increased CEO turnover.[7]

The surge in leveraged buyouts put further pressure on executives to boost shareholder returns. Kohlberg Kravis Roberts' $31 billion takeover of the tobacco and food giant RJR Nabisco in 1989 demonstrated that even the largest U.S. companies were vulnerable to attack from corporate raiders.[8] The result was a rush by diversified giants to restructure before leveraged buyout specialists did it for them. Evidence of "conglomerate discounts"—that the stock market was valuing diversified companies at less than the sum of their parts—provided a further incentive for breakups.[9]

*Turbulence and Transaction Costs* In Chapter 14, we observed that the relative costs of organizing transactions within firms and across markets depend on the conditions in the external environment. Administrative hierarchies are very efficient in processing routine transactions, but in turbulent conditions the pressure of decision making on top management results in stress, inefficiency and delay. As the business environment has become more volatile, specialized companies are more agile than large diversified corporations where strategic decisions require approval at divisional and corporate levels. At the same time, external markets for resources—capital markets especially—have become increasingly efficient. Many diversified companies have spun off their growth businesses because of the greater potential of external capital markets to fund their development.

Outside the mature industrialized countries, the situation is very different. Highly diversified business groups dominate the industrial sectors of many emerging countries: Tata Group and Reliance in India, Charoen Pokphand (CP) in Thailand, Astra in Indonesia, Sime Darby in Malaysia, Grupo Alfa and Grupo Carso in Mexico. One reason for the continued dominance of large conglomerates in emerging market countries may be higher transaction costs associated with their less sophisticated markets for finance, information, and labor that offer diversified companies advantages over their specialized competitors.[10]

*Trends in Management Thinking* Optimism that new tools and systems of financial and strategic management would enable companies to span many different businesses has been replaced by recognition that competitive advantage requires focusing on key strengths in resources and capabilities. Where core resources and

**FIGURE 16.2** Diversification: the evolution of strategy and management thinking

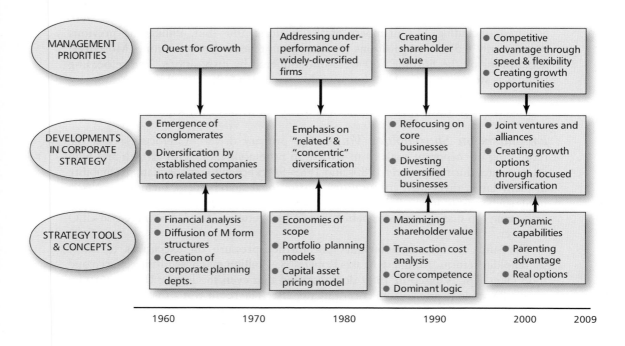

capabilities can be deployed across different product markets, this can support profitable diversification. Hence, the focus of diversification analysis has been to identify the circumstances in which multibusiness activity can create value. Analysis of economies of scope, the transferability of resources and capabilities across industry boundaries, and the role of transaction costs has allowed us to be more precise about these circumstances. Mere linkages between businesses are not enough: the key to creating value is the ability of the diversified firm to share resources and transfer capabilities more efficiently than alternative institutional arrangements. Moreover, it is essential that the benefits of these linkages are not outweighed by the additional management costs of exploiting them. Figure 16.2 summarizes some of the key developments in diversification strategy over the past 50 years.

# Motives for Diversification

A critical development in the transition from diversification to refocusing has been the reordering of corporate objectives. The era of corporate diversification was influenced by two key objectives—growth and risk reduction—neither of which are consistent with the creation of shareholder value.

## Growth

In the absence of diversification firms are prisoners of their industry. For firms in stagnant or declining industries this is a daunting prospect—especially for top management. The urge to achieve corporate growth that outstrips that of a firm's primary industry is an appealing prospect for managers. Companies in low-growth, cash flow-rich industries such as tobacco and oil have been especially susceptible to the temptations of diversification. During the 1980s, Exxon diversified into copper and coal mining, electric motors, and computers and office equipment; RJR Nabisco transformed itself from a tobacco company into a diversified consumer products company. In both cases diversification was highly destructive of shareholder value. Shareholders are quite happy to invest in companies in low growth, even declining industries, so long as these companies throw off plenty of cash flow which shareholders can invest in promising growth companies.

## Risk Reduction

If the cash flows of different businesses are imperfectly correlated, then bringing them together under common ownership reduces the variance of the combined cash flow. However, such risk reduction appeals to managers more than to owners. Shareholders can diversify risk by holding diversified portfolios. Hence, what advantage can there be in companies diversifying for them? The only possible advantage could be if firms can diversify at lower cost than individual investors. In fact the reverse is true: the transaction costs to shareholders of diversifying their portfolios are far less than the transaction costs to firms diversifying through acquisition. Not only do acquiring firms incur the heavy costs of using investment banks and legal advisers, they must also pay an acquisition premium to gain control of an independent company.

The *capital asset pricing model* (CAPM) formalizes this argument. The theory states that the risk that is relevant to determining the price of a security is not the overall risk (variance) of the security's return, but *systematic risk*: that part of the variance of the return that is correlated with overall market returns. This is measured by the security's *beta coefficient*. Corporate diversification does not reduce systematic risk: if three separate companies are brought under common ownership, in the absence of any other changes, the beta coefficient of the combined company is simply the weighted average of the beta coefficients of the constituent companies. Hence, the simple act of bringing different businesses under common ownership does not create shareholder value through risk reduction.[11]

Empirical studies are generally supportive of the absence of shareholder benefit from diversification that simply combines independent businesses under a single corporate umbrella.[12] Unrelated diversification may even fail to lower unsystematic risk.[13]

Special issues arise once we consider the risk of bankruptcy. For a marginally profitable firm, diversification can help avoid cyclical fluctuations of profits that can push it into insolvency. However, diversification that reduces the risk of bankruptcy is beneficial to bondholders (and other creditors) rather than shareholders.[14]

Are there circumstances where reductions in unsystematic risk can create shareholder value? If there are economies to the firm from financing investments internally rather than resorting to external capital markets, the stability in the firm's cash flow that results from diversification may reinforce independence from external capital markets. For ExxonMobil, BP, and the other major oil companies, one of the benefits of extending across upstream (exploration and production), downstream (refining and marketing), and chemicals is that the negative correlation of the returns from these businesses increases the overall stability of their cash flows. This in turn increases their capacity to undertake huge, risky investments in offshore oil production, transcontinental pipelines, and natural gas liquefaction. These benefits also explain why firms pursue hedging activities that only reduce unsystematic risk.[15]

The financial turmoil of 2008–9 has created a new appreciation of the risk spreading benefits of diversification. The seizing up of credit markets towards the end of 2008 was less serious for large firms with diversified cash flows that were less dependent on banks providing working capital.

## Value Creation: Porter's "Essential Tests"

If we return to the assumption that corporate strategy should be directed toward the interests of shareholders, what are the implications for diversification strategy? We have already revisited our two sources of superior profitability: industry attractiveness and competitive advantage. For firms contemplating diversification, Michael Porter expands on these. He proposes three "essential tests" to be applied in deciding whether diversification will truly create shareholder value:

- *The attractiveness test*. The industries chosen for diversification must be structurally attractive or capable of being made attractive.
- *The cost-of-entry test*. The cost of entry must not capitalize all the future profits.
- *The better-off test*. Either the new unit must gain competitive advantage from its link with the corporation, or vice versa.[16]

### The Attractiveness and Cost-of-entry Tests

A critical realization in Porter's "essential tests" is that industry attractiveness is insufficient on its own. Although diversification allows a firm to access more attractive investment opportunities than are available in its own industry, it faces the challenge of entering a new industry. The second test, *cost of entry*, recognizes that for outsiders, the cost of entry may counteract the attractiveness of the industry. Pharmaceuticals, corporate legal services, and defense contracting offer above-average profitability precisely because they are protected by barriers to entry. Firms seeking to enter these industries have a choice. They may acquire an established player, in which case the acquisition price will almost certainly fully capitalize the target firm's profit prospects (especially given the need to pay an acquisition premium over the market price of the target).[17] Alternatively, entry may occur through establishing a new corporate venture. In this case, the diversifying firm must directly confront the barriers to entry protecting that industry.[18]

### The Better-off Test

Porter's third criterion for successful diversification—*the better-off test*—addresses the basic issue of competitive advantage: if two businesses producing different products are brought together under the ownership and control of a single enterprise, is there any reason why they should become any more profitable? Combining different, but related, businesses can enhance the competitive advantages of the original business, the new business, or both. For example:

- Procter & Gamble's 2005 acquisition of Gillette was intended to boost the competitive position of both companies through combining the two companies' global marketing and distribution networks, transferring

Gillette's new product development capabilities to P&G, and increasing both companies' bargaining power relative to retail giants such as Wal-Mart.

- Bank of America's $50 billion takeover of Merrill Lynch in October 2008 to create the world's largest diversified financial services companies was justified by the strengthening of the core businesses of both firms. The combination of Merrill's investment banking business and Bank of America's corporate banking businesses created a massive presence in corporate financial services. The augmenting of Bank of America's retail banking presence with Merrill's huge network of stockbrokers created a broad U.S. platform for wealth management services.[19]

*Primacy of the Better-Off Test*   In most normal circumstances it is only the better-off test that matters. In the first place, industry attractiveness is rarely a source of value from diversification—in most cases, the attractiveness test and the cost-of-entry test cancel each other out.

The second reason why the better-off test normally dominates is that it can make sense for a company to enter an unattractive industry so long as the cost of entry is sufficiently discounted and the better-off test is met. When private equity firm Golden Gate Capital bought Eddie Bauer Inc. in August 2009, the deal was motivated, not by the attractiveness of the retail clothing sector, but by Golden Gate's ability to by the 400-store chain for a mere $286 million, then apply its financial and strategic management capabilities to revitalizing the sportswear chain. Similarly, Disney's acquisition of marvel entertainment, also in August 2009, reflected Disney's desire to exploit the marvel characters in its movie and theme park businessed rather than Disney's desire to invest in the comic industry.

So, let us now explore further into the ways in which diversification can make businesses "better off" through analyzing the relationship between diversification and competitive advantage.

## Competitive Advantage from Diversification

If the primary source of value creation from diversification is exploiting linkages between different businesses, what are these linkages and how are they exploited? The critical linkages are those that arise through the sharing of resources and capabilities across different businesses. In addition, there is the potential for diversification to enhance or exploit a firm's market power—this issue is addressed in the appendix to this chapter.

### Economies of Scope

The most general argument concerning the benefits of diversification focuses on the presence of *economies of scope* in common resources: "Economies of scope exist when using a resource across multiple activities uses less of that resource than when the activities are carried out independently."[20]

*Economies of scope* exist for similar reasons as *economies of scale*. The key difference is that the economies of scale relate to cost economies from increasing output of a *single product*; economies of scope are cost economies from increasing the output of *multiple products*.[21] The nature of economies of scope varies between different types of resources and capabilities.

*Tangible Resources* Tangible resources—such as distribution networks, information technology systems, sales forces and research laboratories—offer economies of scope by eliminating duplication between businesses through creating a single shared facility. The greater the fixed costs of these items, the greater the associated economies of scope are likely to be. Entry by cable TV companies into telephone services and telephone companies into cable TV are motivated by the desire to spread the costs of networks and billing systems over as great a volume of business as possible. Common resources such as customer data bases, customer service centers, and billing systems have encouraged British Gas, a former publicly owned gas utility, to diversify into supplying electricity, fixed-line and mobile telephone services, broadband internet connections, home security systems, home insurance and home appliance repair.

Economies of scope also arise from the centralized provision of administrative and support services to the different businesses of the corporation. Within diversified companies, accounting, legal services, government relations and information technology tend to be centralized—often through *shared service organizations* that supply common administrative and technical services to the operating businesses. Similar economies arise from centralizing research activities in a corporate R&D lab.

*Intangible Resources* Intangible resources such as brands, corporate reputation and technology offer economies of scope from the ability to extend them to additional businesses at low marginal cost.[22] Exploiting a strong brand across additional products is called *brand extension*. Starbucks has extended its brand to ice cream, packaged cold drinks, home espresso machines, audio CDs and books.

*Organizational Capabilities* Organizational capabilities can also be transferred within the diversified company. For example:

- LVMH is the world's biggest and most diversified supplier of branded luxury goods. Its distinctive capability is the management of luxury brands. This capability comprises market analysis, advertising, promotion, retail management, and quality assurance. These capabilities are deployed across Louis Vuitton (accessories and leather goods); Hennessey (cognac); Moet et Chandon, Dom Perignon, Veuve Clicquot, and Krug (champagne); Celine, Givenchy, Kenzo, Dior, Guerlain, and Donna Karan (fashion clothing and perfumes); TAG Heuer and Chaumet (watches); Sephora and La Samaritaine (retailing); and some 25 other branded businesses.

- Sharp Corporation—originally established to manufacture metal products and the Ever Sharp Pencil—developed capabilities in the miniaturization of electronic products. It has developed and introduced a stream of innovative products, beginning with the world's first transistor calculator (1964), the first LCD pocket calculator (1973), LCD color TVs, PDAs, internet viewcams, ultraportable notebook computers, and 3G mobile telephones.

Some of the most important capabilities in influencing the performance of diversified corporations are *general management capabilities*. General Electric possesses strong technological and operational capabilities at business level and it is good at sharing these capabilities between businesses (for example, turbine knowhow between jet engines and electrical generating equipment). However, its core capabilities are in general management and these reside primarily at the corporate level. They include its ability to motivate and develop its managers, its outstanding strategic and financial management that reconciles decentralized decision making with strong centralized control, and its international management capability. Similar observations could be made about 3M. While 3M's capabilities in technical know-how, new product development, and international marketing reside within the individual businesses, it is the corporate management capabilities and the systems through which they are exercised that maintain, nourish, coordinate, and upgrade these competitive advantages.[23]

## Economies from Internalizing Transactions

Although economies of scope provide cost savings from sharing and transferring resources and capabilities, does a firm have to diversify across these different businesses to exploit those economies? The answer is no. Economies of scope in resources and capabilities can be exploited simply by selling or licensing the use of the resource or capability to another company. In Chapter 12, we observed that a firm can exploit proprietary technology by licensing it to other firms. In Chapter 15, we noted how technology and trademarks are licensed across national frontiers as an alternative to direct investment. Similarly across industries: Starbucks' extension of its brand to other products has been achieved primarily through licensing: Pepsi produces and distributes Starbucks Frappaccino; Unilever produces Tazo Tea beverages, Dreyer's produces Starbucks ice cream. Walt Disney exploits the enormous value of its trademarks, copyrights, and characters partly through diversification into theme parks, live theater, cruise ships, and hotels; but it also licenses the use of these assets to producers of clothing, toys, music, comics, food, and drinks, as well as to the franchisees of Disney's retail stores. Disney's income from licensing fees and royalties was over $2 billion in 2005.

Even tangible resources can be shared across different businesses through market transactions. Airport and railroad station operators exploit economies of scope in their facilities not by diversifying into catering and retailing but by leasing out space to specialist retailers and restaurants.

Are economies of scope better exploited internally within the firm through diversification, or externally through market contracts with independent companies? The key issue is relative efficiency: what are the transaction costs of market contracts, as compared with the administrative costs of diversified activities? Transaction costs include the costs involved in drafting, negotiating, monitoring, and enforcing a contract, plus the costs of protecting against exploitation by the partner. The costs of internalization consist of the management costs of establishing and coordinating the diversified business.[24]

Consider the following:

- In the case of Walt Disney Company, it licenses Donald Duck trademarks to Florida's Natural Growers rather than setting up its own orange-juice company; it owns and operates Disneyland and Disney World theme parks but licenses its trademarks and technology to Oriental Land Company, the owner and operator of Tokyo Disneyland.

- Both Mars and Cadbury used their confectionary brands to enter the European ice cream market. Cadbury decided to license its brands to Nestlé; Mars entered the business itself by setting up production and distribution facilities, competing with Unilever and Nestlé. The result was that Cadbury made significant profits from its licenses whereas Mars experienced years of losses or low returns on its investment.

Finding the right answer is complex. It depends on the nature of the resource or capability that is generating the "better off" benefits. If the resource can be traded or licensed out for anything close to its real value—as in the case of the Donald Duck trademark or the confectionery brands, then it is not necessary to enter another business in order to capture the extra profitability. Cadbury captured more profitability by not entering the ice cream-business. If, on the other hand, the resource is one that cannot easily be traded, such as general management capabilities, then it will be necessary to enter the new business in order to create the extra profitability. There is little scope for 3M to deploy its new product development capabilities other than within its own business. Similarly, for Apple Computer, the only way for it to exploit its capabilities in user-friendly design was to diversify outside of its core computer business. Virgin has a separate licensing company but only licenses its brand to companies within the Virgin group. So why doesn't Virgin license its brand to companies it does not own? The answer presumably is that the brand is part of a package of benefits that Virgin offers, some of which could not be traded or licensed. For example, Virgin has developed special marketing skills around its brand, often using the brand and Richard Branson to gain press comment in place of expensive advertising.

## Parenting Advantage

The recognition that it is only certain kinds of economies of scope that justify diversification led Goold, Campbell and Alexander to propose the concept "parenting value added" (an alternative to Porter's better-off test).[25] Parenting value comes from the resources and general management skills possessed by the parent company, holding company or corporate centre that is thinking of diversifying into a new business. In Virgin's case they include the brand, Richard Branson's skill at getting press coverage and Virgin's attractiveness to partners. If these skills add value to a new business, then Virgin should think of entering that business. If the "better-off" value comes from combining manufacturing or sales forces, then Goold and his colleagues argue that it is the skills of the managers in the parent company that make these combinations happen. Hence, they argue that parenting value added explains nearly all successful diversification because parenting is the main resource that is hard to trade and it is the activities of parent-level managers that lower internal transaction costs.

## The Diversified Firm as an Internal Market

We see that economies of scope on their own do not provide an adequate rationale for diversification—they must be supported by potential to economize on transaction costs. In fact, the lower costs of managing transactions internally can offer "better off" efficiencies, even when no economies of scope are present.

*Internal Capital Markets*   Consider the case of financial capital. The diversified firm represents an internal capital market: the corporate allocating capital between the different businesses through the capital expenditure budget. Which is more efficient, the internal capital markets of diversified companies or the external capital market? Diversified companies have two key advantages:

- By maintaining a balanced portfolio of cash-generating and cash-using businesses, diversified firms can avoid the costs of using the external capital market, including the margin between borrowing and lending rates and the heavy costs of issuing new debt and equity.
- Diversified companies have better access to information on the financial prospects of their different businesses than that typically available to external financiers.[26]

Against these advantages is the critical disadvantage that investment allocation within the diversified company is a politicized process in which strategic and financial considerations are subordinated by turf battles and ego building. Evidence suggests that diversified firms' internal capital markets tend to cross-subsidize poorly performing divisions and are reluctant to transfer cash flows to the divisions with the best prospects.[27] However, the efficiency of capital allocation varies greatly across companies. Makron Associates identified several conglomerates with exceptional performance in terms of ten-year shareholder returns. They included GE and Berkshire Hathaway of the U.S., Hutchison Wampoa of Hong Kong, Bouygues and Lagardere of France, Wesfarmers of Australia, ITC of India, and Carso of Mexico. These companies were characterized by: "Strict financial discipline, rigorous analysis and valuation, a refusal to overpay for acquisitions, and a willingness to close or sell existing businesses."[28]

Another form of organization that reduces the transaction costs of external capital markets is the *private equity firm*. These firms raise money into a fund that is then used to buy businesses. Instead of raising money each time they want to buy a business, they do the money raising once. Moreover, they have developed ways of avoiding the agency problems of self-seeking managers. Each fund has to be closed and returned to investors within a set number of years, often 10–14 years. This encourages the managers in the private equity firm to take particular care when allocating money from the fund. They want to make sure that each allocation will produce a good return before the fund is closed. They also give equity stakes to the managers in charge of each business that will pay out when the business is sold. This reduces the motivation for playing politics. Finally, the managers leading the individual businesses do not participate in the management decisions of the private equity firm. Many corporations, in contrast, have the heads of the biggest divisions sitting on the corporate-level management committee (more on this in the next chapter).

*Internal Labor Markets*   Efficiencies also arise from the ability of diversified companies to transfer employees—especially managers and technical specialists—between their divisions, and to rely less on hiring and firing. As companies develop and encounter new circumstances, so different management skills are required. The costs associated with hiring include advertising, time spent in interviewing and selection and the costs of "head-hunting" agencies. The costs of dismissing employees can be very high where severance payments must be offered. A diversified corporation has a pool of employees and can respond to the specific needs of any one business through transfer from elsewhere within the corporation.

The broader set of opportunities available in the diversified corporation as a result of internal transfer may also result in attracting a higher caliber of employee. Graduating students compete intensely for entry-level positions with diversified corporations such as Canon, General Electric, Unilever and Nestlé in the belief that these companies can offer richer career development than more specialized companies.

The informational advantages of diversified firms are especially important in relation to internal labor markets. A key problem of hiring from the external labor market is limited information. A résumé, references, and a day of interviews are poor indicators of how a new hire will perform in a particular job. The diversified firm that is engaged in transferring employees between different positions and different internal units can build detailed information on the competencies and characteristics of its employees. This informational advantage exists not only for individual employees but also for groups of individuals working together as teams. Hence, in exploiting a new business opportunity an established firm is at an advantage over the new firm which must assemble its team from scratch.

## Diversification and Performance

Where diversification exploits economies of scope in resources and capabilities in the presence of transaction costs, it has the potential to create value for shareholders. Diversification that seeks only growth or risk reduction is likely to destroy value. How do these predictions work in practice?

### The Findings of Empirical Research

Empirical research into diversification has concentrated on two major issues: first, how do diversified firms perform relative to specialized firms and, second, does related diversification outperform unrelated diversification?

*The Performance of Diversified and Specialized Firms* Despite many empirical studies since the 1960s, consistent, systematic relationships between diversification and performance are lacking. Beyond a certain threshold, high levels of diversification appear to be associated with lower profitability—probably because of the organizational complexity that diversification creates. Among British companies, diversification was associated with increased profitability up to a point, after which further diversification was accompanied by declining profitability.[29] Several other studies have detected a similar curvilinear relationship between diversification and profitability.[30] McKinsey & Company also point to the benefits of moderate diversification—"a strategic sweet spot between focus and broader diversification." Diversification, they argue, makes most sense when a company has exhausted growth opportunities in its existing markets and can match its existing capabilities to emerging external opportunities.[31]

A key problem is distinguishing *association* from *causation*. If moderately diversified companies are generally more profitable than specialized firms, is it because diversification increases profitability or because profitable firms channel their cash flows into diversifying investments?

The performance effects of diversification depend on the mode of diversification. Mergers and acquisitions involving companies in different industries appear to perform especially poorly.[32]

More consistent evidence concerns the performance results of refocusing initiatives by North American and European companies: when companies divest diversified businesses and concentrate more on their core businesses, the result is typically increased profitability and higher stock market valuation.[33] These findings may reflect a changing relationship between diversification and profitability over time: growing turbulence of the business environment may have increased the costs of managing widely diversified corporations.

*Related and Unrelated Diversification*   Given the importance of economies of scope in shared resources and capabilities, it seems likely that diversification into *related* industries should be more profitable than diversification into *unrelated* industries. Empirical research initially supported this prediction. Rumelt discovered that companies that diversified into businesses closely related to their core activities were significantly more profitable than those that pursued unrelated diversification.[34] By 1982, Tom Peters and Robert Waterman were able to conclude: "virtually every academic study has concluded that unchanneled diversification is a losing proposition."[35] This observation supported one of their "golden rules of excellence":

> *Stick to the Knitting*
> Our principal finding is clear and simple. Organizations that do branch out but stick very close to their knitting outperform the others. The most successful are those diversified around a single skill, the coating and bonding technology at 3M for example. The second group in descending order, comprise those companies that branch out into related fields, the leap from electric power generation turbines to jet engines from GE for example. Least successful are those companies that diversify into a wide variety of fields. Acquisitions especially among this group tend to wither on the vine.[36]

Subsequent studies have clouded the picture: the superiority of related diversifiers may be the result of risk factors and industry influences;[37] unrelated diversification may even outperform related.[38] Several factors may be confusing the relationship. First, related diversification offers greater potential benefits than unrelated but the linkages it involves also create more difficult management problems. (I shall address this issue in the next chapter.) Second, the apparently poor results from unrelated diversification might be the result of poorly performing companies seeking to get far away from their existing businesses.[39] Finally, the distinction between "related" and "unrelated" diversification is not always clear—it may depend upon the strategy and characteristics of individual firms. Champagne and luggage are not obviously related products, but LVMH applies similar brand management capabilities to them both. Let us consider this issue further.

## The Meaning of Relatedness in Diversification

If relatedness refers to the potential for sharing and transferring resources and capabilities between businesses, there are no unambiguous criteria to determine whether two industries are related—it all depends on the company undertaking the diversification. Empirical studies have defined relatedness in terms of similarities between industries in technologies and markets. These similarities emphasize relatedness at the *operational* level—in manufacturing, marketing, and distribution—typically activities where economies from resource sharing are small and achieving them is costly in management terms. Conversely, some of the most important sources of value creation within the diversified firm are the ability to apply common general management capabilities, strategic management systems, and resource allocation processes to different businesses. Such economies depend on the existence of *strategic* rather than *operational* commonalities among the different businesses within the diversified corporation.[40]

- Berkshire Hathaway is involved in insurance, candy stores, furniture, kitchen knives, jewelry and footwear. Despite this diversity, all these businesses have been selected on the basis of their ability to benefit from the unique style of corporate management established by chairman Warren Buffett and CEO Charles Munger.
- Richard Branson's Virgin Group covers a huge array of businesses from airlines to bridal stores. Yet, they share certain strategic similarities: almost all are startup companies that benefit from Branson's entrepreneurial zeal and expertise; almost all sell to final consumers and are in sectors that offer opportunities for innovative approaches to differentiation.

The essence of such strategic-level linkages is the ability to apply similar strategies, resource allocation procedures, and control systems across the different businesses within the corporate portfolio.[41] Table 16.1 lists some of the strategic factors that determine similarities among businesses in relation to corporate management activities.

**TABLE 16.1** The determinants of strategic relatedness between businesses

| Corporate Management Tasks | Determinants of Strategic Similarity |
|---|---|
| Resource allocation | Similar sizes of capital investment projects |
| | Similar time spans of investment projects |
| | Similar sources of risk |
| | Similar general management skills required for business unit managers |
| Strategy formulation | Similar key success factors |
| | Similar stages of the industry life cycle |
| | Similar competitive positions occupied by each business within its industry |
| Performance management and control | Targets defined in terms of similar performance variables |
| | Similar time horizons for performance targets |

*Source:* R. M. Grant, "On Dominant Logic, Relatedness, and the Link Between Diversity and Performance," *Strategic Management Journal* 9 (1988): 641. Reproduced by permission of John Wiley & Sons, Inc.

Unlike operational relatedness, where the opportunities for exploiting economies of scope in joint inputs are comparatively easy to identify—even to quantify—strategic relatedness is more elusive. It necessitates an understanding of the overall strategic approach of the company and recognition of its corporate-level management capabilities.

Ultimately, the linkage between the different businesses within a company may depend upon the strategic rationale of the company. Prahalad and Bettis use the term *dominant logic* to refer to managers' cognition of the rationale that unifies the different parts of the company.[42] Such a common view of a company's identity and *raison d'être* is a critical precondition for effective integration across its different businesses. However, dominant logic needs to be underpinned by economic synergies. Otherwise an appealing dominant logic—such as Allegis Corporation's desire to meet travelers' needs by combining airlines and hotels or General Mills meeting "the needs and wants of the homemaker" by diversifying into toys, fashion clothing, specialty retailing, and restaurants—will fail to translate into real value creation.

## Summary

Diversification is like sex: its attractions are obvious, often irresistible. Yet, the experience is often disappointing. For top management it is a minefield. The diversification experiences of large corporations are littered with expensive mistakes: Exxon's attempt to build Exxon Office Systems as a rival to Xerox and IBM; Vivendi's diversification from water and environmental services into media, entertainment, and telecoms; Royal Bank of Scotland's quest to transform itself from a retail bank into a financial services giant. Despite so many costly failures, the urge to diversify continues to captivate senior managers. Part of the problem is the divergence between managerial and shareholder goals. While diversification has offered meager rewards to shareholders, it is the fastest route to building vast corporate empires. A further problem is hubris. A company's success in one line of business tends to result in the top management team becoming overconfident of its ability to achieve similar success in other businesses.

Nevertheless, for companies to survive and prosper over the long term they must change; inevitably this involves redefining the businesses in which they operate. The world's two largest IT companies—IBM and Hewlett-Packard—are both over six decades old. Their longevity is based on their ability to adapt their product lines to changing market opportunities. Essentially they have applied existing capabilities to developing new products which have provided new growth trajectories. Similarly with most other long established companies: for 3M, Canon, Samsung, and DuPont diversification has been central to the process of evolution. In most cases, this diversification was not a major discontinuity, but an initial incremental step in which existing resources and capabilities were deployed to exploit a perceived opportunity.

If companies are to use diversification as part of their long-term adaptation and avoid the many errors that corporate executives have made in the past, then better strategic analysis of diversification decisions is essential. The objectives of diversification need to be clear and explicit. Shareholder value creation has provided a demanding and illuminating criterion with which to appraise investment in new business opportunities. Rigorous analysis also counters the tendency for diversification to be a diversion— corporate escapism resulting from the unwillingness of top management to come to terms with difficult conditions within the core business.

The analytic tools at our disposal for evaluating diversification decisions have developed greatly in recent years. In the late 1980s, diversification decisions were based on vague concepts of synergy that involved identifying linkages between different industries. We are now able to be much more precise about the need for economies of scope in resources and capabilities *and* the economies of internalization that are prerequisites for diversification to create shareholder value. Recognizing the role of these economies of internalization has directed attention to the role of top management capabilities and effective corporate management systems in determining the success of diversification.

# Self-Study Questions

1   An ice cream manufacturer is proposing to acquire a soup manufacturer on the basis that, first, its sales and profits will be more seasonally balanced and, second, from year to year, sales and profits will be less affected by variations in weather. Will this risk spreading create value for shareholders? Under what circumstances could this acquisition create value for shareholders?

2   Tata Group is one of India's largest companies, employing 203 000 people in many different industries, including steel, motor vehicles, watches and jewelry, telecommunications, financial services, management consulting, food products, tea, chemicals and fertilizers, satellite TV, hotels, motor vehicles, energy, IT, and construction. Such diversity far exceeds that of any North American or Western European company. What are the conditions in India that might make such broad-based diversification both feasible and profitable?

3   Giorgio Armani SpA is an Italian private company owned mainly by the Armani family. Most of its clothing and accessories are produced and marketed by the company (some are manufactured by outside contractors). For other products, notably fragrances, cosmetics, and eyewear, Armani licenses its brand names to other companies. Armani is considering expanding into athletic clothing, hotels, and bridal shops. Advise Armani on whether these new businesses should be developed in-house, by joint ventures, or by licensing the Armani brands to specialist companies already within these fields.

4   General Electric, Berkshire Hathaway and Richard Branson's Virgin Group each comprise a wide range of different businesses that appear to have few close technical or customer linkages. Are these examples of unrelated diversification and do the corporate and ownership links within each of the groups result in the creation of any value? If so, what are the sources of this value creation?

## Appendix: Does Diversification Confer Market Power?

The potential for diversification to enhance profitability by increasing a firm's market power and suppressing competition has been a continuing interest for antitrust authorities in the U.S. and Europe—and more recently in Japan and South Korea. It has been claimed that large diversified companies can exercise market power through four mechanisms:

- *Predatory pricing*. Just as global corporations derive strength from their ability to finance competitive battles in individual markets through cross-subsidization, so multibusiness companies can use their size and diversity to discipline or even drive out specialized competitors in particular product markets through predatory pricing—cutting prices to below the level of rivals' costs. In 2003, following up complaints from AOL, the European Commission fined France Telecom 10 million euros for the predatory pricing of ISP services by its subsidiary, Wanadoo.[43]

- *Bundling*. A diversified firm can extend its monopoly in one market into a related market by bundling the two products together. The U.S. Justice Department claimed Microsoft abused its monopoly power in PC operating systems by bundling its Explorer web browser with Windows, thereby squeezing Netscape from the browser market. The E.U. made a similar case against Microsoft regarding its bundling of its media player with Windows.[44]

- *Reciprocal dealing*. A diversified company can leverage its market share across its businesses by reciprocal buying arrangements. These involve offers of the type: "I'll buy from you if you buy from me." A recent case involved Intel, which refused to supply microprocessors to Intergraph Corporation unless Intergraph licensed certain technology to Intel free of charge.[45] The potential for reciprocal dealing is greatest in those emerging market economies where a few large companies span many sectors.

- *Mutual forbearance*. Corwin Edwards argued that:

When one large conglomerate enterprise competes with another, the two are likely to encounter each other in a considerable number of markets. The multiplicity of their contacts may blunt the edge of their competition. A prospect of advantage in one market from vigorous competition may be weighed against the danger of retaliatory forays by the competitor in other markets. Each conglomerate may adopt a live-and-let-live policy designed to stabilize the whole structure of the competitive relationship.[46]

Game theory shows that such *multimarket competition* is likely to inhibit aggressive action in any one market for fear of triggering more generalized warfare.[47] Empirical evidence suggests that such behavior is most likely among companies that meet in multiple geographical markets for the same product or service—the airline industry, for example.[48] Such tendencies may also exist where diversified companies meet in multiple product markets.[49]

# Notes

1 A. D. Chandler Jr., *Strategy and Structure: Chapters in the History of the Industrial Enterprise* (Cambridge, MA: MIT Press, 1962); R. P. Rumelt, *Strategy, Structure and Economic Performance* (Cambridge, MA: Harvard University Press, 1974); H. Itami, T. Kagono, H. Yoshihara and S. Sakuma, "Diversification Strategies and Economic Performance," *Japanese Economic Studies* 11, no. 1 (1982): 78–110.

2 M. Goold and K. Luchs, "Why Diversify? Four Decades of Management Thinking," *Academy of Management Executive* 7, no. 3 (August, 1993): 7–25.

3 G. F. Davis, K. A. Diekman and C. F. Tinsley, "The Decline and Fall of the Conglomerate Firm in the 1980s: A Study in the De-Institutionalization of an Organizational Form," *American Sociological Review* 49 (1994): 547–70.

4 R. E. Hoskisson and M. A. Hitt, *Downscoping: How to Tame the Diversified Firm* (New York: Oxford University Press, 1994).

5 A. Shleifer and R. W. Vishny, "The Takeover Wave of the 1980s," *Science* 248 (July–September 1990): 747–9.

6 L. G. Franko, "The Death of Diversification: The Focusing of the World's Industrial Firms, 1980–2000," *Business Horizons* (July–August, 2004): 41–50.

7 During 2004-6 CEO turnover reached an all-time high. See Booz Allen Hamilton, "CEO Succession 2006: The Era of the Inclusive Leader," *strategy+business* (Summer 2007): www.strategy-business.com.

8 B. Burrough, *Barbarians at the Gate: The Fall of RJR Nabisco* (New York: Harper & Row, 1990).

9 L. Laeven and R. Levine, "Is there a Diversification Discount in Financial Conglomerates?" *Journal of Financial Economics* 82 (2006): 331–367.

10 T. Khanna and K. Palepu, "Why Focused Strategies May Be Wrong for Emerging Markets," *Harvard Business Review* (July–August, 1997): 41–51; D. Kim, D. Kandemir and S. T. Cavusgil, "The Role of Family Conglomerates in Emerging Markets," *Thunderbird International Business Review* 46 (January, 2004): 7–20.

11 See any standard corporate finance text, for example R. A. Brealey, S. Myers and F. Allen, *Principles of Corporate Finance*, 8th edn (McGraw-Hill, 2006): Chapter 8.

12 See, for example, H. Levy and M. Sarnat, "Diversification, Portfolio Analysis and the Uneasy Case for Conglomerate Mergers," *Journal of Finance* 25 (1970): 795–802; R. H. Mason and M. B. Goudzwaard, "Performance of Conglomerate Firms: A Portfolio Approach," *Journal of Finance* 31 (1976): 39–48; J. F. Weston, K. V. Smith and R. E. Shrieves, "Conglomerate Performance Using the Capital Asset Pricing Model," *Review of Economics and Statistics* 54 (1972): 357–63.

13 M. Lubatkin and S. Chetterjee, "Extending Modern Portfolio Theory into the Domain of Corporate Strategy: Does It Apply?" *Academy of Management Journal* 37 (1994): 109–36.

14 The reduction in risk that bondholders derive from diversification is termed the *coinsurance effect*. See: L. W. Lee, "Coinsurance and the Conglomerate Merger," *Journal of Finance* 32 (1977): 1527–37.

15 S. M. Bartram, "Corporate Risk Management as a Lever for Shareholder Value Creation," *Financial Markets, Institutions and Instruments* 9 (2000): 279–324.

16 M. E. Porter, "From Competitive Advantage to Corporate Strategy," *Harvard Business Review* (May–June 1987): 46.

17 M. Hayward and D. C. Hambrick, "Explaining the Premiums Paid for Large Acquisitions," *Administrative Science Quarterly* 42 (1997): 103–27.

18 A study of 68 diversifying ventures by established companies found that, on average, breakeven was not attained until the seventh and eighth years of operation: R. Biggadike, "The Risky Business of Diversification," *Harvard Business Review* (May–June, 1979): 103–111.

19 Ken Lewis and John Thain, "Creating the Premier Financial Services Company in the World," A joint Bank of America and Merrill Lynch Presentation, September 15, 2008.

20 The formal definition of economies of scope is in terms of "subadditivity." Economies of scope exist in the production of goods $x_1, x_2, \ldots, xn$, if $C(X) < \Re i C i(xi)$ where: $X = \Re i(xi)$

$C(X)$ is the cost of producing all $n$ goods within a single firm

$\Re i C i(xi)$ is the cost of producing the goods in $n$ specialized firms.

See W. J. Baumol, J. C. Panzar and R. D. Willig, *Contestable Markets and the Theory of Industry Structure* (New York: Harcourt Brace Jovanovich, 1982): 71–2.

21 Economies of scope can arise in consumption as well as in production: customers may prefer to buy different products from the same supplier. See T. Cottrell and B. R. Nault, "Product Variety and Firm Survival in Microcomputer Software," *Strategic Management Journal* 25 (2004): 1005–26.

22 There is some evidence to the contrary. See H. Park, T. A. Kruse, K. Suzuki and K. Park, "Long-term Performance Following Mergers of Japanese Companies: The Effect of Diversification and Affiliation," *Pacific Basin Finance Journal* 14 (2006); and P. R. Nayyar, "Performance Effects of Information Asymmetry and Economies of Scope in Diversified Service Firms," *Academy of Management Journal* 36 (1993): 28–57.

23 The role of capabilities in diversification is discussed in C. C. Markides and P. J. Williamson, "Related Diversification, Core Competencies and Corporate

Performance," *Strategic Management Journal* 15 (Special Issue, 1994): 149–65.

24 This issue is examined more fully in D. J. Teece, "Towards an Economic Theory of the Multiproduct Firm," *Journal of Economic Behavior and Organization* 3 (1982): 39–63.

25 M. Goold, A. Campbell and M. Alexander, *Corporate-Level Strategy: Creating Value in the Multibusiness Company* (New York: John Wiley & Sons, Inc., 1994).

26 J. P. Liebeskind, "Internal Capital Markets: Benefits, Costs and Organizational Arrangements," *Organization Science* 11 (2000): 58–76.

27 D. Scharfstein and J. Stein, "The Dark Side of Internal Capital Markets: Divisional Rent Seeking and Inefficient Investment," *Journal of Finance* 55 (2000): 2537–64; V. Maksimovic and G. Phillips, "Do Conglomerate Firms Allocate Resources Inefficiently Across Industries?" *Journal of Finance* 57 (2002): 721–67; R. Rajan, H. Servaes and L. Zingales, "The Cost of Diversity: The Diversification Discount and Inefficient Investment," *Journal of Finance* 55 (2000): 35–84.

28 C. Kaye and J. Yuwono, "Conglomerate Discount or Premium? How Some Diversified Companies Create Exceptional Value," Marakon Associates (2003). www.marakon.com/.

29 R. M. Grant, A. P. Jammine and H. Thomas, "Diversity, Diversification and Performance in British Manufacturing Industry," *Academy of Management Journal* 31 (1988): 771–801.

30 L. E. Palich, L. B. Cardinal and C. C. Miller, "Curvi-linearity in the Diversification-Performance Linkage: An Examination of over Three Decades of Research," *Strategic Management Journal* 22 (2000): 155–74.

31 N. Harper and S. P. Viguerie, "Are You Too Focused?" *McKinsey Quarterly* (2002 Special Edition): 29–37.

32 J. D. Martin and A. Sayrak, "Corporate Diversification and Shareholder Value: A Survey of Recent Literature," *Journal of Corporate Finance* 9 (2003): 37–57.

33 C. C. Markides, "Consequences of Corporate Refocusing: Ex Ante Evidence," *Academy of Management Journal* 35 (1992): 398-412; C. C. Markides, "Diversification, Restructuring and Economic Performance," *Strategic Management Journal* 16 (1995): 101–18.

34 R. P. Rumelt, *Strategy, Structure and Economic Performance* (Cambridge, MA: Harvard University Press, 1974).

35 T. Peters and R. Waterman, *In Search of Excellence* (New York: Harper & Row, 1982): 294.

36 Ibid.

37 H. K. Christensen and C. A. Montgomery, "Corporate Economic Performance: Diversification Strategy versus Market Structure," *Strategic Management Journal* 2 (1981): 327-43; R. A. Bettis, "Performance Differences in Related and Unrelated Diversified Firms," *Strategic Management Journal* 2 (1981): 379–83.

38 See, for example, A. Michel and I. Shaked, "Does Business Diversification Affect Performance?" *Financial Management* 13, no. 4 (1984): 18–24; G. A. Luffman and R. Reed, *The Strategy and Performance of British Industry, 1970-80* (London: Macmillan, 1984).

39 C. Park, "The Effects of Prior Performance on the Choice between Related and Unrelated Acquisitions," *Journal of Management Studies* 39 (2002): 1003–19.

40 For a discussion of relatedness in diversification, see J. Robins and M. F. Wiersema, "A Resource-Based Approach to the Multibusiness Firm: Empirical Analysis of Portfolio Interrelationships and Corporate Financial Performance," *Strategic Management Journal* 16 (1995): 277–300; J. Robins and M. F. Wiersema, "The Measurement of Corporate Portfolio Strategy: Analysis of the Content Validity of Related Diversification Indexes," *Strategic Management Journal* 24 (2002): 39–59.

41 R. M. Grant, "On Dominant Logic, Relatedness, and the Link Between Diversity and Performance," *Strategic Management Journal* 9 (1988): 639–42.

42 C. K. Prahalad and R. A. Bettis, "The Dominant Logic: A New Linkage Between Diversity and Performance," *Strategic Management Journal* 7 (1986): 485–502.

43 "Wanadoo Fined £10m for Predatory Pricing," *Financial Times* (July 17, 2003).

44 "Microsoft on Trial," *Economist* (April 28, 2006) (www.economist.com).

45 E. D. Cavanagh, "Reciprocal Dealing: A Rebirth?" *St. Johns Law Review* 75 (2001): 633–47.

46 US Senate, Subcommittee on Antitrust and Monopoly Hearings, *Economic Concentration*, Part 1, Congress, 1st session (1965): 45.

47 B. D. Bernheim and M. D. Whinston, "Multimarket Contact and Collusive Behavior," *Rand Journal of Economics* 2 (1990): 1–26.

48 In the U.S. airline industry, extensive multimarket contact resulted in a reluctance to compete on routes dominated by one or other of the airlines. See J. A. C. Baum and H. J. Korn, "Competitive Dynamics of Interfirm Rivalry," *Academy of Management Review* 39 (1996): 255–91.

49 S. Jayachandran, J. Gimeno, and P. R. Varadarajan, "The Theory of Multimarket Competition: A Synthesis and Implications for Marketing Strategy," *Journal of Marketing* 63 (July 1999): 49–66.

# 17 Implementing Corporate Strategy: Managing the Multibusiness Firm

*Some have argued that single-product businesses have a focus that gives them an advantage over multibusiness companies like our own—and perhaps they would have, but only if we neglect our own overriding advantage: the ability to share the ideas that are the result of wide and rich input from a multitude of global sources.*

*GE businesses share technology, design, compensation and personnel evaluation systems, manufacturing practices, and customer and country knowledge. Gas Turbines shares manufacturing technology with Aircraft Engines; Motors and Transportation Systems work together on new propulsion systems; Lighting and Medical Systems collaborate to improve x-ray tube processes; and GE Capital provides innovative financing packages that help all our businesses around the globe. Supporting all this is a management system that fosters and rewards this sharing and teamwork, and, increasingly, a culture that makes it reflexive and natural at every level and corner of our Company.*

—JACK WELCH, CHAIRMAN, GENERAL ELECTRIC COMPANY, 1981–2001

# Introduction and Objectives

In the last chapter, I concluded that the case for diversification depends on whether the diversified company can create value by operating across multiple businesses. Chapters 14 and 15 arrived at the same conclusion in relation to vertical integration and multinational operations. Having determined the potential for vertical integration, international expansion, or diversification to create value, the challenge is managing the company to exploit these sources of value. Implementing corporate strategy requires answering the following questions: How should the multibusiness corporation be structured? Through what systems and tools should management exercise control and coordination? What roles do the chief executive and top management team need to fulfill and what styles of leadership are likely to be most effective? Answering these questions requires that we look closely at the activities of the corporate head office and its relationships with the various businesses.

In this chapter we begin by addressing the problem of corporate governance in the large, multibusiness corporation and then go on to examine the main activities through which corporate management creates value, namely: managing the business portfolio, managing individual businesses, managing linkages between businesses, and leading change. We then assess the role of external strategies—mergers, acquisitions and alliances—in developing the corporation.

By the time you have completed this chapter you will be able to:

◆ appreciate the governance issues that impact the work of managers within the large corporation;

◆ recognize the principal organizational features of the multibusiness corporation;

◆ apply the techniques of portfolio analysis to corporate strategy decisions;

◆ understand how corporate headquarters manages its individual businesses through strategic planning and financial control and by managing linkages across businesses;

◆ analyze the fit between a firm's corporate strategy, organization structure, management systems, and leadership style;

◆ analyze the potential for value creation through restructuring a multibusiness corporation;

◆ identify the circumstances in which mergers and acquisitions can create value for a company—and be aware of their pitfalls.

## Governance and the Structure of the Multibusiness Corporation

Chapter 1 introduced the distinction between business strategy and corporate strategy and observed that, within the multibusiness company,[1] corporate management takes primary responsibility for corporate strategy, and business-level management takes primary responsibility for business strategy. This distinction is the key management feature of the multibusiness corporation irrespective of whether the individual businesses are defined vertically (ExxonMobil), geographically (SABMiller), or by product (3M). In these *multidivisional* companies business decisions are located at the business level and the corporate center exercises overall coordination and control. While the multidivisional structure is the dominant organizational form for multibusiness companies, many multibusiness private companies are organized as holding companies (see Strategy Capsule 17.1).

## STRATEGY CAPSULE 17.1

# Alternatives to the Divisional Structure: the Holding Company

Despite the success of the multidivisional structure—especially in the U.S.—it is important to recognize that there are many multibusiness companies that have organizational and governance structures quite different from that of the divisionalized firm. By far the most common is the *holding company*. A holding company is a company that owns a controlling interest in a number of subsidiary companies. The term "holding company" is used to refer both to the parent company and to the group as a whole.

A holding company exercises control over the subsidiary through appointing its board of directors. The individual subsidiaries typically retain high levels of strategic and operational autonomy. A distinctive difference between a holding company and a divisionalized company is in financial integration. A divisionalized company almost always has a centralized treasury that manages cash holdings and hedges foreign exchange for the group as a whole; profits accrue to the corporate head office and operating funds and capital budgets are allocated by head quarters to the divisions. In the holding company each subsidiary manages is a separate financial entity. The parent company provides equity and debt capital to the subsidiary and receives dividends from the subsidiary.

Although the potential for exploiting synergies between businesses is more limited in the holding company than the divisionalized corporation, the holding company structure has important advantages for large family-owned companies. The attractiveness of holding companies is that they allow family dynasties to retain ownership and control of business empires that diversify family wealth across multiple sectors. At the same time their decentralization allows effective management of the group without the need for the parent company to develop tremendous depth of management capability.

Thus, Tata Group—India's biggest business concern with over $60 billion in revenue and over 330 000 employees—is controlled by the Tata family through Tata Sons Ltd., parent company of the group. Among the several hundred subsidiaries, several are leading companies within their industries—including Tata Steel, Tata Motors (owner of Jaguar and Land Rover), Tata Tea (owner of the Tetley brand), and Tata Consulting Services. Twenty-seven Tata companies are publicly listed.

Holding companies are common elsewhere in Asia—including the traditional Japanese *zaibatsu* (Mitsubishi and Mitsui), the Korean *chaebols* (Samsung and Hyundai), and the Hong Kong trading houses (Swire Group, Jardine Matteson and Hutchison Wampoa). In the U.S., bank holding companies are companies that own several banks. Because each bank must be separately regulated and have its own financial reserves, the holding company provides common ownership and control, but not the level of integration that exists within the typical divisionalized corporation.

By allowing the corporate headquarters to specialize in managing corporate issues and divisional units to specialize in managing the individual businesses, the multidivisional structure uses the principles of *modularity* to reconcile integration with decentralized responsiveness (see Chapter 7). However, separating corporate managers from divisional managers and managers from owners gives rise to problems of goal alignment—what referred to as the *agency problem* (see Chapter 7). The stream of corporate scandals of the past nine years—from Enron, WorldCom and Parmalat through to Lehman Brothers, AIG, and the Royal Bank of Scotland—involving acquisitive CEOs presiding over massive destruction of shareholder value raise critical issues over the efficacy of *corporate governance*—the system through which companies are directed and controlled.

## The Theory of the M-form

While Alfred Chandler identified the invention and diffusion of the multidivisional form as critical to the development of the modern corporation (see Chapter 14), Oliver Williamson provided its theoretical rationale.[2] Williamson identified four key efficiency advantages of the divisionalized firm (or, in his terminology, the *M-form*):

- *Adaptation to "bounded rationality."* If managers are limited in their cognitive, information-processing, and decision-making capabilities, the top management team cannot be responsible for all coordination and decision making within a complex organization. The M-form permits decision making to be dispersed.
- *Allocation of decision making.* Decision-making responsibilities should be separated according to the frequency with which different types of decisions are made. The M-form allows high frequency decisions (such as operating decisions) to be made at divisional level and decisions that are made infrequently (such as strategic decisions) to be made at corporate level.
- *Minimizing coordination costs.* In the functional organization, decisions concerning a particular product or business area must pass up to the top of the company where all the relevant information and expertise can be brought to bear. In the divisionalized firm, so long as close coordination between different business areas is not necessary, most decisions concerning a particular business can be made at the divisional level. This eases the information and decision-making burden on top management.
- *Avoiding goal conflict.* In functional organizations, department heads emphasize functional goals over those of the organization as a whole. In multidivisional companies, divisional heads, as general managers, are more likely to pursue profit goals that are consistent with the goals of the company as a whole.

As a result, Williamson believed that the multidivisional form provided a solution to two central problems of corporate governance:

- *Allocation of resources.* Resource allocation within any administrative structure is a political process in which power, status, and influence can triumph over purely commercial considerations.[3] To the extent that the multidivisional company can create a competitive internal capital market in which capital is allocated according to financial and strategic criteria, it can avoid much of the politicization inherent in purely hierarchical systems. The multidivisional company does this through operating an internal capital market where budgets are linked to past and projected divisional profitability, and individual projects are subject to a standardized appraisal process.

- *Resolution of agency problems.* The basic agency problem is that owners (shareholders) desire maximization of the value of the firm, while their agents (managers) are more interested in salaries, security and power. Given the limited power of shareholders to discipline and replace managers and the weakness of boards to control management, the corporate head office of multidivisional firm can act as an interface between shareholders and the divisional managers and enforce adherence to profit goals. With divisions designated as profit centers, financial performance can readily be monitored by the head office and divisional managers can be held responsible for performance failures. According to Williamson, multibusiness companies can be more effective profit maximizers than specialist companies because of two critical advantages of the corporate head office over the board of directors of a single business company: first, the corporate head office has better access to information about the business, second, it is easier for a corporate head office to replace business managers than it is for a board of directors.[4] At General Electric, ExxonMobil, and PepsiCo, this capacity for corporate headquarters to create strongly profit-oriented systems is particularly evident.

## The Challenge of Corporate Governance

Is Williamson right that the corporate head office can be relied upon to act as an "agent of the stockholders whose purpose is to monitor the operations of the constituent parts"? Among diversified firms, it seems that multidivisional structures are more conducive to profitability than alternative structural forms,[5] yet it is also clear that multidivisional structures are no safeguard against agency problems. The most notorious examples of chief executives operating their companies as personal fiefdoms are found among divisionalized, multibusiness corporations—Howard Hughes at Hughes Corporation, Ken Lay at Enron, Dennis Kozlowski at Tyco, Jean-Marie Messier at Vivendi Universal and Fred Goodwin at Royal Bank of Scotland. While the CEOs of diversified companies may avoid emotional commitment to particular businesses, this does not mean that they are more predisposed to share-holder return over the quest for Napoleonic personal grandeur.

Top management's pursuit of personal goals related to the aggrandizement of wealth, power, influence, and status in preference to owners' goals of value maximization are primarily a problem for public companies.[6] The critical problem is that the ability of shareholders to exercise effective control over management is limited by their large number. This creates, first, a coordination problem and, second, an incentive problem—if each shareholder owns only a small fraction of a company and if that company's shares only account for a small fraction of the shareholder's total wealth, then the costs of active engagement are high relative to the likely returns. Disgruntled shareholders typically sell their shares rather than oppose the incumbent management team.

Yet, even in the face of widespread shareholder apathy, the mechanisms and rules through which public companies are governed—in particular the rights accorded to shareholders and the responsibilities applied to companies' boards of directors—reinforce the power of owners relative to that of managers.

*Rights of Shareholders* Company law relating to the rights of shareholders typically covers shareholders' rights to sell their shares, their rights to company information (including access to audited financial statements), their rights to elect and remove members of the board of directors, and their right to share in the profits of the company.

Although seemingly straightforward, these rights are often abrogated by companies. For example, managers are more likely than shareholders to oppose takeover by another company—while shareholders benefit financially, senior executives often lose their jobs. Hence, companies frequently create impediments to hostile takeover either in the form of special voting rights for certain classes of share or "poison pill" defenses. Yahoo! defended against a 2008 takeover bid from Microsoft through a provision that any hostile bid would trigger the creation of a rights issue to existing shareholders. To resist takeover by Mittal Steel, Arcelor attempted to make itself indigestible by arranging a merger with Russian steel giant Severstal.

Managers desire to manipulate their companies' share prices has resulted in misreporting their financial results. Financial misreporting was at the center of the scandals that engulfed Enron and WorldCom in the U.S. and Parmalat and Royal Ahold in Europe.[7] New standards of financial reporting include America's Sarbanes Oxley Act.

The Board of Directors, according to *OECD Principles of Corporate Governance*, has the responsibility to: "...ensure the strategic guidance of the company, the effective monitoring of management by the board, and the board's accountability to the company and the shareholders."[8] This requires that:

- Board members act in good faith, with due diligence and care, in the best interest of the company and its shareholders.
- Board members review and guide corporate strategy, major plans of action, risk policy, annual budgets and business plans; set and monitor performance objectives; and oversee major capital expenditures; select, monitor, and compensate key executives; ensure the integrity of the corporation's accounting and financial reporting systems; and oversee the process of disclosure and communication.

The ability of the board to achieve these goals has been compromised by key impediments:

- The dominance of the board by executive directors—in both the U.S. and U.K. and some other countries, the top management team (the CEO, CFO and other senior executives) are likely to be board members.
- Combining the roles of board chair and CEO—this is common in the U.S., less so in most European companies. United States opinion suggests that splitting board chair and CEO roles is neither an advantage nor disadvantage—it depends entirely upon the attributes of the person doing

the job.[9] However, interlocking boards—where CEOs serve as independent members on one another's boards—does appear to be an unambiguous constraint on board independence.

The harshest criticisms of board oversight have been in relation to management compensation. The escalation of CEO compensation among large public companies since the early 1990s has been little short of staggering. The paradox is that the massive payouts to CEOs have been the result of compensation systems designed to align management goals with those of shareholders—especially through the grant of stock options and emphasis on performance-related bonuses. Yet, some of the biggest executive payouts have been by companies that have experienced shareholder returns that have ranged from indifferent to disastrous (see Table 17.1). Performance bonuses and options packages have been extended down corporate hierarchies to include middle managers as well as the top management team. In the U.K., salary comprised 54% of overall executive compensation as compared with bonuses 24%, and options and long-term incentive plans 22%.[10] Aspects of the poor alignment between executive compensation and shareholder value creation include linking bonuses to short term performance, a failure to correct for overall stockmarket movements, and incentives for creating shareholder value not being matched by penalties for its destruction.[11]

In short, there is little evidence to support Williamson's claim that the large multidivisional firm is a successful solution to the agency problem. While corporate CEOs may be able to avoid the distortions of judgment that result from emotional commitment to a particular business, the evidence suggest that they are far more prone to the delusions associated with hubris and the quest for power, influence and status.

## Other Problems of Divisionalized Firms

Multidivisional structures may also suffer from other problems. In principle, the divisionalized corporation reconciles decentralization with coordination through

**TABLE 17.1** Highest earning CEOs of U.S. companies 2003–7

| CEO | Company | Total 5-year compensation (million $) |
|---|---|---|
| Steve Jobs | Apple | 662 |
| Ray Irani | Occidental Petroleum | 550 |
| Barry Diller | IAC/InterActive Corp. | 462 |
| Larry Ellison | Oracle | 429 |
| Angelo Mozilo | Countrywide Financial | 392 |
| Richard Fairbank | Capital One Financial | 380 |
| Richard Fuld | Lehman Brothers Holdings | 354 |
| Lew Frankfort | Coach | 254 |
| John Chambers | Cisco Systems | 229 |
| Bob Simpson | XTO Energy | 215 |

*Source:*
"Special Report: CEO Compensation," *Fortune* (April 30, 2008).

embracing the principles of modularity (see Chapter 7). Yet, according to Henry Mintzberg, the multidivisional structure suffers from two key rigidities:[12]

- *Constraints on decentralization.* Although operational authority in the M-form firm is dispersed to the divisional level, the individual divisions often feature highly centralized power that arises from divisional presidents' personal accountability to the head office. In addition, the operational freedom of the divisional management exists only so long as the corporate head office is satisfied with divisional performance. As we have seen in the recent financial crisis, divisional underperformance typically results in a speedy end to divisional autonomy as the corporate head office intervenes.
- *Standardization of divisional management.* In principle, each division can adapt itself to the requirements of its business sector. In practice, there are powerful forces for standardizing control systems and management styles across the multidivisional corporation. The imposition by Exxon of its standard financial control systems and hierarchical management style on its IT subsidiary, Exxon Office Systems, was a key factor in the venture's eventual failure. The difficulties that many large, mature corporations experience with new business development often result from applying to new businesses the same management systems designed for existing businesses.[13]

## The Role of Corporate Management

For the multibusiness corporation to be viable, the benefits from bringing businesses under common ownership and control must exceed the costs of the corporate overlay. Indeed, Goold, Campbell and Alexander go further. They propose a tougher hurdle for multibusiness companies: for each and every business within the corporate portfolio, not only must the additional profit from inclusion within the corporate fold exceed the cost of headquarters management, but the net gain should be bigger than that which any other potential corporate parent can offer.[14] (Otherwise it would be profitable to sell the business.) This notion of "parenting advantage"—that a company must be able to add more value to a business than rivals could—raises important issues concerning how multibusiness corporations create value and the tools needed to do so.

We shall focus on four activities through which corporate management adds value within the multibusiness company:

- managing the overall corporate portfolio, including acquisitions, divestments, and resource allocation;
- managing each individual business;
- managing linkages among businesses;
- managing change.

Let us consider each of these activities and establish the conditions under which they create value.

## Managing the Corporate Portfolio

The basic questions of corporate strategy are "what businesses should we be in?" and "how should we manage these business in order to generate as much value from them as possible?" *Portfolio planning models* can assist help managers with both of these questions.

### General Electric and the Development of Strategic Planning

Portfolio planning techniques were one outcome of the pioneering work in corporate strategy initiated by General Electric at the end of the 1960s.[15] GE comprised 46 divisions and over 190 businesses. To manage this sprawling industrial empire more effectively, GE launched a series of initiatives together with Boston Consulting Group, McKinsey & Company, Arthur D. Little, and Harvard Business School. The result was three key developments in strategic management at the corporate level. The first was the identification of *strategic business units (SBUs)*–businesses that were sufficiently self-contained to formulate a separate competitive strategy.[16] The other two were *portfolio planning models* and the *PIMS database,* which we discuss below.

### Portfolio Planning: The GE/McKinsey Matrix

The basic idea of a portfolio planning model is to represent graphically the individual businesses of a multibusiness company in terms of key strategic variables that determine their potential for profit. These strategic variables typically relate to the attractiveness of their market and their competitive advantage within that market. This analysis can guide:

- allocating resources between the businesses on the basis of each business's market attractiveness and competitive position;
- formulating business unit strategy—by comparing the strategic positioning of different businesses opportunities for repositioning (including divestment) can be identified.
- analyzing portfolio balance—a single display of all the company's businesses permits assessment of the overall balance of the portfolio in terms of *cash flow generation* and *growth prospects*;
- setting performance targets on the basis of each business's market attractiveness and its competitive position.

In the GE/McKinsey matrix (see Figure 17.1) the industry attractiveness axis combines market size, market growth rate, market profitability (return on sales over three years), cyclicality, "inflation recovery" (potential to increase productivity and product prices), and international potential (ratio of foreign to domestic sales). Business unit competitive advantage combines: market share, return on sales relative to competitors, and relative position with regard to quality, technology, manufacturing, distribution, marketing, and cost.[17] The strategy implications are shown by three regions of Figure 17.1.

**FIGURE 17.1**  The GE/McKinsey portfolio planning matrix

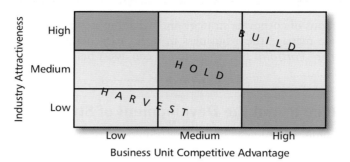

## Portfolio Planning: BCG's Growth-Share Matrix

The Boston Consulting Group's *growth-share matrix* also uses industry attractiveness and competitive position to compare the strategic positions of different businesses. However, it uses a single indicator as a proxy for each of these dimensions: industry attractiveness is measured by *rate of market growth*, competitive advantage by *relative market share* (the business unit's market share relative to that of its largest competitor). The four quadrants of the BCG matrix predict patterns of profits and cash flow and indicate strategies to be adopted (see Figure 17.2).[18]

The simplicity of BCG matrix is both its limitation and its usefulness. It can be prepared very easily and offers a clear picture of a firm's business portfolio in relation to some important strategic characteristics. Moreover, the analysis is versatile—it can be applied to business units and to the positioning of different

**FIGURE 17.2**  The BCG growth-share matrix

| | | | | |
|---|---|---|---|---|
| Earnings: | low, unstable, growing | | Earnings: | high, stable, growing |
| Cash flow: | negative | | Cash flow: | neutral |
| Strategy: | analyze to determine whether business can be grown into a star or will degenerate into a dog | | Strategy: | invest for growth |
| Earnings: | low, unstable | | Earnings: | high, stable |
| Cash flow: | neutral or negative | | Cash flow: | high, stable |
| Strategy: | divest | | Strategy: | milk |

Annual Real Rate of Market Growth (%) — HIGH / LOW

Relative Market Share — LOW / HIGH

products, brands, distribution channels and customers. Though simplistic, it can be useful as a preliminary view before embarking upon a more detailed and rigorous analysis.

However, the simplistic approach of both the BCG and McKinsey business portfolio matrices has resulted in both losing their popularity as analytic tools. Apart from their simplistic approaches to the determinants of industry attractiveness and competitive advantage, there are problems relating to market definition. For example, in the BCG matrix, is BMW's auto business a "dog" because it holds less than 2% of the world auto market, or a cash cow because it is market leader in the luxury car segment? An even greater problem is the implicit assumption that every business in the portfolio is independent—a direct denial of the basic rational for the multibusiness corporation: the synergistic linkages between businesses.[19]

## Portfolio Planning: The Ashridge Portfolio Display

The Ashridge Portfolio Display is based upon Goold, Campbell and Alexander's *parenting advantage* framework.[20] It takes account of the fact that the value creating potential of a business within a company's business portfolio depends not just upon the characteristics of the business (as assumed by the McKinsey and BCG matrices) but also on the characteristics of the parent. The focus, therefore, is on the *fit* between a business and its parent company. The horizontal axis of Figure 17.3 shows the parent's potential for creating additional profit within the business, for example, from applying corporate-level management capabilities to the business, from sharing resources and capabilities with other businesses, from economizing on transaction costs, and so on. The vertical axis measures the potential for value destruction by the

**FIGURE 17.3**  Ashridge portfolio display: the potential for patenting advantage

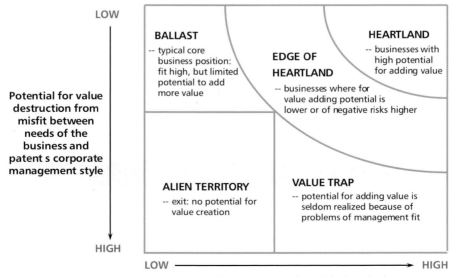

*Source:* Ashridge Strategic Management Centre.

**FIGURE 17.4** Ashridge portfolio display applied to a diversified leisure company

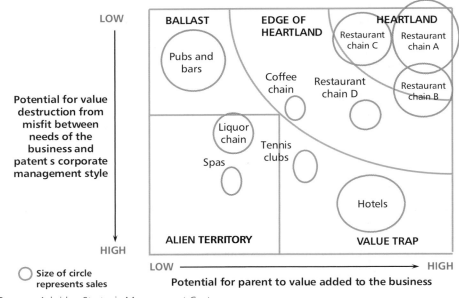

*Source:* Ashridge Strategic Management Centre.

parent—these result both from the costs of corporate overhead and mismatch between the management needs of the business and the management systems and style of the parent. These might include bureaucratic rigidity, incompatibility with top management mindset, politicization of decision making and risks of inappropriate strategic guidance. Figure 17.4 applies the framework to position the businesses of a diversified hospitality company.

The need for assessment of complex issues of fit between the business and the parent and the fact that these assessments inevitably require subjective judgments mean that the Ashridge Display is more difficult to use than GE/McKinsey or BCG matrices. However, this is the reality of the subject matter: creating value from the configuration and reconfiguration of a portfolio of business involves complex issues of fit that requires insight into the fundamental strategic characteristics of the businesses and the nature of corporate management systems and style.

## Managing Individual Businesses

Some of the most important opportunities for corporate headquarters to create value arise from its ability to improve the strategic and operational management of its businesses—what Goold, Campbell, and Alexander call "standalone influence." This influence is exercised through the corporate parent's ability to:

> . . . appoint the general manager of each business and influence management development and succession planning within the businesses. It can approve or reject budgets, strategic plans, and capital expenditure proposals and it can

influence the shape and implementation of these plans and proposals. It can provide advice and policy guidance to the businesses. The parent also influences the businesses by the hints and pressures passed on through both formal and informal line management meetings and contacts, and, more indirectly, through the corporate culture.[21]

The mechanisms through which the corporate headquarters exercises control over individual businesses can be divided into two types. Corporate management can control decisions, through requiring that certain decisions—typically those involving significant resource commitments— are referred upward for corporate approval. For example, the corporate HQ might require that capital expenditure requests that exceed $5 million are approved by the executive committee. Alternatively, corporate management can control businesses through setting and monitoring performance targets, backed by incentives and penalties to motivate their attainment. The distinction is between *input* and *output* control: the company can control the inputs into strategy (the decisions) or the output from strategy (the performance). Although most companies use a combination of input and output controls, there is an unavoidable tradeoff between the two: more of one implies less of the other. If the corporate HQ micromanages divisional decisions, it must accept the performance outcomes that result. If the corporate HQ imposes rigorous performance targets, it must give divisional managers the freedom to make the decisions necessary to achieve those targets.

## The Strategic Planning System

In Chapter 1, I identified corporate strategy as being set at the corporate level and business strategy as set at the business level. In reality, business strategies are formulated jointly by corporate and divisional managers. In most diversified, divisionalized companies, business strategies are initiated by divisional managers and the role of corporate managers is to probe, appraise, amend and approve divisional strategy proposals. The challenge for corporate management is to create a strategy-making process that reconciles the decentralized decision making essential to fostering flexibility, responsiveness, and a sense of ownership at the business level, with the ability of the corporate level to bring to bear its knowledge, perspective, and responsibility for the shareholder interest. Achieving an optimal blend of business-level initiative and corporate-level guidance and discipline is a difficult challenge for the multibusiness corporation. Common to the success of General Electric, ExxonMobil, Samsung, and Unilever is a system of strategic management that has managed this difficult tradeoff between business initiative and corporate control. Strategy Capsule 17.2 describes key elements of the strategic planning process at Exxon.

*Rethinking the Strategic Planning System*   Since the early 1980s, the strategic planning systems of large firms have been bombarded by criticism from academics and consultants. Two features of corporate strategic planning systems have attracted particular scorn:

- *Strategic planning systems don't make strategy.* Ever since Henry Mintzberg attacked the "rational design" school of strategy (see Chapter 1), strategic planning systems have been castigated as ineffective for formulating strategy.

## STRATEGY CAPSULE 17.2

# Strategic Planning at Exxon

Exxon (now ExxonMobil) is the world's biggest company (in terms of revenue and market value) and is the most financially successful oil and gas major. Exxon's strategic planning system has successfully reconciled long-term strategic planning with rigorous, short-term financial control; and strong centralized direction with flexible, responsive, business-level decision making. Exxon's strate-gic planning process follows an annual cycle that is similar to the "generic" strategic planning process outlined in Chapter 6 (see Figure 6.6).

The principal stages of the planning cycle are as follows:

1  *Economic review and energy review* are forecasts of the economy and energy markets prepared in spring by the corporate planning department to provide a basis for strategic planning.

2  *Business plans* are developed during the spring and summer by individual businesses and are aggregated and refined at the divisional level. Their time horizon is ten years for upstream, five years for downstream and chemicals. Prior to discussion, negotiation, and approval by the management committee, the plans are discussed with each division's contact director and evaluated by the corporate planning department (during October).

3  *The corporate plan* results from the aggregation of individual business plans. The approved business and corporate plans then provide the basis for the financial and performance plans (formulated during November).

4  *The financial forecast* comprises forecasts of revenues, operating costs, capital expenditures, interest and other expenses, income, and cash flow for divisions and for the company as a whole over a two-year period.

5  *The operating and capital budgets* are set for the upcoming year (the first year of the plans).

6  *The stewardship basis* comprises annual targets against which the next year's performance by each division will be judged. They include financial objectives, operating targets, safety and environmental objectives and strategy mileposts.

7  *Stewardship reviews*. In February of each year, each division's performance for the previous year is evaluated against its stewardship objectives. These reviews involve presentations by the divisional top management to the management committee.

8  *Investment reappraisals* occur in August and September and involve the divisions reporting back on the outcomes of specific investment projects.

In addition to this annual strategic planning cycle, *Strategic Studies* are *ad hoc* projects by the corporate planning department that address specific issues such as country and product studies and responses to major market, techn-ological, and political changes.

Exxon's strategic management system features clearly defined corporate, divisional, and business unit responsibilities (with matching accountability). At the same time there is close communication and coordination between these levels. This takes place formally through the strategic planning and financial control system and informally through ongoing communication between the management committee (composed of Exxon's executive board members) and the divisional presidents and their management teams. Each member of the management committee is "contact director" for two or three divisions. The dialog between the divisional presidents and the contact directors is a mechanism for knowledge sharing and initiating

strategic changes that adds flexibility to the formal strategic planning process. The result is a system of strategy formulation and performance management that is simultaneously top-down and bottom-up.

Fundamental to Exxon's close integration of financial management with strategic planning is Exxon's emphasis on *stewardship*—a doctrine of managerial responsibility and accountability that makes each executive personally responsible to the corporation and its shareholders.

In particular, formalized strategic planning has been viewed as the enemy of flexibility, creativity and entrepreneurship. Marakon consultants Mankins and Steele have observed that "strategic planning doesn't really influence most companies' strategy."[22] The principal reasons are its rigid annual cycle and its preoccupation with business unit plans—as a result "senior executives . . . make the decisions that really shape their companies' strategies . . . outside the planning process typically in an ad hoc fashion without rigorous analysis or productive debate." The approach they identify at companies such as Microsoft, Boeing and Textron is what they call "continuous, decision-oriented planning" where the emphasis is, first, on analyzing the critical issues that face the company and, second, on decision making. The central feature of the process is that the top management team—the executive committee—drives the strategy-making process.

● *Weak strategy execution.* A major theme of recent years has been the need for more effective strategy execution by large companies. This means a more effective linkage between strategic planning and operational management. Larry Bossidy and Ram Charan point to the key role of *milestones* that can ". . . bring reality to a strategic plan."[23] Thus, to keep Honeywell's strategy for cost cutting in its automotive business on track, managers developed short- and medium-term milestones for shifting production overseas. As was noted in Chapter 2, the *balanced scorecard* is another technique for translating strategy into specific functional and operational targets. Building on their balanced scorecard approach, Kaplan and Norton propose that *strategy maps* are used to plot the relationships between strategic actions and overall goals.[24] To ensure a close linkage between strategic planning and strategy implementation they recommend that companies establish an *office of strategy management*, responsible not just for managing the annual strategic planning cycle but also for overseeing the execution of strategic plans.[25] The risk is that such a unit is the potential for it to conflict with the roles and responsibilities of divisional and business unit managers.

## Performance Control and the Budgeting Process

Most multidivisional companies have a dual planning process: strategic planning concentrates on the medium and long term, financial planning controls short-term performance. Typically, the first year of the strategic plan includes the performance plan for the upcoming year in terms of an operating budget, a capital expenditure budget, and strategy targets relating to market share, output and employment levels, and specific strategic milestones. Annual performance plans are agreed between senior business-level managers and corporate-level managers. They are monitored on a monthly and quarterly basis. At the end of each financial year, they are probed and evaluated in performance review meetings between business and corporate management.

Performance targets emphasize financial indicators (return on invested capital, gross margin, growth of sales revenue) and also include strategic goals (market share, new product introductions, market penetration, quality) and operational performance (output, productivity). Performance targets are usually specified in detail for the next year, with less detailed performance targets set for up to five years ahead. Monthly and quarterly monitoring focuses on early detection of deviations from targets.

Performance targets are supported by management incentives and sanctions. Companies whose management systems are heavily orientated towards demanding profit targets typically use powerful individual incentives to create an intensely motivating environment for divisional managers. At ITT, Geneen's obsession with highly detailed performance monitoring, ruthless interrogation of divisional executives, and generous rewards for success developed an intensely competitive cadre of executives. They worked relentless long hours and applied the same performance demands on their subordinates as Geneen did of them.[26] Creating a performance-driven culture requires unremitting focus on a few quantitative performance targets that can be monitored on a short-term basis. PepsiCo's obsession with monthly market share nourishes an intense, marketing-oriented culture. Chief executive Indra Nooyi observed: "We are a very objective-driven company. We spend a lot of time up front setting objectives and our guys rise to the challenge of meeting those objectives. When they don't meet the objectives, we don't have to flog them because they do it themselves."[27] One executive put it more bluntly: "The place is full of guys with sparks coming out of their asses."[28] Even in businesses where interdependence is high and investment gestation periods are long, as in petroleum, short- and medium-term performance targets can be highly effective. The performance-oriented culture built by former CEO John Browne at BP was based upon a system of performance contracts in which each business unit general manager agrees a set of financial, strategic and operational targets with the CEO.[29] However, as we have observed, performance-based compensation can lead to unanticipated and dysfunctional consequences—especially with regard to prioritizing short-term over long-term performance.

## Balancing Strategic Planning and Financial Control

One implication of the tradeoff between *input control* (controlling decisions) and *output control* (controlling performance) is that companies must choose a balance between strategic planning and financial control. Michael Goold and Andrew Campbell found that the corporate management systems of British multibusiness

**TABLE 17.2** Characteristics of different strategic management styles

| | Strategic planning | Financial control |
|---|---|---|
| *Business Strategy Formulation* | Businesses and corporate HQ jointly formulate strategy. The HQ coordinates strategies of businesses. | Strategy formulated at business unit level. Corporate HQ largely reactive, offering little coordination. |
| *Controlling Performance* | Primarily strategic goals with medium- to long-term horizon. | Financial budgets set annual targets for ROI and other financial variables with monthly and quarterly monitoring. |
| *Advantages* | Effective in managing (a) linkages among businesses, (b) innovation, (c) long-term competitive positioning. | Business unit autonomy encourages initiative, responsiveness, and the development of business leaders. |
| *Disadvantages* | Loss of divisional autonomy and initiative. Conducive to unitary strategic view. Resistance to abandoning failed strategy. | Short-term focus discourages innovation and long-term development. Limited sharing of resources and skills among businesses. |
| *Style suited to:* | Companies with a small number of closely related businesses. In sectors where technology and competition are important and projects are large and long term. | Companies with many businesses across a wide range of industries, and with limited linkages between them. Approach works best in mature, technologically stable sectors where investment projects are relatively small and short term. |
| *U.K. Examples* | BP, BOC, Cadbury-Schweppes, Lex Group, STC, United Biscuits. | Hanson, BTR, General Electric Company, Ferranti, Tarmac. |

*Source:*
Based on M. Goold and A. Campbell, *Strategies and Styles* (Oxford: Blackwell, 1987).

companies emphasized one or the other.[30] The *strategic planning companies* emphasized the longer term development of their businesses and had corporate HQs that were was heavily involved in business-level planning. The *financial control companies* had corporate HQs that emphasized short-term budgetary control and rigorously monitored financial performance against ambitious targets, but had limited involvement in business strategy formulation—this was left to divisional and business unit managers. Table 17.2 summarizes key features of the two styles.

The trend over time has been a growing influence of financial control—even among oil and gas majors (BP in particular), strategic planning has become less concerned with strategic decision making and more focused on managing financial performance.[31]

## Using PIMS in Strategy Formulation and Performance Appraisal

The PIMS (Profit Impact of Market Strategies) project offers corporate managers a set of techniques for appraising the performance of businesses and developing strategies towards them. PIMS grew out of General Electric's internal database and is now maintained by the Strategic Planning Institute.[32] Using information on about 4000 business units, it deploys multiple regression analysis to estimate the impact on profitability of a large number of strategy and market structure variables. PIMS is used by multibusiness companies to assist in two main areas of corporate management:

- *Setting performance targets for business units.* Using the regression coefficients in the PIMS profitability equations allows a business to calculate its "Par ROI"—the return on investment that would be expected for a specific business given its profile of strategic and industry characteristics if its performance were typical of the sample as a whole. "Par ROI" can be used as a benchmark to evaluate profitability and set profitability targets.
- *Formulating business unit strategy.* Using the PIMS regression equations, the effects of changes in business strategy on profitability can be simulated.

The PIMS analysis assumes that the various strategy and market structure variables have independent influences on profitability. The more complex are the interactions between different strategy and market structure variables, the less valid is the guidance based upon the results of large database regression estimates.

## Managing Linkages between Businesses

As we saw in the previous chapter, the main opportunities for creating value in the multibusiness company arise from sharing resources and transferring capabilities among the different businesses within the company. This sharing occurs both through the centralization of common services at the corporate level and through direct linkages between the businesses.

### Common Corporate Services

The simplest form of resource sharing in the multidivisional company is the centralized provision of common services and functions. These include corporate management functions such as strategic planning, financial control, treasury, risk management, internal audit, taxation, government relations and shareholder relations. They also include business services that are more efficiently provided on a centralized basis, such as research, engineering, human resources management, legal services, management development, purchasing and any other administrative services subject to economies of scale or learning. By 2000, shared corporate services accounted for 43% of headquarters staff among large U.K. corporations.[33]

In practice, the benefits of centralized provision of common services tend to be smaller than many corporate managers anticipate. Centralized provision can avoid costs of duplication but there can be little incentive among headquarters staff and specialized corporate units to meet the needs of their business-level customers. The experience of many companies is that corporate staffs tend to grow under their own momentum with few obvious economies from central provision and few benefits of superior services.

As a result, many companies separated their corporate headquarters into two groups: a *corporate management unit* responsible for supporting the corporate management team in core support activities such as strategic planning, finance and legal, and a *shared services organization* responsible for supplying common services such as research, engineering, training, and information technology to the businesses. Market incentives have been created for these shared service organizations by requiring them to supply services on an arm's-length basis to internal operating units, sometimes in competition with independent suppliers.

For example, Alcoa's Global Business Services was created in 2003. It offers financial accounting services; procurement; environment, health and safety services; people services; global credit; and information services. Its 1900 employees are based in Pittsburgh, Monterrey (Mexico), Quebec (Canada), Szekesfehervar (Hungary), Booragoon (Australia), Sao Paulo (Brazil) and Bangalore (India). Its vision is to "deliver valuable services to Alcoa's business and resource units at a cost and quality better than competitive alternatives."[34]

## Business Linkages and Porter's Corporate Strategy Types

Exploiting economies of scope doesn't necessarily mean centralizing resources at the corporate level. Resources and capabilities can also be shared between the businesses. Michael Porter has argued that the way in which a company manages these linkages determines its potential to create value for shareholders.[35] He identifies four corporate strategy types:

- *Portfolio management.* The most limited form of resource sharing is where the parent company simply acquires a portfolio of attractive, soundly managed companies, allows them to operate autonomously, and links them through an efficient internal capital market. The typical organizational structure for portfolio management is the *holding company*—a parent company that owns controlling stakes in a number of (typically unrelated) subsidiaries but, beyond appointing the boards of the subsidiary companies, does not exert significant management control. Investor AB of Sweden (controlled by the Wallenberg family), Koor Industries of Israel and Berkshire Hathaway of the U.S. (headed by legendary investor Warren Buffett) are leading examples. Value is created by acquiring companies at favorable prices, closely monitoring their financial performance and operating an effective internal capital market.

- *Restructuring.* Conglomerates, such as Tyco International and Textron in the U.S., and Tomkins plc and Invensys plc in the U.K., create value primarily by restructuring: acquiring poorly managed companies, then intervening to appoint new management, dispose of underperforming businesses, restructure balance sheets and cut costs. As conglomerates have increasingly restructured themselves into oblivion (either transforming themselves into more focused industrial companies or breaking up entirely) private equity groups—such as Carlyle, KKR, Blackstone, and Texas Pacific in the U.S., and Alchemy and Candover in the U.K.—have increasingly taken on the same restructuring role.[36]

- *Transferring skills.* Organizational capabilities can be transferred between business units. LVMH transfers brand management and distribution capabilities among its different luxury-brand businesses. Sharp transfers its optoelectronics and miniaturization capabilities across a number of consumer, electronic, and office equipment products. Creating value by sharing skills requires that the same capabilities are applicable to the different businesses and also that mechanisms are established to transfer these skills through personnel exchange and best practice transfer.

- *Sharing activities.* Porter argues that the most important source of value arises from exploiting economies of scope in common resources and activities. For these economies to be realized, corporate management must play a key coordinating role, including involvement in formulating business unit strategies and intervention in operational matters to ensure that opportunities for sharing R&D, advertising, distribution systems and service networks are fully exploited. In many countries, Unilever has a single marketing and distribution organization that handles a wide range of different consumer products.[37] The emergence of Samsung Electronics as a global leader in digital consumer products during 2000-4 owed much to its development of advanced design capabilities. These were located in four design centers in London, Tokyo, San Francisco and Seoul and are shared across Samsung's different business units.[38]

## The Corporate Role in Managing Linkages

The closer the linkages among businesses, the greater the opportunities for creating value from sharing resources and transferring capabilities, and the greater the need for corporate headquarters to coordinate across businesses. We noted earlier that the "financial control" style of management occurs mainly in conglomerates where the independence of each business limits the coordinating role of the head office to manage the budgetary process and establish "framework conditions" for divisional planning.

In more closely related companies, such as the vertically integrated oil companies, or companies with close market or technological links (such as IBM, Procter & Gamble, American Express, and Alcoa), corporate management uses a "strategic planning" style, which is likely to involve not only coordination of strategies but also operational coordination to exploit the economies of scope and transferable skills discussed in Chapter 16. Corporate involvement in interdivisional affairs has implications for the size of the corporate headquarters. Berkshire Hathaway, which has almost no linkages among its businesses, has a corporate staff of about 50. Hewlett-Packard, with about the same sales but much closer linkages between its divisions, has close to 3000 employees at its Palo Alto head office. Where business units are linked through their sharing of a common resource or capability then the corporate headquarters is likely to be closely involved in the development and deployment of that resource or capability. For example, Pfizer and Corning have strong corporate R&D groups; Dow has a strong corporate manufacturing function; and Virgin's corporate team plays a key role in managing the Virgin brand.[39]

Developing and sharing resources and capabilities may require *ad hoc* organizational arrangements such as *cross-divisional task forces*. Such task forces might be formed for the introduction and dissemination of total quality management, to reengineer financial management practices, to promote fast-cycle new product development, or to coordinate business development in China.

The CEO can play an important role in initiating and pushing these kinds of cross-business initiatives. Corporate initiatives sponsored by the CEO are a key mechanism for disseminating strategic changes, best practices and management innovations.[40] At General Electric, Jack Welch was an especially effective exponent of period corporate initiatives as drivers of organizational change. These were built around communicable and compelling slogans such as "GE's growth engine," "boundarylessness," "six-sigma quality" and "destroy-your-business-dot-com."

Exploiting linkages between businesses imposes costs. Though Porter may be right that the *potential* for value creation increases as a company moves from a loose, "portfolio management" strategy toward the more integrated, "shared activity" strategy, this potential is not always realized. For example, most attempts at exploiting the potential for cross-selling across different businesses have yielded disappointing results, especially in financial services.[41] Lorsch and Allen point to some of management costs incurred in exploiting linkages between businesses. They compared three conglomerates with three vertically integrated paper companies.[42] The coordination requirements of the paper companies resulted in greater involvement of head office staff in divisional operations, larger head office staffs, more complex planning and control devices, and lower responsiveness to change in the external environment. By contrast, the conglomerates made little attempt to exploit linkages even if they were present:

> The conglomerate firms we had studied seemed to be achieving appreciable degrees of financial and managerial synergy but little or no operating synergy. Some of the firms saw little immediate payoff in this operating synergy; others met with little success in attempting to achieve it.[43]

The success with which the corporate headquarters manages linkages between businesses depends on top management's understanding of the commonalities among its different businesses. Ultimately, these commonalities have their basis in the underlying rationale for the corporation—what C. K. Prahalad and Rich Bettis have called *dominant logic*: "the way in which managers conceptualize the business and make critical resource allocation decisions."[44] The success of the multibusiness corporation depends upon strategic similarity among the different businesses that is consistent with an overall dominant logic.

## Managing Change in the Multibusiness Corporation

Conceptions of the role of corporate management in the multibusiness company have shifted greatly over time. These shifting roles have been associated with different priorities with regard to value creation within the multibusiness corporation. During the 1970s and early 1980s, corporate management was concerned with the creation of large business empires. The motivation was partly growth but also the belief in the power of new tools of strategic and financial management to transcend industry boundaries. During the late 1980s a profound shift in top management priorities occurred and throughout the 1990s the dominant theme was applying the logic and principles of shareholder value maximization to restructure diversified corporate empires. The principal sources of value were pruning business portfolios and exercising "stand-alone" influence to boost the performance of individual businesses. During the present decade the primary challenges have been, first, creating value through exploiting linkages between businesses and improving integration within the corporation; second, increasing responsiveness to external change and accelerating the pace of organizational evolution. These shifts in strategic priorities have been associated with different leadership styles. Let me address each of these two major transitions.

## Value Creation through Corporate Restructuring

During the late 1980s and 1990s, a large proportion of the largest corporations of North America and Europe underwent intense phases of corporate change typically triggered by declining financial performance or some external threat. Given the tendency for most multibusiness corporations to develop through a series of incremental strategy initiatives, periodic corporate restructuring based upon a comprehensive corporate review that appraises individual businesses and review of the overall business portfolio can be critical to revitalization.

McKinsey & Company's *pentagon framework* offers a systematic approach to analyzing the potential for increasing the market value of a multibusiness company through corporate restructuring.[45] The analysis comprises five stages—these correspond to the five nodes of Figure 17.5:

1 *The current market value of the company.* The starting point of the analysis is current enterprise value, which comprises the value of equity plus the value of debt. (As we know from Chapter 2, if securities markets are efficient, this equals the net present value of anticipated cash flow over the life of the company.)

2 *The value of the company as is.* Even without any changes to strategy or operations, it may be possible to value simply by managing external

**FIGURE 17.5** The McKinsey restructuring pentagon

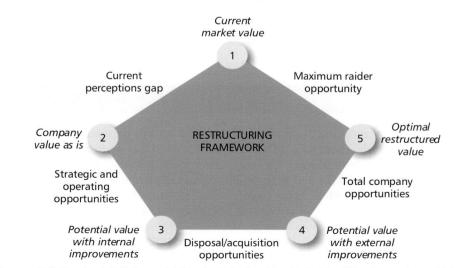

*Source:* T. E. Copeland, T. Koller, and J. Murrin, *Valuation* (New York: John Wiley & sons, Inc., 1990).

perceptions of a company's future prospects. Over the past two decades, companies have devoted increasing attention to managing investor expectations by increasing the quantity and quality of information flow to shareholders and investment analysts and establishing departments of investor relations for this purpose.

3 *The potential value of the company with internal improvements.* As we have seen, corporate management has opportunities for increasing the overall value of the company by making strategic and operational improvements to individual businesses that increase their cash flows. These might include exploiting global expansion opportunities, outsourcing certain activities and cost-cutting opportunities.

4 *The potential value of the company with external improvements.* Having determined the potential value of its constituent businesses, corporate management needs to determine whether changes in the business portfolio can increase overall company value. The key is to apply the principle of parenting advantage: even after strategic and operating improvements have been made, can a business be sold for price greater than its value to the company?

5 *The optimum restructured value of the company.* The previous four steps establish maximum value potential of a company. Assuming that these changes could also be undertaken by an alternative owner of the company, the difference between the maximum restructured value and the current market value represents the profit potential available to a corporate raider.

This type of analysis has been traditionally associated with leveraged buyout specialists and other corporate raiders. Faced with this threat, comprehensive corporate restructuring became widespread among large multibusiness companies (for example, the restructuring wave by the oil majors during 1986–92.)[46]

Leadership style associated with corporate restructuring is indicated by the nicknames given to some of the prominent exponents—"Chainsaw" Al Dunlap (at Scott Paper and Sunbeam), "Neutron" Jack Welch (at General Electric), "Fred-the-Shred" Goodwin (at Royal Bank of Scotland). This points to an emphasis on cost cutting and asset divestment. The leadership mode associated with this approach is characterized by obsessive commitment to the shareholder value maximization and the bottom-line results needed to achieve it, managing through performance targets and an emphasis on performance incentives—both compensation incentives and the threat of termination threats for underperformance.

## Beyond Restructuring: Value Creation from Business Linkages and Innovation

Disillusion with the shareholder value maximization model, diminishing returns to cost cutting, and the need to create new sources of corporate value have resulted in profound shifts in the corporate strategies of multibusiness companies. Increasingly, large multibusiness companies have sought to identify opportunities for innovation, for new product development and for creating value from exploiting new and more sophisticated linkages between companies. Corporate headquarters are concerned less with the problem of control and more with the problem of identifying and implementing the means for creating value within and between their individual businesses. The use of the term "parenting" to describe the corporate role, as opposed to the notion of "systems of corporate control," reflects this shift in thinking.

Changes in the management of multibusiness corporations have included decentralization of decision making from corporate to divisional levels, a shift from formal to informal coordination and a more multidimensional role for the corporate headquarters. From being simply a control center, the corporate HQ acts as a service center, a guide to the future, and a knowledge hub.

Managing transition has been a key role for chief executives. The most celebrated of these "change masters" was Jack Welch, Chairman and CEO of General Electric from 1981 to 2001. Welch's style and the system he created has become a model for other large, multibusiness corporations—not just in North America, but in Europe and Asia too. Strategy Capsule 17.3 outlines Welch's style and methods.

## STRATEGY CAPSULE 17.3

# General Electric: Welch's Reinvention of Corporate Management

Jack Welch's 20 years as Chairman and CEO of General Electric began with an intensive period of restructuring, which transformed the composition of GE's business portfolio through acquisitions and disposals and extended the conglomerate's global reach. Toward the mid-1980s, Welch's attention shifted from the business portfolio to the structure, systems and style of GE. Among the changes he initiated were the following.

- *Delayering*. Welch's fundamental criticism of GE's management was that it was slow and unresponsive. Welch eliminated GE's sector level of organization so that business heads reported directly to him. He pressured them to flatten their management pyramids. Overall, GE's layers of hierarchy were cut from nine or ten to four or five.

- *Changing the strategic planning system*. During the 1970s, GE had developed a systematic and formalized approach to strategy formulation and appraisal. Welch believed that not only was the system slow

and inefficient, it also stifled innovation and opportunism. Welch replaced the staff-led, document-driven process with more personal, less formal but very intensive face-to-face discussions. Instead of data-heavy documents, each business head was asked to produce a slim "play-book" that summarized key strategic issues and actions. Concise answers were required to questions about market dynamics, competitive activity, risks, and proposed GE business responses. These documents became the basis for a half-day review session where business heads and key executives met with the Office of the CEO in an open dialog on strategy and performance.[47]

- *Redefining the role of headquarters*. The changes in the strategic planning system reflected broader changes in the role of the corporate headquarters. Welch viewed headquarters as interfering too much, generating too much paper, and failing to add value. His objective was to "turn their role 180 degrees from checker, inquisitor, and authority figure to facilitator, helper, and supporter" so that decisions could move more quickly: "What we do here at headquarters . . . is to multiply the resources we have, the human resources, the financial resources, and the best practices . . . Our job is to help, it's to assist, it's to make these businesses stronger, to help them grow and be more powerful."[48]

- *The coordinating role of corporate.* A key role of corporate was facilitating coordination across GE's businesses. The Corporate Executive Council was reconstituted to include the leaders of GE's 13 businesses and several key corporate executives. It met two days each quarter to discuss common problems and issues. The Council became an important vehicle for identifying and exploiting synergies. In 1990, Welch launched his concept of the "boundaryless company." This involved blurring internal divisions so that people could work together across functional and business boundaries. Welch aimed at "integrated diversity"—the ability to transfer the best ideas, most developed knowledge and most valuable people freely and easily between businesses:

*Boundaryless behavior is the soul of today's GE . . . Simply put, people seem compelled to build layers and walls between themselves and others, and that human tendency tends to be magnified in large, old institutions like ours. These walls cramp people, inhibit creativity, waste time, restrict vision, smother dreams and, above all, slow things down . . . Boundaryless behavior shows up in the actions of a woman from our Appliances business in Hong Kong helping NBC with contacts needed to develop satellite television service in Asia . . . And finally, boundaryless behavior means exploiting one of the unmatchable advantages a multibusiness GE has over almost any other company in the world. Boundaryless behavior combines 12 huge global businesses—each number one or number two in its markets—into a vast laboratory whose principal product is new ideas, coupled with a common commitment to spread them throughout the company.[49]*

As Welch has shown, managing large-scale organizational change is not simply about top-down decision making. A key component is fostering change processes at lower levels of the organization—GE's "Work-Out" is a prime example. A critical feature of organizational design is building structures and systems that permit adaptation. While CEOs cannot be the primary initiators of change, they need to be alert and responsive to signals. Intel's former CEO, Andy Grove, emphasizes the importance of CEOs identifying *strategic inflection points*—instances where seismic shifts in a firm's competitive environment require a fundamental redirection of strategy.[50] At Intel, such inflection points included the transition from DRAM chips to microprocessors, the decision to focus on its x86 series of microprocessors in favor of RISC architecture, and the decision to replace its faulty Pentium chips.[51]

Above all, CEOs need to be adept at managing contradiction and dilemma. For example:

- companies must strive for efficiency, which requires rigorous financial controls; they must also be innovative and entrepreneurial, which requires autonomy and loose, flexible controls;

- maximizing current performance requires strategies that exploit existing resources and capabilities across different markets; success for the future is dependent on the creation of new resources and capabilities and their deployment in new markets;

- innovation, efficiency, and responsiveness require autonomy for business-level managers; yet the competitive advantage of the multibusiness corporation ultimately depends on integrating resources and capabilities across businesses. Is it possible for companies like Microsoft, Siemens, or Samsung to mesh the resource advantages of the giant corporation with the responsiveness and creativity of small enterprises?

Resolving these dilemmas requires that organizations operate in multiple modes simultaneously. In particular, they need to combine both decentralized flexibility and initiative *and* centralized purpose and integration. The transformation of IBM under Lou Gerstner offers some guidance as to how this can be achieved. Resisting Wall Street pressure to break up IBM, Gerstner was able to combine aggressive cuts in costs and jobs, entrepreneurship, and flexibility through decentralized decision making, and integration of technology and know-how by breaking down barriers both within IBM and between IBM and other companies.[52]

Flexible integration—whether it is sharing capabilities, harmonizing market initiatives in different countries, or collaborating to develop the new products and technologies required—cannot be hierarchically decreed: headquarters does not possess the necessary knowledge to be in the driver's seat. It must happen through horizontal collaboration among the businesses units. This requires that business-level general managers identify not only with their particular businesses, but also with the corporation as a whole. Fostering the necessary identity and direction within the multibusiness corporation is probably the most important task that the CEO must perform.

Creating this sense of identity is much more challenging for a company that spans several businesses than for one whose identity is determined by the products it offers (McDonald's or De Beers). It goes beyond "strategic relatedness" and "dominant logic" and embraces notions of vision and mission—concepts which were identified in Chapter 1 as lying at the foundations of companies' strategy formulation.[53] In the previous chapter, I observed that the luxury goods giant LVMH deploys its core brand management capabilities across many different businesses. Its success in doing so depends critically upon establishing a corporate identity that forms a "cultural glue" between these disparate businesses: "The common cultural trunk is based on the permanent search for quality of the products and the management, human relations based on responsibility and initiative, and rewarding competences and services."[54]

## External Strategy: Mergers and Acquisitions

If the central concern of corporate strategy is managing the scope of the firm, then mergers and acquisitions are key instruments of corporate strategy as they are the principal means by which firms achieve major extensions in the scope of their activities. Mergers and acquisitions also represent one of the greatest paradoxes in strategic management. Given the absence of evidence that acquisitions create shareholder value for the acquiring firm, why is acquisition the preferred means of corporate growth for so many companies?

In Chapter 6 we examined the role of mergers and acquisitions in building the resources and capabilities of the firm (see "Acquiring Capabilities: Mergers, Acquisitions and Alliances"). In the previous chapter we looked at the role of acquisition in diversification strategy. In this chapter our goal is to look more generally at the efficacy of mergers, acquisitions and alliances as instruments of corporate strategy, the circumstances where they can be successful, and how they should be managed.

Acquisitions involve one company purchasing another. This involves the acquiring company making an offer for the common stock of another for a fixed price per share. Acquisitions can be "friendly," that is when they are supported by the board of the target company, or unfriendly, when they are opposed by the target company's board—in the latter case they are known as a *hostile takeover.*

Mergers are where two companies amalgamate to form a new company.[55] This requires agreement by the shareholders of the two companies who then exchange their shares for shares in the new company. Mergers occur when the companies involved are of roughly similar size and strength. Where the companies involved are in different countries, a merger may be preferred to an acquisition for political reasons. Thus, the amalgamations between Daimler Benz and Chrysler, Alcatel and Lucent, and Mittal Steel and Alcelor all took the form of mergers.

Table 17.3 shows the biggest acquisitions of the past decade.

**TABLE 17.3** Deals of the decade: mergers and acquisitions with bid value exceeding $50 billion, 1999–2009

| Year | Purchaser | Purchased | Transaction value (U.S. $ bn.) |
|---|---|---|---|
| 1999 | Vodafone Airtouch Plc. | Mannesmann | 183 |
| 2000 | America Online Inc. | Time Warner | 165 |
| 1999 | Pfizer | Warner-Lambert | 90 |
| 2007 | ABN-AMBRO | Royal Bank of Scotland, Banco Santander, Fortis | 79 |
| 2000 | Glaxo Wellcome Plc. | SmithKline Beecham Plc. | 76 |
| 2004 | Royal Dutch Petroleum Co. | Shell Transport & Trading Co | 75 |
| 1999 | Citicorp | Travelers Group | 73 |
| 2006 | AT&T Inc. | BellSouth Corporation | 73 |
| 2001 | Comcast Corporation | AT&T Broadband & Internet Services | 72 |
| 2009 | Pfizer | Wyeth | 68 |
| 1999 | SBC Communications | Ameritech Corporation | 63 |
| 2004 | Sanofi-Synthelabo SA | Aventis SA | 60 |
| 1999 | Vodafone Group | AirTouch Communications | 60 |
| 2002 | Pfizer Inc. | Pharmacia Corporation | 60 |
| 2007 | Endesa SA | Enel SpA, Acciona SA | 60 |
| 2004 | JP Morgan Chase & Co | Bank One Corp | 59 |
| 2007 | Procter & Gamble | Gillette | 57 |
| 2008 | InBev | Anheuser-Busch | 52 |
| 2008 | Bank of America | Merrill Lynch | 50 |

## Empirical Evidence on Mergers and Acquisitions

The performance effects of mergers and acquisitions have been measured using both shareholder returns (typically the stock market reaction to takeover announcements) and using accounting data on profitability. The only unambiguous evidence is that acquisitions benefit the shareholders of the acquired firms. For acquiring firms, studies show that the returns are either negative or insignificant from zero. Combining the effects on both acquirers and acquirees, the overall picture is one of small gains to mergers—typically around 2% of the combined market value of the companies involved.[56]

Studies that use accounting data measure the actual outcomes of mergers and acquisitions rather than stock market expectations of their results. However, attempts to compare post-merger performance with pre-merger performance are fraught with difficulties— "results from these accounting-based studies are all over the map."[57]

This outcome of several decades of research into the performance effects of mergers and acquisitions—that, overall, the only clear-cut effect is the shareholders of acquired firms gain—is disappointing. Yet it is not altogether unsurprising. Mergers and acquisitions are motivated by multiple factors; they each involve a unique combination of circumstances; and distinguishing their effects from the multiplicity of other influences on company performance is exceptionally difficult.

## When do Mergers and Acquisitions Make Sense?

Inevitably, any lessons about when and how companies should use mergers and acquisitions as instruments of corporate strategy requires analysis of the specific circumstances of the merger or acquisition. Again, empirical research gives us limited insight into these circumstances. Even highly plausible propositions—for example, that horizontal mergers which increase market share result in gains in efficiency and profitability, or that acquisitions of firms in related businesses outperform unrelated acquisitions—fail to gain systematic empirical support.

Beginning with strategic analysis, it seems obvious that a merger or acquisition should be based upon a sound strategic rationale. Yet, it is not always apparent that this is the case. Michael Jensen suggests that CEOs of companies with overvalued equity will make equity financed acquisitions to help support their share price.[58] AOL's merger with Time Warner may reflect this motive. More typical is the propensity of CEOs to vastly overestimate the gains from mergers. Many diversifying mergers within financial services have been motivated by wildly optimistic forecasts of the potential for cross-selling and customers' desire for "one-stop-shopping."

The most common reason that mergers and acquisitions lack a strong strategic rationale is the propensity for imitation. Acquisitions go in waves: the petroleum mergers of the 1998-2002; the 1990s rush for banks and insurance companies to combine; the telecoms urge-to-merge of 1998-2005; and the global consolidation of the beer, pharmaceuticals, and metals sectors during the past decade. In these situations, the propensity of firms to "follow the leader" is reinforced by the fear of being alone at the fringes of the dance floor with only unattractive dancing partners left.

A realistic assessment of the potential gains from a merger or acquisition requires intimate knowledge of the target company. This is a bigger problem for hostile takeovers than for agreed acquisitions. However, even friendly takeovers are still prone to the *lemons problem:* the seller knows much more about the acquisition target than the buyer, so the acquirer can be hoodwinked into overpaying. One year after its acquisition of Jaguar, a Ford executive commented: "If we had known what a terrible shape Jaguar was in, we would never had paid the price we did."

Acquirers can also fall victims of believing their own propaganda—in seeking to persuade the stock market about the benefits of an acquisition, they risk believing their own inflated estimates of potential synergies.

## Postmerger Integration

Case-study evidence shows that some of the most carefully planned mergers and acquisitions can end up as failures because of the problems of managing postmerger integration. The combination of Daimler Benz and Chrysler was exemplary in its premerger planning; the outcome was disastrous. Not only did Chrysler's problems appear to be intractable but Chrysler's demands on the group's top management negatively impacted the core Mercedes-Benz business.[59]

Frequently, it appears that where the potential benefits of mergers and acquisitions are large, the costs and risks of integrations are also large. Thus, Capron and Anand argue that cross-border acquisitions typically have the strongest strategic logic.[60] Yet, the evidence of Daimler-Chrysler, BMW-Rover, and Alcatel-Lucent suggests that when differences in corporate culture are accentuated by differences in national culture, the challenge of post-merger integration becomes immense.

A growing body of literature views acquisition as an organizational capability and points to the need for acquisition capability to be developed through explicit and experiential learning. Acquisition performance tends to increase with experience— although not at first. A learning threshold appears, after which subsequent acquisitions add value.[61] Explicit learning through the codification of acquisition processes also appears to be conducive to acquisition success.[62]

In common with my approach throughout this book, I consider that it is important to separate issues of preacquisition planning and postacquisition management. In the long and rich history of acquisition disasters, poor postacquisition management has been identified as the source of the problem. Yet, in many of these cases the integration problems could have been anticipated: the critical problem was going ahead with the acquisition without adequate assessment of post-merger management problems. Thus, in the case of Quaker Oats acquisition of Snapple ("the billion dollar blunder"), the critical problem—the impediments to integrating Snapple's distribution system with that of Quaker's Gatorade—were evident to the marketing managers and the franchised distributors of the two companies prior to the takeover.[63]

## Summary

Formulating and implementing corporate strategy in the multibusiness company presents complex issues. We must extend our tools of strategy analysis to address challenging issues of organizational design, management control, and coordination between businesses. Developing generic recommendations as to how a multibusiness company should implement its corporate strategy is impossible: each firm is unique in terms of its portfolio of products and markets; its resources and capabilities; its corporate culture, and its administrative heritage. Given these factors, it is hardly surprising that empirical research offers limited guidance as to the correlates of superior performance—close relationships between businesses may or may not lead to higher profitability; sharing resources and capabilities offers economies but also imposes management costs; some mergers create value, others don't.

Managing the multibusiness firm inevitably requires abstracting from the complexities of the large, multifunctional, multiproduct, multinational firm. Tools such as portfolio planning matrices are simplistic but they offer a starting point for addressing the complexity of dealing with the firm as a whole.

The key to this complexity is *strategic fit*. Corporate strategy, business strategy, the external environment, together with the firm's resource, capabilities, structure, systems, leadership style, and culture need to be consistent and closely linked. To get to grips with these issues we need to characterize the firm in terms of its few fundamental features. For example, its strategic rationale can be described by its *dominant logic*,[64] its "personality" and "self-image" can be described by its *organizational identity*,[65] the consistency of its overall configuration by its *corporate coherence*.[66]

Internal fit is not enough: the critical requirement is fit with the external environment. As the business environment changes, so large, multibusiness companies need to adapt. Very often, the scale of this adaptation makes the task impossible. Conglomerates had strategies and structures that fitted well with the business environment of the 1970s. By the mid-1990s almost all of them had been dismantled. As we shall explore in the next chapter, the business environment has entered a new phase of discontinuous change. Large, multibusiness companies face critical challenges of adaption.

## Self-Study Questions

1   Williamson's "M-form" concept argues that the efficiency of the multidivisional firm is the result of (a) the separation of responsibilities between divisional and corporate management and (b) overcoming the "agency problem" of managers pursuing their own interests rather than those of shareholders. How effective are most multibusiness companies in achieving these advantages? Are there other performance advantages associated with multibusiness companies?

2   If you were VP of strategic planning for a large multibusiness company, would you use portfolio planning techniques in your work? If so, for what purposes? If not, why not? Would your preference be to use the GE/McKinsey matrix or the BCG matrix?

3   Identify a poorly performing multibusiness company (examples might include Sony, Time Warner, Bombardier, Pearson, Matsushita, Dubai World, or Tyco). Using the McKinsey

pentagon framework, in which stage do you perceive the greatest opportunities for value creation through restructuring? (Use the company's web site or Hoovers.com to access information on the company.)

4  For technology-based companies, building linkages across different businesses is critical to sustaining competitive advantage. Select a technology-based company that you are familiar with (possibilities might include Microsoft, HP, Apple Computer, Canon, Sony, or Finmeccanica), then identify how linkages between businesses are currently being exploited and identify opportunities for additional exploitation of cross-business linkages.

# Notes

1  A *multibusiness company* is a company that comprises multiple business units. These business units may comprise different vertical activities, different geographical units, or different product sectors.

2  O. E. Williamson, *Markets and Hierarchies: Analysis and Antitrust Implications* (New York: Free Press, 1975) and O. E. Williamson, "The Modern Corporation: Origins, Evolution, Attributes," *Journal of Economic Literature* 19 (1981): 1537–68.

3  J. L. Bower, *Managing the Resource Allocation Process* (Boston: Harvard Business School Press, 1986).

4  Williamson, "The Modern Corporation," op. cit.

5  See, for example, P. Steer and J. Cable, "Internal Organization and Profit: An Empirical Analysis of Large U.K. Companies," *Journal of Industrial Economics* 21 (September 1978): 13–30; H. Armour and D. Teece, "Organizational Structure and Economic Performance: A Test of the Multidivisional Hypothesis," *Bell Journal of Economics* 9 (1978): 106–22; D. Teece, "Internal Organization and Economic Performance," *Journal of Industrial Economics* 30 (1981): 173–99.

6  Among private companies, the key governance problem is typically one set of owners (for example, the founding family) enriching themselves at the expense of the other owners. See J. C. Coffee, "A Theory of Corporate Scandals: Why the U.S. and Europe Differ" *Columbia Law School Working Paper* No. 274 (March, 2005).

7  R. M. Grant and M. Visconti, "The Strategic Background to Corporate Accounting Scandals," *Long Range Planning* 39 (August 2006): 361–83.

8  *OECD Principles of Corporate Governance* (Paris: OECD, 2004).

9  "Splitting the Chairman and CEO Roles," *Business Week* (January 10, 2008): http://www.businessweek .com/managing/content/jan2008/ca2008018_642807 .htm, accessed July 8, 2009.

10  M. J. Conyon, S. I. Peck, L. E. Read and G. V. Sadler, "The Structure of Executive Compensation Contracts: The U.K. Evidence," *Long Range Planning* 33 (August 2000): 478–503.

11  See for example: P. Bolton, J. Scheinkman and W. Xiong, "Pay for Short-term Performance: Executive Compensation in Speculative Markets," NBER Working Paper 12107 (March 2006); M. C. Jensen and K. J. Murphy, "Remuneration: Where We've Been, How We Got Here, What are the Problems," ECGI-Finance Working Paper 44 (2004).

12  H. Mintzberg, *Structure in Fives: Designing Effective Organizations* (Englewood Cliffs, NJ: Prentice Hall, 1983): Chapter 11.

13  J. Birkinshaw and A. Campbell, "Know the Limits of Corporate Venturing," FT Summer School, *Financial Times* (August 10, 2004).

14  M. Goold, A. Campbell, and M. Alexander, *Corporate-Level Strategy: Creating Value in the Multibusiness Company* (New York: John Wiley & Sons Inc., 1994).

15  *General Electric: Strategic Position—1981*, Case No. 381-174 (Boston: Harvard Business School, 1981): 1.

16  McKinsey & Company has recently reconceptualized SBUs as *value cells*. See M. Giordano and F. Wenger, "Organizing for Value" *Perspectives on Finance and Strategy* No. 18 (McKinsey & Company, Summer, 2008).

17  For a fuller discussion of the GE/McKinsey matrix see: "Enduring Ideas: The GE-McKinsey Nine-box Matrix," *McKinsey Quarterly* (September 2008).

18  For a fuller discussion of the BCG matrix see: B. Henderson, "The Experience Curve Reviewed: IV. The Growth Share Matrix or Product Portfolio," Boston Consulting Group (1973). www.bcg.com/publications/ files/Experience_Curve_IV_Growth_Share_Matrix_1973 .pdf

19  Booz Allen Hamilton claim that "dog" businesses can offer promising potential (H. Quarls, T. Pernsteiner and K. Rangan, "Love Your Dogs," Booz Allen Hamilton, March 15, 2005).

20  Goold, Campbell, and Alexander, *Corporate-Level Strategy* op. cit.

21  Ibid.: 90.

22  M. C. Mankins and R. Steele, "Stop Making Plans; Start Making Decisions," *Harvard Business Review* (January 2006): 76–84.

23 L. Bossidy and R. Charan, *Execution: The Discipline of Getting Things Done* (New York: Crown Business, 2002): 197–201.

24 R. S. Kaplan and D. P. Norton, "Having Trouble With Your Strategy? Then Map It," *Harvard Business Review* (September–October 2000): 67–76.

25 R. S. Kaplan and D. P. Norton, "The Office of Strategy Management," *Harvard Business Review* (October 2005): 72–80.

26 Geneen's style of management is discussed in Chapter 3 of R. T. Pascale and A. G. Athos, *The Art of Japanese Management* (New York: Warner Books, 1982).

27 Tuck School of Business, CEO Speaker Series, September 23, 2002.

28 "Those Highflying PepsiCo Managers," *Fortune* (April 10, 1989): 79.

29 BP, "Performance Contracts" (www.bp.com/genericarticle?Id=25&contentId=2000476).

30 M. Goold and A. Campbell, *Strategies and Styles* (Oxford: Blackwell, 1987).

31 R. M. Grant, "Strategic Planning in a Turbulent Environment: Evidence from the Oil and Gas Majors," *Strategic Management Journal* 24 (2003): 491–518.

32 Information on PIMS analysis and the PIMS database is available from: http://pimsonline.com/index.htm.

33 M. Goold, D. Pettifer and D. Young, "Redesigning the Corporate Center," *European Mangement Review* 19, no. 1 (2001): 83–91.

34 IQPC, "Most Admired Shared Service Organizations, 2005" (www.iqpc.com).

35 M. E. Porter, "From Competitive Advantage to Corporate Strategy," *Harvard Business Review* (May–June 1987): 46.

36 "Going Private," *Business Week* (February 27, 2006).

37 F. A. Maljers, "Corporate Strategy from a Unilever Perspective," in F. A. J. van den Bosch and A. P. de Man (eds.) *Perspectives on Strategy: Contributions of Michael E. Porter* (Boston: Kluwer, 1997): 35–45.

38 "How Samsung became a Global Champion," *Financial Times* (September 5, 2004).

39 M. Goold, D. Pettifer and D. Young, op. cit.

40 J. Darragh and A. Campbell, "Why Corporate Initiatives Get Stuck," *Long Range Planning* 34 (January 2001): 33–52.

41 "Cross-selling's Elusive Charms," *Financial Times* (November 16, 1998): 21.

42 J. W. Lorsch and S. A. Allen III, *Managing Diversity and Interdependence: An Organizational Study of Multidivisional Firms* (Boston: Harvard Business School Press, 1973).

43 Ibid.: 168.

44 C. K. Prahalad and R. Bettis, "The Dominant Logic: A New Linkage Between Diversity and Performance," *Strategic Management Journal* 7 (1986): 485–502.

45 T. Copeland, T. Koller and J. Murrin, *Valuation: Measuring and Managing the Value of Companies*, 3rd edn (New York: John Wiley & Sons, Inc., 2000).

46 R. Cibin and R. M. Grant, "Restructuring Among the World's Largest Oil Companies," *British Journal of Management* 7 (December 1996): 411–28.

47 *General Electric: Jack Welch's Second Wave (A)*, Case No. 9-391-248 (Boston: Harvard Business School, 1991).

48 Jack Welch, "GE Growth Engine," speech to employees (1988).

49 "Letter to Share Owners," General Electric Company 1993 Annual Report (Fairfield, CT, 1994): 2.

50 A. S. Grove, *Only the Paranoid Survive: How to Exploit the Crisis Points that Challenge Every Company* (New York: Bantam, 1999).

51 R. A. Burgelman and A. Grove, "Strategic Dissonance," *California Management Review* 38 (Winter, 1996): 8–28.

52 L. V. Gerstner, *Who Says Elephants Can't Dance?* (New York: Harper Business, 2002).

53 Albert, S. and Whetten, D. A. (1985) "Organizational identity". In Cummings, L. L. and M. M. Staw (eds.) *Research in Organizational Behavior*, 7, 263–95.

54 *LVMH: Building Star Brands*, ICFAI Case MKTA016 (2004); R. Calori, "How Successful Companies Manage Diverse Businesses," *Long Range Planning* 21 (June, 1988): 85.

55 In everyday usage, the term "merger" is often used to refer to both mergers and acquisitions.

56 S. N. Kaplan, "Mergers and Acquisitions: A Financial Economics Perspective," University of Chicago, Graduate School of Business Working Paper (February, 2006). Also, Paul A. Pautler, "Evidence on Mergers and Acquisitions," Bureau of Economics, Federal Trade Commission (September 25, 2001).

57 S. N. Kaplan, "Mergers and Acquisitions," op. cit.: 8.

58 M. Jensen, "Agency costs of overvalued equity." Working paper, Harvard Business School (2004).

59 "DaimlerChrysler: Stalled," *Business Week* (September 10, 2003).

60 L. Capron and J. Anand, "Acquisition-based Dynamic Capabilities," in C. E. Helfat, S. Finkelstein, W. Mitchell, M. A. Peteraf, H. Singh, D. J. Teece and S. G. Winter, *Dynamic Capabilities* (Malden, MA: Blackwell, 2007): 80–99.

61 S. Finkelstein and J. Haleblian, "Understanding Acquisition Performance: The Role of Transfer Effects" *Organization Science* 13 (2002): 36–47.

62 M. Zollo and H. Singh, "Deliberate Learning in Corporate Acquisitions: Post-acquisition Strategies and Integration Capabilities in U.S. Bank Mergers," *Strategic Management Journal* 24 (2004): 1233–56.

63 C. E. Helfat *et al.*, *Dynamic Capabilities*, op. cit.: 57–62.

64 C. K. Prahalad and R. Bettis, "The Dominant Logic" op cit.

65 B. Kogut and U. Zander, "What Firms Do? Coordination, Identity and Learning", *Organization Science* 7 (1996): 502–18.

66 D. J. Teece, R. Rumelt, G. Dosi and S. G. Winter, "Understanding Corporate Coherence: Theory and Evidence," *Journal of Economic Behavior and Organization*, 23 (1994): 1–30.

# 18 Current Trends in Strategic Management

*There are things we know we know. We also know there are known unknowns—We know there are some things we do not know. But there are also unknown unknowns: the ones we don't know we don't know.*

—DONALD RUMSFELD, U.S. SECRETARY OF DEFENSE, 2000–6

*In theory there is no difference between theory and practice. In practice there is.*

—YOGI BERRA, PLAYER AND COACH, NEW YORK YANKEES, 1946–64, 1976–85

# Introduction

With the world mired in the worst economic downturn since the 1930s, it has become increasingly clear that the first decade of the twenty-first century has marked a fundamental break point both in global economic history and in the development of the business enterprise. Our challenge in this chapter is to assess what has changed in the business environment, what the implications for strategic management are, and what concepts and tools can help managers guide their businesses through these turbulent times.

We are in uncharted waters and, unlike the other chapters of this book, this chapter will not equip you with proven tools and frameworks that you can deploy directly in your own companies or in case analysis. The approach is exploratory. My goal is to identify the forces that are reshaping the environment of business, to introduce you to some of the concepts and approaches that are influencing current thinking about strategy, and to draw lessons from leading-edge companies about strategies, organizational forms, and management styles that may prove effective during this era of rapid, unpredictable change.

## The New External Environment of Business

Since the financial crisis claimed its first major corporate casualty, Lehman Brothers, in September 2008, followed by the world's first sovereign state, Iceland, four weeks later, business leaders and politicians alike have surveyed the precarious world economy with shocked disbelief. Yet, for all the drama and tragedy of the banking crisis of 2008–9, it would appear that breakup of the world economic order began at the beginning of the decade rather than the end.

The NASDAQ stock market index hit its all time high on March 10, 2000. The ensuing meltdown of internet, technology, media and telecom stocks was the first evidence that U.S. credit expansion would not be enough to sustain the investment bubbles that had built up during the roaring 1990s.

The first major external shock of the decade was the terrorist attacks of September 11. The train of events that followed—the invasions of Afghanistan and Iraq, and further bombings in Bali, Madrid, London and Mumbai—had a major impact on world trade, financial flows, political tensions and risk perceptions.

Two months later, Enron, one of America's most successful and admired companies of the 1990s, entered bankruptcy. This was the first of a series of financial scandals that was to engulf companies on both sides of the Atlantic and revealed the downside of the aggressive pursuit of shareholder value through leverage, financial engineering and high-powered management incentives.

Unprecedented market turbulence was particularly evident in commodities and foreign exchange. In the two years up to July 2008, NYMEX crude oil rose from $49 to $147 a barrel before dropping to $37 before year end. Ship charter rates showed even more extreme gyrations: driven by booming Chinese demand for raw materials, bulk carrier daily rates reached a peak of $233 988 on June 5, 2008, before collapsing to $3670 five months later. In the foreign exchange markets, daily fluctuations of 5% between major currencies became quite normal during 2006–9.

The natural world has also emerged as a source of instability. A slew of scientific evidence suggests that climate change has reached "tipping point," triggering rapidly accelerating global warming accompanied by greatly increased risks of natural disasters.

At present we still have little idea as to the likely outcome of the present economic downturn—efforts to draw parallels with the Great Depression of the 1930s, the oil-shock of the early 1970s, or Japan's "lost decade" of the 1990s only emphasize the unique features of each of these major economic downturns. But whatever the length and depth of the current recession, a few general features of the prevailing business environment can be identified.

## The Economy: Volatility and Low Growth

While the response of the world economy to the massive monetary and fiscal initiatives introduced by governments and international organizations remains unknown, one certainty does exist: even if successful, these policies will saddle all the world's leading economies with levels of public debt that are unprecedented in peacetime. Thus, even if the current expenditures on refinancing banks, acquiring "toxic securities," and supporting failing industrial enterprises are successful, the costs of servicing public debt will inevitably be major drag on future economic growth.

Meanwhile, it seems highly likely that the levels of volatility and unpredictability that we have experienced in recent years will continue into the future. A key feature of the global economy is the high level of interconnectedness that results from high levels of trade, internationalization of financial markets, flexibility of exchange and interest rates, and speed of communication. As predicted by systems theory, high levels of interconnectedness increase the tendency for the system to amplify small initial movements in unpredictable ways.

Shifts in the global balance of economic power will continue to undermine the ability of the leading industrial nations to control these disruptive forces. The rise of the BRIC countries is creating a multipolar world where the Old Order—the U.S., the E.U. and Japan and the institutions they created (the World Bank, IMF and OECD) are less able to offer global leadership. Looking ahead to 2025, the U.S. National Intelligence Council predicts:

> The international system—as constructed following the Second World War— will be almost unrecognizable . . . owing to the rise of emerging powers, a globalizing economy, an historic transfer of relative wealth and economic power from west to east, and the growing influence of non-state actors.[1]

## Technology

Despite overblown expectations concerning the ability of new digital and com-munications technologies to create a "New Economy," we have witnessed a tran-sition from an industrial economy to a knowledge economy, where software rather than hardware is the primary source of value. The digitally driven knowledge revolution also creates what Brian Arthur calls the "casino of technology," where markets are transformed and established market leaders deposed.[2] The ability of two maverick entrepreneurs operating out of Estonia, Niklas Zennstrom and Janus Friis, to initiate revolutions in two industries—recorded music through their Kazaa file sharing system and telephony through their Skype VoIP telephony service—exemplifies the disruptive potential of new internet-based business models.[3]

Digital technologies are also causing competition to intensify the dissolution of industry barriers. In hand-held devices, Nokia cell phones, Apple iPods, Nintendo Gameboys, Palm PDAs, and RIM's BlackBerry smartphones are increasingly sharing functions and increasingly competing in a shared marketplace.

## Societal Pressures

For organizations to survive and prosper requires that they adapt to the values and expectations of society—what organizational sociologists refer to as *legitimacy*.[4] One of the profoundest impacts of the recent financial crisis on business may be implications for the legitimacy of particular types of business—which influences acceptability among consumers, motivation of employees, willingness of investors and financiers to provide funding, and government support. Loss of social legitimacy may be as great a threat to the survival of commercial and investment banks as their weak balance sheets.[5]

The notion that the business enterprise is a social institution which must identify with the goals and aspirations of society has been endorsed by several leading management thinkers—including Peter Drucker, Charles Handy and Sumantra Ghoshal.[6] The implication is that when the values and attitudes of society are changing, so must the strategies and behaviors of companies.

While anti-business sentiment has for the most part been restricted to the fringes of the political spectrum—neo-Marxists, environmentalist and anti-globalization activists—the corporate scandals of the early part of the decade (Enron, Worldcom, Parmalat) and the financial crisis of 2008–9 have moved disdain for business corporation and their leaders into the mainstream of public opinion. Three issues have been paramount: equity, ethics and environmental sustainability.

Equity issues have been fueled by the growing income disparity within organizational hierarchy. In 1980 the multiple of CEO compensation to that of first-tier employees within U.S. companies was around 40. By 2000, that ratio had risen to 400 in many U.S. companies. Increasingly, claims that bloated CEO bonuses and option packages were justified by the dictates of "the market" or the need to align top management incentives with shareholder value creation were no longer credible. However, it was the payoffs earned by top executives and star traders at failing financial institutions such as Merrill Lynch and Royal Bank of Scotland that turned disquiet into popular outrage.

Similarly with ethical issues. While the offences that put Michael Milken (the "junk-bond king") and Martha Stewart ("America's favorite housewife") behind bars seem modest transgressions, recent examples of rogue executive behavior are far more shocking, whether grossly extravagant (John Thain's $1200 trash bin for his office at Merrill Lynch), criminal (Bernard Madoff), or both (Allen Stanford).

Finally, as public concern over the degradation of the natural environment grows, so businesses are increasingly pressured to adopt strategies and actions that are conducive to environmental sustainability.[7]

Adapting to society's growing demands for fairness, ethics and sustainability presents challenges for business leaders that extend beyond the problems of reconciling societal demands with shareholder interests. Should a company determine unilaterally the values that will govern its behavior, or does it seek to reflect those of the society in which it operates? Companies that embrace the values espoused by their founders are secure in their own sense of mission and can ensure a long-term consistency in their strategy and corporate identity (for example, Walt Disney Company and Wal-Mart with respect to founders Walt Disney and Sam Walton). However, there is a risk that these values become out of step with those of the society as a whole or with the requirements for business effectiveness. Thus, Marks & Spencer's paternalism towards employees and suppliers became a source of rigidity rather than competitive advantage. Conversely, seeking to embrace the concerns and values of society presents the challenge of identifying what these are in a society characterized by diversity and rapid change. These increasing societal pressures have reinforced the attractions of private status: between 1998 and 2008, the number of companies listed on the NYSE fell from 2722 to 1978.

## Managing in an Economic Crisis

When demand falls as quickly as it has between the fourth quarter of 2008 and third quarter of 2009, and credit markets seize up, business as normal gives way to crisis management. The problem, for most companies, is managing under conditions which are unlike anything in living memory, where the outlook is uncertain, and even the current situation is difficult to recognize, let alone comprehend. The evidence available so far points to several key themes and areas of management action which can help companies navigate their way through these troubled times.

*New Top Management Requirements*  When events are moving at unprecedented speed, the time intervals between obtaining information, analyzing information, taking decisions and implementing those decisions need to be tightly compressed. Management consultant Ram Charan identifies the need for "management intensity": plans and progress must be revisited on a daily basis and every top executive must be involved, visible, and in continuous conversation with employees, customers and suppliers. Management intensity requires:

> . . . immersion in the business's operational details and the day-to-day competitive climate the business is facing, along with hands-on involvement and follow-through . . . Surviving a volatile environment requires frequent operational adjustments . . . your guiding principle should be: Head in, hands on. Only in this way will you be able to anticipate what's coming next and respond quickly and appropriately.[8]

The implication is that normal management processes must be bypassed—this can be facilitated by creating an alternative top management structure dedicated to crisis management. In December 2008, LG Electronics established a crisis war room comprising senior executives from LG's five business units, its eight regional headquarters and key functional areas. The team developed 11 key action items and every business unit was required to set up task-force teams to implement them.[9]

Other companies have adapted existing crisis management structures (see Strategy Capsule 18.1).

*Dual Strategies: Surviving Today, Competing for Tomorrow* We discussed *dual strategies* in Chapter 1. Strategic management involves making the most of the firm's existing resources and capabilities to maximize performance in the present while also developing to meet the requirements of the future. In times of crisis this conflict becomes more much more acute. The economic crisis has foreshortened management time horizons for most companies. The greater the impact of the downturn, the more firms are likely to be focusing their energies on surviving the present. The danger, however, is that in retrenching to secure survival,

---

## STRATEGY CAPSULE 18.1
# Crisis Management at DuPont

DuPont's CEO Chad Holliday was alerted to the spread of the subprime crisis when, on a visit to Japan, a major customer there announced cash flow concerns. A meeting with senior managers on his return to Wilmington, Delaware, resulted in a fragmentary but consistent picture of an accelerating downturn: sharp falls in orders by automakers for paint, falling occupancy rates for local hotels, etc. Holliday activated DuPont's Corporate Crisis Management Plan, which had last been initiated on the September 11, 2001. The next day the 17 standing committees met at DuPont HQ for four days of meetings. The committees assigned to security and safety issues were stood down, while the remaining teams worked on initial financial, operational and HR responses. To alert all employees, DuPont's chief economist and the head of its pension fund prepared a communication to employees on the business outlook, which also addressed pension fund issues. Within 10 days of initiating the crisis plan all DuPont employees had had a face-to-face meeting with a manager who outlined expectations with regard to cost cutting.

The initial measure involved heavy cutbacks of discretionary costs such as travel, consultants, overtime and outside contracts. But as the financial situation continued to deteriorate it became clear that additional measures would be needed. Together with his COO and CFO, Holliday had meetings with each of DuPont's 14 leaders to discuss their responses to the crisis. With evidence that cost cutting and cash conservation measures were not being implemented fast enough the top trio introduced sharply reduced targets for cost and working for the remainder of 2008 and first quarter of 2009.

Revised sales projections allowed a reassessment of capacity and labor requirements. On December 4, 2008 DuPont announced a series of plant closures, the elimination of 4000 contractors, and 2500 job losses.

Within six weeks Du Pont had achieved a major financial and operational repositioning of its entire company.

*Source:* Based on Ram Charan, *Leadership in the Era of Economic Uncertainty* (New York: McGraw-Hill, 2009)

for example by cutting back investments in technology, facilities, brands and people, companies will undermine their future competitiveness. One of the great challenges of managing in a downturn is to safeguard core capabilities and to make shrewd investments to prepare for the next upturn. Firms that perform best across economic cycles tend to be those which adjust activity levels early on in a downcycle, then invest in technology, human resources, and acquisitions at the depth of a recession.[10] However, timing is difficult. Recessions offer unique opportunities for acquiring resources on the cheap—however, as Bank of America discovered in its opportunistic acquisition of Merrill Lynch, moving too early may result in overpaying.

*Adjusting Performance Criteria* Emphasis on survival rather than long run profitability or growth has implications for the performance criteria a firm adopts to set targets and monitor performance. When battling for survival many of the conventional indicators—earnings per share for example—lose relevance. Standard indicators of solvency—debt/equity, excess of assets over liabilities, current ratio—take second place to indicators of liquidity such as cash reserves and free cash flow. When so many asset markets—for real estate, industrial equipment, or debt instruments—suffer from lack of trading volume, a liquidity problem can easily become a solvency problem. During recession cash is king, which means planning and monitoring of cash flows and cash balances. Tatum, the financial consulting firm recommends: "focus on managing the funds that are available . . . This requires the company to maintain a meaningful 13-week cash flow forecast, tracking and regularly updating the forecast to perpetually keep it running one quarter ahead, reflecting new information as it is gleaned."[11] Active cash management requires careful management of receivables, which must go beyond the numbers. What is the financial health of individual customers? Which ones are being unusually slow in settling their invoices? When cash flows are uncertain, contingency planning is essential—will suppliers extend lengthen payment periods what nonbank sources of credit are available, which assets can be sold?

*Linking Environment Scanning to Financial Management* A key feature of the 2008–9 downturn was a high level of uncertainty as managers sought to make sense of a mass of confusing economic and financial information—all of which pointed to rapid deterioration, but none of which was helpful in indicating the depth or length of the recession. Given human propensities to interpret new information in the light of individual emotional disposition, prior belief structures and outright denial, top management access to real time information from the periphery of the organization and group processes to interpret that information are critical. Cisco's corporate information systems allow senior executives to track orders from around the world on a real time basis and quickly identify potential deviations from budgets. Lego uses a monthly meeting of senior managers—the "operations board"—to pool knowledge of what is happening in its various markets and take a view about what is likely to happen in the 12 months to come.[12] Given the impossibility of forecasting, scenarios and simulations can be valuable ways of thinking about the future and exploring its implications. Early in the financial crisis, J. P. Morgan Chase examined the effect of a 50% fall in the stock market and 10% unemployment on its budgets. Lego generated a number of different scenarios as part of its 2009 budget and developed contingency plans for each scenario so that it can react swiftly to emerging events.

*Innovative Approaches to Strategy* Recessionary times offer opportunities for doing things differently—as well as opportunities for acquiring assets at fire-sale prices. Cash-strapped consumers offer a willing market for companies that can offer superior value propositions. According to Peter Williamson and Ming Zeng, companies that adapt low-cost technical solutions can quickly take market share from established market leaders. China's BYD now leads the world market for lithium ion batteries after developing a battery that uses lower cost materials and can be manufactured using a lower cost process. Another Chinese company, Zhongxing Medical, has developed a direct digital radiography scanner using a less sophisticated technology that allows it to undercut GE and Philips by about 75%. By developing products for emerging market countries, Western MNCs can find innovative low-cost customer solution. In India, HP has developed its *Shop Owner's Management Assistant*, a low-cost Linux-based device for inventory management and billing. Designed for India's mom-and-pop stores, HP is now discovering a global market for the product.[13]

The key to developing promising new strategies during a severe recession, according to Richard Rumelt, is to recognize that a serious economic downturn is not part of a normal business cycle but is a *structural break*: a point where trends become discontinuous and established cause-and-effect relationships break down.[14] Such periods are often associated with massive industrial change—some established industries go into terminal decline but others flourish. The Great Depression of the 1930s coincided with the golden years of Hollywood, the rise of air travel and the emergence of many branded consumer goods, including ready-to-eat breakfast cereals. Investment banking will never be the same and the auto industry may never bounce back, yet in the new networked, big-government economy struggling to save the ecosystem, massive opportunities are available in water supply systems, waste management, high-speed rail systems, alternative energy, next generation wireless services, healthcare, and crime prevention.

# New Directions in Strategic Thinking

## Reorienting Shareholder Value Maximization

As outlined in Chapter 1, the late twentieth century saw a broad acceptance of shareholder value maximization as the dominant goal of firms. The pursuit of shareholder value has resulted in major gains in cost efficiency and a wave of corporate restructuring involving divestment, outsourcing and delayering. During the present decade, the unremitting quest for shareholder value has also had unforeseen and undesired consequences. Rather than maximize the flow of profits on which stock market valuation depended, many companies had focused excessively on short-term earnings, while others had gone further and had attempted to directly manage their stock market valuations through smoothing fluctuations in reported earnings and, in some cases, artificially manipulating financial statements. The alleged alignment of management incentives with shareholder value through grants of stock options and bonuses to senior managers have, for many companies, become a mechanism for the enrichment of executives at the expense of shareholders.

However, none of these outcomes implies that the goal of maximizing the value of the firm is misguided. Maximizing shareholder value is essentially about maximizing the present value of economic profit over the lifetime of the firm. The key issue is how it is translated into strategy. The problem for many public companies is that shareholder value creation was interpreted by management to mean the management of a firm's stock market value. Management cannot create stock market value—only the stock market can do that. What management can do is to generate the stream of profits that the stock market capitalizes into market value. The danger is that CEO obsession with their companies' share price can divert them from the task of long-term profit maximization. Indeed, as I argued in Chapter 2, the critical focus of top management should be less on profits and more upon the factors that drive profits: operational efficiency, customer satisfaction, new product development and the like.

The implication is not that firms abandon shareholder value maximization in favor of some woolly notion of stakeholder satisfaction but that they should focus more determinedly on identifying the basic drivers of value creation and seek to manage them. Following this line of reasoning, the answer to the present crisis of confidence among business leaders lies not in some new model of capitalism but in refocusing upon the fundamentals of strategic management.

The corporate disasters of the present decade from Enron to Citigroup, Lehman Brothers and Royal Bank of Scotland have their roots in strategies that were a poor fit both with the key success factors of the industries within which the firms operated and with their resources and capabilities. The universal banking model pursued by Citigroup rested upon dubious assumptions about supply-side and demand-side economies of scope. RBS's acquisition-based growth strategy never adequately addressed the question of how cost savings from integrating the target firms would match the acquisition premiums that were paid.

The most powerful antidote to the triple threat of corporate empire building, CEO hubris, and unwarranted faith in new business models is fundamental strategic analysis: strate-gies which build value are those which are based upon choosing markets whose structural characteristics can support profitability over the long term, creating com-petitive advantage through matching internal strengths to emerging success factors and maintaining the flexibility to adapt to unexpected changes.

## Managing Options

Deploying shareholder value maximization also means recognizing that shareholder value derives not only from the net present value of profits, but also from *real options*. During turbulent times, options are likely to become increasingly important as sources of value. A failure to take account of option value has been a critical flaw in the ways in which the shareholder value model has been applied. In the interests of reducing cost of capital and boosting after-tax profits, firms have substituted debt for equity. In doing so they have simultaneously reduced options: highly leveraged firms have fewer opportunities to take advantage of unexpected investment opportunities (including acquisition). In the event of an unexpected downturn, highly leveraged firms may experience a catastrophic lack of strategic options.

Analysis of strategy in terms of option-creation has focused on particular types of strategic decisions—for example, R&D decisions,[15] acquisitions,[16] and alliance formation.[17] However, application of real options thinking to strategic analysis at a broader level has been limited to broad generalizations, such as the value of flexibility. If we are to take on board options thinking more widely, then we need to reconsider many of our core strategy models and strategy techniques. For example:

- Industry analysis has taken the view that decisions about industry attractiveness depend on profit potential. However, if industry structure becomes so unstable that forecasting industry profitability is no longer viable, it is likely that industry attractiveness will depend much more on option value. From an options perspective, an attractive industry is one that is rich in options—for example, an industry that produces a number of different products is comprised of multiple segments, has many strategic groups, utilizes a diversity of alternative technologies and raw materials, and where internal mobility barriers tend to be low. Thus, consumer electronics, semiconductors, packaging, and investment banking would seem to be more attractive in terms of options than electricity or steel or car rental.

- An options approach also has major implications for the analysis of resources and capabilities. In terms of option value, an attractive resource is one that can be deployed in different businesses and support alternative strategies. Owning a patent on a breakthrough in nanotechnology is likely to offer greater option value than owning a blast furnace. Similarly with capabilities: highly specialized capabilities such as expertise in the design of petrochemical plants offers less option potential than expertise in the marketing of fast-moving consumer goods. Dynamic capabilities are important because they can create new options: "Dynamic capabilities are the organizational and strategic routines by which firms achieve new resource combinations as markets emerge, collide, split, evolve, and die."[18]

## Seeking More Complex Sources of Competitive Advantage

Focus on strategy fundamentals does not necessarily lead to simple strategies. In many industries, increasing pressure of competition and the entry of firms with unassailable cost advantages requires that established players access new sources of profitability. As we observed in Chapter 7, there are few competitive advantages that are sustainable over a significant period of time in today's dynamic business environment. Ultimately, the only sustainable competitive advantage is the ability to create new sources of competitive advantage. A key fear of companies that have maintained both profitability and market share over periods of many years is their capacity to build layers of competitive advantage—for example, Toyota, Wal-Mart, 3M, Canon, Swatch and L'Oreal. These companies have meshed the diverse performance goals of cost efficiency, differentiation, innovation, responsiveness and global learning. As we shall see, reconciling the different requirements of different performance dimensions imposes highly complex organizational challenges that are pushing companies to fundamentally rethink their structures and management systems.

Thus the ability of some companies to combine multiple capabilities recalls Isaiah Berlin's classification of intellectuals into foxes and hedgehogs: "The fox knows many things; the hedgehog knows one big thing."[19] Despite Jim Collins' praise for companies that have a single penetrating insight into the complexities of their business environments, it appears that companies that have built their strategy on such insight often have difficulty in fending off new competitors: Toys-R-Us with its big-box retailing, Dell with its direct sales model, AOL with dial-up internet access.[20]

## The Challenge of Strategic Fit: Complementarity and Complexity

Central to just about everything in this book is the notion of *strategic fit*. Strategy must *fit* with the business environment and with resources and capabilities; strategy must *fit* with structure; the individual components of strategy must *fit* one with another; organization structure must *fit* with management systems . . . We have examined these issues of fit intuitively using logic to explore individual relationships ("in a commodity market, the dominant strategy will be to be a cost leader"). However, two areas—the *economics of complementarity* and *complexity theory*—offer approaches to the analysis of strategic fit that not only offer vastly increased rigor but have troubling implications for strategy formulation and implementation.

*Complementarity* Complementarity research addresses the linkages among a firm's management practices such that adopting an apparently superior practice is likely to be ineffective or even counterproductive—the key is a system-wide shift to a new configuration of management practices. Much of the research has addressed the transition from mass manufacturing to lean manufacturing—reorganizing production processes achieves little without simultaneous adaptation of a wide range of human resource practices.[21] Similarly, a six-sigma quality management program is likely to be of little value unless it is accompanied by adjustments in incentives, recruitment policies, product strategy, and capital budgeting practices.

At one extreme, recognition of complementarities in management practices implies a retreat from rules and generalizations in formulating and implementing of strategy in favor of particularism: every firm is unique and must create a unique combination of strategic variables and management practices. In practice, the implications of complementarity are less stark. While every firm is unique, management choices tend to converge to a limited number of *configurations*. Thus, successful adaptation among large European companies was associated with a small number of configurations of organizational structure, processes and boundaries.[22]

*Complexity Theory* Organizations—like the weather, ant colonies, flocks of birds, human crowds, and seismic activity—are *complex systems* whose behavior results from the interactions of a large number of independent agents. This behavior has a number of interesting features:

- *Unpredictability*. The behavior of complex adaptive systems cannot be predicted in any precise sense. There is no tendency to stable equilibria; cascades of change are constantly interacting and reshaping competitive landscapes. Patterns of change tend to follow *power-law distributions*: small changes typically result in small consequences but may also trigger major movements—dropping grains of sand onto a sand pile results in small movements interspersed by occasional major landslides.[23]
- *Self-organization*. Complex systems—especially biological and social systems—have a capacity for self-organizing. A bee colony or shoal of fish shows coordinated responses to external threats and opportunities without anyone giving orders. Humans too can often do as well as bees and ants in organizing themselves, adapting to change and creating new structures and

systems without any formal authority. Quite sophisticated synchronized behavior can be achieved through adopting just a few simple rules. For human organizations there are three main requirements for self-organization: *identity* that permits a common sense-making process within the organization, *information* that provides the possibility of synchronized behavior, and *relationships* that are the pathways through which information is transformed into intelligent, coordinated action. The more access individuals have to one another, the greater the possibilities for organized activity.[24]

● *Inertia and chaos*. Evolutionary processes can produce orderly outcomes where change is so limited that the system falls into stasis, or disorder leading to chaotic outcomes. In between is an intermediate region where disturbances produce both small and large shifts (with a power-law distribution) that achieves the most rapid evolutionary adaptation. These results point to the advantages of systems that are positioned at the *edge of chaos*—they are capable of small, localized adaptations, but also have the potential to make larger leaps toward higher *fitness peaks*.[25] The implications of these ideas for strategic management are radical and far-reaching. Complexity implies that business is inherently unpredictable—not only is it impossible to forecast the business environment but managers cannot predict with any certainty what the outcomes of their actions will be. The concept of the CEO as the peak decision maker and strategy architect is not only unrealistic—it is undesirable. Managers must rely on the self-organizing properties of their companies. The critical issues are how can they select the structures, systems, and management styles that will allow these self-organizing properties to generate the best outcomes? Some of the recommendations arising from applications of complexity theory to strategic management include:[26]

● *Setting up conditions for both incremental and radical change*. Kaufman's *NK model* (and the *fitness landscapes* that it generates) is a widely used tool for exploring the implications among choices of strategy, organizational form, and management behavior.[27] Achieving the highest level of adaptive performance typically requires a combination of incremental changes with occasional radical leaps. Management systems can be designed to encourage these outcomes. For example the reorientation of companies' strategic planning systems from resource allocation decisions to agreeing performance targets is likely to encourage incentives for incremental measures—cost reduction and continuous improvement—while establishing conditions where serious performance shortfalls trigger corporate intervention involving major strategic changes. NK models also show that the optimal balance between incremental and radical management measures depend upon the degree of interdependency of the organizational environment: the stronger the linkages, the more rugged the landscape, and the greater the need for major strategic leaps to move to new performance peaks.

● *Establishing simple rules*. If the coordinated behaviors of complex systems (e.g. the flying formations of flocks of birds) can be simulated with a few simple rules, it seems feasible that companies can be managed by a few simple rules and very little managerial direction. For instance, rather than plan strategy in any formal sense, rules of thumb in screening opportunities ("*boundary rules*") can locate the company where the opportunities are richest. Thus, Cisco's acquisitions strategy is guided by the rule that it will acquire companies with fewer than 75 employees of which 75% are engineers. Second, rules can designate a common approach to how the company will exploit opportunities ("*how-to rules*"). Thus, Yahoo! has a few rules regarding the look and functionality of new web pages, but then gives freedom to developers to design new additions. Third, companies have rules to determine priorities in resource allocation ("*priority rules*").[28] Jack Welch's corporate initiatives at GE—"Be number 1 or number 2 in your industry," "Six-sigma," "Destroy-your-business-dot-com"—fulfilled a similar role. They were not directives, but guidelines to stimulate and focus decentralized adaptation.[29]

- *Accelerating evolution through flexibility.* Organizational structures tend to ossify over time as power centers build and interactions become institutionalized. Periodic large-scale corporate reorganizations are not enough: to exploit innovation and entrepreneurial initiative, flexibility in organizational structure is essential. Eisenhardt and Brown use the term "patching" to describe a process in which new organizational units are continually being created, merged, and redefined to foster initiative.[30] Achieving flexibility may require leaving structures only partially defined. This may be especially effective in assisting collaboration between different business units within a company. Rather than attempt to manage business unit linkages from the corporate level, it may be better for corporate to create a context within which businesses can co-evolve. This requires allowing considerable autonomy to business units while keeping their boundaries porous to permit a multiplicity of voluntary collaborations between individuals across the businesses. Walt Disney Company exemplifies co-evolution between different internal divisions. Disney's *The Lion King* movie spawned videos, theme park attractions, a stage musical, and over 150 kinds of merchandise. These spinoffs were not planned by corporate strategists; they occurred through voluntary cooperation across Disney's different divisions.[31]

- *Using adaptive tension to position at the edge of chaos.* If too little tension produces inertia and too much creates chaos, the challenge for top management is to create a level of adaptive tension that optimizes the pace of organizational change and innovation. Bill McKelvey interprets Jack Welch's management style from a complexity viewpoint—by imposing initiatives ("be number 1 or number 2 in your industry") and powerful performance incentives—he turned up the level of pressure in the organization to the point where changes began occurring spontaneously.[32]

Applications of complexity theory to strategy management add analytic depth to Mintzberg's arguments in favor of *emergent* approaches to strategy making. Mintzberg's critique of the "rational design" school of strategy emphasized the superiority of decentralized strategy making that embraced intuition and responsiveness.[33] Complexity theory provides an intellectual basis for emergence in strategy making. Changes in large companies' strategic planning practices in recent years—reduced formality, emphasis on performance goals, focus on direction rather than content—are consistent with the tenets of complexity theory.[34]

*Analyzing Linkages within the Firm* Porter and Siggelkow observe that common to both complementarity and complexity approaches to linkages among a firm's activities is the concept of *contextuality*—the benefits from any particular activity depend upon what other activities are taking place.[35] In Chapter 8, I observed that one implication of this idea is that imitation of a firm's competitive advantage becomes more difficult: imitating a particular resource or process is unlikely to do the trick. However, Porter and Siggelkow's main contribution is the recognition of different types of linkage and their implications for management. Two dimensions are important:

- Generic activities *versus* strategy-specific activities. Some management activities have performance effects that are independent of other activities— for example using computers for managing accounting systems is optimal for virtually all firms. For other activities, how they are configured depends upon the other choices that the firm makes. Thus, the optimal employee incentive system depends upon a number of strategic choices.

- Generic interactions *versus* contextual interactions. The interactions between management activities can also be different across firms. Some activities may interact in the same way for all firms. For example, the benefits from flexibility in manufacturing will tend to increase with increased product differentiation for all firms. For other pairs of activities, interactions may be different across firms—depending either on the levels of the two activities, or on choices regarding other activities.

## Redesigning the Organization

As business environments become more complex, more competitive and less predictable, survival requires that companies perform at a higher level with a broader repertoire of capabilities. Building multiple capabilities and achieving excellence across multiple performance dimensions requires managing dilemmas that cannot be resolved as simple tradeoffs. A company must produce at low cost, while also innovating; it must deploy the massed resources of a large corporation, while showing the entrepreneurial flair of a small startup; it must achieve high levels of reliability and consistency while also being flexible. All of these dilemmas are aspects of the underlying conflict between achieving operational efficiency today and adapting for tomorrow. Reconciling these conflicts within a single organization presents huge management challenges. We know how to devise structures and incentive systems that drive cost efficiency; we also know the organizational conditions conducive to innovation. But how on earth do we do both simultaneously?

Changes in organizational design are being driven by two major forces: first, the need for organizations to deploy more capabilities developed to a higher level; second, the need to respond quicker to external change.

### Capability-based Structures

In Chapter 6, we noted that organizational design has been dominated by the requirements of cooperation rather than coordination. As a result, hierarchical structures have emphasized control and the need for unitary lines of command. Once we acknowledge that building outstanding capabilities is the primary goal of organizational design then the emphasis shifts to the need to achieve effective coordination. If we accept that most enterprises need to deploy multiple capabilities and the coordination needs of different capabilities vary, it follows that our organizational structure must encompass different patterns of interaction. Hence, most business enterprises are unlikely to be successful with a unitary structure and will need to encompass multiple structures.

*Beyond Unitary Structures* Developing multiple capabilities requires that organizational members coordinate in different ways for different purposes, which requires structures that simultaneously support multiple patterns of coordination.[36] Matrix structures—organizing to develop capabilities around businesses, geographical markets and functions—have been around for a long time. But these dimensions of the traditional matrix relate primarily to operational activities. The literature on organizational learning knowledge management distinguishes productive activities according to whether they are building the firm's stock of knowledge or deploying that knowledge: the former is referred to as *exploration*, the latter as *exploitation*.[37] When exploration activities were carried out by specialized functions—R&D, market research, strategic planning—organizations could simply differentiate these departments to meet the organizational requirements of exploration. Increasingly, however, these functions are not the preserve of specialized departments but are diffused across the organization.

Adding exploration activities—product development teams, innovation initiatives, communities of practice—on top of the standard dimensions of the organizational matrix requires additional structures to support coordination. Structures directed towards acquiring new knowledge and promoting change within the formal organization have been described as *parallel learning structures*.[38] They are designed to foster communication and interaction, but typically involve little specialization or rules. For example:

- 3M has a parallel structure for new product development whereby individuals are encouraged, to "bootleg" time, materials, and use of facilities to work on new product ideas. Promising new products that emerge from this informal structure are ultimately taken up by the formal structure.
- The "Work-Out" program implemented by Jack Welch at GE was a parallel structure designed to effect change within the formal structure. During Work-Out sessions the norms that governed the formal organization were suspended, and free interchange of ideas was encouraged.
- IBM's massive online *"Innovation Jam"* (more on this later) creates a temporary organization that administers a biannual, 72-hour online session involving tens of thousands of contributors from inside and outside the company, then harvesting the results.[39]

*Team-based, Project-based and Process-based Structures* The structures needed to support coordination are different from those required to ensure compliance and control. Increased reliance on teams reflects the recognition that routines require patterns of interaction that are spontaneous and poorly understood—hence, they cannot be "managed" in any directive sense. Flexible, team-based structures can achieve the kinds of adaptable integration that are the basis of dynamic capabilities, yet beyond some very basic requirements of team structure we know little about the dynamics of team interaction.[40]

More companies are organizing their activities less around functions and continuous operations and more around time-designated projects where a team is assigned to a specific project with a clearly defined outcome and a specified completion date. While construction companies and consulting firms have always been structured around projects, a wide range of companies are finding that project-based structures featuring temporary cross-functional teams charged with clear objectives are more able to achieve innovation, adaptability, and rapid learning than more traditional structures:

- About half of Google's employees—including almost all of its software engineers—are organized into teams comprising three or four people. Team leadership revolves, individuals work on multiple teams, and individuals can move between teams without HR approval. According to Shona Brown, Google's head of operations: "If at all possible, we want people to commit to things, rather than be assigned to things . . . If you see an opportunity, go for it."[41]
- W. L. Gore, the supplier of Gore-Tex and wide a range of hi-tech fabric products, also has a team-based structure with minimal top-down direction—there are no formal job titles and leaders are selected by peers. Employees ("associates") may apply to join particular teams and it is up to the team members to choose new members. The teams are self-managed and team goals are not assigned from above but are agreed through team commitments. Associates are encouraged to work on multiple teams.[42]

Non-hierarchical, team-based organizations can achieve high levels of innovation, flexibility and employee motivation. But absence of hierarchical control can also produce chaos. Oticon, the Danish manufacturer of hearing aids, initiated radical decentralization, abolished most formal controls, and reorganized around over 100 self-directed project teams.[43] Within six years, lack of coordination, confused incentives, and excessive internal politicking caused Oticon to dismantle much of its "spaghetti organization" and reinstitute hierarchical control.[44]

To improve coordination across, between and within organizational capabilities has encouraged companies to align their structures more closely with their internal *processes*. While business process reengineering directs attention to the microstructure of processes, a focus on organizational capabilities fosters an integrated view of processes that explores how individual processes fit together in sequences and networks of complementary activities. For example, a company's order fulfillment process may span a whole chain of activities from supplying information to potential customers, to customer selection and ordering, to manufacturing, through to distribution. Similarly, the customer relations process embraces the entirety of a company's interactions with its customers through marketing and after-sales services. These macro processes often extend beyond the company: supply-chain management links internal logistics with those of suppliers and suppliers' suppliers. Volvo reorganized ordering, production planning, supply chains, distribution, and dealer relations into an integrated "order fulfillment process" with the goal of a 14-day cycle between customer order and customer receipt of a customized automobile.[45]

## Organizing for Adaptability

The need for organizations to coordinate in multiple ways for multiple purposes inevitably means that company structures become more complex. Despite the propensity for CEOs to echo Thoreau in their call to "simplify, simplify," typically the emphasis has been, first, replacing formal systems by informal systems; second, relying less on continuous supervision and more on setting performance goals against which individuals are periodically appraised.

*Hands-off Management* Complexity theory supports the idea that organizations may be able to do complex things without necessarily resorting to complex structures. Notions of *self organization* and the power of *simple rules* support the idea that human beings are capable of interesting in complex patterns without the need for managers telling them what to do. Loosening the structure may be a critical step towards building the *ambidextrous organization*—one that can combine multiple capabilities and accommodate both gradual change and occasional revolutionary leaps.[46]

The paradox of simplicity is that reducing complexity at the formal level can foster greater variety and sophisticated coordination at the informal level. At GE, Jack Welch's emphasis on "Speed, Simplicity, Self-confidence" resulted in reformulating control systems around just a few performance indicators and using periodic corporate initiatives ("growth," "boundarylessness," and "six-sigma") to drive change. Yet, this paring down of formal systems fostered more complex patterns of coordination and collaboration within GE.[47] In general, the greater the potential for reordering existing resources and capabilities in complex new combinations, the greater the potential for "consensus-based hierarchies" that emphasize horizontal communication over "authority-based hierarchies" that emphasize vertical communication.[48]

*Identity* Substituting informal structures and systems for formal structures and systems requires focus on organizational context over organizational structure. To manage the organizational context includes influencing social and behavioral norms but these depend on some shared cognition of what the organization is and an emotional attachment towards what the organization represents. These ideas are components of what has been termed *organizational identity*—a collective understanding of what is presumed core, distinctive, and enduring about the character of an organization.[49] A strong consensus around organizational identity provides a powerful basis for coordinated action that permits flexibility and responsiveness to be reconciled with continuity and stability. At some point, organizational identity becomes are impediment to rather than a facilitator of change. (IBM's identity as a vertically integrated supplier of mainframe computers to large organizations hampered adaptation to microcomputing, networking, and web-based computing.) Organizational identity creates an important linkage between a firm's internal self-image and its market positioning. With the increase of symbolic influences on consumer choices, the linkage between product design, brand image, and organizational identity becomes increasingly important. For companies such as Nokia, Apple, Alessi, and Bang & Olufsen, product design is an important vehicle for establishing and interpreting organizational identity.[50]

*Breaking Down Corporate Boundaries* Even with informal coordination mechanisms, modular structures and sophisticated knowledge management systems there are limits to the range of capabilities that any company can encompass. Indeed, converging technologies and the need for rapid new product development means that outsourcing capabilities is often preferable to developing them internally. The implication is less distinction between what happens within the firm and what happens outside it. Interfirm networks, as we saw in the previous chapter, permit stable yet flexible patterns for integrating the capabilities of different firms while also sharing risks. "Contingent workforces"—comprising people who work for companies but are not covered by long-term employment contracts—similarly permit access to a wide range of skills while avoiding fixed costs.

While localized networks of firms—such as those that characterize Italy's clothing, furniture, and industrial machinery industries—offer potential for building trust and interfirm routines, web-based technologies permit much wider networks of collaboration. The open innovation efforts described in this book—Procter & Gamble's "Connect & Develop" approach to new product development and IBM's "Innovation Jam" (see Chapter 12)—both point to the power of ICT technologies to enable firms to draw upon ideas and expertise across the globe. Increasingly innovation requires the combination of very different technologies: the Nike + iPod Sport Kit involving sensors in Nike running shoes providing real time information that can be read on an Apple iPod is just one example of a phenomenon that is breaking down barriers between industries as well as between companies.[51] Cisco Systems has pioneered the development of web-based business integration with its suppliers, customers, and collaborations. The collaborative potential of the internet is most strongly revealed in open-source communities that build highly complex products such as Linux and Wikipedia through global networks of individual collaborators.[52]

Interfirm networks facilitate the design and production of complex products that require a wide range of technical and commercial capabilities in sectors subject to rapid change. In automobiles, fashion clothing, aerospace, machine tools, and telecom equipment, networks allow each firm to specialize in a few capabilities while providing the close linkages needed to integrate these different capabilities. The flexibility of these linkages offers the potential for the capabilities resident within an interfirm network to be reconfigured in order to adapt quickly to external change.[53]

## New Modes of Leadership

Changing external conditions, new strategic priorities, and different types of organization call for new approaches to leadership. The era of restructuring and share-holder focus has been associated with "change-masters"[54]—highly visible, individualistic, often hard-driving management styles of CEOs such as Lee Iacocca at Chrysler, John Browne at BP, Michael Eisner at Disney, and Rupert Murdoch at News International. These leaders have been, first and foremost, strategic decision makers, charting the direction and redirection of their companies, and making key decisions over acquisitions, divestments, new products and cost cutting. The changing circumstances of management I have outlined imply that the "buck-stops-here" peak decision-making role may no longer be feasible, let alone desirable. One simple observation is that most companies are too complex for the CEO to be able to access the information necessary to act as peak decision maker. Recent contributions to the literature on leadership point to business leaders that are capable of creating an organizational environment consistent with the company's strategic needs—including the potential for rapid evolution.

Gary Hamel argues the need to redefine the work of leadership:

> The notion of the leader as a heroic decision maker is untenable. Leaders must be recast as social-systems architects who enable innovation . . .
>
> In Management 2.0, leaders will no longer be seen as grand visionaries, all-wise decision makers, and ironfisted disciplinarians. Instead, they will need to become social architects, constitution writers, and entrepreneurs of meaning. In this new model, the leader's job is to create an environment where every employee has the chance to collaborate, innovate, and excel.[55]

If strategy is founded in organizational identity and common purpose, and if organizational culture is the bedrock of capability, then a key role of top management is to clarify, nurture and communicate the company's purpose, *heritage*, personality, values, and norms. To unify and inspire the efforts of organizational members, leadership requires providing meaning to people's own aspirations. Ultimately this requires attention to the emotional climate of the organization.[56]

If business leadership is less about decision making and more about guiding culture, identity, and vision, then the managers will require different knowledge and skills. Research into the psychological and demographic characteristics of successful leaders has identified few consistent or robust relationships—successful leaders come in all shapes, sizes, and personality types. However, research based upon McClelland's *competency modeling* methodology pointed to the role of a set of personality attributes that have been referred to by Daniel Goleman as *emotional intelligence*.[57] These comprise: *self-awareness*—the ability understand oneself and one's emotions, *self-management*—control, integrity, conscientiousness, and initiative; *social awareness*—particularly the capacity to sense others' emotions (empathy) and *social skills*—communication, collaboration and relationship building.

Jim Collins' concept of "Level 5 Leadership" also emphasizes individual qualities—notably a combination of personal and intense resolve.[58] This combination allows business leaders to avoid the hubris and megalomania associated with outsized egos and to devote themselves to team building and organizational development. Philip Morris's Joseph Cullman, Kimberley-Clark's Darwin Smith, Nucor's Ken Iversen, P&G's L.G. Laffey, and IBM's Sam Palmisano are all transformational leaders who did not succumb to the cult of personality.

Probably the greatest error in Western thinking about leadership in organizations is the heavy emphasis on the role of individuals. Tappin and Cave argue that *team leadership* is best suited to today's troubled times where the top management team members are bound together by close bonds of fellowship. Their model is the Nokia leadership team that comprised Jorma Ollila, Matti Alahuhta, Pekka Ala-Pietilä, Sari Baldauf, and his replacement as president and chief operating officer, Olli-Pekka Kallasvuo. An effective top management team comprises, ideally, just three or four people who share extensively and openly, who have specialized roles but are also able to cover for one another.[59]

However, it is important to acknowledge that, despite the urge to uncover "the secrets of leadership," there is no dominant model of leadership or profile of the successful leader. The main lesson from empirical research is that successful leadership is associated with many different leadership approaches and many different leader characteristics. At the same time, different situations will respond to different leadership approaches. In responding to the present crisis, it is notable that several of the leadership trends that we have identified have gone into sharp reverse for many companies. In order to take fast decisive actions to cut costs, conserve cash and shore up balance sheets, many companies have recentralized management and moved to a much more interventionist and directive top management style.

## Summary

In responding to the environments in which their companies find themselves, business leaders experience two major difficulties. First, the outlook for the future is highly uncertain—for many countries, 2009 saw the fastest decline in economic activity since 1930. How the world economy will develop during the second decade of the twenty-first century is unknown. Even in the short-term we do not know how deep the present recession will be, how long it will last, whether governments' monetary and fiscal initiatives will work, or what the political consequences will be. Looking longer term, there is the potential for the recent crisis to lead to fundamental changes in the capitalist system.

Second, the capacity for managerial action has been confounded by a conflict between short term and longer term forces. Over the longer term, several forces for change are influencing our thinking about strategy and management in general. These include increasing competition (arising in particular from internationalization), turbulence, technology and changing social attitudes. In the short term the overwhelming priority is surviving the present downturn.

The central problem is that the two sets of challenges require responses that are often conflicting. While meeting the challenges of increased competition and technological change is likely to require developing new capabilities, survival requires intense focus on cash conservation that is likely to inhibit all forms of investment. Similar observations can be made about styles of leadership. Complex organizations operating at high levels of evolutionary fitness require leaders that foster decentralized adaptation and initiative.

Yet, effective responses to the financial crisis of 2008–9 necessitated radical shifts in strategy that have necessitated, in most companies, a dramatic recentralization of power in order to "circle the wagons."

In many ways this dilemma of reconciling short-term survival with longer term fitness is merely an extreme example of the paradoxes that almost define the challenge of management in the twenty-first century. Several years have passed since Charles Handy identified paradox as the fundamental feature of business—and, indeed society. Yet it is only recently that the challenges of reconciling cost cutting with innovation, global integration with local differentiation, scale with responsiveness, and systematization with improvisation have been acknowledged.

At the same time, emerging concepts and theories—complexity thinking, self-organization, real options, organizational identity, open-source innovation and distributed leadership—offer the potential for us to augment our existing standard tools of strategic management. Even more encouraging is the fact that experimentation and innovation at the coal-face of management practice is offering new approaches to dealing both with old problems and with emerging ones. Radical corporate initiatives such as IBM's "Innovation Jam," Google's emergent approach to business development, and W. L. Gore's self-managed teams tend to be found among companies whose survival is not under serious threat. But even among firms that are primarily focused upon survival, management actions are going beyond conventional approaches to restructuring and cost cutting. These include novel forms of financing which are independent of traditional financial institutions, new approaches to employee relations, scenario-based financial planning, and building strategy around options rather than projects.

One of the challenges for strategic management scholars is to be alert to the initiatives and innovations that are being developed across a vast array of different firms, to identify the critical features of these initiatives and innovations, and to deploy the tools of management and social science theory to draw out their significance and potential for diffusion. A key consequence of this type of activity is that, while strategic management continues to draw heavily on concepts and theories drawn from economics, sociology, psychology, biology, systems theory, and other disciplines, in addressing current issues then is scope for strategic management to take on a leading role in developing new conceptual thinking.

Of course, many of the ideas that have developed over recent years—including the characteristics of the "new economy," the potential for employee stock options to resolve agency problems, and the potential for "decoupling" from the world market have been shown to be empty. This reinforces my belief that our basic tools of strategy analysis—industry analysis and the analysis of resources and capabilities—remain valid and robust. At the same time, there is vast potential for developing new thinking about management—not just in relation to strategy but also in terms of the role of people within organizations, the relationships among companies themselves, and those between companies and government.

# Notes

1 U.S. National Intelligence Council, *Global Trends 2025:L A Transformed World* (Washington DC, November, 2008): www.dni.gov/nic/NIC_2025_ project.html, accessed July 8, 2009.

2 W. B. Arthur, "Increasing Returns and the New World of Business," *Harvard Business Review* (July–August 1996): 101–8.

3 "The Skype Guys," *Time* (April 30, 2006).

4 A. Y. Lewin, C. B. Weigelt and J. D. Emery, "Adaptation and Selection in Strategy and Change" in M. S. Poole and A. H. van de Ven (eds.), *Handbook of Organizational Change and Innovation* (New York: Oxford University Press, 2004): 108–60.

5 S. Jonsson, H.R. Greve, and T. Fujiwara-Greve, "Undeserved Loss: The Spread of Legitimacy Loss to Innocent Organizations in Response to Reported Corporate Deviance," *Administrative Science Quarterly*, 54 (2009): 195–228.

6 P. F. Drucker, *Managing in the Next Society* (London: St. Martin's Press, 2003), S. Ghoshal, C. A. Bartlett and P. Moran, "A New Manifesto for Management," *Sloan Management Review* (Spring 1999): 9–20; C. Handy, *The Age of Paradox* (Boston: Harvard University Press, 1995).

7 "Sustainable Business," *Financial Times* (October 9, 2006): special section.

8 "Head in, Hands on: Ram Charan on How to Lead Now," *Harvard Management Update,* (Harvard Business School: February 11, 2009).

9 "LG Considers Job Cuts Overseas," *Korean Times* (February 9, 2009): http://www.koreatimes.co.kr/www/ news/biz/2009/02/123_39214.html, accessed July 8, 2009.

10 P. Bromiley, P. Navarro and P. Sottile, "Strategic business cycle management and organizational performance: a call to action," *Strategic Organization.* 6 (2008): 207–19.

11 C. Jamison, "What Every Board Director Should Know About Financial Leadership During a Recession," Tatum LLC (2009): www.tatumllc.com.

12 "Managing in the Fog," *Economist* (February 28, 2009): 71–2.

13 P. J. Williamson and M. Zeng, "Value-for-Money Strategies for Recessionary Times," *Harvard Business Review* (March, 2009):

14 R. P. Rumelt, "Strategy in a Structural Break," *McKinsey Quarterly* (December, 2008): 24–31.

15 R. G. McGrath, "A Real Option Logic for Initiating Technology Positioning Investment," *Academy of Management Review* 22 (1997): 974–96.

16 H. T. J. Smit, "Acquisition Strategies as Option Games," *Journal of Applied Corporate Finance* (2001): 79–89.

17 M. J. Leiblein and D. D. Miller, "An Empirical Examination of the Effect of Uncertainty and Firm Strategy on the Vertical Boundaries of the Firm," *Strategic Management Journal* 24 (2003): 839–60.

18 K. M. Eisenhardt and J. A. Martin, "Dynamic Capabilities: What are They?" *Strategic Management Journal* 21 (2000): 1105–21.

19 I. Berlin, *The Hedgehog and the Fox* (New York: Simon & Schuster, 1953).

20 J. Collins, *Good to Great* (New York: HarperCollins, 2001).

21 K. Laursen and N. J. Foss, "New Human Resource Management Practices, Complementarities and the Impact on Innovation Performance," *Cambridge Journal of Economics* 27 (2003): 243–63.

22 R. Whittington, A. Pettigrew, S. Peck, E. Fenton and M. Conyon, "Change and Complementarities in the New Competitive Landscape," *Organization Science* 10 (1999): 583–600.

23 P. Bak, *How Nature Works: The Science of Self-organized Criticality* (New York: Copernicus, 1996).

24 M. J. Wheatley and M. Kellner Rogers, *A Simpler Way* (San Francisco: Berrett-Koehler, 1996).

25 P. Anderson, "Complexity Theory and Organizational Science," *Organization Science* 10 (1999): 216–32.

26 Among the sources I draw upon are: S. L. Brown and K. M. Eisenhardt, *Competing on the Edge: Strategy as Structured Chaos* (Boston: Harvard Business School Press, 1998); W. McKelvey, "Energizing Order-creating Networks of Distributed Intelligence: Improving the Corporate Brain," *International Journal of Innovation Management* 5 (June, 2001): 132–54; D. A. Levinthal, "Adaptation on a Rugged Landscape," *Management Science* 43 (1997): 934–50.

27 S. A. Kaufman, *The Origins of Order: Self Organization and Selection In Evolution* (New York: Oxford University Press, 1993).

28 For discussion of the role of rules in strategy making, see K. M. Eisenhardt and D. Sull, "Strategy as Simple Rules," *Harvard Business Review* (January–February 2001): 107–16.

29 W. McKelvey, "A Simple Rule Approach to CEO Leadership in the 21st Century" (Paper presented at the ISUFI Conference, Ostuni, Italy, September 11–13, 2003).

30 K. M. Eisenhardt and S. L. Brown, "Patching: Restitching Business Portfolios in Dynamic Markets," *Harvard Business Review* (May–June 1999): 72–84.

31 K. M. Eisenhardt and D. C. Galunic, "Coevolving: At Last, a Way to Make Synergies Work," *Harvard Business Review* (January–February 2000): 91–101.

32 W. McKelvey, "A Simple Rule Approach to CEO Leadership," op. cit.

33 H. Mintzberg, *The Rise and Fall of Strategic Planning* (New York: Free Press, 1994); H. Mintzberg, B. Ahlstrand and J. Lampel, *Strategy Safari: A Guided Tour through the Wilds of Strategic Management* (New York: Free Press, 1998).

34  R. M. Grant, "Strategic Planning In a Turbulent Environment: Evidence from the Oil Majors," *Strategic Management Journal* 24 (2003): 491–518.

35  M. E. Porter and N. Siggelkow, "Contextuality Within Activity Systems and Sustainable Competitive Advantage," *Academy of Management Perspectives* 22 (May, 2008): 34–56.

36  J. Strikwerda, "The Emergence of the Multidimensional Organization" (April, 2008). Available at SSRN: http://ssrn.com/abstract=1077363, accessed July 8, 2009.

37  J. G. March, "Exploration and Exploitation in Organizational Learning," *Organization Science* 2 (1991): 71–8.

38  G. Bushe and A. B. Shani, *Parallel Learning Structures* (Reading, MA: Addison-Wesley, 1991).

39  O. M. Bjelland and R. C. Wood, "An Inside View of IBM's 'Innovation Jam,'" *MIT Sloan Management Review* (Fall, 2008): 32–40.

40  J. R. Katzenbach and D. K. Smith, "The Discipline of Teams," *Harvard Business Review* (March–April, 1993): 111–20.

41  G. Hamel and W. Breen, *The Future of Management* (Boston: Harvard Business School Press, 2007): Chapter 6.

42  Ibid: Chapter 5.

43  D. Ravasi and G. Verona, "Organizing the Process of Knowledge Integration: The Benefits of Structural Ambiguity", *Scandinavian Journal of Management* 17 (2001): 41–66.

44  N. J. Foss, "Internal Disaggregation in Oticon: An Organizational Economics Interpretation of the Rise and Decline of the Spaghetti Organization" (Department of Industrial Economics and Strategy, Copenhagen Business School, October, 2000).

45  S. Hertz, J. K. Johansson and F. de Jager, "Customer-focused Cost Cutting: Process Management at Volvo," *Journal of Supply Chain Management* 6, no. 3 (2001): 128–41.

46  C. A. O'Reilly III and M. L. Tushman, "The Ambidextrous Organization," *Harvard Business Review* (April, 2004): 74–81. M. L. Tushman and C. A. O'Reilly III, "The Ambidextrous Organization: Managing Evolutionary and Revolutionary Change," *California Management Review* 38, no. 4 (Summer, 1996): 8–30.

47  "Jack Welch and the General Electric Management System," in R. M. Grant, *Cases to Accompany Contemporary Strategy Analysis,* 6th edn (Oxford: Blackwell, 2008).

48  J. A. Nickerson and T. R. Zenger, "The Knowledge-based Theory of the Firm—A Problem-solving Perspective," *Organization Science* 15 (2004): 617–32.

49  D. A. Gioia, M. Schultz and K. G. Corley, "Organizational Identity, Image and Adaptive Instability," *Academy of Management Review* 25 (2000): 63–81.

50  D. Ravasi and G. Lojacono, "Managing Design and Designers for Strategic Renewal," Long Range Planning, 38, No. 1. (February, 2005): 51–77.

51  "Apple and Nike, Running Mates," *Business Week* (May 24, 2006).

52  A. Wright, "The Next Paradigm Shift: Open Source Everything" *Brighthand.com* (July 9, 2008): http://www.brighthand.com/default.asp?newsID=14348, accessed July 8, 2009.

53  R. Gulati, N. Nohria and A. Zaheer, "Strategic Networks," *Strategic Management Journal* 21 (2000): 203–15.

54  R. M. Kanter, *The Change Masters* (New York: Simon & Schuster, 1983).

55  G. Hamel, "Moon Shots for Management?" *Harvard Business Review* (February 2009): 91-98.

56  J. C. Collins and J. I. Porras, *Built to Last* (New York: Harper Business, 1996).

57  D. Goleman, "What Makes a Leader?" *Harvard Business Review* (November–December 1998): 93–102. See also: J. C. Hayton and G. M. McEvoy,. "Developing and Assessing Professional and Managerial Competence" *Human Resource Management* 45 (2006): 291–4.

58  J. Collins, "Level 5 Leadership: The Triumph of Humility and Fierce Resolve," *Harvard Business Review* (January 2001): 67–76.

59  S. Tappin and A. Cave, *The Secrets of CEOs: 150 Global Chief Executives Lift the Lid on Business, Life and Leadership* (London: Nicholas Brealey Publishing, 2008).

Note: page numbers in *italic* refer to illustrations and tables.